Correspondence

Theodor W. Adorno and
Gershom Scholem

Correspondence

1939–1969

Edited and with an Introduction by
Asaf Angermann

Translated by
Paula Schwebel and Sebastian Truskolaski

polity

Originally published in German as *"Der Liebe Gott wohnt im Detail" Theodor W. Adorno / Gershom Scholem Briefwechsel 1939–1969*, herausgegeben von Asaf Angermann

The translation of this work was supported by a grant from the Goethe-Institut.

Polity Press
65 Bridge Street
Cambridge CB2 1UR, UK

Polity Press
101 Station Landing
Suite 300
Medford, MA 02155, USA

ISBN-13: 978-1-5095-1045-0

A catalogue record for this book is available from the British Library.

Library of Congress Cataloging-in-Publication Data
Names: Adorno, Theodor W., 1903-1969, author. | Scholem, Gershom, 1897-1982, author. | Angermann, Asaf, 1978- editor. | Schwebel, Paula, 1981- translator. | Truskolaski, Sebastian, translator.
Title: Correspondence : 1939 - 1969 / Theodore W. Adorno and Gershom Scholem ; edited by Asaf Angermann ; translated by Paula Schwebel and Sebastian Truskolaski.
Description: Medford : Polity, [2020] | Originally published in German as "Der Liebe Gott wohnt im Detail": Briefwechsel 1969-1969. Herausgegeben von Asaf Angermann © Suhrkamp Verlag Berlin 2015. | Includes bibliographical references and index. | Summary: "Thirty years of epistolary friendship between two towering figures of the 20th century"-- Provided by publisher.
Identifiers: LCCN 2020005504 (print) | LCCN 2020005505 (ebook) | ISBN 9781509510450 (hardback) | ISBN 9781509510498 (epub)
Subjects: LCSH: Adorno, Theodor W., 1903-1969. Correspondence Selections English. | Scholem, Gershom, 1897-1982. Correspondence. | Authors, German--20th century--Correspondence. | Intellectuals--Germany--Correspondence. | Germany--Intellectual life--20th century.
Classification: LCC B3199.A34 A4213 2020 (print) | LCC B3199.A34 (ebook) | DDC 193 [B]--dc23
LC record available at https://lccn.loc.gov/2020005504
LC ebook record available at https://lccn.loc.gov/2020005505

Typeset in 10.5 on 12 Sabon by
Servis Filmsetting Ltd, Stockport, Cheshire
Printed and bound by TJ Books Ltd, Padstow, Cornwall

For further information on Polity, visit our website: politybooks.com

Contents

Introduction

"Overall, my memory of this might involve much retrospective fantasy," Theodor W. Adorno reminisced about his first encounter with Gershom Scholem, which must have taken place sometime around 1923.

> Anyway, the setting was the Frankfurt Civic Hospital; it seems to me that it was the garden. He was wearing a bathrobe, if I didn't retroactively make that up, associating it with the impression of a Bedouin prince, which he invoked in me with his blazing eyes – at a time when I was blissfully ignorant of the situation in the Near East. It was this ignorance that made me irreverently say to him that I was envious of his imminent travel to Palestine – it was nothing other than the emigration itself. I imagined the Arab girls to be so appealing, wearing copper chains on their slender ankles. Scholem responded, in that truly down-to-earth Berlin dialect, which he kept through forty-five years of Zion and which the great Hebraist, as a rumor has it, faithfully preserved even in his Hebrew pronunciation: "Well, then you could readily get a knife stuck between your ribs."[1]

This recollection, which may seem to be rather sexist and orientalist, filled, however, with fascination and admiration, featured in Adorno's congratulatory article on Scholem's seventieth birthday in December 1967. The concrete occasion for that first encounter was a visit to Siegfried Kracauer, the philosopher and cultural critic, who, as Scholem later recalled, had been hospitalized that day for a "minor malady." Kracauer was a mutual friend of Adorno and Walter Benjamin, and it was Benjamin who had brought Scholem along for the hospital visit. For his part, Scholem was hardly aware of Adorno's presence at that visit and was only reminded of it by

Adorno decades later.[2] For Adorno, Scholem not only represented the Jewish sage – knowledgeable in all matters religious, especially regarding the mystical and esoteric – but he also seemed to be the conduit to a realm of cognition that transcends the given social reality, with its instrumental mores. Adorno's nebulous memory of their first encounter includes such esoteric, mystical, and indeed orientalist elements, which he associated with Scholem's life and work, as well as the latter's harsh, pragmatic words of caution: getting carried away with such fantasies could result in being knifed between the ribs. Adorno, the rational critic of irrational society, sought an alternative to instrumental rationality in Scholem's worldview, while Scholem, the renowned scholar of Jewish mysticism, was himself never weary of warning of mysticism's temptations and dangers.[3] "It was my first information about the conflict that reverberates in the world today," Adorno concluded his reminiscence, which he published in the widely read German-language Swiss newspaper *Neue Zürcher Zeitung* six months after the Arab–Israeli "Six-Day War" of June 1967.

The first brief encounter at the Frankfurt Hospital was followed by a decade and a half in which there was no communication whatsoever between Adorno and Scholem. However, each of them was virtually present in the other's exchanges with their mutual friend Walter Benjamin. Benjamin's continuous efforts to bring about an amicable relationship between his two close friends were often met with suspicion, skepticism, and presumably also some envy. Scholem – who had known Benjamin since 1915, when the two were eighteen and twenty-three years old, respectively – persistently resisted any closer bond with Adorno. Adorno, born in 1903, met Benjamin in 1923 in Frankfurt, either during a sociology seminar that both attended – Adorno as a student, Benjamin while pursuing his *Habilitation* (a second doctorate required in Germany for academic posts) – or else at a meeting arranged by Kracauer in a Frankfurt café. Adorno was not able to recall which of these occasions occurred first.[4] Scholem had also lived for a short time in Frankfurt, before leaving for Palestine to pursue his Zionist political belief in a new Jewish national beginning. He had arrived in Frankfurt from Berlin in April 1923 and stayed until August of that year, before returning to Berlin, from which he left for Palestine in September.[5] During that brief stay in Frankfurt, in which his fleeting first encounter with Adorno took place, there was ample opportunity for the two to develop a more substantial personal or scholarly relationship. Not only were Adorno and Scholem mutual friends of Benjamin's, but they also socialized in intersecting intellectual circles. Both Benjamin and Kracauer, alongside, for example, Erich Fromm and Leo Löwenthal – all four would later belong to the wider circle around the Frankfurt Institute of Social Research – attended the Freies Jüdisches Lehrhaus ("Free Jewish House of Learning"), an institute for Jewish education established in 1920 by philosopher Franz Rosenzweig in Frankfurt. Among other attendees – who were at the same time instructors, as the Lehrhaus was based on communal learning rather than teacher-centered classes – were Martin Buber and Ernst Simon, as well as Scholem, who taught and studied Kabbalistic texts in Hebrew while there. Adorno kept his distance from the happenings at the Lehrhaus, however. Born to a Jewish father and a Catholic mother, Adorno entertained no particular interest in Jewish matters, religious, cultural, or otherwise. In fact, he reportedly referred derisively to his friends Fromm and Löwenthal as "*Berufsjuden*" ("professional Jews"), on account of their involvement in the Lehrhaus.

Scholem, for his part, made no effort to conceal his disdain for Adorno. "A strange reluctance kept me from an encounter with Adorno, which was due at that time and which he probably expected," he recalled almost half a century later.[6] "I wrote Walter about this. He replied that my reserved remarks about Adorno could not keep him from drawing my attention to Adorno's recently published first work on Kierkegaard."[7] Adorno's first book, *Kierkegaard: Construction of the Aesthetic*, was published in 1933 – "on the very same day in which Hitler seized the dictatorship," as Adorno himself noted.[8] The book, based on Adorno's *Habilitation*, which was written under the direction of the theologian Paul Tillich, was considerably indebted to the method that Benjamin had developed in his own work, *Origin of the German Trauerspiel*, based on his failed effort at a *Habilitation*. Benjamin's method involved reading material and social phenomena allegorically so as to decipher their hidden "truth-content."[9] Both Benjamin and Scholem received the page proofs of Adorno's Kierkegaard book before publication. Following months of Benjamin's persistent attempts to persuade Scholem to read Adorno's book, Scholem finally wrote to Benjamin, in October 1933: "to my mind the book combines a sublime plagiarism of your thought with an uncommon chutzpah, and it will ultimately not mean much for a future, objective appraisal of Kierkegaard, in marked contrast to your analysis of the *Trauerspiel*. I regret that our opinions probably differ in this matter."[10] Whether Scholem's scathing critique of the book was motivated by political aversion due to Adorno's Marxist approach (which Scholem generally rejected, although he critically tolerated Benjamin's own Marxist positions), because of Adorno's detachment from Frankfurt's Jewish circles and from Judaism altogether (which Scholem interpreted as assimilatory and opportunistic self-denial), or perhaps motivated by his envy of Adorno's close friendship with Benjamin, the latter's attempts to establish an amicable and productive relationship between these two great Jewish-German minds repeatedly led to a dead end. At least this was the case when both men lived in Frankfurt, surrounded by the same friends, arguably concerned with similar questions of identity, tradition, and prejudice.

This state of affairs had dramatically changed a few years later, on the other side of the Atlantic, as the world was sinking into murderous chaos. Adorno and Scholem encountered each other again in New York in 1938. Adorno had just arrived in the city, joining Horkheimer at the Institute for Social Research's new incarnation in exile at Columbia University, and also working on the Princeton Radio Research Project directed by an Austrian-Jewish émigré, sociologist Paul Lazarsfeld. Scholem traveled to New York from Jerusalem – via Paris, where he saw Benjamin for the last time – to deliver the Hilda Stich Stroock Lectures on Jewish mysticism at the Jewish Institute of Religion. On the ship from France, Scholem met Paul Tillich. It was Tillich who succeeded in initiating the contact between Adorno and Scholem, despite the difficult premises. Scholem reported to Benjamin on March 25, 1938: "Wiesengrund wasn't aboard the ship, and he hasn't been in touch with me either. However, I did meet with Tillich and his wife, who are resolutely determined to bring me together with Horkheimer and Wiesengrund, with whom, they said, they are very close, which placed me in a somewhat embarrassing position."[11]

But, as soon as the meeting took place, both sides readily overcame their predispositions. Scholem's disdain and mistrust of Adorno was transformed into a careful appreciation motivated by the discovery of mutual interests (although he retained an unrelenting aversion toward Horkheimer). Adorno's animadversion toward Scholem's demonstrative Jewish-theological approach, while not overcome, was softened by the latter's enthusiasm for those radical, heretical dimensions of Judaism which might have resonated, to some extent, with the drives behind the project of critical theory. Both eagerly conveyed their impressions of that meeting, and of each other, to Benjamin. Their accounts shed much light on the origins and foundations of the long-lasting and wide-ranging dialogue that ensued. On May 6, just a few weeks after his arrival in New York, Scholem wrote to Benjamin that he:

> was able to establish a very sympathetic relationship [with Wiesengrund-Adorno]. I like him immensely, and we found quite a lot to say to one another. I intend to cultivate relations with him and his wife quite vigorously. Talking with him is pleasant and engaging, and I find it possible to reach agreement on many things. You shouldn't be surprised by the fact that we spend a great deal of time mulling over your situation.[12]

Benjamin responded from Paris two months later: "I was pleased to see that some things go smoothly as soon as my back is turned. How many complaints have I heard *de part et d'autre* about you and Wiesengrund! And now it all turns out to have been much ado about nothing. Nobody is more pleased about that than I am."[13]

Decades later, Scholem explained his sudden change of heart at these meetings, further elucidating his perspective on the beginning of his friendship with Adorno:

> The good spirit that prevailed in the meetings between Adorno and me was due not so much to the cordiality of the reception as to my considerable surprise at Adorno's appreciation of the continuing theological element in Benjamin. I had expected a Marxist who would insist on the liquidation of what were in my opinion the most valuable furnishings in Benjamin's intellectual household. Instead I encountered here a man who definitely had an open mind and even a positive attitude toward these traits, although he viewed them from his own dialectical perspective.[14]

Adorno reported to Benjamin on this remarkable meeting in a letter from March 1938:

> You may find this hard to believe, but the first time we got to meet him [Scholem] was at the Tillichs. . . . Not exactly the best atmosphere in which to be introduced to the Sohar; and especially since Frau Tillich's relationship to the Kabbala seems to resemble that of a terrified teenager [*Backfisch*: also, literally, fried fish] to pornography. The antinomian Maggid was extremely reserved towards me at first, and clearly regarded me as some sort of dangerous arch-seducer. . . . Needless to say, nothing of the kind was actually said, and Scholem contrived to sustain the fiction, with considerable brash grace, that he knew nothing at all about me except that a book of mine had been published by the blessed Siebeck [publisher of Adorno's book on Kierkegaard]. Nevertheless, I somehow succeeded in breaking the spell and he began to show some kind of trust in me, something which I think will continue to grow.
>
> We have spent a couple of evenings together, as the ringing in your ears has presumably already told you by now; once on our own, in a discussion which touched in part upon our own last conversation in San Remo concerning theology, and in part upon my Husserl piece, which Scholem read with great care, as if it were some intelligence test. We spent the second evening in the company of Max, and Scholem, who was in great form, regaled us in detail with the most astonishing things in connection with Sabbatian and Frankist mysticism; a number of which, however, sounded so clearly reminiscent of some of Rosenberg's notions about "the people," that Max was seriously concerned about the prospect of more

of this kind actually appearing in print. It is not altogether easy for me to convey my own impression of Scholem. This is indeed a classic case of the conflict between duty and inclination. My personal inclination comes into play most strongly when he makes himself the advocate [*Anwalt*] of the theological moment of your, and perhaps I might also say of my own, philosophy.[15]

It is remarkable, though perhaps not surprising, that in this letter Adorno critically and presciently diagnoses exactly what Scholem would write years after his death, namely of the theological element not only in Benjamin's but also in his – Adorno's – own thought. Already during their first conversations, Adorno and Scholem discovered that they shared much more with each other than they had initially themselves presumed. Scholem displayed what seems to be a genuine and profound interest in Adorno's work. Although he dismissed the main thesis of Adorno's Kierkegaard book and accused its author of plagiarism, Scholem was indeed intrigued by the materialist, dialectical reading of a theological thinker. Adorno's work on Husserl, which began as his dissertation and continued – with various versions of papers published along the way – until the publication in 1956 of his book on Husserl, *Zur Metakritik der Erkenntnistheorie* [trans. as *Against Epistemology: A Metacritique*], seems to have sparked Scholem's own philosophical interest. Scholem's initially critical and often dismissive approach toward Adorno's work (in letters to Benjamin and others) was increasingly overturned, and he ultimately came to discover a common language with the dialectical social philosopher. His interest in Adorno's work, although motivated at first by Benjamin and the proximity to his work, largely transcends their shared interest in all things Benjamin. Adorno and Scholem's correspondence reveals, for the first time, the full scope of the thematic resonance that they found with each other.

Adorno, for his part, was – cautiously – fascinated by Scholem's work on religious mysticism and its heretical, transgressive offshoots. Baptized as a Catholic and raised in an assimilated Jewish family, which kept its distance from anything "professionally Jewish," Adorno was never a religious thinker, and even less so a Jewish thinker – at least not conspicuously. His interest in Kierkegaard's theological thought was philosophical and predominantly aesthetic. Furthermore, as a harsh critic of irrationality and the occult, Adorno had an attitude toward Kabbalah and the mystical dimensions of life that could not, at first glance, have been more apprehensive. But in Scholem's writings he did not perceive an irrational relapse into mythical thinking of the sort he critically diagnoses, for example, in *Minima Moralia*, as occultism. "The tendency to occultism," he notes there, "is a symptom of regression in consciousness. This has lost the power to think the unconditional and to endure the conditional."[16] On the contrary, Scholem's work on mysticism represented for Adorno an alternative to the all-consuming power of instrumental reason, a realm of possibilities beyond the given social order and the limitations that this social order imposed on thought and the imagination. As Adorno understood Scholem's project, mysticism does not necessarily seek to transcend the given reality in order to escape to an imaginary realm outside of it. Rather than fleeing the conditional into a regressive and escapist form of metaphysical surrogate for this world, it translated concrete, material, earthly life into mystical categories, thereby allowing for a critical perspective on this life.

At the time of their first encounter in 1938, Scholem had already published a significant body of work on various aspects of Jewish mysticism. His Munich dissertation, a German translation of the Bahir, the first book of the Kabbalah, was published in 1922. His annotated German translation of a chapter from the Zohar, the most central book of the Kabbalah, furnished with his detailed introduction on the book's historical and conceptual aspects, was published in 1935. In his lectures at the Jewish Institute of Religion in New York, held at the time of his first conversations with Adorno, Scholem elaborated on this topic, which was the subject, in part, of their discussion. But at that time Scholem was enthusiastically pursuing pioneering research into another dimension of Jewish mysticism, namely heretical messianism. In 1937, he published a text that would become a signpost of modern scholarship on Sabbatianism and Frankism, the Jewish heretical movements of the seventeenth and eighteenth centuries that followed the self-proclaimed messiahs Sabbatai Sevi (1626–1676) and Jacob Frank (1726–1791), respectively. "Mitzvah ha-ba'ah ba'averah" – literally: a commandment fulfilled by transgression – initially published only in Hebrew, was translated into English only decades later, in 1971, as "Redemption through Sin."[17] Aware of the subject's delicate, controversial dimensions and its inflammatory potential, Scholem insisted on keeping a discussion of its topic within the boundaries of Jewish communities. He published an abbreviated, expurgated German version of the text, excluding all the transgressive and contentious elements.[18] The Sabbatian and Frankist movements, Scholem explained, drew from Kabbalistic cosmogonic theories, especially Lurianic Kabbalah – the teachings of Rabbi Isaac Luria of Safed in the sixteenth century – on the notions of good and evil, and concluded that, in order to achieve redemption in times of exile and catastrophe, the messiah and his followers are commanded to transgress prevailing norms and laws, to commit evil deeds, overturning divine law and religious commandments. The original Hebrew text discusses such transgressions in detail – from moral crimes to forbidden sexual acts and religious blasphemies, culminating in apostasy: Sabbatai Sevi converted to Islam, Jacob Frank to Christianity. The followers of both, however, retained their Jewish faith beneath the ostensive practice of their newly acquired religions as crypto-Jews, forever the subject of suspicion and aversion. But the need to transgress the given law, to challenge predominant morality for the sake of true redemption and liberation, was the main motif of Scholem's own modern rendering of the Sabbatian and Frankist doctrines. This was the subject of Scholem's conversations in New York with Theodor and Gretel Adorno, attended by Max Horkheimer, who, as noted above, feared that such scholarship might only affirm certain anti-Semitic prejudices (the year was 1938), and he was "seriously concerned about the prospect of more of this kind actually appearing in print." Adorno himself, however, must have been better able to relate to Scholem's theory, in particular to its disobedient, anti-normative, and anti-authoritarian – one might also suggest: anarchist – elements. Additionally, Scholem's historical reading of heretical messianism emphasized the materialistic, social, and psychological aspects of such soteriological theories. Rather than explaining them from a merely theological point of view, Scholem offered an interpretation that analyzed the heretical mysticism of the Sabbatian and Frankist movements – as well as Lurianic Kabbalah in which they originated – as giving expression to the material, social, and psychological needs of the exiled Jewish communities. Later on, in his autobiography *From Berlin to Jerusalem*, he in fact referred to Adorno and the Frankfurt School as a latter-day incarnation of such heretical sects.[19]

Nevertheless, whereas the personal meetings transformed Scholem's perception of Adorno, enabling him to transcend his initially skeptical premises and suspicions, Adorno, for his part, experienced this encounter as more complex. Along with his fascination for Scholem's anarchist mystical theories and his respect for the latter's erudition in both German philosophy and Jewish history, Adorno was also somewhat perplexed by his theological – one might add, arguably, political-theological – worldview. Specifically, as he noted in his report to Benjamin, Adorno was definitely uneasy about Scholem's heavy-handed effort to advance the theological element in Benjamin's – and in his own – thought. Scholem, Adorno suspected, claimed authority not only over Benjamin's thought, which conspicuously merged theology with materialism, but also over Adorno's own philosophy, in which – despite numerous theological references and metaphors – theology ultimately plays a rather marginal role.

Such proximities of interest and differences of perspective did, however, allow Adorno and Scholem to establish a fruitful and profound dialogue. At the same time, it is important to note that their differences and dissensions were initially expressed only covertly, mainly in letters to Benjamin. After Benjamin's death, they were transmuted into a less tangible, underlying tenor of the exchange. As the correspondence shows, these differences were not detrimental to their relationship but contributed, rather, to the sensitive and nuanced communication. They added an underlying facet of irony that continuously conceals but never eliminates the discrepancies. Precisely because of these proximities and differences, much is left unsaid in the correspondence. What the authors agree on is assumed as a given; what they disagree about is softened in order to avoid confrontations. Although continuously kept at bay, however, the tensions – interpersonal and, more substantially, theoretical, conceptual, and perspectival – are hard to overlook. The correspondence therefore requires a form of active reading between the lines, of filling in the gaps with information available through other sources. What the authors write to each other gains an additional dimension once it is read in the light of their exchanges with Benjamin and others, as well as their published and unpublished writings.

Benjamin's suicide in 1940 – which took place when he was attempting to escape the Nazi occupation of France but was turned back at the French border in Port-Bou, Spain – deeply affected his two close friends. Their correspondence, which began a year before Benjamin's death, grew more intense as they shared reports about his precarious situation, and their concerns about his fate became grave. After his death, their recently forged friendship was strengthened by their mutual efforts to preserve Benjamin's legacy. Adorno and Scholem joined forces in the project of editing and publishing Benjamin's writings and letters. Although not completely unknown, Benjamin's work eluded widespread public attention during his lifetime. His numerous newspaper articles and literary reviews, along with the four books he published between 1920 and 1928 (with an annotated edition of letters written by German intellectuals, entitled *Deutsche Menschen* [German men and women], in 1936), could not have guaranteed him the reputation he enjoyed in the succeeding decades. This reputation is entirely indebted to his friends' efforts – against all odds and in the face of countless obstacles. The correspondence provides extensive evidence of the struggles Adorno and Scholem undertook to establish Walter Benjamin as the outstanding seminal figure of modern European thought that he has meanwhile become. Readers familiar with Benjamin's work may find it surprising to discover in the correspondence that, without Adorno and Scholem's monumental efforts and harsh struggles, Benjamin's writings – and his status as an intellectual figure – would most likely have been doomed to oblivion. It is perhaps no exaggeration to suggest that Walter Benjamin as we know him today, as a writer, philosopher, and cultural critic, is, to a certain degree, a "product," a "creation" fashioned by his two close friends. Not only did Adorno and Scholem struggle to bring Benjamin's writing into the light of the public, they were also concerned with each and every detail of the way Benjamin – both the man and his work – would be received and perceived. As editors of the first publication of his collected writings, they made careful choices as to which texts to include and how to present them, bringing to the fore those writings that they considered significant and representative of his thought and omitting those that they would rather not have seen published. In any event, this was the harsh critique leveled at the two editors following the publications of Benjamin's collected writings and correspondence. They were charged with manipulating the content and the reception of his work, reclaiming his thought as either too Marxist or too theological. Wherever one falls with respect to these accusations, the correspondence between Adorno and Scholem shows that their editorial work, and their efforts to establish Benjamin's intellectual legacy, involved substantial theoretical and practical debates on how to decipher, interpret, and present his thought.

In 1950, Adorno published Benjamin's *Berlin Childhood around 1900*, a collection of literary, autobiographical aphorisms, which Benjamin intended, without success, to publish in book form. (Some of these aphorisms were published in journals, most of them pseudonymously).[20] Adorno edited the book based on the manuscript he had previously received from Benjamin and on their earlier conversations. He also wrote an afterword, which he did not sign. The volume was published by the newly established Suhrkamp Verlag, as the second title in its prestigious series Bibliothek Suhrkamp. It was a colossal commercial failure.[21] A first collection of Benjamin's writings, under the modest title *Schriften* [Writings], was published a few years later, edited by Gretel and Theodor Adorno, together with Friedrich Podszus, the editor for Suhrkamp. They were substantially assisted by Scholem, who, as Adorno writes in the introduction (this time signed with his name), "provided the manuscripts of the early writings and altogether contributed to the realization of the project with his advisory participation."[22] The two-volume edition was published in 1955, making Benjamin's work available to a broader audience for the first time. In the following years, Adorno collaborated with Scholem on an edited collection of Benjamin's letters. Published in 1966, the collection received significant attention and led to a wide-ranging discussion of Benjamin's life and work. Whereas Benjamin's early writings had received hardly any attention, and the publisher – reluctant to avoid another unmarketable Benjamin volume – balked even at the idea of a volume collecting his letters, the response to this publication was spectacular. In fact, the debates on Benjamin's legacy were so intense – especially among the German student movements, which were overwhelmingly inspired by his thought – that Adorno actually felt compelled to lock Benjamin's manuscripts away inside a vault – far from the madding crowd. It was at this point that Adorno and Scholem were accused – by the political student movements in Berlin and West Germany, and by literary scholars and journalists, even in East Germany – of manipulating the reception of Benjamin's work according to their own views. The main concern of these critics was that Adorno and Scholem had overemphasized the theological moment in Benjamin's thought at the expense of his Marxism. Whatever the historical truth in the case might be, if it is at all determinable, the correspondence testifies to its authors' unwavering commitment to establish Benjamin's legacy, against all odds, while defending their own authority, as editors and self-appointed estate managers, against attacks from a multiplicity of sides.

Whereas, at the outset of their correspondence, Benjamin was the connecting link between Adorno and Scholem, after his death he becomes the missing – yet ever present – link. Likewise, the correspondence between Adorno and Scholem is the hitherto missing angle in a triangle. It completes a triangle that began in 1980, when Scholem edited for publication his own exchange with Benjamin from the years 1933 to 1940. The impetus behind this publication was the unearthing of his own correspondence with Benjamin, previously considered lost. Scholem learned in 1966 that large portions of this correspondence with Benjamin had survived in Paris and were stored in the East German archives. As it turned out, Scholem's earlier letters to Benjamin, left in the latter's Berlin apartment, were confiscated by the Gestapo, but the letters sent to Benjamin in Paris were discovered – in boxes related to the *Pariser Tageszeitung*, a journal of German émigrés in Paris – by the Red Army. They were transferred to Moscow from Paris, and from there they were sent to the East German Central Archives in Potsdam. Later on, they were moved to the Literary Archives in East Berlin, which Scholem visited in 1966. More than ten years elapsed before Scholem received copies of these letters, in 1977, which made possible the publication – edited and annotated by Scholem – of his own correspondence with Benjamin. The correspondence between Adorno and Benjamin constituted the next angle of the triangle. It includes letters from 1928, when Benjamin lived in Berlin and Adorno in Frankfurt, until Benjamin's death in 1940. From the years preceding Benjamin's escape to Paris, only

Benjamin's letters survived. Adorno's pre-1934 letters, like Scholem's – presumably left behind in Benjamin's Berlin apartment – are irretrievably missing. The correspondence, edited by Henri Lonitz from the Frankfurt Adorno archive, was published by Suhrkamp in 1994, as the first volume of Adorno's correspondences with friends, colleagues, and his parents.

The present volume, which formally completes the triangle, was originally published in 2015 as the eighth volume in the series of Adorno's collected correspondence. As Jürgen Habermas wrote in his review of the German volume, the correspondence is "documentation of one of the finest hours of German-Jewish intellectual history – after the Holocaust . . . a reminder of the widely ramified network of relationships between a grand generation of German-Jewish intellectuals – including rivalries and viciousness in this small academic-literary world in which Ernst Bloch and Georg Lukács, Martin Buber and Siegfried Kracauer, Helmuth Plessner, Hannah Arendt, and Herbert Marcuse lived next-door to one another" (*Die Zeit*, April 2015). The volume virtually begins where the two others end. Already in the second letter of the correspondence, Scholem writes: "I am extremely worried about the fate of Walter Benjamin, from whom I have received very troubling news from Paris."[23] The following letters discuss possibilities for saving Benjamin's life, until in the fifth letter, from October 1940, Adorno conveys that "Walter Benjamin has taken his life."[24] From there, efforts are made to understand the exact circumstances of Benjamin's death and to rescue his work and legacy. Despite the authors' diverging viewpoints of Benjamin's thought, they succeed in overcoming their differences to unfold a comprehensive – critical, but constructive – conversation regarding the substance, meaning, and power of Benjamin's work.

Nevertheless, the intellectual relationship between Adorno and Scholem encompasses far more than their joint efforts to establish and sustain their mutual friend's legacy. The present correspondence documents their substantial, wide-ranging, and far-reaching dialogue. In particular, it shows that Adorno and Scholem read each other's work with serious interest and enthusiastically reported to each other of their reading experiences. Adorno, the Marxist social philosopher and cultural critic, emerges as a dedicated reader and admirer of Scholem's work on Jewish mysticism. As he reported to Scholem, Adorno read the latter's *Major Trends in Jewish Mysticism* (based on Scholem's 1938 New York lectures and published in 1941) "repeatedly [and] internalized it as well as anyone can who does not speak Hebrew. In substance, I was most powerfully moved by the chapter on Lurianic mysticism, the basic concepts of which appear infinitely productive to me."[25] It is not surprising, therefore, that Kabbalistic motifs found their way into Adorno's own writings. Scholem, the anti-Marxist historian of religion, read Adorno's various writings with great care, often critically – but respectfully and constructively – pointing out problems and difficulties and not hesitating to suggest his own interpretations of his friend's work. Having read *Minima Moralia: Reflections from a Damaged Life*, Adorno's first book to be published in post-war Germany, a collection of social and cultural critical aphorisms on life in late capitalism, Scholem was inclined to assign the book to the long tradition of esoteric writings of negative theology: "I am not sure," he wrote, "whether I always fully grasped your intentions, which, in keeping with a great esoteric tradition, lie hidden within the dialectic; nonetheless, your treatise appears to me to be one of the most a remarkable documents of negative theology."[26] Adorno, for his part, responded that, "as for [the] reading of my book of aphorisms in terms of a negative theology, I have no objections, provided that this reading remains as esoteric as the subject itself. If, however, one translates the book straightforwardly into theological categories . . . then neither the book nor, presumably, the categories feel quite at ease."[27] Instead of rejecting each other's work from their divergent and, arguably, opposed perspectives on life, philosophy, and scholarship, Adorno and Scholem both chose to make each other's work applicable to their own. Accordingly, the correspondence sheds light on Adorno's hitherto unknown interest in Kabbalah and its impact on his own thought and writings. It also reveals Scholem's interest in critical theory, as well as the dialectical-materialist dimensions of his own scholarship on Jewish mysticism.

The letters comprising this volume provide a rare insight into a relationship that spans thirty years in a most turbulent time in history. The correspondence begins in 1939, only a year after Adorno's arrival in the US from England, where, having escaped Nazi Germany, he had spent the years between 1934 and 1938 unsuccessfully attempting to establish a scholarly career at the University of Oxford. It ends in 1969, with Adorno's death during a summer vacation in Switzerland. The underlying tone of the letters is implicitly shaped by the protagonists' divergent portentous life decisions and responses to the rise of anti-Semitism and Nazism in Germany. Scholem's wish for a new life of Zionist self-determination motivated him as a young man, as early as 1923, to emigrate from his native Germany to the unknown shores of Palestine. This decision remains constantly at odds with Adorno's preference to remain in his hostile homeland for as long as possible, temporarily relocating when no alternative was at hand, first to England, and then to the United States, and returning to his home city of Frankfurt in 1949, only four years after the war ended.[28]

These personal and political choices were arguably related to – influenced by and influencing – the philosophical, historical, social, and political questions addressed in Adorno's and Scholem's scholarships. Scholem's decision to leave his native Germany behind and begin a new life in what he considered to be the promised land of the Jewish people was a political decision supported by and anchored in his scholarly work. For his part, Adorno continuously reflected philosophically on the meaning of life in exile, as well as on the meaning of a life in Germany in the wake of the Nazi Holocaust. During his years in exile, he made collaborative efforts with Max Horkheimer to understand – from the perspective of a philosophy of history – the *Urgeschichte* – that is, the primordial, underlying conception of history that could give an account of the relapse from progress to regression, from Enlightenment to destructive irrationality, as was elaborated in the *Dialectic of Enlightenment* (1944/1947).[29] After his return to Germany, Adorno sought to elucidate not only the mechanisms that lead to fascism and authoritarianism but also the methods for educating the masses, in particular the younger generations, to resist and combat prejudice and oppression.[30]

Thematically, the correspondence begins with an in-depth textual analysis, namely, Adorno's own interpretation of the Zohar, the Kabbalistic "Book of Splendor."[31] Adorno refers to Scholem's own translation, which the two discussed during their first conversations in New York, a copy of which Scholem sent to Adorno after his return to Jerusalem. The chapter translated by Scholem is entitled "Sitrei Torah" [The secrets of the Torah]. It provides a mystical interpretation of the biblical story of the world's creation in Genesis.[32] Now it was Adorno's turn to suggest his own interpretation – and this interpretation is not only illuminating in itself, it also provides a lens for understanding some of Adorno's most central concepts. In his reading of Scholem's translation, Adorno presents two substantial remarks: one concerns, as he writes, the history of philosophy, while the other concerns epistemology. Although the relation to Adorno's own work is not conspicuous at first glance, a close examination will reveal the intrinsic relation between his reading of the text and his own work from the same time: the "philosophical fragments" that will comprise his seminal *Dialectic of Enlightenment*, co-authored with Horkheimer just a few years later. The proximity raises the question as to whether Adorno "ha[s] not read out of it anything other than what [he has] read into it," as he is willing to admit, or whether these ideas found their way – directly or indirectly – into the reflections that constitute the *Dialectic of Enlightenment*'s main theses.

Firstly, Adorno detects in the Zohar chapter a proximity between Jewish mysticism and the Neoplatonic gnostic tradition. He aligns the

Zohar with the Western tradition of gnostic metaphysics, in which knowledge of the unknowable is sought in a negative way, through a search for the "remainders" of a presumed original experience, without presupposing such an experience. Adorno calls this a process of disintegration and emphasizes that, for him, the concept of disintegration carries no pejorative implications. On the contrary, understanding the process of disintegration is a most valuable method for a philosophy of history that seeks to detect historical truth by examining its demise. Although not explicitly stated in the letter, Benjamin's theories of truth and allegory – as presented in *Origin of the German Trauerspiel* are most decisive here: both Adorno and Scholem were familiar with it (Adorno, in fact, held seminars on the book in the early 1930s in Frankfurt), and it arguably shaped their views on the concept of historical truth. For Adorno, such disintegration of experience and truth is the process that generates myth. When truth and experience can no longer be recognized or communicated in their immediacy, they tend to be translated into myth. These are the historical origins of myth and of mythical thinking. These are, at the same time, the very mystical truths and experiences that the Enlightenment sought to annihilate, but failed to do so, since it could revert back to myth only by creating ever newer mythologies. Adorno describes this process here as "the transformation of spiritualism into myth." This, in a nutshell, is the argument that will be unfolded in the *Dialectic of Enlightenment*'s diagnosis, namely that "Myth is already enlightenment, and enlightenment reverts to mythology."[33]

Secondly, Adorno asks about the nature of symbolic representation in Jewish mysticism – namely, whether the symbols conceal a hidden reality which can become tangible through a process of deciphering that would allow us to see reality as it is, or whether we can only face an endless chain of symbols: as he puts it, "whether there is any ground in this hierarchy of symbols or whether it represents a bottomless fall."[34] The latter case raises the question of what Adorno calls "the context of delusion" [*Verblendungszusammenhang*]. This concept, which will become ever more central and decisive in Adorno's work, in the *Dialectic of Enlightenment* and in subsequent writings, is introduced here for the first time. It concerns the epistemological question as to the possibility of seeing beyond social and ideological delusion. If we are continuously being deceived by the mechanisms of power and domination, and if these mechanisms affect, first and foremost, our consciousness and our ability to see clearly and critically, then how is it possible to "see through the delusion"? This epistemological but, at the same time, social and political question is one of the most essential questions both in Adorno's work and in the Frankfurt School's critical theory overall. It is noteworthy that it is developed here, probably for the first time, by means of an interpretation of the Zohar.

It is fair to suggest that, while Adorno has never truly delved into the depths of Kabbalistic mysticism – or, for that matter, of any theological doctrine as such – he was indeed interested in its content and familiar with its ideas to the extent that he could reappropriate them for his own philosophical purposes. As noted above, having read Scholem's *Major Trends in Jewish Mysticism*, Adorno acknowledged the significance and productive potential of Lurianic Kabbalah. Initially developed by Rabbi Isaac Luria (1534–1572) in the community of Safed, located in the Galilee region of Palestine, and further articulated by his disciples (Luria himself produced no written texts; his teachings were transcribed by his disciples), Lurianic Kabbalah is a mystical theory of redemption. It provides a cosmogonic theory of the world's creation, as formed by an omnipotent God and shattered by His very omnipotence. Such shattering is deemed a crisis of destruction, which places the potential of mending and restitution in the hands of human beings. Metaphysical redemption depends, accordingly, on human agency. Luria calls it "*Tikkun*," mending. Although it is impossible to assert with absolute evidence, there is good reason to consider Adorno's final aphorism of *Minima Moralia* to be a response to such Lurianic metaphysics of shattering and restitution:

> The only philosophy which can be responsibly practiced in face of despair is the attempt to contemplate all things as they would present themselves from the standpoint of redemption. Knowledge has no light but that shed on the world by redemption: all else is reconstruction, mere technique. Perspectives must be fashioned that displace and estrange the world, reveal it to be, with its rifts and crevices, as indigent and distorted as it will appear one day in the messianic light.[35]

Beyond the use of theological, soteriological, and arguably Kabbalistic terminology, it seems that Adorno's very argument on the scope of redemption provides a response – which requires human agency and action – to what he perceives as "damaged life": the destruction of natural, individual life by late capitalism and its ideology. Viewed from this perspective, the subject of Adorno's book of aphorisms largely resonates with the destruction of divine powers in the mystical story of the world's creation in Luria's Kabbalistic metaphysics. In both cases – and this point is crucial to Adorno as much as it is crucial for Luria – metaphysical, theological redemption depends on ethics: on human, moral action.

To what extent, however, and in what sense can one speak of messianism in Adorno's philosophy? And how much of it is indeed indebted to Scholem's scholarship? This is one of the central and most intriguing questions that emerge from their correspondence. There are numerous hints and indications in Adorno's writings and throughout the correspondence, which call for various interpretations. But one version of messianism is decidedly pertinent in this context, namely that of heretical messianism. Before reading any of Scholem's published texts, Adorno learned at first hand of Scholem's research on the topic during their first conversations. Adorno had most likely not received a copy of Scholem's German text on the topic from 1937 (a copy of which Scholem sent to Benjamin), but he had read the relevant chapters in *Major Trends*. He also kept track of Scholem's papers for the Eranos conference, an annual meeting of scholars of religion, which took place in Ascona, Switzerland. Scholem participated regularly in these meetings and published his papers in the *Eranos Yearbook*. From the mid-1950s onward, Scholem's main research papers were first presented at these conferences, and published in the *Eranos Yearbook*, before finding their way into his own published collections of articles. Adorno attested to collecting and reading these works, some of which – especially on the topic of messianism, as he wrote – meant a great deal to him personally.[36]

An opportunity for Adorno to learn more about these matters presented itself in 1963. Scholem, who was probably inclined to make Adorno aware of the proximity between heretical messianism and the latter's own project of critical theory, suggested that he could contribute an article to the *Festschrift* celebrating Adorno's sixtieth birthday. The title of his initial suggestion was "Heretical Messianism and Jewish Society," implying a connection between his research on Sabbatianism and Adorno's social philosophy. The paper, included in the volume *Zeugnisse: Theodor W. Adorno zum 60. Geburtstag* [Testimonials: for Theodor W. Adorno's 60th birthday], edited by Max Horkheimer, was eventually entitled "Die Metamorphose des häretischen Messianismus der Sabbatianer in religiösen Nihilismus im 18. Jahrhundert" [The metamorphosis of the Sabbatians' heretical messianism into religious nihilism in the 18th century].[37] This is a remarkable but underexplored text. In it, Scholem seems to be conducting historical research into the formation of Frankism and its radical doctrine of unlawfulness and transgression as a means to redemption; however, under the guise of historical scholarship, he brings to light some remarkable affinities between this heretical doctrine and Adorno's own philosophy. For example, Scholem emphasizes the Frankists' understanding of the existing social order as governed by unjustified, oppressive laws. Therefore, Frank and his followers believed it to be the task of the individual to question, challenge, and transgress these laws. In this text, Scholem conjoins heretical theology with the critique of unjust laws and oppressive social normativity. The Frankist anti-authoritarian movement, Scholem surmises, resonates with some aspects of Adorno's philosophy – those aspects, one may assume, to which Scholem could relate positively, namely the anarchist dimensions of critical theory, which, by contesting the existing social order, aspired to a certain vision of utopian life.

In most cases, Adorno and Scholem maintained an amicable, gentle tone in their replies to each other, often suppressing and concealing dissensions and disagreements. But such dissensions and disagreements belong to the overall conversation, both on personal and on scholarly matters. Scholem, in particular, did not spare his critique of Adorno's writings, especially when they touched upon two matters about which he had profound views: Marxism and Zionism. The latter was particularly important to Scholem. The *Dialectic of Enlightenment*'s analyses of myth, culture, and human history conclude with a chapter entitled "Elements of Anti-Semitism." Overall, the book's topics largely converge with Scholem's various scholarly and historical-political interests. However, while Scholem generally accepted the premises and the arguments of the first historical-philosophical chapters on the dialectics of progress and regression and on the relation between myth and enlightenment, he was infuriated by the analysis of modern anti-Semitism in the book's final chapter. He left Adorno's queries about his response to the book unanswered, but he did study the text thoroughly, as the notes that he wrote in his own copy of the book and on the back of one of Adorno's letters attest.

In the sixth thesis of the "Elements of Anti-Semitism," Adorno and Horkheimer contend that[38]

> Only the liberation of thought from power, the abolition of violence, could realize the idea which has been unrealized until now: that the Jew is a human being. This would be a step away from the anti-Semitic society, which drives both Jews and others into sickness, and toward the human one.[39]

"Awful in his Marxist mendacity," Scholem commented. "So in Zion the Jew cannot be a human being?" Adorno and Horkheimer's insistence on the essential separation between thinking and power as the foundation of emancipation and the abolition of violence appears opposed to Scholem's understanding of Zionism as a recoupling of thought and power. Instead of liberating thought from its entanglement with power, thereby redeeming Jews from their continual subjection to those in power, as Adorno and Horkheimer demand, Scholem views Zionism as itself a reclamation of power, placing it in the hands of a Jewish political sovereignty. Scholem never expresses his critique explicitly in his letters to Adorno (and one may presume that it never became a subject of personal conversations either). Nonetheless, the matter continues to haunt their exchanges in a subterranean fashion. At the same time, Scholem was pleased to detect what he considered to be his own influence on Adorno's writings. When, in the chapter on anti-Semitism, Adorno and Horkheimer explain that "Reconciliation is Judaism's highest concept, and expectation its whole meaning,"[40] Scholem notes on the page margin: "Das hat er von mir" – "this he got from me."

To be sure, it is uncertain whether Adorno and Horkheimer – particularly Horkheimer, with whom Scholem shared a deep mutual antipathy – gained this knowledge from Scholem. However, Scholem's influence cannot be overlooked in Adorno's later writings. While it is debatable whether ideas such as in the aphorism from *Minima Moralia* cited above do indeed allude to Kabbalistic texts, Adorno's late *magnum opus* of 1966, *Negative Dialectics*, unquestionably draws on Scholem's scholarship to explicate some of the main tenets of Adorno's central question on the possibility of philosophy after the Holocaust. At the beginning of the book's final part, under the title "Meditations on Metaphysics" and its opening section "After Auschwitz," Adorno writes:

> One of the mystical impulses secularized in dialectics was the doctrine that the intramundane and historic is relevant to what traditional metaphysics distinguished as transcendence – or at least, less gnostically and radically put, that it is relevant to the position taken by human consciousness on the questions which the canon of philosophy assigned to metaphysics.[41]

Scholem, who had also thoroughly read and extensively annotated *Negative Dialectics*, noted in the margin next to these lines: "Kabbalah." Indeed, it was a central characteristic of mystical theories, including – but not limited to – Jewish Kabbalistic theories (Christian mysticism, and even the Christian reception of Kabbalah may be counted in this view),[42] to emphasize that actions and events that take place on earth, committed by human beings, effect and shape transcendence – that is, they have an impact on the divine. The intersection and interaction between worldly and transcendent entities play central roles in Kabbalah. Adorno introduces this mystical idea into his own re-evaluation of metaphysics: the catastrophe of the Holocaust makes it evidently clear, for Adorno, that worldly events shape the structure of metaphysics, of any realm beyond the here and now, and of any possible understanding of this realm. Understanding this context and the allusion to mystical impulses that connect the worldly with the transcendent sheds special light on Adorno's unique concept of metaphysics. Against Scholem's anti-Marxist view, such an intersection between concrete-material and abstract-metaphysical (or theological) elements conspicuously corresponds to Marx's historical dialectics, on which Adorno elaborates here. Adorno's concept of metaphysics, in its substantive difference from the long tradition of metaphysical thought in the Western canon, does not exclude the temporal, historical, material elements – the "intramundane" – from metaphysics. Metaphysics, for Adorno, is the study not of immediate and absolute essences and categories but, rather, of contingencies, eventualities, and possibilities.

Furthermore, in Adorno's emphasis on the mediated character of metaphysics – that is, on the fact that no metaphysics can ever claim to be immediate, unrelated to given, contingent historical and material matters – he draws again from theories of Jewish mysticism. "It has been observed," he argues, "that mysticism . . . establishes social traditions and comes from tradition, across the lines of demarcation drawn by religions that regard each other as heretical. Cabbala, the name of the body of Jewish mysticism, means tradition. In its farthest ventures, metaphysical immediacy did not deny how much of it is not immediate."[43] In his own copy of the book, Scholem noted in the margin next to these lines "Scholem." Indeed, it was Scholem who explained – in his first letter to Adorno, in response to the latter's own remark on the Zohar – that the literal meaning of Kabbalah is tradition, emphasizing its historically mediated character over any understanding of primordial immediacy. Kabbalah, similar to Adorno's philosophy, seeks not to understand any absolute proto-historical or meta-historical essence or experience but, rather, to draw an idea of transcendence – of material and utopian possibilities – from given historical experience, handed down over times and generations. Against this backdrop, Adorno's social philosophy and metaphysics, as a theory of political redemption and emancipation, may indeed appear to follow in the footsteps of the mystical heretics whom Scholem explored in his scholarship.

In addition – and not unrelated – to their scholarly interests, the experience of the Holocaust and the analysis of its meaning played a significant role in Adorno's and Scholem's thought and writings, though with divergent emphases and implications. For Adorno, the Holocaust marked the line of demarcation, after which it becomes impossible to continue adhering to any theory of meaning that does not take into metaphysical, philosophical consideration the historical events of the destruction. For Scholem, however, the Holocaust does not mark any line of demarcation at all: he viewed it as the radical but imminent result of a long process of Jewish assimilation, self-oblivion, and loss of agency. It is nevertheless remarkable that, despite – or perhaps because of – the radical impact of these events on the life of both authors (Scholem's brother Werner, a communist politician in the Weimar Republic, was deported to the Buchenwald concentration camp in 1938 and executed by the Nazis in 1940), their letters do not include an assessment or an interpretation of the meaning of the Holocaust, personally, historically, or ideologically. This, too, remains a decisive underlying facet of their exchange. In the post-war years, one of the central questions in their published writings, as much as in their private correspondence, concerns their relation to Germany and the possibility of a German-Jewish dialogue. Here, the biographical differences could not be more conspicuous. On behalf of the Hebrew University of Jerusalem, Scholem traveled to Europe in the post-war years to examine the situation of Jewish books and manuscripts that were either looted by the Nazis or left behind by their persecuted, and in most cases exterminated, owners. His first journey took place in 1946, as part of a two-man delegation alongside Avraham Yaari of the National Library in Jerusalem. Their expedition included cities that were centers of Jewish life and culture before the war, which were subsequently covered in debris and destruction. Beginning their journey in London and Paris, Scholem and Yaari traveled to Zurich, Prague, Frankfurt, Offenbach, Heidelberg, Munich, and Berlin. Scholem was devasted by the situation he faced in Europe. For one thing, he felt that it was impossible for him to accomplish the task he was assigned. He was deeply disappointed by the failure to find many of the manuscripts he was seeking and by the disarray of the depots housing the books whose original owners could not be identified. He was also dismayed by the unwillingness of the personalities responsible for the materials to allow for their transfer to the National Library in Jerusalem, which he had hoped to arrange. However, beyond the professional discontent and frustration, it was the humanitarian situation of the survivors that most appalled him. The visits to destroyed synagogues and communities, and to camps of displaced persons, left Scholem with a most distressing impression – not only on account of the concrete situation of the survivors but also concerning the very idea of the possibility of Jewish life in Germany. The visit had a long-lasting negative effect on Scholem's psyche, and it also seems to have affected his overall health. It took him a long time to recover, and some argue that he never fully recovered from the trauma of the visit. His wife Fania wrote of his personal situation after his return from the journey:

> He returned to the Land of Israel physically exhausted and mentally depressed. He would lie down for most of the day, doing nothing, hardly

> speaking with anyone, and only occasionally repeat sentences like: "The Jewish people has been murdered, has ceased to exist, only smoldering stumps are left, with no strength or direction. Their source of nourishment no longer exists, the people has been cut off at the root. And we in Israel, a handful of people, the remnant (*sheerit hapletah*), will we really find the strength to build the creative, free society, not materialistic, for the sake of whose formation we came here? Maybe we won't succeed in the task and we will degenerate, because we are bereft of our nation, we are orphaned." He was prostrate on his bed, going from couch to couch in his house, without finding repose for himself. Scholem refused to be consoled and he only became himself again and recovered a year later.[44]

In the years that followed, Scholem was increasingly involved in debates on German-Jewish relations. Consistent with his position from the 1920s and 1930s, but with an added dimension of bitter disillusionment, he was critical and dismissive of the very idea of a "German-Jewish dialogue." That is, he was not only critical of the possibility of renewing and preserving such a dialogue after the Holocaust, but he was profoundly skeptical of the very thought that such a dialogue had ever existed. In 1964, he wrote explicitly,

> I deny that there has ever been such a German-Jewish dialogue in any genuine sense whatsoever, i.e., as a historical phenomenon. It takes two to have a dialogue, who listen to each other, who are prepared to perceive the other as what he is and represents, and to respond to him. Nothing can be more misleading than to apply such a concept to the discussions between Germans and Jews during the last 200 years. This dialogue died at its very start and never took place.[45]

Scholem maintained this argument over various discussions and publications in the post-war years. For a long time after his journey in search of the lost and looted libraries, he avoided further visits to Germany, and refrained particularly from any public appearances. This applied, however, specifically to Germany. In fact, the situation proved to be rather complex, since Scholem increasingly discovered that the main audience for his developing scholarship could not be limited to the Hebrew University or, for that matter, to the newly established State of Israel. Remarkably, only a few years after the end of the Second World War, and only one year after the establishment of the State of Israel, where Scholem had been one of the leading academic figures, he gradually – intentionally or not, consciously or not – transferred the centerpiece of his scholarly activities to Europe – not to Germany, but to Switzerland, and indeed to the German language. Beginning in 1949, he delivered most, if not all, of his substantial work at the Eranos conferences in Ascona and published it in German in the *Eranos- Yearbook*. Despite his own objections and against all odds, Scholem practically returned after the war to his native German culture, motivated by both pragmatic reasons of potential readership and publication context and by a certain disillusionment with the Zionist project he so eagerly pursued earlier in his life.[46]

Despite his gradual return to his native language and to European intellectual surroundings, Scholem nevertheless refused to speak publicly in Germany and to publish his German writings with a German publisher. In 1953 he wrote to Adorno that he deemed it impossible to speak in Germany after the war.[47] Three years later, Adorno informed Scholem of newly acquired funds for the initiative to hold at the Goethe University of Frankfurt guest lectures by distinguished scholars on central topics in Judaism.[48] The first speaker was Leo Baeck, in 1956. When Adorno formally invited Scholem to deliver a lecture in Frankfurt, Scholem responded: "Perhaps it is the time to speak up. I will think about it." (In German: "Vielleicht ist es an der Zeit, mal den Mund zu öffnen. Ich denke darüber nach." Literally: "Perhaps it is time to open the mouth. I will think about it.") Scholem eventually agreed. He delivered the Loeb Lectures on the Kabbalah in Safed in July 1957, speaking for the first time publicly in post-war Germany.

It was also Adorno's suggestion that motivated Scholem to publish again in Germany. Until the early 1960s, he published his German-language work with the Swiss publisher Rhein Verlag, directed by his friend Daniel Brody, which was also the publisher of the *Eranos Yearbooks*. Adorno personally introduced Scholem to Peter Suhrkamp, director of Suhrkamp Verlag, but Scholem initially rejected the idea of having his books of essays on Jewish mysticism published with Suhrkamp, maintaining that he was already committed to Rhein Verlag. However, a few years later, Siegfried Unseld, who replaced Peter Suhrkamp as director of Suhrkamp Verlag after the latter's death, proposed, once again, that Scholem publish a small volume of essays to be made available to a large German readership. This time Scholem accepted the offer. His first volume of essays, entitled *Judaica*, appeared with Suhrkamp Verlag in 1963, followed by five additional volumes under the same title (*Judaica II–VI*), alongside licenced editions of previously published works with Rhein Verlag. This marked the completion of Scholem's reluctant and critical return to Germany. Nevertheless, he did not discard his critique of the "myth of a German-Jewish dialogue," which was the title of an essay (originally published in 1964) included in the second of the *Judaica* volumes in 1970, alongside other essays on German-Jewish relations and the (im)possibility of Jewish life in Germany.

In contrast, Adorno's practical and theoretical response to the Holocaust and to the questions concerning German-Jewish relations was, at least at the outset, an antithesis to Scholem's. Adorno, for whom emigration to Palestine was never even a consideration, spent the years from 1933 to 1949 in exile. But as early as 1949, only four years after the end of the war, he decided to return to Germany. The decision is significant, especially in the light of Adorno's own diagnosis, which he still maintained ten years later, namely that "National Socialism lives on, and even today we still do not know whether it is merely the ghost of what was so monstrous that it lingers on after its own death, or whether it has not yet died at all, whether the willingness to commit the unspeakable survives in people as well as in the conditions that enclose them."[49] It is difficult to determine exactly what motivated Adorno and Horkheimer to return to their homeland so soon, relatively speaking, after the end of the war. Adorno himself suggested various reasons – ranging from what he considers his close, intimate relationship with the German language to his sense of moral and political responsibility to circumvent a return of the catastrophe.[50] Fifteen years after he had left Germany and eleven years after his arrival in the United States, Adorno returned to Frankfurt in October 1949. It was five months after the post-war Federal Republic of Germany was established in the areas occupied by the American, British, and French allies in West Germany. Frankfurt, the center of German finance, was located in the American Zone of Occupation. This might have given Adorno, a Frankfurt native, the sense of some continuity between his American and German experiences.

During his years in exile in America, Adorno participated in numerous research projects and was prolific in producing texts that would prove highly influential; alas, no prospect of an academic career was in sight for him. After returning to German academia in 1949, he initially only replaced Horkheimer, whose pre-war professorship at the University of Frankfurt had been renewed but who had not yet returned to the city to take up the position. Only in 1953 was Adorno offered an ordinary professorship. In the time between his return and his formal appointment, he traveled to the United States twice to participate in research activities and to cultivate further his research and scholarly contacts, but also – especially with the long stay from October 1952 to August 1953 – first and foremost in order to ensure that he retained his newly acquired naturalization as a US citizen.[51] Despite his commitment to return to Germany and to contribute to post-war enlightenment, and political education in particular, his uncertainty was still significant enough to necessitate these journeys. Adorno's long-term professional instability and insecurity in American exile was at odds with Scholem's secure and influential position in his newly adopted homeland in Palestine. This might have held implications for the differences between their views on diasporic life and the question of a return to Germany. After emigrating in 1923, Scholem initially worked as a librarian, directing the departments of Hebrew and Judaica at the Jerusalem National Library. But, shortly after the Hebrew University of Jerusalem was formally established in 1925, he was appointed as a lecturer, and in 1933 he was promoted to a full professorship of Jewish mysticism. It is noteworthy that this is the very year in which the Nazis revoked Adorno's license for academic teaching. Scholem's profound ideological faith in the Zionist idea as a solution to all theological, social, and political problems of the Jews was also, even more substantially, at odds with Adorno's skepticism about any such ideological, nationalist, and particularist solutions. The Holocaust and the Jewish catastrophe only strengthened Scholem's views on the need for a national Jewish home, whereas they only intensified Adorno's skepticism about such absolute solutions, deepening his worries about the threat of nationalism of any sort.

Such differences in worldviews are tacitly present throughout Adorno and Scholem's entire correspondence. Both aware of the fundamental discrepancies in their political thought, particularly regarding German-Jewish life, the two men remained cautious not to let these differences harm their friendship. But the differences were insurmountable: Scholem opted for a decisively particularist worldview, in which Jewish life and responsibility for fellow Jews were at the center of any ethical and political consideration, while Adorno, wary and vigilant of any such kind of political bias, held on to a universalist position – especially in reflections on the ethical meaning and political lessons to be learned from the experience of the Holocaust. He famously contended: "A new categorical imperative has been imposed by Hitler upon unfree mankind: to arrange their thoughts and actions so that Auschwitz will not repeat itself, so that nothing similar will happen."[52]

In his new role as a philosopher and public intellectual in post-war Germany, Adorno was increasingly dedicated to the task of educating the new generation of Germans to think critically, both philosophically and politically: not to accept unquestioned authorities, not to be tempted by any form of social prejudice or political chauvinism. He was committed to a "new categorical imperative" that would make a recurrence of the Holocaust impossible. Whereas Scholem's scholarly and political efforts focused on strengthening the Jewish moral and political consciousness in the form of Jewish nationalism, Adorno emphasized the necessity of a prevention of the recurrence of Auschwitz – that is, of the Jewish catastrophe (one should keep in mind here that, in Auschwitz, not only Jews were murdered) – and of anything "similar": "so that nothing similar will happen." Adorno was never content with a purely particularistic position. The new ethical responsibility, engrained in him by the experiences of the Holocaust, was for him, unlike for Scholem, universal. Such discrepancies also suggest themselves at the level of their intended readership: Adorno's writings, especially following his return to Germany, were aimed first and foremost at a German audience. From the late 1950s onward Adorno regularly, and enthusiastically, participated in radio conversations, progressively assuming the role of an engaged public intellectual. Scholem, who equally enjoyed the role of a public intellectual in the newly established State of Israel, was engaged in social and political matters of Israeli society. He published on matters of Jewish and Israeli politics, some of which were far removed from his immediate scholarly research on mysticism, such as the formation of Israeli political parties, dialogue with the Arab states, Israeli education, and the political-theological meaning of the Jewish diaspora. But over time Scholem's intended audience changed, along with his change of attitude regarding the prospect of public appearances and publications in Germany. His texts were now addressed predominantly to a German readership (not exclusively Germans, but readers of the German language) – and this shift of focus implied a shift of content as well.

In their letters from the 1960s, Adorno and Scholem both express a remarkable change of heart, resulting, presumably, from changing social and political constellations. Adorno, eager to return to his German homeland after the war in order to reform and educate the German masses to critical thought and enlightenment, was increasingly alienated in what was simultaneously his native and new-found home. A new generation of students, profoundly influenced by his critical theory and by his call for anti-authoritarian progressive thinking, now charged him, their own educator, with conservatism, bigotry, and resignation.[53] Struggling, since his return, with the national conservative tendencies in post-war West-German society, in which regime change had done little to alter the actual balance of power since many public offices continued to be filled by the very same people who had held them during the Nazi era, Adorno found himself in a new and unexpected situation in the late 1960s. His own students, demanding a full de-Nazification and a thorough democratic reform of German public universities, as well as protesting against the Vietnam War and the colonial politics in developing countries, now demanded their teacher's support and solidarity. Although Adorno supported many of these causes, he was reluctant to participate in what he considered barbaric and violent demonstrations of power, and he compared the students' revolts to fascist brutality. In December 1968, he reported to Scholem: "[A]ll hell has literally broken loose here, with a Walpurgis Night of the students, in which the pseudo-revolution is spinning out of control in the most ludicrous actions . . . they are committing atrocities."[54]

In what both Adorno and Scholem might have described as a dialectical paradox, toward the end of the 1960s their views and their experiences somewhat transformed and crossed paths: Scholem, who for decades had been reluctant to participate in any dialogue with German audiences, and who addressed his writings almost exclusively to Jewish, mostly Israeli, readers, now enthusiastically published his writings with Suhrkamp Verlag, held public lectures at the University of Frankfurt, and even recorded speeches and lectures to be broadcasted on German radio. Adorno, initially eager to return to the "new" Germany and to assume academic and political-pedagogic responsibilities there, now found himself disillusioned and isolated, a stranger in his own land, estranged by his own students. In addition to these developments at the university, Adorno experienced a form of overt and aggressive anti-Semitism during these years. As the correspondence reveals for the first time, Adorno even faced concrete and intimidating murder threats. Beginning in 1965, he received letters from a person of German origin and Ecuadorian citizenship, who initially expressed admiration for his work and sought his advice on intellectual matters, as well as his support in the professional quest for academic employment in both Germany and Israel. The letters then escalated to anti-Semitic clichés, complaining that all academic positions were occupied by Jews, whereas a man of German origins – "although," as he emphasized, he "hadn't personally murdered any Jews" – remained unemployed.[55] In 1967, the man threatened to murder Adorno should the latter not assist him in securing academic employment. He then announced his intention to travel to Jerusalem to commit murderous attacks. Adorno shared his knowledge of the matter and his concerns with Scholem. He also reported the information to the German authorities, who located and arrested the man. But Adorno, out of compassion, eventually dropped the charges against him, having realized that he suffered from mental illness. The case is significant not only biographically but also in a broader perspective, since the man's threats and anti-Semitic letters allow for a better understanding of the scope of anti-Semitism in post-war Germany, giving expression to widespread views and opinions on Jews, notwithstanding the process of "de-Nazification." It was precisely the man's mental illness and instability that allowed him openly to express views that were widely shared but socially suppressed and therefore only reluctantly and rarely overtly articulated.

As the violent and hostile events at the university were escalating, Adorno died of a heart attack while on vacation in August 1969. His untimely and sudden death occurred during an intense and momentous time of significant developments, both in a social-political perspective and within the scope of his friendship with Scholem. The final letters in the correspondence document in detail Adorno's hitherto largely unknown plans of a journey to Israel. In November 1968 he received a formal invitation from the Israeli National Council of Culture and Art to deliver lectures on music at a festival in Tel Aviv. In consultation with Adorno, Scholem enhanced the invitation with an offer to hold an additional lecture and a seminar at the Hebrew University of Jerusalem. Adorno was enthusiastic and at the same time reluctant to undertake the visit, which he considered "eminently encumbered."[56] Whereas questions of scheduling remained a subject of endless negotiations, the content of Adorno's prospective lectures was essentially established. Presenting his work for the first time to an Israeli audience, Adorno intended to deliver lectures on two topics he had deemed most relevant and most representative of his thought: one lecture was either to address a topic from his recently published *Negative Dialectics*, preferably the book's final chapter, "Meditations on Metaphysics," which discusses the possibility and the meaning of philosophical thought after the Holocaust, or else to discuss ideas from his work in progress, *Aesthetic Theory*, which was published posthumously. The second lecture was meant to concern his philosophy of music, either his philosophical interpretation of Mahler or that of Schoenberg, with a preference for the latter, who, Adorno wrongly assumed, was less known in Israel. The language in which Adorno was to speak presented another dilemma. Although it was rather probable that the audience would consist mostly of academics of European background – native German speakers and natives of other countries who had mastery in the German language – delivering a lecture in German in 1960s Israel might have been seriously offensive to many survivors. "Naturally, it is easier for me to speak about very difficult and complex things in German than in English," he wrote to Scholem, "but I would under no circumstances want to commit any kind of mistake. Precisely when one lives in Germany, one may not forget even for a moment what happened."[57] Although it was repeatedly postponed – in his very final letter to Scholem from May 1969, Adorno still considered scheduling the journey for September 1970 – the visit was ultimately rendered impossible by Adorno's sudden death. Nevertheless, what remains as pressing as ever are the theoretical – and hypothetical – questions concerning the probable reception and discussion of Adorno's thought in Israel, in particular regarding the possibility of philosophy after the Holocaust and of dealing with the German past.

Scholem traveled to Frankfurt for Adorno's funeral immediately after Adorno's death. In the following years he continued to pursue his fruitful relationships with Suhrkamp Verlag and other German contacts, including, first and foremost, Gretel Adorno, his friend's widow. Scholem produced a host of new material to be published in German in the 1970s. He continued to publish his collected essays with Suhrkamp in the *Judaica* volumes, alongside autobiographical work, which included *Walter Benjamin: The Story of a Friendship* (1975), his own autobiography *From Berlin to Jerusalem* (1977), and the edition of his correspondence with Benjamin (1980). Despite his profoundly negative experiences in the immediate post-war years, when he traveled to Europe in search of the destroyed Jewish libraries, Scholem was frequently in Europe, and especially in Germany, in his last years. It is also noteworthy that his collection of texts about Walter Benjamin, published in 1983, a year after his death, as well as the fourth volume in the *Judaica* series, published the following year, were both edited by Rolf Tiedemann, Adorno's student and assistant, the co-editor of both Adorno's and Benjamin's *Gesammelte Schriften* [Collected works], and subsequently the director of the Adorno Archive in Frankfurt.

Rolf Tiedemann was the first scholar ever to write a doctoral dissertation on Benjamin's work. As Tiedemann's doctoral advisor, Adorno arranged a first meeting between Tiedemann and Scholem during one of the latter's numerous visits to Frankfurt in the early 1960s. Tiedemann maintained a close working relationship with Scholem, especially after 1968 as work on the edition of Benjamin's writings began. He was one of the few people who witnessed at first hand the relationship between Adorno and Scholem in its later phase. In what could be seen as almost the mirror image of Adorno's alienation in his own homeland, Tiedemann could attest to Scholem's rediscovery of post-war Germany and of his increasing alienation and frustration in his adopted homeland of Israel. Despite Scholem's rejection of the "myth" of German-Jewish dialogue, he expressed a most welcoming attitude toward young Germans and their newly discovered interest in matters of Jewish thought, theology, and history. He was, indeed, open to dialogue. "After Scholem's death," Tiedemann wrote, "I have encountered in Israel friends of his, German Jews who were unwilling ever again to set foot on German land and who were unable to understand why he traveled to Germany so often."[58] At the same time, he gives an account of Scholem's ever more problematic situation in Israel and his changing attitude toward its politics. Although internationally recognized as the leading scholar of Jewish mysticism and nationally respected not only as a scholar but also as a public intellectual and the president of the Israeli Academy of Sciences, Scholem had grown ever more powerless in Israel, where there was a growing sense of hostility toward the ideas that he represented. Paradoxically or not, after the 1967 war and the occupation of the West Bank, a growing messianic movement of right-wing Zionist nationalists settled in the Occupied Territories, holding on to many of the ideas that he discussed in his work and embodied in his existence: ideas concerning the mystical and messianic origins of Jewish political rebirth and sovereignty. It was probably "Scholem's Golem" – his own creation coming to life against his own intention – that turned against what he claimed to believe in and pursue.[59] Tiedemann wrote that, in his final years, Scholem seemed desperate about the situation in his homeland and to have lost any hope in the Zionist project that he had supported for his entire life: "Perhaps for the first time ever," Tiedemann noted, "I comprehended what that hope is, of which Benjamin wrote that we have been given it only for the sake of the hopeless ones."[60]

Just as Scholem carefully assisted Tiedemann and his co-editor Hermann Schweppenhäuser in their work on the edition of Benjamin's writings, so was Tiedemann most helpful and supportive in the edition of the original German version of the present volume. He dedicatedly clarified matters that remained uncertain and graciously elucidated aspects that required personal knowledge of the events and individuals involved. In particular, he helped to shed light on a matter that had remained so obscure over the years that all the available sources either contained misguided information or were insufficient to determine its historical truth – that is, until Tiedemann clarified it for the present edition.[61] The matter in question concerns Paul Klee's painting *Angelus novus*, to which Benjamin prominently alluded in his thesis "On the Concept of History" and which eventually became emblematic of both his life and his thought.

Benjamin purchased the painting in 1921, and its long and winding road began on the way from Munich to Berlin, where Benjamin had initially left it with Scholem until he could find a permanent residence in the latter city. After his escape from Germany, the painting was brought, by a Berlin acquaintance of Benjamin's, to him in Paris. In his flight from Nazi-occupied Paris in 1940, Benjamin cut the painting out of its frame and stowed it in a suitcase in which he had also stored his papers. A friend, the French intellectual George Bataille, who then worked as a librarian in the French Bibliothèque nationale, hid the suitcase there, where it survived the war. After the war, the suitcase was sent to Adorno in America, and he brought the painting back with him to Germany in 1949. Yet, the question of who was to gain possession of the painting after Benjamin's death remained undetermined over the years. In a will written when he contemplated suicide in 1932, Benjamin initially bequeathed it to Scholem. But, since he did not pursue his desperate plan at that time, the painting was eventually bequeathed, together with his other belongings, to his son Stefan Benjamin, who was living as a bookseller in London.[62] In 1961, Adorno happily reported to Scholem of Stefan Benjamin's consent to lend him the painting "for life, while also stipulating that it should be mine if I survive him."[63] However, it was eventually Stefan Benjamin who survived Adorno. After Adorno's death in 1969, the painting remained in the house on Kettenhofweg in Frankfurt where he had lived with wife Gretel.[64] Either during his visit to Frankfurt to attend Adorno's funeral, or shortly thereafter, Scholem asserted his claim of ownership against Stefan Benjamin. According to Tiedemann, this led to a bitter dispute, which could not be settled until Stefan Benjamin's sudden death in February 1972.[65] After Stefan Benjamin's death, Scholem impelled Siegfried Unseld, then director of Suhrkamp Verlag, to remove the painting from Gretel Adorno's house and to keep it at his place. Unseld, eager to settle the matter, flew to London to reach an agreement with Janet Benjamin, Stefan's widow (an agreement she reportedly still considered unjust in the following years). In July 1972, Scholem visited Frankfurt again to participate in a conference commemorating Walter Benjamin's eightieth birthday, on the occasion of which the first published volumes of Benjamin's *Gesammelte Schriften* were presented. Scholem presented at the conference a paper entitled "Walter Benjamin and His Angel," which included an account of the painting's history from the time that Benjamin purchased it until its return to Germany with Adorno. At the conclusion of this visit, Scholem added another ironic twist to the painting's tumultuous history when he – apparently cutting it out of its frame again and sewing it into his jacket – smuggled it, concealed from the Israeli customs duty officials, from Germany to Israel.[66] Subsequently, it hung in his own apartment in Abarbanel Street in Jerusalem. After Scholem passed away in 1982, the painting was given as "a gift of Fania and Gershom Scholem" to the Israel Museum in Jerusalem – a gift that was "financially made possible" by a weighty donation from the art dealers John and Paul Herring and the philanthropists Jo Carole and Ronald Lauder. It is perhaps emblematic to the triangular and tri-continental relationship of Adorno, Benjamin, and Scholem that the long story of the *Angelus novus*, designated as the angel of history, began in Germany, continued in America, and ended up – through power plays, instrumental interests, and possibly some possessive trickery – in Jerusalem.

Does the history of the painting *Angelus novus* correspond to the concept of history presented in the theses inspired by the painting's subject? Does the angel of history, whose "face is turned toward the past [and] where a chain of events appears before *us*, *he* sees one single catastrophe,"[67] represent the painting's tumultuous history and the painting owner's turbulent biography? Or is he perhaps even emblematic of the German-Jewish catastrophe? Benjamin's angel encounters the storm that prevents him from going back to the past, "mak[ing] whole what has been smashed," and redeeming the past's promise from the destructive storm of progress, of an unrelenting thrust into the future. Benjamin's intention here, like that of his friends Adorno and Scholem, is by no means anti-progressive or conservative but, rather, heretical. The angel – a figure that was arguably inspired by the Kabbalistic images studied by Scholem and that was inarguably influential for Adorno's critical theory of the Enlightenment's progress and regression – represents the wish, introduced by Benjamin in an earlier thesis, to "brush history against the grain." It is, accordingly, the task of the historical materialist to critically challenge and counteract the seemingly unwavering, unalterable course of history. The angel of history is a figure in which Scholem's heretical mysticism converges with Adorno's heretical social critique, contesting prevailing presumptions about the relationship between tradition and progress, myth and reason, religion and materialism. By heretically disputing simple binaries in religion, philosophy, and society, and by carefully attending to complex dialectical relationships and setting these in new and radically non-conforming constellations, Benjamin's angel of history – the painting and the figure depicted in it – thus represents a substantial point of intersection between Scholem's and Adorno's life and thought.

"Among certain Jews, all of whom are great authors in German," Rolf Tiedemann wrote in his "Reminiscence of Scholem," "at first in Bloch, then in Benjamin and Adorno, and even in Scholem, we find a word that no German dictionary knows: *Eingedenken* [remembrance]. According to Benjamin, *Eingedenken* makes 'every second . . . the small gateway . . . through which the messiah might enter' to 'awaken the dead.'"[68] This notion originates, according to Benjamin, from the Jewish prohibition on inquiring into the future: "the Torah and the prayers instructed them in remembrance."[69] It is precisely such remembrance – a concept that, for Benjamin, draws equally on Jewish sources (presumably mediated by Scholem) and on Marcel Proust – that makes possible a different concept of the future, different from any that is positively calculable (Benjamin differentiates it from the soothsayers' concept of the future) and allows for a messianic concept, anchored in a remembrance of the past, which facilitates a radically different, revolutionary and utopian future. Tiedemann connects precisely this messianic, utopian concept to Scholem's perception of the concrete past and future of German-Jewish life. In a sense that may apply as well to Adorno's view, he wrote: "I think, for the sake of such *Eingedenken*, that Scholem was time and again willing to also speak with us" – that is, with the generation of Germans, the very generation that Adorno sought to educate to autonomous thinking, individuality, and responsibility, and which Scholem rediscovered after his disenchantment with his own "metaphysics of youth."

* * *

Rolf Tiedemann passed away in July 2018. His meticulous work on the editions of the writings of Benjamin and Adorno, as well as some of Scholem's, is invaluable in that, without it, it would be impossible to imagine how – and if at all – their work would have been available to contemporary readers in such masterfully prepared critical editions. As I mentioned earlier, the present volume greatly benefited from Tiedemann's support and advice. I would like to dedicate it to his memory and legacy.

Michael Schwarz, of the Berlin Dependance of the Adorno Archive within the Walter Benjamin Archive at the Akademie der Künste, endorsed and supported this project from its pre-conception stages and closely accompanied the work up to its current rendering into English. He has provided innumerable suggestions and invaluable advice on both conceptual and historical matters. The present volume, initially conceived in conversations with Michael Schwarz, would be inconceivable without his support. Erdmut Wizisla and Ursula Marx from the Benjamin Archive in Berlin – where the Adorno Archive Dependance is located and where much of the work on this volume was conducted – were most helpful in the research for the edition and were always available with advice and suggestions. Christoph Gödde and Henri Lonitz from the Frankfurt Adorno Archive helped in deciphering Adorno and Scholem's almost illegible handwriting and provided information that was crucial for the annotations. Professor Jan Philipp Reemtsma and Joachim Kersten of the Hamburger Stiftung zur Förderung von Wissenschaft und Kultur supported the project institutionally and financially. Thomas Sparr, Eva Gilmer, Petra Hardt, and Nora Mercurio of Suhrkamp Verlag assisted in both editorial and practical matters. John Thompson and Elise Heslinga at Polity Press were most helpful in the preparation of the English edition of the volume. Willi Goetschel, Paul-Mendes Flohr, and Moshe Zuckermann accompanied the work on this project from its very early stages and provided substantial assistance in both theory and practice. Further, I wish to thank the many friends and colleagues who were supportive with advice, suggestions, and information at the various stages of work on the edition: Daniel Abrams, David Biale, Dirk Braunstein, Steven Fraade, Paul Franks, Peter E. Gordon, Christine Hayes, Hannan Hever, Rahel Jaeggi, Martin Jay, Marie Luise Knott, Zvi Leshem (at the Scholem Archive and Library in Jerusalem), Stefan Litt (at the Israel National Library in Jerusalem), Christoph Menke, Michael L. Morgan, Teresa Muxeneder (at the Arnold Schönberg Center in Vienna), Adalbert and Brita Rang, Nuria Schoenberg-Nono, Paula Schwebel, Zvi Septimus, Yfaat Weiss, Kenneth Winkler, and Jörg Wyrschowy (at the Deutsches Rundfunkarchiv, Frankfurt am Main).

Asaf Angermann

Notes

1 Theodor W. Adorno, "Gruß an G. Scholem," *Neue Zürcher Zeitung*, December 2, 1967; repr. in *Gesammelte Schriften*, 20.2 (Frankfurt am Main: Suhrkamp, 2003), p. 479 [my translation].

2 Gershom Scholem, *Walter Benjamin: The Story of a Friendship*, trans. Harry Zohn (New York: Schocken Books 1988), p. 118.

3 See David Biale, "The Threat of Messianism: An Interview with Gershom Scholem," *New York Review of Books*, August 14, 1980.

4 Theodor W. Adorno, "Erinnerungen" (1964), in *Gesammelte Schriften*, 20.1, p. 173.

5 Gershom Scholem, *From Berlin to Jerusalem: Memories of My Youth* (New York: Schocken Books 1988), pp. 153–61.

6 Scholem, *Walter Benjamin: The Story of a Friendship*, p. 191.

7 Ibid.

8 Theodor W. Adorno, *Kierkegaard: Construction of the Aesthetic*, trans. Robert Hullot-Kentor (Minneapolis: University of Minnesota Press, 1989); Adorno, "Notiz," in *Gesammelte Schriften*, 2, p. 261.

9 Walter Benjamin, *Origin of the German Trauerspiel*, trans. Howard Eiland (Cambridge, Mass.: Harvard University Press, 2019).

10 *The Correspondence of Walter Benjamin and Gershom Scholem, 1932–1940*, ed. Gershom Scholem, trans. Gary Smith and Andre LeFevere (New York: Schocken Books, 1989), p. 84. Wiesengrund was Adorno's original paternal last name, substituted in the first year of emigration with his mother's Italian last name Adorno.

11 Benjamin and Scholem, *Correspondence*, p. 214.

12 Ibid., pp. 218–19.

13 Ibid., p. 226.

14 Scholem, *Walter Benjamin: The Story of a Friendship*, p. 215.

15 Theodor W. Adorno and Walter Benjamin, *The Complete Correspondence 1928–1940*, ed. Henri Lonitz, trans. Nicholas Walker (Cambridge, MA: Harvard University Press, 2001), pp. 248–9.

16 Theodor W. Adorno, *Minima Moralia: Reflections from Damaged Life*, trans. Edmund Jephcott (London and New York: Verso, 2005), p. 238.

17 Gershom Scholem, "Redemption through Sin," in *The Messianic Idea in*

Judaism and Other Essays on Jewish Spirituality (New York: Schocken Books, 1995), pp. 78–141.

18 Gershom Scholem, "Zum Verständnis des Sabbatianismus: Zugleich ein Beitrag zur Geschichte der Aufklärung" [Towards an understanding of Sabbatianism: a contribution to the history of the Enlightenment], in *Almanach des Schocken Verlags auf das Jahr 5697* (Berlin: Schocken, 1936), pp. 30–42.

19 Scholem, *From Berlin to Jerusalem*, p. 131.

20 See Walter Benjamin, *Berliner Chronik/Berliner Kindheit um neunzehnhundert*, ed. Burkhardt Lindner and Nadine Werner - *Walter Benjamin Werke und Nachlaß – Kritische Gesamtausgabe* Vol. 11.2 (Berlin: Suhrkamp, 2019), pp. 7–57, esp. pp. 29–57. Eng. trans. as *Berlin Childhood around 1900*, trans. Howard Eiland (Cambridge, MA: The Belknap Press of Harvard University Press, 2006).

21 Benjamin, *Berliner Chronik/Berliner Kindheit um neunzehnhundert*, p. 49.

22 Theodor W. Adorno, "Einleitung," in Walter Benjamin, *Schriften*, Vol. I, p. xxvii.

23 Letter 2, 4.6.1939, p. 7 in this volume.

24 Letter 5, 8.10.1940, p. 14 in this volume.

25 Letter 15, 9.5.1949, p. 42 in this volume.

26 Letter 22, 22.2.1952, p. 59 in this volume.

27 Letter 23, 13.4.1952, p. 60 in this volume.

28 Theodor W. Adorno, "On the Meaning of Working through the Past," in *Critical Models: Interventions and Catchwords*, trans. Henry W. Pickford (New York: Columbia University Press 1998), pp. 89–103.

29 Theodor W. Adorno and Max Horkheimer, *Dialectic of Enlightenment: Philosophical Fragments*, trans. Edmund Jephcott (Stanford, CA: Stanford University Press, 2002).

30 Theodor W. Adorno, "Education after Auschwitz," in *Critical Models*, pp. 191–204.

31 Letter 1, 19.4.1939.

32 Gershom Scholem, *Die Geheimnisse der Schöpfung: Ein Kapitel aus dem kabbalistichen Buche Sohar* (1935) (Frankfurt am Main: Insel, 1971). Scholem entitled the second edition from 1936 – the edition he actually sent to Adorno – "The Secrets of Creation" ("Die Geheimnisse der Schöpfung").

33 Adorno and Horkheimer, *Dialectic of Enlightenment*, "Preface," p. xviii.

34 Letter 1, 19.4.1939.

35 Adorno, *Minima Moralia*, Aphorism 153: "Finale," p. 247.

36 Letter 94, 7.11.1960.

37 Gershom Scholem, "Die Metamorphose des häretischen Messianismus der Sabbatianer in religiösen Nihilismus im 18. Jahrhundert", in *Judaica 3* (Frankfurt am Main: Surhkamp, 1970).

38 In fact, it was Horkheimer who drafted the chapter's aphorisms, later completed with Adorno's additions. See Stefan Muller-Doohm, *Adorno: A Biography* (Cambridge, UK, and Malden, MA: Polity, 2005), p. 280.

39 Adorno and Horkheimer, *Dialectic of Enlightenment*, p. 165.
40 Ibid.
41 Adorno, *Negative Dialectics*, trans. E. B. Ashton (London and New York: Continuum, 1973), p. 361.
42 In his lectures on Metaphysics from 1965, the time of writing the book, Adorno speaks of "the mystical doctrine – which is common to the Cabbala and to Christian mysticism such as that of Angelus Silesius – of the infinite relevance of the intra-mundane, and thus the historical, to transcendence, and to any possible conception of transcendence." Adorno, *Metaphysics: Concept and Problems*, ed. Rolf Tiedemann, trans. Edmund Jephcott (Stanford, CA: Stanford University Press, 2001), p. 100.
43 Adorno, *Negative Dialectics*, p. 372.
44 Fania Scholem, "Beshulei ha'hakdamah' ha'avudah shenitgaltah," in Gershom Scholem, *Shabtai Tzvi vehatnu'ah hashabta'it beiyemei chaiyav*. 2nd edn, Tel Aviv: Am Oved, 1988, pp. 27–9; trans. and cited in Noam Zadoff, *Gershom Scholem: From Berlin to Jerusalem and Back*, trans. Jeffrey Green (Waltham, MA: Brandeis University Press, 2018), p. 144.
45 Gershom Scholem, "Against the Myth of the German-Jewish Dialogue," in *On Jews and Judaism in Crisis*, ed. Werner J. Dannhauser (New York: Schocken Books, 1976), pp. 61–2.
46 See Zadoff, *Gershom Scholem: From Berlin to Jerusalem and Back*.
47 Letter 32, 9.7.1953.
48 Letter 53, 9.3.1956.
49 Adorno, "The Meaning of Working through the Past," p. 90.
50 Adorno, "On the Question: 'What is German?" in *Critical Models*, pp. 205–14, and "The Meaning of Working through the Past."
51 Letter 23, 13.4.1952, p. 60 in this volume.
52 Adorno, *Negative Dialectics*, p. 365.
53 Adorno, "Resignation," in *Critical Models*, pp. 289–93.
54 Letter 216, 11.12.1968, p. 380 in this volume.
55 Letter 191, 18.9.1967 – annotation, p. 323 in this volume.
56 Letter 220, 21.3.1969, p. 387 in this volume.
57 Ibid., p. 388 in this volume.
58 Tiedemann, "Erinnerung an Scholem," in Scholem, *Walter Benjamin und sein Engel*, ed. Rolf Tiedemann (Frankfurt am Main: Surhkamp, 1983), p. 213.
59 See Benjamin Lazier, *God Interrupted: Heresy and the European Imagination between the World Wars* (Princeton, NJ, and Oxford: Princeton University Press, 2008), pp. 191–200.
60 Tiedemann, "Erinnerung an Scholem," p. 215; citation from Benjamin's "Goethe's Elective Affinities," trans. Stanley Corngold, in Walter Benjamin, *Selected Writings* (Cambridge, MA: Harvard University Press, 5 vols, 2004–6), Vol. 1, p. 356.
61 Just as he writes of Scholem, Tiedemann himself also preferred to read the published book rather than page proofs. Upon the publication of the German edition of the correspondence, he enthusiastically commented

on the edition and commented that the annotation regarding the history of the *Angelus novus* after Adorno's death, based on available sources, is incorrect. He then elucidated the matter in an e-mail to me from May 2015 – a month after the publication of the German original edition – which is the source and the basis of the full account of the painting's history, published here for the first time.

62 See annotation to letter 110, 24.10.1961.

63 Letter 110, 24.10.1961.

64 Available sources on the matter all include misguided information. For example, even Stefan Müller-Doohm's outstandingly erudite and lucid biography of Adorno inaccurately notes that he owned only a reproduction of the painting, while the original was in the possession of Gershom Scholem (Stefan Müller-Doohm: *Adorno: A Biography*, trans. Rodney Livingstone, Cambridge, UK, and Malden, MA: Polity, 2005, p. 571n92).

65 Rolf Tiedemann in a letter to the editor, May 2015.

66 See Uwe Johnson and Eberhardt Klemm, Brief vom 19. Juli [1972], cited in Erdmut Wizisla, "Ossian an Béla: Über Benjamin und Bloch – Aus dem Briefwechsel zwischen Uwe Johnson und Eberhardt und Erika Klemm," in Michael Hofmann, with Ingo Breuer and Torsten Pflugmacher (eds), *Johnson-Jahrbuch*, Vol. 11, 2004, pp. 11–28 (here p. 23). I thank Erdmut Wizisla, director of the Bertolt Brecht and the Walter Benjamin Archives in Berlin, for this information.

67 Walter Benjamin, "On the Concept of History," in *Selected Writings*, Vol. 4, p. 392.

68 Tiedemann, "Erinnerung an Scholem," p. 214. Tiedemann intersects here thesis A from the supplement to the text (Benjamin, *Selected Writings*, Vol. 4, p. 397), dropped in its final version, with thesis IX (p. 392); see also note 28 on the text (p. 400).

69 Benjamin, "On the Concept of History," Vol. 4, p. 397.

1 ADORNO TO SCHOLEM
NEW YORK, 19.4.1939

290 Riverside Drive 13D
N.Y. City

19 April 1939

Dear Mr. Scholem:

It isn't just rhetoric if I tell you that the translation of the Zohar section that you sent me has brought me the greatest pleasure that a gift has given me in quite some time. Please don't take this claim to be presumptuous – far be it from me to pretend that I could seriously rise to the task of reading this text. But it is of such a kind that its very indecipherability is a part of the pleasure that it gave me. I think I can say, in any case, that with the help of your afterword, I have at least attained a clearer topological idea of it. It is something like when you go up into the high mountains in the hopes of glimpsing chamois and, as a nearsighted city dweller, you fail to spot them. But then an experienced guide gives you a precise description of the places where the chamois roam, and you are at last so familiarized with their true habitat that you think you must be able to discover the rare creature in the flesh at any moment. Indeed, the summer vacationer can't presume to extract anything more from a landscape, the authentic experience of which yields to nothing less than the risk of one's life.

Still, I would like to say two things, even if they're completely foolish. The first concerns my astonishment at the relation between this text and the Neoplatonic–gnostic tradition. This connection was the last thing I had expected to see. I had imagined the Zohar to be the most inward and hermetic product of the Jewish spirit, as it were. But I now find that, in its very foreignness, it is most enigmatically intertwined with Western thought. If the Zohar indeed represents the Jewish document in an eminent sense, then, at any rate, it does so in the mediated sense in which the *Galut* constitutes the Jewish fate. This seems to me to have far-reaching implications, because the work thus enters into philosophical-historical connections that the uninitiated would not dream of when hearing the word Kabbalah. And perhaps it is not too bold to ask whether the metaphysical intuitions, the sediment of which this text presents, are not better grasped under the philosophical-historical aspect of a "disintegration" of Western gnosis – and you know perfectly well that, for me, the concept of disintegration entails nothing in the least bit pejorative – rather than that of of religious "*Ur*-experience." As the trustee of the great commentaries, you are probably as skeptical as I am of "*Ur*-experiences," which I cannot believe in for philosophical reasons, any more than I can imagine the life of truth as anything other than mediated. It often seemed to me as though the force of this text was due to disintegration itself; and perhaps such a dialectic could contribute something to the understanding of that moment which you so forcefully emphasize: the transformation of spiritualism – I almost want to say acosmism, in keeping with your interpretation – into mythology. This would bring us very close to what our talks in the summer were about, namely, the question of mystical nihilism. The spirit, which, out of the act of creation, expels the world, calls up the demons, against whom the world was set as a limit.

The other question is of an epistemological nature, so to speak – although it is of course related, in subject matter, to the mythical form of absolute spiritualism. The section that you have translated is an interpretation of the story of Creation as a "symbol." The language into which the symbol is translated, however, is itself a mere language of symbols – a point which calls to mind Kafka's remark that all of his writings are symbolic, but only in the sense that they should be interpreted through ever new symbols in an endless series of steps. The question that I want to put to you is whether there is any ground in this hierarchy of symbols or whether it represents a bottomless fall. Bottomless because, in a world which knows nothing but spirit, and in which even alterity is determined as spirit's mere self-externalization, the hierarchy of intentions knows no end. One might also say: there is nothing other than intentions. If I may refer to Benjamin's old theorem of the intentionless character of truth, which does not represent a final intention but rather calls a halt to the flight of intentions, then, in face of the Zohar text, the question of myth's context of delusion [*Verblendungszusammenhang*] imposes itself in turn. As much as the totality of the symbolic may seem to be the expression of the expressionless, does it not succumb to nature precisely because it knows nothing of the expressionless – or nature, I would almost say, in an authentic sense?

As you can see, and as is probably not otherwise possible with a text like this, I have not read out of it anything other than what I have read into it, and perhaps I'm even more captivated by the spell of the writing than my comments make it seem. But what is beyond doubt for me is that the force emanating from this text only becomes productive in the moment when it is transposed into the force of critique; and I would have understood very little of your intentions unless the faithfulness of your insistence led of its own accord to critique. Perhaps in this context I might ask you how you view the positions laid out in my little Kierkegaard book, which are, after all, inseparable from the questions discussed here.

I would also like to add that I was deeply and strangely moved by the idea of the immediately transient angels. And one last thing: the connection between your concerns and Benjamin's has never been as present to me as it has been on this reading. If, in the Ur-*Arcades*, Benjamin had the intention of presenting a certain historical state of the world as a "symbol" of a process in which this world, in the flesh, as it were, traverses the space of hell in time, then this is not so far removed from the gist of your text. I must confess that I am still, to this day, extremely moved by this thought. But I am also still entirely in the dark about how it might be sustained in the face of that critique of spiritualism on which, if I'm not mistaken, you, Benjamin and I concur. I hardly see any other option but to postpone such questions *ad Kalendas graecas*.

Gretel sends her kindest regards.

In heartfelt affinity
always yours
Teddie Wiesengrund

Original: typescript with Scholem's handwritten note: "Adorno-Wiesengrund / 290 Riverside Drive, 13 D / NY City"; Gershom Scholem Archive, The National Library of Israel, Jerusalem. First published in Rolf Tiedemann (ed.), *Frankfurter Adorno Blätter* V (Munich: Edition Text + Kritik, 1998), pp. 144–8. An excerpt of this letter appears in translation in *Gershom Scholem: A Life in Letters*, ed. and trans. Anthony David Skinner (Cambridge, MA: Harvard University Press, 2002), pp. 298-299.

the translation of the Zohar section that you sent me: Subsequent to their initial meetings in New Year the previous year – during which Scholem spoke to Theodor and Gretel Adorno about his work on the Zohar, one of the most important works of Jewish mysticism, and its translation into German – Scholem sent Adorno a copy of the second, private bibliophilic edition, put out by Schocken, of *Die Geheimnisse der Tora: Ein Kapitel aus dem Sohar* [The secrets of the Torah: a chapter from the Zohar] (Berlin, 1936). The first edition had been published in 1935 as volume 40 of the "Bücherei des Schocken Verlags" with the different title, *Die Geheimnisse der Schöpfung: Ein Kapitel aus dem Sohar* [The secrets of creation: a chapter from the Zohar]. Remarks about the New York conversations appear in Adorno and Scholem's letters to Benjamin. On the 6th of May 1938, Scholem wrote from New York: "In the meantime, I saw Wiesengrund on three occasions and Horkheimer once, at Wiesengrund's insistence, just a few days ago. H. seemed to be bored stiff by me (but he put on a good show), which I couldn't say about Wiesengrund, with whom I was able to establish a very sympathetic relationship. I like him immensely, and we found quite a lot to say to one another. I intend to cultivate relations with him and his wife quite vigorously. Talking with him is pleasant and engaging, and I find it possible to reach agreement on many things. You shouldn't be surprised by the fact that we spend a great deal of time mulling over your situation. In short, I found myself pleasantly disappointed by this couple." See *The Correspondence of Walter Benjamin and Gershom Scholem, 1932–1940*, ed. Gershom Scholem, trans. Gary Smith and Andre Lefevere

(New York, Schocken Books, 1989), pp. 218–19; for Adorno's full account of the meeting, see *The Complete Correspondence of Walter Benjamin and Theodor W. Adorno, 1928–1940*, ed. Henri Lonitz, trans. Nicholas Walker (Cambridge, MA: Harvard University Press, 2001), pp. 248-53. On the 24th of April 1939 Gretel Adorno wrote to Benjamin: "About 2 weeks ago we had a great surprise: Scholem sent the Sohar [*sic*] section from Jerusalem." See *Gretel Adorno and Walter Benjamin: Correspondence, 1930–1940*, ed. Henri Lonitz and Christoph Gödde, trans. Wieland Hoban (Cambridge: Polity, 2008), p. 258.

Galut: Hebrew: exile, Jewish diaspora.

the transformation of spiritualism: Adorno is presumably thinking of the following passage from "Zum historischen Verständnis des Sohar" [Toward a Historical Understanding of the Zohar], Scholem's introduction to his book *Die Geheimnisse der Schöpfung* [The secrets of creation] (1935): "It was only with the collapse of that stratum of life and belief in which the Kabbalah was able to represent a historical force that the splendor of the Zohar also faded; and later, in the revaluation of the Enlightenment, it became the "book of lies," considered to have obscured the pure light of Judaism." See *Zohar: The Book of Splendor: Basic Readings from the Kabbalah*, ed. Gershom Scholem, trans. Ralph Marcus (New York: Schocken Books, 1977), p. ix.

Kafka's remark that all of his writings are symbolic: Not determined.

Benjamin's old theorem of the intentionless character of truth: In the "Epistemo-Critical Prologue" to his *Origin of the German Trauerspiel*, Benjamin wrote: "The object of knowledge, an object determined in conceptual intention, is not truth. Truth is an intentionless being formed from ideas. The comportment appropriate to truth is therefore an entering and disappearing into it, not an intending and knowing. Truth is the death of intention . . . Thus the structure of truth calls for a kind of being that, in its intentionlessness, resembles the simple being of things, although in its constancy it would be superior." See Benjamin, *Origin of the German Trauerspiel*, trans. Howard Eiland (Cambridge, Mass.: Harvard University Press, 2019), p. 12.

the question of myth's context of delusion *[Verblendungszusammenhang]*: This question, which remained central to Adorno throughout his life, and which converges with Scholem's work, is treated early on in his lecture on "The Idea of Natural History" and in his book on Kierkegaard, which Adorno had introduced in the context of his first conversations with Scholem. In "The Idea of Natural History" Adorno wrote: "Just as the element of semblance is an aspect of every myth, indeed just as the dialectic of mythical fate is in every instance inaugurated by semblance in the forms of hubris and blindness, so the historically produced elements of semblance are always mythical." Adorno, "The Idea of Natural History," trans. Robert Hullot-Kentor, in *Things Beyond Resemblance: Collected Essays on Theodor W. Adorno* (New York: Columbia University Press, 2006, pp. 252–69), p. 268. The connection between myth and the "context of delusion," which Adorno associates with the dialectic between the domination of nature and the fall into nature, constitutes the centre of the sixth chapter of his book on Kierkegaard, "Reason and Sacrifice." See Adorno, *Kierkegaard: Construction of the Aesthetic*, trans. Robert Hullot-Kentor (Minneapolis: University of Minnesota Press, 1989), pp. 106–122.

my little Kierkegaard book: Adorno's *Kierkegaard: Construction of the Aesthetic* – a reworked version of his 1931 *Habilitation* thesis at the University of Frankfurt – was originally published in Tübingen, 1933, and subsequently reprinted in Adorno's *Gesammelte Schriften 2: Kierkegaard, Konstruktion des Ästhetischen* ed. Rolf Tiedemann et al. (Frankfurt am Main: Suhrkamp, 1974). For an English translation, see Theodor W. Adorno, *Kierkegaard: Construction of the Aesthetic*, ed. and trans. Robert Hullot-Kentor (Minneapolis: University of Minnesota Press, 1989). As Adorno notes in the Preface to the second edition, his book was published on the same day that Hitler seized power (*GS* 2, p. 261). Following their conversations in New York, Adorno sent Scholem a copy of his book with the following inscription: "May this little book solicit you, dear Gerhard Scholem, to put in a good word for your Th. Wiesengrund-Adorno at the right place, at the right time. New York, 28 July 1938."

immediately transient angels: The Zohar contains the following interpretation of Psalm 104:14: "*Who makes the grass grow for the behemah* – the behemoth crouching on a thousand mountains, which grow that grass for her every day. *Grass* is the angels ruling momentarily, created on the second day, existing as food for this *behemah*, for there is fire consuming fire." *The Zohar* (Pritzker edn, Vol. 1), trans. Daniel C. Matt (Stanford, CA: Stanford University Press, 2004), 1:18b; see Scholem, *Die Geheimnisse der Schöpfung* [The secrets of creation], p. 77.

Benjamin's ... Ur-Arcades: The early drafts of Walter Benjamin's *Arcades Project* (1927–9) include some notes that refer to "the time of hell." See Benjamin, "First Sketches: Paris Arcades I," in *The Arcades Project*, ed. Rolf Tiedemann, trans. Howard Eiland and Kevin McLaughlin (Cambridge, MA: The Belknap Press of Harvard University Press, 1996), pp. 825–868; see pp. 842–43 for a particular instance.

2 SCHOLEM TO ADORNO
JERUSALEM, 4.6.1939

Prof. Dr. G. Scholem

Jerusalem, on the 4.6 39.
28, Abarbanel Road

Dear Mr. Wiesengrund,

Your letter of April 19th, which took at least 4 weeks to arrive, has brought me sincere enjoyment. Your comments on the gift that you were presented constitute a wholly suitable honorarium. Since, in any case, there is nobody who could seriously measure up to the task of reading Kabbalistic texts, the only thing that separates us is a little bit of philology.

Your astonishment at the connection with the Neoplatonic–gnostic tradition will dissipate as soon as you kindly peruse the relevant texts by your humble servant. If I can still dig up a copy of my 1929 essay "Zur Frage nach der Entstehung der Kabbala" [On the question of the formation of the Kabbalah] I will send it to you by registered mail. In it, the Neo-Platonic gnostic tradition is properly illuminated in its connection to the Kabbalah. Of course, what is uncanny and attractive about these texts lies precisely in the extent to which the most original products of Jewish thought are of an assimilatory nature. All of these questions invariably lead to paradoxes, that is, precisely to dialectical connections, about which I'm no less astonished than you, even though I have been seeking to unravel their mystery for nearly 20 years. The astonishing thing about any such rational form of mysticism lies in the enigmatic interrelation between tradition and experience, although, of course, I would cautiously dispense with so bold a term as *Ur*-experience. The fact that Jewish mysticism points to this interrelation in its very name appears to have escaped you. Kabbalah, in translation, means tradition rather than *Ur*-experience; and all along, the Kabbalists, even the greatest visionaries among them, have asserted the commentary-character of their insights with a vigor that is worthy of the utmost respect. The fact that Gnosticism, of all things, provides the common thread leading through this labyrinth demonstrates just how tricky the pertinent connections really are.

Your 2nd question concerning the nature of the symbolic in the Zohar is not so easy to answer. The texts tolerate a commentary in both of the directions that you offer as alternatives. I, myself, tend towards the view that, in the minds of the Kabbalists, there is <u>no</u> ground to the hierarchy of symbolic strata. I hope to deal with this in depth one day, in very strange connections. You are completely right when you suspect that, for a man such as the author of the Zohar, there is no longer anything like nature in the authentic sense. This is the only way in which a medieval Jew could confront the phenomenon of nature, unless he was simply a Scholastic.

I apologise for not speaking of your Kierkegaard book today for the simple reason that I have not yet understood it. You may find it ridiculous that I, of all people, have such difficulties reading a book that, compared with the Zohar, you would probably consider harmless. Nevertheless, it is so. I have only understood some parts, from which I have yet to be able to form an exact image of your position. It may also be that, for me, the approach was particularly unexpected when brought to bear on Kierkegaard. And so I have merely wandered through your book with eyes, mouth, and ears wide open, having admired you much more than I've understood you.

Has an issue of the *Zeitschrift für Sozialforschung* actually appeared in the meantime? What about your Husserl critique? The last issue that I have is Vol. 7, nos. 1/2.

I am extremely worried about the fate of Walter Benjamin, from whom I have received very troubling news from Paris. Do you not see any possibility of setting him on his feet for a number of years? I would very much like to invite him to Palestine for an extended period, but the practical implementation of this plan has come up against great difficulties, which I unfortunately underestimated at first. Does the Institute intend to keep him on for the foreseeable future? I was quite shocked when I heard that the Baudelaire piece would not be printed, even though, upon reading the sections that were sent to me, I also had considerable misgivings. The colors appeared to me as having been imposed rather too starkly, and the methodology was also questionable at times. But as it stands, there is gradually no place left in the wide world for a man like him to publish. This dismal perspective weighs very heavily on my soul.

I would be very glad to hear a few words from you.

Please greet the Tillichs and Goldsteins for me occasionally, and pass on my cordial regards to your wife, as to you.

Yours,

Gerhard Scholem

Original: typescript; Theodor W. Adorno Archive, Frankfurt am Main. First published in Gershom Scholem, *Briefe I: 1914–1947*, ed. Itta Shedletzky (Munich: C.H. Beck, 1994), pp. 274-76. An excerpt of this letter appears in translation in *Gershom Scholem: A Life in Letters*, ed. and trans. Anthony David Skinner (Cambridge, MA: Harvard University Press, 2002), pp. 300–1.

"*Zur Frage nach der Entstehung der Kabbala*": See Scholem, "Zur Frage der Entstehung der Kabbalah" [On the question of the formation of the Kabbalah], *Korrespondenzblatt des Vereins zur Gründung und Erhaltung einer Akademie für die Wissenschaft des Judentums*, Vol. 9 (1928): 4–26.

Kierkegaard book . . . I have not yet understood it: Scholem had already read the book in 1933, after being urged to do so by Walter Benjamin. On the 24th of October 1933 he wrote to Benjamin: "I have thus far read about two-thirds of the book on Kierkegaard by Wiesengrund – whose name I just read next to 50 others on the official list of people dismissed from [the University of] Frankfurt – and to my mind the book combines a sublime plagiarism of your thought with an uncommon chutzpah, and it will ultimately not mean much for a future, objective appraisal of Kierkegaard." See *The Correspondence of Walter Benjamin and Gershom Scholem, 1932–1940*, ed. Gershom Scholem, trans. Gary Smith and Andre Lefevere (New York: Schocken Books, 1989), p. 84.

an issue of the Zeitschrift für Sozialforschung: The *Zeitschrift für Sozialforschung*, the journal put out by the Institute for Social Research, was published by the Librairie Félix Alcan (Paris) from 1933 to 1939. The double issue, nos. 1/2, Vol. VII, was published at the beginning of 1939.

your Husserl critique: Scholem is probably referring to Adorno's essay "Zur Philosophie Husserls" [On Husserl's philosophy], which was slated for publication in the *Zeitschrift*, although it never appeared there. See Adorno, "Zur Philosophie Husserls," in *Gesammelte Schriften 20.1: Vermischte Schriften* [Miscellaneous writings], ed. Rolf Tiedemann et al. (Frankfurt am Main: Suhrkamp, 1986), pp. 46–118.

the fate of Walter Benjamin, from whom I have received very troubling news from Paris: Benjamin had reported to Scholem, in his letters dated the 14th of March and the 8th of April 1939, about the impending loss of his stipend as a result of the Institute's stock market losses, about the European situation and the necessity of leaving Paris for New York and about the role that the Institute would need to play in facilitating this move. (See *The Correspondence of Walter Benjamin and Gershom Scholem*, pp. 248–9 and 251–4.)

Do you not see any possibility of setting him on his feet for a number of years?: Starting in 1934, the Institute for Social Research, under Max Horkheimer's leadership, had granted Walter Benjamin a stipend that guaranteed his livelihood during his time in Paris. Additionally, Benjamin was commissioned to write articles for the *Zeitschrift für Sozialforschung*. On the 14th of March 1939 Benjamin wrote to Scholem: "Horkheimer informs me that the Institute is facing enormous difficulties. Without stating a definite date, he is preparing me for the end of the financial stipend that has been my sole subsistence since 1934. Your eyes didn't deceive you, nor did your humble servant think for a moment that they had. All the same, I didn't foresee a catastrophe. As their letter indicates, these people had not been living on interest, as one would assume in the case of a foundation, but on the capital. The major portion of this is said to be still in existence but frozen, and the rest is supposed to be about to dry up." See *The Correspondence of Walter Benjamin and Gershom Scholem*, p. 248. On this point, see letter no. 5 in this volume. See also Christoph Gödde and Henri Lonitz, "Das Institut für Sozialforschung / Gretel Adorno, Adorno und Horkheimer," in *Benjamin-Handbuch: Leben–Werk–Wirkung* [Benjamin handbook: life–work–impact], ed. Burkhardt Lindner (Stuttgart: J. B. Metzler, 2006), pp. 92–106.

invite him to Palestine: Scholem had long harbored the plan to invite Benjamin to Palestine. Between November 1934 and March 1935, Benjamin and Scholem discussed the possibility of a visit, lasting four to eight weeks, during which Benjamin would have stayed with Scholem or his friends, in the hope that something "could be done in the way of a private lecture series . . . which would bring in a few pounds of pocket money" (*The Correspondence of Walter Benjamin and Gershom Scholem*, p. 151). However, Benjamin postponed his visit, hoping to meet Horkheimer and Pollock during their trip to Europe. Some years later, when his situation in Paris began to worsen, he returned to this idea. In his aforementioned letter of the 14th of March 1939, Benjamin wrote to Scholem: "I was pleased to see that, without knowing my present prospects, you have kept my visit to Palestine in mind. The way things are shaping up now, the question of whether or not it will be possible to assure me of sustenance in Palestine for a number of months has become important" (ibid., p. 249). In his memoir Scholem recalls the following: "In response to this letter, which left nothing to be desired in the way of gravity, I made an attempt among a small circle of people in Jerusalem to raise the sum that might make possible Benjamin's aforementioned sojourn. The situation at that time hardly could have been more unfavorable. The only dependable person who was ready to contribute an appropriate amount of money was the painter Anna Ticho, whom I had introduced to Benjamin in Paris a year earlier; he had made a great impression on her. Thus I could not promise him anything really definitive." See Scholem, *Walter Benjamin: The Story of a Friendship*, trans. Harry Zohn (New York: NYRB Classics, 2003), pp. 274–5.

the Baudelaire piece: Benjamin's essay "The Paris of the Second Empire in Baudelaire," which was written in large part while visiting Brecht in Denmark during the summer, was rejected by the editors of the *Zeitschrift für Sozialforschung*. Adorno justified this rejection in a letter dated the 10th of November 1938, in which he asked for an amended version of the text, which subsequently appeared in the *Zeitschrift für Sozialforschung* under the title "On Some Motifs in Baudelaire." See Walter Benjamin, "The Paris of the Second Empire in Baudelaire," in *Selected Writings*, Vol. 4: *1938–1940*, ed. Howard Eiland and Michael Jennings (Cambridge, MA: The Belknap Press of Harvard University Press, 2006), pp. 3–92; *The Complete Correspondence of Walter Benjamin and Theodor W. Adorno, 1928–1940*, ed. Henri Lonitz, trans. Nicholas Walker (Cambridge, MA: Harvard University Press, 2001), pp. 280–287; and Benjamin, "On Some Motifs in Baudelaire," in *Selected Writings*, Vol. 4, pp. 313–55.

the Tillichs and Goldsteins: Scholem is referring to the couples Paul and Hannah Tillich and Kurt and Eva Goldstein. The theologian and philosopher of religion Paul Tillich (1886–1965) was professor of theology at the University of Frankfurt from 1929 to 1933. Tillich was dismissed from his post in 1933 for publishing criticisms of the Nazi regime. He immigrated to New York, where he taught at the Union Theological Seminary. In February 1931 Adorno completed his *Habilitation*, *Konstruktion des Ästhetischen in Kierkegaards Philosophie* [Construction of the aesthetic in Kierkegaard's philosophy] under Tillich's supervision. Hannah Tillich (1896–1988) was a writer, whose works were written in English. The psychiatrist and neurologist Kurt Goldstein (1878–1965) knew Adorno from Frankfurt. In a letter to Benjamin, dated the 4th of March 1938, Adorno describes his first meeting with Scholem in New York in the presence of the Tillichs and the Goldsteins: "You may find this hard to believe, but the first time we got to meet him [Scholem] was at the Tillichs, together with Goldstein and his new wife. Not exactly the best atmosphere in which to be introduced to the Sohar; and especially since Frau Tillich's relationship to the Kabbala seems to resemble that of a terrified teenager [Backfisch] to pornography." *The Complete Correspondence of Walter Benjamin and Theodor W. Adorno, 1928–1940*, ed. Henri Lonitz, trans. Nicholas Walker (Cambridge, MA: Harvard University Press, 2001), p. 248.

3 SCHOLEM TO ADORNO
JERUSALEM, 15.4.1940

פרופ" ד"ר גרשם שלום
ירושלים, רחביה
Jerusalem 15.4.1940
28, Abarbanel Road

In case you wish to reply to your humble servant, please indicate the language in which the letter is written on the envelope. This is required by the censor!

Dear Mr. Wiesengrund-Adorno

Last week, after a rather long but evidently safe journey, your friendly package containing of the most recent issue of the *Zeitschrift für Sozialforschung* finally arrived. Many thanks for having thought of me. I never received the previous issue, unfortunately, so my series is interrupted. If at some point you could stick a spare copy in an envelope for me that would be very kind! So much for the *schnorring* part! Regarding the contents, I can only say that in many respects this issue was of truly great interest to me. Since I lack all musical prerequisites, I can't judge your essay except to say that I value its philosophical perspective, insofar as I could distill it from the musical. I only regret that your Husserl critique, which I had looked forward to for a long time, appears to have disappeared into some kind of oblivion. Do publish it eventually – there are more readers for it than you think. Among the most fantastical readings was Schlesinger's paper – here one truly feels as though one were in a madhouse. Only in Hitler's Germany have I encountered such a load of unadulterated chatter, whose manifest purpose is none other than a few physicists – thank God they still exist – seeking to keep their jobs, a purpose for which they are prepared to make free with all of the phrases in the world. One can really only see this as a parody. Obviously, nobody in this whole ghostly affair actually believes that the theoretical discourse of physics has much to gain by appealing to Stalin's "latest essay" – I, for one, could only hold my head in my hands. The notion of a philosophy that begins with Lenin's lightweight booklet against Mach instead of the *Theaetetus* or *Parmenides* is no laughing matter. According to their methods, the Russians ought really to have the author killed for this gruesome compromise of their natural-philosophical standards.

It is unclear to me why Horkheimer released his essay on the Jews and Europe, which is so obviously entirely inadequate to the issue. After all, he does not treat the specificity of this "and" at all; and what he does claim seems to concern the function of the Jews in general. I was disappointed that I could find nothing in his piece to advance the desperate state of the discussion surrounding the Jewish question. It is not enough to rehash in today's words Marx's essay "On the Jewish Question" (which was already feeble and biased a hundred years ago); and regarding the overly allegorical twist at the end, with its Delphic recommendation concerning what we should actually do, in a positive sense – I confess to you that I have little use for it! I hope that you are not angry with me for expressing this opinion.

I am very worried about Walter Benjamin, from whom I have heard nothing, even in answer to my inquiries, since early December 1939. He wrote quite regularly at first following his return to Paris, and I was doubly delighted by the offprints of his works. If you know anything, please write to me. Every communication is so difficult these days – sometimes a letter to Paris takes 10 days to arrive, other times it takes 30. Might something have gotten in his way again?

Do you ever see the Tillichs? If so, please say hello for me. We are still alive here and I am working with the gallows leisure that I learned from the gallows humor. All cordial regards to you and your wife from your

Gerhard Scholem

Original: manuscript with printed and hand-annotated letterhead; Theodor W. Adorno Archive, Frankfurt am Main. First published in Scholem, *Briefe I: 1914–1947*, ed. Itta Shedletzky (Munich: C.H. Beck, 1994), pp. 280-81. An excerpt of this letter appears in translation in *Gershom Scholem: A Life in Letters*, ed. and trans. Anthony David Skinner (Cambridge, MA: Harvard University Press, 2002), pp. 305–6.

the most recent issue of the Zeitschrift für Sozialforschung: This refers to the double issue, nos. 1/2 Vol. VIII (Paris: 1939), which came out after a "considerable delay" (according to a note appended to the issue). It contained, among other pieces, Adorno's "Fragmente über Wagner" [Fragments on Wagner] (pp. 1–49), Benjamin's "On Some Motifs in Baudelaire" (pp. 50–91), as well as his "Introduction" to Jochmann (pp. 92–114), Horkheimer's "The Jews and Europe" (pp. 115–37), and Rudolf Schlesinger's essay "Neue sowjetrussische Literatur zur Sozialforschung III: Moderne Physik und Philosophie" [New Soviet literature and social research III: modern physics and philosophy] (pp.187–208).

the previous issue: Scholem is referring to the double issue nos. 1/2, Vol. VII (Paris: 1939), mentioned in letter no. 2 in this volume.

your essay: Adorno's essay "Fragmente über Wagner" includes what would become the first, the sixth, and the final two chapters of his subsequent monograph *In Search of Wagner*, trans. Rodney Livingstone (London and New York: Verso, 1981).

Horkheimer ... essay on the Jews and Europe: In a letter dated February 1940, Scholem wrote to Benjamin:

> You want to know my opinion of Horkheimer's essay "The Jews and Europe."After repeated readings of the pages in question, I don't find it difficult to formulate in a readily understandable manner: this is an entirely useless product in which, astonishingly enough, *nothing* beneficial and new is to be discovered. The author has neither any conception of the Jewish problem nor any interest in it. ... The man explains nothing at all – except a cliché that one has been able to read for years in every provincial Jewish newspaper aimed at the man in the street, namely, that in the totalitarian state the Jews have been deprived of the old economic foundations of their existence. ... The *style* of Horkheimer's writings has always made me uncomfortable because of a certain brash insolence in its instrumentation, and in this essay that insolence has unfortunately found its way home in the most exact sense of the word. *This* Jew is the last person who is able to provide us with an unsentimental analysis (but one that hits the heart of the matter itself and not its most decayed emblems) of "The Jews and Europe," the genuine question that concerns *us*, you and me, equally and decisively. As an exhortation addressed to the Jews in the Second World War, the essay leaves one "as disconsolate as the speech of ghosts," to quote Benjamin. (See *The Correspondence of Walter Benjamin and Gershom Scholem, 1932–1940*, trans. Gary Smith and Andre Lefevere (New York, Schocken Books, 1989), pp. 264–5)

Compare to Gershom Scholem, *Walter Benjamin: The Story of a Friendship*, trans. Harry Zohn (New York: Jewish Publication Society, 1981), pp. 277–80.

See also Max Horkheimer, "The Jews and Europe," in *Critical Theory and Society: A Reader*, ed. Stephen Eric Bronner and Douglas MacKay Kellner (New York: Routledge, 1989), pp. 77–94.

Marx's essay "On the Jewish Question": See Karl Marx, "On the Jewish Question," in *Karl Marx: Selected Writings*, ed. David McLellan (Oxford: Oxford University Press, 2000), pp. 46–63.

Walter Benjamin, from whom I have heard nothing ... since early December 1939: The last letter that Scholem received from Benjamin is dated the 11th of January 1940. See *The Correspondence of Walter Benjamin and Gershom Scholem*, pp. 262–4.

4 ADORNO TO SCHOLEM
NEW YORK, 16.7.1940*

T. W. Adorno
429 West 117th Street
New York City

July 16, 1940.

Air-Mail

Professor Dr. Gerhard Gershom Scholem
Abarbanel Road
Jerusalem, Pal.

Dear Mr. Scholem,

Thank you very much for your kind letter of April 15. I am sending you under separate cover the copy of our periodical which did not reach you. The new issue is about to appear and you will receive it as soon as possible.

Today I wish to write you on behalf of Walter Benjamin whose fate worries me just as much as it worries you. He has managed to escape from Paris to Lourdes, which is in the unoccupied zone of France. His present address is 8 Rue Notre Dame, Lourdes. There is no immediate danger, but due to the development in France any fear with regard to the fate of Jewish refugees is more than justified. Therefore, we are trying desperately and with all means at our disposal, to realize Walter's immigration into this country. It would be a great help if you would write a testimony about Walter Benjamin as both a personality, scholar and philosopher, if possible, with special reference to the way in which his thinking is bound up with the Jewish tradition. Could you please let us have this testimony with six copies, each of them signed by you with all your titles and degrees, on official paper, and written in English? The more glowing this testimony will read the better it will be for Walter. It would also facilitate matters if you would send it by air-mail, normal mail to and from Palestine takes months and there are no more months to be lost.

Incidentally, do you know Mrs. Cecilia Razovsky in New York? If so, it might be a good idea, if you think it advisable, if you would write to her immediately with regard to Walter. I am getting in touch with her now hoping that she might be helpful in the matter of Walter's immigration. She has obtained for him a very excellent American affidavit as early as January and I hope that she will take a further

* Original letter in English.

interest in him. I judge that your authority with her is incomparably greater than mine. Horkheimer has had to leave for the west in official Institute matters which will keep him there for several months. He has put me in charge of Walter's case and I need not tell you that we are going to do everything in our power in order to save him.

Is there any chance of your coming to this country in the near future? For innumerable reasons I shall be very happy if you would come.

With kindest regards also from Gretel,

yours ever

T. W. Adorno

Original: typescript; Gershom Scholem Archive, The National Library of Israel, Jerusalem. First published in *Frankfurter Adorno Blätter* V (Munich: Edition Text + Kritik, 1998), pp. 148–9. An excerpt of this letter appears in translation in: *Gershom Scholem: A Life in Letters*, ed. and trans. Anthony David Skinner (Cambridge, MA: Harvard University Press, 2002), p. 306.

Mrs. Cecilia Razovsky in New York . . . affidavit: Cecilia Razovsky (1891–1968) was a social worker and author who worked for various organizations supporting Jewish immigrants to the US. She was a member of the National Refugee Service and the National Council of Jewish Women. In January 1940 she organized an affidavit for Walter Benjamin – a financial guarantee provided by Milton Starr from Nashville, Tennessee. See *The Complete Correspondence of Walter Benjamin and Theodor W. Adorno, 1928–1940*, ed. Henri Lonitz, trans. Nicholas Walker (Cambridge, MA: Harvard University Press, 2001), the note on p. 324, and p. 332.

5 ADORNO TO SCHOLEM NEW YORK, 8.10.1940

8 October 1940.

Dear Mr. Scholem,

Walter Benjamin has taken his life. He had received his American visa in Marseille, a permanent appointment* to the Institute, and everything was in order; only, the French denied him, and everyone else, an exit visa. He then attempted to cross the border at Port Bou along with several women, three of whom I know by name: Mrs. Grete Freund, Dr. Biermann and Mrs. Hedi Gurland, all now in Lisbon. After what was evidently a terribly strenuous journey on foot and great difficulties caused by the French, the refugees arrived in Port Bou. From there they were supposed to be sent back to France, but

* original in English

they requested, and were granted, a night's rest. During this night, Walter took morphine. (Probably this was on the 23rd of September, in the evening). He died the following evening and was buried on Wednesday. The others were <u>not</u> sent back and all arrived safely in Lisbon. So Walter killed himself after he had already been saved. Fear of deportation, of a French concentration camp, and perhaps also of the physical exertion, for which he was unfit, brought him to do it. But even this is hardly an adequate explanation, since he must have known that, for him, as for many others, a way out would have been found. After all, he possessed ample financial means and was backed by America. The end is so dreadful and senseless that any consolation and any explanation are equally in vain.

I urgently implore you to write me. I simply do not know how things can go on after Walter's death, and communication from you would be infinitely important. Could you not come here again?

Yours ever

Teddie Wiesengrund-Adorno

Original: typescript with handwritten note by Scholem: "290 Riverside Drive / New York City"; Gershom Scholem Archive, The National Library of Israel, Jerusalem. First published in Rolf Tiedemann (ed.), *Frankfurter Adorno Blätter* V (Munich: Edition Text + Kritik, 1998), pp. 149–50.

Mrs. Grete Freund: Grete Freund (b. 1895–?) was a friend of the attorney Carina Birman. She was the financial director of the leftist, Berlin-based journal *Das Tage-Buch*. After 1933 the journal was published in Paris as *Das Neue Tage-Buch*. The journal drew contributions from such figures as Walter Benjamin, Max Brod, Thomas Mann, Klaus Mann, and Franz Mehring, among others.

Dr. Biermann: Adorno's spelling. The attorney Carina Birman (1895–1996) worked as a legal advisor at the Austrian embassy in Paris from 1926 to 1938. She was active on behalf of artists and intellectuals who were under threat due to the political situation. By inventing a fictitious arts festival in Mexico, she was able to secure numerous visas from the Mexican ambassador. In 1940 she and Walter Benjamin were part of the same group of refugees fleeing from France to Spain over the Pyrenees. From 1942 she lived in New York, where she resumed her legal practice. She eventually became one of the first women to serve on the Supreme Court in Washington, DC. See Carina Birman, *The Narrow Foothold* (London: Hearing Eye, 2006).

Mrs. Hedi Gurland: Adorno's spelling. Henny Gurland (1900–1952) was a photographer who worked for the social-democratic newspaper *Vorwärts* during the early 1930s. Following a house search by the Nazis in 1933 she fled, first to Brussels and then to Paris. In September 1940 she tried to cross the border into Spain, along with a small group of people, including Walter Benjamin. Like Benjamin, she did not obtain a French exit permit and was refused entry. Henny Gurland witnessed Benjamin's suicide and made arrangements for his burial. In July 1944 in New York, she married the philosopher and social psychologist Erich Fromm (1900–1980), who had been a member of the Institute during the 1930s. In 1950 the couple moved to Mexico in order to treat Henny Gurland's arthritis, which she developed following an illness, at the radioactive springs at San José Purua. She died of her condition in 1952. See Rainer Funk, *Erich Fromm: His Life and Ideas*, trans. Ian Portman and Manuela Kunkel (New York: Continuum, 2000, pp. 120–7).

Probably this was on the 23rd of September, in the evening: Benjamin ingested the poison on the 25th of September in the evening. He died the following night around 10 p.m.

6 SCHOLEM TO ADORNO
JERUSALEM, 11.11.1940

Jerusalem, on the 11 of November, 1940.
Abarbanel St. 28

Dear Mr. Adorno,

As is unfortunately often the case with letters from America, your letter of the 16th of July took a very long time to arrive. Sometimes letters get here after four weeks, sometimes after four months. And so I received your call for help on behalf of Walter Benjamin a few days before I received Hanna Stern's terrible message from southern France about our friend's suicide. She informs me that Walter had obtained a US visa, evidently thanks to your efforts, and that he was not allowed to cross into the Spanish border town. Hanna Stern gave me no address for herself, so I cannot write to her. She tells me that she too had only heard the news from Walter's sister after a four-week delay. I suppose that you either already have more direct news about the details, or that such information may be more easily obtained from New York than from here. I needn't tell you what Benjamin's death means for us, and how much it matters to me to find out every possible detail in connection with his final days. I believe that it is the duty of his friends to rescue his papers, in whatever way the current circumstances allow, and to ensure the arrangement of a dignified memorial. The events of world history are such that, amidst all this terrible turbulence, the loss of one brilliant person is scarcely noticed; and yet there are enough people for whom the memory of this deceased will remain unforgettable. Please write to me regarding anything you hear or are able to find out. If Benjamin's own papers have not survived and been sent to New York, then I suppose that I am the only person in possession of a relatively complete collection of his writings. Perhaps a time will come when this precious legacy can be put to use. He must have had far more with him in manuscript form than he ever published, and I do not need to tell you how important it is to me to know that these things might be in a safe place.

It is inconceivable that I must write you this letter instead of the one that you requested. You may already know this – I briefly reported it to Prof. Arthur Rosenberg, with whom you may occasionally get together (if so, please send him my regards) – that my brother Werner also met his death, under unexplained circumstances, in the Buchenwald concentration camp, after being imprisoned there for more than seven years.

I hope to hear from you soon. Please do not let the difficulties in communication deter you – perhaps your next letter will be lucky and will arrive within four weeks. I do not share your hope of seeing me in America in the foreseeable future. I am thoroughly preoccupied here and do not anticipate leaving Palestine any time soon. During the summer I completed my big English book *Major Trends in Jewish Mysticism*, which will probably go to print soon, and I hope you can get hold of a copy. It is intended for an American audience, and contains an elaboration of the lectures that I held there. I will dedicate it to the memory of our friend, for whom it was already intended during his lifetime.

I have received the copy of the *Zeitschrift für Sozialforschung* that you sent me and hope to acquire the forthcoming issues when they are out.

I cannot write any more today and only ask that you and your wife accept my best regards.

Yours,

Gerhard Scholem

Original: typescript; Theodor W. Adorno Archive, Frankfurt am Main. First published in Scholem, *Briefe I: 1914–1947*, ed. Itta Shedletzky (Munich: C.H. Beck, 1994), pp. 281–82. An excerpt of this letter appears in translation in *Gershom Scholem: A Life in Letters*, ed. and trans. Anthony David Skinner (Cambridge, MA: Harvard University Press, 2002), pp. 308–9.

Hanna Stern's . . . message from southern France: The philosopher Hannah Arendt (1906–1975) was married from 1929 to 1937 to the philosopher Günter Stern, who later went by the name of Günter Anders. She informed Scholem of Benjamin's death in a letter dated the 21st of October 1940: "Walter Benjamin took his own life on September 26th in Port Bou on the Spanish frontier. He had an American visa, but on the twenty-third, the only people that the Spanish allowed to pass the border were those with "national" passports. . . . The report of his death took nearly four weeks to reach both his sister and us." See *The Correspondence of Hannah Arendt and Gershom*

Scholem, ed. Marie Luise Knott, trans. Anthony David (Chicago: University of Chicago Press, 2017) p. 4 (translation slightly modified to correct the date given for Benjamin's suicide).

Walter's sister: Walter Benjamin's sister, Dora (1901–1946), was born in Berlin, where she studied economics and psychology. She completed a doctorate at the University of Greifswald and subsequently worked as a social worker. From 1934 she lived in Paris. Between 1935 and 1938 Benjamin stayed with her on numerous occasions. In 1935 she developed a severe case of ankylosing spondylitis (AS). After being interned at Gurs, and following several unsuccessful attempts to obtain a US visa, she managed to escape to Switzerland in 1942. Despite her illness she worked for the *Schweizer Hilfswerk für Emigrantenkinder* [Swiss relief agency for refugee children], as well as other aid organizations. She died of her condition in Zurich in June 1946. See Gershom Scholem, "Ahnen und Verwandte Walter Benjamins" [Walter Benjamin's ancestors and relatives], in *Walter Benjamin und sein Engel: Vierzehn Aufsätze und kleine Beiträge* [Walter Benjamin and his angel: fourteen essays and minor pieces], ed. Rolf Tiedemann (Frankfurt am Main: Suhrkamp, 1983), pp. 128–57, esp. p. 145; see also Gershom Scholem, *Walter Benjamin: The Story of a Friendship*, trans. Harry Zohn (New York: NYRB Classics, 2003), p. 250.

a relatively complete collection of his writings: Scholem's archive contains the vast majority of Benjamin's published works, as well as some manuscripts.

Prof. Arthur Rosenberg: Arthur Rosenberg (1889–1943), a historian and member of the KPD [German Communist Party] was a member of the Reichstag until 1928. In 1933 he fled to England via Zurich, and in 1937 he immigrated to New York.

my brother Werner: Werner Scholem (1895–1940) was a KPD politician and a member of the Reichstag. In 1917 he was arrested for taking part in an anti-war demonstration and was later sentenced to nine months in prison for *lèse-majesté*. In 1924 he was elected as a Reichstag representative for the KPD. In 1926 he was expelled from the party, though he remained a member of the Reichstag until 1933. The Nazis arrested him that year, and he was shot in the Buchenwald concentration camp in 1940. See Mirjam Zadoff, *Werner Scholem: A German Life*, trans. Dona Geyer (Philadelphia: University of Pennsylvania Press, 2018). Gershom Scholem learned of his brother's death in a letter from his mother. See *Gershom Scholem: A Life in Letters*, ed. and trans. Anthony David Skinner (Cambridge, MA: Harvard University Press, 2002), pp. 306-7.

my big English book: See Gershom Scholem, *Major Trends in Jewish Mysticism* (Jerusalem: 1941; rev. edn., New York: Schocken, 1995). The book is based on a series of lectures that Scholem gave at the Jewish Institute of Religion in New York in 1938 as part of the "Hilda Stich Stroock Lectures."

7 ADORNO TO SCHOLEM
NEW YORK, 19.11.1940

19 November 1940

Dear Mr. Scholem,

I received your telegram. There is no longer any possible doubt about Walter's death. We have received reports by letter from various parties; we also know that he has been buried in Port Bou. I am enclosing a copy of a letter from the lady with whom he attempted to cross the border.

Apparently the events unfolded as follows: Walter, who had been complaining of a heart condition for about six months, was unfit for the exertions caused by the 12-hour hike through the mountains. He suffered a heart attack. From this he seems to have recovered, and is said to have led the small group with astonishing energy. But, even so, it was evidently too much for him. My brother-in-law, Egon Wissing, who, as you may know, is Benjamin's cousin – and someone with whom he was together for much of the harshest period of his exile in the south of France – told me that, during a hike in the mountains of Monte Carlo, Walter came down with altitude sickness and it was only with the greatest difficulty that he could be brought back to Monte.

What occurred after the crossing of the Spanish border was of such a nature that Walter's depleted physical strength was insufficient to withstand it. The Spaniards threatened to send the entire group back to France the following morning. Walter is reported to have categorically declared that he was staying and not walking on. He didn't hold out until the morning but took morphine during the night. When one of the ladies attempted to bribe the border guards the following morning – successfully, by the way – Walter told her what he had done and and then immediately lost consciousness. A physician who had been summoned refused to pump Walter's stomach, as he had apparently suffered a brain haemorrhage and was already dying. In all likelihood this physician was a nitwit – or worse. In any case, it does not appear as though any serious action was taken. Walter then died in the evening, one day after he had taken the poison. His travel companion, Mrs. Gurland, stayed with him until the very end and seems to have behaved very decently. She also took care of funeral arrangements and bought a grave for 5 years.

There can be no doubt that Walter would have been rescued had he only held out for another 12 hours. We were already looking for an apartment for him. He had also been made a permanent member of the Institute and he knew that. All that is humanly possible would have been done to take care of him materially. He also had an American visa. If he had only just telegraphed us, we could have officially intervened as an American institution. He had already crossed out of France, and the Spaniards haven't sent a single person back in earnest; evidently, only some subalterns made threats in order to pocket bribes. Walter had sufficient financial means, but he seems only to have had a small part of his money on him. He knew that he could count on us materially, however, so it is impossible that the question of money played any significant role. He also had with him letters of recommendation from high-ranking French clerics to Spanish ones. But he made no use of these and also did not request a doctor. It is all completely incomprehensible – as if he was seized by a stupor and sought as though to extinguish himself, as someone who had already been rescued. It is a chain of catastrophes that can scarcely be imagined. I have no words to express to you what this means for us; it has altered our mental and empirical existence to the innermost core, and has gripped Gretel and me with an apathy, which will probably only reach its limit with our own actual demise.

We had a ceremony at the Institute, and Pollock read an excerpt from one of the French *Arcades* drafts that Horkheimer and I had translated, and he spoke of Walter in words truly commensurate to his significance. But what's the use now, when it is as if the only guarantor of hope has been taken away.

Walter's manuscripts appear to be safe, and we are doing everything we can to bring them here. I will write to you in further detail as soon as I myself know more. It goes without saying that everything will be done by us to save what can be saved. Some pieces are at the Institute, some are at our place, and some are at Wissing's. The most important thing, it seems to me, is to collect as many of Benjamin's texts as are accessible to us, with the ultimate goal of putting together a complete edition. I would like to ask you to help us by sending copies of everything that is available to you. We are missing two of Benjamin's major texts: the piece on Hölderlin, of which he often spoke to me, but which I have never read, and the extraordinarily important work on fate and character from *Die Argonauten*, with which I am familiar. Do you have those? I also lack the dissertation, although that should not be too hard to access.

As you probably know, our journal now appears in English. However, we are preparing a final German volume that will be mimeographed and distributed in limited numbers. Among other things, it will contain Horkheimer's piece on state capitalism and my essay on George and Hofmannsthal. It is of vital importance to us to include an unpublished text by Benjamin in this issue. We have considered the French *Arcades* exposé, although perhaps something can be found that represents Walter more quintessentially. Can you think of anything? I vividly remember a letter about Kafka that you read to us here. Would you make that available to us? What else could be considered? The Hölderlin piece? Aside from the wonderful Baudelaire essay that we printed, we have a second, older manuscript, parts of which we could publish if need be – even though it does not compare in quality to the printed piece. We also have large parts of the handwritten *Berlin Childhood* manuscript, but too much of that has already appeared in newspapers.

I repeat my question as to whether you could not secure another invitation from the Jewish Theological Seminary. Frankly, you are just about the only person in the old world in whose rescue I still take an interest after Walter's death. Please excuse this clunky confession; the world no longer permits one to speak in allusive terms. Surely it must be possible for you to come here. I am quite certain of a British victory, but the nature of whatever may unfold between today and such a victory is such that I prefer not to associate it with the thought of you.

All that is cordial, also from Gretel

in loyal affinity

yours

Teddie Wiesengrund-Adorno

Original: typescript, with the copy of a letter from Grete Freund; Gershom Scholem Archive, The National Library of Israel, Jerusalem. First published in Rolf Tiedemann (ed.), *Frankfurter Adorno Blätter* V (Munich: Edition Text + Kritik, 1998), pp. 150–3.

your telegram: Not preserved.

a letter from the lady: See Grete Freund's letter to an unknown addressee, Lisbon, the 9th of October 1940, in Walter Benjamin, *Gesammelte Schriften* V.2, ed. Rolf Tiedemann (Frankfurt am Main: 2015), pp. 1194–5.

My brother in law, Egon Wissing: The physician, Egon Wissing (1900–1984) worked at the Institute for Cancer Research in Moscow in the mid-1930s. Later he immigrated to the United States, where he worked at the Massachusetts Memorial Hospital in Boston. Wissing was Benjamin's maternal cousin. In the spring of 1940 he married the dentist Liselotte Karplus (1909–1998), Gretel Adorno's sister.

Pollock: The economist and sociologist Friedrich Pollock (1894–1970) was a co-founder of the Institute for Social Research and a lifelong friend of Max Horkheimer's. He completed his doctorate in 1923, followed by his *Habilitation* in 1928, both at the University of Frankfurt. Pollock was the Institute's chief administrator and financial officer. After immigrating to Switzerland in 1933, he directed the Institute's Geneva branch. In 1934 he went to Paris and then to New York, where he resumed his work for the Institute while also teaching at Columbia University. In 1950 he returned to Germany and the following year became an adjunct professor of political economy and sociology at the University of Frankfurt, where he was tenured in 1958.

the French Arcades *drafts*: See Walter Benjamin's French exposé, "Paris, capitale du XIXe siècle" [Paris, capital of the XIXth century], in *The Arcades Project*, ed. Rolf Tiedemann, trans. Howard Eiland and Kevin McLaughlin (Cambridge, MA: The Belknap Press of Harvard University Press, 1996), pp. 14–26.

Walter's manuscripts appear to be safe: See letter no. 10 in this volume.

the piece on Hölderlin: See Walter Benjamin, "Two Poems by Friedrich Hölderlin," in *Selected Writings*, Vol. 1: *1913–1926*, ed. Marcus Bullock and Michael W. Jennings (Cambridge, MA: The Belknap Press of Harvard University Press, 1996), pp. 18–36.

fate and character from Die Argonauten: See Walter Benjamin, "Schicksal und Charakter," *Die Argonauten*, 1/10–12 (1921); "Fate and Character," in *Selected Writings*, Vol. 1: *1913–1926*, ed. Marcus Bullock and Michael W. Jennings (Cambridge, MA: The Belknap Press of Harvard University Press, 1996), pp. 201–6.

the dissertation: Walter Benjamin's dissertation *The Concept of Art Criticism in German Romanticism* first appeared in 1920 as the fifth volume of the *Neue Berner Abhandlungen zur Philosophie und ihrer Geschichte* [New Berne essays on philosophy and its history], a series edited by Richard Herbertz for the A. Francke Verlag. See Walter Benjamin, "The Concept of Criticism in German Romanticism," in *Selected Writings*, Vol. 1: *1913–1926*, ed. Marcus Bullock and Michael W. Jennings (Cambridge, MA: The Belknap Press of Harvard University Press, 1996), pp. 116–200.

a final German volume: A special issue of the *Zeitschrift für Sozialforschung*, titled "Walter Benjamin zum Gedächtnis" [In memory of Walter Benjamin] was published by the Institute in Los Angeles in 1942. The issue contained Benjamin's theses "On the Concept of History," a "Bibliographische Notiz" [bibliographic note] about Benjamin's works, as well as essays by Horkheimer ("Vernunft und Selbsterhaltung" [Reason and self-preservation] and "Autoritärer Staat" [The authoritarian state]), and Adorno's essay "George und Hofmannsthal. Zum Briefwechsel: 1891-1906" [George and Hofmannsthal: On the Correspondence 1891–1906].

a letter about Kafka: Benjamin's letter to Scholem, dated the 12th of June 1938, consists of two parts. The first part consists of a discussion of Max Brod's Kafka biography, followed by Benjamin's own reflections on Kafka. In the second part of the letter, Benjamin explained his intention to write up his views on Kafka separately, so as to "keep it presentable" in order for Scholem to "give it to [the publisher, Salman] Schocken" with a view to possible publication. See *The Correspondence of Walter Benjamin and Gershom Scholem, 1932–1940*, ed. Gershom Scholem, trans. Gary Smith and Andre Lefevere (New York, Schocken Books, 1989), pp. 220–226, here p. 226. Schocken, however, was not interested. On Salman Schocken, see the relevant note accompanying letter no. 31 in this volume.

Baudelaire essay . . . a second, older manuscript: Adorno is referring to the version of "The Paris of the Second Empire in Baudelaire," which had been rejected by the *Zeitschrift für Sozialforschung*. See Walter Benjamin, "The Paris of the Second Empire in Baudelaire," in *Selected Writings*, Vol. 4: *1938–1940*, ed. Howard Eiland and Michael W. Jennings (Cambridge, MA: The Belknap Press of Harvard University Press, 2006), pp. 3–92. (See also letter no. 2 in this volume, and the relevant note).

parts of the handwritten Berlin Childhood *manuscript*: Adorno is referring to the so-called Felizitas-Exemplar [Felicitas copy], Benjamin's handwritten draft, which was first published in facsimile in *Werke und Nachlass 11: Berliner Chronik / Berliner Kindheit um neunzehnhundert* [Works and writings from the estate 11: Berlin chronicle / Berlin childhood around 1900], ed. Burkhardt Lindner (Frankfurt am Main: Suhrkamp, 2019). Most of the pieces collected in *Berlin Childhood around 1900* first appeared between December 1932 and August 1934 in the newspapers *Frankfurter Zeitung* and *Vossische Zeitung* and in 1938 in the exile journal *Maß und Wert*. See "Berlin Childhood around 1900," in *Selected Writings*, Vol. 3: *1935–1938*, ed. Howard Eiland and Michael W. Jennings (Cambridge, MA: The Belknap Press of Harvard University Press, 2002), pp. 344–413.

8 SCHOLEM TO ADORNO
JERUSALEM, 17.7.1941

Jerusalem, 17-7-41
Abarbanel R^{d}, 28

Dear Mr. Adorno

I am writing you these few lines in the hope that they will reach you – an acquaintance of mine who is travelling to Cuba will send them to you.

I don't know whether the letters that I wrote you following Walter's death, and my response to your letter from the end of '40 ever reached you! I haven't heard from you in six months, and perhaps stuff of yours has gotten lost. I very much hope to hear, at length, from you and your wife! Among other things, I sent you a copy of the letter about Kafka, as you had asked me. In the meantime, I have obtained the address of Walter's wife (who has entered into a pseudo-marriage). Just imagine: she knew nothing of Walter's death until now! You can reach her at: Mrs. Dora Morser, 62 Leinster Square, London W. 2 – in actuality, she is living in the country, since the house has been destroyed. Stefan has been <u>interned</u> in Australia and would like to go to America. Perhaps you and your friends can help him from there.

We are well. We are still here, and I am working. My big English book, which I mentioned to you, is all but printed – but who knows when copies will arrive in America. I will have a copy sent to you directly from here – perhaps, if it suits you, you could even announce it in the *Zeitschrift*! It will be sufficiently interesting to you, that I predict! Meanwhile, I continue to work a lot. The war has moved away from us, surprisingly enough, so you can consider us to be living in tolerable safety for the time being. But we do not hear much from the outside world. If you want to make me happy, send me a few journals from over there on occasion! I received the first English edition of your journal and am studying it with great interest. I am waiting for the next issues.

With cordial regards for your wife and you

yours Gerhard Scholem

Original: manuscript; Theodor W. Adorno Archive, Frankfurt am Main.

An acquaintance who is travelling to Cuba: Not verified.

the address of Walter's wife: In 1938 Walter Benjamin's ex-wife, Dora Sophie Benjamin, née Kellner (1890–1964), married the South African businessman Harry Morser in London.

Stefan has been <u>*interned*</u> *in Australia*: Walter and Dora's son, Stefan Rafael Benjamin (1918–1972), initially lived in San Remo and London with his mother. During the Second World War he was interned in Australia. He returned to London after the War, where he worked as an antiquarian book dealer.

9 SCHOLEM TO ADORNO JERUSALEM, 25.1.1942*

28 Abarbanel Road – Jerusalem

25–I–1942

My dear Wiesengrund – I just got Nr. II of the last year of the *Studies in Social Science*. Nr. I never got here – as no letter of yours has ever reached me since last January. I wonder if you have forgotten me. I wrote you several times, for the last time in July. It would be good to hear from you. I sent you a copy of Walter Benjamin's letter on Kafka – no reply. Meanwhile my book has appeared in English, *Major Trends in Jewish Mysticism*, dedicated to Walter B's memory.

* Original postcard in English.

Please get in touch with The Jewish Institute of Religion (40 West 68th street) – especially with Dr. Sh. Spiegel there – in order to secure a copy for you (600 copies have been sent there). Of course, the book may not arrive in New York before April. It surely will interest you. Kind regards to you and your wife

yours Gerhard Scholem.

Original: postcard (manuscript); Theodor W. Adorno Archive, Frankfurt am Main.

dedicated to Walter B's memory: Scholem's book contains the following dedication: "TO THE MEMORY OF / WALTER BENJAMIN / (1892–1940) / THE FRIEND OF A LIFETIME / WHOSE GENIUS UNITED / THE INSIGHT OF THE METAPHYSICIAN / THE INTERPRETATIVE POWER OF THE CRITIC / AND THE ERUDITION OF THE SCHOLAR / DIED AT PORTBOU (SPAIN) / ON HIS WAY INTO FREEDOM."

The Jewish Institute of Religion . . . Dr. Sh. Spiegel: Shalom Spiegel (1899–1984), born in Austria-Hungary, was a high-school teacher in Haifa, Palestine, from 1923 to 1928. In 1929 he immigrated to New York, where he became professor of medieval Hebrew literature at the Jewish Theological Seminary. On the 8th of January 1941 Scholem wrote to Spiegel: "The most important recent event is the death of my friend Walter Benjamin, who took his life while fleeing over the border from France to Spain. I'll never recover from this terrible blow. I received a detailed letter from Dr. Wiesengrund-Adorno, the only one in New York who still writes me. I was able to surmise from this letter the awful depth of this tragedy." See *Gershom Scholem: A Life in Letters*, ed. and trans. Anthony David Skinner (Cambridge, MA: Harvard University Press, 2002), pp. 311–12.

10 ADORNO TO SCHOLEM
LOS ANGELES, 19.2.1942*

T. W. Adorno
316 So. Kenter Ave,
Brentwood Heights,
Los Angeles, Calif.

19 February 1942.

Dear Mr. Scholem:

I got your letter of July 1941 and the post card which reached us via Cuba only here and did not hear from you in the meantime. The last letter of yours I got I answered immediately and nothing

* Original letter in English.

in between has reached me, also not the copy of Walter's letter on Kafka.

The most important thing I have to write you is that two suit cases with manuscripts and books of Walter have reached us in New York. A friend of his, Dr. Dohmke, brought them over here. He told us many things about the reasons for Walter's death, some of which sounded rather fantastic. According to Dohmke Walter had decided to take his life anyway and had probably killed himself even if he had safely come to Lisbon. This is supposedly due partly to his fear to lose his independence and unique intellectual position he had in France (a consideration which of course is entirely baseless, since nobody ever had thought of curtailing in the least his originality or to charge him with any routine work), partly to an absolutely unimportant literary affair he had with a man called Krafft, who incidentally right now is in Jerusalem (the issue is the priority of the discovery of Jochmann). But all this cannot possibly explain what has happened and it remains as senseless, as completely beyond any reconciliation as ever before.

I made a complete catalogue of the content of these suit cases. It becomes much more complete with regard to the last years than to Walter's earlier period. Still, there are comparatively few things which I did not know. The most important ones are a selection of exceedingly bold notes bearing the title Zentralpark [Central Park] (a double entendu referring to the importance of these notes as well as to his plans to come to New York) which evidently should be the nucleus for the last big section of the Baudelaire book which never was written. There are also the historico-philosophical theses of spring 1940 which you probably know. There is, however, not a single trace of the huge material of the Passagenarbeit [Arcades Project] which doubtless exists somewhere. There are rumors that he has deposited this material at the Bibliothèque Nationale in Paris. There is a certain hope that they may hibernate there and that we can get hold of them after the war. Among the books is the very rare *Argonauten* volume, containing the study Schicksal und Charakter [Fate and Character] which I did not know but which is a kind of blue print of the whole of Walter's philosophy, and also a study on Dostoevsky's *Idiot*. His early study on Hölderlin, however, as far as I know an interpretation of "Patmos" which I never read but for which he himself expressed great esteem, was not among the manuscripts. Do you own it?

The whole question of an edition of Walter's works can be approached only after the war. Happily enough, however, there are several people who have a kind of Benjamin archive. Besides his own material, our private material and the extensive material of the

Institute, Walter's old friend Cohn has a pretty complete archive which he certainly would make available. I feel confident that you also have many things which are otherwise unaccessible and if we combine our efforts it should be possible to reconstruct Walter's oeuvre to rather a great extent. What we plan to do right now is to bring out a mimeographed German issue of our *Zeitschrift* dedicated to the memory of Walter which will contain his own historico-philosophical theses (the last text which he finished) a study on the dialectics of reason which Horkheimer and I completed right now and my own study on George and Hofmannsthal which was the last of my things that Walter knew and endorsed. I am looking forward to your reading the study on reason which I feel very strongly will be a surprise to you in more than one respect.

I gave order to send you everything of our periodical that has appeared in English. So far there are out three English issues: the one which contains my article on Kierkegaard's doctrine of love, the "Communication issue" and the issue on state capitalism with Horkheimer's Art and Mass Culture and my Spengler. Did you get all this? I wrote, apart from that, rather an extensive study "Philosophy of Advanced Music" which is going to appear in the *Journal of Aesthetics* and a study of Thorstein Veblen, so far unpublished.

Is your book out? Please let me have it as soon as possible. The fact that you have completed a chef d'oeuvre is one of the very few positive things which I find in life.

We have moved to California in fall. There are a good many reasons which caused us to take this decision. The most important is that we hope to find the time here to finally bring in the harvest of our theoretical efforts for so many years, which in New York was practically impossible. Here Horkheimer and I can devote our whole time to writing, practically undisturbed. It is more beautiful here than we ever imagined – the working conditions are simply ideal. We have a very nice little house and an old car, see very few people and devote ourselves to the dianoetic virtue which is anyway the one thing that makes any sense in this world of ours. The idea that Walter could – and would! – certainly be here with us and would find the calm to complete his things without worries if he had had a little more patience drives me crazy. Even his Brecht is quite close and if he had insisted upon seeing him daily we could have driven him there in five minutes.

Probably the fact that so many of your letters have been lost is due to the language in which they were written. I therefore write in English today and ask you to excuse the deficiencies of this communication with the desire to communicate with you at all. It might be a good idea if you would write me back in English as well.

I send you wholeheartedly my best wishes and am longing for your letter. Kindest regards also from Gretel.

Most cordially yours,

Teddie W. Adorno

Original: typescript; Gershom Scholem Archive, The National Library of Israel, Jerusalem. First published in Rolf Tiedemann (ed.), *Frankfurter Adorno Blätter* V (Munich: Edition Text + Kritik, 1998), pp. 153–6. An excerpt of this letter appears in *Gershom Scholem: A Life in Letters*, ed. and trans. Anthony David Skinner (Cambridge, MA: Harvard University Press, 2002), p. 313.

two suit cases with manuscripts and books of Walter ... Dr. Dohmke, brought them over here: Adorno's spelling. Martin Domke (1892–1980), a friend of Walter Benjamin's, worked until 1933 as a lawyer in Berlin, where he belonged to the circle around Bertolt Brecht. He immigrated to Paris in 1933 and then to the USA in 1941, where he initially worked as a lawyer specializing in international commercial law. From 1950, he worked as an adjunct professor of jurisprudence at New York University. Domke collected works by the natural scientist and author Georg Cristoph Lichtenberg (1742–1799). He commissioned Benjamin to catalog the collection. This commission produced the so-called Lichtenberg file, the groundwork for the Lichtenberg bibliography.

unimportant literary affair...with a man called Krafft ... the discovery of Jochmann: In 1939 Walter Benjamin published "The Regression of Poetry," his selected excerpts from an essay of that title by the forgotten German author Carl Gustav Jochmann (1789–1830), with Benjamin's Introduction. The piece appeared in the *Zeitschrift für Sozialforschung*, Vol. 8, pp. 92–114. Werner Kraft (1896–1991) (Adorno's misspelling) had drawn Benjamin's attention to this author in 1937. Benjamin, for his part, had told Horkheimer, whom Kraft had contacted via mail, that he had become aware of Jochmann independently of Kraft.

Zentralpark [Central Park]: Written between 1939 and 1940, the fragments known as *Central Park* were first published in Theodor W. Adorno and Walter Dirks (eds), *Sociologica: Aufsätze, Max Horkheimer zum sechzigsten Geburtstag gewidmet* [Sociologica: essays for Max Horkheimer on his sixtieth birthday] (Frankfurt am Main: Europäische Verlagsanstalt, 1955); See Benjamin, "Central Park," in *Selected Writings*, Vol. 4: *1938–1940*, ed. Howard Eiland and Michael W. Jennings (Cambridge, MA: The Belknap Press of Harvard University Press, 2006), pp. 161–99. For an overview of the publication history, see Benjamin, *Gesammelte Schriften I.3*, ed. Rolf Tiedemann and Hermann Schweppenhäuser (Frankfurt am Main: Suhrkamp, 1974), pp. 1216–19.

historico-philosophical theses of spring 1940: Benjamin's theses "On the Concept of History," written between 1939 and 1949, first appeared in the mimeographed edition *Walter Benjamin zum Gedächtnis* [In memory of Walter Benjamin] (1942). See Benjamin, "On the Concept of History," in *Selected Writings*, Vol. 4: *1938–1940*, ed. Howard Eiland and Michael W.

Jennings (Cambridge, MA: The Belknap Press of Harvard University Press, 2006), pp. 389–400.

Passagenarbeit [Arcades Project]... Bibliothèque Nationale in Paris: The manuscripts comprising *The Arcades Project* were in fact hidden at the Bibliothèque Nationale de France by Georges Bataille (1897–1962). See Rolf Tiedemann and Hermann Schweppenhäuser's editorial remarks in Benjamin, *Gesammelte Schriften I.2* (Frankfurt am Main: Suhrkamp, 1974), p. 759.

Argonauten ... *Schicksal und Charakter [Fate and Character]*: See letter no. 7 in this volume.

a study on Dostoevsky's Idiot: Benjamin's short text "Dostoevsky's *The Idiot*," written in 1917, was first published in 1921 in the Heidelberg-based journal *Die Argonauten*. See Benjamin, "Dostoevsky's *The Idiot*," in *Selected Writings*, Vol. 1: *1913–1926*, ed. Marcus Bullock and Michael W. Jennings (Cambridge, MA: The Belknap Press of Harvard University Press, 1996), pp. 78–81.

early study on Hölderlin ... an interpretation of "Patmos": Benjamin's essay "Two Poems by Friedrich Hölderlin" treats the poems "Dichtermut" [The poet's courage] and "Blödigkeit" [Timidity] and not, as Adorno mistakenly assumed, the "Patmos" hymn (see letters nos. 11 and 18 in this volume). See Benjamin, "Two Poems by Friedrich Hölderlin," in *Selected Writings*, Vol. 1: *1913–1926*, ed. Marcus Bullock and Michael W. Jennings (Cambridge, MA: The Belknap Press of Harvard University Press, 1996), pp. 18–36.

Walter's old friend Cohn: The businessman Alfred Cohn (1892–1954) was a close schoolfriend of Walter Benjamin's. In 1921 he married Benjamin's first fiancée, Grete Radt.

mimeographed German issue of our Zeitschrift dedicated to the memory of Walter: See letter no. 7 and the relevant note in this volume.

three English issues: This refers to *Studies in Philosophy and Social Science*, Vol. 8/3 (1939), Vol. 9/1, "the Communication issue" (1941), and Vol. 9/2, "the issue on state capitalism" (1941). Of the three pieces that Adorno names by title, his essay, "On Kierkegaard's Doctrine of Love" appeared in Vol. 8/3, pp. 413–429; Horkheimer's "Art and Mass Culture" appeared in Vol. 9/2, pp. 290–304 (reprinted in Max Horkheimer, *Critical Theory: Selected Essays* (New York: Continuum, 2002, pp. 273–90); and Adorno's "Spengler Today" appeared in Vol. 9/2, pp. 305–325.

"Philosophy of Advanced Music": At the time of writing this letter, Adorno had only planned the Schoenberg chapter of his *Philosophy of New Music*. However, this did not appear in the *Journal of Aesthetics*. The text was expanded to include a section on Stravinsky and was published by J.C.B. Mohr (Paul Siebeck) in Tübingen in 1949.

a study of Thorstein Veblen: See Theodor W. Adorno, "Veblen's Attack on Culture," in *Studies in Philosophy and Social Science*, Vol. 9/3 (1941), pp. 389–413; reprinted in *Prisms*, trans. Samuel Weber and Shierry Weber (Cambridge, MA: MIT Press, 1981), pp. 73–94.

Is your book out?: Scholem's *Major Trends in Jewish Mysticism* was published in Jerusalem in 1941. See letter no. 6 and the relevant note in this volume.

We have moved to California in fall: The Adornos followed Horkheimer to Los Angeles, where a planned work on materialist logic was to be written.

11 SCHOLEM TO ADORNO
JERUSALEM, 27.3.1942

G. SCHOLEM
28, Abarbanel Rd.,
JERUSALEM-Rehavia.

Jerusalem, March 27, 1942*

Dear Mr. Adorno,

To my delighted surprise, your airmail letter of 19.2. reached me yesterday. I am responding right away in the hope that the journey in the opposite direction will also only take four weeks. For the sake of convenience, I am writing in German rather than English, since I am convinced that the loss of my previous letters had nothing to do with the language in which they were written. But you should continue doing as you like.

The loss of my letters from the beginning of last year is very painful to me. I had sent you a synopsis of what I possess of Benjamin's literary estate. I am, of course, very interested in facilitating the collection of all of Benjamin's writings in a safe place in America for a possible edition after the war. Naturally, what you write about this possibility is extremely interesting to me. To repeat myself: I probably have the most extensive collection of his works, aside from what he himself had, which seems to be lost. With the exception of his contributions to the journal *Der Anfang* (1912–14), I essentially have everything written since 1915 that he has published, aside from a few insignificant minutiae or occasional writings, copies of which should be easy to obtain. All of his important reviews and critical essays are with me. With respect to the unpublished writings, I only have these in part, of course. I never received the historical-philosophical theses from the spring of 1940, so I look forward to seeing the text that you have with doubled excitement. By contrast, I do have what appears to be the only remaining copy of his 1915 Hölderlin essay, which, as you correctly note, he always saw as of the greatest importance. This is esoteric literature in the most eminent sense, exceedingly condensed and profound. It is not, as you believe, a commentary on Hölderlin's "Patmos," but, rather, an investigation of the two poems

* Date in English in the original.

"Dichtermut" [The poet's courage] and "Blödigkeit" [Timidity], and the relationship between them. In a publication of his literary estate, it would have to appear first. Of his early work, I also have the "Metaphysics of Youth" – the magnum opus of the youth movement, which remained incomplete – only two out of the six sections have been fully elaborated ("The Conversation" and "The Diary"). In addition, I have a whole file of unpublished essays from the years of our joint studies 1916–1919, including the manuscript "On the Program of the Coming Philosophy," from 1918, as well as "On Language as Such and on the Language of Man" – a 23-page letter written to me in 1916. Parts of the latter were taken up verbatim into the book on the origin of the *Trauerspiel.* Of course, given the current state of the postal service, I cannot entrust these unique items to the mail. Perhaps it could be arranged for me to have them transcribed here. Unfortunately my financial situation could not withstand such strains; however, I have had copies of the Hölderlin essay and the letter on Kafka made, which I will send to you by regular post. You will have to wait some months for them to arrive, however. It would be very nice if the commemorative volume that you mention could be out by the 15th of July, Walter's 50th birthday. I have no objections if you would like to include the letter that he wrote to me about Kafka.

It would likewise be exceedingly important to compile Benjamin's correspondence. During his early years, there must have been no small number of noteworthy exchanges with various people about whom I know; but these letters may not have been preserved. On the other hand, I can't imagine that there isn't a complete collection somewhere of his correspondence with Dora, Ernst Bloch (ugh, ugh . . . or do you happen to have some particular affection for this person?), the lady Lacis, Florens Christian Rang, Hessel, Wolfgang Heinle, and others. I've saved all of the letters he wrote to me in the past 25 years, and I suppose that my letters to him (I only made copies in 3 or 4 cases) might be found somewhere in his literary estate. His letters to me total more than 300. One of his most notable exchanges was with Mr. Kraft, whom you mention, but after a supposed quarrel between them in 1921, Kraft – entirely unbidden, and to Walter's great perplexity – returned all of his letters, so they probably remained behind in Germany and got lost. Many of these letters were long treatises on literary and aesthetic questions. Perhaps there is some way to collect copies of all these materials in one place? By the way, the piece on Dostoevsky's *Idiot*, which you mention, played a very important role in both of our lives; along with "Fate and Character," it is, without a doubt, his most concealing and, at the same time, most revealing piece from the years after he wrote the text on Hölderlin. Any investigation into the volume that Benjamin prepared of works by his childhood friend Edwin Heinle, who committed suicide on the 10th of August 1914, would also be of the utmost significance. He wanted to write a lengthy introduction to accompany it, but based on his letters, it was never clear to me whether he did so or not.

I'm very curious about your work, and I would ask you to send it to me regularly. Of the three English editions of your journal, I have received only the first and the third, but not the one in the middle. I have already asked you to re-send it once. It's a real pity that we cannot discuss your essays verbally, because in writing, it simply isn't feasible. Let me just say that I have been reading them with the greatest sympathy, both in agreement and disagreement. I am very sorry that your work on Husserl, which I saw in manuscript in New York, has not been published. I would have liked to have a copy of it. Of course, the same limitations apply to the possibility of a face-to-face exchange about my book, about which I'm even more sorry! My book came out 4 months ago (comprised of almost 30 octavos) and almost the entire print run has gone to America. I have urged my friend Spiegel in New York to send you a copy as soon as the book arrives for distribution, either for review in the *Zeitschrift* or simply for your private use. If you have not received it by April or May, I will send you a separate copy from here, which, hopefully, at any rate, will reach you. I have to be brief today, so I have one final question: do you or Horkheimer know any theoretical political economists over there (maybe from the émigré circles) who could be recommended for an appointment to the economics department of our university? In contention are Jews with a feeling for the endeavor in Palestine and for the problems of this country. I figured that maybe you could give me some useful suggestions. I may have written to you that I will hold the deanship of the faculty of humanities this year and next.

If you could possibly send me a catalog of the texts by Benjamin that are in your and your friends' possession, I could then compare and supplement it with my own. Do you think that could be done? I conclude with warmest wishes for your wife and for you. It is now four years since we sat together in New York. What worlds and what memories lie in between! Greetings to all of our mutual acquaintances, and especially to Hanna Arendt-Blücher, about whom I'm only sorry that she is not sitting here with us. In the hope of seeing you again, most cordially, yours

Gerhard Scholem

Original: typescript; Theodor W. Adorno Archive, Frankfurt am Main. First published in Scholem, *Briefe I: 1914–1947*, ed. Itta Shedletzky (Munich: C.H. Beck, 1994), pp. 286-288. An excerpt of this letter appears in translation in *Gershom Scholem: A Life in Letters*, ed. and trans. Anthony David Skinner (Cambridge, MA: Harvard University Press, 2002), p. 314.

the journal Der Anfang *(1912–14)*: The journal *Der Anfang* appeared in Berlin between 1908 and 1914 (from 1911 on, with the subtitle *Vereinigte Zeitschriften der Jugend* and from 1913–14, with the subtitle *Zeitschrift der Jugend.*) *Der Anfang* was the journal of the circle around the pedagogue Gustav Wyneken and the Youth Movement in which Benjamin was involved between 1910 and 1914. Starting in 1910 Benjamin wrote poems and prose pieces for the journal, which he published under the pseudonym "Ardor."

"Metaphysics of Youth": Scholem's transcript is the only surviving copy of Benjamin's text "Metaphysics of Youth." See Benjamin, "Metaphysics of Youth," in *Selected Writings*, Vol. 1: *1913–1926*, ed. Marcus Bullock and Michael W. Jennings (Cambridge, MA: The Belknap Press of Harvard University Press, 1996), pp. 6–17.

the period of our joint studies 1916–1919: Benjamin, who had begun his studies in philosophy, German, and art history in Freiburg im Breisgau, transferred to the University of Berlin in 1915, where Scholem was studying mathematics from 1915 to 1917. Benjamin moved in 1916 to Munich and in 1917 to Berne (see letter no. 36 in this volume).

"On the Program of the Coming Philosophy," from 1918: Here too, Scholem's transcript is the only surviving copy of Benjamin's text. See Benjamin, "On the Program of the Coming Philosophy," in *Selected Writings*, Vol. 1: *1913–1926*, ed. Marcus Bullock and Michael W. Jennings (Cambridge, MA: The Belknap Press of Harvard University Press, 1996), pp. 100–110.

"On Language as Such and on the Language of Man" – a 23-page letter written to me in 1916: As Benjamin writes to Scholem on the 11th of November 1916, the piece had begun as a letter to Scholem "that ended up being eighteen pages long." See *The Correspondence of Walter Benjamin 1910–1940*, ed. Theodor W. Adorno and Gershom Scholem, trans. Manfred R. Jacobson and Evelyn M. Jacobson (Chicago: University of Chicago Press, 1994), p. 81. It was subsequently developed into an essay in its own right. See Benjamin, "On Language as Such and on the Language of Man," in *Selected Writings, Vol. 1: 1913–1926*, ed. Marcus Bullock and Michael W. Jennings (Cambridge, MA: The Belknap Press of Harvard University Press,1996), pp. 62–74.

Ernst Bloch: Benjamin and Scholem became acquainted with the philosopher Ernst Bloch (1885–1977) during their time together in Switzerland. Parts of the correspondence have been preserved. See Ernst Bloch: *Briefe 1903-1975*, Volume 2, ed. Karola Bloch, Jan Robert Bloch, Anne Frommann (Frankfurt am Main: Suhrkamp, 1985), pp. 649–68.

The lady Lacis: The Latvian actress and director Asja Anna Ernestowna Lācis (1891–1972) met Benjamin in Capri in 1924. On the 7th of July 1924 he wrote to Scholem: "I made the acquaintance of a Russian revolutionary from Riga, one of the most splendid women I have ever met" (*The*

Correspondence of Walter Benjamin 1910–1940, ed. Theodor W. Adorno and Gershom Scholem, trans. Manfred R. Jacobson and Evelyn M. Jacobson (Chicago: University of Chicago Press, 1994), p. 245). Between 1928 and 1929 they lived together in Berlin. Walter Benjamin's book *One-Way Street* bears the dedication "This street is named Asja Lacis street after her who as an engineer cut it through the author." See Benjamin, "One-Way Street," in *Selected Writings*, Vol. 1: *1913–1926*, ed. Marcus Bullock and Michael W. Jennings (Cambridge, MA: The Belknap Press of Harvard University Press, 1996), pp. 444–88.

Florens Christian Rang: Benjamin had been acquainted with the theologian and writer Florens Christian Rang (1864–1924) since 1920. See Walter Benjamin: *Gesammelte Briefe II, 1919-1924*, ed. Henri Lonitz and Christoph Gödde (Frankfurt am Main: Suhrkamp, 1996), p. 158, as well as Lorenz Jäger, *Messianische Kritik. Studien zu Leben und Werk von Florens Christian Rang* (Cologne: Böhlau, 1998).

Hessel: The writer, translator, and editor Franz Hessel (1880–1941) was a close friend of Benjamin's during the 1920s. Together they translated two volumes of Proust's *In Search of Lost Time*. See Walter Benjamin "Franz Hessel" in Benjamin, *Gesammelte Schriften III*, ed. Hella Tiedemann-Bartels (Suhrkamp: Frankfurt a.M., 1972), pp. 45–46.

Wolfgang Heinle: The poet Wolf Heinle (1899–1923) was the younger brother of the poet Friedrich (Fritz) Heinle (1894–1914), with whom Benjamin had been friends, from his student days in Berlin until the latter's suicide. See Walter Benjamin: *Gesammelte Briefe I, 1910–1918*, ed. Henri Lonitz and Christoph Gödde (Frankfurt am Main: Suhrkamp, 1995), pp. 119–122.

the volume . . . Edwin Heinle: This refers to the works of the poet Fritz Heinle, which Benjamin kept (see letter no. 10). In his will Walter Benjamin wrote: "My entire estate contains in addition to my own writings primarily the works of the brothers Fritz and Wolf Heinle . . . These comprise not only the Heinles' manuscripts but also my edited handwritten copies of their works." See Gershom Scholem, *Walter Benjamin: The Story of a Friendship*, trans. Harry Zohn (New York: NYRB Classics, 2003), p. 236. The works of both Heinle brothers stayed behind in Berlin when Benjamin left Germany and were thus lost.

your work on Husserl: See letter no. 2 and the relevant note in this volume.

Hanna Arendt-Blücher: Hannah Arendt and Heinrich Blücher (1899-1970) were married in Paris in 1940. From 1952, Blücher taught philosophy at Bard College.

12 SCHOLEM TO ADORNO
JERUSALEM, 30.9.1942

האוניברסיטה העברית
THE HEBREW UNIVERSITY

Jerusalem 30 September 1942 ירושלים
28 Abarbanel Road

Dear Mr. Wiesengrund-Adorno,

All of my attempts to get in contact with you have failed, for reasons inexplicable to me. I wrote to you in California and New York by registered Air-Mail* – and nothing. I heard from Hanna Blücher that you've published a volume dedicated to the memory of Walter Benjamin, a copy of which, unfortunately, I did not receive, as much as I have been waiting for it. In the spring I sent you a transcript of Benjamin's Hölderlin essay, but I have no certainty as to whether it reached you, in light of the great difficulties this summer. In short, since your little letter from California, I have heard nothing further from you.

Meanwhile, my English book, by some miracle, arrived in America (600 copies) sometime in July, and my friend Professor S. Spiegel at the Jewish Institute of Religion has your name on the list of those for whom copies have been reserved. If you have yet to receive a copy, simply contact him directly at the Institute (40 West 68 Street), and refer to my letter. And when you've read it, write to me if you've learned something peculiar. I am currently working on a major history of the Sabbatian movement, which I told you about in New York. I am writing in Hebrew, but there is a good chance that the book will be translated into English.

I wrote to you in the spring with an extensive survey of the works by Benjamin that are in my possession, especially the unpublished ones. Dora has written to me from England, following my urgent appeal, promising that she will write up all of the biographical details concerning Walter's life that are known to her alone, or that she is, at any rate, best equipped to comment on – especially from the years 1912 to 1923.

Here we are healthy, remarkably isolated from the rest of the world, and we feel something like the finger of God in the extraordinary fate of Palestine.

* Original in English.

To your wife and you all that is cordial,
yours Gerhard Scholem

Original: manuscript with printed and hand-annotated letterhead; Theodor W. Adorno Archive, Frankfurt am Main.

a major history of the Sabbatian movement . . . in Hebrew: Scholem's Hebrew book שבתי צבי והתנועה השבתאית בימי חייו first came out in 1957. An English edition followed in 1973 (see letter no. 59 and the relevant note in this volume). See Gershom Scholem, *Sabbatai Sevi: The Mystical Messiah, 1626–1676*, trans. R. J. Zwi Werblowsky (Princeton, NJ: Princeton University Press, 2016). Scholem told Gretel and Theodor Adorno about his research into the Sabbatian movement in New York in 1938, as Adorno recounts to Benjamin in a letter dated the 4th of March 1938: Scholem "regaled us in detail with the most astonishing things in connection with Sabbatian and Frankist mysticism; a number of which, however, sounded so clearly reminiscent of some of Rosenberg's notions about 'the people,' that Max was seriously concerned about the prospect of more of this kind actually appearing in print." See *The Complete Correspondence of Walter Benjamin and Theodor W. Adorno, 1928–1940*, ed. Henri Lonitz, trans. Nicholas Walker (Cambridge, MA: Harvard University Press, 2001), p. 249. Gretel's addition to the same letter reads: "Please forgive your Felicitas a rather cheeky question: is Scholem himself a Frankist, or does he actually believe everything he says?" (ibid, p. 253).

13 SCHOLEM TO ADORNO
JERUSALEM, 28.10.1943

האוניברסיטה העברית
THE HEBREW UNIVERSITY

28, Abarbanel Rd.
Jerusalem 28 October 1943 ירושלים

Dear master of Los Angeles and wise woman!

For the sake of speed I am writing in German. Yesterday I received the letter from your wife, dated the 22nd of August 1943, from which I have learned: a) that of all my mail (addressed to the Institute in New York), only my letter from February of '43, whose content I cannot recall, has reached you; b) that I have not received a single one of the letters mentioned by your wife; and c) that the copy of my tome that I sent you from here never arrived, but that you did get the second copy through Spiegel, thank God! To this I should add that, earlier this year, a letter that I had sent you on the 1st of April 1942, containing a copy of the letter that Walter Benjamin had written to me about Kafka, was returned to me as undeliverable by the postal service in Los Angeles. Since I sent my book on the same day, registered* as it were, it's a mystery to me why that wasn't returned as well. About the copy of the special issue on Benjamin, I never heard (through Spiegel!) saw or received anything!! What now?? Shall we cease all postal communication, or do we stand a chance?

I greatly hoped to find out two things from you: about the condition and prospects of Benjamin's literary estate – in my lost letters, I sent list upon list of the unpublished manuscripts that are in my possession – and about your situation over there, regarding which I'm entirely unclear. What are you doing on behalf of the Institute on such distant shores as Los Angeles? From your wife's few words, about which I'm doubly delighted – after more than two years! – I can see that at the Institute you are dealing with anti-Semitism, about which I can only offer you condolences. As an old historian, I sadly no longer believe that the social sciences have anything relevant to contribute on this theme. I have become increasingly convinced, unfortunately, that only the metaphysicians have something useful to say on this topic; a conviction caused not only by the hideous nonsense produced by all parties on this topic – as I've found for years, and most recently in the American papers that I've happened to get my hands on (most of which don't come here!) – but also (please allow this frankness between us) by the equally annoying and vacuous article on the Jewish question, with which Horkheimer disgraced himself in the *Zeitschrift* at the outset of the war. I suppose that only you and the devil – or, better still, his grandmother – could clarify what is supposed to come out of a "cooperation" with the dreadful assimilationists from the American Jewish Committee. No offense, but two days ago I read two issues of this committee's journal and was stunned by their idiocy and mendaciousness. They reminded me of old, and of the oldest non-sellers from 1910. So I ask you, very sincerely, to please adequately enlighten me about your work!

And what does Your Highness think of my book? Not even your wife, a Jewish child, has read it – though I would have assumed that it would doth excite her, as any dialectical truth!! How foolish I look. And here I was thinking that your journal would run a review by someone like Leo Straus or Marcuse. Never?

I'm currently writing a book (in Hebrew) about the matters treated in the Sabbatianism chapter of my *Anglicum*, which I believe I told you about in New York. Other than that I am well. After two years

* Original in English.

I am finally rid of the deanship of the faculty of the humanities, and for a year I won't sit on any committees. After the war I'd like to come over again for a year. I'm just waiting for your invitation. In the meantime you should write to me, magnanimously and at length; and send me something to read from America, including the English editions of the *Zeitschrift*, of which I only ever received the second.

Cordial regards to you both
yours, G. Scholem

Original: manuscript with printed and hand-annotated letterhead; Theodor W. Adorno Archive, Frankfurt am Main. First published in Scholem, *Briefe I: 1914–1947*, ed. Itta Shedletzky (Munich: C.H. Beck, 1994), pp. 290–91. An excerpt of this letter appears in translation in *Gershom Scholem: A Life in Letters*, ed. and trans. Anthony David Skinner (Cambridge, MA: Harvard University Press, 2002), p. 317 (in which the excerpt is mistakenly dated the 28th of January 1943).

your wife's letter from the 22nd of August 1943: Gretel Adorno's letter to Scholem has not been preserved.

my letter from February of '43: Scholem's letter has not been preserved.

at the Institute you are dealing with anti-Semitism: In collaboration with the Berkeley Public Opinion Study Group, the Californian branch of the Institute for Social Research began working on a joint research project on anti-Semitism in 1943, which led to the study, *The Authoritarian Personality* (1949/1950). See Letter no. 15 and the relevant note in this volume.

the Jewish question ... Horkheimer: On Horkheimer's essay, see letter no. 3 in this volume.

this committee's journal: Between 1938 and 1945, the journal of the American Jewish Committee was called *Contemporary Jewish Record*. In November 1945 it was renamed *Commentary*.

that your journal would run a review: A review of Scholem's book did not appear in the *Zeitschrift für Sozialforschung*.

Leo Straus: Scholem's spelling. Leo Strauss (1899–1973) was a political philosopher, who worked as a professor in the philosophy departments of the New School for Social Research in New York (1938-1949) and the University of Chicago (1949–1958).

Marcuse: Herbert Marcuse (1898–1979) was a philosopher and sociologist who belonged to the inner circle of the Institute for Social Research. In 1934 he immigrated to the USA, where he initially worked as a member of the Institute for Social Research at Columbia University, and then at the Office of Strategic Services in Washington, DC. From 1954 he was professor of philosophy at Brandeis University and from 1964, he was professor of political science at the University of California, San Diego.

a book (in Hebrew) about . . . Sabbatianism chapter of my Anglicum: The eighth lecture in Scholem's book *Major Trends in Jewish Mysticism* (see letter no. 6 in this volume) is titled "Sabbatianism and Mystical Heresy." See Scholem, *Major Trends in Jewish Mysticism* (Jerusalem: 1941; rev. edn., New York: Schocken, 1995), pp. 287–324.

14 SCHOLEM TO ADORNO
JERUSALEM, 4.7.1945

Jerusalem, 4 July 1945
Abarbanel Rd., 28

My dear Mr. Adorno,

After having heard nothing from you for probably three years, I was delighted this morning to receive the issue of the *Zeitschrift* dedicated to the memory of Walter Benjamin, which, by the way, Hanna Arendt had already prepared me to expect. I gather that the sparse note with greetings from A. is from you, and I wanted to waste no time in thanking you for the package. I read your essay therein on George and Hofmannsthal with great interest (at least, I immediately attributed it to you), and I would like to comment on it. Your piece made quite an impression on me, and, if, as I suspect, its inclusion in this volume is meant to be a productive example of your commitment to Benjamin's approach, then it seems to me to have been very successful. Surely you won't hold it against me if I, as a hopeless non-Marxist, believe I have perceived something in your analysis that was also quite evident in Benjamin's case, and that I frequently pointed out to him; namely, while many of your deepest insights are bound up with your anarchistic élan and anarchistic tendency, these are not quite at home with the method that you have adopted here. But it is also the case that a lot leaps out along the way, and if I understand Marxism in Benjamin's sense, as an esoteric method of true theology, then there is probably much to be said for the *sacrificium* that this method requires – a *sacrificium* which seems, above all, to prohibit the dialectical blasting open of the concept of society as an immanent and enclosed sphere. (A high price for philosophers, which gives the works of the "critical theorists," insofar as I have understood them, an aftertaste of "dynamite held in reserve.") Your account of the specific societal dialectic behind the clichés draping these two men is extraordinarily exciting. Even more exciting, however, are Benjamin's theses, which are truly a legacy in ciphers – the sort that only a metaphysician in the vein of Edgar Allan Poe could have devised. Did people over there have nothing to say when they read these? Or: were they not even read?

From the bibliography I can see that there is a group of essays by our friend that I do not have, and of which I was not aware. Are the manuscripts listed under the section of this title all extant? Are they with you? Out of this group I only have the Goethe essay and perhaps "Painting and Photography," although at the moment I'm unsure whether or not B. asked me to return this to him back then. I'm certain I have the Goethe piece.

In the meantime I have written a book, sent it to you, and received confirmation from your wife that it arrived. This was the last sign of life I had from you, and I'm sufficiently puzzled by it. I will spend the next three months working on the second edition, which is to be expanded by a third. It is supposed to be printed over there in the USA.

If you want to do something for me, please get me Marcuse's book on Hegel, which I have tried in vain to acquire here. What's more, you really should write to me yourself sometime. Until then, best regards and thanks to your wife and you

yours Gerhard Scholem

Original: manuscript; Theodor W. Adorno Archive, Frankfurt am Main. First published in Gershom Scholem, *Briefe I: 1914–1947*, ed. Itta Shedletzky (Munich: C. H. Beck, 1994), pp. 299–300. An excerpt of this letter appears in translation in *Gershom Scholem: A Life in Letters*, ed. and trans. Anthony David Skinner (Cambridge, MA: Harvard University Press, 2002), pp. 325–6.

the sparse note with greetings from A: Adorno's laconic dedication, written (in English) in pencil, reads "For Scholem / Regards / A."

your essay on George and Hofmannsthal: Adorno's essay "George and Hofmannsthal: On the Correspondence 1891–1906" first appeared in 1942 in the mimeographed volume "Walter Benjamin zum Gedächtnis" [In memory of Walter Benjamin] (see letter no. 7 in this volume). It was later included in the collection *Prismen: Kulturkritik und Gesellschaft* (1955); see *Prisms*, trans. Samuel Weber and Shierry Weber (Cambridge, MA: MIT Press, 1981), pp. 187–226.

Benjamin's theses: Scholem is referring to Benjamin's theses "On the Concept of History." See Benjamin, "On the Concept of History," *Selected Writings*, Vol. 4: *1938–1940*, ed. Howard Eiland and Michael W. Jennings (Cambridge, MA: The Belknap Press of Harvard University Press, 2006), pp. 389–400.

the sort that only a metaphysician in the vein of Edgar Allan Poe could have devised: Scholem is alluding to Poe's stupendous ability to decipher codes and cryptograms – an ability that is reflected in stories such as "The Gold-Bug."

Goethe: See Walter Benjamin, "Goethe's *Elective Affinities*," in *Selected Writings*, Vol. 1: *1913–1926*, ed. Marcus Bullow and Michael W. Jennings

(Cambridge, MA: The Belknap Press of Harvard University Press, 1996), pp. 297–360.

"Painting and Photography": Scholem is referring to the second "Pariser Brief: Malerei und Photographie" [Parisian letter: painting and photography], which remained unpublished during Benjamin's lifetime. See "Letter from Paris (2): Painting and Photography" in Walter Benjamin, *Selected Writings*, Vol. 3: 1935–1938, ed. Howard Eiland and Michael W. Jennings (Cambridge, MA: The Belknap Press of Harvard University Press, 2002), pp. 236–248.

Marcuse's book on Hegel: Scholem probably requested a copy of Herbert Marcuse's *Reason and Revolution: Hegel and the Rise of Social Theory* (London: Oxford University Press, 1941). It is possible, though less likely, that he is referring here to Marcuse's earlier book on Hegel, published in German in 1932, *Hegels Ontologie und die Grundlegung einer Theorie der Geschichtlichtkeit* (Frankfurt am Main: Vittorio Klostermann, 1932; *Hegel's Ontology and the Theory of Historicity*, trans. Seyla Benhabib, Cambridge, MA: MIT Press, 1987). Scholem owned a copy of *Reason and Revolution* in its original 1941 English edition and a copy of *Hegels Ontologie* in its 1968 second German edition. Therefore, although it is impossible to determine with certainty which of the books is meant here, it is more likely the former.

15 ADORNO TO SCHOLEM
SANTA MONICA, 9.5.1949

T. W. Adorno
803 Yale St. (new address) 9 May 1949
Santa Monica, Calif.

Dear Mr. Scholem,

I have Leo Löwenthal to thank for your address. I also heard from him that you have bitterly complained about me, and with the utmost right. Above all else, I am writing to you today to ask sincerely for your forgiveness. While I can't excuse my silence, I might be able to explain it to a certain extent. It isn't just the workload, which has certainly been extreme in the past few years, since I – like Horkheimer – have had to wrest the possibility of doing anything theoretical from a heap of empirical research and administrative duties, such as the management of the very extensive Berkeley project. On top of this, I have also intermittently been disturbed by serious health problems, like diabetes and a heart condition. But the real reason is likely that, having at one point failed to respond in depth to an important and encumbered letter of yours, my feelings of guilt got in the way of any attempt to re-establish contact with you. I was about to write to you on countless occasions, but each time, I recoiled. At the deepest level, the insurmountable shock caused by Benjamin's death probably plays a part in this – at any rate, my relationships to the few people with whom he was close have been paralysed during the last few years.

Is there any chance of your coming here? It will be far more pleasant here than in New York in the months to come, and I could imagine a really fruitful get-together – at least for me. There would be an endless amount to discuss – above all your book, which I never wrote to you about, but which I've read repeatedly. I think that I can say without hubris that I have internalized it as well as anyone can who does not speak Hebrew. In substance, I was most powerfully moved by the chapter on Lurianic mysticism, the basic concepts of which appear infinitely productive to me. There is so much that I would have liked to ask you about this, especially as regards the speculative background of your own theology and its connection to Benjamin.

Equally pressing are the questions in connection with Benjamin's estate. At the beginning of last year, I finally received the *Arcades* material that had been hidden in the Bibliothèque Nationale. I worked through it in the minutest detail last summer, which brought certain problems to light that I need to discuss with you. For today, let me at least indicate to you what these are. The gravest of these is the extraordinary retreat of expressed theoretical ideas as compared to the formidable hoard of quotations. This can be explained, in part, through the idea, which is explicitly expressed (and which, incidentally, I find problematic) that the work can only be "assembled" ["*montiert*"] – that is, that the quotes can be set in relation to each other in such a way that the theory leaps out of it without the need for any accompanying interpretation. If this were at all possible, then Benjamin alone would have been able to achieve it. But, on this point, I remain committed to the standpoint of the Hegelian *Phenomenology of Spirit*, namely, that the movement of the concept, of the thing itself, is at the same time the explicitly thinking movement of the onlooking subject. Only the authority of sacred texts could be opposed to such a conception, but precisely this idea is avoided in the *Arcades* work. If, as I would have it, one does not take Benjamin's montage plan entirely *à la lettre*, then it is likely the case that Benjamin gave considerable thought to the innumerable quotes, but wrote down as little of this as a composer notates the instrumentation that he remembers by sound when putting down an idea. The vast majority of the theoretical content that has been noted down in the convolutes is already entered into in the piece on Baudelaire and in the theses "On the Concept of History."

A further difficulty lies in the fact that, although there is a general plan, and although the material has been painstakingly divided into sections according to keywords, there is no concretely elaborated schema whatsoever, which would allow one to carry out its construction in the manner that he intended. On the other hand, the unorganized publication of the material would not help at all, since, as it stands, the work's intention does not leap out. Accordingly, I would like us to give in-depth consideration as to what can be done if we want both to remain strictly faithful to the material and to present something meaningful.

Let me just add that we are quite well. Have you received the *Dialectic of Enlightenment* by Horkheimer and me? If not, I'll be happy to send you a copy. Another small, yet very encumbered book of mine, *Philosophy of New Music*, is about to be published by Mohr in Tübingen. I would very much like you to read the manuscript of my extensive, unpublished book of aphorisms, *Minima Moralia*. You probably know that the Institute's research on anti-Semitism is about to be published by Harpers. You should find a lot in this as well.

I bid you once more to not repay like with like, and to let me hear from you soon.

In heartfelt affinity,

yours,

[Adorno]

Original: typescript (carbon copy); Theodor W. Adorno Archive, Frankfurt am Main. First published in Rolf Tiedemann (ed.), *Frankfurter Adorno Blätter* V (Munich: Edition Text + Kritik, 1998), pp. 157–9.

I have Leo Löwenthal to thank for your address: The sociologist of literature Leo Löwenthal (1900–1993) was a member of the Institute for Social Research in Frankfurt and later in New York. From 1949 he was the director of the research department at the radio broadcaster, Voice of America. From 1956 he was professor of sociology at the University of California, Berkeley. In Frankfurt, Löwenthal belonged to the circle around Franz Rosenzweig's Freies Jüdisches Lehrhaus [Free Jewish House of Learning], which is where he first met Scholem.

my silence: Adorno had not replied to Scholem's previous four letters. In a letter to Hannah Arendt, dated the 6th of August 1945, Scholem wrote: "Four weeks ago I got the Institute's volume on Benjamin, with a laconic dedication from Wiesengrund. Thanks so much for this. I credit you and your efforts for the book. For years now I haven't heard a thing from Wiesengrund, and why this is so, I can't say. At first there was no end to his declarations of friendship; then, suddenly, total silence." See *The Correspondence of Hannah Arendt and Gershom Scholem*, ed. Marie Luise Knott, trans. Anthony David (Chicago: University of Chicago Press, 2017) p. 33.

empirical research ... Berkeley project: In 1945, when Horkheimer became the director of the research department at the American Jewish Committee

New York, the Institute for Social Research began to collaborate with the Berkeley Public Opinion Study Group – a group of scientists from the University of California, Berkeley – on a research project on anti-Semitism in the USA. The results were published as part of a book series titled "Studies in Prejudice," which was edited by Max Horkheimer and Samuel H. Flowerman. The first volume, *The Authoritarian Personality*, by Theodor W. Adorno, Else Frenkel-Brunswik, Daniel J. Levinson, and Nevitt Sanford, was published by Harper & Brothers, New York, in 1950.

an important and encumbered letter of yours: See letter no. 12 in this volume.

chapter on Lurianic mysticism: Under the title "Isaac Luria and his School," the seventh lecture treats Lurianic mysticism in sixteenth-century Safed. See Gershom Scholem, "Isaac Luria and his School," in *Major Trends in Jewish Mysticism* (Jerusalem: 1941; rev. edn., New York: Schocken, 1995), pp. 244–86. The central terms of Lurianic mysticism discussed in Scholem's book are: *tsimtsum* (צמצום, God's self-contraction, which, according to Scholem, is a metaphor for exile); *shevirah*, or *shevirat ha-kelim* (שבירה, שבירת הכלים, the breaking of the vessels, the *Sefiroth*, in which God's light was supposed to be contained); and *tikkun* (reparation, restoration – a metaphor for redemption, according to Scholem). Arguably, an echo of the latter can be found in "Finale," the final aphorism from *Minima Moralia*: "The only philosophy which can be responsibly practised in face of despair is the attempt to contemplate all things as they would present themselves from the standpoint of redemption. . . . Perspectives must be fashioned that displace and estrange the world, reveal it to be, with its rifts and crevices, as indigent and distorted as it will appear one day in the messianic light." See Adorno, *Minima Moralia: Reflections From Damaged Life*, trans. Edmund Jephcott (London: New Left Books, 1974), p. 247.

At the beginning of last year, I finally received the Arcades *material that had been hidden in the Bibliothèque Nationale*: Georges Bataille, who had hidden Benjamin's manuscripts at the Bibliothèque Nationale during the war, handed the papers to Benjamin's friend, the writer Pierre Missac, in 1945. Missac had the papers sent to Adorno with the wife of an official at the American embassy in Paris. See Rolf Tiedemann and Hermann Schweppenhäuser's editorial afterword in Walter Benjamin, *Gesammelte Schriften I.2*, ed. Rolf Tiedemann and Hermann Schweppenhäuser (Frankfurt am Main: Suhrkamp, 1974, pp. 751–96), p. 759.

general plan: Adorno is referring to the exposé "Paris, the Capital of the Nineteenth Century." See *The Arcades Project*, ed. Rolf Tiedemann, trans. Howard Eiland and Kevin McLaughlin (Cambridge, MA: The Belknap Press of Harvard University Press, 1996), pp. 3–13.

the material has been painstakingly divided into sections according to keywords: Benjamin had drawn up an overview of the "Aufzeichnung und Materialien" [Notes and materials, or "Convolutes" in the English translation], which divided the material according to section headings. See *The*

Arcades Project, ed. Rolf Tiedemann, trans. Howard Eiland and Kevin McLaughlin (Cambridge, MA: The Belknap Press of Harvard University Press, 1996), p. 29.

Have you received the Dialectic of Enlightenment *by Horkheimer and me?*: Horkheimer and Adorno's *Dialectic of Enlightenment* was published by Querido in Amsterdam in 1947. A copy of the first edition can be found in the Scholem library. It contains numerous marginal notes of a critical nature in Scholem's handwriting.

Philosophy of New Music: See letter no. 10 in this volume.

the manuscript of my extensive, unpublished book of aphorisms, Minima Moralia: Adorno's *Minima Moralia: Reflections from Damaged Life* was first published by Suhrkamp, Frankfurt am Main, in 1951. While a copy of the first edition of *Minima Moralia* can be found in the Scholem library, the manuscript of this text cannot be found there.

16 SCHOLEM TO ADORNO
JERUSALEM, 5.1.1951

האוניברסיטה העברית בירושלים
THE HEBREW UNIVERSITY, JERUSALEM

Jerusalem, 5 Jan. 1951
28 Abarbanel St.

Dear Sir, teacher of wisdom and colleague,

Yesterday I received the *Berlin Childhood* from Suhrkamp, and I would also like to thank you for your effort in connection with the publication of this text. I had the manuscript here in Jerusalem towards the end of 1932, and, over the course of our correspondence, Walter Benjamin wrote to me that he would follow my advice to secrete [sekretieren] the section "Awakening of Sexuality." (If I am not mistaken, my argument was that the only appearance of Judaism in this context amounted to a completely perverse image, especially in the eyes of a non-Jewish readership. After all, in our (and also his) childhood experiences, Judaism, however denatured it may have been, also appeared in different, unexpected and exciting settings. Consequently, one should either treat this phenomenon in a more differentiated way, or one should not treat it publicly at all.) You may be better equipped to explain how the piece found its way into the manuscript after all. Apart from that, it is strange that the piece "Krumme Strasse," which was published in *Maß und Wert* in July of 1938, is now missing from the book. Did it remain unknown to you? It is also a pity that the marvellous double dictum [Doppelsatz] at the end of "The Sock" – another piece printed in *Maß und Wert*, with its foreshadowing of Benjamin's later attitude towards the truth in poetry – was lost during the revisions, when it was taken up into "Cabinets," the text included here. Could it be that this section, published in 1938 – long after the completion of the manuscript – stems from a subsequent reworking and shortening? As far as I know, he rewrote many pieces seven or eight times.

I suspect that you wrote the beautiful afterword with the concluding "Hölderlin." I am very moved by all of this, although, frankly, I do not find the air surrounding the scenes of B.'s presentation to be deathly. As much as this turned out to be true, the presentation expresses little of that here (and rightly so, I would say). The irretrievable, to which you rightly appeal, is precisely not the deathly.

I would be very pleased if the path has now been cleared for the publication of further volumes. If, when the time comes, I can be of any help in supplying materials, you may certainly count on me.

With repeated thanks and best regards, also to your wife

yours

Gerhard Scholem

Original: manuscript with printed letterhead; Theodor W. Adorno Archive, Frankfurt am Main. First printed in Gershom Scholem, *Briefe II: 1948–1970*, ed. Thomas Sparr (Munich: C. H. Beck, 1995), p. 23.

Berlin Childhood: *Berlin Childhood* was the first work of Benjamin's to be published by Suhrkamp. It appeared in 1950, and contained an unsigned afterword, which was in fact written by Adorno. See Walter Benjamin, *Gesammelte Schriften IV.2*, ed. Tillman Rexroth (Frankfurt am Main: Suhrkamp, 1991), pp. 964–70.

my advice to secrete [sekretieren] the section "Awakening of Sexuality": Scholem's letter, in which he urges Benjamin to "secrete" this section, has not been preserved. In an editorial note on his correspondence with Benjamin (which is included only in the German edition) Scholem wrote: "I urged him to secrete this piece because it was the only one in the whole book that made explicit reference to Judaism, thus creating a false impression. If he had broached the topic of his Jewish experiences in other pieces too, then I would have had no objections to his including the piece; but in isolation it wouldn't have been right." See *Walter Benjamin / Gershom Scholem: Briefwechsel, 1933–1940*, ed. Gershom Scholem (Frankfurt am Main: Suhrkamp, 1980), p. 37. In a letter dated the 28th of February 1933, Benjamin refers to "Awakening of Sexuality" as "the one deleted on your advice." See *The Correspondence of Walter Benjamin and Gershom Scholem, 1932–1940*, ed. Gershom Scholem, trans. Gary Smith and Andre Lefevere (New York, Schocken Books, 1989), p. 28.

"Krumme Strasse": The piece was first published in the bi-monthly journal *Maß und Wert*, Vol. 1, no. 6 (July/August 1938), which was edited by Thomas

Mann and Konrad Falke. See Benjamin, "Berlin Childhood around 1900," in *Selected Writings*, Vol. 3: *1935–1938*, ed. Howard Eiland and Michael W. Jennings (Cambridge, MA: The Belknap Press of Harvard University Press, 2002), pp. 372–4.

the marvellous double dictum [Doppelsatz] at the end of "The Sock": The first edition of *Berlin Childhood*, edited by Adorno, contained the piece "Cabinets," which overlaps with "The Sock," which was included in later editions, in parts. However, the final double dictum at the end of "The Sock" is not included in "Cabinets" and was published only in later versions of *Berlin Childhood*. "I could not repeat the experiment on this phenomenon often enough. It taught me that form and content, veil and what is veiled, are the same. It led me to draw truth from works of literature as warily as the child's hand retrieved the sock from 'the pocket'" (Benjamin, "Berlin Childhood," p. 374). For "Cabinets," see "Berlin Childhood," pp. 401–4.

the beautiful afterword with the concluding "Hölderlin": In his afterword to *Berlin Childhood* Adorno cites Friedrich von Matthisson's poem "Das Feenland" [The fairyland] without, however, naming the title or the author. Before quoting the poem, Adorno writes: "Comfortingly, the explosion of despair lays bare the fairyland, which is spoken of in an apocryphal poem attributed to Hölderlin." See Adorno, "Nachwort zur *Berliner Kindheit um 1900*" [Afterword to Berlin Childhood around 1900], in *Gesammelte Schriften 20.1*, ed. Rolf Tiedemann et al. (Frankfurt am Main: Suhrkamp, 1986), p. 172.

the air surrounding the scenes of B.'s presentation: Adorno's afterword reads, "A deathly air permeates the scenes poised to awaken in Benjamin's depiction." See Adorno, *Gesammelte Schriften 20.1*, ed. Rolf Tiedemann et al. (Frankfurt am Main: Suhrkamp, 1986), pp. 170–72, here p. 171.

17 ADORNO TO SCHOLEM
FRANKFURT AM MAIN, 15.1.1951

15 Jan. 1951

Dear Mr. Scholem,

Kindest thanks for your letter of the 5th of January, which I received today to my great delight. It is a real pity that we could not talk through the problems of *Berlin Childhood* while I was preparing it for publication. I was unaware of the agreement to secrete "Awakening of Sexuality," and neither the two original manuscripts nor the typescript contain any indication to that effect. I would have gladly taken your objection into account, since I also never felt quite comfortable with the the piece myself. On the other hand, I did not want to remove it on my own authority. The piece "Krumme Strasse" is unknown to me; it is neither contained in the manuscripts, nor do I own that issue of *Maß und Wert*. If you have it, it could be earmarked for a reissue, or possibly for inclusion in the projected edition. Also unknown to me is the piece "The Sock," which, as you write, has melded with "Cupboards." It cannot be ruled out that "The Sock" is a later piece; but then he has not included this version in the collection of manuscripts.

A few words about the formulation of a "deathly air" surrounding the scenes of *Berlin Childhood*: I clearly recall using this phrase in conversation with him, and I know that it met with his approval. He in turn used the phrase of the person who abandons his class without finding a way into another one. At the very least, this is not formulated *ex post facto*. Indeed, if I am not very mistaken, childhood does not mean something that is irretrievable simply in the sense of memory; but rather in the sense that the very forces that shattered the continuity of life, the unity of experience, unleashed in Benjamin those opposing forces through which he took possession of that which had been, not only empirically, but also intelligibly lost. The overexposed memory images from *Berlin Childhood* were gained at no lesser cost than the loss of that *mémoire involontaire*, the theory of which he laid out in the piece on Baudelaire. However, my emphasis on the catastrophic background in the little afterword was motivated by the will to fend off any cosy, idyllic misreadings – in contrast, say, to the calm and refined genre represented by Hessel and his Berlin book – so as to impose on the reception from the first moment the dignity befitting the matter.

Apart from this, little can be said as yet about the work's reception. The reviews that have appeared to date, by Rychner, Sternberger, and the exacting connoisseur Peter von Haselberg, are enthusiastic; however – in the publisher's opinion – they are what in English is called awe-inspiring,* such that they hinder the circulation of this book rather than helping it along. I sincerely hope that the projected edition will come to pass this year, and I would already like to ask you to send me anything that you would like to see included from the earlier period, and that I don't have, especially the piece on Hölderlin. By the way, do you think the essay "On Language as Such and on the Language of Man" should be included? I would opt for it. We have published a small announcement in the *Times Literary Supplement*, calling on people to send us any missing pieces by Benjamin, and there have already been some results.

In the meantime, the theses "On the Concept of History" have appeared in the December issue of Fischer's *Neue Rundschau*, alongside an essay of mine with which you are familiar, and framed by some

* Original in English.

pieces by Gide and Valéry. It looks quite dignified and I think it would have pleased him. If you don't have this issue, please let me know.

Meanwhile, Stefan has given me authorization for the publication of the Suhrkamp edition. We are also in continuous contact with Dora Sophie.

We hope that you are well and that we will hear from you again soon.

The kindest regards, also from Gretel,

your sincerely devoted
T. W. Adorno

Original: transcript with Scholem's handwritten note: "Kettenhofweg 123, Frkf. a.M."; Gershom Scholem Archive, The National Library of Israel, Jerusalem. First published in Rolf Tiedemann (ed.), *Frankfurter Adorno Blätter* V (Munich: Edition Text + Kritik, 1998), pp. 160–3.

"Krumme Strasse" . . . inclusion in the projected edition: The piece "Krumme Strasse" [Krumme Street] was included in the 1955 edition of Benjamin's *Schriften*, Vol. I, ed. Theodor W. Adorno et al. (Frankfurt am Main: Suhrkamp, 1955), pp. 643–4.

mémoire involontaire, the theory of which he laid out in the piece on Baudelaire: Benjamin develops his interpretation of Proust's notion of "mémoire involontaire" in "On Some Motifs in Baudelaire." See Walter Benjamin, *Selected Writings*, Vol. 4: *1938–1940*, ed. Howard Eiland and Michael W. Jennings (Cambridge, MA: The Belknap Press of Harvard University Press, 2006), pp. 313–55, esp. pp. 315–17, 335–8.

Hessel . . . his Berlin book: See Franz Hessel, *Walking in Berlin: A Flaneur in the Capital*, trans. Amanda DeMarco (Cambridge, MA: MIT Press, 2017).

The reviews that have appeared to date: See Max Rychner, "Nachgelassene Prosastücke von Walter Benjamin" [Posthumous prose pieces by Walter Benjamin], *Die Tat*, 15/321 (25.11.1950), p. 13; Dolf Sternberger, "Walter Benjamins Prosa" [Walter Benjamin's prose], *Die Gegenwart*, 5/23 (1.12.1950), pp. 2–3; Peter von Haselberg discussed the book in a radio broadcast of the Nord-West-Deutscher Rundfunk.

a small announcement: On the 5th of January 1951 the following announcement appeared (in English) under the title WALTER BENJAMIN, in the "Letters to the Editors" section of the London-based *Times Literary Supplement* (no. 2553, p. 7): "Sir, – In co-operation with the Suhrkamp Verlag, Frankfurt am Main I am preparing an edition of selected writings of the philosopher and essayist Walter Benjamin, who died in 1940 when he attempted in vain to escape from France. Although I saved a large part of Benjamin's publications and manuscripts with the help of various persons interested in his works, my collection is not complete. In particular, some of his writings of the early twenties, and his own poems are missing. It would be of great help if any of your readers possessing Benjamin material would communicate with me. Any assistance thus obtained would be highly appreciated by both publisher and editor. PROFESSOR T. W. ADORNO. Institute for Social Research at the University of Frankfurt, 34 Senckenberganlage, Frankfurt a.M."

December issue of Fischer's Neue Rundschau: Benjamin's theses on the philosophy of history appeared under the title "Über den Begriff der Geschichte" [On the concept of history], alongside Adorno's essay "Charakteristik Walter Benjamins" [A portrait of Walter Benjamin] in *Neue Rundschau*, 61/4 (1950), pp. 560–70. See Adorno, "A Portrait of Walter Benjamin," in *Prisms*, trans. Samuel Weber and Shierry Weber (Cambridge, MA: MIT Press, 1981), pp. 227–42.

pieces by Gide and Valéry: "Literarische Erinnerungen und Gegenwartsprobleme" [Literary memories and present-day problems] by André Gide, and "Nachgelassene Fragmente zu 'Mon Faust'" [Posthumous fragments of 'My Faust'] by Paul Valéry.

Stefan: Stefan Benjamin – Walter Benjamin's son. See letter no. 8 in this volume.

Dora Sophie: Dora Sophie Benjamin, Walter Benjamin's former wife. See letter no. 8 in this volume.

18 ADORNO TO SCHOLEM
FRANKFURT AM MAIN, 18.2.1951

18 Feb. 1951

Dear Mr. Scholem,

A few days ago I received a hectographed copy of Benjamin's essay "Two Poems by Friedrich Hölderlin: 'The Poet's Courage' and 'Timidity'," which Bernhard Reichenbach sent me from England. Please kindly let me know whether this work is identical with the Hölderlin essay in your posession, which I had always assumed deals with the "Patmos" hymn.

I also received, following the announcement in the *Times Literary Supplement*, a rather strange letter from a certain Mr. Belmore, who refers to himself as a friend from Benjamin's youth. The letter is quite hostile, but at the very least it shows, in the form of vexation, that its author was affected by Benjamin's incomparability, and perhaps that means more than the naïve enthusiasm of appreciation.

In *Merkur*, in the meantime, the peculiar Mr. Bense has let his views on *Berlin Childhood* be heard. This man, by no means a transparent figure, told me a year ago that, in the summer of 1940, there had been a plan in the circles of the German general staff that were familiar with Benjamin's name to rescue Benjamin by sticking him into a field hospital as a care assistant. Supposedly this plan involved Ernst Jünger, who – immediately after the war – did in fact convey to me, via Eduard Roditi, how much Benjamin had meant to him. I am only writing these things to you in the imagination of the *tiens*, *tiens*, with which Benjamin would have reacted to such reports.

With the most cordial regards from us both,

yours

T. W. Adorno

Original: typescript; Gershom Scholem Archive, The National Library of Israel, Jerusalem. First published in Rolf Tiedemann (ed.), *Frankfurter Adorno Blätter* V (Munich: Edition Text + Kritik, 1998), pp. 163–4.

Bernhard Reichenbach: Bernhard Reichenbach (1888–1975) was a communist politician and journalist. From 1912 until 1914 he studied in Berlin, where he was a member of the Jugendbewegung [Youth movement] and the Freien Studentenschaft [free student body], as well as a co-editor of the journal *Der Aufbruch*. He knew Benjamin from this period. Later he became a member of the Communist Party of Germany, the KPD, of the Communist Workers' Party of Germany, the KAPD, and in 1925, he joined the Social Democratic Party of Germany, the SPD. In 1935 he immigrated to the United Kingdom, where he joined the Labour Party. After 1945 he worked in London as a correspondent for German newspapers and radio broadcasters.

Belmore: Scholem added the following notation to the letter: "i.e. = Herbert Blumenthal." Herbert William Belmore (1893–1978) was a childhood friend of Benjamin's from his time in the youth movement. He was born in Hopetown, South Africa, and grew up in England and Germany, where he attended the same school as Walter Benjamin. After spending the years of the First World War in England and Switzerland, he worked as an antiquarian in Rome. In 1939 he moved to England, where he studied, while working as a librarian in London. His MA theses, entitled "Rilke's Craftsmanship" was published by Blackwell in 1954. In 1959 he returned to Rome, where he worked as a translator. During the 1960s he wrote several articles about Walter Benjamin in English. See letter no. 122 in this volume.

Bense . . . on Berlin Childhood: See Max Bense, "Walter Benjamin und seine Literatur" [Walter Benjamin and his literature], *Merkur*, 5/36.2 (February 1951): 181–4.

in the summer of 1940, there had been a plan . . . to rescue Benjamin: When asked about Bense's account during a 1973 interview with Rolf Tiedemann, Ernst Jünger replied: "I consider it possible that such a campaign on behalf of Walter Benjamin took place, or could have been attempted from the [hotel] Majestic, because I recall similar cases, which I have to some extent also mentioned in my diaries. However, I could not have participated in this plan since I was not yet in Paris in the summer of 1940, but was with an infantry regiment. A number of people, whose traces were to be more or less erased, were taken care of by those that had been charged with the protection of art and literary relations." (Letter from Ernst Jünger to Rolf Tiedemann, dated 25.6.1973; see Tiedemann (ed.), *Frankfurter Adorno Blätter* V (Munich: Edition Text + Kritik, 1998), p. 164, incl. notes).

Eduard Roditi: Edouard Roditi (1910–1992) was a French-American writer and art critic. The person who is supposed to have conveyed this plan to Roditi is unknown.

19 SCHOLEM TO ADORNO
JERUSALEM, 20.2.1951

האוניברסיטה העברית
THE HEBREW UNIVERSITY

Jerusalem 28 Abarbanel Rd. ירושלים

20 February 1951

Dear Mr. Adorno,

I thank you for your letter, which was left lying, because in the wake of a general epidemic of flu etc., I spent some time with a mild case of pneumonia. In the meantime, through a friend in London, I – who cannot come by any German periodicals in Israel – also received the issue of N.R. with the two pieces by and about Benjamin. You have certainly taken an important step with this. I have read your portrait [of Walter Benjamin] several times. It would be presumptuous of me to claim that I have understood all that is in it, but, from what I could fathom, I found much to be not only true and fitting but also very well said. Due to my personal experience, I was quite moved by what you said about the promise of happiness, the – I would have to say – magical implications of Benjamin's thinking. You brought that out marvellously. In his essay "On the Program of the Coming Philosophy," which he wrote towards the end of 1917, he even tried to formulate the systematic framework for this promise. Your attempt to specify the meaning of his materialist endeavors, and to present their own rather catastrophic dialectic, concerns a point that is, of course, no less central. It is curious, and perhaps clearer to you than to me, that of the two categories which previously played such an important role in his Theologoumena – namely revelation and redemption – it is the latter that has been retained *expressis verbis* in his turn to "materialism," while the former, which is most clearly (and consciously) related to his most essential method (and perhaps also concern), namely the commentary of texts, is no longer mentioned. Has it disappeared in this process of transformation, or has it merely been concealed (as I almost suspect)? The pride with which he appeals to the utopian image of theology, while its existential (or better: substantial?) quality disappears, must be related to the reason for this turn, and I have thought about it more than once.

While I do not need to trouble you for the issue of N.R., I would be grateful if you could send me your essay on the critique of Husserl, which has since been published, I've heard. I remember reading it with great interest in 1938 when it was still in Ms. form, and I should very much like to have it.

Since I don't know how best to proceed with the pieces by B. that remain only with me, I would first like to see whether I will come to Europe again in the foreseeable future (which, by the way, I don't think is likely), where I could give you the relevant materials directly for transcription instead of entrusting them to the postal service. Here everything is currently so expensive that I cannot have copies made. Perhaps it will be possible to get some microfilms manufactured in the coming months. Still, it is possible that I'll have to go to Paris one more time to complete my work on the libraries of former Jewish institutions, which has been underway for five years now. In this case, I could take everything with me, and we could meet in Paris. In Germany, my part is done, I hope, and I'm no longer fond of travelling there!

With best regards, also for your wife,

yours Gerhard Scholem

Original: aerogram (manuscript) with printed letterhead; Theodor W. Adorno Archive, Frankfurt am Main.

what you said about the promise of happiness: In his essay on Benjamin, Adorno writes that Benjamin's philosophy "resides neither in magical effects, which were not foreign to him, nor in an 'objectivity,' denoting the disappearance of the subject in those constellations. It stems rather from a quality which intellectual departmentalization otherwise reserves for art, but which sheds all semblance when transposed into the realm of theory and assumes incomparable dignity – the promise of happiness." See Adorno, "A Portrait of Walter Benjamin," in *Prisms*, trans. Samuel Weber and Shierry Weber (Cambridge, MA: MIT Press, 1981), p. 230.

your essay on the critique of Husserl: An early draft of the fourth chapter from Adorno's *Metacritique of Epistemology* had been published in *Archiv für Philosophie*, 3/4 (1949), under the title "Zur Philosophie Husserls" [On Husserl's philosophy]. See Adorno, *Against Epistemology: A Metacritique*, trans. Willis Domingo (London: Blackwell, 1982), pp. 186–234.

my work ... on the libraries of former Jewish institutions: During the first years of the post-war period, Scholem frequently traveled to Europe

(Germany, France, England, Switzerland, Czechoslovakia) on behalf of the Hebrew University in search of the Jewish libraries and collections that had been seized by the Nazis.

20 SCHOLEM TO ADORNO JERUSALEM, 25.2.1951

February 1951

Dear Mr. Adorno,

Three hours ago I dropped a letter for you into the mailbox, and I am now writing you just a few lines in response to your letter of the 18th of February. Of course the Hölderlin essay, which has now apparently reached you, is the one on "Dichtermut" [The Poet's Courage] and "Blödigkeit" [Timidity]. I'd already written in 1942 to correct your mistaken assumption that the essay is on "Patmos," although the letter, along with a transcription of the piece, set off on its journey to you but never arrived. What do you make of this strange text (which, if I am not mistaken, was written in the winter of 1913/1914)? At the time, W. B. was studying with Rickert, which can hardly be overlooked.

Mr. Belmore is identical with Herbert Blumenthal, a friend from Walter Benjamin's youth, who played a lively part in the "discussion groups" held by the circle around *Der Anfang* and the "youth movement." He had transcriptions of various pieces. Since he was a British national by birth, of German-Jewish provenance, he left Germany in 1914. In 1915 W. B. met with him one last time in Switzerland, and since then, they had no further contact. Since I only met W. B. in June of 1915, I know of him only through Walter and Dora's stories. Dora has, I think, met with him in England once or twice, or maybe she corresponded with him there. In 1949 she spoke to me about him with great disappointment.

By the way, I've forgotten to ask, who is the "existentialist overlord" whom you cite? I should like you to give me *chapter and verse** of this fine pronouncement.

The idea that Ernst Jünger, through his military connections, could have kidnapped Walter Benjamin from the dungeons of the Gestapo, and that he could have brought him, like himself, to a place of safety – Paris or something – is so naive and so comical that one would want to laugh, if one were not reminded of the poison that Benjamin had prepared for just the first phase of such an adventure. It is roughly equivalent to Jünger's naïveté when, in his immortal writings, he

* Original in English.

is astonished and indignant that, wherever possible, the résistance shot down his French friends who practiced "cross-cultural understanding" between France and Germany. These, Mr. Adorno, are the readers before whom these writings will now appear. I dread to think that we, to speak in Benjaminian terms, "will provide the comfort."

Yours, G. Scholem

Original: aerogram (manuscript) dated by postmark; Theodor W. Adorno Archive, Frankfurt am Main. First published in Gershom Scholem, *Briefe II: 1948–1970*, ed. Thomas Sparr (Munich: C. H. Beck, 1995), p. 24.

a transcription of the piece . . . never arrived: In his letter of 16.12.1945 to Hannah Arendt, which contained a transcript of Benjamin's Hölderlin essay, Scholem writes of his refusal to send Adorno this piece since the latter had been ignoring his letters. See *The Correspondence of Hannah Arendt and Gershom Scholem*, ed. Marie Luise Knott, trans. Anthony David (Chicago: University of Chicago Press, 2017), p. 38.

Rickert: Heinrich Rickert (1863–1936) was a philosopher and a founding figure of the south-western school of neo-Kantianism. From 1912 to 1913 Benjamin attended Rickert's lectures in Freiburg, and was influenced for a time by his thinking.

the "existentialist overlord" whom you cite: In his essay "Portrait of Walter Benjamin," Adorno writes: "The perfidious reproach of being 'too intelligent' haunted him throughout his life; an Existentialist overlord had the effrontery to defame him as being 'touched by demons,' as though the suffering of a person dominated and estranged by the mind should be considered his metaphysical death sentence, merely because it disturbs the all-too-lively I–Thou relationship." See Adorno, *Prisms*, trans. Samuel Weber and Shierry Weber (Cambridge, MA: MIT Press, 1981), p. 231. In the letter that follows in this volume, Adorno provides information about the person to whom he was referring. The "all-too-lively I-Thou relationship" alone was, for most readers, a clear reference to Martin Buber.

I dread to think that we, to speak in Benjaminian terms, "will provide the comfort": Scholem's words could not be verified to be a quotation from Benjamin.

21 ADORNO TO SCHOLEM
FRANKFURT AM MAIN, 4.3.1951

4 March 1951

Dear Mr. Scholem,

Please accept my sincerest thanks for both of your letters. The fact that you liked my essay on Benjamin is a source of immense gratification for me, and it is dampened only by the fact that you found some of it not easily accessible. However, since you are – so to speak – the reader, qua transcendental subject, to whom the essay is addressed, I cannot imagine that any potentially murky passages will not dissolve under your gaze. I am especially pleased that you agree with what I wrote about the promise of happiness. I neither discussed this point with him, nor am I familiar with the piece on "The Program of the Coming Philosophy"; here the matter itself seems to have spoken. With regard to his position on the category of revelation, I am inclined to your view that it is not a matter of surrendering the intention, but rather of concealment. Or of a disappearance, rather, in the mystical sense – that he intended to incorporate the power of revelation entirely into the profane – while, most recently, in the short theological-political fragment, he conceived of the concept of redemption in entirely transcendent terms. Of course, matters are different with the element of theology, which you call existential or substantial. For here we are, in fact, dealing with – what is for him – a critical intention (not merely triggered by German Heideggerese). I tried to work that out in the essay by treating the categories that Benjamin omitted. For this philosophy, everything that is called I, person, subject, individual, is radically dissolved in the tension between the ambiguously mythical being of nature and the mythical self – the name – as he would have put it in the past, and properly speaking, the negative aspect of the labor of the Benjaminian concept lies here. I believe that only if one seizes and rescues his "un-humanity" out of its theoretical centre, just as he had done with the un-human Kraus, can one do him justice without trivializing his position. Naturally, I would not presume to suggest that I have managed to do this in my essay.

The piece on Hölderlin is exciting and significant, even if, like some of the other early writings, it suffers from a certain "abstractness" – from what I would almost like to call an unfortunate infatuation with logic – which he overcame completely around the time of the baroque book. Of course the piece must be included in the collection.

The existential overlord is none other than Mr. Buber. Of course the old Talmudist didn't have his sanctimonious invective printed, but he used it in a conversation with Kracauer. Nevertheless, I've never forgotten this utterance, and even just recently, I avoided an encounter with him.

The idea that the Jüngers and Benses will not only be Benjamin's readers but that they will also try to monopolize him is as dire to me as it is to you. On the other hand, however, it would not be possible to stop the German publication just so that it would remain immune to this fate. Not only the linguistic complexion of Benjamin's oeuvres, but also their subject matter, broadly construed, rules out the possibility that they might adequately unfold in any other language. However, if a Hebrew edition would be possible after the German one, this would of course be a stroke of luck.

I share your view that *unica* must not, under any circumstances, be entrusted to the postal service. At the same time, we should not wait for your uncertain trip to Europe. I would therefore be grateful if you could send me a list of the unpublished pieces of which only a single copy exists. Please also indicate the approximate length of each piece and suggest what you would include in the collection. I would ask you to send me those texts of which there are duplicates by registered mail; regarding the transcription of others, I'm confident that, together with Suhrkamp, we will find a solution.

In the coming days I will send you the Husserl essay from the *Archiv für Philosophie*, as well as the *Minima Moralia*, which has just been published.

Hopefully, you have recovered from your pneumonia. The semester has ended, and I hope that I will get to do some theoretical work during the holidays.

Kindest regards from both of us

yours

T. W. Adorno

Original: typescript; Gershom Scholem Archive, The National Library of Israel, Jerusalem. First published in Rolf Tiedemann (ed.), *Frankfurter Adorno Blätter* V (Munich: Edition Text + Kritik, 1998), pp. 164–7.

more recently, in the short theological-political fragment: Adorno evidently believed that this early fragment was written at a later date.

just as he had done with the un-human Kraus: Benjamin's 1931 essay "Karl Kraus" consists of three parts: I. Cosmic Man [*Allmensch*], II. Demon, and III. Monster [*Unmensch*]. See Walter Benjamin, *Selected Writings, Vol. 2.2: 1931–1934*, ed. Michael W. Jennings, Howard Eiland and Gary Smith (Cambridge, MA: Belknap Press of Harvard University Press, 2005), pp. 433–458.

The existential overlord is none other than Mr. Buber: During the early 1920s, the philosopher of religion Martin Buber (1878–1965) worked at the Freies Jüdisches Lehrhaus [Free Jewish House of Learning], an institution founded by Franz Rosenzweig in Frankfurt. In 1924 he became a lecturer at the University of Frankfurt, where, in 1930, he became an honorary professor. In 1933, when the Nazis seized power, Buber resigned from his position. In 1938 he immigrated to Jerusalem, where he became professor of social psychology at the Hebrew University. Buber's early writings about Judaism and Zionism – especially his "Three Speeches on Judaism" (1911) – deeply influenced Scholem. In subsequent years, however, Scholem distanced himself from Buber's philosophy.

in a conversation with Kracauer: The philosopher, author, cultural critic, and journalist Siegfried Kracauer (1889–1966), a close friend of Adorno's, taught at the Freies Jüdisches Lehrhaus [Free Jewish House of Learning] during the 1920s, in which context he became acquainted with Buber. In 1926 Kracauer published a critical review in the *Frankfurter Zeitung* of Buber and Rosenzweig's German translation of the Bible, which led to a confrontation between them. See Siegfried Kracauer, "The Bible in German: on the Translation by Martin Buber and Franz Rosenzweig," in *The Mass Ornament: Weimar Essays*, ed. Thomas Y. Levin (Cambridge, MA: Harvard University Press, 1995), pp. 189–202; see also the anonymously published note: "Die Bibel auf Deutsch – epochal" [The Bible in German – epochal], in Siegfried Kracauer, *Werke*, Vol. 5.2: *Essays, Feuilletons, Rezensionen 1924–1927*, ed. Inka Mülder-Bach et al. (Berlin: Suhrkamp, 2011), pp. 386–8; and the rejoinder "Gegen wen?" [Against whom?], ibid. pp. 388–90. In "The Bible in German," pp. 200–1, Kracauer writes:

> The problem raised by the translation is that of *religious renewal* in general. Spellbound by the word of such renewal, movements, circles, and groups have arisen and, out of a sometimes tenuous, sometimes closer contact with extant faiths, have endeavored to proclaim a shift in Being. The rendering of Scripture into German, which cannot be separated from the current state of this religious renewal, provides an indication of the dangers to which such movements are subject. It could be that in their "move into reality" those groups might in fact miss what is real in the visible external world. It could be that they think they are entering that reality with their lives, whereas in fact they are leaving public reality to take care of itself in order to save their own private existence. It could be that they believe they are serving the truth, whereas in fact they have no idea how to find truth in all its actuality. For today access to truth is by way of the profane.

a Hebrew edition: The first of Benjamin's writings to appear in Hebrew was a translation of his artwork essay, in 1983, followed by a translation of his essay on Baudelaire in 1989. A first two-volume edition of Benjamin's collected writings, edited by Jürgen Nirad, Nissim Calderon, and Rina Klinov, and translated by David Singer, was published in 1992 (Vol. 1) and 1996 (Vol. 2) by the HaKibbutz HaMeuchad Publishing House, Tel Aviv.

22 SCHOLEM TO ADORNO
JERUSALEM, 22.2.1952

Dear Mr. Adorno,

I am writing to you following a prolonged illness which befell me last spring, shortly after receiving your letter and your book. I had to undergo surgery and I just didn't have the strength to take up correspondence. This is the reason for my long silence. Now that I've finally been restored to health, I would like to thank you – however belatedly

– for the *Minima Moralia*. I'm not sure whether I thoroughly grasped your intentions, which, in the best esoteric tradition, lie hidden within the dialectic; but I think I perceive in your treatise one of the most remarkable documents of negative theology. Of course, I have a lot on my mind here, but I am hoping that, along with other matters, there may be an opportunity to discuss it with you in person. For I see a certain chance that I might come to Europe this summer, and it's possible that I will have to come to Germany once more for archival matters, so I'd like to know whether we could meet in Frankfurt in September (beforehand is out of the question). If so, then I would try to busy myself in Fr. for a few days, if I can finance it (which is a problem this time) without getting myself into difficulties. For obvious reasons, I cannot give any lectures in Germany – I'll have to find some other way. Since I would be travelling from Basel to Hamburg, Berlin, and Amsterdam, a stopover in Frankfurt would work well. So tell me what you think about this. What about further plans concerning W. B.'s estate? I could take the necessary papers with me for transcription, if you haven't already obtained all of them by some other means.

I am so deeply in debt, as far as my correspondence goes, that I must hope you will excuse my brevity, judge it with leniency, and tolerate it with a view to an in-person encounter.

With cordial regards, also to your wife,

yours

Gerhard Scholem

I hope the old address is still correct and that this reaches you!

Original: aerogram (manuscript), dated by postmark; Theodor W. Adorno Archive, Frankfurt am Main. First published in Gershom Scholem, *Briefe II: 1948–1970*, ed. Thomas Sparr (Munich: C. H. Beck, 1995), pp. 29–30.

archival matters: As of 1946, Scholem had been commissioned by the National Library of Israel to search for lost and confiscated Jewish writings in Europe.

23 ADORNO TO SCHOLEM
FRANKFURT AM MAIN, 13.4.1952

123 Kettenhofweg, Frankfurt/Main
13 April 1952

Dear Mr. Scholem,

I was very happy to finally hear from you again, and, as sorry as I am about the reason for your silence, your long illness, I am relieved in a barbarous way that it doesn't appear to be based on displeasure with what I've published. As for your reading of my book of aphorisms in terms of a negative theology, I have no objections, provided that this reading remains as esoteric as the subject itself. If, however, one translates the book straightforwardly into theological categories – as the good Mr. Thieme has done in the *Frankfurter Hefte* – then neither the book nor, presumably, the categories feel quite at ease. Well, you know this better than I do. This makes my wish to speak with you all the more urgent. But this comes up against a serious problem. In September – and I must ask you to treat this matter with the utmost discretion – I will hardly be here anymore. The three-year deadline set for naturalized Americans runs out around this time, and I will have to show my face over there [in America] for a while. This is quite aside from the fact that I initiated a rather serious and urgent research project project there; incidentally, I already spent some hectic weeks in Los Angeles last fall. As things stand, it looks as though we'll be leaving in August; I'll have to stay here for the semester anyway.

I hope to have gotten the Benjamin project underway by then, despite the perplexing circumstance that, with consistently enthusiastic reviews, also on radio, *Berlin Childhood* hasn't really permeated the book market, presumably because of the trauma that asserts itself in this country as soon as the name Berlin is heard.

What is missing from among the important pieces, as far as I can tell right now, is the volume of *Die Argonauten* which includes "Fate and Character" and the essay on *The Idiot*. Benjamin always attached particular importance to this essay, since he saw it as a kind of key, as laying his cards on the table like almost none other. I do own a copy myself, but, as with the rest of my library, I cannot get to it because it's in Los Angeles. It would be great if, without going to too much trouble, you could send me a typewritten copy. I would not expect you to hand over the volume itself, of course, which has presumably become quite rare by now.

Please be so kind as to keep me apprised of your plans. Perhaps it will work out [to see each other] after all, and I would be very happy about that. I just wouldn't want you to adjust your arrangements to suit my at least <u>very</u> uncertain German late summer.

Are you considering revisiting your – *sit venia verbo* – hermitage in New York in the foreseeable future?

With cordial regards, also from Gretel

always yours

Teddie Adorno

Original: typescript with handwritten note from Scholem: עניתי (replied) 26 May; Gershom Scholem Archive, The National Library of Israel, Jerusalem.

First published in Rolf Tiedemann (ed.), *Frankfurter Adorno Blätter* V (Munich: Edition Text + Kritik, 1998), pp. 167–8.

Thieme . . . in the Frankfurter Hefte: See Karl Thieme, "Apokalypse unserer Zeit" [Apocalypse of our time], *Frankfurter Hefte*, 6/12 (December 1951), pp. 944–6. In his book review, the protestant theologian and historian Karl Thieme (1902–1963) put Adorno's *Minima Moralia* in the context of Christian apocalyptical theology.

The three-year deadline: For the reasons outlined in the letter, from mid-October 1952 to late August 1953 Gretel and Theodor Adorno were in Los Angeles, where Adorno worked as director of research at the Hacker Foundation in Beverly Hills.

I initiated a . . . research project: During his time in Los Angeles, Adorno worked on two projects: the first was a content analysis on the function of horoscopes in American newspapers, using the astrology column of the *Los Angeles Times* as an example. See Adorno, "The Stars Down to Earth: The Los Angeles Times Astrology Column. A Study in Secondary Superstition," *Jahrbuch für Amerikastudien*, Vol. 2, ed. Walther Fischer (Heidelberg: Deutsche Gesellschaft für Amerikastudien, 1957), pp. 19–88. Now in *The Stars Down to Earth and other Essays on the Irrational in Culture*, ed. Stephen Crook (London: Routledge, 1994), pp. 46–171. The second was an investigation of the sociological significance of the new medium of television. First published as "How to Look at Television," *The Quarterly of Film, Radio, and Television,* Vol. VIII (spring 1954), pp 214–35. A reworked German version was included in the 1963 volume *Eingriffe* [Interventions], under the heading "Fernsehen als Ideologie." Now as "Television as Ideology," in *Critical Models: Interventions and Catchwords*, trans. Henry Pickford (New York: Columbia University Press, 1998), pp. 59–70. See also Adorno, "Scientific Experiences of a European Scholar in America," ibid., pp. 215–42, esp. pp. 237–9.

Berlin Childhood *hasn't really permeated the book market*: On the 14th of February 1951, the German news weekly *Der Spiegel* published a survey, conducted among publishers, regarding the successes and failures of the previous year. The article notes the following: "Out of the Suhrkamp books, Walter Benjamin's *Berlin Childhood around 1900* was the least successful." Peter Suhrkamp is quoted as saying: "Since these compressed miniatures, these crystallized childhood memories, are so hard for readers to crack – not least because their linguistic form is extremely precise, seamless, and hard – even for well-versed readers, it may take a long time to digest these pieces. However, I believe that they will open up in retrospect and will come to appear like miracles." See "Zwischen Staub und Parfüm: Büchermarkt 1950" [Between dust and perfume: the book market 1950], *Der Spiegel*, 14.2.1951, pp. 32–34, here p. 33.

the volume of Die Argonauten, *which includes "Fate and Character" and the essay on* The Idiot: See the references in the relevant notes to letters nos. 7 and 10 in this volume.

24 SCHOLEM TO ADORNO
JERUSALEM, 26.5.1952

26 May 1952

Dear Mr. Adorno,

I am responding briefly to your letter of the 13th of April, because, on the one hand, I can tell you that, *deo volente*, I will come to Europe in August (although I will be in Switzerland, where I have various plans, until the 31st of Aug.); and, on the other hand, because I hope that this news may persuade you to organize your trip in such a way that we might meet in person after all. After this, it is not to be expected that I will come to Europe, to say nothing of America, for a long time. From the 19th to the 27th of August I will be in Ascona (Eranos convention), then in Zurich until the 31st. From there, I could come directly to Frkft. in early September, in case you are still there. If you leave before, then the question is whether we can possibly still meet in Switzerland before the 19th of August. I am already writing to you about my arrangements, as far as I can be sure of them. Please consider what you can do in this situation.

If we did meet, I would bring you the issue of *Die Argonauten* personally so you could have the essays photographed right away. To do so here would be far too expensive for me at the moment!

I have to fit in two other rendezvous with American friends in August. Therefore I would be grateful to hear from you soon about our chances [of meeting]. Everything else is better discussed orally!

With cordial regards, also to your wife,
your very devoted
Gerhard Scholem

Original: aerogram (manuscript); Theodor W. Adorno Archive, Frankfurt am Main.

Ascona (Eranos convention): The Eranos convention, a meeting place for intellectuals from all disciplines, has been held in the Swiss town of Ascona since 1933. From 1949 on, Scholem participated in the annual meeting almost every summer.

25 ADORNO TO SCHOLEM
FRANKFURT AM MAIN, 6.7.1952

T. W. Adorno
123 Kettenhofweg
Frankfurt a. M.

6 July 1952

Professor Gerhard G. Scholem
28 Abarbanel St.
Jerusalem

Dear Mr. Scholem,

If I am just now responding to your letter of the 26th of May, it is only because I had to wait before informing you to see how things unfolded here. In fact, matters have now developed in such a way that we will be returning to America only in mid-October – but then without any doubt. So we could meet here in Frankfurt in early September, and I would be wholeheartedly glad if you could come. Please plan your trip accordingly, and let me know soon so I can also make arrangements.

I'd be very happy, of course, if you could give me the issue of *Die Argonauten* when you're here so that the essays can be transcribed immediately.

A fortnight ago I had a rather pleasant radio conversation with Kerenyi about myth and enlightenment; we thought fondly of you. Admittedly, I am not otherwise terribly well-disposed toward the Jung circle. A blatantly anti-Semitic review of *Minima Moralia*, by a fossil of an independent scholar named Brock, appeared in the *Neue Schweizer Rundschau*. It's a pity that I can't be present when you give these people a piece of your mind.

With the most cordial regards, also from Gretel,

your loyal

T. W. Adorno

Original: typescript with Scholem's handwritten notes (in Hebrew and German) on *Dialectic of Enlightenment*; Gershom Scholem Archive, The National Library of Israel, Jerusalem. First published in Rolf Tiedemann (ed.), *Frankfurter Adorno Blätter* V (Munich: Edition Text + Kritik, 1998), pp. 169–70.

Radio conversation with Kerenyi about myth and enlightenment: Karl Kerényi (1897–1973) a Hungarian historian of religion and classical philologist, lived in Switzerland from 1943. From 1948 he was a member of the C.G. Jung Institute in Zurich, and he took part in the Eranos conferences from 1941. Adorno and Kerényi conducted their radio conversation in 1952. See "Theodor W. Adorno und Karl Kerényi, Mythologie und Aufklärung: Ein Rundfunkgespräch" [Theodor W. Adorno and Karl Kerényi, myth and enlightenment: a radio conversation], *Frankfurter Adorno Blätter* V (Munich: Edition Text + Kritik, 1998), pp. 89–103.

The Jung circle: Most of the participants of the Ascona conferences belonged to the circle of scholars around the Swiss psychiatrist Carl Gustav Jung (1875–1961), the founder of analytical psychology. Jung's activities as president of the Deutsche Allgemeine Gesellschaft für Therapie [German Public Society for Therapy] (1933–40), as well as his statements about Jews and Judaism during the 1930s, were interpreted as anti-Semitic.

A blatantly anti-Semitic review of Minima Moralia: See Erich Brock, "*Minima Moralia*: Das Buch der kleinsten sittlichen Verantwortung" [*Minima Moralia*: the book of the smallest ethical responsibility], *Neue Schweizer Rundschau*, 19/7 (7 November 1951), p. 450. See also *Frankfurter Adorno Blätter* V (Munich: Edition Text + Kritik, 1998), p. 170 (note).

Scholem's handwritten notes on Dialectic of Enlightenment:

לויכוח על ספרו: רק פרק ד' עמ' 208–215 בגדר ויכוח רציני
השאר דברי הבל מרכסיסטיים! וכן 219/20
עם פרק ו,' הניתוח הפסיכואנליטי, לא אוכל לעשות
כלום! (רק עמ' 234 משהו רציני): (Versöhnung)
furchtbar in seiner Marxschen Verlogenheit p. 235 oben, also in Zion kann der Jude kein Mensch sein??

[Translation:]

On the debate about his book: Only Chapter IV, pp. 208–215, is a serious debate.
Everything else is Marxist nonsense! Also 219/20.
I have no use for the psychoanalytic analysis in chapter VI. (Only p. 234 contains something serious): (reconciliation)
Awful in its Marxist mendacity, p. 235 at the top, so the Jew cannot be a human being in Zion??

In the margin of the letter, Scholem noted his impressions of the chapter "Elements of Anti-Semitism: Limits of Enlightenment" from *Dialectic of Enlightenment*. The page numbers he gives pertain to the first edition from 1947, where p. 235 at the top states:

> Only the liberation of thought from power, the abolition of violence, could realize the idea which has been unrealized until now: that the Jew is a human being. This would be a step away from the anti-Semitic society, which drives both Jews and others into sickness, and toward the human one. Such a step would fulfil the fascist lie by contradicting it: the Jewish question would indeed prove the turning-point of history. By conquering the sickness of the mind which flourishes on the rich soil of self-assertion unhampered by reflection, humanity would cease to be the universal anti-race and become the species which, as nature, is more

than mere nature, in that it is aware of its own image. The individual and social emancipation from domination is the countermovement to false projection, and no longer would Jews seek, by resembling it, to appease the evil senselessly visited on them as on all the persecuted, whether animals or human beings. (Theodor W. Adorno and Max Horkheimer, *Dialectic of Enlightenment*, ed. Gunzelin Schmid Noerr, trans. Edmund Jephcott (Stanford, CA: Stanford University Press, 2002), p. 165)

26 SCHOLEM TO ADORNO
JERUSALEM, 8.7.1952

8 July 1952

Dear Mr. Adorno,

I received no response to my last letter regarding our possible encounter, so I am writing to you again. I depart here on the 5th of August. I'll be in Zurich for about a week (c/o Dr. Erich Katzenstein, Mühlebachstr. 140), and again from the 28th to the 30th of August (in a hotel). If nothing comes up, I'll come to Frankfurt on the 2nd of September on my way north.

How are things now with you and your plans? Please send a word.

I'd also like to see Mr. Suhrkamp and Mr. Podschus while I'm in Frankfurt, to whom you may wish to give my best regards.

One week from today would have been W. B.'s sixtieth birthday!

Cordial regards to your
wife and you
yours
G. Scholem

Original: aerogram (manuscript); Theodor W. Adorno Archive, Frankfurt am Main.

Dr. Erich Katzenstein: Erich Katzenstein (1893–1961) was a Swiss neurologist. Scholem met him in Ascona in 1949 when he first lectured at the Eranos conference. Since then, Gershom and Fania Scholem maintained a close friendship with Katzenstein and his wife, Nettie Sutro-Katzenstein, a historian and refugee aid. See Gershom Scholem, *Briefe III: 1971–1982*, ed. Itta Shedletzky (Munich: C. H. Beck, 1999), p. 181.

Mr. Suhrkamp: Peter Suhrkamp (1891–1959) was a publisher and the founder of the Suhrkamp Verlag. See letter no. 33 in this volume.

Mr. Podschus: Scholem's spelling. Friedrich Podszus (1899–1971) was a writer, translator, and – at this point in time – an editor at Suhrkamp.

27 SCHOLEM TO ADORNO
JERUSALEM, 11.7.1952

11 July 1952

Dear Mr. Adorno,

The day before yesterday I sent you a short letter, which must have crossed paths at the airport with yours, which just arrived. I am very glad that we will meet after all. I wrote to the Hotel National (at the train station) to ask if they could reserve an en-suite room for me from the 2nd of Sept. on. Perhaps you could be so kind as to check if the reservation is in order.

I'll bring *Die Argonauten* with me.

I plan to be in Frankfurt from the 2nd until Friday the 5th of Sept. – at the very latest until Sunday the 7th. If something unforeseen should come up, this could shift, at the most, by a few days (perhaps by one week).

Kerenyi is a decent guy. His mythology provides food for thought, although stylistically it does not come close to Schwab's – the German is too scattered. Nevertheless, it is objectively (and in its intention) very fascinating.

I think you might be confusing some things here: as far as I know, the *N. Schweizer Rundschau* is quite opposed to Jung. Perhaps I'll have the opportunity to help establish the connections if, as I intend to do, I wind up meeting with Stössinger or Rychner. I depart on the 5th of August.

Cordial regards to you both

yours G. Scholem

Original: aerogram (manuscript); Theodor W. Adorno Archive, Frankfurt am Main.

Kerenyi . . . His mythology: See Karl Kerényi, *The Gods of the Greeks*, trans. Norman Cameron (London and New York: Thames & Hudson, 1951).

Schwab: See Gustav Schwab, *Gods and Heroes of Ancient Greece: Myths and Epics of Ancient Greece*, trans. Werner Jaeger (New York: Pantheon Books, 1946).

Stössinger: The journalist, publisher, and translator Felix Stössinger (1889–1954) was born in Prague and grew up in Vienna. During the 1920s he wrote predominantly political journalism. Following his escape to Switzerland in 1942, Stössinger and his wife were interned there. After being freed, he continued to live in Zurich, where he worked primarily for the *Neue Schweizer Rundschau*, as well as *Aufbau*, a German-Jewish weekly based in New York.

Rychner: As the editor of the *Neue Schweizer Rundschau*, the journalist and writer Max Rychner (1897–1965) was in contact with Walter Benjamin. See letter no. 86 in this volume.

28 ADORNO TO SCHOLEM
FRANKFURT AM MAIN, 19.8.1952

19 August 1952

Prof. Dr. T. W. Adorno

Prof. Dr. G. Scholem
c/o Casa Gabriella;
Eranos
Ascona, Switzerland

Dear Mr. Scholem,

Kindest thanks for your card. The Hotel National, where we had already inquired at the time, explained to my secretary that, in early September, they could only accommodate guests from the trade fair, and that your request to reserve a room would have been denied. Subsequently we made a reservation for you at the Festhalle guesthouse. Just now, however, my secretary received confirmation from the Hotel National that your room has been reserved after all, and from the 31st of August. They received your letter of the 17th of August, but the reservation cannot be changed to the 1st of September. We've cancelled the room at the Festhalle guesthouse.

Incidentally, I'll be away for a few days and will only return around noon on the 1st of September. I hope that this will not disrupt your plans, however, and I am looking forward to seeing you again.

With the most cordial regards,
always yours
[Adorno]

Original: typescript (carbon copy); Theodor W. Adorno Archive, Frankfurt am Main. First published in Rolf Tiedemann (ed.), *Frankfurter Adorno Blätter V* (Munich: Edition Text + Kritik, 1998), p. 170.

29 ADORNO TO SCHOLEM
FRANKFURT AM MAIN, 11.10.1952

INSTITUTE FOR SOCIAL RESEARCH
AT THE JOHANN WOLFGANG GOETHE
UNIVERSITY

FRANKURT A.M.
SENCKENBERG-ANLAGE 26
11 October 1952

T.W. Adorno

Dear Mr. Scholem,

I assume that you are still in Europe, but I don't have your address, and I suppose that my letter will reach you more quickly if I send it to Jerusalem than if it were to chase after you via Dora Benjamin's address.

There are two things at issue, which are connected to the Benjamin edition. First: Suhrkamp wants to include *Berlin Childhood* in the collection. Now, I recall that you once told me that you have a piece – I think it was called "Krumme Lanke" – which is not included in the manuscript that I have at hand and which is entirely unfamiliar to me. I would like to include it in the final edition, and I'd be very grateful if you could send a copy to Suhrkamp, indicating that it belongs to the *Childhood*. On the other hand, you mentioned that you and Benjamin had agreed at the time that the piece "Sexual Awakening," which I also do not find especially successful, should be secreted. I'll see to this, although perhaps it would be helpful if you told Suhrkamp that there was an agreement on this point between you and Benjamin.

Second, there is a much more fundamental matter. I have adopted your view that it would be very nice to include in the edition whatever is possible from the individual drafts of the *Arcades* material. According to the preliminary calculation of the scope, it looks as though there would be room to do so. However, Suhrkamp has certain reservations, namely, that this material is publishable only as part of a "critical" edition, otherwise [it] might compromise the [current edition's] unified image, and the like. I have mobilized every conceivable argument against this view – above all, of course, that it seems decisive to me to provide an adequate idea of Benjamin's *chef d'oeuvre*, and that, since at least three of the longer, more developed texts from the *Arcades* complex are to appear ("Paris, Capital of the Nineteenth Century," the theses "On the Concept of History," and "Baudelaire" – and perhaps also some developed but as yet unpublished passages from the section on Baudelaire), the fragmentary materials would certainly be supported by such a connection, as is the case with the Empedocles drafts in the decent Hölderlin editions. Furthermore, following Suhrkamp's suggestion, I have agreed to write a separate introduction for the *Arcades* complex so as to establish the context, insofar as this is possible. Podszus seems to concur with my opinion. However, Suhrkamp is still undecided, and I have the feeling that if you intervened again in this direction, it would be very beneficial to the matter. It is partly to do with material problems, namely the enlarged reproduction of the *Arcades* materials. Since the idea of trying, in spite of everything, to work with the handwritten materials, comes from you, your intervention would be all the more legitimate. I would be extraordinarily grateful if you could write as soon as possible, since the preparations are supposed to be finished by Christmas and the whole thing will likely go to press in the spring.

I have entrusted the Benjamin material to Suhrkamp so as not to expose it to the risk of a 6000-mile journey by post. This has the added advantage that further pieces can be included in the edition, in addition to the ones that I have already identified, should more space become available.

So, we are leaving next Thursday. From the 16th to the 21st of October my address will be Hôtel Régina, 2 Place des Pyramides, Paris. Around the end of the month I'll be in New York for a few days, c/o Institute of Social Research, 90 Morningside Drive, New York 27, N.Y. From the 10th of November, at the latest, my permanent address will be: 803 Yale St., Santa Monica, California.

With kindest regards, also to your wife, also from Gretel,

Most cordially
always yours
Teddie Adorno

P.S.
The address of Peter Suhrkamp is: Frankfurt a. M., Schaumainkai 53.

Original: typescript with printed letterhead; Gershom Scholem Archive, The National Library of Israel, Jerusalem. First published in Rolf Tiedemann (ed.), *Frankfurter Adorno Blätter* V (Munich: Edition Text + Kritik, 1998), pp. 170–2.

Benjamin edition: This refers to the two-volume edition of Benjamin's *Schriften*, which was published in 1955 by Theodor and Gretel Adorno with the participation of Friedrich Podszus.

individual drafts from the Arcades material: "The three longer, more developed texts named here were included in the *Schriften*, whereas the unpublished ... passages from the section on Baudelaire – i.e. from the first piece on Baudelaire, "The Paris of the Second Empire in Baudelaire" – were left out, as were the notes and drafts comprising the actual *Arcades* material. Only *Central Park*, individual notes from the section on Baudelaire, was taken up into the *Schriften*" (Rolf Tiedemann, note on the first edition).

enlarged reproduction of the Arcades materials: "Adorno supposed that only a photographic magnification of Benjamin's microscopic handwriting would allow for the *Arcades* materials to be deciphered" (Rolf Tiedemann, note on the first edition).

30 SCHOLEM TO ADORNO
JERUSALEM, 16.6.1953

16 June 1953

Dear Mr. Adorno,

I might understand your sending of the fragment on music and language as a kind of letter to my kabbalistic conscience, and as you can see, such appeals have an immediate effect on my writing nerves, should these exist. I am expecting you soon in my course on the linguistic theory of the Kabbalists (in which music has so far been neglected, for the forgivable reasons of my lack of ability). The difficulty of your theory, to the extent that I – a complete philistine – can presume to say anything about it, lies in what is unintuitable in the essence of God's name (as you use it). It seems questionable how, in the spirit of your attempt, this could make itself audible. In the audible, after all, the name – also in its "configurations" – could only be <u>omitted</u>, not <u>fulfilled</u>. How music should accomplish this, I do not know.

We are going to Switzerland for some weeks on the 1st of August, where I will crown my trip with an Eranos lecture on the Golem – it is not every day that one gets to conclude a lecture with a spoonerism on the relation between a speaker and his topic!! That must be enjoyed. I have no business in Germany this time, nor any money to go there. Are you coming back to Europe in the summer? As it stands I only know for sure that we will be in Zurich from the 16th to the 23rd of September. At the end of the month, or early in October, I want to fly back – my wife will take a detour to Florence and will return by boat. Perhaps we will meet somewhere?

Cordial regards to your wife and you

yours

Gerhard Scholem

Original: aerogram (manuscript); Theodor W. Adorno Archive, Frankfurt am Main.

fragment on music and language: See Adorno, "Music and Language: A Fragment," in *Quasi una Fantasia*, trans. Rodney Livingstone (London:

Verso, 1998), pp. 1–6. A carbon-copy of the typescript of this piece was enclosed in the letter to Scholem.

in my course on the linguistic theories of the Kabbalists: Scholem spoke on the linguistic theories of the Kabbalists at the Eranos conference in 1970. See "The Name of God in the Linguistic Theory of the Kabbala," trans. Simon Pleasance, *Diogenes*, 20/79 (1972), pp. 59–80. Further details of the course have not been verified.

Eranos lecture on the Golem: During the Eranos conference in 1953, Scholem spoke about "Die Vorstellung vom Golem in ihren tellurischen und magischen Beziehungen [The Idea of the Golem in its telluric and magical relations]; see now "The Idea of the Golem" in *On the Kabbalah and its Symbolism*, trans. Ralph Manheim (New York: Schocken Books, 1965), pp. 158–204. The special edition of this piece, which was sent to Adorno, contains the handwritten dedication "Kind regards from London! G. Scholem."

31 ADORNO TO SCHOLEM
SANTA MONICA, 1.7.1953

T. W. Adorno
803 Yale Str.
Santa Monica, Calif. 1 July 1953

Dear Mr. Scholem,

Kindest thanks for your letter of the 16th of June. I very much hope that we will have the opportunity to discuss the questions that you have raised *ad vocem* "Music and Language" – and much else – for we have the definite intention of coming to Europe in the course of August. At the moment, however, I can't anticipate the exact dates.

I'll probably have so much to do in Frankfurt that a journey to Switzerland is rather improbable, although it is extraordinarily tempting to me, as I have a superstitious faith in the air of the Engadin. Yet I am all the more hopeful that you might, in the end, take a detour through Frankfurt. After all, there are more than enough reasons for it – not only the joyful one that we might meet again, but also the sad one of the crisis concerning the matter of the Benjamin edition. I attach a copy of the letter that I sent to Suhrkamp in response to the note in which he declares that he is stepping back from the plan. At the very least we should make a concerted, common effort to save the project. Perhaps it would not be bad if you could feel out Schocken to see whether he might be interested in a German edition. I dare not judge the difficulties of a Hebrew translation – which, in any case, no one else but you could undertake – although I imagine these difficulties to be extraordinary. Please do not mention anything about this alternative plan to Suhrkamp, since we shouldn't give up so easily on this matter, and we must proceed with the utmost diplomacy to realize the edition in spite of everything. Incidentally, in keeping with your intentions, we have prepared a series of notes from the *Arcades* material for inclusion in the edition.

Do drop me a few lines soon.

With the most cordial regards, also from Gretel,

yours

Teddie Adorno

Original: typescript; Gershom Scholem Archive, The National Library of Israel, Jerusalem. First published in Rolf Tiedemann (ed.), *Frankfurter Adorno Blätter* V (Munich: Edition Text + Kritik, 1998), pp. 173–4.

copy of the letter: On 25.6.1953, Peter Suhrkamp wrote the following to Adorno: "Dear Teddie Adorno – on the 20th of June I sent you a plan for Walter Benjamin's *Gesammelte Schriften*. You have not been able to comment on this yet. In the meantime this has become unnecessary, as I have stepped back from this plan and from the publication of the *Gesammelte Schriften* altogether. This will startle you. You can be assured that I did not reach this decision easily. Moreover, you musn't think that this has occurred during the past 4 or 5 days. The dispute goes back further." The reason for the decision was the high cost of a critical edition given the difficulty of the texts and the state of the material. See Suhrkamp's letter, Podszus's statement, and Adorno's response, dated 30.6.1953, in *"So müßte ich ein Engel und kein Autor sein." Adorno und seine Frankfurter Verleger: Der Briefwechsel mit Peter Suhrkamp und Siegfried Unseld* ["So I would have to be an angel, not an author." Adorno and his Frankfurt publishers: the correspondence with Peter Suhrkamp and Siegfried Unseld], ed. Wolfgang Schopf (Frankfurt am Main: Suhrkamp, 2003), pp. 99–111.

Schocken: The department store owner and publisher Salman Schocken (1877–1959) founded the Schocken Verlag in Berlin in 1931. In 1933 he immigrated to Palestine, where he continued running the publishing house, as well as acquiring the newspaper *Haaretz*. Schocken was friends with Gershom Scholem. See letter the relevant note in letter no. 7 in this volume.

32 SCHOLEM TO ADORNO
JERUSALEM, 9.7.1953

9 July 1953

Dear Mr. Adorno,

I am responding to your letter right away. Yesterday morning I wrote to Suhrkamp, whose letter I received only five days ago, entirely in the spirit of your letter: I think an intermediary way is conceivable. (In case of doubt, I would – in B.'s spirit, as you rightly say – forego including, in particular, the notes to the dissertation and the notes to the piece on Baudelaire, without <u>any</u> scruples of the sort expressed by P.) Confidentially, I'd like to tell you the following: unfortunately, since I am traveling on personal business this time, and, moreover, with my wife, I am so short of money that I could only afford the detour to Frkft. a.M. (which would only be conceivable in late September) if the sum of approx. $100 were to be made available for this purpose. If you see any possibility of procuring this sum for me, then I could come over and we could appear <u>together</u>. (I would have to keep my wife in Switzerland for longer if I were to go back and forth instead of returning directly – I cannot bring her to Germany for passport-related reasons). You will understand that I am sharing this point with you only. Last year this was not a problem; this year I have to consider every Franc. Off the bat, speaking in Germany is still completely impossible for me, so I cannot seek any funding through such channels. It would have to come from somewhere else. If not, we will have to settle for brief, written statements. In my estimation, Schocken <u>is out</u> as far as alternative plans are concerned. I am under no illusion, his great speeches notwithstanding. Despite everything, I will of course see what might be done if I happen to meet him in Switzerland (although this is unlikely).

All the best,

yours Gerhard Scholem

P.S. Should this letter only come into your hands after the 20th, please send your response to Zurich instead, c/o Dr. Erich Katzenstein, Mühlebachstrasse 140, where I will find it.

Original: aerogram (manuscript); Theodor W. Adorno Archive, Frankfurt am Main.

P: Friedrich Podszus, who had reported Suhrkamp's wish to exclude notes and annotations in a letter to Adorno. See *"So müßte ich ein Engel und kein Autor sein." Adorno und seine Frankfurter Verleger: Der Briefwechsel mit Peter Suhrkamp und Siegfried Unseld* ["So I would have to be an angel, not an author." Adorno and his Frankfurt publishers: the correspondence with Peter Suhrkamp and Siegfried Unseld], ed. Wolfgang Schopf (Frankfurt am Main: Suhrkamp, 2003), p. 102.

33 ADORNO TO SCHOLEM
FRANKFURT AM MAIN, 18.9.1953

INSTITUTE FOR SOCIAL RESEARCH
AT THE JOHANN WOLFGANG GOETHE
UNIVERSITY

FRANKURT A.M.
SENCKENBERG-ANLAGE 26

T.W. Adorno

18 September 1953

Professor Dr. G. Scholem
c/o Dr. Erich Katzenstein
Zurich
Mühlebachstr. 140

Dear Mr. Scholem,

Well, after overcoming some complications and feeling rather enervated, I have happily arrived here and resumed my activities. In the meantime, a regular professorship has been created for me, which gives my work at the university a permanent framework.

It goes without saying how very important, as well as very nice, it would be to see you. However, at the moment I cannot organize a guest lecture for you at the Institute on account of the holidays; nobody would come. Things would be easier at the university, as part of the philosophy seminar, but this too would be possible only after the 1st of November, and I don't know if you'll still be here by then. Is there any other possibility – perhaps on the radio? Please be so kind as to let me know as soon as possible. On the 26th I have committed to opening the Darmstadt talks and chairing the discussion on the first day, and in the back of my mind there stirs the faint hope that you might join us.

Regarding the Benjamin edition, I have good, though not yet decisive, news to report – albeit cautiously, and with the utmost discretion towards Suhrkamp and Podszus. In a long conversation with me, Suhrkamp has agreed to resume discussions and not to treat the issue as a *causa judicata*, and Podszus – I spoke with each of them separately – was also quite forthcoming. If there isn't some hidden and more genuine motive behind this whole tempest in a teacup – namely, trepidation over the economic risks – then I have no doubt that the whole thing will come together in the spring after all. Since the Schröder edition, which was very expensive, turned out to be a success, against my expectations, and the dreaded economic fears did not materialize, the situation seems to have been caused by little more than ephemeral tensions within the publishing house. Of course it would be very good if you could be present for the decisive discussion. This will only be possible after the 28th; there is no talking to Suhrkamp before that because of the book fair. Incidentally, he is not in good health. He never fully recovered from what happened to him in the concentration camp, such that he literally exists in the borderline situation that has become such a sorry metaphor in the mouths of the philosophers.

Gretel sends her regards to you, also to your wife, whom we would love to meet.

Please be so kind as to respond quickly.

Most affectionately, always

Teddie Adorno

Original: typescript with printed letterhead; Gershom Scholem Archive, The National Library of Israel, Jerusalem. First published in Rolf Tiedemann (ed.), *Frankfurter Adorno Blätter* V (Munich: Edition Text + Kritik, 1998), pp. 174–5.

a regular professorship has been created: On 1.7.1953 Adorno was appointed as a permanent extraordinary professor of philosophy and sociology in the Faculty of Philosophy at the Goethe University Frankfurt.

opening the Darmstadt talks and chairing the discussion on the first day: During his opening lecture at the Darmstadt talks in 1953, Adorno gave a presentation entitled "Individuum und Organisation" [Individual and organization]. See Adorno, *Gesammelte Schriften 8: Soziologische Schriften 1*, ed. Rolf Tiedemann et al. (Frankfurt am Main: Suhrkamp, 1972), pp. 440–56.

the Schröder edition, which was very expensive: Rudolf Alexander Schröder (1878–1962) was a German writer, poet, and translator. The complete edition of his writings was the first such collection published by the newly founded Suhrkamp Verlag. See Schröder, *Gesammelte Werke in Fünf Bänden* (Frankfurt am Main: Suhrkamp, 1952).

what happened to him in the concentration camp: Peter Suhrkamp was arrested by the Gestapo in April 1944 because of alleged high treason and treason. After the trial was suspended, he was taken into custody in the concentration camp at Sachsenhausen. He was released two weeks later, in February 1945, at the peak of a severe case of pneumonia. See Siegfried Unseld and Helene Ritzerfeld (eds), *Peter Suhrkamp: Zur Biographie eines Verlegers in Daten, Dokumenten und Bildern* [Peter Suhrkamp: on the biography of a publisher in dates, documents and images] (Frankfurt am Main: Suhrkamp, 1975), pp. 101–6.

34 SCHOLEM TO ADORNO
ZURICH, 22.9.1953

Kurhaus Rigiblick
Zurich
22 Sept. 1953

Dear Mr. Adorno,

I have just received your letter and am replying immediately. I am very glad to hear about the good prospects of which you write for the Benjamin edition, and I am hopeful that it will come to fruition in friendly agreement – even with some compromises. As you know, I am firmly of the opinion, in this case, that an incomplete edition is better than no edition, and so – to the extent that it lies within your powers of persuasion – I fully endorse your approach of not letting matters founder over "*technicalities.*"* Unfortunately, as I've already told you, I cannot afford the journey. I do not wish to speak. Accordingly I will have to forego the trip. I do not know what the Darmstadt talks are, of course, but I wish you all the best with these. You'll receive a copy of my Eranos lecture on the problem of the Golem when it's published. Have I sent you the one about the *Shekinah*?

I am flying back to Israel on the 2nd of October. Until then you can reach me here; otherwise, you'd better write back to Jerusalem.

Cordial regards, also to your wife, and to the gentlemen, Suhrkamp and Podszus.

Yours,

Gershom Scholem

Original: manuscript; Theodor W. Adorno Archive, Frankfurt am Main.

my Eranos lecture on the problem of the Golem: A special edition of the lecture is not part of Adorno's estate.

Have I sent you the one about the Shekinah?: Scholem's lecture at the 1952 Eranos conference, titled, "Zur Entwicklungsgeschichte der kabbalistischen Konzeption der Schechinah" [On the history of the development of the kabbalistic conception of *Shekinah*], appeared in the *Eranos Jahrbuch 1952*, Vol. 21: *Mensch und Energie* [Man and energy], ed. Olga Fröbe-Kapteyn (Zurich: Rhein, 1953), pp. 45–107. It was re-edited under the title "*Schechina*; das passiv-weibliche Moment in der Gottheit" in Gershom Scholem, *Von der mystischen Gestalt der Gottheit* (Zürich: 1962, p. 135–191). See: Gershom Scholem, "The Feminine Element in Divinity", in *On the Mystical Shape of the Godhead: Basic Concepts of the Kabbalah* (Schocken Books: New York, 1991), pp. 140–96.

* Original in English.

35 SCHOLEM TO ADORNO
JERUSALEM, 18.12.1953

האוניברסיטה העברית בירושלים
THE HEBREW UNIVERSITY, JERUSALEM

18 Dec. 1953

Dear Mr. Adorno,

I haven't heard from you for three months and I do not know whether an amicable agreement has been reached regarding Walter Benjamin's writings. It would be very nice if you could let me know where things stand. It is a pity that I was so restricted in my movements this time around.

I am enclosing a copy of a major new piece of mine, which could now appear in French. I hope that this address is sufficient for the postal service to find you – I don't know if you've changed your old postal address.

Next year I'll be on *sabbatical leave*,* and my wife and I will likely find ourselves a quiet place, in England or in Switzerland, where I'll be able to write without disturbance. This time our circumstances will be more favorable. I intend to come to Europe toward the end of March or in early April.

All the best to you and your wife,
from your
Gerhard Scholem

Original: aerogram (manuscript) with printed letterhead; Theodor W. Adorno Archive, Frankfurt am Main.

a copy of a major new piece of mine: See Gershom-Gerhard Scholem, "Le Mouvement sabbataïste en Pologne" [The Sabbatian movement in Poland], *Revue de l'Histoire des Religions*, 143/1 (1953), pp. 30–90 [Part 1]; 143/2 (1953), pp. 209–232; 144/1 (1953), pp. 42–77 [Part 2].

* Original in English.

36 SCHOLEM TO ADORNO
JERUSALEM, 5.1.1954

האוניברסיטה העברית בירושלים
THE HEBREW UNIVERSITY, JERUSALEM

5 Jan. 1954

My dear Sir,

You have not responded to my letter; but instead (or in anticipation thereof?) today I received your essay on Kafka, to which I was delighted to dedicate a first reading while summoning my courage ahead of a seminar on the Kabbalah of Moses Cordovero. Many thanks for this. These pages really make one think; and you can receive a well-deserved wreath for the Lessing quote. That's really something. While reading your piece, I realize that I lack any knowledge of Mr. Sade, which I previously believed to be superfluous, since having taken note of his colleagues from the other barricade. It seems, however, that the leap from Masoch to Sade was premature, and that a stay in Europe should have been dedicated to such enlightenment. Not this year, of course, since I will be busy with quite different matters. Indeed, my wife and I intend to go to Berne in two to three months, where an affiliation with none other than the University of Muri seems certain – and what could compete with that? As I probably already told you, we can stay between six and eight months; and since, this time, I have declined an offer from America to go to California and slave away at lecturing, I can devote this great holiday to more serious matters. In the meantime, I do hope to hear from you about how the Benjamin edition is coming together.

This time, it's well and truly winter here.

Many thanks and best wishes to you and your wife

from your

Gerhard Scholem

Original: aerogram with printed letterhead; Theodor W. Adorno Archive, Frankfurt am Main.

essay on Kafka: Adorno's essay "Notes on Kafka," written between 1942 and 1953, first appeared in *Die Neue Rundschau* in 1953 and was included in 1955 in the collection *Prismen*. See *Prisms*, trans. Samuel Weber and Shierry Weber (Cambridge, MA: MIT Press, 1981), pp. 253–71.

seminar on the Kabbalah of Moses Cordovero: The Kabbalist Rabbi Moses Cordovero (1522–1570) was one of the most important representatives of the Kabbalah in Safed. A teacher of the mystic Isaac Luria (see letter no. 15 in this volume), he wrote an extensive commentary on the book of Zohar. His central, systematic work *Pardes Rimmonim* (Hebrew: Garden of pomegranates), was written in 1548 and published in Kraków in 1592. See Scholem, *Major Trends in Jewish Mysticism* (Jerusalem: 1941; rev. edn., New York: Schocken, 1995), pp. 244–86. Details of Scholem's seminar have not been verified.

the Lessing quote: Adorno cites his source in the essay: "In the Eighth Part of the Axiomata directed against the orthodox chief pastor Goeze, by an author Kafka esteemed highly, Lessing, there is the story of a 'discharged Lutheran preacher from the Pfalz'" (Adorno, "Notes on Kafka," p. 265).

Mr. Sade ... his colleagues from the other barricade ... from Masoch to Sade: The writer and politician Donatien Alphonse Francois de Sade (1740–1814), author of the novels *Justine, or the Misfortunes of Virtue* (1787) and *Juliette, or Vice Amply Rewarded* (1796), is frequently discussed in Adorno's writings. Scholem appears to have contrasted him with the writer Leopold Ritter von Sacher-Masoch (1836–1895), author of the novella *Venus in Furs* (1870), thus alluding to the opposition of sadism and masochism. In his essay on Kafka, Adorno refers to the relation between the works of Kafka and Sade. See "Notes on Kafka," p. 164. See also Adorno and Max Horkheimer, "Excursus II: Juliette or Enlightenment and Morality," in *Dialectic of Enlightenment*, trans. Edmund Jephcott (Stanford, CA: Stanford University Press, 2002), pp. 63–93.

an affiliation with none other than the University of Muri: Scholem is referring to the fictional "University of Muri," which he and Benjamin had invented, named after the area of Berne where the two had lived as neighbours for three months in 1918. See the note to letter no. 71 (18.9.1918) in *The Correspondence of Walter Benjamin 1910–1940*, ed. Theodor W. Adorno and Gershom Scholem, trans. Manfred R. Jacobson and Evelyn M. Jacobson (Chicago: University of Chicago Press, 1994), p. 134.

37 ADORNO TO SCHOLEM
FRANKFURT AM MAIN, 6.1.1954

INSTITUTE FOR SOCIAL RESEARCH
AT THE JOHANN WOLFGANG GOETHE
UNIVERSITY

FRANKURT A.M.
SENCKENBERG-ANLAGE 26
Kettenhofweg 123
6 January 1954

T.W. Adorno

Dear Mr. Scholem,

Kindest thanks for your letter of 18.12. I would like nothing better than to tell you something positive about the publication of Benjamin's writings. But this is still not the case. Even though, in line with your intentions, I made every conceivable concession to Suhrkamp regarding the trifling, technical issues surrounding the publication, he has made no positive commitment. He keeps referring to the disagreement with Podszus, which has long since been resolved – and in keeping with his wishes, no less. However, since I know Suhrkamp quite well, I'd say it's unwise to force the issue – one has to wait and also mobilize some outside aides. I'm optimistic *à la longue*, since the publishing house has recently enjoyed some very, very large commercial successes, which should make it easier for Suhrkamp to balance the risk that the Benjamin edition represents. I have no doubts that, in the end, there are material considerations behind this unexpected and somewhat irrational difficulty; and when these considerations dissipate I believe that Suhrkamp will go ahead with the project after all. Naturally, we mustn't wait too long, especially so as not to let a situation arise in which he could produce this reaction "too late." But you can count on the fact that I am looking into it. Initially I was offended – not without success, I think.

Thanks kindly for your essay. I haven't gotten around to reading it yet, but I'm looking forward to it. En route, it must have crossed paths with my Kafka piece, which, of all the things I've written since the Kierkegaard book, reveals certain fundamental positions most openly. I would be very keen to hear your thoughts, if you find the time and the inclination to take to heart the product, which has been worked according to the *Landjäger* principle – that is to say, it has been stuffed like a hard sausage.

I am overjoyed that you are coming to Europe for an extended period. Of course we must meet, whether in Switzerland or, should it be possible to lure you here with books and manuscripts, in Germany. As it stands, we intend to go on a lengthy holiday in August (something that hasn't happened for years). Moreover, there is the hope that I might be invited to give a lecture in Rome this April. Please be so kind as to keep me updated with full details of your movements.

One more thing: I don't know whether you are aware that Arnold Schoenberg – without question the most significant and, for this reason, the most feared composer of our time – composed a series of biblical, pointedly Jewish works during his late period. Among them is a *Kol Nidre*, of which his wife recently played me a record in Los Angeles – a piece of overwhelming luminosity, quite unknown as yet; the *Survivor of Warsaw*, with the *Sh'ma Yisrael* at the end; and the fragmentary opera *Moses und Aron*, with the indescribable *Dance around the Golden Calf*. I have no doubt that this music has its proper place in Israel. On the other hand, it is about as different from ordinary synagogue music as Kafka is from a rabbi. I can only imagine the kind of folkloristic nonsense that will be thrown at Schoenberg, who does not draw on traditional melodies but who connects to the Jewish tradition in a subterranean and hence all the more magnificent way. I am telling you these things because I can imagine that your authority might put you in a position to do something decisive on this front. Besides, there is likely no shortage of musicians in Israel who would support you, if necessary, against the cantors. I would truly view it as a joyful duty if there were something I could do to help. You may be interested to know that, during his last phase, Schoenberg felt increasingly drawn to Jewish mysticism, as Kolisch told me. Perhaps you've come across my essay on Schoenberg, which appeared in *Die Neue Rundschau* about a year ago.

All that is cordial to you and your wife, also from Gretel,

yours

Teddie Adorno

Original: typescript with printed letterhead; Gershom Scholem Archive, The National Library of Israel, Jerusalem; see Rolf Tiedemann (ed.), *Frankfurter Adorno Blätter* V (Munich: Edition Text + Kritik, 1998), pp. 176–8.

disagreement with Podszus: See the relevant note in letter no. 31 in this volume.

should it be possible to lure you here with books and manuscripts, in Germany: Adorno is referring to Scholem's trips to Europe in the name of The National Library of Israel, during which he looked for Jewish texts that had been confiscated or lost during the war (see letter no. 19 in this volume).

in Rome this April: In January 1954 Adorno received an invitation to take part in an international conference on contemporary music, which took place in Rome from the 4th to the 15th of April 1954. Initially, Adorno accepted the invitation and suggested speaking on "Das Altern der Neuen Musik" [The aging of the New Music]. However, after further consideration and further correspondence with the organizer, Nicolas Nabokov, Adorno canceled his appearance. He presented the lecture "Das Altern der Neuen Musik" on the radio (Süddeutscher Rundfunk) in April 1954. See "The Aging of the New Music" in *Essays on Music*, ed. Richard Leppert, trans. Susan Gillespie (Berkeley: University of California Press, 2002), pp. 181–202.

Arnold Schoenberg: Adorno had been acquainted with the composer and theorist of music Arnold Schoenberg (1874–1951) since studying composition in Vienna with Alban Berg.

Kol Nidre: Hebrew: "all vows": a Jewish prayer spoken at the synagogue on the eve of Yom Kippur (the Day of Atonement). Schoenberg set the prayer to music in 1938, *Kol Nidre*, Op. 39.

his wife: In 1924 Schoenberg married Gertrud Kolisch (1898–1987), the sister of Rudolf Kolisch. Under the pseudonym Max Blonda, she wrote the libretto to Schoenberg's opera *Von heute auf morgen* [From one day to the next]. After Schoenberg's death she founded the publishing house, Belmont Music Publishers, which dealt primarily with Schoenberg's work.

the Survivor of Warsaw, *with the* Sh'ma Yisrael *at the end*: Schoenberg's cantata *A Survivor from Warsaw*, Op. 46 (1947), treats the uprising in the Warsaw Ghetto and its subsequent suppression in April–May 1943. At the end of the piece the choir sings the Jewish prayer *Sh'ma Yisrael* ("Hear O Israel") in Hebrew.

the fragmentary opera Moses und Aron *with the indescribable* Dance around the Golden Calf: Schoenberg composed the first two acts of the opera *Moses und Aron* as early as 1930–2 and completed the third act in 1937. He abandoned the project, however, during his American exile. The fragmentary opera was first performed in 1954, after his death. The biblical story of the "dance around the golden calf" (Exodus 32: 1–4) is portrayed in the third scene of the second act. Adorno's essay "Sacred Fragment: Schoenberg's 'Moses und Aron'" is dedicated to Gershom Scholem. See *Quasi una Fantasia: Essays on Modern Music*, trans. Rodney Livingstone (London: Verso, 1999), pp. 224–48. See also letter no. 127 in this volume.

Kolisch: The violinist, conductor, and theorist of music Rudolf Kolisch (1896–1978) was a student of Schoenberg's and a friend of Adorno's. From 1939 to 1941 he taught at the New School for Social Research in New York.

my essay on Schoenberg: See Theodor W. Adorno, "Arnold Schoenberg (1874–1951)," *Die Neue Rundschau*, 64/1 (1953), pp. 80–104. In 1955 Adorno included the piece in his essay collection *Prismen. Kulturkritik und Gesellschaft* [Prisms: Cultural critique and society]. See *Prisms*, trans. Samuel Weber and Shierry Weber (Cambridge, MA: MIT Press, 1981), pp.147–72.

38 ADORNO TO SCHOLEM
FRANKFURT AM MAIN, AFTER 6 JANUARY 1954

INSTITUTE FOR SOCIAL RESEARCH
AT THE JOHANN WOLFGANG GOETHE
UNIVERSITY

FRANKURT A.M.
SENCKENBERG-ANLAGE 26
January 1954

T.W. Adorno

Dear Mr. Scholem,

Kindest thanks for your letter, which has crossed with mine en route. It was a great pleasure for me, especially because you were the first to recognize the scope of my Lessing discovery – something of which I am quite proud.

I am writing to you today for a very peculiar reason. The January issue of *MERKUR* includes some fragments from the estate of a certain writer, Franz Baermann-Steiner, which I not only find quite extraordinary in themselves, but which also coincide with my own Kafka interpretation on decisive points. Until now I was unaware of this man's existence, not to mention his writings, and he would hardly have been aware of me. The most important passages are on page 40 of the January edition of *MERKUR*. My feeling is that this is someone who is relevant for you in the highest degree. Perhaps you could do something to get his work published in Hebrew? I know the publisher of these fragments in passing through some correspondence. His name is Dr. H. G. Adler. His address is:

96, Dalgarno Gdns., London W.10.

I have written to Adler and mentioned your name – but perhaps you'll get in touch with him yourself.

So, hopefully we will see each other quite soon.

With heartfelt affinity
always yours
Teddie Adorno

Original: typescript with printed letterhead; Gershom Scholem Archive, The National Library of Israel, Jerusalem. First published in Rolf Tiedemann (ed.), *Frankfurter Adorno Blätter* V (Munich: Edition Text + Kritik, 1998), p. 178.

my Lessing discovery: See letter no. 36 in this volume.

The January issue of MERKUR . . . Franz Baermann-Steiner: The writer, poet, and ethnologist Franz Baermann Steiner (1909–1952) came from Prague. After the war he was a lecturer in Oxford and London. His main ethnological work, *Taboo*, was published in English (posthumously, 1956) but his German writings remained largely unknown at that time. See Franz Baermann Steiner, "Aus dem Nachlass" [From the estate], *Merkur*, 8/71.1 (1954), pp. 32–41.

H. G. Adler: The writer and poet H. G. Adler (1910–1988) was born in Prague. After completing his studies and obtaining his doctorate at the German University in Prague, he worked for the German-language broadcaster of Czechoslovakia. In 1942 he was deported to the concentration camp at Theresienstadt and in 1944 to Auschwitz. After the war he wrote works of prose, collections of poems, and, above all, studies on the Theresienstadt concentration camp. See *Gershom Scholem: A Life in Letters*, ed. and trans. Anthony David Skinner (Cambridge, MA: Harvard University Press, 2002), p. 396; see also Adorno, "Über H. G. Adler" [On H. G. Adler], in *Gesammelte Schriften 20.2: Vermischte Schriften* [Miscellaneous Writings], ed. Rolf Tiedemann et al. (Frankfurt am Main: Suhrkamp, 1986), p. 495.

I have written to Adler: In his letter to Adler, dated January 1954, Adorno writes:

The occasion for the resumption of our correspondence, which was unfortunately interrupted in August of 1951, is your publication of fragments from the estate of Franz Baermann-Steiner.

The impression that I received was quite extraordinary. First, on account of the material itself, which has a quality that is very seldom found. – It is symptomatic of the state of the world that one only learns of such a man, to whom one truly feels a deep connection, after his passing. But then, also, for a reason that is essential to me: his Kafka interpretation coincides with mine in a startling manner – in contrast to almost everything that has been written about Kafka to date. I am enclosing my essay on Kafka, which appeared in *Die Neue Rundschau* in December. If you compare the note "Kafka and the Old Testament" with the beginning of my piece, and especially if you compare the subsequent "Similarities to Dostoevsky" with the beginning of the ninth chapter (as well as the eighth), then you will be no less astonished than I was. My idea of Kafka's antinomian theology corresponds absolutely with Steiner's thesis that redemption "is neither wanted by this order nor willed by it." And the mythical deity I speak of is none other than the gnostic demiurge mentioned by Steiner. I cannot tell you how happy I am to find speculations of this sort confirmed by someone who couldn't possibly have known of my efforts, just as I was unaware of his. Is it immodest to ask you if Steiner did know my work? I want to thank you sincerely for publishing this piece.

Naturally, everything must be done to ensure that Steiner's work is made public. The obvious thing for me to do would be to approach my publisher, Suhrkamp; however, I am reluctant to do so at the moment because I am making every conceivable effort to ensure that the work of my friend Benjamin is published, and I cannot get in the way of this plan. But I will write today to Professor Schoeps in Erlangen, who has worked on Kafka, suggesting that he should publish more of Steiner's work in his journal. Moreover, I will write to my friend Scholem, a professor of Kabbalah in Jerusalem. I hope that these interventions will lead to something. (Carbon copy of typescript, Theodor W. Adorno Archive, Frankfurt am Main)

39 SCHOLEM TO ADORNO
JERUSALEM, 24.1.1954

האוניברסיטה העברית בירושלים
THE HEBREW UNIVERSITY, JERUSALEM

24.I.1954

Dear Mr. Adorno,

Many thanks for both of your letters. To my knowledge, Schoenberg has already been widely performed here, years ago, although I am not at all versed in this subject. In response to your letter about the article in *Merkur*, I can say nothing, since this journal only arrives here after several months' delay (if it arrives at all), and I haven't seen it for a long time. I hardly read any German journals, and there isn't really any opportunity to do so in Israel. You may not be entirely clear about the degree of almost complete estrangement between everything that happens here and what happens there.

In late March we will go – that is to say, we will fly – to England (via Holland?), where we will probably stay for several months: at least until August. I do not intend to come to the continent before mid-August; then we might go to Ascona for 2 weeks.

I hope you will be successful in your plans with Suhrkamp – I fear that, if things don't happen soon, it will be too late. The background of the matter is entirely incomprehensible to me.

Might you be able to arrange for the German textbook, published by S., to be sent to me? It is said to have been very successful, I heard from a London friend.

All the best to you and your wife

yours

Gerhard Scholem

Original: aerogram (manuscript) with printed letterhead; Theodor W. Adorno Archive, Frankfurt am Main.

Schoenberg has already been widely performed here, years ago: Arnold Schoenberg's symphonic poem *Pelleas and Melisande* (Op. 5) was performed in Tel Aviv as early as 1939 by the Palestine Orchestra. The conductor was Hermann Scherchen. A "Schoenberg Festival" took place in Israel on the occasion of the composer's 70th birthday in 1944. As part of the festivities, the symphony orchestra played his Suite for String Orchestra, and the radio orchestra recorded further pieces, which were subsequently broadcast. In 1949, on the occasion of Schoenberg's 75th birthday, two public concerts were held, in which both *Ode to Napoleon* (Op. 41) and *Piano Pieces* (Op. 33) were performed. The performances were followed by further broadcasts on Israeli radio. The events were organized by the Berlin-born German-Israeli musicologist Peter Gradenwitz (1910–2001), who was personally acquainted with Schoenberg. Schoenberg was named honorary president of the Israeli Academy of Music in Jerusalem shortly before his death.

the German textbook: See Oskar Loerke and Peter Suhrkamp (eds), *Deutscher Geist: Ein Lesebuch aus Zwei Jahrhunderten* [German spirit: readings from two centuries], 2 vols, revised and expanded edition (Frankfurt am Main: Suhrkamp, 1953).

40 ADORNO TO SCHOLEM
FRANKFURT AM MAIN, 5.4.1955

INSTITUTE FOR SOCIAL RESEARCH
AT THE JOHANN WOLFGANG GOETHE
UNIVERSITY

FRANKURT A.M.
SENCKENBERG-ANLAGE 26
5 April 1955

T.W. Adorno

Dear Mr. Scholem,

Today I have good news to report: Suhrkamp is going to publish an extensive two-volume Benjamin edition. It was quite an odyssey to get this far. You're familiar with the old song and dance from before. The subsequent development was as follows: Dr. Wild, the uncommonly nice head of the strictly Catholic publisher Kösel, who is very sympathetic to our undertaking, took an interest in Benjamin, looked at the materials, and decided, considering his publishing house's particular readership, that he could not publish it. He then passed the materials on to Beck, where he energetically intervened on our part, as did my friend Arnold Hauser (the author of the excellent *Sozialgeschichte der Literatur und Kunst* [Social history of literature and art]). This resulted in the miracle that Beck, in itself a rather conservative publishing house, in fact undertook to publish the Benjamin edition, albeit in a somewhat abridged form, compared with the expansive plans that I had devised with Suhrkamp and Podszus. Now, Suhrkamp had never definitively rejected the project; indeed, he had asked me to offer him the option before I signed a contract with anyone else. When I received a copy of the contract, signed by Beck, I kept my promise and showed it to Suhrkamp, and within two days he decided to go ahead with it after all. I decided to go with Suhrkamp for many reasons, but above all because this way we'll be able to include a lot more material. With the help of Wild, I was able to get out of the agreement with Beck without consequences.

The edition is already being typeset. Initially, of course, this applies only to those materials that already exist in book form. All manuscripts will be carefully proofread by us before they're typeset. Gretel and I will act as editors.

Moreover, by way of an opening act to the full edition, *One-Way Street* is to appear in the "Bibliothek Suhrkamp" series, in a respectable edition of 5000 copies. It is still uncertain whether *Berlin Childhood* and *One-Way Street*, the two texts that have recently appeared separately, will also be included in the edition. Suhrkamp is for it; I am reluctant, as I'd rather leave room for other things. Besides, I do not want to create unnecessary competition for the books that have already come out.

I'm approaching you with a request today. Suhrkamp has asked me to also include biographical details in my introduction. I think it would be most in keeping with Benjamin's wishes if this were to occur in tabular form, as rigorously and soberly as possible. I know a lot, but not everything. Would it be possible for you to relay the central dates to me, to the extent that you are familiar with them? I will also approach Dora about this – though of course we cannot securely rely on her memories – and Ernst Schön, and wherever there are divergences we will clarify them together. I'd be grateful if you could respond quickly, since the whole edition is supposed to come out in the early autumn, and the introduction and biographical notes have to go to print in June.

Many thanks in advance.

I do not need to tell you how happy I am about this development. Only last year we would have hardly thought it possible that two big publishing houses would be fighting over the Benjamin edition.

All that is cordial to you and Fanja, also from Gretel.

Your old

Teddie Adorno

Original: typescript with printed letterhead; Gershom Scholem Archive, The National Library of Israel, Jerusalem. First published in Rolf Tiedemann (ed.), *Frankfurter Adorno Blätter* V (Munich: Edition Text + Kritik, 1998), pp. 179–81.

Dr. Wild: Adorno discussed the idea of publishing a Benjamin edition through Kösel with Friedhelm Kemp (1914–2011). After the war, Heinrich Wild (1909–1975) directed the publishing house and opened it also to non-Catholic authors.

my friend Arnold Hauser: Arnold Hauser (1892–1978) was a German-Hungarian sociologist of art and literature. In 1953 Beck had published his two-volume *Sozialgeschichte der Kunst und Literatur* [Social history of art and literature]. See Günther Schiwy, Arnold Hauser and Theodor W. Adorno, "Zeugnisse einer Freundschaft" [Testimonials of a friendship], in *Der Aquädukt, 1763–1988: Ein Almanach aus dem Verlag C. H. Beck im 225. Jahr seines Bestehens* [The Aqueduct, 1763–1988: an almanac from the C. H. Beck Verlag in the 225th year of its existence] (Munich: C. H. Beck, 1988), pp. 507–14.

One-Way Street: Walter Benjamin's book *One-Way Street* first appeared with Rowohlt in 1928. It was reissued as part of the "Bibliothek Suhrkamp" series in 1955.

Ernst Schön: Adorno's spelling. The musician, poet, and translator Ernst Schoen (1894–1960), a friend of Walter Benjamin's youth, lived primarily in Berlin. Later on he lived in Frankfurt, where he worked as a programming director for the radio. From 1933 until 1952 he lived in England. Thereafter he returned to East Berlin. See Sabine Schiller-Lerg, "Ernst Schoen (1894–1960): Ein Freund überlebt: Erste biographische Einblicke in seinen Nachlass" [Ernst Schoen (1894–1960): a friend survives: first biographical insights into his estate], in *Global Benjamin*, ed. Klaus Garber and Ludger Rahm (Munich: Fink, 1999), vol. 2, pp. 982–1013. See also letter no. 98 in this volume.

41 SCHOLEM TO ADORNO
JERUSALEM, 1.5.1955

1 May 1955

Dear Mr. Adorno,

Your letter of April 5th, containing the good news about the Benjamin edition, reached me only 3 days ago upon my return from Rome, where I had been since April 14th to attend a conference for historians of religion (rubbish). I cannot explain why I didn't get it until the 13th. I have now looked through part of the papers for you, the ones from before I left Germany. I am enclosing a table of dates that may be useful to you. After 1923, I spent only a month with Benjamin in Paris (August, 1927), and later in Berlin; in February 1938, I spent another week with him in Paris. If you are interested in a table based on dates from the letters he sent me from 1923 to 1940, I can try to put one together. But perhaps such dates are of no interest to you. If I can answer any specific questions, do send them to me. Of course, from 1915 to 1923, Dora was with him almost all of the time – the marriage deteriorated around 1920, but until their divorce in 1929, which took the cruellest form, they remained very close, even during the 5 years following 1924, when he had a liaison with Asja Lacis (whose acquaintance I never made). I kept track, through our correspondence, of his journeys and wanderings after 1924. Naturally, this correspondence retains much more of W. B.'s longstanding orbits around the Jewish sphere – his repeated attempts to penetrate it, and the plans to bring him to Jerusalem – than is discernible in his other writings. Surely you are aware that, in 1928 and 1929, Dr. Magnes, the chancellor of the university in Jerusalem, offered him a stipend to live in Jerusalem for a year, which W. B. accepted. The plans were foiled by events surrounding the divorce and maybe by other things of which I am not aware.

Concerning significant dates, perhaps I should have mentioned that in December 1922 W. B. paid a visit to Franz Rosenzweig (who was already very ill at that point).

If the book comes out in September, I will (most likely) be in Frankfurt, where I intend to stay for about a week. If I know that you will be there, I can probably arrange to meet you. (Is the book supposed to come out in time for the book fair?) I will go to Switzerland around the 20th of August. I'll stay in Europe for a maximum of two months, probably less, and I will also have to go to Paris.

Please accept my congratulations for the success of your efforts. Warmest wishes to you both, also from my wife.

Yours G. Scholem.

W. B.

15.7.1892	Berlin
	Rural boarding school in Thuringia (Haubinda, I think)
	Ascanian High School in Berlin.
1912	Abiturium
1912	University studies at Berlin and Freiburg (1913)
until 1914	Active in Wyneken's *Anfang* (pseudon. Ardor), in the "Speakers' halls" of the youth movement in Berlin (where he was the dominant figure in the discussions)
	First journey to Paris (summer 1913)
	Friendship with Fritz Heinle (who, along with his wife, took his own life in Göttingen at the outbreak of the war)
Summer semester 1914	Chairman of the Freie Studentenschaft [Free student movement] at the Uni. of Berlin. (The speech he gave when taking over the position is partly reproduced in his essay "The Life of Students," in *Das Ziel*, I). When the war broke out he resigned his chairmanship.
August 1914	Following Heinle's suicide he volunteered to join the war effort in Berlin but was refused.
Summer or autumn 1914	Engagement to Grete Radt (broken off around autumn 1915).
Autumn 1914	Writes the Hölderlin essay.
Until summer 1915	Studies in Berlin
April 1915	Journey to Geneva (with Dora [?], at that time Dora Pollak, née Kellner)
	[I met him at the end of May 1915]

End of October 1915	Goes to Munich (where Dora lived in Seeshaupt). *Attachment** to Dora, starting in spring 1916. Until Christmas 1916
Beginning of 1917	
Berlin April 1917	Marries Dora (in Berlin) May – June in Bavaria
Beginning of July 1917 – Oct. 1919	Switzerland (resident in Berne) [I was with them from May 1918 until September 1919. "University of Muri"]. Start of the relationship with Ernst Bloch.
April 1918	Birth of his [only] son Stefan.
July 1919	Doctorate under Herbertz in Berne.
Winter 1919 – 1920	in Austria
March 1920 – June 1921	Berlin (Plans for a *Habilitation* in Berne foiled by inflation; on the scholastic philosophy of language)
May	Falls out with parents; lives with Gutkind at their house in Grünau. W. B. attempts to learn Hebrew.
July 1921	Heidelberg *Angelus Novus* plans (contract for the publication of this journal with Weißbach 7.VIII.21 [This summer and autumn mark one of the high points in W. B.'s life and hopes!] Negotiations concerning this journal.
End of August – September 1921	With Dora in Breitenstein (Semmering).
Since 1921	Close friendship with Florens Chr. Rang, whom he had known since 1916 or 17.
October 1921 – Autumn 22	Berlin Prepares *Angelus Novus* [The plan finally failed in September 1922 when the first issue was already typeset and the publisher pulled out.]
Summer 1922	Writes the essay on Elective Affinities.

* Original in English.

Winter 1922–1923	Heidelberg, Frankfurt, Breitenstein.
1923	Frankfurt am Main *Habilitation* plans? [This is the last time I spent several months with him before my departure for Palestine]

Original: manuscript with Scholem's handwritten tabular curriculum vitae of Walter Benjamin's life: Theodor W. Adorno Archive, Frankfurt am Main. First published in Gershom Scholem, *Briefe II: 1948–1970*, ed. Thomas Sparr (Munich: C. H. Beck, 1995), pp. 35-6 (without the curriculum vitae). An excerpt of this letter appears in translation in *Gershom Scholem: A Life in Letters*, ed. and trans. Anthony David Skinner (Cambridge, MA: Harvard University Press, 2002), p. 368.

conference for historians of religion: See Raffaele Pettazzoni (ed.), *Atti dell'VIII Congresso Internazionale di Storia delle Religioni* [Proceedings from the VIII International Congress of Historians of Religion] (Florence: Sansoni, 1956).

Dr. Magnes, the chancellor of the university in Jerusalem: Judah Leon Magnes (1877–1948) was born in San Francisco and trained as a rabbi in Cincinnati. Subsequently he studied philosophy in Berlin and Heidelberg. In 1903 he returned to the United States, worked as a rabbi in New York, and went on to co-found the American Jewish Committee. In 1922 Magnes immigrated to Palestine, where he was initially chancellor of the Hebrew University (1925–35) before subsequently becoming its president (1935–48). In the summer of 1927 he met with Scholem and Benjamin in Paris, where he encouraged Benjamin to immigrate to Palestine and to take up teaching at the Hebrew University. In a letter to Hugo von Hofmannsthal, dated 17.03.1928, Benjamin wrote: "My friend Scholem, who is a professor of the philosophy of the Kabbalah at the University of Jerusalem, arranged for me to meet the permanent rector of the university, Dr. Magnes. We had a very comprehensive conversation, after which my plan to devote myself to Hebrew for the first time took on the definitive shape in which you became acquainted with it and encouraged it. Dr. Magnes is now very much inclined to obtain a subsidy for me through one of the usual channels for such things." See *The Correspondence of Walter Benjamin 1910–1940*, ed. Theodor W. Adorno and Gershom Scholem, trans. Manfred R. Jacobson and Evelyn M. Jacobson (Chicago: University of Chicago Press, 1994), pp. 328–9.

Franz Rosenzweig: The philosopher of religion and historian Franz Rosenzweig (1886–1929) directed the Freies Jüdisches Lehrhaus [Free Jewish House of Learning] in Frankfurt from 1920. His principal philosophical work, *The Star of Redemption*, was published in 1921. Together with Martin Buber, he translated the Bible into German (see letter no. 21 in this volume). Scholem knew Rosenzweig, and the two men engaged in a critical exchange of ideas concerning Judaism and Zionism.

42 ADORNO TO SCHOLEM
FRANKFURT AM MAIN, 9.5.1955

INSTITUTE FOR SOCIAL RESEARCH
AT THE JOHANN WOLFGANG GOETHE
UNIVERSITY

FRANKURT A.M.
SENCKENBERG-ANLAGE 26
9 May 1955

T.W. Adorno

Dear Mr. Scholem,

A thousand thanks for your letter. Once again, we narrowly missed each other. We were also in Italy – in Tuscany – from the 7th to the 18th of April, and, had we known that you were in the area, we could have met somewhere halfway, around Perugia, say.

The information you sent was enormously helpful to me and I am profoundly grateful. Dora has also promised to make everything she has available to us. Ernst Schön, on the other hand, has declined to help – presumably because he is angry that the edition will appear in the Western zone and not with the savage tribes to whom he is apparently committed. As a matter of fact, the edition is supposed to be ready in time for the book fair, although I am not quite sure if Peter Suhrkamp will pull it off in time. The contract stipulates that my introduction must be finished by the 15th of July. It will wind up being far more modest than my big essay, since it is only intended to support the edition and W. B., not to decipher his philosophical project.

Throughout August, if all goes smoothly, we will most likely be in Switzerland – in the Engadin. I can't quite say where we will be in September, but, with enough notice, I can certainly arrange to be here at the same time as you.

You should also be interested to learn that a substantial part of W. B.'s communication with Rang has surfaced. We are very seriously mulling over the possibility of putting together a volume of correspondence. Of course that would only be possible on the condition that you would make what you have available. Gretel and I also possess a very extensive set of letters.

Just these quick lines for today – do write to us soon. Regarding some of the references, I will probably have to ask you for explanations; also, I will need your advice as to whether some references should even be included in the biography, insofar as they concern third parties.

Cordial regards to you and your wife, also from Gretel,
always yours
Teddie Adorno

Original: typescript with printed letterhead; Gershom Scholem Archive, The National Library of Israel, Jerusalem. First published in Rolf Tiedemann (ed.), *Frankfurter Adorno Blätter* V (Munich: Edition Text + Kritik, 1998), p. 181.

Ernst Schön ... declined to help: Adorno's spelling. In his response to Adorno's request, Ernst Schoen wrote the following, on the 28th of April 1955:

> I was very glad to glean from your letter that Walter Benjamin's writings are now finally – and very belatedly – to be granted their proper place in the form of a coherent edition. I am eagerly looking forward to *One-Way-Street* as well as the two other volumes.
>
> I regret all the more that I cannot contribute anything to the biographical notes you are preparing. If I were ever to join the ranks of the memoirists, I might have some things to say about our "dramatic reading group" during our early school years; about a high school senior "Beer Newspaper," which caused a defamation trial and led to the founding of *Der Anfang*; about our reunion, the student movement, the strangely entangled youthful relationships that surrounded us; and about the countless hours on Delbrückstraße, at Lutter and Wegener in Frankfurt, and lastly in Paris, during which we conversed endlessly – conversations that were interrupted only when we read our own works out loud to each other. Yet these memories also involve other people and events, and they have nothing explicitly biographical about them. Above all, however, I am separated from them by an abyss, which, to this day, we are all attempting to bridge – an effort that may well persist until our days are numbered, only to then be carried on by others. These considerations, even more than being daily overworked, make it impossible for me to grant you the assistance you requested. (Typescript, Theodor W. Adorno Archive, Frankfurt am Main)

my introduction: For Adorno's introduction to Benjamin's *Schriften* from 1955, see Adorno, "Introduction to Benjamin's *Schriften*," *Notes to Literature*, trans. Shierry Weber Nicholsen (New York: Columbia University Press, 1992), Vol. 2, pp. 220–32.

my big essay: See letter no. 7 in this volume, and the accompanying note.

43 SCHOLEM TO ADORNO
JERUSALEM, 14.5.1955

14 May 1955
Jerusalem

Dear Mr. Adorno,

It is indeed a great pity that we didn't meet in Italy – we could have discussed so much that would be useful for the introduction to the forthcoming edition, and it is possible to say many things in person that one cannot easily put in writing. For instance, I would have liked to tell you about the circumstances under which my personal acquaintance with W. B. came about in 1915, which had something of the extravagant *quid pro quo* that played such an important role at several pivotal points in his biography.

If you tell me now when the book fair will take place (towards the end of September?), then I could arrange to be in Frankfurt for a few days during this time. It would really be something if we could celebrate the publication of the edition together. In fact, I could be there from the 15th to the 20th of September; this is what I had intended; but I can postpone it, if necessary. If these dates suit you, I suggest that you have a room booked for me at the Hotel National right away – later on it gets terribly busy and it becomes difficult to get a decent room. I would rather pay a little bit more and have a proper hotel for these few days.

My first stop in Europe will be the Eranos conference, which begins on the 24th of August (although I may arrive five days before). Afterwards, I am going to Sils Maria in the Engadin, where I intend to vacation for about ten days, from the 3rd of September. I have already booked my stay there. If you were to extend your visit to the Engadin somewhat, then we could also meet there. Sils is truly the most tranquil and temperate place, and that is exactly what I have been wanting. It is not possible for me to come to Europe any earlier.

Regarding an edition of W. B.'s letters, a friendly agreement with at least some of the more important addressees would probably have to be reached. I'm gladly prepared to speak with you and Suhrkamp about this. I myself have about 300 letters, many of them exceedingly brilliant; but whether guys like Brecht and Bloch will hand over theirs seems doubtful to me. (W's letters to me are no picnic for Bloch, but they contain enthusiastic praise for Brecht). Naturally, the Jewish side of things plays an extraordinarily important role in the letters to me.

Do the letters to Hofmannsthal exist? And is Ernst Schön in the Soviet sector, as I believe I'm led to understand from your insinuation?

I am, of course, always at your disposal should you require further clarification on biographical matters, provided that they are within my field of expertise.

Today, along with your letter, I received the *Prisms* volume. Although I have not yet had an opportunity to look at it, I would, nevertheless, like to express my thanks to you for sending it.

In the meantime, I am including some more biographical information for 1924 – I notice now, as I am looking through the letters, how telling the contrast in our academic "careers" was: at exactly the same time as W.'s *Habilitation* was so shamefully rejected in Frkft. with the "help" of Schulz and Cornelius, I received an offer to join the recently founded university in Jerusalem, to which I tried so hard for many years to have him appointed. In the end, the fact that nothing came of this, despite all the golden bridges, was because of his inner resistance to such work being greater than he cared to admit to himself. Negotiations concerning his appointment to a chair for (German?) literature in Jerusalem took place throughout 1928, supported by brilliant reports about him (from A. Brecht, Hofmannsthal, and F. Strich). But in the fall of 1928, when the university made the money available, enabling him to devote one year solely to the study of Hebrew, the whole undertaking flickered out, with postponements *ad infinitum* from his side. Besides the inner qualms (to which he never admitted), Asja Lacis, who had returned to Berlin by the end of 1928, was very visibly behind all this. Time and again he planned a trip to Palestine, and time and again he put it off.

Unfortunately all of my letters to W. B. have been lost – they stayed behind in Berlin and Paris. I kept outlines and copies of only two letters, sent consecutively in March and May of 1931 – I had completely forgotten about the first of these. Since the subject dealt with in these letters – Walter Benjamin's "materialist" production – may be of significance for your interests and your introduction, I pulled myself together and am sending you some enlarged copies, which I would ask you to return to me in the summer.

4 pages from me dated the 30th of March 1931
2 pages: W.'s response dated the 17th of April 1931
2 pages: my response to this letter dated the 6th of May 1931

Given the extreme care that you will find devoted to the precise formulation of these letters, it seems right to me that you should take note of them. Perhaps these rather intimate discussions lie outside the area you've staked out for yourself; if not – *tant mieux*. In any case, I wanted to bring the atmosphere of certain discussions to life using the only example available to me. Aside from this, I have only one long letter on Zionism, of which he himself made me a copy.

Please excuse these lengthy messages, with which I only hope to serve a good cause.

With best wishes for the success of this edition,

yours

Gerhard Scholem

1927 "The Idea of a Mystery"

"To represent history as a trial in which man, as an advocate of dumb nature, brings charges [*Klage*] against all Creation and cites the failure of the promised Messiah to appear. The court, however, decides to hear witnesses for the future. Then appear the poet, who senses the future; the artist, who sees it; the musician, who hears it; and the philosopher, who knows it. Hence, their evidence conflicts, even though they all testify that the future is coming. The court does not dare to admit that it cannot make up its mind. For this reason, new grievances keep being introduced, as do new witnesses. There is torture and martyrdom. The jury benches are filled with the living, who listen to the human prosecutor and the witnesses with equal distrust. The jury members pass their duties on to their heirs. At last, the fear grows in them that they might be driven from their places. At the end, the entire jury has fled; only the prosecutor and the witnesses remain."*

This note accompanied a letter, dated the 18th of November 1927, when he was suffering from severe jaundice. At the end of the letter he writes: "As a patient's angel, I have Kafka by my bed. I am reading *The Trial.*"

Hofmannsthal to Rang, on the 20th of November 1923
[From a copy made for me by W. B.]

["]Please do not expect me to comment at any length on the, frankly, incomparable essay by Benjamin, which you were kind enough to send me. All I can say is that it made an epochal impact on my inner life, and that my thinking – to the extent that it was not wholly absorbed by my own work – could barely disengage from it. What to me is most wonderful, to speak only of seemingly outward things, is how the unparalleled penetration of a secret is presented with such great beauty. This beauty springs forth from an utterly self-assured and untainted thinking, the likes of which I have seldom encountered. Should this man be young, that is, younger in years than I, then I would be greatly moved by his maturity. The connection with your world has gripped me; what a blessing to behold something of this sort. . . . If, through you, I attain the permission – most earnestly sought – to publish this piece in the *Beiträge*, then those readers who are receptive to spiritual things will immediately feel compelled to make a connection with your contribution ["Goethe's Blessed Longing," G. S.]. I hope that this can accomplish an essential part of what you had in mind when planning to found a journal [*Angelus Novus*, G. S.] with Mr. Benjamin."

* Walter Benjamin, "The Idea of a Mystery," in *Selected Writings*, Vol. 2.1: *1927–1930*, ed. Michael Jennings, Howard Eiland and Gary Smith (Cambridge, MA: The Belknap Press of Harvard University Press, 1999), p. 68.

April 1924 – November
Journey through Italy (with the Gutkinds; sojourn of several months in Capri until the 10th of October. This is where he met Asja Lacis in the middle of June 1924, with the emotional and intellectual consequences that are familiar to you).

On 7.VII he wrote me a line from Capri, which probably warrants quoting:
"All sorts of things have happened here that could only really be communicated in person – that is, if I were to take a trip to Palestine or if you were to take a possibly more legitimate trip to Capri. What happened was not for the best in terms of my work [on the *Trauerspiel* book as a *Habilitation*, G. S.], which was dangerously interrupted, nor, perhaps, for the best in terms of the rhythm of bourgeois life, which is indispensable to every project; absolutely for the best [!] in terms of a vital liberation and intense insight into the actuality of radical communism. I made the acquaintance of a Russian revolutionary from Riga, one of the most splendid women I have ever met."*

I do not need to explain to you the significance of this sentence for W's biography. If you like, you can quote it. In his subsequent letters to me he cited the strong impression that Lukács' book had made on him, which, starting with political considerations, arrived at epistemological insights that are – at least in part – "very familiar and confirming to me."

1925 Berlin and Frkft.
Failure of the Frankfurt *Habilitation*. By April the *Trauerspiel* book was ready for printing.

August – end of October 1925 Spain, Italy
(on a freight ship from Hamburg to Naples)
November 1925, Riga (Mlle Lacis)
Winter 1925/1926, begins work on Proust
Mid-March – October 1926 Paris
(In 1926 W. B. wrote his first Marxist attempt, the article, Goethe, which had been commissioned for the Russian encyclopaedia, but which was never collected.)

* See *The Correspondence of Walter Benjamin 1910–1940*, ed. Theodor W. Adorno and Gershom Scholem, trans. Manfred R. Jacobson and Evelyn M. Jacobson (Chicago: University of Chicago Press, 1994), p. 245.

6 December – 1 February 1927	Moscow
February – March 1927	Berlin
April – September 1927	Paris (I spent two extended periods with him here, in April and August–September)
From October 1927	Berlin

From 1927: begins work on the *Paris Arcades*

1928: Moscow again commissions the article, Goethe for their Great Encyclopaedia, which he rewrote, in a *tour de force*, during the autumn of 1928.

Test subject for Dr. Joel's hashish experiments.

January 1930	One month in Paris.
1929 – 1930	Divorce proceedings.
2 November 1930	Death of W.B.'s mother.

I take it that you are familiar with the events after 1930.

Original: manuscript, with Scholem's handwritten copies of Benjamin's text "The Idea of a Mystery" (1927), the letter from Hugo von Hofmannsthal to Florens Christian Rang, dated 20.11.1923, and the continuation of the tabular CV of Walter Benjamin; Theodor W. Adorno Archive, Frankfurt am Main.

Eranos conference: Scholem's lecture, held at the Eranos conference in 1955, was first published as "Seelenwanderung und Sympathie der Seelen in der jüdischen Mystik" [The transmigration of souls and the sympathy of the soul in Jewish mysticism], in *Eranos-Jahrbuch 1955*, Vol. 24: *Der Mensch und die Sympathie aller Dinge* [Man and the sympathy of all things], ed. Olga Fröbe-Kapteyn (Zurich: Rhein, 1956), pp. 55–118. See Scholem, "Gilgul: The Transmigration of Souls," in *On the Mystical Shape of the Godhead: Basic Concepts in the Kabbalah*, trans. Joachim Neugroschel (New York: Schocken Books, 1991), pp. 197–250.

guys like Brecht and Bloch: Five letters to Brecht were included in the edition of the letters. Of Benjamin's letters to Bloch, only one survives in full, dated Paris, 29.03.1937, as well as a draft from late December 1934. See Henri Lonitz and Christoph Gödde (eds), *Walter Benjamin: Gesammelte Briefe V, 1935–1937* (Frankfurt am Main: Suhrkamp, 1999), pp. 496–8; *Walter Benjamin: Gesammelte Briefe IV, 1931–1934* (Frankfurt am Main: Suhrkamp, 1998), pp. 554–6.

Do the letters to Hofmannsthal exist?: Sixteen letters to Hugo von Hofmannsthal were included in the two-volume edition of the letters; a further four were included in the edition of Benjamin's *Gesammelte Briefe*.

the Prisms *volume*: See Adorno, *Prisms*, trans. Samuel Weber and Shierry Weber (Cambridge, MA: MIT Press, 1981).

W.'s Habilitation was so shamefully rejected in Frankfurt with the "help" of Schulz and Cornelius: Benjamin's text was met with incomprehension on the parts of Franz Schultz and Hans Cornelius, which foreshadowed the rejection of his *Habilitation* application. Accordingly, Benjamin withdrew his text.

reports about him (from A. Brecht, Hofmannsthal, and F. Strich): In support of his plan to appoint Benjamin to a chair at the Hebrew University in Jerusalem, the university's chancellor – J. L. Magnes – requested opinions on Benjamin from renowned German literary scholars. See Benjamin's letter to Scholem dated 23.4.1928, as well as Scholem's editorial note, in *The Correspondence of Walter Benjamin 1910–1940*, ed. Theodor W. Adorno and Gershom Scholem, trans. Manfred R. Jacobson and Evelyn M. Jacobson (Chicago: University of Chicago Press, 1994), pp. 332–4. In his note (p. 334), Scholem wrote: "Magnes was soliciting letters of recommendation from Germanists in support of the plan to get WB an appointment at the University of Jerusalem." For Benjamin's letter to Hofmannsthal dated 5.5.1928, see: *The Correspondence of Walter Benjamin 1910–1940*, p. 334. The recommendation by Fritz Strich (1882–1963), scholar of German literature, has since been published in Jane O. Newman, "Aus dem (Jerusalemer) Archiv: Fritz Strich to Judah Magnes on Walter Benjamin, 26 March 1928" [From the (Jerusalem) archive: Fritz Strich to Judah Magnes on Walter Benjamin, 26 March 1928], *Trajekte: Zeitschrift des Zentrums für Literaturforschung Berlin*, 13 (2006), pp. 4–7.

4 pages from me dated the 30th of March 1931: See *The Correspondence of Walter Benjamin 1910–1940*, pp. 373–6.

2 pages: W.'s response dated the 17th of April 1931: See *The Correspondence of Walter Benjamin 1910–1940*, pp. 376–8.

2 pages: my response to this letter dated the 6th of May 1931: See *The Correspondence of Walter Benjamin 1910–1940*, pp. 378–9.

a long letter on Zionism: The first part of Scholem's letter to Benjamin on Zionism is included in Scholem, *Walter Benjamin: The Story of a Friendship*, trans. Harry Zohn (New York: NYRB Classics, 2003), pp. 215-220

44 ADORNO TO SCHOLEM
FRANKFURT AM MAIN, 17.5.1955

17 May 1955

Th. W. Adorno

Dear Mr. Scholem,

One more request for today:

You mentioned to me that you have in your possession a piece from *Berlin Childhood* that is not included in the published version – I think it is called "Krumme Lanke." I do not have this piece, nor do I know it. Since *Berlin Childhood* is supposed to come out again in the new two-volume edition, it would be very nice if we could incorporate it. Would you be so kind as to send me a transcript as soon as possible?

A thousand thanks in advance and all that is cordial

from your

[Adorno]

Original: typescript (carbon copy); Theodor W. Adorno Archive, Frankfurt am Main. First published in Rolf Tiedemann (ed.), *Frankfurter Adorno Blätter* V (Munich: Edition Text + Kritik, 1998), p. 182.

"*Krumme Lanke*": See letters nos. 16 and 17 in this volume.

45 SCHOLEM TO ADORNO
11.6.1955

האוניברסיטה העברית בירושלים
THE HEBREW UNIVERSITY, JERUSALEM

11 June 1955

Dear Mr. Adorno,

I am wondering why you have not confirmed receipt of the extensive delivery of papers, photocopies, etc., or of the accompanying letter that was sent to you (via airmail) over a month ago; and why you have not responded to my suggestion of a possible visit to Frkft. This worries me, indeed. I sent you these materials so that you could use them in your work on the biography. What happened? Did you not receive the package? Please drop me a line.

Cordial regards,

yours, Gerhard Scholem

Original: aerogram, manuscript with printed letterhead; Theodor W. Adorno Archive, Frankfurt am Main.

46 ADORNO TO SCHOLEM
FRANKFURT AM MAIN, 15.6.1955

INSTITUTE FOR SOCIAL RESEARCH
AT THE JOHANN WOLFGANG GOETHE
UNIVERSITY

FRANKURT A.M.
SENCKENBERG-ANLAGE 26
15 June 1955

T.W. Adorno

Dear Mr. Scholem,

Upon returning from Munich, I found your note of the 11th of June. Everything has arrived; I thank you a thousand times. Rest assured, I will make use of your materials with the greatest conscientiousness and care. I would have already tackled the introduction were it not for the fact that some materials, promised by Dora, are still pending. I am going to remind her of this again. In the meantime, I have written a lengthy announcement for *One-Way Street* (which has been reissued in a separate volume, as you know). It will be aired on local radio in July. As soon as I receive a fair copy I will have the piece sent to you, with the request that you tell me whether, in your opinion, it could be used as an introduction for the complete edition. It will have to be quite different from the long essay in *Prisms*; namely, it will have to serve as a kind of bridge for the reader, or – should one not be so keen on such a point of contact – it will at least have to shed light on the *differentia specifica* of Benjamin. I am still waiting for a *brainstorm*,* an idea of form for how to achieve what is almost impossible. But perhaps you will find a starting point in the radio lecture. Of course it is not broad enough in itself to give an indication of the <u>whole</u>, since it is limited to *One-Way Street*; but the question is whether one central aspect, when picked out effectively, could not achieve more than an all too vague totality. Benjamin himself would surely have shared this view, although, naturally, this should not commit us to anything as far as our editorial strategy goes.

I had a copy of *One-Way Street* sent to you immediately – I hope it has reached you. This edition seems more dignified to me than the rather gaudy one by Rowohlt, the typographic audacity of which seems quite out of date today.

Once again, many thanks for your help. The typesetting is coming along nicely. Gretel is reviewing proofs around the clock – currently those for the baroque book.

All that is cordial to you and your wife from us both,

your faithful

Teddie Adorno

* Original in English.

Original: typescript with printed letterhead; Gershom Scholem Archive, The National Library of Israel, Jerusalem. First published in Rolf Tiedemann (ed.), *Frankfurter Adorno Blätter* V (Munich: Edition Text + Kritik, 1998), pp. 183–4.

Dora . . . I am going to remind her of this again: Adorno wrote to Dora Sophie Morser on the same day. However, judging by the surviving correspondence, he did not receive a reply.

a lengthy announcement for One-Way Street: first published in *Texte und Zeichen*, 1/4 (1955), pp. 518–22; See Adorno, "Benjamin's *One-Way Street*," in *Notes to Literature*, trans. Shierry Weber Nicholsen (New York: Columbia University Press, 1992), Vol. 2, pp. 322–7.

baroque book: See Walter Benjamin, *Origin of the German Trauerspiel*, trans. Howard Eiland (Cambridge, Mass.: Harvard University Press, 2019).

47 SCHOLEM TO ADORNO
JERUSALEM, 3.7.1955

Jerusalem, 3 July 1955
28 Abarbanel St.

Dear Mr. Adorno,

Kind thanks for your letter, and for sending your lecture on *One-Way Street*. Since, even by straining my imagination, I can't envisage the supposed readership for Benjamin's writings in Germany in 1955, I'll have to refrain from advising you as to the viability of this method of introducing W.B. Anyhow, *a priori* I would not have thought of anything other than a pragmatic introduction; surely this would open up enough perspectives on the work. But, as I said, I am far too disoriented regarding the current situation to make a judgment.

At the end of September, a large auto show is taking place in Frkft. a.M., and, far and wide, there are no decent hotels available. As such, I will in all likelihood have to cancel my trip there at this time. Maybe I will come later. In any case, it would be nice if we could meet in Switzerland.

With cordial regards to your wife and you
yours,
Gerhard Scholem

Original: manuscript; Theodor W. Adorno Archive, Frankfurt am Main.

48 SCHOLEM TO ADORNO
JERUSALEM, 16.8.1955

האוניברסיטה העברית בירושלים
THE HEBREW UNIVERSITY, JERUSALEM

16.8.1955

Dear Mr. Adorno,

I am going to Europe tomorrow and can be reached during the coming 5 weeks

a) until the 2nd of September — Ascona, Casa Tamaro
b) until the 14th of Sept. — Sils Maria, Hotel Alpenrose
c) until the 22nd of Sept. — Zurich, Kurhaus Rigiblick

In all likelihood, I will then either go on to London via Berlin, or – in case I do not come to Germany at all – via Paris. I will be in London until the 17th of October.

Perhaps I will hear from you or meet with you. Maybe you will pass through Zurich while I am there?

Best regards to you both,
yours,
G. Scholem

Original: aerogram (manuscript) with printed letterhead; Theodor W. Adorno Archive, Frankfurt, am Main.

49 SCHOLEM TO ADORNO
ASCONA, 24.8.1955

Ascona, 24.8.1955

Dear Mr. Adorno,

I will be in Ascona, Casa Tamaro, until the 2nd of September. Afterwards, I possibly wanted to go to the Engadin as well. How long will you be in Sils Maria? Maybe I will still meet you there? From the 14th of September, I will be at the Kurhaus Rigiblick in Zurich for one to two weeks.

When will the edition be published? Will it be in September or October? Is there a fixed publication date?

I will be in London from the 5th to the 17th of October, by the way. It is still unclear whether or not I will come to Germany.

So let me know.

Cordial regards to your wife and you
yours,
Gerhard Scholem

Original: manuscript; Theodor W. Adorno Archive, Frankfurt am Main.

50 SCHOLEM TO ADORNO
ASCONA, LATE AUGUST 1955

Dear Mr. Adorno,

Many thanks for your messages. I am sorry that the dates for our possible reunion are turning out to be so inconvenient. I will be down here until Friday morning and will arrive in Sils only after your departure; and since from the 5th of October I have to be in London, where I will give some lectures around the middle of the month, I seriously doubt whether I will be able to stop off in Frankfurt on the way back – if at all, then only very briefly. On the 22nd of October, I am flying back to Israel. Should I be available for three days in September before I go to Paris, I will write to you. The difficulty is that Frkfrt. is completely overcrowded at this time.

I hope you will be able to return to Jerusalem the photocopies of the papers that I sent you. I am eagerly awaiting the publication of the collection and am in awe at the speed with which it is being printed.

Best wishes to your wife and you,
cordially yours,
Gerhard Scholem

Original: manuscript, no location or date; Theodor W. Adorno Archive, Frankfurt am Main. Regarding the dating: Scholem was at the Eranos conference in Ascona until the 1st of September.

your messages: there is no record of surviving letters from Adorno to Scholem in the period between June 1955 and March 1956.

down here: Scholem was spending time in Ascona, a town located at the lowest point in Switzerland.

London . . . lectures: Scholem had been invited to the University of London. The lecture series was published the following year, under the title "The Meaning of the Torah in Jewish Mysticism." See *On the Kabbalah and its Symbolism*, trans. Ralph Manheim (New York: Schocken Books, 1969), pp. 32–86.

51 SCHOLEM TO ADORNO
LONDON, 6.10.1955

6 Oct 1955

Cumberland Hotel
Marble Arch,
London, W.1

Dear Mr. Adorno,

Would you please be so kind as to let me know, by return of post or by *cable*,* whether you would be available if I came to Frankfurt on Tuesday the 18th of October (this is the only date that is available to me). I have to make the arrangements now. If I can catch a flight that arrives in the early afternoon, then we could see each other for a few hours, especially in the evening. I will be busy in London on Monday and have to travel on to Zurich early on Wednesday.

I would be glad to see Suhrkamp too.

In case it's a yes, may I ask you to immediately book a room for one night (18/19 Oct.) in a good hotel right by the train station (National, Baselerhof, or the like), and kindly to let me know where I will be staying? It is always so busy there that I would rather not be at the mercy of contingencies.

I hope to receive W. B.'s writings on this occasion.

Should you not be available, or are out of town, or in case I don't hear from you, I will take a direct flight to Zurich and Tel Aviv. I therefore ask that you respond quickly.

To your wife and you
cordial regards
yours,

Gerhard Scholem

Please write my name on the address very clearly!

Original: manuscript; Theodor W. Adorno Archive, Frankfurt am Main.

52 SCHOLEM TO ADORNO
LONDON, 14.10.1955

14 Oct. 1955

Dear Mr. Adorno,

According to my itinerary, I should arrive on Tuesday at 3 o'clock in the afternoon (BEA 490), so I should be at the hotel around 4 o'clock.

* Original in English.

Unfortunately, there have been delays in air traffic during the past days due to fog, and I can only hope that I will have more luck with my flight around noon.

Cordial regards to you both
yours
G. Scholem

Original: manuscript; Theodor W. Adorno Archive, Frankfurt am Main.

53 ADORNO TO SCHOLEM
FRANKFURT 9.3.1956

PROF. DR. THEODOR W. ADORNO

FRANKFURT AM MAIN
KETTENHOFWEG 123
9 March 1956

Professor Dr. Gerhard Scholem
The Hebrew University
Jerusalem/Israel

Dear Mr. Scholem,

I am writing to you today regarding a matter that is very close to my heart.

As you may know, the University of Frankfurt has been granted a sizeable sum – 20.000 DM [German marks] per year for five years – to organize lectures on central aspects of Judaism by scholars of the highest possible rank. I hardly have to tell you how glad I would be if you would take part in this affair. The lectures are named *Loeb Lectures** after the donor; the ceremonial opening, in keeping with an act of representation, took place in the crowded auditorium on the 22nd of February, with the aged Leo Baeck as a keynote speaker.

I would like to ask you today, unofficially and non-bindingly, whether you would like to participate. A single lecture or a series of, say, three would be equally conceivable. Of course I would prefer the latter option. As the subject area, I imagined the Kabbalah. With regard to the audience, it would be advisable to focus on the relationship between the Kabbalah and a truly topical philosophical speculation. However, this is merely a suggestion, and it is entirely up to you should you wish to remain in the realm of the strictly historical. You would be certain to have a sizeable and attentive audience. The remuneration promises to be very adequate, which is unfortunately not

* Original in English

something that one can otherwise say about academic lectures. The important thing, though, is that you would speak during the coming term, i.e. before the 1st of August. Perhaps you could arrange your European plans so as to arrive a little earlier than usual, so that you could give the lectures before you go to Switzerland.

As I said, this is simply an inquiry on my part. However, if you were to agree, then I am quite certain that I could arrange for an official invitation.

This time it is you who has been silent for a long time – you have not written to me regarding the Benjamin edition; nor have I heard a word about it from Dora. I am pleased to be able to tell you that its success, both in literary terms and with respect to sales, has greatly exceeded expectations. There can be no doubt that Benjamin's name has been restored in just the way that we had hoped. The publisher is almost "out of the woods," so Stefan can also count on a material return.

My friend Georg Solti, the general musical director here, is traveling to Israel on Monday for six weeks, along with his wife, to conduct 25 concerts. I warmly recommend him to you. It is no exaggeration when I say that I think of him as being the most significant among the young generation of conductors. I do not make affirmations like this lightly, and I have a decent international overview. These concerts may really mean something. I mentioned you to the Soltis, and I expect that they will reach out to you. If not, it would be nice if you contacted them. He is a Hungarian-Jewish émigré, she is Swiss – both are politically completely sound and personally very pleasant.

Very cordially, also to your wife, and also from Gretel,

always yours

Adorno

Original: typescript with printed letterhead; Gershom Scholem Archive, The National Library of Israel, Jerusalem.

The lectures are named Loeb Lectures *after their donor*: The donor of the Loeb Lectures was Eda Kuhn Loeb (1867–1951). Loeb was born into a German-Jewish family in Cincinnati and lived in New York. As a philanthropist, she supported universities, libraries, and hospitals. Thanks to Horkheimer's efforts, the foundation headed by Loeb set up the Loeb Lectures in the Faculty of Philosophy at the University of Frankfurt in 1956. The lectures were supposed to treat Jewish history, religion, and philosophy in order to reestablish these themes at German universities.

Leo Baeck: Rabbi Leo Baeck (1873–1956) was an important representative of Reform Judaism. He was ordained as a rabbi at the Hochschule für die Wissenschaft des Judentums [Higher Institute for the Science of Judaism], after completing his doctoral studies under Wilhelm Dilthey. After 1933 he became president of the official organization representing Jews in Germany, the Reichsvertretung der Juden in Deutschland [the Reich deputation of German Jews]. In 1943 he was deported to the Theresienstadt concentration camp. After liberation, Baeck moved to London, where he became chairman of the Council of Jews from Germany. From 1948 to 1953 he was Professor at the Hebrew Union College in Cincinnati. Baeck held the inaugural Loeb Lecture, on the 22nd of February 1956, on the theme of "Revolution and Rebirth."

My friend Georg Solti, the general musical director here: The conductor Georg Solti (1912–1997), who, from 1937, had been Arturo Toscanini's assistant in Salzburg, spent the duration of the war in Switzerland. In 1946 he was appointed as the general musical director of the Bavarian Opera, and in 1951, of the Frankfurt Opera. In 1961 he became the general musical director of the Royal Opera House in London. Georg Solti was married to Hedwig Oeschli as of 1946.

54 SCHOLEM TO ADORNO
JERUSALEM, 4.4.1956

28, Abarbanel St.
4 April 1956

האוניברסיטה העברית בירושלים
THE HEBREW UNIVERSITY, JERUSALEM

Dear Mr. Adorno,

Today a certain Mrs. Sholty called me from Tel Aviv, cited your name, and claimed that you wrote to me. However, since I did not receive anything from you, I am assuming that the alleged letter remained in the realm of good intentions. That is a pity, of course. But since I should also have written to you long ago, yet failed to do so, it seems that we are even, as it were. Aside from the completion of my opus vol. 1, I dedicated this winter to a reading of Benjamin's *Schriften*. It was very exciting to read it all together. I cannot imagine how the response has been and would love to hear from you about this. I read your introduction with great admiration, by the way – even at the points where I would draw the lines quite differently. There is a lot in there. It is a shame that there are quite a lot of typos in the text as a result of the quick printing. "For the *record**" it would have been good to include the dates for when the two early manuscripts were written.

* Original in English.

I have yet to receive the materials that I sent you (e.g. the copies of the letters). If they are lying around at your place, or at Podszus', perhaps you would be so kind as to pack them up and return them to me.

It is dark here, but by no means as gloomy as it appears to our corresponding friends abroad. Indeed, I cannot find a single person who would bet against my "peace" prognosis on war with the Arabs. What is more: I accepted an invitation from Brown University, Providence, to be a Visiting Professor in Religious Studies for 1956/57 – something that I would not ordinarily do. We intend to come to Europe in the summer – 20.8 – 5.9 (if peace actually prevails) – and to travel from there to America, where we plan to stay until June. I will have almost complete peace and quiet over there, an ideal state. Perhaps we will see you on the Swiss battle scene? That would be very nice. We have something of a plan to stop off in Germany on our way back. Perhaps it is the time to speak up. I will think about it.

To your wife and you
cordial regards
your old reader
Gerhard Scholem

À propos reading: is your Husserl out in the meantime?

Original: aerogram with printed letterhead; Theodor W. Adorno Archive, Frankfurt am Main.

Mrs. Sholty: This spelling seems to refer to the Hungarian pronunciation of Solti, the name with which she must have introduced herself over the phone.

I did not receive anything from you: Adorno's letter of 9.3.1956 hadn't reached Scholem when Mrs. Solti called. He received it two days later. See letter no. 55 in this volume.

my opus vol. 1: Scholem's Hebrew book on Sabbatai Sevi – שבתי צבי והתנועה השבתאית בימי חייו – was published by Am Oved, Tel Aviv, in 1957. See letter no. 12 in this volume.

war with the Arabs: In the spring of 1956 the conflict between Israel and Egypt had escalated. The attacks launched from Egyptian territory, and the closure of the Suez Canal for Israeli ships, led to the Suez War some months later, which involved Great Britain and France. See letter no. 60 in this volume.

invitation from Brown University: On 4.3.1954 Scholem received an invitation to serve as a Visiting Professor of Biblical Literature at Brown University, Providence, Rhode Island, during the academic year of 1954/55. Since Scholem had made an effort to receive such an invitation 18 months previously, but had, in the interim, made plans in London for his sabbatical year, he asked the president of Brown University, Dr. Henry M. Wriston, if the invitation could be postponed by two years. The official invitation followed in May of 1956 for the academic year of 1956/57. In a letter to Prof. Samuel T. Arnold, the provost of Brown University, dated 31.5.1956, Scholem suggested two courses for this year: a weekly, two-hour graduate seminar for students with knowledge of Hebrew, and a monthly lecture series on some aspects of Jewish mysticism in the wider context of the history of religion, in particular, of mysticism.

your Husserl: Adorno's *Zur Metakritik der Erkenntnistheorie: Studien über Husserl und die phänomenologischen Antinomien* was published by Kohlhammer, Stuttgart, in 1956. His dedication in Scholem's copy reads: "For Gerhard Scholem, in heartfelt affinity, Teddie Adorno / Frankfurt, 10 July 1957." See Adorno, *Against Epistemology – A Metacritique: Studies in Husserl and the Phenomenological Antinomies*, trans. Willis Domingo (London: Polity Press, 2013).

55 SCHOLEM TO ADORNO
JERUSALEM, 6.4.1956

האוניברסיטה העברית
THE HEBREW UNIVERSITY

Jerusalem 6 April ירושלים
28 Abarbanel

Dear Mr. Adorno,

Our letters crossed paths in the most providential way! I wrote to you the day before yesterday to say that we are coming to America, where I am to stay for one year; and now I receive your request regarding the Loeb Lectures. I am responding immediately – since I am very sorry that you sent such a letter, which concerns specific dates – by <u>ordinary</u> mail; because of this, it was en route for <u>four weeks</u> instead of 4 days! You should not have done that, or else your secretary deserves a bitter reprimand!

I have spoken to my wife about the aspect of principle in this matter. The framework of the Loeb Lectures (of which I know nothing, and have only learned about from you) may indeed be appropriate for a first public appearance in Germany, twelve years after the end of the war. If the conditions really correspond to what you suggest (I would certainly have to know further particulars), then I would, in principle, be prepared to accept such an invitation, although, naturally, <u>not this</u> year – that is impossible for <u>technical</u> reasons. I cannot leave Israel before mid-August, as my book is being typeset and I am busy with corrections. However, 1957 would be a different matter. I should actually remain in the USA after the end of the academic year, where considerable offers were made to me for the summer. This is where the material moment enters into the calculation. If the offer were to enable me to leave the USA in mid-June, then I could accept an invitation to give one or, conceivably, three lectures. I cannot commit to a topic at this moment. We could discuss this in Switzerland or on some other occasion (it looks like we will be in Zurich and Ascona from the 14th of August to until the 1st or 3rd of September, but no longer than that). Because of my schedule for 1957, however, it is essential that I receive the invitation to hold these lectures for the academic year of 1956–57 (summer term) in good time, i.e. this summer.

My intention next year was, in fact, to stop off in Oxford on my journey back and not to return east until the autumn.

I hope this information will allow you to clarify matters and to make use of this opportune moment. In any case, I thank you very sincerely for your initiative, and I will be very glad if – in good time – it will yield satisfactory results for both of us.

I am extremely happy to hear the good news about the Benjamin edition.

To both of you, all that is cordial

yours, G. Scholem

Original: manuscript with printed letterhead; Theodor W. Adorno Archive, Frankfurt am Main.

56 ADORNO TO SCHOLEM
FRANKFURT AM MAIN, 18.4.1956

INSTITUTE FOR SOCIAL RESEARCH
AT THE JOHANN WOLFGANG GOETHE
UNIVERSITY

FRANKURT A.M.
SENCKENBERG-ANLAGE 26
18 April 1956

T.W. Adorno

Professor Gerhard Scholem
The Hebrew University

Jerusalem/Israel

Dear Mr. Scholem,

I found your letter upon returning from Vienna, and I am very glad about your positive answer. I spoke about this matter right away with Horkheimer, who is on a retreat in Baden-Baden, and who is just as pleased as I am. It would be good if we could stay in touch regarding possible dates in 1957. Of course it would have to be during the semester, so either between the 1st of May and the end of June, or after the 1st of November. However, waiting until 1958 does seem too long to me. The financial side of things would probably depend on the scope of what you propose to do here. Perhaps, therefore, you could let me know concretely what you are thinking about. I have no doubts that we will find a solution that will satisfy you.

As far as our plans are concerned, we will probably spend all of August at the Waldhaus in Sils Maria again. I have been invited to go to Alpbach in the first days of September to give some lectures; but perhaps we could arrange to see each other. In any case, do send me your news soon.

To you and your wife all that is cordial, also from Gretel,

always yours

Teddie Adorno

Original: typescript with printed letterhead; Gershom Scholem Archive, the National Library of Israel, Jerusalem.

Vienna: On the 12th of April Adorno gave the lecture "The Function of Counterpoint in New Music" (see *Sound Figures*, trans. Rodney Livingstone (Stanford, CA: Stanford University Press, 1999), pp. 123–44), and also spoke on the radio about "New Music, Interpretation, Audience" (see *Sound Figures*, pp. 29–40).

Alpbach ... lectures: The *Europäisches Forum Alpbach* [European Forum Alpbach], founded in 1945 as the *Internationale Hochschulwochen* [International University Weeks], is an international conference on science, economics, and politics which takes place annually in the Tyrolean mountain village of Alpbach. Adorno had agreed to speak at the event but canceled because of ill health. On the 7th of September he wrote to Alexander Auer, the secretary general of the Austrian College: "Dear Mr. Auer, I feel compelled to tell you how sorry I am that I could not make it to Alpbach – I looked forward to this visit enormously and my own selfish regrets are almost greater than those caused by having let you down. However, I was overworked to such a degree that I was truly on the verge of what could only be called a complete collapse – something one can barely imagine if one has not personally gone through it. In this condition the thought of preparing such a substantial lecture during the short vacation period was a '*nightmare*'"* (carbon copy of typescript, Theodor W. Adorno Archive, Frankfurt am Main). Alexander Auer's suggested theme had been "Konsumwelt – Reklame – Kulturindustrie" [The world of consumption – advertising – culture industry].

* Original in English.

57 SCHOLEM TO ADORNO
JERUSALEM, AFTER 18.4.1956

האוניברסיטה העברית בירושלים
THE HEBREW UNIVERSITY, JERUSALEM

INSTITUTE OF JEWISH STUDIES — המכון למדעי היהדות

Dear Mr. Adorno,

I am responding to your letter of the 18th of April right away. July 1957 is the only possible period for the lecture series in Fr. I will be back in Jerusalem by November. I don't understand your question concerning the scope of what I could do. You yourself asked if I would give one lecture or three. I responded: in principle I could give three, as per your suggestion. It would be premature to settle on a topic. I am considering issues, such as the origins of the Kabbalah, or a specific group (Safed?), or an analysis of certain ideas (Hasidism, not in the vein of Buber?). I cannot commit to something at the moment; in any case, I would first have to know the exact conditions.

We will probably fly to America on the 1st or 2nd of September. Before that we will probably be in Zurich for 2 days. From the 20th–30th of August we will be in Ascona.

With best wishes for you and your wife,

yours,
Gerhard Scholem

Original: manuscript with printed letterhead; Theodor W. Adorno Archive, Frankfurt am Main.

one lecture or three: Scholem's Loeb Lectures on the theme of the Kabbalah in Safed took place in Frankfurt on the 12th, 15th, and 17th of July, 1957.

58 ADORNO TO SCHOLEM
FRANKFURT AM MAIN, 30.4.1956

INSTITUTE FOR SOCIAL RESEARCH
AT THE JOHANN WOLFGANG GOETHE
UNIVERSITY

FRANKURT A.M.
SENCKENBERG-ANLAGE 26
30.4.1956

Dear Mr. Scholem,

Kindest thanks for your lines. I would like, firstly, to confirm our arrangement formally. We are counting on you to deliver three lectures in July 1957 as part of the Loeb Lectures. The general theme would be the Kabbalah; the specific topic would, of course, be up to you. Naturally, my personal wish would be that the choice is made with an eye to the audience hearing something about the enormous intellectual scope of such matters, not least in a philosophical sense – I was thinking, therefore, of Lurianic mysticism. Of course, something on Hasidism, especially coming from you, would also be wonderful.

Do write to me soon. Horkheimer, who is also very pleased about your acceptance, will send you the official invitation in due course. He will also write to you about material matters. The fulfilment of this plan means more to me than I can tell you.

Other than that, I am happy to report that my Husserl book – which is now called *Die philosophischen Antinomien* [The philosophical antinomies], and is subtitled *Zur Metakritik der Erkenntnistheorie* [On the meta-critique of epistemology] – is finally being typeset, at the same time as a little musicological book of mine, titled *Dissonanzen – Musik in der verwalteten Welt* [Dissonances: music in the administered world]. I am very happy that I was able to get this wrapped up before the new semester breaks loose, bringing with it, among other things, a big lecture series by all sorts of people on the occasion of Freud's 100th birthday.

Did the meeting with Solti, whose wife I saw yesterday, work out in the end?

Perhaps things in Switzerland will somehow work out this summer after all. We will probably spend August up in the Waldhaus in Sils Maria again, and in the first days of September, I will probably speak at the Austrian College in Alpbach. But, if we work out the dates exactly, it should be possible to arrange for some overlap – unless, of course, you would prefer to come to Sils Maria for a few days towards the end of August, which I hardly need to recommend to you.

All that is heartfelt to you both, also from Gretel,

always yours,

Teddie Adorno

Original: typescript with printed letterhead; Gershom Scholem Archive, The National Library of Israel, Jerusalem.

Lurianic mysticism: Lurianic mysticism was a Kabbalistic doctrine developed by the Safed-based mystic, Isaac Luria (1536–1572). See letter no. 15 in this volume.

something on Hasidism: Despite the fact that Scholem treated the theme of Hasidism in a chapter of his book *Major Trends in Jewish Mysticism*, it was widely considered to be Martin Buber's particular area of interest. See Scholem, "Martin Buber's Interpretation of Hasidism," in *The Messianic Idea in Judaism*, trans. Michael A. Meyer (New York: Schocken Books, 1971), pp. 228–50.

official invitation: Horkheimer wrote to Scholem on the 4th and 13th of June 1956:

4 June 1956

Professor Gershom Scholem
The Hebrew University
Institute of Jewish Studies
Jerusalem
Israel

Most esteemed, dear Mr. Scholem!

Please excuse me for only writing to you now, long after Mr. Adorno's letter of the 30th of April regarding your lectures in the summer term.

I am now in a position to invite you, in the name of the dean of the Faculty of the Humanities, to hold three lectures in July 1957 on a topic of your choosing. If this is agreeable to you, perhaps you could speak for 45 minutes and subsequently hold a colloquium. However, we would also be satisfied if you chose to limit yourself to lecturing.

In terms of an honorarium, we can offer you 500 DM [German marks], in addition to travel and accommodation expenses. I hope that this arrangement, which is in keeping with what we offer other visiting professors, is satisfactory for you.

If you respond in the affirmative, as I hope will be the case, I will await the specifications of your topic. You are quite free to choose one title, or indeed three, for the lectures. Whatever you select will be of interest to us. Your audience will, in all likelihood, be comprised of professors and students in theology, philosophy, history, and sociology.

I hardly need to tell you how glad we are to be hosting you. As far as I am concerned, our meeting in New York remains vivid in my memory and I am pleased that we will be able to pick up where we left off on this occasion.

With friendly regards, I remain
your very devoted
[Max Horkheimer]

Copy: Professor Dr. Adorno
Institute for Social Research
Frankfurt a. Main.

The letter was followed by a telegram : "13 June 1956 / Professor Dr. Gershom Scholem / The Hebrew University / Institute of Jewish Studies / Jerusalem, Israel / Dear Mr. Scholem! /I have just sent you the following telegram: / *Re my letter June 4th lecture fee 1.500 not five hundred [/] kindly excuse error. Cordially Horkheimer** / The error occurred because

* Original in English.

we accidentally accounted for one lecture, rather than three. / With friendly regards / your very devoted / [Max Horkheimer]

[Copy:]

Professor Dr. Adorno
Institute for Social Research
Frankfurt a. Main

a little musicological book: Adorno's book *Dissonanzen: Musik in der verwalteten Welt* [Dissonances: music in the administered world] came out in the "Kleine Vandenhoeck" series in Göttingen in 1956. See Adorno, *Gesammelte Schriften 14: Dissonanzen / Einleitung in die Musiksoziologie* [Dissonances/ Introduction to the Sociology of Music], ed. Rolf Tiedemann et al. (Frankfurt am Main: Suhrkamp, 2003), pp. 7–167.

a big lecture series ... on the occasion of Freud's 100th birthday: The Sigmund Freud Memorial Lectures were organized with the cooperation of the Universities of Frankfurt and Heidelberg. The opening ceremony took place on the 6th of May. The keynote lecture, "Freuds psychoanalytische Krise" [Freud's psychoanalytic crisis], was given by Erik H. Erikson. The lecture series spanned the entire summer term. See *Freud in der Gegenwart. Ein Vortragszyklus der Universitäten Frankfurt und Heidelberg zum hundertsten Geburtstag* [Freud in the present: a lecture cycle at the Universities of Frankfurt and Heidelberg on Freud's hundredth birthday], ed. Theodor W. Adorno and Walter Dirks (Frankfurt am Main: Europäische Verlagsanstalt, 1957).

59 SCHOLEM TO ADORNO
JERUSALEM, 21.5.1956

האוניברסיטה העברית בירושלים
THE HEBREW UNIVERSITY, JERUSALEM

Dear Mr. Adorno,

Many thanks for your note of the 30th of April; also, I received the photocopies.

I would like to draw your attention, once again, to the fact that I prefer to arrange in advance what an invitation should say, so as to avoid subsequent disappointment. Should Frkfrt. send an invitation whose terms I find unacceptable then this would create an unpleasant situation – this has already happened to me in the case of another invitation from America to give three such lectures. But you may proceed as you see fit. I will consider possible themes.

We are tentatively booked on a flight from Zurich to N.Y. on the 2nd of September, although I am not yet certain of the final dates.

As I observe with pleasure, we are in competition regarding our publications. My tome – the thickest book I've written to date – is also not to be underestimated, even if it has more to do with the phenomenology of Antinomianism than with the phenomenological antinomies. If I find a translator, I would like to see it published in English. A portion of my last 15 years can be found in it.

Best regards to you both,

yours,

G. Scholem

P.S. – A friendly reminder: it is important to me that, in all official correspondence and announcements, I am referred to only by my legal name, Gershom Scholem (as it appears in my passport), and not by the German Gerhard.

Original: aerogram, manuscript with printed letterhead; Theodor W. Adorno Archive, Frankfurt am Main.

the photocopies: Copies of the Benjamin manuscripts belonging to Scholem.

the thickest book I've written to date: The original Hebrew version of Scholem's book comprised 842 pages. The English edition – *Sabbatai Sevi: The Mystical Messiah, 1626–1676*, trans. R. J. Zwi Werblowsky – was published by Princeton University Press in 1973 as part of the Bollingen series. The book was reissued in 2016. In England, it was published by Routledge & Kegan Paul (London).

my legal name, Gershom Scholem: Scholem's birth name was Gerhard. Since his immigration to Palestine, however, he primarily used his Jewish name, Gershom. See Adorno's letter to Horkheimer dated 30.5.1956: "May I remind you of the invitation to Scholem. It would probably be best if you wrote to him first regarding the financial arrangements surrounding the three lectures he would like to give. As soon as an agreement is reached on this point, the official invitation can be sent. / It is especially important to him that he is announced as Gershom, not as Gerhard. There's nothing one can do about this." See *Theodor W. Adorno/Max Horkheimer: Briefwechsel*, Vol. IV: *1950–1969*, ed. Henri Lonitz and Christoph Gödde (Frankfurt am Main: Suhrkamp, 2006), p. 356.

60 ADORNO TO SCHOLEM
FRANKFURT AM MAIN, 28.11.1956

PROF. DR. THEODOR W. ADORNO

Frankfurt Am Main
Kettenhofweg 123
28.11.1956

Professor Dr. Gerhard Scholem
Brown University
Department of Religious Studies

Providence R.I.
USA

Dear Mr. Scholem,

I would like to send you a copy of my book on Husserl, which has come out, in the meantime, under the title *On the Meta-Critique of Epistemology*. However, since I am not sure if this address (which I received from Horkheimer's secretary, and to which I am sending these words) is still current, and since I am loath to send the book on an endless journey, I would be very grateful if you could forward me your next address (or addresses) so that I can send it to you.

Meanwhile I held a long and extremely encumbered lecture on Hegel at the Freie Universität in Berlin to coincide with the start of the semester and, at the same time, to mark the anniversary of Hegel's death. I will now expand this lecture and it will be published as a stand-alone piece. I think that the result may interest you. I have hardly ever spoken so directly.

What is happening with the German edition of your great book? I keep hearing, also in Switzerland, that it is supposed to come out, but, as of yet, I have been unable to find out where and with whom. Are you having it translated or will you prepare the German edition yourself? Without wanting to be presumptuous: I would seriously urge you to opt for the latter. When a text by our sort is retranslated into German, as it were, it causes so much trouble, and one winds up having to do so much work on it, that – in the end – it is more economical to undertake the process of rethinking it into German for oneself (and it can't be about less than this with works that make such emphatic demands). But presumably this is a question of time for you, as well as one about the extent to which it is inwardly possible for you to use German for such a significant and authoritative text about central Jewish matters. At any rate, in the German context, the book would be of the utmost importance. This dawned on me during my recent re-engagement with Schelling.

I would only like to add that I am one of a very few people who consider the actions of Israel, France, and England to be right and fortunate, even now, after the two Western powers have retreated when faced with Mr. Khrushchev's threateningly crooked little finger. For now, in spite of everything, Israel's overall situation should have improved considerably.

All that is heartfelt, also
from Gretel,

your old
Adorno

Original: typescript with printed letterhead and a handwritten note by Scholem: 17 December עניתי (replied); Gershom Scholem Archive, The National Library of Israel, Jerusalem.

a long and extremely encumbered lecture on Hegel . . . to mark the anniversary of Hegel's death: Adorno gave a lecture at the Freie Universität in Berlin on the 14th of November 1956 to mark the 100th anniversary of Hegel's death. The lecture was first published by Suhrkamp in Frankfurt am Main under the heading "Aspekte der Hegelschen Philosophie" [Aspects of Hegel's philosophy]. In 1963 the piece was taken up in the collection *Drei Studien zu Hegel* [Three Studies on Hegel]. See *Hegel: Three Studies*, trans. Shierry Weber Nicholsen (Cambridge, MA: MIT Press, 1993), pp. 1–52.

What is happening with the German edition of your great book?: Scholem personally prepared the German edition of *Major Trends in Jewish Mysticism*, which was published as *Die jüdische Mystik in ihren Hauptströmungen* by Rhein Verlag, Zurich, in 1957.

the actions of Israel, France, and England: In July 1956, the Suez Canal Company, which had been founded and operated by Great Britain and France, was nationalized by the Egyptian government under Gamal Abdel Nasser. Consequently, marine access for British and French ships, which was important for crude oil supplies, was in danger of being cut off. Along with Israel, which was subject to regular attacks by Egypt, the three states launched a military strike, which began with the Israeli invasion of the Sinai peninsula in October 1956, with full support from the British and French armies.

after the two Western powers have retreated when faced with Mr. Khrushchev's threateningly crooked little finger: In November 1956, under the leadership of Nikita Khrushchev, the Soviet Union threatened to intervene in the Middle East, to side with Egypt, and to use nuclear weapons.

61 SCHOLEM TO ADORNO
PROVIDENCE, 17.12.1956

Deprt. of Rel. Studies

17 December 1956

BROWN UNIVERSITY
PROVIDENCE 12, RHODE ISLAND

Dear Mr. Adorno,

Please excuse the delay in responding to your letter of the 28th of Nov., which I was very glad to receive. I was traveling a lot (even though this is my permanent address as long as we are in the USA), and I was so inundated with work that I left mail unanswered. I had to write up my Eranos lecture before Christmas, since I spoke off the cuff without a manuscript in Ascona, and I hadn't gotten around to it in Jerusalem. (I was busy with the corrections for my opus on Sabbatai Sevi).

We are going to New York for 14 days, but from early January until mid-May my address will be the one that you are currently using. From the 18th of May to the 3rd of June we will be in New York again and will possibly fly directly to Europe from there. If nothing comes up, I expect to be in Frankfurt with my wife between roughly 8th and the 24th/ 25th of July, from where I'll be flying back to Israel directly for a conference. However, unless events determine otherwise, I may return to Europe for another 3 months. I would prefer it if you did not send your new publications here; I am busy preparing the German edition of my book – the one you have been looking forward to – and I have neither the time nor the requisite level of attention to devote to them right now. Instead, you may hand them to me in Frankfurt. In any case, congratulations on the publication of this book.

If I manage to finish my book on time, it will come out with Rhein in Zurich next autumn (1957). They have a licensing agreement with Metzner (in Frankfurt), which will be publishing a licensed German edition. For my part, I am only dealing with Rhein.

It is quiet here; I am sitting in a beautiful *office*,* and I can take contemplative walks. I am also using the time to study things for which I cannot consult the relevant literature in Jerusalem (on all manner of sects).

Please be in touch. I only hope that the situation in Israel doesn't upset all our plans, including the visit to your vicinity.

* Original in English.

Cordial regards, also to your wife
yours,
Gershom Scholem

Original: manuscript with printed letterhead; Theodor W. Adorno Archive, Frankfurt am Main.

my Eranos lecture: Scholem's 1956 Eranos lecture was first published as "Schöpfung aus Nichts und Selbstverschränkung Gottes" [Creation out of nothing and the self-contraction of God], in *Eranos-Jahrbuch 1956*, Vol. 25: *Der Mensch und das Schöpferische* [Man and the creative], ed. Olga Fröbe-Kapteyn (Zurich: Rhein, 1957), pp. 87–119. Repr. in Scholem, *Über einige Grundbegriffe des Judentums* [On some fundamental concepts in Judaism] (Frankfurt am Main: Suhrkamp, 1970), pp. 53–89.

agreement with Metzner: The licensed edition of Scholem's *Die jüdische Mystik in ihren Hauptströmungen* [Major trends in Jewish mysticism] was published in the Federal Republic of Germany by Alfred Metzner, Frankfurt am Main, in 1957.

62 SCHOLEM TO ADORNO
PROVIDENCE, 18.3.1957

Brown University
Providence 18.III.57.
12, Rhode Island

Dear Adorno,

As our journey to your oh-so-German dominion appears to be taking shape, I am writing to duly prepare you. We want to be in Berlin from the 3rd to the 9th of July. Do you happen to know somebody there who is actually worth meeting? Otherwise, I will just promenade with my wife along the Spree, where I was born, and I will show her Walter Benjamin's house in Grunewald.

From the 10th to the 24th of July we plan to be in Frankfurt where, until the 19th, I will hold my lectures.

On the 24th I will go by myself to Israel, where I am urgently needed for 14 days, leaving my tearful wife to her own devices, wherever she may choose to go. Perhaps she will go to Sils Maria, which she enjoyed enormously. She does not want to commit, though. For my part, I will come back to Switzerland in early August, where I intend to stay for three months. I hope that these arrangements will also be of some interest to you.

We will stay in Providence for two more months, where news concerning your plans can reach us.

Hopefully we can discuss all other matters in person. Please do not forget that my copy of your Husserl book is with you. I hope that we can celebrate the handover.

Cordial regards to you and your wife,

yours, G. Scholem

Original: typescript; Theodor W. Adorno Archive, Frankfurt am Main.

Walter Benjamin's house in Grunewald: The house at Delbrückstraße 23 in Berlin-Grunewald was Benjamin's parents' last address. At the time that this letter was written, the house no longer existed.

63 ADORNO TO SCHOLEM
FRANKFURT AM MAIN, 26.3.1957

PROF. DR. THEODOR W. ADORNO

FRANKFURT AM MAIN
KETTENHOFWEG 123
26.3. 1957

Dear Mr. Scholem,

Kindest thanks for your letter of the 18th of March. I think the one from the 17th of December also remains unanswered.

I'm very glad that our agreement stands, that you will be here between the 10th and 24th of July, and that you will hold your lectures until the 19th.

We were in Berlin again for a week and found it to be quite interesting – much more relaxed than is usual in the Federal Republic, even if it's all a bit uncanny. It has the feel of a Potemkin village, which is especially noticeable around the memorial church. The only person I know there who would probably be of genuine interest to you is the current director of the Ecclesiastical College of Music, Professor Smend. He is without question the most significant Bach scholar alive today. That may be of little interest to you, in and of itself; however, his way of working, the questions he poses, the downright unbelievable discovery that the B minor Mass is not a work but a "collection," greatly reminded Gretel and me of certain features of your work. So I can well imagine the appeal to you of this indescribably erudite man, whose genius for philological detective work was forged in the conception of sacred texts, only then to throw a spanner in their works. As a church leader, his behavior in the Third Reich was irreproachable. He was severely persecuted and went into hibernation as a librarian in the State Library.

Did you know that Horkheimer is in America? I'm not exactly sure where he is right now – possibly in Beverly Hills, or maybe back in New York. In the latter case, of course, a meeting could easily be arranged. The address at which he can always be reached is:

90 Morning Side Drive
New York 27, N.Y.

The Husserl book waits abidingly. It seems to be having quite an effect, by the way, especially where I would have least expected it: among the heads of the Husserl archive.

All that is heartfelt to you and your wife, also from Gretel,

your old

Teddie Adorno

I assume you do know that a Hasidic movement in Brooklyn has become quite a talking point.

Original: typescript with printed letterhead and handwritten postscript; Gershom Scholem Archive, The National Library of Israel, Jerusalem.

the current director of the Ecclesiastical College of Music, Professor Smend: The Protestant theologian and Bach scholar Friedrich Smend (1893–1980) was, since 1945, professor of hymnology and liturgics at the Kirchliche Hochschule Berlin-Zehlendorf [Institute of Higher Education in Ecclesiastics Berlin-Zehlendorf].

the downright unbelievable discovery that the B minor Mass is not a work but a "collection": See Friedrich Smend, "Luther und Bach," in *Bach-Studien: Gesammelte Reden und Aufsätze* [Bach studies: collected speeches and essays], ed. Christoph Wolff, (Kassel: Bärenreiter, 1969), pp. 153–75. Regarding the thesis mentioned here, see pp. 165–169.

90 Morning Side Drive: Adorno's spelling.

The Husserl book ... effect ... among the heads of the Husserl archive: Reviews published at the time that this letter was written have not been verified. However, on the 11th of February 1957, the Husserl editor, Rudolf Boehm, sent Adorno an offprint of his essay "Karl Löwith und das Problem der Geschichtsphilosophie" [Karl Löwith and the Problem of the Philosophy of History], with the dedication: "As a small expression of great admiration after reading the Introduction to the *Metakritik der Erkenntnistheorie* [Against Epistemology], from the editor of the 'First Philosophy' of Husserl.'"

64 ADORNO TO SCHOLEM
FRANKFURT AM MAIN, 18.12.1957

PROF. DR. THEODOR W. ADORNO

FRANKFURT AM MAIN
KETTENHOFWEG 123
18 December 1957

Professor Dr. Gershom Scholem
The Hebrew University
Jerusalem / Israel

Dear Mr. Scholem,

This is just a quick word of thanks – what the late Husserl would have called a "formal indication" – for the receipt of your magnum opus. It is really most imposing; and however paradoxical and frivolous this may sound, now that it has appeared in German, I do feel as if it is much more at one with itself than in the English version – as if it had been taken out of its cellophane wrapper. The effect that can be expected from it, especially in Germany, should be extraordinary. For my part, I will do what I can to contribute to this effect. Naturally, I must add that I am qualified to comment on this matter neither from the perspective of Jewish studies nor from that of comparative religious history; I am limited to what I can discern philosophically in the book. But perhaps you might welcome an emphasis on this dimension, especially with Benjamin in mind. It goes without saying that I want, at the very least, to allude to these connections. So far, an essay in the *Neue Deutsche Hefte* has been agreed upon, and I think that I will also get a chance to have my say in the highly influential *Frankfurter Allgemeine Zeitung*. They have just invited me to do so.

Other than that, all there is to say at my end is that I have been under incredible pressure during the past three months, mainly because Max has gone to America again for a couple of months. Nevertheless, I managed to get quite a lot done; among other things, a series of short Proust commentaries to mark the completion of the edition published by Suhrkamp. It includes a piece on Proust and Anatole France, which really made me think of you and our conversation about the latter. At bottom it concerns nothing less than the Enlightenment as the rescue of theology. In this regard, I recommend that you read the little chapter on the death of Bergotte from the translation of *The Prisoner*, which Suhrkamp hopefully sent you, and which refers directly to Anatole France. It's on pages 269 to 278.

All the best and cordially to you and Fanja, from both of us,

your loyal

Teddie Adorno

Original: typescript with printed letterhead; Gershom Scholem Archive, The National Library of Israel, Jerusalem.

"formal indication": The term "formal indication" comes not from Husserl but, rather, from Martin Heidegger. See Martin Heidegger, *Phenomenological Interpretations of Aristotle: Initiation into Phenomenological Research*, trans. Richard Rojcewicz (Bloomington: Indiana University Press, 2001), pp. 25–28.

essay in the Neue Deutsche Hefte . . . Allgemeine Zeitung: Adorno did not review Scholem's book in either publication.

a series of short Proust commentaries: Adorno's "Short Proust Commentaries" were originally presented as lectures for the Hessischer Runkfunk and the Süddeutscher Runkfunk and were published in 1961 in the second volume of *Notes to Literature*. See *Notes to Literature*, Vol. 2, trans. Shierry Weber Nicholsen (New York: Columbia University Press, 1992), pp. 174–84.

The Prisoner: *The Prisoner* is the fifth part of Marcel Proust's *In Search of Lost Time*. The seven-volume German translation by Eva Rechel-Mertens was published between 1953 and 1957 by Suhrkamp in Frankfurt am Main and Rascher in Zurich. See Marcel Proust, *In Search of Lost Time*, Vol. 5: *The Prisoner and the Fugitive*, trans. Carol Clark (New York and London: Penguin, 2003).

65 SCHOLEM TO ADORNO
JERUSALEM, 26.1.1958

האוניברסיטה העברית בירושלים
THE HEBREW UNIVERSITY, JERUSALEM

26 Jan. 1958

Dear Adorno,

Sincere thanks for your letter of the 18th of December. My response is delayed because I developed an eye condition when I had the Asian flu, and only now am I allowed to write again. I am very glad that you want to write about my little book; I hope to learn something from your comments. Of course the German original (which – *nebbish* that I am – I prepared myself) reads quite differently from the English version, however respectable the latter may be.

Perhaps, with a bit of luck, we can arrange a meeting in Switzerland? I am coming directly to the Eranos conference, which starts on the 14th of August. But afterwards I am staying in Ascona for a month before going to Paris. Maybe you'll come down into the valley from Sils at the end of August? That would be a convenient time, for me, at any rate.

I am enjoying the stay in my library in the mild Jerusalem winter. The long journey must now be digested.

Cordial regards to your wife and you, from your

Gerhard Scholem

Original: aerogram (manuscript) with printed letterhead; Theodor W. Adorno Archive, Frankfurt am Main.

Eranos conference: Scholem's 1958 Eranos lecture was first published as "Die Lehre vom 'Gerechten' in der jüdischen Mystik" [The doctrine of the "righteous one" in Jewish mysticism], in *Eranos Jahrbuch 1958*, Vol. 27: *Mensch und Frieden* [Man and peace], ed. Olga Fröbe-Kapteyn (Zurich: Rhein, 1959), pp. 237–97. See Scholem, "Tsaddik: The Righteous One," in *The Mystical Shape of the Godhead: Basic Concepts in the Kabbalah*, trans. Joachim Neugroschel (New York: Schocken Books, 1991), pp. 88–139.

66 SCHOLEM TO ADORNO
JERUSALEM, 29.5.1958

29 May '58

Dear Adorno,

Today I sent you my latest Eranos lecture, wherein you will find my remarks on Kafka (253–4), which we spoke about last year.

[The issue of] *Commentary* containing an essay of mine should have reached you in April.

I haven't heard from you since December. Did you receive my letter? I still haven't heard even a single echo from Germany about my book.

It is rumored here that chairs in Jewish studies are being established [in] Frkt., Berlin, and Hamburg. Hopefully you will get somebody who is worth his salt!

Best wishes to you both,

yours, G. Scholem

Original: postcard (manuscript); Theodor W. Adorno Archive, Frankfurt am Main.

my latest Eranos lecture: Scholem's 1957 Eranos lecture was first published as "Religiöse Autorität und Mystik" [Religious authority and mysticism], in: *Eranos-Jahrbuch 1957*, Vol. 26: *Mensch und Sinn* [Man and sense], ed. Olga Fröbe-Kapteyn (Zurich: Rhein, 1958), pp. 243–78. See Scholem, "Religious Authority and Mysticism" in *On the Kaballah and its Symbolism*, trans. Ralph Manheim (New York: Schocken Books, 1965), pp. 5–31.

remarks on Kafka: Scholem's "Religious Authority and Mysticism" contains the following passage: "The word of God must be infinite, or to put it another way, the absolute word is in itself meaningless, yet is *pregnant* with meaning. Under human eyes it enters into significant finite embodiments, which mark innumerable layers of meaning. Thus mystical exegesis, this *new* revelation imparted to the mystic, has the character of a key. The key itself may be lost, but an immense desire to look for it remains alive. In a day when such mystical impulses seem to have dwindled to the vanishing point, they still retain an enormous force in the work of Franz Kafka" (p. 12).

[The issue of] Commentary *containing an essay of mine*: Scholem, "Jewish Messianism and the Idea of Progress: Exile and Redemption in the Cabala," *Commentary*, 25/4 April, 1958, pp. 298–304; repr. as "The Messianic Idea in Kabbalism," in Scholem, *The Messianic Idea in Judaism and Other Essays on Jewish Spirituality*, pp. 37–48.

67 SCHOLEM TO ADORNO
JERUSALEM, 17.7.1958

האוניברסיטה העברית בירושלים
THE HEBREW UNIVERSITY, JERUSALEM

INSTITUTE OF JEWISH STUDIES — המכון למדעי היהדות

17 July 1958

Dear Adorno,

I thank you sincerely for sending a copy of your *Notes to Literature*, the pages of which I will peruse when things settle down here. (As you can imagine, we are currently quite preoccupied with the outside world). So far, I have understood most of your essay on Eichendorf, which I find quite admirable.

I am currently preparing this year's Eranos lecture. I sent you the previous one, if for no other reason than for the sake of the conclusion, which invites certain thoughts. I hope that you received it.

Will we see each other in Europe? I am going to Switzerland on the 11th of August (if world events permit it) and will be reachable at the Hotel Tamaro in Ascona. Until then, you can reach me here.

With cordial thanks and regards to you and your wife

yours,

Gerhard Scholem

Original: manuscript with printed letterhead; Theodor W. Adorno Archive, Frankfurt am Main.

Notes to Literature: The first volume of *Noten zur Literatur* was published in 1958 as volume 47 of the "Bibliothek Suhrkamp" series in Berlin and Frankfurt am Main.

essay on Eichendorf: Scholem's spelling. Adorno's essay, "Zum Gedächtnis Eichendorffs" [In memory of Eichendorff], was originally a lecture prepared for the Westdeutscher Rundfunk on the 100th anniversary of Eichendorff's death in November 1957. It was first published in the journal *Akzente*, 5/1 (1958), pp. 73–95, and was included in 1958 in the first volume of *Notes to Literature*. See *Notes to Literature*, Vol. 1, trans. Shierry Weber Nicholsen (New York: Columbia University Press, 1991), pp. 55–79.

this year's Eranos lecture: Regarding Scholem's lecture at the Eranos Conference in 1958, see letter no. 65 in this volume.

for the sake of the conclusion: At the end of his essay on "Religious Authority and Mysticism" (pp. 29–30), Scholem comments on a claim by the Hasidic Rabbi Mendel Torum of Rymanów, according to which the people of Israel – upon receiving the Ten Commandments on Mount Sinai – heard God's voice, however:

> the people were overwhelmed, they could no longer endure the divine voice. Thus they had been obliged to receive the remaining Commandments through Moses. Moses alone was able to withstand the divine voice. . . . All that Israel heard was the *aleph* with which in the Hebrew text the first Commandment begins. . . . To hear the aleph is to hear next to nothing; it is the preparation for all audible language, but in itself conveys no determinate, specific meaning. Thus, with his daring statement that the actual revelation to Israel consisted only of the aleph, Rabbi Mendel transformed the revelation on Mount Sinai into a mystical revelation, pregnant with infinite meaning, but without specific meaning. In order to become a foundation of religious authority, it had to be translated into human language. . . . In this light every statement on which authority is grounded would become a human interpretation, however valid and exalted, of something that transcends it.

68 ADORNO TO SCHOLEM
FRANKFURT AM MAIN, 1.8.1958

PROF. DR. THEODOR W. ADORNO

FRANKFURT AM MAIN
KETTENHOFWEG 123
1 August 1958

Dear Scholem,

Sincerest thanks for your letter of the 17th of July. It is something of a consolation to me that you like the piece on Eichendorff, whose "positivity" has enjoyed a kind of success that I find quite uncanny.

For now I just want to quickly inform you that we are going to Switzerland today and will be staying at the Waldhaus in Sils Maria again. We are going to be staying throughout August, and it would be very nice if we could meet again – hopefully up here in Sils; we will probably avoid coming down into the valley for even a day, for, if there is one thing that we are stingy with, it is the alpine air. From roughly the 20th of August, Horkheimer will also be at his new house in Montagnola near Lugano (telephone: 2 – 6997), and perhaps it will work out for you to see each other.

Above all, though, I hope that we can keep up our ritual and stroll around together at the Chastè.

You may also be interested that a doctoral thesis on Benjamin is now being written under my supervision – an effort at a complete overview of his aesthetics. The man who is writing it, named Thiedemann, is one of my most talented students, without a doubt. Aside from the dissertation, he has taken it upon himself to present a coherent account of Benjamin's theories on the sociology of art in the graduate seminar on sociology next semester, which will treat the sociology of art. A byproduct of his work, he told me yesterday, will be a decent Benjamin bibliography, the likes of which is long overdue.

All that is cordial to you and your wife, also from Gretel,

your loyal
Adorno

Original: typescript with printed letterhead; Gershom Scholem Archive, The National Library of Israel, Jerusalem.

a doctoral thesis on Benjamin . . . Thiedemann: Adorno's spelling. Rolf Tiedemann (1932–2018) a philosopher, literary theorist, and later the editor of Benjamin and Adorno's writings, wrote the first doctorate on Benjamin, which he completed in 1964 under the supervision of Adorno and Horkheimer. See Rolf Tiedemann, *Studien zur Philosophie Walter Benjamins* [Studies on Walter Benjamin's philosophy] (Frankfurt am Main: Suhrkamp, 1965); see also Tiedemann, *Mystik und Aufklärung: Studien zur Philosophie Walter Benjamins* [Mysticism and enlightenment: studies on Walter Benjamin's philosophy](Munich: Edition Text + Kritik, 2002).

a decent Benjamin bibliography: See Rolf Tiedemann, "Beiträge zu einer Benjamin-Bibliographie" [Contributions to a Benjamin bibliography], *Studien zur Philosophie Walter Benjamins* [Studies on Walter Benjamin's philosophy] (Frankfurt am Main: Suhrkamp, 1965), pp. 162–209.

69 ADORNO TO SCHOLEM
FRANKFURT AM MAIN, 25.9.1959

PROF. DR. THEODOR W. ADORNO

FRANKFURT AM MAIN
KETTENHOFWEG 123
25.9.1959

Professor Dr. Gershom Scholem
The Hebrew University
Jerusalem

Dear Mr. Scholem,

I just wanted to let you know that, during a meeting a few days ago, the new head of Suhrkamp, Dr. Unseld, finally agreed to publish a selection of Benjamin's correspondence in the scope of approximately 250 to 300 pages. I wanted to ask if you would be prepared to take over the editorship with me. If so, we would have to agree on how to formulate the introduction.

The call for people to contribute letters by Benjamin will be published by Suhrkamp through a number of prominent channels, including *Aufbau* in New York, which is most likely to reach people who may still have something of significance. In the meantime, I have learned that Benjamin's letters to Bloch have apparently been lost, although this would have to be double-checked. Of course it would also be important to get in touch with Dora. I will leave it up to you to judge whether it would be better for you or for me to contact her. I have also compiled a list of those who may be presumed to have letters in their possession, and in the next weeks, I will send them all requests for contributions. I do not have an address for Kohn, who, if he is still alive, is surely one of the most important sources. This is another reason why I would be grateful for a sign from you. It is also worth considering whether we should contact Werner Kraft. I am of the opinion that today, 20 years after Benjamin's death, their old feud should be put to rest.

Moreover, and without wishing to influence the outcome, I raised the issue with Unseld of a possible German edition of your collected – dare I say – systematic essays on the Kabbalah, and he took a keen interest in the matter. I recommend that you get in touch with him. After all, it would be very nice if you published your material with the publisher of the Benjamin edition.

I have had my new book on music, *Sound Figures*, sent to you. Perhaps you'd be so kind as to confirm whether you've received it? If I am not mistaken, the piece on Anton von Webern might, in a surprising way, be of interest to you. If the opportunity presents itself, by the way, don't forget to share with me what you've compiled by way of musical speculations of Jewish mysticism.

We were very happy to see you in Sils Maria and are looking forward to next time.

With the kindest regards, also from Gretel,

your old

Teddie Adorno

Original: typescript with printed letterhead; Theodor W. Adorno Archive, Frankfurt am Main.

the new head of Suhrkamp Verlag: The publisher Siegfried Unseld (1924–2002) directed Suhrkamp until his death.

an address for Kohn: Adorno's spelling. Alfred Cohn (1892–1954) was a lifelong friend of Walter Benjamin's. Adorno was apparently unaware of Cohn's death.

my new book on music, Sound Figures: Adorno's book *Klangfiguren: Musikalische Schriften I* [Sound figures: musical writings I] was first published by Suhrkamp in Berlin and Frankfurt in 1959. See *Sound Figures*, trans. Rodney Livingstone (Stanford, CA: Stanford University Press, 1999).

the piece on Anton von Webern: Presumably Adorno has the following passage from his essay in mind (*Sound Figures*, p. 94, translation slightly modified):

> In Hegel's *Phenomenology* we encounter at one point the disconcerting phrase "fury of disappearance." Webern's work converted this into his angel. The formal law presiding over his composing, in all its stages, is that of shrinkage: his pieces appear from the very first day to have the same sort of substance that one usually finds at the end of a historical process. Webern shares with Walter Benjamin a penchant for the micrological and the confidence that the concrete concentration of a fulfilled moment is worth more than any amount of development that is merely ordained abstractly from the outside. The handwriting [Handschriften] of the two men, the philosopher and the musician who was fanatically tied to his material, two men who did not know each other or even very much about each other, was nevertheless very similar. Both were like letters received from a kingdom of dwarfs, in miniature format, which always looked as if they had been reduced from something of vast dimensions.

70 SCHOLEM TO ADORNO
JERUSALEM, 16.11.1959

האוניברסיטה העברית בירושלים
THE HEBREW UNIVERSITY, JERUSALEM

FACULTY OF HUMANITIES הפקולטה למדעי הרוח

16 November 1959

Dear Mr. Adorno,

Only now, after returning from Poland and Scandinavia, am I getting around to answering your letter of the 25th of September, which arrived during our journey. So please excuse the date.

In principle I am prepared to take over the editorship with you in the matter of a selection of W. Benjamin's letters for Suhrkamp. We just have to determine whether it would be possible, in praxi, to organize such a collaboration, or at least to arrange for a joint viewing of the materials amassed. This, then, would be a question of the concrete conditions.

Regarding the requisite public call for contributions from people in possession of these letters, we could both be named as prospective editors.

Re Kohn (I assume you mean Cohn, the husband of Grete Radt and brother of Jula), it would have to be established whether he is still alive. With regards to Dora (hopeless, in my opinion), we might both have to write to her together. I have had no contact with her for 5 years. She will be turning seventy on the 6th of January 1960.

Kraft only has about 10 letters from the 1930s, which he would make available to us. On one misguided occasion he returned all of the earlier letters (1915–1923) to W. B., which is a pity indeed.

Rhein is publishing my collected essays. I already have a contract, so I cannot go with Suhrkamp!

Bloch vol. III is a quixotic mix of occasionally wonderful pages and revolting and mendacious chatter. If only I had the time!!

In haste, with cordial regards

yours,

Gerhard Scholem

P.S. – Poland was very interesting.

Original: manuscript with printed letterhead; Theodor W. Adorno Archive, Frankfurt am Main. First published in Gershom Scholem, *Briefe II: 1948–1970*, ed. Thomas Sparr (Munich: C. H. Beck, 1995), p. 49.

I assume you mean Cohn, the husband of Grete Radt and brother of Jula: Grete Radt (1891–1979) was engaged to Benjamin for some time; she married Alfred Cohn in 1921. Jula Radt-Cohn (1894–1981), a sculptor, was Alfred Cohn's sister. In 1925 she married Fritz Radt, Grete Radt's brother. She was close friends with Benjamin from 1912 to 1915 and from 1921 to 1933. Benjamin's piece "Goethe's Elective Affinities" (in *Selected Writings*, Vol. 1: *1913–1926*, ed. Marcus Bullow and Michael W. Jennings (Cambridge, MA: The Belknap Press of Harvard University Press, 1996), pp. 297–360) is "Dedicated to Jula Cohn." See also Gershom Scholem, "Walter Benjamin and his Angel," in *On Jews and Judaism in Crisis*, ed. Werner J. Dannhauser (New York: Schocken Books, 1976), p. 221.

Bloch vol. III: Scholem is referring to the third and final volume of Ernst Bloch's *The Principle of Hope* (1959). See *The Principle of Hope*, Vol. 3, trans. Neville Plaice, Stephen Plaice, and Paul Knight (Cambridge, MA: MIT Press, 1995).

71 ADORNO TO SCHOLEM
FRANKFURT AM MAIN, 23.11.1959

PROF. DR. THEODOR W. ADORNO

FRANKFURT AM MAIN
KETTENHOFWEG 123
23 November 1959

Dear Mr. Scholem,

I thank you very sincerely for your letter and for agreeing to tackle the edition of the letters with me. I think the *modus procedendi* is going to be relatively straightforward, at least initially. I suggest that you work through your materials and that I work through mine, and that each of us compile a selection of what is available to him, to be sent to the other for review. At the same time I will see to it that the project is announced in the most important newspapers, and I will write to a number of people from a list that I've drawn up. Like you, I have not been in contact with Dora for some years; however, there is absolutely no tension between us. I would make the question as to who contacts her depend on whose intervention promises the best results. There can be no doubt that you know Dora better than I do; then again, it is precisely this familiarity that causes certain tensions. I, on the other hand, have a degree of credit with her on account of the Benjamin edition. I do not want to proceed with this important matter without your consent – not least because, through Dora, it might be possible to obtain the most decisive letters. I'd like to leave the decision about who will write to her up to you. I will take action as soon as I hear from you. In the meantime, I will convey to Suhrkamp your agreement, in principle, to participate in the project. As far as the introduction is concerned, I would like to write a first draft and then send it to you, if you agree, for critique and elaboration. But, unfortunately, we're a long way away from that point.

I am very glad to hear that your collected essays are forthcoming, although I am a little sad that they won't be published by Suhrkamp, since I would have expected this collection to have had an extremely intense effect in this country, which could also have reached beyond academic circles. Nevertheless, I understand your reservations quite well.

To you and Fanja all that is cordial, also from Gretel,

your old

Teddie Adorno

Original: typescript with printed letterhead; Gershom Scholem Archive, The National Library of Israel, Jerusalem.

your collected essays: Adorno is referring to Scholem's essay collection *On the Kaballah and its Symbolism*, first published in Zurich in 1960.

72 SCHOLEM TO ADORNO
JERUSALEM, 6.12.1959

Jerusalem, 6 December 1959

Dear Mr. Adorno,

Many thanks for your letter. I do not know whether it will be so simple to find a mode of cooperation, and, moreover, whether a volume of this relatively limited range (250–300 pages) could begin to do justice to the material. Perhaps we should insist, if necessary, on a greater scope?

For now, I will do the following: eliminate those letters that can, *prima facie*, not be included, and bring the remainder – which should be rather extensive – to Europe for joint consultation and selection, in case no earlier opportunity presents itself.

Problems arising right away are as follows:

1) Should the selection also serve to give a kind of biographical overview (excluding the most private chapters, which must be ruled out *a priori*)?
2) Travel logs?
3) Critical remarks about living people (for example, the letters to me contain many disparaging comments about Bloch)?

After all, the letters contain lots of the above, in addition to the wealth of remarks about people and books (which sometimes, understandably, contradict each other).

It will, at times, be necessary to include only the especially remarkable sections of some letters. If only complete letters are to be included, then quite a lot of material must immediately be ruled out (for the reasons listed under points (1) and (3), above).

I am not able to transcribe the letters. I would have to bring the originals with me, and whatever is to be included would have to be photographed or copied by the publisher.

I will ask Buber, Kraft, and Kitty Marx-Steinschneider about their letters and whether they will make them available. Kitty M. has some very beautiful letters from him.

I do not know whether I will make it to Europe in 1960; it is quite possible, but in any case, not before the 20th of August. In this case I would come for the conference of historians of religion in Marburg (11–17 September), where I am supposed to give a lecture. If it is at all affordable, I could come to Frankfurt before or after. I say this, tentatively, for your information. (Might Suhrkamp pay for the hotel?)

To conclude, a friendly question and a request for information: Is the following sentence to be found in Hegel: "God dwells in the detail" – and exactly where is it in his work, if he uses it at all? I seem to remember reading this line as a quote from Hegel in one of your pieces. I have also come across it elsewhere. For instance, it is sometimes attributed to Flaubert, as well as being Aby Warburg's motto. I would be grateful if you could shed some light on this matter for me.

In the meantime, cordial regards to you and your wife

yours, Gershom Scholem

P.S. – Regarding the prospective collection, I'd ask that you contact Dora (although I suspect it is hopeless). But in any event, I will congratulate her on her 70th birthday (on the 6th of January 1960). Hopefully she is alive and well.

Original: manuscript; Theodor W. Adorno Archive, Frankfurt am Main.

Kitty Marx-Steinschneider: Kitty Marx-Steinschneider (1905–2002) was a mutual friend of Scholem's and Benjamin's. She was the niece of Scholem's friend, Moses Marx, and his sister Esther, who was the wife of the Israeli novelist S. J. Agnon. At Scholem's request, she visited Walter Benjamin before emigrating from Germany to Palestine in 1933. See Scholem, *Walter Benjamin: The Story of a Friendship*, trans. Harry Zohn (New York: NYRB Classics, 2003), pp. 246–248; see also *The Correspondence of Walter Benjamin and Gershom Scholem, 1932–1940*, ed. Gershom Scholem, trans. Gary Smith and Andre Lefevere (New York: Schocken Books, 1989), p. 27, n.1.

conference of historians of religion in Marburg: Scholem's lecture at the "X. Internationaler Kongress für Religionsgeschichte" [Tenth International Congress on the History of Religion] in Marburg was published under the title "Die krypto-jüdische Sekte der Dönmeh 'Sabbatianer' in der Türkei" [The crypto-Jewish sect of the Dönmeh "Sabbatians" in Turkey], *Numen*, no. 7 (1960), pp. 93–122; repr. in *On the Messianic Idea in Judaism and Other Essays on Jewish Spirituality*, pp. 142–66.

"God dwells in the details" . . . Aby Warburg's motto: As is made clear in the subsequent letter, this phrase is not attributable to Hegel. However, it can indeed be traced back to the art and cultural historian Aby (Abraham Moritz) Warburg (1866–1929). Warburg introduced methods from the natural sciences into the humanities and established iconography as a cultural-historical discipline. After 1909 his collection of books was developed into an interdisciplinary cultural-historical library, which became a unique centre of study – first in Hamburg and, after 1933, in London. Scholem had been very impressed by Warburg's cultural-historical methods and had been in contact with the circle around Warburg's library. In his autobiography, *From Berlin to Jerusalem* (trans. Harry Zohn, New York: Schocken Books, 1980, p. 131), he writes: "I used to define the three groups around the Warburg library, Max Horkheimer's Institut für Sozialforschung [Institute for Social Research], and the metaphysical magicians around Oskar Goldberg as the three most remarkable 'Jewish sects' that German Jewry produced. Not all of them liked to hear this."

73 ADORNO TO SCHOLEM
FRANKFURT AM MAIN, 17.12.1959

PROF. DR. THEODOR W. ADORNO

FRANKFURT AM MAIN
KETTENHOFWEG 123
17 December 1959

Dear Mr. Scholem,

Please accept the kindest thanks for your letter. Without being particularly sanguine about it, I do not think that the difficulties of our communication concerning the edition of Benjamin's letters will be as great as you fear. With regard to extending the scope of the volume, I will certainly inquire about it, but I doubt that I will be successful. Since it cannot be expected that such a book will reach a wide readership, the publisher will probably not be prepared to invest that much in it. At the same time, I do not want to let the project founder on this point. A good deal can be accommodated in 300 pages.

I am happy with the *modus procedendi* that you suggest.

Regarding your questions:

1. I do <u>not</u> envisage the volume as containing much biographical information. In fact, I would only consider this dimension as part of the selection process insofar as it is directly connected with the philosophical content [of Benjamin's work].

2. I do not see Benjamin's travel writings as his forte; they have something violent about them, a sensuous quality that is to some extent commanded by reflection. In any case, I wouldn't place great emphasis on these texts, unless we stumble across something especially beautiful. If this is the case, then, of course, I also wouldn't be puritanical about it.
3. I would exclude critical remarks about living persons, as is customary, but I would indicate the exclusions with ellipses. Above all, I do not want this volume to pick on Bloch, who is having enough of a hard time as it is. Without question, that would also not have been Benjamin's intention.

I am as little afraid of contradictions within this volume as elsewhere, and I quite agree with you that, on occasion, we should include only certain passages from the letters.

I am happy to write to Dora.

The thought of you transporting all the original material before having it transcribed worries me a little. My suggestion would be for Suhrkamp to pay for the transcriptions in Israel so that you can bring copies and keep the originals. If you agree, then I will be glad to speak to Suhrkamp about this.

A detailed consultation in mid-September would suit me. We would have to speak to the publisher about funding.

I would be very grateful if you could contact the people you name in your letter; at any rate, it would be impossible for me to write to Buber. Who, by the way, is Kitty Marx-Steinschneider?

Finally, in response to your question: to my knowledge, the phrase "God dwells in the details" is <u>not</u> in Hegel, and I never claimed this to be the case. One could, of course, interpret Hegel's view that totality cannot be grasped immediately but only as mediated through its individual moments in this sense. However, such a view does not match the pithiness of this formulation. As far as I know, this phrase is attributed to Aby Warburg, and I have never heard anyone else credited with inventing it. It is more fitting than anything else as a motto for Benjamin.

That's all for today.

To you and Fanja all the best, also from Gretel,

your loyal

Teddie Adorno

Original: typescript with printed letterhead; Gershom Scholem Archive, The National Library of Israel, Jerusalem.

the phrase "God dwells in the details" . . . is more fitting than anything else as a motto for Benjamin: In his subsequent essay on Walter Benjamin from 1965, Scholem writes: "That the greatest is revealed in the smallest, that – as

Aby Warburg used to say – "The Lord God dwells in the detail": these were fundamental truths to him in many ways." See Scholem, "Walter Benjamin," in *On Jews and Judaism in Crisis*, ed. Werner J. Dannhauser (New York: Schocken Books, 1976), p. 177. Scholem's 1959 lecture "The Science of Judaism – Then and Now" ends with the following words: "By genuine scholarly immersion into facts and circumstances we may be able to reorganize and reconstruct the whole from its smallest parts. Such an immersion must not shrink from the insight expressed in the magnificent saying ascribed to Aby Warburg: *Der liebe Gott wohnt im Detail* (The Lord God dwells in the detail)." See *The Messianic Idea in Judaism*, trans. Michael A. Meyer (New York: Schocken Books, 1971), p. 313. This saying plays a central role in Scholem's thinking more generally. It corresponds to the Hebrew word שכינה ("Shekhinah"), which means both divinity and indwelling and has a special significance in Kabbalah. See Scholem, "Shekhinah: The Feminine Element in Divinity," in *On the Mystical Shape of the Godhead*, trans. Joachim Neugroschel (New York: Schocken Books, 1997), pp. 140–96. Scholem also uses another variant of the phrase, "the dear Lord is to be found in the details." See Jacob Taubes, "Der liebe Gott steckt im Detail: Gershom G. Scholem und die messianische Verheißung" [The dear Lord is to be found in the details: Gershom G. Scholem and the messianic promise], in *Der Preis des Messianismus: Briefe von Jacob Taubes an Gershom Scholem und andere Materialien* [The price of messianism: letters from Jacob Taubes to Gershom Scholem and other materials], ed. Elettra Stimilli (Würzburg: Könighausen & Neumann, 2006), pp. 25–31.

74 SCHOLEM TO ADORNO
JERUSALEM, 28.12.1959

28 Dec. 1959

Dear Mr. Adorno,

Thank you very much for your letter of the 17th of December. Of course I am happy to speak to the people in Israel who are in possession of letters from Benjamin (including Buber), and I do not anticipate any difficulties on that front. Kitty Marx is a friend of mine, with whom W. B. was particularly taken; she visited him in Berlin – at my request – shortly before she immigrated to Palestine.

I fear that you are not quite clear about the main difficulty of transcribing B.'s letters when you suggest that I should bring copies to Europe. There is <u>nobody</u> here who would be prepared to transcribe these letters, which are, for the most part, written in <u>tiny</u>, tightly crammed characters. I do not see how this can be done at all, except, in part, by having <u>enlarged</u> photographic prints made, on the basis of which transcriptions might be possible. I simply do not have the time to dictate these letters to be typed by someone. Even I often find them exceedingly difficult to read. I am not fit, for now, to tackle the technical challenge that thus presents itself. This is why I considered, if need be, taking the material with me, further reduced through another review.

It is not entirely certain whether I will come this year. But something else is certain: if I come, it will be in the middle of the difficult time of the fair. It would be best if you could reserve an en-suite room for me right away, just in case. The dates in question are either the 4th – the 11th of September (i.e. the week before the conference in Marburg) or the 17th – 27th of September, ten days after the conference. The "Hessische Hof" was very pleasant last time, and it's close to your apartment. I think that the publisher should pay for my stay. I would come by myself.

If I were unable to come, then we would surely be able to meet in 1961.

The sentence that I believed to have been by Hegel (and which we've all heard in the name of Warburg) appears verbatim (for the first time?) in a letter of Flaubert's.

Cordial regards to you both

yours,

Gershom Scholem

P.S. I see now that the 1960 Eranos conference ends on the 25th of August. That means that the earlier date would be much better for me than the later one. It would be better in any case.

Original: manuscript; Theodor W. Adorno Archive, Frankfurt am Main.

in a letter of Flaubert's: To date, and to the best of our knowledge, nobody has been able to find the source of this statement. It remains unclear whether anyone else makes this connection.

the 1960 Eranos conference: At the 1960 Eranos conference, Scholem spoke on "Die mystische Gestalt der Gottheit in der Kabbala" [On the Mystical Shape of the Godhead in the Kabbalah]. The lecture was published in: *Eranos Jahrbuch 1960*, Vol. 29: *Mensch und Gestalltung* [Man and formation], ed. Olga Fröbe-Kapteyn (Zurich: Rhein, 1961), pp. 139–82. See Scholem, "Shi'ur Komah: The Mystical Shape of the Godhead," in *On the Mystical Shape of the Godhead: Basic Concepts in the Kabbalah*, trans. Joachim Neugroschel (New York: Schocken Books, 1991), pp. 15–55.

75 SCHOLEM TO ADORNO
JERUSALEM, 8.2.1960

האוניברסיטה העברית בירושלים
THE HEBREW UNIVERSITY, JERUSALEM

FACULTY OF HUMANITIES — הפקולטה למדעי הרוח

8 Feb. 1960

Dear Mr. Adorno,

I am still waiting for a response to my previous letter. I expect to come to Europe from the 10th to the 18th of September in order to attend the conference in Marburg. The week before would work very well for us.

Just one urgent request: I have found somebody who is able to read Benjamin's handwriting well and who is prepared to transcribe the texts. Is the publisher prepared to cover costs within a reasonable limit? Approximately 300 typed pages (likely more, not less). Please let me know. This work will, in any case, have to be done somewhere, and this way we would avoid the precarious issue of transporting the original manuscripts – plus, I can check the texts here.

With cordial regards and in a hurry,

yours,

G. S.

Many thanks for your Faust essay!

P.S. Meridian Books (New York) have just written to me to say that *["]the difficulties of negotiating with Suhrkamp . . . make it necessary for us to drop the idea [of the Benjamin essays]."** I had written on the 14th of XI in connection with our conversation, to agree to make the selection. It is a mystery to me what happened here.

Original: manuscript with printed letterhead; Theodor W. Adorno Archive, Frankfurt am Main.

Faust essay: See Adorno, "Zur Schlußszene des Faust" [On the final scene of Faust], first published in *Akzente*, 6/6 (1959), pp. 567–75, with the following remark on p. 576: "I once teased Walter Benjamin about his predilection for unusual and out-of-the-way material by asking him when he planned to write an interpretation of Faust, and he immediately parried by saying that he would do so if it could be serialized in the *Frankfurter Zeitung*. The memory of that conversation occasioned the writing of the fragments published here."

* Original in English.

The quotation is taken from the editors' afterword to the German edition of *Notes to Literature*: *Gesammelte Schriften 11: Noten zur Literatur* (Frankfurt am Main, 2003), p. 698. For the English translation, see Adorno, "On the Final Scene of Faust," in *Notes to Literature*, Vol. 1, trans. Shierry Weber Nicholsen (New York: Columbia University Press, 1991), pp. 111–20.

Meridian Books (New York): There had been a plan for an English language edition of Benjamin's essays to be published by the American publisher Meridian Books.

76 ADORNO TO SCHOLEM
FRANKFURT AM MAIN, 17. 2.1960

PROF. DR. THEODOR W. ADORNO

FRANKFURT AM MAIN
KETTENHOFWEG 123
17 February 1960

Dear Mr. Scholem,

Please accept my sincerest thanks for your letter, which I received yesterday, and at the same time, please accept my apologies that the previous one still remains unanswered. The academic term took such a turbulent turn last week, and I got buried under so many silly tasks that I did not get around to the most urgent matters.

I am very glad that we will see each other in September. Miss Olbrich will make reservations for you right away so so that no calamity occurs.

I immediately communicated our suggestion of having Benjamin's letters transcribed on your end, and at the publisher's expense, although, admittedly, I did not reach Unseld himself. Of course that would be the best option by far. Perhaps you could send them a rough estimation of the cost. It won't cost the world, and I cannot imagine that it will pose any serious obstacle.

The American matter is incomprehensible to me. Nothing happened besides what we discussed in Sils Maria, namely: that you and I will prepare the edition, and that Mrs. Hannah Arendt is, under no circumstances, to be involved in the project in any way. In their last letter to Suhrkamp, Meridian Books provided an interim report to the effect that their head of operations would get in touch, and this was then followed by a long silence. There have been no difficulties as far as Suhrkamp is concerned. I asked the lady in charge of foreign licencing, Miss Ritzerfeld, to contact you directly on this matter. By the way, something similar happened to me with a big American publisher, Beacon Press: they had already offered me a contract and quoted me an honorarium; then, following my agreement in principle, there was a period of long silence, followed by an impudent letter saying that they were withdrawing from the whole project. My suggestion would be that you do not relent on the matter of the Benjamin edition and that you simply explain that it is not about difficulties caused by Suhrkamp, but only about respecting our conditions – and, God knows, they are not that complicated. In the case of Hannah Arendt, though, I am intransigent – not only because of my own disdain for this lady, whom I consider to be an old washer-woman, but above all because I know how Benjamin felt about her and her erstwhile husband.

During the first days of March, as soon as I can breathe again, I will get the cogs moving with regard to the Benjamin letters. It would be good if you could let me know by then if you have any more names or any other suggestions.

The Kempskian review was very humane; I asked him to send it to you. As you well know, he did his doctorate under me. He is one of the candidates who is under serious consideration for the associate professorship in philosophy that has opened up here. In this connection, it would be good to get your opinion on him, possibly in the form of a separate letter, which I could present to the faculty. However, if you don't know Kempski well enough, I do not want to burden you with this.

Incidentally, Mr. Rothenberg has written – not to me, but to my secretary (not that she provoked this in any way) – indicating that he would be sending another letter. Apparently he wants to repeat his Frankfurt coup in all seriousness. Of course, it would be best if he could be stopped in Israel from doing so, in a friendly yet decisive manner. For obvious reasons, it's not exactly comfortable for me to reject him here; but, after everything you've told me about him, I would have no other choice.

All that is cordial, also from Gretel, and also to Fanya,

your old

Adorno

Original: typescript with printed letterhead; Gershom Scholem Archive, The National Library of Israel, Jerusalem.

Miss Olbrich: Elfriede Olbrich (1923–2006) was Adorno's secretary from 1956.

The American matter: Adorno is referring to the plan for an English-language edition of Benjamin's essays to be put out by Meridian Books, New York.

Hannah Arendt: Arendt prepared the first English-language edition of Benjamin's selected essays: Walter Benjamin, *Illuminations: Essays and Reflections* (New York: Harcourt, 1968).

Miss Ritzerfeld: Helene Ritzerfeld (1914–2000) was Suhrkamp's first employee. From 1959 she was head of the publishing house's department for rights and licencing.

Beacon Press: Founded in 1854 by the American Unitarian Association, Beacon Press published Herbert Marcuse's *One-Dimensional Man* (1964), among other titles. Adorno's writings were not published by Beacon.

Hannah Arendt . . . her erstwhile husband: Hannah Arendt's first husband, Günther Stern (1902–1992; later called Günther Anders), was a second cousin of Walter Benjamin's. Anders's *Habilitation*, supervised by Paul Tillich at the University of Frankfurt, was rejected following Adorno's intervention. See Konrad Paul Liessmann, "Hot Potatoes: Zum Briefwechsel zwischen Günther Anders und Theodor W. Adorno" [Hot Potatoes: On the correspondence between Günther Anders and Theodor W. Adorno], in the *Zeitschrift für Kritische Theorie*, no. 6 (1998), pp. 29–38.

The Kempskian review: The philosopher and legal scholar Jürgen von Kempski Rakoszyn (1910–1998) was an advisor in matters concerning international law at the Deutsches Institut für außenpolitische Forschung [German Institute for Research in Foreign Policy] in Berlin in 1939. In 1951 he completed his doctorate, under Adorno's supervision, on the American pragmatist Charles Sanders Peirce. In 1961 he held an honorary professorship in the logic of the social sciences at the University of Munich, which followed teaching posts in Hannover and Hamburg. In 1981 he was named director of the Institut für Methdoden- und Strukturforschung [Institute for the Study of Methods and Structures] at the Ruhr-University in Bochum. Von Kempski reviewed the German edition of Scholem's book *Major Trends in Jewish Mysticism*. See Jürgen von Kempski Rakoszyn, "Jüdische Mystik und Kabbala" [Jewish mysticism and Kabbalah], *Neue Deutsche Hefte*, Vol. 63 (1959), pp. 627–30. For Scholem's letter to von Kempski, dated 6.4.1960, see Scholem, *Briefe II: 1948–1970*, ed. Thomas Sparr (Munich: C. H. Beck, 1995), pp. 54–6. See also Jürgen von Kempski's review of Scholem's *Judaica*, "Gershom Scholem und das deutsch-jüdische Gespräch" [Gershom Scholem and the German-Jewish conversation], *Merkur*, 28/7 (1974).

Rothenberg: Beno Rothenberg (1914–2012), born in Frankfurt, was a photographer and archeologist. He immigrated to Palestine in 1933. Famed for his documentation of the state's early years, he is considered one of the most important photographers in the history of Israel. As an archeologist, Rothenberg contributed to the discovery of King Solomon's copper mines in the Timna valley in Israel's northern Negev desert during the 1950s. In 1973 he founded the Institute for Archaeo-Metallurgic Studies at University College London. Rothenberg intended to write his doctorate under Adorno and Horkheimer.

77 ADORNO TO SCHOLEM
FRANKFURT AM MAIN, 22.2.1960

PROF. DR. THEODOR W. ADORNO

FRANKFURT AM MAIN
KETTENHOFWEG 123
22 February 1960

Dear Mr. Scholem,

As a postscript to my letter: Suhrkamp told me that they are happy to cover the costs of having Benjamin's letters transcribed, provided that these are not unusually high. It would probably be best if you got in touch with them directly. I am confident that this issue can be readily resolved.

Kempski has already sent you his review, at my request. He is a great admirer of your works.

Most cordially,
always yours
Adorno

Original: typescript with printed letterhead; Gershom Scholem Archive, The National Library of Israel, Jerusalem.

78 ADORNO TO SCHOLEM
FRANKFURT AM MAIN, 2.3.1960

PROF. DR. THEODOR W. ADORNO

FRANKFURT AM MAIN
KETTENHOFWEG 123
2 March 1960

Dear Mr. Scholem,

I have, in the meantime, vigorously sprung into action on the matter of Benjamin's correspondence. Letters have been written to:

Dora Morser – Ernst Schoen – Martin Domke – Adalbert Rang – Pierre Bonnasse (Missac) – Dr. Willi Haas – Dr. Hirsch, on account of Hofmannsthal (S. Fischer Verlag) – Dr. Werner Kraft.

Bloch will be here at Suhrkamp next week to give a lecture. I will have the opportunity to discuss the plan with him in depth, although I doubt whether he has that much and also whether he will give us what he does have.

I have not written to Kohn yet because I do not have a current address for him and because Gretel, despite all her rummaging, was unable to find an old one. I fear the worst: that he fell into the hands of the Nazis. Should I be mistaken, and should you have any idea of how to get in touch with him, please let me know right away. It would probably be best if you wrote to those friends of Benjamin's, whose names you sent me, a lady among them, but whom I don't know.

I hope that the whole thing will progress quickly and that we will soon have enough that we will be able to start sorting through the material. It would be nice if we could arrive at final decisions when we meet in autumn.

Most cordially, also to Fanya, and also from Gretel,

always yours,

Adorno

Original: typescript with printed letterhead and Scholem's handwritten note, reading "Gustav Glück"; Gershom Scholem Archive, The National Library of Israel, Jerusalem.

Martin Domke: Regarding Walter Benjamin's friend, Martin Domke, see letter no. 10 in this volume.

Adalbert Rang: The pedagogue, Adalbert Rang (1928–2019), grandson of Walter Benjamin's friend, the theologian and writer Florens Christian Rang (see letter no. 11 in this volume), studied in Frankfurt under Adorno, among others. In 1968 he became professor of pedagogy at the Pedagogical University in Berlin, and at the University of the Arts, Berlin, as well as at the University of Amsterdam. Rang's thesis was published in the Institute for Social Research's book series *Frankfurter Beiträge zur Soziologie* [Frankfurt contributions to sociology]: Adalbert Rang, *Der politische Pestalozzi* [The political Pestalozzi] (Frankfurt am Main: Europäische Verlagsanstalt, 1967). See also Adorno's foreword to Rang's thesis: "Adalbert Rang: Der politische Pestalozzi", in *Gesammelte Schriften 20.2: Vermischte Schriften* [Miscellaneous Writings], ed. Rolf Tiedemann et al. (Frankfurt am Main: Suhrkamp, 1986), pp. 664–666.

Pierre Bonnasse (Missac): Pierre Bonnasse (1910–1986), who went by the pseudonym of Pierre Missac, was a friend of Walter Benjamin's from his time in Paris. In 1947 he published a translation of "On the Concept of History" in the journal *Les Temps Modernes*, which is considered to be authoritative. See Pierre Missac, *Walter Benjamin's Passages*, trans. Shierry Weber Nicholsen (Cambridge, MA: MIT Press, 1995).

Dr. Willi Haas: Adorno's spelling. Willy Haas (1891–1973) was a critic of literature, film, and theatre. He also wrote screenplays. He was the founder of the journal *Literarische Welt*, which published some of Walter Benjamin's work.

Dr. Hirsch, on account of Hofmannsthal (S. Fischer Verlag): Rudolf Hirsch (1905–1996) was an art historian and publisher, who, from 1954 to 1963, was the director of S. Fischer Verlag. He was also an important collector of manuscripts by Hofmannsthal and a connoisseur of his work.

Gustav Glück: The banker Gustav Glück (1902–1973) was a close friend of Walter Benjamin's in the 1930s. Until 1938, he was the director of the international department of the Reichskreditgesellschaft [Imperial Credit Society]. In 1938 he immigrated to Argentina. After the war he became a member of the directorial board at Dresdner Bank in Frankfurt am Main. Glück helped Benjamin receive his honoraria from German journals in France. See *The Correspondence of Walter Benjamin 1910–1940*, ed. Theodor W. Adorno and Gershom Scholem, trans. Manfred R. Jacobson and Evelyn M. Jacobson (Chicago: University of Chicago Press, 1994) p. 376.

79 SCHOLEM TO ADORNO
JERUSALEM, 6.3.1960

6 March 1960

האוניברסיטה העברית בירושלים
THE HEBREW UNIVERSITY OF JERUSALEM

Dear Adorno,

Sincere thanks for your letters. The transcription of the letters addressed to me has indeed already begun, but it is a sizeable chunk of work – even for somebody who can read the handwriting, microscopic or otherwise.

I am keeping the week from the 4th to the 11th of September free for Frankfurt. Please thank Miss Olbrich for her letter and for her efforts. She should definitely secure the reservation that she mentioned at the Palmgarten Hotel. I do not want to stay at the Festhalle Guesthouse. She can still change the reservation, should she, in the meantime, find a single, en-suite room in a good hotel. Will the publisher at least cover the cost of the hotel? (I do not want to make my trip depend on this, but it doesn't strike me as an unreasonable request.)

What about the letters to Gustav Glück? I heard (from you? Or someone else?) that he survived and became the director of a bank in Vienna or Berlin.

Dr. Alfred Cohn (with a C, not a K), if he is alive, could probably be tracked down through Schön. I never had any direct contact with him (having only met him in Paris with W. B. in 1927).

Is Suhrkamp issuing a call, as is commonly the case? Perhaps somebody, e.g. from the circle around *Der Anfang*, will get in touch. (Herbert Blumenthal, for instance, lives in England under a goyish name, which Dora probably knows).

I have already spoken to Kraft and Buber (positive). (And Rychner, whom you're still missing).

Help from Ernst Bloch would be very welcome. Perhaps, if you have a chance, you should say this to him, in both of our names. In case you see him, please say hello to him from me.

The New York situation has now become clear to me: they lost interest when the prospect of making a profit became questionable. However, <u>after</u> I agreed, they did <u>not</u> write to Suhrkamp <u>at all</u>, but rather wrote to me directly with a rejection letter, which allowed for two possible interpretations.

Cordial regards,

yours, G.S.

P.S.

I don't know any of Kempski's writings, so I can't offer you an informed opinion. I am glad to hear from you that he has sent his review.

Original: aerogram (manuscript) with printed letterhead; Theodor W. Adorno Archive, Frankfurt am Main.

the circle around Der Anfang: See letter no. 11 in this volume.

Herbert Blumenthal: Herbert Belmore. See letter no. 18 in this volume.

80 ADORNO TO SCHOLEM
FRANKFURT AM MAIN, 18.3.1960

PROF. DR. THEODOR W. ADORNO

FRANKFURT AM MAIN
KETTENHOFWEG 123
18 March 1960

Dear Scholem,

Today I am just sending along a quick interim report regarding the state of the Benjamin letters.

I have yet to hear anything from Dora. My letter to Schoen was returned as undeliverable; anyway, Bloch told me that he now lives in the Eastern Zone. Admittedly, I have no idea how I can get his address. This is all the more troubling since, according to Bloch as well, he is the only person who may have an address for Cohn. Bloch, who was here and sends his sincere regards, has lost all of his letters from Benjamin. He also claimed that he is in the habit of destroying the letters he receives after reading them, which hardly seems credible. We will get the letters to Hofmannsthal; Hirsch, from S. Fischer Verlag, confirmed this for me today. As regards the French correspondents, I had appealed to Missac, actually Pierre Bonnasse, who recently visited me here, and whom you also know. He is the only person who knows the names of everyone under consideration. But I still don't have his response. Kraft wrote to me to say that he is in direct contact with you and that he is having his letters transcribed for you. I received a friendly letter from Willi Haas to the effect that his entire correspondence has been destroyed. Gustav Glück now lives in Frankfurt and is a manager at the Dresdner Bank. I saw him briefly yesterday. Today he and his wife are coming to our place, and I will have an opportunity to discuss the project with him. I will unquestionably receive the young Rang's material. I have not received a reply from Domke. I have not yet written to Wissing or Kracauer – in both cases I have certain psychological inhibitions, which I am sure you understand.

The results so far are not exactly thrilling, but I do think that we will find enough to make our project viable. Hopefully Suhrkamp has since confirmed that they are covering the cost of transcribing your letters.

That is all for today. I am under the wholly unfamiliar and inhumane pressure to complete a book which, against my intentions, has already been announced. You can imagine how I feel about this.

To you and Fanya all the best, also from Gretel,

your old

Adorno

Original: typescript with printed letterhead; Gershom Scholem Archive, The National Library of Israel, Jerusalem.

Missac: Pierre Missac visited Scholem in Jerusalem, as he wrote to Adorno on the 5th of June 1959. On the 12th of April he replied to Adorno's request for letters from Benjamin: "I found 4 letters, all from the years '38 and '39. Unfortunately they are without interest and concern merely practical arrangements for appointments. Only one letter, written in October 1939, could be of historical significance. In it, he describes his situation and speaks of the hope for impending liberation. Of course the letters are at your disposal and I look forward to receiving your instructions on this matter." For Benjamin's letter to P. Missac from the 29th of October 1939, see *Walter Benjamin: Gesammelte Briefe VI, 1938–1940*, ed. Henri Lonitz and Christoph Gödde (Frankfurt am Main: Suhrkamp, 2000), pp. 348–9.

Wissing: Regarding Egon Wissing, see letter no. 7 in this volume.

Kracauer: Regarding Siegfried Kracauer, see the Editor's Introduction and letter no. 21 in this volume.

to complete a book: Adorno is referring to his book on Mahler, which was first published by Suhrkamp in Frankfurt in 1960. See Adorno, *Mahler: A Musical Physiognomy*, trans. Edmund Jephcott (Chicago: University of Chicago Press, 1992).

81 SCHOLEM TO ADORNO
JERUSALEM, 29.3.1960

האוניברסיטה העברית בירושלים
THE HEBREW UNIVERSITY, JERUSALEM

FACULTY OF HUMANITIES הפקולטה למדעי הרוח
29 March 1960

Dear Adorno,

I am writing in connection to your message about Mr. Benno Rothenberg's activities, re obtaining a doctorate in his own particular way. I must inform you that Mr. R. turned up here, some three weeks ago, declaring to the faculty secretary that he is in possession of a doctorate from Frankfurt a.M. and that he is now preparing to attain the same honours from Oxford. Mr. R.'s mendacity has come to light, accidentally, through your communication; I can only conclude from your letter that this is yet another example of his numerous dubious operations (although the motives are as yet unclear). I don't know how one can put an end to his game, although it is surely necessary to do so. The fact that he has spuriously presented himself as being in possession of a doctorate from your university should make it easier for you to refuse any further attempts by him. Should it be necessary, you can attain proof of the situation in the form of an official statement from the dean of the faculty, Professor N. Rottenstreich. My (emeritus) colleague, Prof. Bergmann, has undertaken to advise him to give up on his Frankfurt plans. B. told me that R. visited him last week and proclaimed that he had completed his doctorate *magna cum laude* under your supervision, and that the "the examination had been child's play." As proof, he dug out an invitation to the written (?) examination. Bergmann is still of the opinion that he is a highly gifted person in a philosophical=logical sense, but that he is a man suffering from *moral insanity** and *pseudologia phantastica* (grandiose qualifications).

Kraft gave me his letters, which are, in part, highly interesting and worthy of publication.

It is unclear to me whether a public call to people in possession of Benjamin's letters has or will be issued in the literary journals, as is properly the norm. You could formulate such a call in both of our names.

With cordial regards, also to your wife

yours,

G. Scholem

* Original in English.

Original: manuscript with printed letterhead; Theodor W. Adorno Archive, Frankfurt am Main.

Professor N. Rottenstreich: Scholem's spelling. The Israeli philosopher Natan Rotenstreich (1914–1993) was one of the most important scholars of the humanities at the Hebrew University in Jerusalem. Together with Shmuel Hugo Bergman, Rotenstreich translated into Hebrew the works of Immanuel Kant, as well as other important philosophical texts. He made significant contributions to the development of philosophy in Israel. From 1958 to 1962 he was dean of the Faculty of Humanities, and from 1965 to 1969 he was rector of the Hebrew University.

My (emeritus) colleague, Prof. Bergmann: Scholem's spelling. The Israeli philosopher Shmuel Hugo Bergman (1883–1975) was a close friend of Scholem's. Born in Prague, he went to school with Franz Kafka. After studying in Prague and Berlin, he immigrated to Palestine in 1920, where he was involved in the establishment of the Hebrew University in Jerusalem. In 1928 he was appointed to a chair in philosophy at that institution. From 1935 to 1938 he was the rector of the university. His translations of major philosophical works into Hebrew, as well as his own philosophical writings, significantly shaped the discipline of philosophy in Israel.

82 ADORNO TO SCHOLEM
FRANKFURT AM MAIN, 6.4.1960

PROF. DR. THEODOR W. ADORNO

FRANKFURT AM MAIN
KETTENHOFWEG 123
6 April 1960

Dear Scholem,

Kindest thanks for your letter of the 29th of March, which I found after coming back from a few days of vacation.

Regarding the matter of the Benjamin letters, I can report that Glück no longer has any letters; they had been stashed at a friend's and were destroyed during an air raid. The young Rang – Florenz Christian's grandson – who, by the way, is writing his dissertation under my supervision, and is a very talented and likeable person – recently brought me [Benjamin and Rang's] complete and extensive correspondence. However, given the difficulties that we are having procuring materials, I did not want to take on the responsibility of storing the letters myself. Accordingly, I asked him to hold on to them for the time being and to make them available to us once we establish whether the collection is actually viable.

I still have not received a reply from Dora or from Domke. Bonnasse will see what he can scrape together among French friends.

Rebus sic stantibus, the question now arises as to the feasibility of our plan. My feeling is that, in spite of it all, the material that has been saved – your letters, those to Hofmannsthal, Rang, Kraft, Gretel and me – are sufficient to put together a small volume. The fact that so much has been destroyed is part of the Benjaminian fate, and one would have to address these circumstances in the introduction. I, for my part, would like to continue with the project but will not discuss it with Suhrkamp until I know your *votum*. Given the failures to date, it seems unlikely to me that we will find much more than what we already have.

Mr. Rothenberg is a dangerous swindler. I told you in the summer, long after you and I had spoken in Sils Maria, that he wrote to me and asked me to conceal the whole thing from you. In the meantime, he has also attempted to get in contact with my secretary. I think it would be easiest if I were to write up a brief account of the situation on the Department of Philosophy's official letterhead, sending you a few copies to use at your discretion. Conceivably, one should also give Oxford the requisite information about Mr. Rothenberg. Since I know the people in the Philosophy Department there quite well, that would be no trouble at all.

To you and Fanya all the best, also from Gretel,

your old

Adorno

Original: typescript with printed letterhead and the official letter from Adorno regarding the Rothenberg matter; Gershom Scholem Archive, the National Library of Israel, Jerusalem.

Florenz: Adorno's spelling.

the Department of Philosophy's official letterhead ... Rothenberg: In his function as director of the Department of Philosophy, Adorno wrote the following on the 6th of April:

> As I have recently learned, Mr. Beno Rothenberg is claiming to have attained a doctorate from the University of Frankfurt am Main. This claim is untrue.
>
> The situation is as follows: some time ago, Mr. Rothenberg approached my colleague, Horkheimer, and myself inquiring about the possibility of writing his doctorate under our supervision. Given the persecution that Mr. Rothenberg was, without question, subject to, the matter was discussed at the faculty level, despite the fact that it was unclear whether the candidate fulfilled the preconditions for the pursuit of further study – especially as regards to his *Abitur* [high-school diploma]. Mr. Rothenberg then submitted a doctoral thesis on logical problems in Franz Brentano's work – apparently a manuscript that had been written some time ago. Our impression was not unfavorable. Since Mr. Horkheimer and I are not

specialists in logistics, we sought the counsel of an expert in this field; he too was satisfied with the result. Consequently, we recommended to the faculty that the thesis be accepted. In his oral examination, however, Mr. Rothenberg demonstrated such an utter lack of philosophical knowledge – notably in those areas that he himself had cited as his specialization – that he failed; and this in spite of the fact that the examiners were really as accommodating as they could be. Mr. Rothenberg tried, with the greatest artfulness, to wriggle out of the situation and named all manner of reasons for his failure. However, the result allowed no doubt as to his shortcomings, above all with respect to his lack of factual knowledge. All of the examiners – the Dean, in addition to the departmental representatives and committee members – conferred at length on the matter, as the incident was exceedingly embarrassing. In the end, however, we were forced to confirm the negative result. I cannot deny that, in light of this oral examination, it seems highly doubtful to me that Mr. Rothenberg in fact wrote the dissertation that he himself submitted.

I ask that you rigorously oppose any attempt on Mr. Rothenberg's part to present himself as having completed a doctorate in Frankfurt. It is characteristic of his behavior that, after his failed exam, he wrote to me asking that I not report this outcome to my friend and colleague Gerhard Scholem – apparently because he was already planning to portray the situation dishonestly to serve his interests.

Theodor W. Adorno

Professor Dr. Th. W. Adorno
Professor of Philosophy

83 SCHOLEM TO ADORNO
JERUSALEM, 6.4.1960

האוניברסיטה העברית בירושלים
THE HEBREW UNIVERSITY OF JERUSALEM

FACULTY OF HUMANITIES הפקולטה למדעי הרוח

6 April 1960

Dear Adorno,

It may interest you to know that Kraft told me that he has transcripts of most of Walter Benjamin's correspondence with Rang. Should you find that the complete correspondence is no longer in the possession of his heirs – Kraft tells me that some of it seems to have been lost – it will, at any rate, still be accessible to us in this way. I will have a look at it sometime soon. It is bound to include some very important pieces.

I also want to draw your attention to Ferdinand Cohrs, a friend from Benjamin's youth from his time in the *Freie Studentenschaft* [free student movement]. As I recall from the discussions surrounding the *Angelus Novus*, Benjamin stayed in contact with him later on as well and placed great importance on his collaboration. Cohrs is still alive and working as a pastor in Lüneburg, as I can see from Friedrich Hielscher's rather wild autobiography, which I recently read in part. Perhaps you could get in touch with him.

Cordial regards

yours,

Gerhard Scholem

Please pass on the enclosed to your secretary.

Original: typescript with printed letterhead and handwritten postscript; Theodor W. Adorno Archive, Frankfurt am Main.

Ferdinand Cohrs: The theologian and pastor Ferdinand Cohrs (1893–1966) was friends with Benjamin during their time together in the *Freie Studentenschaft* [free student movement]. Later on, Cohrs studied theology in Göttingen. After the First World War he worked as a pastor in Lower Saxony. From 1937 to 1945 he was the director of studies at the Domkandidatenstift seminary in Berlin, and from 1945 until his retirement he worked as a pastor in Lüneburg. See *Walter Benjamin: Gesammelte Briefe I, 1910-1918*, ed. Henri Lonitz and Christoph Gödde (Frankfurt am Main: Suhrkamp, 1995), pp. 224–6.

Friedrich Hielscher's . . . autobiography: The journalist and philosopher of religion Friedrich Hielscher (1902–1990) was the founder of the nichtchristlichen Freikirche [non-Christian free Church]. For his autobiography, see Friedrich Hielscher, *50 Jahre unter Deutschen* [50 years among Germans] (Hamburg: Rowohlt, 1954).

84 ADORNO TO SCHOLEM
FRANKFURT AM MAIN, 21.4.1960

INSTITUTE FOR SOCIAL RESEARCH
AT THE JOHANN WOLFGANG GOETHE
UNIVERSITY

FRANKURT A.M.
SENCKENBERG-ANLAGE 26
FRANKFURT AM MAIN, 21.4.1960
tel. 772147 and 772195
21 April 1960

Dear Scholem,

Kindest thanks for your letter.

The young Rang has already told me that part of the Rang letters are with Kraft, so we shouldn't have any difficulties on that front. Meanwhile I have also written to Kracauer and Cohrs. Still no response from Dora, although my letter has also not been returned, so I presume she's still at the old address.

Most cordially, also from Gretel,

yours,

Adorno

Original: typescript with printed letterhead; Gershom Scholem Archive, The National Library of Israel, Jerusalem.

I have written to Kracauer and Cohrs: Adorno wrote to Kracauer on the 7th of April 1960. See *Theodor W. Adorno / Siegfried Kracauer: Correspondence 1923–1966*, ed. Wolfgang Schopf, trans. Susan Reynolds and Michael Winkler (Cambridge: Polity, 2020), pp. 344–346. Kracauer replied on the 30th of April: "Unfortunately, I have no Benjamin letters for you. There are probably some very old ones lying around somewhere – I don't know where – and they would certainly not be of any significance. The lack of correspondence arises from the fact that during our émigré years in Paris – and then up to the end in the South – we were together without interruption" (ibid., p. 346). See, however, *Walter Benjamin, Briefe an Siegfried Kracauer: Mit vier Briefen von Siegfried Kracauer an Walter Benjamin* [Walter Benjamin, letters to Siegfried Kracauer: with four letters from Siegfried Kracauer to Walter Benjamin], ed. Rolf Tiedemann and Henri Lonitz (Marbach am Neckar: Marbacher Schriften 279, Deutsche Schillergesellschaft, 1987). Adorno wrote to Ferdinand Cohrs on the 21st of April 1960, and Cohrs replied on the 16th of June 1960: "I still hope to find letters from Walter Benjamin. Due to the war and the period thereafter, my papers – and especially my letters – are in a state of terrible disarray. I will have to look for them." Ultimately, only one letter from Benjamin, from 1922, could be found. See *Walter Benjamin: Gesammelte Briefe II, 1919–1924*, ed. Henri Lonitz and Christoph Gödde (Frankfurt am Main: Suhrkamp, 1996), pp. 256–8.

85 SCHOLEM TO ADORNO JERUSALEM, 21.4.1960

Jerusalem, the 21st of April 1960.

Dear Adorno,

I thank you for your letter from the 6th of April, as well as for the documentary statement regarding Mr. Benno Rothenberg. I will see to it that it is disseminated widely and in the appropriate places – you can count on this. I will also have a copy put in his personal *file** at the university.

* Original in English

With regard to your question about the Benjamin letters, it seems to me that we will have no difficulties at all putting something together from the material at hand. We will likely have too much rather than too little. As I probably wrote to you, Kraft has made his letters from the thirties, the only ones he still has, available to me. They are very interesting. Regarding the letters to me, which may be eligible for selection, in part or in full, I don't know yet whether I will have transcriptions available by August. I have selected 120 out of the 300 or so; of course, these alone would fill a whole volume, since some of them are very long. It might be the only material available from the early period. I was able to get Mrs. Steinschneider, the former Kitty Marx, to do the transcriptions for us. Of course, the pay is in no way adequate for the time and effort required, given the difficulty of deciphering the microscopic script, but she will certainly do it. She is going away in mid-June, however, and I doubt that I fill find someone else to do it before my departure. Anyhow, I expect to receive transcripts of some 80 to 90 letters. (She only has evenings to work on them).

Why haven't you written to Rychner? And to Willy Haas, who now lives in Hamburg? It might be possible to find more letters of significance from Benjamin's youth if we could get hold of Herbert Belmont, formerly Blumenthal, who now lives in England, and who was friends with Benjamin during the Wyneken days (until 1914). And why don't you want to have an open call issued – in both our names, or in the name of the Suhrkamp Verlag – in the newspapers and literary journals, as we had planned? How would you assess your chances of walking straight over to East Berlin and intervening with Mrs. Brecht there? Is this completely out of the question? Couldn't Bloch help in this matter? He [Benjamin] wrote quite a number of letters to André Gide. Shouldn't they be part of Gide's estate? And what about his friend Germaine Krull in Paris? And Pierre Klossowski, who surely has letters from him, and who is merrily publishing away in the French journals – partly through Catholic prayer, partly through analyses of the Marquis de Sade? I have retained no clear memory of Mr. Klossowski, even though Benjamin presented him to me in person in 1938. By contrast, the memory of Arthur Koestler has only left me with disgust.

I see from a letter from your secretary, Miss Olbrich, that the room in Frankfurt has been reserved from the 4th to the 10th of September; however, I will probably need it until the 11th, which is when I clear off for Marburg.

This is all for today.

With cordial regards to you both,

yours,

Gerhard Scholem

Original: aerogram, typescript; Theodor W. Adorno Archive, Frankfurt am Main.

Benno Rothenberg: Scholem's spelling.

Herbert Belmont: Scholem is referring to Herbert Belmore, born Blumenthal.

intervening with Mrs. Brecht: Helene Weigel (1900–1971) was an actress and the director of the Berliner Ensemble, which she co-founded with her husband, the playwright and poet, Bertolt Brecht (1898–1956), who had been one of Walter Benjamin's closest friends. Helene Weigel also had a friendly relationship with Benjamin. In 1966, Weigel corresponded with Benjamin's sister-in-law, Hilde Benjamin (1902–1989) – who was minister of justice in the GDR from 1953 to 1967 – to clarify the legal situation of Benjamin's papers and to enable the publication of his works in the GDR. See Erdmut Wizisla, *Walter Benjamin and Bertolt Brecht: The Story of a Friendship*, trans. Christine Shuttleworth (London: Verso, 2016), p. 22.

André Gide: Benjamin had been friends with the writer and 1947 Nobel Prize laureate, André Gide (1869–1951), since the 1920s. See Benjamin, "André Gide and Germany," in *Selected Writings*, Vol. 2.1: *1927–1930*, ed. Michael W. Jennings, Howard Eiland, and Gary Smith (Cambridge, MA: The Belknap Press of Harvard University Press, 2005), pp. 80–4. See also Benjamin, "Conversation with André Gide," ibid., pp. 91–7.

Germaine Krull: The Parisian photographer Germaine Krull (1897–1985) was friends with Benjamin, Horkheimer, and Pollock. Only one of Benjamin's letters to her, dated the 16th of May 1938, has survived. See *Walter Benjamin: Gesammelte Briefe VI, 1938–1940*, ed. Henri Lonitz and Christoph Gödde (Frankfurt am Main: Suhrkamp, 2000), pp. 83–4.

Pierre Klossowski: Benjamin got acquainted with the writer, philosopher, translator and painter Pierre Klossowski (1905–2001) in Paris through their mutual friend Georges Bataille. Klossowski, who had translated works by Heidegger, Hölderlin, Kafka, Nietzsche, and Wittgenstein into French, also translated into French Benjamin's essay "The Work of Art in the Age of its Technological Reproducibility," which first appeared in the *Zeitschrift für Sozialforschung*, 5/1 (1936), pp. 40–66; now in Benjamin, *Gesammelte Schriften I.2*, ed. Rolf Tiedemann and Hermann Schweppenhäuser (Frankfurt am Main: Suhrkamp, 1974), pp. 710–39. For an English translation of the second, expanded version of Benjamin's essay, see Walter Benjamin, *Selected Writings*, Vol. 3: 1935-1938, ed. Howard Eiland and Michael W. Jennings (Cambridge, M.A.: the Belknap Press of Harvard University Press, 2002), pp. 101-33. See also *The Complete Correspondence of Walter Benjamin and Theodor W. Adorno, 1928–1940*, ed. Henri Lonitz, trans. Nicholas Walker (Cambridge, MA: Harvard University Press, 2001), pp. 122–5.

Arthur Koestler: The writer Arthur Koestler (1905–1983) was born in Budapest and immigrated to Palestine in 1926, where he worked as a journalist. In 1930 he moved to Berlin and in 1933 to Paris, where he met Benjamin. From 1939 to 1940, Koestler was interned in France. In 1944 he returned to Palestine and continued his work as a journalist. In 1949 he moved to England.

86 SCHOLEM TO ADORNO JERUSALEM, 8.5.1960

Jerusalem, 8 May 1960

Dear Adorno,

I sent Max Rychner an exchange that I had with Walter Benjamin regarding a letter addressed to him. A copy of this letter survives in my possession, since W. B. sent it for my attention. To my great surprise, Rychner cannot remember ever having received such a letter; he asked me if it's possible that it was never sent. However, given the state of the material, that is quite impossible. At the same time, Rychner wrote that he would be happy to make the letters he received from W. B. available to us, even though there are only a few short letters. I think I will ask him to send transcripts to both of us – that is, if he plans to have transcripts made at all. Maybe you could also write him a few friendly lines?

Do you know if there are letters to Albert Salomon, who spoke out in favor of W. B.'s *Habilitation* in Frankfurt at the time? As you know, he teaches at the New School in New York and described himself to me as a great admirer of both the man and his writings.

Cordial regards

yours,

[Not signed]

Original: aerogram (typescript); Theodor W. Adorno Archive, Frankfurt am Main.

I sent Max Rychner an exchange that I had with Walter Benjamin regarding a letter addressed to him: In 1931, Max Rychner sent Walter Benjamin his article on the Marxist book by Bernard von Brentano, *Kapitalismus und schöne Literatur* [Capitalism and belles-lettres] (Hamburg, 1930). Rychner inscribed the copy with the Latin proverb "Dic, cur hic" ("Say why you are here"), which, according to Scholem, referred to Marxism. Benjamin sent Scholem a copy of his response to Rychner, dated the 7th of March 1931. See *The Correspondence of Walter Benjamin 1910–1940*, ed. Theodor W. Adorno and Gershom Scholem, trans. Manfred R. Jacobson and Evelyn M. Jacobson (Chicago: University of Chicago Press, 1994), pp. 371–3. In the letter, Benjamin explains his relationship to Marxism and asks Rychner "to see in me not a representative of dialectical materialism as a dogma, but a scholar to whom the *stance* of the materialist seems scientifically and humanely more productive in everything that moves us than does that of the idealist." In his response, dated the 30th of March 1931, Scholem criticizes Benjamin by saying that he is engaged "in an unusually intent kind of self-deception" (ibid., p. 373). See also Benjamin's letter to Scholem, dated the 6th of May 1934, and Scholem's letter to Benjamin, dated the 20th of June 1934, in *The Correspondence of Walter Benjamin and Gershom Scholem, 1932–1940*, ed. Gershom Scholem, trans. Gary Smith and Andre Lefevere (New York: Schocken Books, 1989), pp. 109–12, 115–18.

Albert Salomon: The sociologist and political scientist Albert Salomon (1891–1966) was born in Berlin and studied in Berlin, Freiburg, and Heidelberg. From 1928 to 1931 he was the editor of the journal *Gesellschaft*. In 1933 Salomon immigrated to Switzerland, and in 1935, to the USA. From 1935 he was professor of sociology at the New School for Social Research in New York.

87 ADORNO TO SCHOLEM
FRANKFURT AM MAIN, 18.5.1960

PROF. DR. THEODOR W. ADORNO

FRANKFURT AM MAIN
KETTENHOFWEG 123
18 May 1960

Dear Scholem,

Kindest thanks for your message. I will gladly write to Rychner again.

Are you not confusing Albert Salomon with Gottfried Salomon? The latter was in Frankfurt at the time and spoke out in support if Benjamin's *Habilitation*, within the constraints of his powerlessness. Then again, I know that Albert Salomon also knew Benjamin well. I will only write to Albert Salomon once we've ruled out any confusion.

As you know, I did not receive any reply from Dora. Do you think I should write to her again, or would it be better if you wrote to her? I will see Unseld in the coming days and I will convey to him our mutual *votum* that we are able to produce a respectable volume of correspondence, despite the relatively narrow range of correspondents.

All that is cordial, also from Gretel,

from your old
Adorno

Original: typescript with printed letterhead and Scholem's handwritten note: "Write to Julien Green re: letters. They were friends"; Gershom Scholem Archive, The National Library of Israel, Jerusalem.

I will gladly write to Rychner again: In his letter to Rychner, which was written that day, Adorno writes: "My friend Scholem has contacted you requesting that you make your letters from Benjamin available to us for a projected collection of correspondence that we are preparing for the Suhrkamp Verlag. I would like, for today, emphatically to add my name to his request. Quite aside from their content, it seems to me to be of a certain strategic importance that Benjamin's correspondence with Hofmannsthal and with you is duly included in the collection, since the all-too-enthusiastic appropriation of Benjamin's legacy by the ladies and gentlemen of the Eastern Zone must be avoided at all costs. It goes without saying that we would look after the originals with the utmost care and that we would return them to you as soon as they've been transcribed" (carbon copy of typescript; Theodor W. Adorno Archive). Rychner replied on the 21st of May saying that he had sent the letters to Scholem.

Gottfried Salomon: The sociologist and economist Gottfried Salomon-Delatour (1892–1964) was born in Frankfurt am Main. He studied there, in Darmstadt and in Saarbrücken. In 1925 he became associate professor at the University in Frankfurt. From 1933 to 1940 he taught at the Sorbonne in Paris and from 1941 in New York. In 1958 Salomon returned to Frankfurt.

88 SCHOLEM TO ADORNO
JERUSALEM, 19.5.1960

Dear Adorno – to my great surprise and displeasure, it now turns out that (as a member of the executive board of the *Int. Ass. for History of Relig**) I must be in Marburg for meetings from Friday the 9th of September. That shortens my time frame by 2 days! Can you move our meeting forward accordingly? I can be in Frkft. on the 2nd of September, if a) you are available and b) the hotel reservations can be changed accordingly (2–9 Sept.). Please let me know as soon as possible if this change of plans is feasible. I had otherwise planned to be in Zurich or Munich from the 1st to the 4th of Sept., but these plans can be changed.

Cordial regards,
yours
G. S.

Original: postcard (manuscript) dating by postmark; Theodor W. Adorno Archive, Frankfurt am Main.

* Original in English.

89 SCHOLEM TO ADORNO
JERUSALEM, 9.6.1960

Jerusalem, the 9th of June 1960.
Abarbanel Rd. 28

Dear Adorno,

I have, as yet, received no response to my request to change the dates of my visit to Frankfurt. I have to go to Marburg on the evening of the 8th of September, where I must attend preliminary meetings of the executive board of the Association for the History of Religion on the morning of the 9th and on the 10th. Accordingly, I suggested that I could come to Frankfurt on the 2nd of September so that we could, in any event, have six days together. I thought of bringing the materials I've collected to Europe, to the extent that they will have been transcribed, and possibly having them sent to you in Sils Maria from Switzerland. If that does not leave you enough time, I could possibly have the transcripts sent from here, say, by the end of July; however, airmail is a costly undertaking. I will have some 200 typed pages of my own letters by then, as well as the letters from Kraft, Buber, and Rychner, transcripts of which I already have.

On account of my travel plans, I'd be grateful for a quick response. By the way, the Israeli mission in Cologne has reserved an en-suite room for me in Frankfurt for this period, at the Park-Hotel on Wiesenhüttenplatz. Presumably, this would cost me less than a double room at the Hotel Palmengarten. Do you have some idea which of the two is preferable? Perhaps the Palmengarten Hotel is better on account of its proximity to your house, which might justify the difference in price? In any case, I'll have to change the reservation, whichever hotel I decide on.

The Salomon about whom I wrote is, in fact, Albert Salomon, as I said.

Have any steps been taken with regard to Julien Green, who has letters from Walter Benjamin? Ernst Lewy, a professor of comparative linguistics in Dublin, who may still be alive, or whose estate might be accessible, was also engaged in an interesting correspondence with him for a time. You never responded to my request regarding an open call to people in possession of letters.

Cordial regards to you and your wife,

yours,

Gershom Scholem

Original: typescript; Theodor W. Adorno Archive, Frankfurt am Main.

Julien Green: Julien Green (1900–1998) was a French-American writer. Benjamin held Green's writings in high regard and he wrote about them on several occasions. See Benjamin, "Julien Green," in *Selected Writings*, Vol. 2.1, *1927–1930*, ed. Michael W. Jennings, Howard Eiland and Gary Smith (Cambridge, MA: The Belknap Press of Harvard University Press, 2005), pp. 331–6. See also *The Correspondence of Walter Benjamin 1910-1940*, ed. Theodor W. Adorno and Gershom Scholem, trans. Manfred R. Jacobson and Evelyn M. Jacobson (Chicago: University of Chicago Press, 1994), pp. 356–7.

Ernst Lewy: The Budapest-born linguist Ernst Lewy (1881–1965) was professor of Finno-Ugric languages at the University of Berlin until 1935. In 1937 he immigrated to Ireland, and from 1939 he taught at University College Dublin. Benjamin was friends with Lewy, whose writings he admired, especially his book *Zur Sprache des alten Goethe: Ein Versuch über die Sprache des Einzelnen* [On the language of the old Goethe: an essay on the language of the individual] (Berlin: P. Cassirer, 1913). See *The Correspondence of Walter Benjamin 1910–1940*, pp. 132–4. See also *Walter Benjamin: Gesammelte Briefe* I, 1910–1918, ed. Henri Lonitz and Christoph Gödde (Frankfurt am Main: Suhrkamp, 1995), pp. 469–71, for passages that have been omitted from the English translation of this letter.

90 ADORNO TO SCHOLEM
FRANKFURT AM MAIN, 10.6.1960

PROF. DR. THEODOR W. ADORNO

FRANKFURT AM MAIN
KETTENHOFWEG 123
10 June 1960

Dear Scholem,

Kindest thanks for your card.

I am not quite sure when I will be returning to Frankfurt. I will be available for certain only from the 5th of September. Miss Olbrich will be able to make hotel reservations with her usual virtuosity. So, please let me know what your plans are.

In other news, in addition to the volume of correspondence, Suhrkamp will publish Benjamin's book of letters, *Deutsche Menschen* [German men and women], as part of the "Bibliothek Suhrkamp" series next year. I am to write an introduction for it, although at most it will wind up being an epilogue. In order to avoid the book being too slim, my suggestion was to include with it the Jochmann text, along with Benjamin's very significant introduction. Due to its nature, this would be an excellent fit for the volume – it is conceived on exactly the same ground as the collection of letters. What do you think of such an addendum? And, first and foremost, do you think that Kraft, with whom Benjamin fell out over the Jochmann matter, will object to it? I can hardly imagine that this would be the case after everything that has happened; but, at the same time, I would be grateful for your advice, since I do not want to tear open this awkward old issue again.

Most cordially
always yours
Adorno

Original: typescript with printed letterhead; Gershom Scholem Archive, The National Library of Israel, Jerusalem.

Deutsche Menschen: The first edition of Walter Benjamin's collection of letters was published under the pseudonym, Detlef Holz. See Detlef Holz, *Deutsche Menschen: Eine Folge von Briefen* [German men and women: a series of letters] (Lucerne: Vita Nova, 1936). The letters collected in this volume are by major German figures and stem from the period between 1783 and 1883. Benjamin first published them at irregular intervals in the *Frankfurter Zeitung* in 1931–2. The first edition published under Benjamin's own name appeared with Suhrkamp in 1962. See Walter Benjamin, "Deutsche Menschen," in *Gesammelte Schriften IV: Kleine Prosa / Baudelaire Übertragungen* [Minor prose / Baudelaire translations], ed. Tillman Rexroth (Frankfurt am Main: Suhrkamp, 1991), pp. 149–233. See also Benjamin, *Werke und Nachlass: Kritische Gesamtausgabe*, Vol. 10: *Deutsche Menschen* [works and writings from the estate: complete critical edition, Vol. 10: German men and women], ed. Momme Brodersen (Frankfurt am Main: Suhrkamp, 2008).

an epilogue: See Adorno, "On Benjamin's *Deutsche Menschen, a Book of Letters*," in *Notes to Literature*, Vol. 2, trans. Shierry Weber Nicholsen (New York: Columbia University Press, 1992), pp. 328–33.

the Jochmann text, along with Benjamin's very significant introduction: See the following letter in this volume.

91 SCHOLEM TO ADORNO
JERUSALEM, 26.6.1960

האוניברסיטה העברית בירושלים
THE HEBREW UNIVERSITY OF JERUSALEM

26 June 1960.

Dear Adorno,

I am writing in response to your question from the 10th of June regarding the inclusion of Benjamin's essay on Jochmann in the new edition of *Deutsche Menschen* [German men and women]. I spoke with Kraft to gauge his reaction and got the following decisive impression: Kraft discovered the man and his writings, pointed them out to Benjamin, lent him the book, and proceeded to produce his own major work on this topic, about the existence of which you're surely in the picture, according to what he told me. He would reconcile himself to such a publication morally, if I may express it thus, if you would duly acknowledge this circumstance in your foreword (or in your afterword – I don't know at which point in the book your remarks are to appear): namely, [first], that Benjamin owes the inspiration for his piece, and, indeed, his acquaintance with the phenomenon of Jochmann, to Werner Kraft; and second, that this author [Kraft] has since produced a major study on this topic. It seems that Kraft wants to publish this extensive work, and for good reason. But if Benjamin's piece were to appear without any reference to him, he would perceive this as a moral curtailment of his own position, which would not be conducive to the publication of his book. Conversely, things would be different for him if you included such a remark in your text as could prove helpful to his cause.

This is as far as my own inquiries have gone. I would advise you to heed this suggestion and to avoid any misunderstanding by settling on the wording of your remark directly with Kraft. I think that in this way all sides and interests would be served in the most dignified and cleanest manner.

With cordial regards
yours
G. Scholem

P.S. – The above refers to B.'s essay. The reissue of [Jochmann's] text would surely have to depend on whether Kraft's book foresees the inclusion of Jochmann's piece. This I do not know. If K. is planning such a re-edition, then you absolutely cannot, in my opinion, interfere with his plans at this point. You would have to obtain his explicit consent so as to avoid a major annoyance.

Original: aerogram (typescript) with printed letterhead and handwritten postscript; Theodor W. Adorno Archive, Frankfurt am Main.

Werner Kraft . . . a major study on this topic: Only in the 1963 edition of Benjamin's *Schriften* did Adorno write the following in a footnote: "At the beginning of the 1930s, Werner Kraft rediscovered Jochmann, an author who had been forgotten in all but name. Impressed by this discovery, in 1939 Walter Benjamin published his essay on "The Regression of Poetry" in the *Zeitschrift für Sozialforschung*, arguing for Jochmann's historico-philosophical significance. Werner Kraft has written a major monograph on Jochmann years ago, which has not been published to date." See Rolf

Tiedemann and Hermann Schweppenhäuser's editorial remarks in Walter Benjamin, *Gesammelte Schriften II.3*, ed. Rolf Tiedemann and Hermann Schweppenhäuser (Frankfurt am Main: Suhrkamp, 1977), pp. 1392–402. For Kraft's book, first published in 1972, see *Carl Gustav Jochmann und sein Kreis: Zur deutschen Geistesgeschichte zwischen Aufklärung und Vormärz* [Carl Gustav Jochmann and his circle: on German intellectual history between the Enlightenment and the "Vormärz"] (Munich: C. H. Beck, 1972).

The reissue of [Jochmann's] text: The text was, in fact, republished by Kraft. See Carl Gustav Jochmann, *Die Rückschritte der Poesie und andere Schriften* [The regression of poetry and other writings], ed. Werner Kraft (Frankfurt am Main: Insel, 1967).

92 ADORNO TO SCHOLEM
FRANKFURT AM MAIN, 4.7.1960

PROF. DR. THEODOR W. ADORNO

FRANKFURT AM MAIN
KETTENHOFWEG 123
4 July 1960

Dear Scholem,

Please excuse the delay in my response to your letter from the 9th of June. I was in Vienna when it arrived, where, at the invitation of the City, I gave the anniversary lecture marking the 100th birthday of Gustav Mahler. Some of it certainly would have been of interest to you. The Mahler book is being typeset.

Regarding the date of your arrival: the 2nd of September, which you suggest, is a bit problematic. It is not impossible that I will be back by then, but it is by no means certain. It depends on arrangements with friends in Switzerland, which I cannot at all foresee at the moment. If you are here on that day, and I am too, then it will be wonderful, of course. However, I would not make our meeting depend on this alone; instead, I would absolutely aim to reserve one day after the 5th of September, since we have a number of important things to discuss. Miss Olbrich will make the necessary arrangements regarding your accommodation.

As for the handling of the Jochmann affair, I envisaged it exactly as you describe. Of course this would require Unseld's agreement; however, I don't think that he would object to anything I might write in my afterword. You can fully reassure Mr. Kraft on this point. I am surely as anxious as he is that this unfortunate story doesn't flare up again. According to Soma Morgenstern, it soured even the last weeks of Benjamin's life. Moreover, I am not even sure if I will actually include the Jochmann piece and Benjamin's introduction to it in the book of letters. Although it fits the bill in spirit and in content, it diverges from it in form (after all, the pieces are not letters), to say nothing of the fact that, in length, it stands out too much from the rest. Naturally, including Benjamin's introduction would make sense only if it were accompanied by the Jochmann piece, which he selected, and which really is quite significant. This too would have to be cleared in advance with Kraft, and I greatly welcome the measures that you are taking on this point. If he should veto it, then I would drop the entire Jochmann plan. I, for one, had hoped to contribute something to a posthumous reconciliation in this matter by the fact that a reference to Kraft's book would benefit its prospects for publication. You are probably not aware of the fact that I already tried some years ago, emphatically, but without success, to find a home for his manuscript.

I have some very good news to report regarding our volume of correspondence. All the letters that Benjamin addressed to Hofmannsthal were found with the latter's heirs, and Mrs. Zimmer has made them available to us. I have already received the originals through Hirsch. This, of course, is quite substantial. Cohrs has also answered in a very friendly manner, promising to hand over his material – he thinks he has something. I haven't been in contact with Albert Salomon since I last saw him in New York some twenty years ago. It would be best if you wrote to him, and to Lewy too. To my knowledge, the open call to submit letters from Benjamin was issued by the publisher some time ago. I had placed the matter in Unseld's hands; hence my silence. For my part, I had limited myself to individual correspondences, and, considering what has happened during the past 25 years, the result is not so bad.

Today I want to ask you how we should go about putting an end to the process of gathering materials. I am of the opinion that it wouldn't be good to draw the matter out for too long. Otherwise, it would be all too easy to get caught up in a kind of bad infinity. If projects of this sort are delayed too much, they are often beset by calamity. My suggestion would be that we conclude the collecting stage at our meeting in September and then discuss guidelines for the selection and problems surrounding the introduction – that is, unless you have any other especially abundant or important sources that you wish to pursue. Benjamin never told me that he was in direct contact with Julien Green, although of course that doesn't mean anything. I can ask Bonnasse to try to get in touch with Green. I don't know whether he is currently living in France or America.

We will be in Sils Maria again at the usual time. Will there be a chance of seeing you there? We would be very glad, if so.

To you both all the best, also from Gretel, from

your old

Adorno

Original: typescript with printed letterhead and Scholem's handwritten note: "J. Green / 52 bis Rue de Varenne / Paris"; Gershom Scholem Archive, The National Library of Israel, Jerusalem.

lecture marking the 100th birthday of Gustav Mahler: Adorno's lecture "Mahler: Wiener Gedenkrede" [Mahler: Viennese memorial speech] first appeared in the *Neue Zürcher Zeitung* in July 1960. It was later included in the collection *Quasi una Fantasia*: *Musikalische Schriften II* [Musical writings II] (1963). See Adorno, "Mahler," in *Quasi una Fantasia: Essays on Modern Music*, trans. Rodney Livingstone (London: Verso, 1998), pp. 81–110.

The Mahler book is being typeset: Adorno's monograph on Mahler first appeared in 1960 as Vol. 61 of the "Bibliothek Suhrkamp" series. See Adorno, *Gustav Mahler: A Musical Physiognomy*, trans. Edmund Jephcott (Chicago: University of Chicago Press, 1996).

According to Soma Morgenstern: Details of Soma Morgenstern's apparently oral remarks have not been verified. The journalist and writer Soma Morgenstern (1890–1976) was friends with Benjamin and Adorno. He was born in Galicia and from 1912 lived in Vienna, where he was the feuilleton correspondent for the *Frankfurter Zeitung*. He fled from Vienna to Paris in 1938. After a period of internment and escape he arrived in New York in 1941. See *The Correspondence of Walter Benjamin 1910–1940*, ed. Theodor W. Adorno and Gershom Scholem, trans. Manfred R. Jacobson and Evelyn M. Jacobson (Chicago: University of Chicago Press, 1994), pp. 599–600, 628; *The Correspondence of Walter Benjamin and Gershom Scholem, 1932–1940*, ed. Gershom Scholem, trans. Gary Smith and Andre Lefevere (New York: Schocken Books, 1989), pp. 253, 386–8. See also *The Complete Correspondence of Walter Benjamin and Theodor W. Adorno, 1928–1940*, ed. Henri Lonitz, trans. Nicholas Walker (Cambridge, MA: Harvard University Press, 2001), p. 161.

Mrs. Zimmer: Christiane von Hofmannsthal (1902–1987) married the Indologist Heinrich Zimmer (1890–1943), in 1928. They immigrated in 1938 to England and in 1940 to the USA, where Heinrich Zimmer taught at Columbia University.

whether he is currently living in France or America: Julien Green left France in 1940 and went to the USA. In 1945 he returned to Paris, where he lived until his death. However, he refused to adopt French citizenship and remained a US national.

93 SCHOLEM TO ADORNO
JERUSALEM, 14.7.1960

האוניברסיטה העברית בירושלים
THE HEBREW UNIVERSITY OF JERUSALEM

Jerusalem, 14.7.1960.

Dear Adorno,

Many thanks for your letter from the 4th of July. My assumption was that we would read or go through the materials together, rather than merely deciding on guidelines for selection. The latter, of course, could easily be achieved in one day, whereas the former could not. In any case, I have now confirmed my reservation at the Park Hotel on Wiesenhüttenplatz from the 2nd to the 8th of September, which makes the reservation at the Hotel Palmengarten obsolete. Please kindly convey this information to Miss Olbrich and ask if she would be so good as to cancel the reservation she made for me there. Should you only be available from the 5th, I could still make good use of the time in Frankfurt, for instance, by dictating the letters that remain to be transcribed to someone, who could perhaps be provided to me by Suhrkamp. I don't think that I'll finish with the transcriptions of the letters before I come. In any case, I'll bring along a selection of the un-transcribed material.

By the way, Julien Green's address is: 52 bis, Rue de Varennes, Paris.

After I received your letter, I spoke with Kraft about the Jochmann matter. He would have no objection to the inclusion of the Jochmann text along with the essay, as long as he can be assured that the circumstances that I outlined in my last letter will be duly highlighted in a manner that is acceptable to him. Should you decide to include these pieces in the projected volume, it would be best if you wrote to Kraft directly, referring to my conversation with him on this matter. His address is Alfassi St. 31.

I am happy to hear that you will be receiving Benjamin's letters to Hofmannsthal. I am unclear as to whether you have the complete correspondence with Rang. I only have the extracts that his son sent to Werner Kraft at the time – very interesting, of course. I will see Albert Salomon in New York, where I'm going for a week in October.

I will be here until the 14th of August. It would be best if we could speak on the phone some evening after the 15th of August once I have arrived in Ascona. We can make further arrangements then. To the extent that I have them, I'll bring the materials with me. I fear that I won't have a chance to come up to Sils Maria this time, although miracles have been known to happen – especially to those who wait for them. Let me conclude with this bit of untimely theology and also with cordial regards for your wife and you.

yours,

G. Scholem

Original: aerogram (typescript) with printed letterhead; Theodor W. Adorno Archive, Frankfurt am Main.

Rue de Varennes: Scholem mistakenly added an *s* to the address by hand.

94 ADORNO TO SCHOLEM
FRANKFURT AM MAIN, 7.11.1960

PROF. DR. THEODOR W. ADORNO

FRANKFURT AM MAIN
KETTENHOFWEG 123
7 November 1960

Dear Scholem,

I am very grateful to you for your book. It's lovely that these pieces are finally united; among them, I am missing only the one on messianism. Out of all of your publications in the past few years, it has meant the most to me personally; but, after all, the series will be continued. Moreover, it is surely true that, wherever there is an inner continuity of production, as is the case in this volume, such individual pieces acquire a completely different status; they begin to sparkle differently than when they appear in isolation. This struck me greatly upon re-reading [the pieces collected here].

Meanwhile, my Mahler book has hopefully gotten into your hands. Even though it is perhaps excessively close to the material, and is therefore too specialized in musical terms, I could imagine that this work will touch on things that matter a great deal to you, albeit from unexpected angles. I would therefore be especially happy if you undertook to read it. I have by no means gained the right distance from the book yet; but, for me to consider it successful, even the purely musical analyses must point beyond themselves; the technical facts must be made to speak.

Unseld has, in the meantime, published the notice regarding the Benjamin correspondence in the most important journals and newspapers. Incidentally, I have some very good news to report regarding our plan. At my request, Pollock, during his short trip to America, looked in New York and Los Angeles, and was able to dig up and bring back all of Benjamin's letters addressed to the Institute *qua* Institute, which is to say to Horkheimer and Pollock – quite a considerable bundle. Gretel is currently sorting through it and pre-selecting such things as might be suitable for publication according to our guidelines. It is already clear that, despite everything that has happened, we have more material worthy of publication than we can accommodate in the projected volume. The problem is thus no longer the acquisition, but the selection of material. This has its comforts, of course.

May I remind you that you wanted to write to Ernst Schoen? Without question, it would be better if this came from you than from me. He seems to have *gravamina* against me, which are connected to my anti-Soviet position, whereas he will hardly at all associate you with this issue.

All that is cordial to you and Fanya, also from Gretel,

always yours,

Adorno

Meanwhile I received a number of photocopies of letters to Bernard von Brentano – among them some interesting ones.

Original: typescript with printed letterhead and handwritten postscript; Gershom Scholem Archive, The National Library of Israel, Jerusalem.

your book: Scholem's *Zur Kabbala und ihrer Symbolik* came out with Rhein Verlag in Zurich, 1960. See *On the Kabbalah and its Symbolism*, trans. Ralph Manheim (New York: Schocken Books, 1996).

the one on messianism: Scholem's lecture at the 1959 Eranos conference was first published as "Zum Verständnis der messianischen Idee im Judentum" [Toward an understanding of the messianic idea in Judaism], in *Eranos-Jahrbuch 1959*, Vol. 29: *Die Erneuerung des Menschen* [The renewal of man] ed. Olga Fröbe-Kapteyn (Zurich: Rhein, 1960), pp. 193–239. See "Toward an Understanding of the Messianic Idea in Judaism," in *The Messianic Idea in Judaism*, trans. Michael A. Meyer (New York: Schocken Books, 1971), pp. 1–36.

Pollock: See letter no. 7 in this volume and the relevant note.

Bernard von Brentano: The writer, playwright and journalist Bernard von Brentano (1901–1964) worked at the *Frankfurter Zeitung*'s Berlin office from 1925 to 1930 and in Moscow from 1930 to 1932. In 1933 he immigrated to Switzerland, where he worked for the *Neue Zürcher Zeitung* and the *Weltwoche*.

95 SCHOLEM TO ADORNO
JERUSALEM, 28.11.1960

Jerusalem, 28 November 1960

Dear Adorno,

I thank you sincerely for the receipt of your Mahler. I will immerse myself in it, to the extent that my meagre powers permit, so as to follow the traces of your allusions. Regrettably, at the moment, I am not entirely capable of such concentration, since Fania has unfortunately come down with an eye disease, which is putting a strain on what little leisure time I have. She has an infection of the iris, which is really quite unpleasant.

Of course I wrote to Ernst Schoen, as we discussed, and – you will laugh – also received an answer, which arrived last week. It is a long, rather friendly letter, in which you come up only implicitly. He wrote that he has letters from Walter Benjamin dating from 1913 to 1920, of which he is prepared to give me about a dozen, "putting into loyal hands by way of a loan those letters, namely, which could be of 'general interest,' theoretically speaking." I will respond of course by saying that, in keeping with what was agreed with Suhrkamp, we do not want to exclude personal matters, and that he should send me all of the material. He writes: "I am prepared to loan you these letters, whereby I will entrust the selection of relevant material from among them to your critical editorship, on the sole condition that no one besides you touches them. Please do let me know whether you agree to this proposal." Needless to say, I will agree to this condition, which, I suspect, also reflects your views. This way we will actually get our hands on something. I will then have copies made here. I'll write to him in the coming days. By the way, he shared with me the biographical information that he and his wife are finally leaving Germany in March or April and relocating to northern Italy. I'll try to set up a rendezvous with him over the summer.

Incidentally, I would be interested to know whether you or Horkheimer ever published any arguments with Lukács. I cannot recall having read anything of that sort in the *Zeitschrift für Sozialforschung*. Chronologically, this would presumably fall into an earlier period. I am asking because I have just collated my *Lukácsiana* from the various sections of my library, which took me on a metaphysical slide from the loftiest spheres into the abyss of chatter. It occurred to me, while browsing, how utterly nebulous the profound essays from *Forms of the Soul of* 1910 would seem to a contemporary reader. That is all for today. Cordial regards,

yours

Gershom Scholem

Original: aerogram (typescript); Theodor W. Adorno Archive, Frankfurt am Main. First published in Gershom Scholem, *Briefe II: 1948–1970*, ed. Thomas Sparr (Munich: C. H. Beck, 1995), pp. 74–5.

for the receipt of your Mahler: Scholem's copy contains a dedication from Adorno, which reads: "My dear Scholem, as a small token of heartfelt attachment, from his Adorno / Frankfurt, September 1960."

I wrote to Ernst Schoen: See Scholem's letters to Ernst Schoen, dated 27.10.1960 and 28.11.1960. For the former, see Scholem, *Briefe II: 1948–1970*, ed. Thomas Sparr (Munich: C. H. Beck, 1995), pp. 70–3; for the latter, see: *Gershom Scholem: A Life in Letters*, ed. and trans. Anthony David Skinner (Cambridge, MA: Harvard University Press, 2002), pp. 379–381.

Forms of the Soul: Scholem's rendering of the title. See György Lukács, *Soul and Form*, ed. John T. Sanders and Katie Terezakis, trans. Anna Bostock (New York: Columbia University Press, 2010). The first German edition appeared as Georg Lukács, *Die Seele und die Formen* (Berlin: Egon Fleischel, 1911).

96 ADORNO TO SCHOLEM
FRANKFURT AM MAIN, 2.12.1960

PROF. DR. THEODOR W. ADORNO

FRANKFURT AM MAIN
KETTENHOFWEG 123
2 December 1960

Dear Scholem,

Kindest thanks for your letter.

The thing with Schoen is really very odd. I never did anything to harm him, nothing that could even remotely be interpreted that way. I lack any key for [understanding] his behavior, and I do not consider him so stupid as to project our political differences onto our personal relationship. It's nothing new that, over the course of a life, one can lose old friends; but it is somewhat hurtful that it should be so pointless and random. Once our heist is completed, would it be too much to ask you to interpellate, should the opportunity present itself? Incidentally, I am of the opinion that, once you have made a selection of the letters addressed to Schoen, I should – at the very least – see them, as has been the case with all of the other material. Since Schoen knows very well that we are preparing the edition together, he can hardly object to this. Of course, nothing in the letters will be changed. It's in the nature of the work that, under certain circumstances, we will omit passages that appear to be too personal or are otherwise irrelevant. What's more, such omissions would have to be indicated by means of ellipses. In the meantime, the public call has been issued very prominently in the *Neue Rundschau*. However, I have yet to receive anything but a few letters to Bernard Brentano, which, I believe, I've already told you about.

Two years ago, I wrote and published a major and very encumbered piece directed against Lukács, entitled "Extorted Reconciliation," which appeared in *Monat* (November or December 1958). I cannot imagine that I didn't send it to you; or perhaps it got lost in the mail? In case you don't know it, or in case you don't have a copy, I will, of course, send you one. It will also be included in my new book of essays, the second volume of *Notes to Literature*, which I have just completed with a piece on Beckett. The volume will come out in the fall of 1961. In substance, I completely agree with you on Lukács. My thoughts on his later work are included in the essay; but, as seems to be the rule, the earlier things are also affected by the later ones and become bad. Even a book such as the *Theory of the Novel*, which once greatly impressed us all, shows a reactionary potential today, which has fully unfolded only through the blessings of the Eastern bloc. I also find *Soul and Form* to be unbearably high-minded drivel, à la 1910. His best work probably remains the piece on reification from *History and Class Consciousness*. The whole book has just been reissued in French, and Lukács immediately rushed to disown it with insults that were both zealous and fatuous. The dangerous thing about this man is that the prestige of his early work is sufficiently great to earn his later writings a degree of attention and respect, even if they are really nothing but M*u*rxist pulp fiction. This includes the huge tome about Hegel, which professes to discover things that everyone who has seriously read the Nohl edition of the early theological writings already knows. It could handily have been said in an essay of 30 pages, instead of being manipulated to reach a quota of 700 pages or more. Well, in my text, you will find that I have said these things as ruthlessly as is necessary. Since the trash that he has been producing for close to forty years is still read as revelation by sections of academic youth, I believed that I shouldn't bow to the dominant suggestion: "not a word against Lukács." After all, he attacked all of us – and especially me – in his book on Socialist Realism, and I do not see why I should put up with his junk in silence, only for no one to lay a finger on him.

We are sad to hear that Fanya is unwell and wish her eyes a speedy and complete recovery.

Most cordially, also from Gretel,

always yours

Adorno

Original: typescript with printed letterhead; Gershom Scholem Archive, The National Library of Israel, Jerusalem.

"Extorted Reconciliation": Adorno's critical confrontation with Lukács's book, *The Meaning of Contemporary Realism*, first appeared as "Erpreßte Versöhnung: Zu Georg Lukács *Wider den mißverstandenen Realismus*" [Extorted reconciliation: on Georg Lukács's *The Meaning of Contemporary Realism*], *Der Monat*, 11/122 (November 1958), pp. 37–49. In 1961 it was included in the second volume of *Notes to Literature*. See Theodor W. Adorno, "Extorted Reconciliation," in *Notes to Literature*, Vol. 2, trans. Shierry Weber Nicholsen (New York: Columbia University Press, 1992), pp. 216–40.

my new book of essays, the second volume of Notes to Literature: The second volume of Adorno's *Notes to Literature* appeared in Berlin and Frankfurt am Main as Vol. 71 of the "Bibliothek Suhrkamp" series in 1961.

just completed with a piece on Beckett: See Adorno, "Trying to Understand *Endgame*," in *Notes to Literature*, Vol. 1, trans. Shierry Weber Nicholsen (New York: Columbia University Press, 1991), pp. 241–76.

Theory of the Novel: Adorno is referring to Georg Lukács's book *Theory of the Novel*, which was first published in Stuttgart in 1916 as a special edition of the journal *Zeitschrift für Ästhetik und allgemeine Kunstwissenschaft*. The work was republished in the form of a book by Paul Cassirer, Berlin, in 1920. See Lukács, *Theory of the Novel: A Historico-Philosophical Essay on the Forms of Great Epic Literature*, trans. Anna Bostock (Cambridge, MA: MIT Press, 1974). In this influential text, Lukács uses the concept of "second nature" in a manner that decisively shaped Critical Theory. Adorno cites Lukács's book in his early lecture on "The Idea of Natural History" from 1932, in Robert Hullot-Kentor, *Things Beyond Resemblance: Collected Essays on Theodor W. Adorno* (New York: Columbia University Press, 2006), pp. 252–69.

the piece on reification from History and Class Consciousness: First published as Georg Lukács, "Die Verdinglichung und das Bewußtsein des Proletariats," in *Geschichte und Klassenbewußtsein: Studien über marxistische Dialektik* (Berlin: Malik, 1923). See "Reification and the Consciousness of the Proletariat," in *History and Class Consciousness: Studies in Marxist Dialectics*, trans. Rodney Livingstone (Cambridge, MA: MIT Press, 1971), pp. 83–222.

The whole book has just been published in French ... insults: Georg Lukács, *Histoire et conscience de classe: Essais de dialectique marxiste*, trans. Kostas Axelos and Jacqueline Bois (Paris: Éditions de Minuit, 1960). Lukács responded to the French edition of this work, which was published against his will, with the "insults" referenced here, in "Une declaration de G. Lukács concernant l'edition française d'*Histoire et Conscience de Classe*" [A statement by G. Lukács on the French edition of *History and Class Consciousness*], *Arguments*, IV/20 (1960), p. 61.

Murxist: As in the original.

the huge tome about Hegel: See György Lukács, *The Young Hegel: Studies in the Relations between Dialectics and Economics*, trans. Rodney Livingstone (Cambridge, MA: MIT Press, 1976).

the Nohl edition: See *Hegels theologische Jugendschriften: Nach den Handschriften der Königlichen Bibliothek in Berlin* [Hegel's early theological writings: according to the manuscripts of the Royal Library in Berlin], ed. Dr. Hermann Nohl (Tübingen 1907). For an English edition, see G. W. F. Hegel, *Early Theological Writings*, trans. T. M. Knox (Philadelphia: University of Pennsylvania Press, 1975).

book on Socialist Realism: See Lukács, *The Meaning of Contemporary Realism*, trans. John Mander and Necke Mander (London: Merlin Press, 1972).

97 SCHOLEM TO ADORNO
JERUSALEM, 6.12.1960

Jerusalem, 6.XII.1960

Dear Adorno,

Your letter of 2 XII already arrived yesterday, on my birthday, and I thank you very much for it.

As with everything else, transcripts of the letters sent to me by Schoen will, of course, be presented to you. His condition was formulated so as to suggest that he does not wish for "somebody else," besides me, to see the originals. This I promised him. If all goes well, we should have no difficulties. If the opportunity to meet him in person should present itself, I will of course interpellate as to his personal disposition toward you. In the meantime, I am waiting for the parcel that he promised.

I did not, at any rate, receive your essay on Lukács. I think it will suffice for me to wait until it appears in your new book next autumn. If you happen to have a spare copy of *Der Monat*, which you would care to send to me, I will, of course, be very happy. As I recall, the *Theory of the Novel* is so profound that it comes out again at the other end. When I first read it, I did not understand one syllable. However, that has to do with my limited powers of reception. Later I had a few sparks of understanding. In 1952, I inherited the exceedingly rare book from the literary estate of a friend. The huge tome about Hegel always annoyed me. I worked out that one could reduce the volume of the book by roughly half simply by leaving out the ornamental epithets that accompany every mention of Dilthey.

Unfortunately, the condition of my wife's eyes has not improved and she's very depressed. An iris infection is especially unpleasant, even with the present-day magic potions that she's swallowing.

With cordial regards,

yours,

G. Scholem

Original: aerogram (typescript); Theodor Adorno Archive, Frankfurt am Main.

98 ADORNO TO SCHOLEM
FRANKFURT AM MAIN, 14.12.1960

PROF. DR. THEODOR W. ADORNO

FRANKFURT AM MAIN
KETTENHOFWEG 123
14 December 1960

Dear Scholem,

Yesterday, to my great horror, I read the announcement of Ernst Schoen's death in the *Frankfurter Zeitung*. There can be no doubt as to the identity. Hansi signed the announcement, which was formulated in an extremely ostentatious way. It's a truly uncanny coincidence. What is especially strange is that Hansi writes that he died as a victim of National Socialism. He emigrated, after all, just like me. We saw each other a lot in England, and, aside from the material difficulties posed for us by the first years of immigration, he got through this time fairly well. The only explanation might be that he really did suffer from hunger during those years and that this damaged his health, or that some Nazis did something nasty to him now, although I can hardly imagine that. In all likelihood, Hansi, who is a thoroughly irresponsible character, wanted to appear important and to elevate Ernst, without thinking at all about the gravity of her formulation.

After the strange way that both the Schoens acted towards me in recent years, I am unsure as to whether or not I should express my condolences. To remain silent runs counter to an old friendship; to write could be tactless and may appear as ingratiating. Please give me your advice.

I am sad that the matter of Fanya's eyes is so bothersome and I sincerely wish her a speedy recovery.

All the best to you both, also from Gretel,

Your old

Adorno

Original: typescript with printed letterhead; Gershom Scholem Archive, The National Library of Israel, Jerusalem.

Hansi: Johanna (Hansi) Schoen, née Countess Rogendorf (1898–1992), was Ernst Schoen's wife. See letter no. 40 in this volume; see also Sabine Schiller-Lerg, "Ernst Schoen (1894–1960): Ein Freund überlebt: Erste biographische Einblicke in seinen Nachlass" [Ernst Schoen (1894–1960): a friend survives: first biographical insights into his estate], in *Global Benjamin: Internationaler Walter-Benjamin-Kongress 1992*, ed. Klaus Garber and Ludger Rehm (Munich: Fink, 1999), pp. 982–1013, here 993-4.

99 SCHOLEM TO ADORNO
JERUSALEM, 20.12.1960

האוניברסיטה העברית בירושלים
THE HEBREW UNIVERSITY OF JERUSALEM

Jerusalem, 20 Dec., 1960.

Dear Adorno,

Yesterday, along with your letter, I received a printed copy of Ernst Schoen's obituary from Berlin, presumably from his wife. All it says is: "A poet and friend of mankind is mourned by all." I will write to her today and can only hope that she will send the letters promised to me by her husband. My letter to him left here on the 28th of November, so it should have reached him just a week or so before he died. I don't know what he died of; I suspect a heart attack. He was 66 years old. Regarding your question as to whether or not you should express your condolences, I would absolutely advise you to do so. In a case where whatever one does could be the wrong thing, it's only right that one should follow one's immediate, positive feeling. If his wife does not like your letter, or, indeed, any utterance from you, then she will remain silent; but under no circumstances should you remain silent.

By the way, Mr. Beno Rothenberg turned up here at the office of the dean with a letter from your dean of philosophy, dated June 1960, which indicates that the dean's office is prepared to permit Mr. Rothenberg to repeat his doctoral viva. Apparently, the dean's office knew nothing about your note from April 1960, which we have here. Wouldn't it be advisable to officially draw the attention of the dean's office to your letter in some appropriate way, indicating that you felt compelled to write it after Mr. R. circulated that he had completed his doctorate in Frankfurt? Our dean, Prof. Rotenstreich, who knows R. quite well, did not hold back in telling him what he thought of his lying and fraudulent behavior. R. declared to our dean that he has the intention of going to Frankfurt this summer and proceeded to tell all manner of tall tales – for instance, that he was not told ahead of the viva what he'd be examined on. Of course, Rotenstreich told him flat out that this was a lie, which contradicts the regular protocols of such an examination. Incidentally, Rotenstreich says that the thesis really is R.'s work, but that he wrote it in the 30s, perhaps as a seminar paper for Bergmann, the contents of which he himself, apparently, no longer knows.

My wife's eyes are better now and we hope she'll make a complete recovery.

With cordial regards to you both,

yours,

G. Scholem

Original: aerogram (typescript with printed letterhead; Theodor W. Adorno Archive, Frankfurt am Main.

100 ADORNO TO SCHOLEM FRANKFURT AM MAIN, 9.1.1961

PROF. DR. THEODOR W. ADORNO

FRANKFURT AM MAIN
KETTENHOFWEG 123
9 January 1961

Dear Mr. Scholem,

Once more regarding Rothenberg: the dean told me that Rothenberg did not contact him again. Presumably he spread this around in Israel only to convey the impression that his case was still in progress. In any case, he is brazen enough to dare to turn up again. In order to deflect a supremely embarrassing situation for all parties, I'd be especially grateful if you – or the chair of your faculty, who recently spoke with R. – could explain to him, in a friendly manner, that he would be well advised definitively to abandon his Frankfurt plans. You'd be doing me a real favor.

I gladly followed your advice and wrote what was in my heart to Hansi Schoen.

I'm deep into my text against Heidegger, in which I do not mince words – not even politically.

To you and Fanya all that is cordial, also from Gretel,

your old

Adorno

Original: typescript with printed letterhead; Gershom Scholem Archive, The National Library of Israel, Jerusalem.

text against Heidegger: Adorno is referring to *The Jargon of Authenticity*, which was published in 1964. See *The Jargon of Authenticity*, trans. Knut Tarnowski and Frederic Will (London: Routledge & Kegan Paul, 1973).

101 SCHOLEM TO ADORNO
JERUSALEM, 16.1.1961

16 Jan. 1961

Dear Adorno,

The dean has spoken to Mr. R. and has advised him not to embark on any adventures in Frankfurt. I do not know whether it will be of any use. I, myself, maintain no relationship with this particular champion!

I am still waiting for a response from Mrs. Schoen regarding my request to send me Walter Benjamin's letters, if possible.

What I understand of your Mahler book, I am enjoying!

By the way, I'd like to arrange my holidays in August so that I might be in Sils Maria from the 3rd to the 14th of August. If you and your wife were planning to go there again, it would be a good opportunity to meet and discuss the letters. I have a strong desire to breathe that clean air again, and I have the time for it.

As you buckle down with Heidegger, I'm trying to wrap up my *Origins of the Kabbalah*, finally, after 40 years of preparation.

Cordial regards to you both,

yours,

G. Scholem

Original: manuscript; Theodor W. Adorno Archive, Frankfurt am Main.

Origins of the Kabbalah: Scholem's *Ursprung und Anfänge der Kabbala* [Origins and beginnings of the Kabbalah] was first published in Berlin in 1962 as the third volume of the series "Studia Judaica: Forschungen zur Wissenschaft des Judentums" [Studia Judaica: research on the science of Judaism]. *Origins of the Kabbalah*, ed. R. J. Zwi Werblowsky, trans. Allan Arkush (Princeton, NJ: Princeton University Press, 1990).

102 ADORNO TO SCHOLEM
FRANKFURT AM MAIN, 7.3.1961

PROF. DR. THEODOR W. ADORNO

FRANKFURT AM MAIN
KETTENHOFWEG 123
7 March 1961

Dear Scholem,

I am enclosing a carbon copy of a letter from the unspeakable Mr. Rothenberg, along with my dilatory response. I would be grateful if, by the time I return from my lecture tour, you could let me know, if need be, after consulting with the dean, how I can rid myself of this gentleman once and for all. I would be especially pleased if, by this time, I could receive some official document allowing us to conclude this matter, from the side of the faculty, in a definitively negative way. It is typical of Mr. Rothenberg that he has the insolence to repeat that the oral viva is a mere formality in Israel; what he is withholding is that this custom presupposes a familiarity with the candidate which is built up over many years through their participation in seminars. By contrast, and one must say, fortunately, Mr. Rothenberg was unknown to all of us. Through this small omission, Mr. Rothenberg's statement, though true in itself, turned into a fraudulent move.

The notice on Benjamin in *Aufbau* is unspeakable. It's as if Karl Kraus had invented it, but as is well known, he did not invent anything; rather, precisely because of this, what he quoted became an invention. If you send a firmly worded response to them, I will be thrilled and will sign it. Perhaps you could send it to me: from the 13th to the 22nd of March I'll be in Paris (Hôtel Lutetia, 49, Boulevard Raspail), and from the 23rd of March until the 16th of April I'll be in Rome (Villa degli Aranci, Via Oriani). The joy of the trip, and of the lovely invitation from the Collège de France, is sullied somewhat by the miserable state that I find myself in of being totally overworked. During the past semester, I did the absolutely insane thing of writing a very encumbered text on ontology and dialectics, in addition to everything else. It is, in fact, finished; but so am I. It will be published next year, either on its own or in combination with other dialectical meditations – I have high hopes for it.

Be well; please accept the most cordial regards, also from Gretel, and also to Fanya, and write a line soon.

Your loyal

Adorno

Original: typescript with printed letterhead and copy of the letter from Beno Rothenberg to Adorno, dated 5.3.1961, as well as Adorno's response, dated 7.3.1961; Gershom Scholem Archive, The National Library of Israel, Jerusalem.

a carbon copy of a letter from the unspeakable Mr. Rothenberg, along with my dilatory response: Rothenberg had asked Adorno for a private meeting regarding his "rehabilitation." He assured Adorno that he never claimed to have completed a doctorate. Adorno responded that he had to "ascertain some things here, and to correspond with Israel," before being able to give him a binding answer.

my lecture tour: During his trip, Adorno kept a diary with short entries. See *Adorno: Eine Bildmonographie* [A monograph in images], ed. Henri Lonitz, Christoph Gödde, and Michael Schwarz (Frankfurt am Main: Suhrkamp, 2003), pp. 253–73.

invitation from the Collège de France: The three lectures on ontology and dialectics that Adorno held at the Collège de France are part of the preliminary work for *Negative Dialectics* (1966). The first part of the book stems from the first two lectures. See Adorno, "Part One: Relation to Ontology," in *Negative Dialectics*, trans. E. B. Ashton (London: Routledge, 1973), pp. 61–131. In the "Notes" to his book (not included in the English translation), Adorno writes that "a thoroughly reworked and expanded [version of the third lecture] is the basis of the second part." See "Notiz" [Note], in *Gesammelte Schriften 6: Negative Dialektik / Jargon der Eigentlichkeit* [Negative Dialectics/ The Jargon of Authenticity] (Frankfurt am Main: 1974), p. 409. See also Adorno, "Part Two: Concepts and Categories," in *Negative Dialectics*, pp. 134–207.

with other dialectical meditations: The third chapter of the third part of *Negative Dialectics* is titled "Meditations on Metaphysics." See Adorno, "III: Meditations on Metaphysics," in *Negative Dialectics*, trans. E. B. Ashton (London: Routledge, 1973), pp. 361–408.

103 SCHOLEM TO ADORNO
JERUSALEM, 2.4.1961

2 April 1961

Dear Adorno,

Many thanks for your letter of the 7th of March. I can send you no official document regarding Rothenberg because Mr. R's fibbing was not "official" in nature, so to speak, but unfolded in a semi-private way. He told the faculty secretary, Mr. Abiram, that he passed his doctorate and that, in order to obtain his diploma, he needed only to submit a character reference from the police in Jerusalem, who were causing him difficulties (!!!). He backpedalled only after being confronted about having lied – he had presented the invitation to the oral examination as proof! – and then he claimed that he had just been too embarrassed to tell the truth. (He wanted to sound out whether they'd admit him to the doctoral programme in archaeology in Jerusalem, and so he hoped to make an "impression."[)] The archaeologist here, Prof. Mazar (the rector), whom he mentioned to you, rejected this out of hand. I showed the letters from you and R. to the dean (Rottenstreich) who said that, if R. had wanted to create the impression (his formulation was, admittedly, very cautious) that either he or Mazar had, in conversation, encouraged him to pursue this matter further, then it was a shameless lie. Rottenstreich told me, moreover, that he had sharply rebuked R. for his fraudulent behavior, which is in keeping with previous incidents, and had advised him to desist, once and for all, from this kind of behaviour. The unfortunate thing is that R., who is a very good photographer, is as addicted to titles as he is unreliable; but clearly this cannot be helped. That's all that I can report on this matter.

I am going to London tomorrow morning. My new address is on the envelope. What do you think about a meeting in Sils Maria between the 1st and the 14th of August? I could use this time (before Ascona) to relax.

Have a good rest, and greet yourself and your wife warmly,

from your G. Scholem

Original: aerogram (manuscript); Theodor W. Adorno Archive, Frankfurt am Main.

Mr. Abiram: The archeologist Joseph Aviram (b. 1916) was secretary of the Faculty of the Humanities at the Hebrew University in Jerusalem from 1954 to 1969.

Prof. Mazar: The archeologist and historian Benjamin Mazar (1906–1995) was one of the founders of biblical archeology at the Hebrew University in Jerusalem. From 1952 to 1961 he was rector of the university.

Rottenstreich: Scholem's spelling.

London . . . new address: G. Scholem / Warburg Institute / Woburn Square / London W.C.1.

104 SCHOLEM TO ADORNO
LONDON, 9.5.1961

London, 9 May

Dear Adorno,

I hope that you have returned to work somewhat rested, and I also hope that we will be able to meet. I have rented a room at the Margna in Sils Maria from the 1st to the 14th of August and will be very glad if I see you both there.

I spoke to Dora again here and told her about our volume of Benjamin's correspondence. This time she told me a different story, namely, that she hardly had anything with her in San Remo – the older letters stayed in Berlin and were lost because she had to flee (which, to my knowledge, is not true – she had lots of time to prepare for her departure) – and that what she did have was thrown away by the people in San Remo after she left. Dora is now over 71 and apparently her memory has suffered in recent years. In any case, I see no chance of us getting anything out of her. That aside, she was very happy to hear about the project. She promised that she'd send me the address for Herbert Baumont, formerly Blumenthal, who is now an English teacher in Rome, although she has yet to keep this promise. *I keep pressing her.** The situation is not helped by the fact that a deep rift has emerged recently between her and her son, the reasons for which I have yet to understand.

With cordial regards to your wife and you,

yours,

Gershom Scholem

Original: typescript; Theodor W. Adorno Archive, Frankfurt am Main.

San Remo: Walter Benjamin's ex-wife, Dora Sophie Benjamin, ran a guest-house in San Remo, which was initially called Villa Emily and soon thereafter Villa Verde. Walter Benjamin stayed there on several occasions after 1934. At the start of 1939, Dora and her son, Stefan Benjamin, fled from San Remo to London. See *The Complete Correspondence of Walter Benjamin and Theodor W. Adorno, 1928–1940*, ed. Henri Lonitz, trans. Nicholas Walker (Cambridge, MA: Harvard University Press, 2001), pp. 58, 279.

Baumont: Scholem is referring to Herbert Belmore.

105 ADORNO TO SCHOLEM
FRANKFURT AM MAIN, 10.5.1961

PROF. DR. THEODOR W. ADORNO

FRANKFURT AM MAIN
KETTENHOFWEG 123
10 May 1961

Dear Scholem,

Your letter of the 2nd of April reached me in Sicily during my long trip, which included, among other things, my lectures

* Original in English.

on ontology and dialectics at the Collège de France and at the University of Rome. I hope that you will understand and forgive me for responding only today; in addition to being rich in beautiful impressions, the trip was exhausting as a result of my many academic commitments.

I gave your letter to our dean today to determine whether there are legal grounds for preventing Mr. Rothenberg from repeating his exam. After careful examination of the university's laws, Mr. Rammelmeyer is of the opinion that this is not possible, since Mr. Rothenberg was originally admitted [to the examination], and since the charges against him – God knows they are justified – were never submitted in a legally binding form. From your letter, I fear that you also see no such option. All that is left, then, is the hope that someone in Jerusalem, once again, can have an effect upon Rothenberg and can impede his plans. The whole thing is especially distressing, since nobody wants to fail someone who was persecuted by the Nazis, of course, and undoubtedly Mr. Rothenberg is shrewdly exploiting precisely this for his own benefit.

We are very much looking forward to seeing you again in August. As has become our custom, we will trot up to Sils Maria like mountain cattle, probably at the end of July, and will remain there throughout August. We'll be staying at the Waldhaus again. Perhaps you could let me know if your plans remain the same, and also if and when in September we can start our discussions regarding Benjamin's letters.

I received no response from Hansi Schoen to my letter.

Most cordially, also from Gretel,

always yours,

Adorno

I just received your letter from the 9th of May – kindest thanks. A Mr. Belmore contacted me in Rome, introducing himself as an old friend of Benjamin's, and as someone who is in possession of letters. Perhaps he and Beaumont (Blumenthal) are one and the same. I have his address. I am very sorry to hear about Dora.

Most cordially!

Original: typescript with printed letterhead and handwritten postscript, as well as Scholem's handwritten note in Hebrew, reading "14.6.61 עניתי (answered)"; Gershom Scholem Archive, The National Library of Israel, Jerusalem.

Mr. Rammelmeyer: The Slavist and literary scholar Alfred Rammelmeyer (1910–1995) was a professor of Slavic philology at the University of Frankfurt from 1958.

106 SCHOLEM TO ADORNO
LONDON, 14.6.1961

UNIVERSITY OF LONDON
THE WARBURG INSTITUTE
WOBURN SQUARE, LONDON W.C.1
TELEPHONE LANGHAM 9663

14 June 1961

Dear Adorno,

I am just writing to you now since I needed first to get a clearer sense of my plans, in accordance with the state of my work.

I will be at the Hotel Margna from the 1st to the 14th of August, where we will enjoy some days off. The question is whether we can also devote some time to W. B.'s letters then. Besides that, I am available for a meeting with you to do preliminary work during the week of the 8th to the 15th of October, and I'm prepared to come to Frkfrt. during this time – September won't work. To be on the safe side, I've already made a reservation at the Park Hotel (where I stayed last year). Will you also be able to set your plans accordingly? I might try to cover the expenses of the trip by giving a lecture in Frkfrt. and perhaps another one in Düsseldorf. I just needed to retract my rejection of an invitation to speak in Germany from the "Friends of the University of Jerusalem." I have to be in Zurich from the 17th to the 20th of October and must return to Jerusalem from there. This is the best and most efficient way for me to fit in a visit to Frkfrt.

I am going to Oxford for a week tomorrow, but I hope to see Mrs. Schoen when I get back to London; she has written to me. Today I am giving a big lecture here on "Buber's Interpretation of Hasidism," which I could possibly repeat in Germany. (A sharp, albeit polite, critique).

I am enclosing a copy of the letter from W.B. that Hannah Arendt made available to me. It's practically the last one we have from him, and, with its fabulous quote from Rochefoucauld, it fits well at the end of our collection. It's the only one she has.

Cordial regards to you both

yours,

Scholem

Original: manuscript with printed letterhead; Theodor W. Adorno Archive, Frankfurt am Main.

"Buber's Interpretation of Hasidism": A modified version of Scholem's lecture at the Institute of Jewish Religion at University College London was first published as "Martin Buber's Hasidism – A Critique," *Commentary*,

32/4 (October 1961), pp. 305–16. See also "Martin Buber's Interpretation of Hasidism," in *The Messianic Idea in Judaism and Other Essays on Jewish Spirituality* (New York: Schocken Books, 1971), pp. 228–50.

fabulous quote from Rochefoucauld: Walter Benjamin's letter to Hannah Arendt from Lourdes (8.7.1940) contains a quote from François de la Rochefoucauld's *Portrait du Cardinal de Retz* (1675): "La paresse l'a soutenu avec gloire, durant plusiers années, dans l'obscurité d'une vie errante et cachée." Benjamin's letter to Arendt was included in the two-volume collection. See *The Correspondence of Walter Benjamin 1910–1940*, ed. Theodor W. Adorno and Gershom Scholem, trans. Manfred R. Jacobson and Evelyn M. Jacobson (Chicago: University of Chicago Press, 1994), p. 637. A translation of this passage is included in "Chronology," the editors' afterword to Benjamin's *Selected Writings*, Vol. 4: *1938–1940*, ed. Howard Eiland and Michael W. Jennings (Cambridge, MA: The Belknap Press of Harvard University Press, 2006), p. 442: "His idleness sustained him in glorious style for many years, in the obscurity of an errant and secluded life."

107 ADORNO TO SCHOLEM
FRANKFURT AM MAIN, 22.6.1961

PROF. DR. THEODOR W. ADORNO

FRANKFURT AM MAIN
KETTENHOFWEG 123
22 June 1961

Dear Scholem,

Kindest thanks for your letter.

So we will see each other in Sils Maria. As far as my plans go, the fact that you have moved your visit to Frankfurt to October is all the more convenient, since, in early September, I am teaching at the Darmstadt Courses for New Music, and I'll also have to leave again in mid-September. On the other hand, we really have tranquility around the time that you suggest, and I think that we will be able to bring about a definitive decision regarding the selection of Benjamin's letters.

The letter to Arendt is interesting, especially because it is certainly one of the latest that can still be tracked down. At the same time, I do not want to be in the debt of this woman, who, as you know, has made efforts to take Benjamin's oeuvre under her wing. Moreover, the personal parts of this letter would require some explanation, which could only be provided by Mrs. Arendt; I do not know who Madame P. or Fritz are, at any rate. But we should save this complex for our meeting.

I don't have to tell you how excited I am about your piece on Buber.

I did not hear a word from Mrs. Schoen. It is also entirely unclear to me what is meant in the obituary by the claim that Schoen died as a victim of National Socialism. I believe that the memory of the victims is far too serious a matter to be abused for such an effect. But Mrs. Schoen is apparently lacking the necessary sensitivity for such matters.

I hope you have a nice time in England. I almost envy you a bit for Oxford. I have not been there for almost a quarter of a century and I have the most grateful memories of it, even though it was a time when I had more than one reason to feel the sting of immigration most painfully.

All that is cordial, also from Gretel,

always yours

Adorno

Original: typescript with printed letterhead; Gershom Scholem Archive, The National Library of Israel, Jerusalem.

who Madame P. or Fritz are: In his letter to Arendt, dated 8.7.1940, Benjamin writes: "Mrs. P. found her husband again. It seems he was in rather bad shape. We received news from Fritz, but it appears that he has not yet been liberated." See *The Correspondence of Walter Benjamin 1910–1940*, ed. Theodor W. Adorno and Gershom Scholem, trans. Manfred R. Jacobson and Evelyn M. Jacobson (Chicago: University of Chicago Press, 1994), p. 637. Madame P. presumably means Mrs. Pollack; the translators of Benjamin's correspondence suggest that Fritz means "the psychiatrist Fritz Fraenkel, a friend of W.B. who lived in the same house in Paris" (ibid., note 2).

Oxford: In July 1934 Adorno enrolled as an "advanced student" in philosophy at Merton College, Oxford. Until his immigration to New York in 1938, he lived, alternately, in Oxford and London; however, until 1937 he regularly returned to Germany during vacations.

108 SCHOLEM TO ADORNO
LONDON, 4.10.61

UNIVERSITY OF LONDON
THE WARBURG INSTITUTE
WORBURN SQUARE, LONDON W.C.1
TELEPHONE LANGHAM 9663

4 Oct. '61

Dear Adorno,

Both of you will perhaps be pleased to hear that my wife will accompany me to Frankfurt this time.

We will arrive in Fr. on Sunday afternoon (the 8th of October) and will be staying at the Parkhotel, Wiesenhüttenplatz.

I tried to call Horkheimer twice from Ascona but could not reach him. Perhaps we can get together this week. We will be in Frankfurt for a week, so we should manage to look through at least some of the material together.

What do you think about Ernst Bloch's ultimate exodus from the East? It's very pleasing, *after all*!* Is he in your neck of the woods?

I hope to receive word from you at the hotel.

Cordial regards to you both

yours,

Scholem

Original: manuscript with printed letterhead; Theodor W. Adorno Archive, Frankfurt am Main.

Ernst Bloch's ultimate exodus from the East? . . . Is he in your neck of the woods?: Because of his critical stance toward the government of the GDR in connection with the Hungarian uprising of 1956, among other things, Ernst Bloch was forced to retire from the University of Leipzig in 1957. He was prohibited from teaching or publishing. In 1961 he did not return from a visit to West Germany, having been appointed visiting professor of philosophy at the Eberhard Karls University in Tübingen.

109 ADORNO TO SCHOLEM
FRANKFURT AM MAIN, 6.10.1961

, on the 6.10.61.

Dear Scholem,

Kindest thanks for your letter. We are sincerely happy that you are both coming. We will be expecting you both for supper on Monday evening at 7. The Glücks are also coming. On Wednesday evening, all four of us are invited to Unseld's place for dinner.

Please come to the Institute at half past ten on Monday morning so that we can begin talking about the Benjamin material. I have studied it intensively over the past few weeks.

To you both all that is cordial, also from Gretel

yours,

[Adorno]

Original: typescript (carbon copy); Theodor W. Adorno Archive, Frankfurt am Main.

* Original in English.

110 ADORNO TO SCHOLEM
FRANKFURT AM MAIN, 24.10.1961

PROF. DR. THEODOR W. ADORNO

FRANKFURT AM MAIN
KETTENHOFWEG 123
24 October 1961

Dear Scholem,

Hopefully you both got home safely.

Today I am enclosing a note with answers to the handful of questions that remained unanswered during our last meeting. I hope that this will suffice. At the same time, perhaps I may remind you that you kindly offered to send me your text against Mr. Schoeps.

In Tübingen – there was no correlation between the efforts expended and the objective results obtained, since most of the participating schools are so hostile to one another that they frown upon even having to articulate their positions in one another's presence – I was with Bloch a number of times. I also saw him at the cocktail party thrown by Unseld on the occasion of the book fair. My impression was very positive. He has the good instinct to refuse any renegade advertising and simply, matter-of-factly, to do his work. Only his wife is something of a liability; she's best compared to a mean-spirited goose, even when roasted. Alas, the prominence of their escape has filled her with a new *élan vital*.

I received an exceptionally friendly and nice letter from Stefan Benjamin, who – in keeping with the alternative suggestion that I'd presented to him – has agreed to lend me the Klee for life, while also stipulating that it should be mine if I survive him.

My work on the letters is proceeding in the agreed-upon way. Hopefully we are far enough along that we will be able to put together the final manuscript during our next meeting.

To you and Fanja all that is cordial, also from Gretel,

your old,

Adorno

Original: typescript with printed letterhead; Gershom Scholem Archive, The National Library of Israel, Jerusalem.

a note: Not preserved.

your text against Mr. Schoeps: Scholem's "Offener Brief an den Verfasser der Schrift *Jüdischer Glaube in dieser Zeit*" [Open letter to the author of *Jewish Faith in these Times*] was addressed to the historian of religion Hans-Joachim Schoeps (1909–1980). It was first published in *Bayerische Israelitische Gemeindezeitung*, 8/16 (15.8.1937), pp. 241–3, and was reprinted in *Briefe I: 1914–1947*, ed. Itta Shedletzky (Munich: C. H. Beck, 1994), pp. 467–71.

In this open letter, Scholem refers to the book based on Schoeps's dissertation *Jüdischer Glaube in dieser Zeit: Prolegomena zur Grundlegung einer systematischen Theologie des Judentums* [Jewish faith in these times: prolegomena towards the foundation of a systematic theology of Judaism] (Berlin, 1932). Scholem criticizes Schoeps's attempt to present Judaism in the categories of systematic theology, which he associates with Protestantism and – in turn – with liberal, assimilated Judaism. Against this, Scholem argues as follows: "This attempt, although legitimate as such, currently takes place on the skewed and false plane of liberalism. It will have to be repeated precisely at that point when the Jews will have become Jews again, rather than hybrid creatures, with a double existence in self-deception. It will have to be repeated, that is, at the level of truth (its gaze directed toward the centre of its own peoplehood, rather than from the perspective of its dissolution). Perhaps this view will be more important to advance in Palestine than in Germany (although even this is not entirely certain for me)." (*Briefe I*, p. 470)

In Tübingen: The meeting of the German Sociological Association took place in Tübingen from the 19th to the 21st of October 1961. The theme was "The Logic of the Social Sciences." The meeting marked the beginning of the so-called positivism dispute in German sociology. On this occasion, Adorno was engaged in a fundamental debate on the methods and positions of the social sciences, particularly with Karl Popper. See Adorno, "Introduction," in *The Positivist Dispute in German Sociology*, trans. Glyn Adey and David Frisby (London: Heinemann, 1976), pp. 1–67.

Klee: The small watercolor painting *Angelus Novus* was painted by Paul Klee (1879-1940) in Munich in 1920 and was presented for the first time in May and June of that year in an extensive Klee exhibition at the Hans Goltz Gallery in Munich. Benjamin, who was not in Munich at that time, might have seen it at a small Klee exhibition which took place in Berlin in April 1921. It was then returned to the Goltz Gallery in Munich, where Benjamin purchased it during his visit to Scholem in May and June 1921. Not having a permanent address in Berlin at that time, he initially left the painting in Munich with Scholem, who sent it to him in Berlin in November of that year. Benjamin left Berlin for Paris in March 1933, and the painting was brought to him by a female acquaintance from Berlin in 1935. When he had to escape Paris in June 1940 because of the Nazi occupation, Benjamin cut the picture out of its frame and stowed it in one of the two suitcases in which he stored his papers. These suitcases were then hidden in the Bibliothèque Nationale by an acquaintance of Benjamin, the French intellectual and author Georges Bataille, who worked there as an archivist. After the war, the suitcases were sent to Adorno in America. Adorno then brought the painting back with him to Frankfurt, where it was hanging in his apartment. Questions of ownership plagued the painting from early on. When Benjamin contemplated suicide in 1932, he wrote a will in which he bequeathed the painting to Scholem. However, since Benjamin did not take his life at that time, the will was ultimately considered void. Thus, when Benjamin did take his own life during his attempt to flee France in 1940, the painting was formally inherited by his son, Stefan Benjamin, who, as Adorno reports in this letter, lent Adorno the painting for life. After Adorno's death, the painting remained in the Adornos' house with his widow Gretel Adorno. Stefan Benjamin ultimately survived Adorno, passing away three years after him in 1972. After Adorno's death, and even more intensely after Stefan Benjamin's death, the question of ownership of the painting arose again, in particular for Scholem; see the Editor's Introduction in this volume pp. xxxvi–xxxvii.

111 SCHOLEM TO ADORNO
JERUSALEM, 5.11.1961

Jerusalem on the 5.XI.1961

Dear Adorno,

We got back in one piece and are readjusting to life in this world. In the meantime, inflation has increased, as has the number of students. Those who do not come now will never hear my course again; it is being transcribed in shorthand so that my critics will have something to laugh at. The whole thing is happening on my own initiative, however.

Kind thanks for your letter. The transcripts of W.B.'s letters to me are still with Suhrkamp, which is supposed to send them to me, along with the letters to Belmore, once they are finished. I will then begin to prepare them for print. I will add a few more letters from the material addressed to me, which I will have transcribed.

I am enclosing a transcription of my open letter to Schoeps from the summer of 1932 since I do not possess any print copies other than my own. Since my lady has already copied the editorial remarks, I did not want to withhold these from you. The editor was Ludwig Feuchtwanger of Duncker & Humblot, who also published Ernst Bloch's *Spirit of Utopia*. I am confident that the text will interest you. I don't think that I'd be able to express my opinion more clearly today than I did back then, to the extent that, at such an advanced age, I still have one (on these matters, anyway*).

In the meantime, all the best to you and your wife, from

your

G. Scholem

* Even so, and without thinking about it, I announced last August that my theme for the Eranos conference in 1962 would be "Tradition as a Religious Category in Judaism" (in case I can make it, that is).

Original: typescript with handwritten postscript; Theodor W. Adorno Archive, Frankfurt am Main.

Ludwig Feuchtwanger: Although trained as a lawyer, Ludwig Feuchtwanger (1885–1947) worked as an editor at Duncker & Humblot Verlag from 1915 to 1933. From 1925 to 1937 he was also on the editorial staff of the *Bayerische Israelitische Gemeindezeitung*, in which Scholem's open letter to Schoeps was published in 1932.

"Tradition as a Religious Category in Judaism": Scholem's lecture at the 1962 Eranos conference was published under the title "Tradition und Kommentar als religiöse Kategorien im Judentum" [Tradition and commentary as religious categories in Judaism], in *Eranos-Jahrbuch 1962, Vol. 31: Der Mensch, Führer und Geführter im Werk* [The human, leader and led, in the work], ed. Adolf Portmann (Zurich: Rhein, 1963), pp. 19–48. See Scholem, "Revelation and Tradition as Religious Categories in Judaism," in *The Messianic Idea in Judaism*, trans. Michael A. Meyer (New York: Schocken Books, 1971), pp. 228–303.

112 ADORNO TO SCHOLEM
FRANKFURT AM MAIN, 13.11.1961

PROF. DR. THEODOR W. ADORNO

FRANKFURT AM MAIN
KETTENHOFWEG 123
13 November 1961

Dear Scholem,

Kindest thanks for your letter and for the open letter to Schoeps. I find the latter to be extraordinarily important on a variety of points, above all, on the constitutive role of tradition. For some time I have also been concerned with this matter, although from a different point of view, namely, that of epistemology. Apart from the marvellous formulation about the concrete, which I already knew from the Benjamin correspondence, I was especially deeply moved by the agreement that prevails between us in our polemical stance against the existential sphere. My Kierkegaard book was, in truth, already an attack on existentialism, the crimes of which were still, at the time, broad blown, as flush as May* [*in seiner Sünden Maienblüte*]. What you say against the attempt of translating theology into the mere immediacy of the relationship, as far as the traditional unfolding of doctrinal content is concerned, I arrived at from a completely different angle, namely, from the untruth of the existentialist standpoint as such, which passes off the immediacy of subjective experience as something transcendent through false pretences and adulation. It is

* See William Shakespeare, *Hamlet*, Act 3, scene 3. The German comes from A.W. Schlegel's translation of Shakespeare's *Hamlet*. See August Wilhelm Schlegel, *Hamlet* (Frankfurt a.M.: Fischer Verlag, 2008), Act 3, scene 3, p. 84.

easy to say why I place such importance on this coincidence: if one arrives at the same central point from such different angles, then it is a sign of the truth of what is being said. My aversion to existentialism, which I've harboured since I read the dialectical theologians and Buber's *I and Thou*, is based primarily on a linguistic experience, by the way. It would not surprise me if this were also your initial impulse. I am currently preparing a text, *The Jargon of Authenticity*, in which I hope to drive home some of these points theoretically.

Since the open letter has been published, I assume that you won't mind if I have it transcribed so that I can quote exactly from it when an opportunity presents itself. As soon as the transcription is complete you will get it back, of course.

The work on the Benjamin letters is also progressing well on our side. I don't think that any further major problems will present themselves. Regarding the issues that you are dealing with, I just want to say two things for today: first, that Willi Wiegand, whom I really liked a great deal, died a few days ago; and, second, that – if I recall correctly – there is an unfriendly remark about Helmuth Plessner in one of the letters addressed to you, in which he is characterized as subaltern, or the like. Since Plessner is still alive, and since he is not only one of the most decent professors in Germany today but also one of the least subaltern – his only defect is, frankly, an almost mythical laziness – I would like to spare him this insult. He is a man with a keen sense for the sorts of things we are working on, and for that reason alone, one shouldn't hurt his feelings.

The *Frankfurter Zeitung*'s literary supplement included a genuinely friendly and enthusiastic essay by Benno Reifenberg on *Illuminations*, along with a lovely reproduction of a photograph of Benjamin. That the authority of Benjamin's work is visibly increasing, by itself and of its own accord, is one of the few exhilarating experiences in my life presently; it will also be a boon for our edition.

Otherwise, I have more aggravation than is good for me, and, at the present moment, it is more than I can handle, psychologically. I have no other remedy for this, besides working doggedly.

Most cordially to you and Fanya, also from Gretel,

yours,

Adorno

Original: typescript with printed letterhead; Gershom Scholem Archive, The National Library of Israel, Jerusalem.

the marvellous formulation about the concrete: "After all, the absolutely concrete is the non-fulfillable as such, whose absoluteness conditions its infinite reflection in the contingency of consummation." See Gershom Scholem, *Briefe I: 1914–1947*, ed. Itta Shedletzky (Munich: C. H. Beck,

1994), pp. 469–70. On the 17th of July 1934, Scholem had written the following to Benjamin: "The *nonfulfillability* of what has been revealed is the point where a *correctly* understood theology (as I, immersed in my Kabbalah, think, and whose expression you can find more or less responsibly formulated in that open letter to Schoeps you are familiar with) coincides most perfectly with that which offers the key to Kafka's work." See *The Correspondence of Walter Benjamin and Gershom Scholem, 1932–1940*, ed. Gershom Scholem, trans. Gary Smith and Andre Lefevere (New York: Schocken Books, 1989), p. 126.

My Kierkegaard book . . . an attack on existentialism: In his early book on Kierkegaard (see letter no. 1 in this volume), Adorno engages in depth with existentialism, above all, with Martin Heidegger's *Existenzphilosophie*. See Adorno, "Chapter 4: Concept of Existence," in *Kierkegaard: Construction of the Aesthetic*, trans. Robert Hullot-Kentor (Minneapolis: University of Minnesota Press, 1999), pp. 68–85.

the dialectical theologians: The Protestant theologian Karl Barth (1886–1968) is considered the principal representative of so-called dialectical theology. See Karl Barth, *The Epistle to the Romans*, trans. Edwyn C. Hoskyns (Oxford: Oxford University Press, 1968). In a later essay, "Kierkegaard Once More," Adorno writes: "Dialectical theology in its entirety was what succeeded Kierkegaard; in Karl Barth it was also that of his resoluteness." See "Kierkegaard Once More," trans. Jensen Suther, *Telos*, no. 174 (2016), p. 60.

Buber's I and Thou: Martin Buber's influential book *Ich und Du* was first published by Insel Verlag, Leipzig, in 1923. See *I and Thou*, trans. Walter Kaufman (New York: Touchstone Books, 1970).

Willi Wiegand: Willy Wiegand (1884–1961) was a typographer and co-founder of the publishing house Bremer Presse.

remark about Helmuth Plessner: The philosopher and sociologist Helmuth Plessner (1892–1985) was the principal representative of philosophical anthropology. He was friends with Adorno and covered Adorno's professorship during the latter's stay in America from 1952 to 1953. From 1952 until his retirement in 1962 he was a professor of sociology at the University of Göttingen. On the relationship between Plessner, Adorno, and Scholem, see Monika Plessner, *Die Argonauten auf Long Island: Begegnungen mit Hannah Arendt, Theodor W. Adorno, Gershom Scholem und anderen* [The Argonauts on Long Island: encounters with Hannah Arendt, Theodor W. Adorno, Gershom Scholem and others] (Berlin: Rowohlt, 1995). The passage in Benjamin's letter reads: "Recently, one of the three hundred new Cologne privatdocents, [Helmuth] Plessner, gave a talk at the Kant Society on the epistemological significance of linguistic philosophy. It was not on a very high level, of course, but its content was mostly very relevant." See *The Correspondence of Walter Benjamin 1910–1940*, ed. Theodor W. Adorno and Gershom Scholem, trans. Manfred R. Jacobson and Evelyn M. Jacobson (Chicago: University of Chicago Press, 1994), p. 168.

essay on Illuminations *by Benno Reifenberg*: Benno Reifenberg's review of *Illuminations*, the collection of Benjamin's selected writings published by Siegfried Unseld, appeared in the *Frankfurter Allgemeine Zeitung* on 11.11.1961. According to Reifenberg, the collection offers "a wider audience the opportunity to become acquainted with the work of an original thinker, a highly critical spirit, a sensitive soul. Anyone who dares can be assured of the cleansing power of this encounter."

113 SCHOLEM TO ADORNO
JERUSALEM, 19.11.1961

Dear Adorno,

Just a quick note to say that of course you don't have to return the copy of my open letter – it was intended for you. I'm glad that you'll be able to do something with it.

The day before yesterday I also sent you my famous *Commentary* essay on Buber's interpretation of Hasidism (famous only to the extent that a piece which has just come out, and which is bound to cause a big stir, can already be famous). Please don't return that either; rather, pass it around diligently!!

I am half stupefied at the moment from working on the index to my latest tome, which I have to prepare by myself. On this account, my words are lame, as Job (who appears to have undergone something similar) put it.

Yours,

Gerhard Scholem

Original: aerogram (manuscript), dated by postmark; Theodor W. Adorno Archive, Frankfurt am Main.

working on the index to my latest tome: Scholem presumably means his book *Origins of the Kabbalah* (see the reference in letter no. 101 in this volume).

114 SCHOLEM TO ADORNO
JERUSALEM, 10.4.1962

10 April 1962

Dear Adorno,

I have taken the liberty of sending you my book on the origin of the Kabbalah, not because you have to read it, but so that you can see what's been plaguing me! This is what my *opera* look like!

On Sunday and Monday, the 3rd and 4th of June, I will pass through Frankfurt, spending two evenings there. I would like to spend one evening with you, and with Horkheimer, if he happens to be in Fr., and the other with Unseldt. It is all the same to me how you divide this up. I am flying back to Israel on Tuesday the 5th – I used an invitation to a colloquium in Paris to make this little detour through F. possible.

I have fallen behind with my work on Benjamin because my eyes have been seriously overstrained. I have to be careful. Nevertheless, I hope to be able to work intensively on this during the summer.

Many cordial regards to your wife and you

yours,

Gershom Scholem

Original: aerogram (manuscript); Theodor W. Adorno Archive, Frankfurt am Main.

Unseldt: Scholem's spelling.

colloquium in Paris: In late May, Scholem took part in a colloquium on heresy and society at the École des Hautes Études in Paris. See *The Correspondence of Hannah Arendt and Gershom Scholem*, ed. Marie Luise Knott, trans. Anthony David (Chicago: University of Chicago Press, 2017), p. 200.

115 ADORNO TO SCHOLEM
FRANKFURT AM MAIN, 18.4.1962

PROF. DR. THEODOR W. ADORNO

FRANKFURT AM MAIN
KETTENHOFWEG 123
on the 18th of April, 1962

Dear Scholem,

Sincere thanks for your letter of the 10th of April, which I received upon my return from Bregenz, where I went, all alone, for a few meagre days off. The best thing about this was the chance to indulge in some healing and relaxing silence. The *Origins of the Kabbalah* has also arrived, and I would like to express my sincerest thanks for this gift, which is extraordinary in every sense. There is something thoroughly impressive about it, even at the first glance with which one attaches oneself to it. Alas, I will have time to read it only after the end of the semester; this one has been packed beyond belief with all sorts of obligations. It will be interrupted by a trip to Vienna that Gretel and I are planning during the week of Pentecost. I'm very happy that you are coming at the start of June. Sunday evening would be preferable for me; Monday is not as good; the following Tuesdays are always so exhausting that, out of reasons of labor economy, I have to go to bed with the birds the night before. I'm not sure about Horkheimer yet, although I'd like to think that he would be available as well, since he planned to spend the following semester lecturing. Since his retirement, some weeks ago, he has clearly been enjoying teaching more than he did previously. I'd rather keep the meeting with Unseld separate.

At our end, the work on the Benjamin volume is coming along nicely. I'll tell you more about it then [when we meet]. By the way, *Deutsche Menschen* [German men and women], the volume of letters that Benjamin edited and commented on during his exile, was recently reissued, along with a short epilogue by me, which involved as much effort on my part as a major essay. I think Suhrkamp will automatically send it to you; if this is not the case (Unseld is currently away), please let me know, and you will receive it right away. You will also be receiving the small collection of sociological essays that Horkheimer and I recently edited. Of course you will already know most of it. We are just waiting to receive our author copies.

To you and Fanya all that is cordial, also from Gretel

your old

Adorno

Original: typescript, with an enclosed copy of Adorno's dream note from the 13th of April 1962, with the following dedication: "My dear Scholem, cordially / from his Adorno / October 1962"; Gershom Scholem Archive, The National Library of Israel, Jerusalem.

Adorno's dream note: See Theodor W. Adorno, *Dream Notes*, ed. Christoph Gödde and Henri Lonitz, trans. Rodney Livingstone (Cambridge: Polity, 2007), pp. 65–8.

Since his retirement, some weeks ago: Since May 1956, Horkheimer had been seeking early retirement due to the fact that he was repeatedly subjected to antisemitic attacks by his colleagues. The administration granted him permission to take sabbatical semesters until his retirement came through. However, Horkheimer only made use of this option on one occasion.

the small collection of sociological essays: See Max Horkheimer and Theodor Adorno, *Sociologica II: Reden und Vorträge* [Sociologica II: speeches and lectures] (Frankfurt am Main: Europäische Verlagsanstalt, 1962).

116 ADORNO TO FANIA SCHOLEM
FRANKFURT AM MAIN, 10.9.1962

10 September 1962

Dear Fanja,

Could you please be so kind as to let us know whether Gerhard has already had his surgery, whether it went well, and at which hospital he is staying? We are thinking of him, and of you both, and of course we send him all our best wishes, to the extent that he can receive them at present. If you permit the mythical expression: we're keeping our fingers crossed for him.

We'd be very grateful for a quick word from you, however brief.

All that is cordial, also from Gretel,

your loyal

[Adorno]

Original: typescript (carbon copy); Theodor W. Adorno Archive, Frankurt am Main.

Gerhard . . . surgery: See the following letter in this volume.

117 FANIA SCHOLEM TO GRETEL AND THEODOR ADORNO
ZURICH, 12.9.1962

Zurich, 12.9.62

Dear Adornos,

The operation was a success, so the worst is almost over; its outcome was the revelation of a little quarry – stones that are as uneven as the temperament of their producer, who is lying here, not exactly happy, occasionally letting out sighs of protest. He is not cut out for this kind of thing. The doctors are very satisfied and we hope to look towards a somewhat happier future in a few days. Gerhard has gratefully received your good wishes and sends you both his most cordial regards. Best thanks and regards from my side as well

yours Fania

Original: manuscript, with the following note: "c/o Hospital of the Red Cross / 18 Gloriastr. / Zurich"; Theodor W. Adorno Archive, Frankfurt am Main.

118 ADORNO TO SCHOLEM
FRANKFURT AM MAIN, 4.10.1962

PROF. DR. THEODOR W. ADORNO

FRANKFURT AM MAIN
KETTENHOFWEG 123
4 October 1962

Dear Scholem,

This is truly *good news** and I heartily congratulate you on your speedy recovery. I was somewhat concerned, indeed – at our age one never knows how the heart will hold up in such cases; but luckily it all went well in the end.

I am very glad that, after all this, you will still come for a few days, not least because of the Ehrlich affair. We have heard such unfavorable – indeed, alarming – things about him that we have come to have serious misgivings. On the other hand, a faculty decision has already been made, and if his appointment should proceed despite our retroactive veto, as it were, it would be extremely bad. This makes it all the more important for you to state your views on this matter, once again, in conversation with the most important faculty members. After the faculty caused the greatest of difficulties for a highly gifted *Habilitation* candidate of ours (you know him, Schweppenhäuser) for not having sat his exam in ancient Greek, Horkheimer and I hardly find it reasonable that they would appoint someone to a professorship in Jewish studies who does not speak Hebrew. I will intercede in this vein once again before your arrival.

Of course, something will be set up for you at the Institute, as was already arranged between us. It's just a pity that I will already have to be in Münster on the 22nd and 23rd, since I am giving the keynote lecture (on the dialectic of progress) at the philosophers' conference there. Incidentally, the 19th of October is a Friday and the 20th is a Saturday. Such events [as your talk at the Institute] cannot take place on Saturdays. As far as I can tell, it would be best if we could do it on Friday evening, although I do not know whether you can already be put under this kind of pressure that evening. In the worst-case scenario, you would have to do the affair without my being there. I would see to it, however, that someone from the University, such as Mr. Rüegg, would stand in for me.

Horkheimer flew to New York yesterday. He intends to stay there for only fourteen days and will most likely already be back by the 17th; but, even setting aside the fact that he sometimes tends to change his arrangements at the last minute, when it comes to such long journeys

* Original in English.

one can, of course, never know exactly. I'd say that there's a good chance he'll be here, but I can't promise you with absolute certainty.

I'll be going away again tomorrow for a week on a belated holiday; but there will still be enough time for us to make all the necessary arrangements.

I am thrilled by the topic of "Heretical Messianism and Jewish Society."

I am making reasonably good progress on what is currently my main project, although the whole thing has gotten a bit out of my control and, in order to submit a strictly organized text, it will need to be completely reworked again. But at least there will be something there to rework, and when it comes to something so exposed, that is also not nothing.

Once again, wishing you a speedy recovery and looking forward to seeing you very soon.

All that is cordial to you both, also from Gretel,

your old

Adorno

Original: typescript with printed letterhead; Gershom Scholem Archive, The National Library of Israel, Jerusalem.

the Ehrlich affair: Ernst Ludwig Ehrlich (1921–2007) was a historian and scholar of Judaism. He studied at the Lehranstalt für die Wissenschaft des Judentums [Higher Institute for the Science of Judaism] in Berlin from 1940 until the institute's closure in 1942. After the closure of the institute and a period of forced labor, he managed to escape to Switzerland in 1943. In 1950 he completed his doctorate in Basel. From 1955 he taught Jewish studies at the universities in Frankfurt am Main, Berlin, Zurich, Berne, and Basel. From 1958 he was the general secretary of the Christian-Jewish Committee of Switzerland, and from 1961 to 1994 he was the European director of B'nai B'rith. In 1963, Ehrlich was appointed to an endowed associate professorship in Jewish studies at the University of Frankfurt. See *Theodor W. Adorno / Max Horkheimer: Briefwechsel Vol. IV, 1950–1969*, ed. Henri Lonitz and Christoph Gödde (Frankfurt am Main: 2006), pp. 465–6.

Schweppenhäuser: The philosopher Hermann Schweppenhäuser (1928–2015) studied at the Goethe University in Frankfurt under Adorno and Horkheimer before becoming Adorno's assistant and a research associate at the Institute for Social Research. In 1956 he completed his doctoral dissertation, under Adorno and Horkheimer, on Martin Heidegger's theory of language. See Hermann Schweppenhäuser, *Studien über die Heideggersche Sprachphilosophie* [Studies on Heidegger's philosophy of language] (Munich: Edition Text + Kritik, 1988). In 1962, he was appointed to the newly established professorship in philosophy at the Pedagogical University in Lüneburg (later: Leuphana University Lüneburg). With Rolf Tiedemann, Schweppenhäuser edited Walter Benjamin's *Gesammelte Schriften* from 1972 to 1989.

in Münster ... the keynote: Adorno's lecture "Fortschritt" [Progress], given at the philosophers' conference in Münster on the 22nd of October 1962, was first published in *Argumentationen: Festschrift für Josef König* [Argumentations: commemorative volume for Josef König], ed. Harald Delius and Günther Patzig (Göttingen: Vandenhoeck & Ruprecht, 1964). See "Progress," in *Critical Models: Interventions and Catchwords*, trans. Henry W. Pickford (New York: Columbia University Press, 1998), pp. 143–60.

such as Mr. Rüegg: Walter Rüegg (1918–2015) was professor of sociology at the Goethe University in Frankfurt between 1961 and 1973. From 1972 to 1986 he had a professorship at the University of Berne.

"Heretical Messianism and Jewish Society": This refers to Scholem's contribution to a collection issued on the occasion of Adorno's 60th birthday. See Scholem, "Die Metamorphose des häretischen Messianismus der Sabbatianer in religiösen Nihilismus im 18. Jahrhundert" [The metamorphosis of the heretical messianism of the Sabbatians into religious nihilism in the 18th century], in *Zeugnisse: Theodor W. Adorno zum 60. Geburtstag* [Testimonies: for Theodor W. Adorno on his 60th birthday], ed. Max Horkheimer on behalf of the Institute for Social Research (Frankfurt am Main: Suhrkamp, 1963), pp. 20–32; repr. in Scholem, *Judaica 3: Studien zur Jüdischen Mystik* [Judaica 3: studies in Jewish mysticism] (Frankfurt am Main: Suhrkamp, 1970), pp. 198–217.

119 SCHOLEM TO ADORNO
ZURICH, 4.10.1962

4.10.62

Dear Adorno, I don't know which false dates you read in my card.

I arrive on Sunday afternoon around 5:10 by train, and will be staying at the Parkhotel – so that's the 14th of October.

Any late afternoon suits me for [my lecture at] the Institute (ideally around <u>5pm</u>, if that's possible), e.g. Tuesday or Wednesday, the 16th or 17th of October?

In haste, cordially

yours Scholem

Zurich
Mühlebachstr. 140
c/o Dr. Katzenstein

Original: manuscript; Theodor W. Adorno Archive, Frankfurt am Main.

120 ADORNO TO SCHOLEM
FRANKFURT AM MAIN, 10.10.1962

PROF. DR. THEODOR W. ADORNO

FRANKFURT AM MAIN
KETTENHOFWEG 123
10 October 1962

Dear Scholem,

Kindest thanks for your letter. I sincerely beg your forgiveness for the confusion I have caused. Ordinarily I have my affairs in good order, but the burden of my current commitments exceeds my capacity; not least, because I have yet to write a single word of my Münster lecture, which is, after all, a big responsibility, and I can only actually work if I am capable of organizing my time in a sensible manner. So, again, please don't be cross with me.

The 16th and 17th would not be so good for your lecture because I probably have to stand in for Horkheimer, once again, who has agreed to something that he is now, on account of his absence, unable to do – a discussion on the aesthetics of film in Mannheim. If I actually do wind up having to go, I would have to leave in the afternoon on the 16th and stay there all day on the 17th. Under these circumstances, it would be most convenient if we could schedule your lecture and the discussion to follow on the afternoon of the 18th, around 5 o'clock, at the Institute. This would have the additional advantage of allowing for slightly more publicity. Otherwise, we could do it on the 15th – although perhaps that would be somewhat too soon for you (as it would be for me) – or on the morning of the 16th; but, as I said, the 18th would be the best by far. Should that not suit you for whatever reason, I would ask you to telegraph me.

So, *a bientôt*, and all that is cordial, also to Fanja

yours,

Adorno

Original: typescript with printed letterhead; Gershom Scholem Archive, The National Library of Israel, Jerusalem.

a discussion on the aesthetics of film in Mannheim: Adorno took part in a panel discussion on the theme, "Demands on Film," which was organized by the Gruppe Junger Deutscher Film [Young German film group] during the Internationalen Filmwoche [International film festival]. Besides Adorno, the participants included Richard Erny, Alexander Kluge, Edgar Reitz, Joseph Rovan, Haro Senft, and Hans-Rolf Strobel. A transcript of the discussion was published in Ralph Eue and Lars Henrik Gass, eds, *Provokation und Wirklichkeit: Das Oberhausener Manifest und die Folgen* [Provocation and reality: the Oberhausen manifesto and its consequences] (Munich: Edition Text + Kritik, 2012), pp. 27–47.

121 SCHOLEM TO ADORNO
ZURICH, 11.10.1962

11 Oct. 62

Dear Adorno,

The 18th of October suits me as well, and I can be available for this from 5 to 7 without any difficulties.

By the way, as I told you (and also Horkheimer, again), I don't want to get actively involved in Ehrlich's case, especially following the recent faculty decision. They'll have to take responsibility for this themselves. I feel no urge to comment on people I do not know.

I am spending the evening of the 15th with Unseldt. That leaves Sunday and/or Thursday evening for us. Should you not have to go to Mannheim, we can – of course – also meet on the other dates, if that would be more convenient for you.

In haste and cordially
yours,
Scholem

Original: manuscript; Theodor W. Adorno Archive, Frankfurt am Main.

Unseldt: Scholem's spelling.

122 ADORNO TO SCHOLEM
FRANKFURT AM MAIN, 6.11.1962

PROF. DR. THEODOR W. ADORNO

FRANKFURT AM MAIN
KETTENHOFWEG 123
6 November 1962

Dear Scholem,

Mailing the Schelling caused all manner of problems. It's now been sent off as an insured parcel. Unfortunately you will have to pay some import duty on it. But no other means of sending it could be found, despite Miss Olbrich's best efforts. Hopefully the whole thing won't cause you more trouble than enjoyment.

In the meantime, Mr. Belmor[e], who now resides in Rome, sent me a piece on Benjamin, which I find to be pure impudence – I will send it to you separately. Some fine friend. I wouldn't bother you with this matter if it didn't raise the question as to whether such a man should be dignified by having the letters addressed to him published. The decision, of course, is in your hands.

Perhaps I might take this opportunity to remind you of the young Mathias Thomae, who will be contacting you. And is it indiscreet to ask what headway you've made with [your work on] Hirschfeld? Have you discovered his likeness and solved his family secret? Gretel and I were delighted to find a lecture of yours announced on the radio, the protagonist of which could be none other than him. Most cordially from us both, also to Fanya,

always yours,

Adorno

Original: typescript with printed letterhead; Gershom Scholem Archive, The National Library of Israel, Jerusalem.

Mailing the Schelling: Adorno is referring to F. W. J. v. Schelling, *Werke: Auswahl in drei Bänden* [Works: selection in three volumes], ed. Otto Weiss (Leipzig: Fritz Eckardt, 1907). The first volume contains a dedication from Adorno, which reads: "For Scholem / as a small token / of friendship from his / Teddie Adorno / Frankfurt, October 1962."

Mr. Belmor[e] . . . a piece on Benjamin: In July 1962, Benjamin's childhood friend Herbert Belmore (see letter no. 18 in this volume) published a short statement (in English) on the current "vogue for Benjamin in Germany" in the journal *German Life and Letters*. Counter to this *Zeitgeist*, Belmore writes of his personal acquaintance with Benjamin:

> Walter Benjamin was completely self-centred, the absolute, and therefore naive egoist, and this quality, together with a certain lack of common sense, lies at the centre of his failings; without these limitations he might well have become a figure of European importance. So much had to be said to approach the phenomenon Walter Benjamin; if he was a genius, he was a broken one. Enough remains in his writings to gauge the quality of his mind, a mind unique in the German landscape of his time. . . . Not much can be said in a short article on Walter Benjamin the philosopher. He is not an easy author: whatever he looks at becomes involved in the true sense of the word – convoluted. With relish he burrows into the centre of the onion and starts peeling it from the inside, not without, in the process, damaging some of its tissues. . . . Philosophy pervades more or less Benjamin's literary work, as literature pervades his philosophical writings; he has given us purely literary works, but hardly anything that might be called purely philosophical. (Herbert Belmore, "Walter Benjamin," *German Life and Letters*, 15/4 (July 1962), pp. 309–13)

Mathias Thomae: Matthias Thomae (1944–2012 [?]) was the son of Jutta Burger-Thomae (1920–1991), who had worked at the Institute for Social Research, where – among other things – she contributed to a project entitled "Schuld und Abwehr: Eine qualitative Analyse zum *Gruppenexperiment*" [Guilt and defense: a qualitative analysis for the *group experiment*]. See Theodor W. Adorno, *Guilt and Defense: On the Legacies of National*

Socialism in Postwar Germany, ed. and trans. Jeffrey K. Olick and Andrew J. Perrin (Cambridge, MA: Harvard University Press, 2010).

Hirschfeld ... his likeness: Scholem researched the life and work of the German-Jewish mystic Ephraim Joseph Hirschfeld (1758–1820). See Scholem, "Ein verschollener jüdischer Mystiker der Aufklärungszeit: E. J. Hirschfeld" [A forgotten Jewish mystic of the Enlightenment era: E. J. Hirschfeld], in *Leo Baeck Institute Yearbook* 7 (1962), pp. 247–78. On Hirschfeld's *likeness*, see the following letter in this volume.

a lecture ... on the radio: On 7.10.1962 the Norddeutscher Rundfunk aired Scholem's lecture entitled "Tradition und Kommentar als religiöse Kategorien im Judentum" [Tradition and commentary as religious categories in Judaism], which was delivered and recorded at the 1962 Eranos conference. See letter no. 111 and the relevant note in this volume.

123 SCHOLEM TO ADORNO
JERUSALEM, 12.11.1962

האוניברסיטה העברית בירושלים
THE HEBREW UNIVERSITY OF JERUSALEM

12 November 1962

Dear Adorno,

Thanks a lot for your letter. I made further progress with Hirschfeld in Darmstadt; but I'm expecting the main surprise to be in Copenhagen, where I'll slide in the next chance I get to visit Europe. Unfortunately, I have not yet discovered the portrait – that's something to look forward to. The lecture is indeed on him. It depicts the first stage of my journey of discovery as it has shaped up until May of this year.

Many thanks, again, for the prospective Schelling. I'm happy to pay some duty on it, although I'm puzzled as to why you didn't simply label it as a print document and send it in one or two parcels. But this isn't a serious problem. Years ago, I owned the first 6 volumes of the new edition, but I traded them, *horribile dictu*, for a rare book on gnosis. That was, of course, a lunacy, brought on by the fact that I'd acquired these volumes very cheaply – for what, by current standards, would amount to a whopping 18 DM [German marks].

Re: Mr. Belmore's piece on Benjamin – he sent this to me in manuscript some time ago. It upset me less than you because I realize the rather particular situation of this man and his relationship to Walter Benjamin. At any rate, I don't see this as a reason for not publishing the precious early letters to him. In such matters, I am largely capable of not giving a damn in the interest of the cause.

In the coming days, the introduction to Benjamin's *Trauerspiel* book is going to be photographed for Suhrkamp, and it will be relayed to Boehlich right away. I have a nearly complete manuscript of the book, in its first, unrevised edition, and it really is a most interesting text. By the way, I also have the *Ur*-manuscript of the essay on Karl Kraus, in much the same condition.

Mr. Thomae still hasn't gotten in touch.

With cordial regards to you both,

yours,

G. Scholem

Original: aerogram (typescript with printed letterhead; Theodor W. Adorno Archive, Frankfurt am Main.

Boehlich: The journalist and translator Walter Boehlich (1921–2006) was an editor for Suhrkamp from 1957 to 1968. In this capacity, he also worked on the collection of letters edited by Adorno and Scholem.

essay on Karl Kraus: See letter no. 21 in this volume.

124 SCHOLEM TO ADORNO
JERUSALEM, 13.12.1962

Jerusalem, on the 13th of December, 1962

Dear Adorno,

I am confirming to you, and thus indirectly to Ms. Olbrich as well, that I have received the three volumes of Schelling. They arrived safely yesterday and have already been set in their proper place, which was no small feat, since everything has been crammed in for a long time, and space first had to be made for such an ample gift. I am very happy to have these writings.

Do you want me to return Belmore's essay on Walter Benjamin? It's at your disposal. Incidentally, you may be interested to know that the Schoenfließ family tree, which I recently viewed, revealed to my surprise that Walter Benjamin was the first cousin of Gertrud Kolmar. Their mothers were sisters. Indeed, two notable descendants from the same grandparents. I had no idea about this; I recall only that he once wrote a letter to me in which he spoke with great admiration about the poems of Gertrud Kolmar. In 14 days I am going away for a little follow-up treatment in Tiberias. We are otherwise both quite well. The outside world is making itself known through all manner of Christmas greetings, which are falsely applied to us. In Tiberias, I will study the Aramaic translation of the Sermon on the Mount – perhaps something will come of it.

With cordial regards and repeated thanks,

yours,

Gerhard Scholem

Please, no more books – my room is also already flooded.

Cordial regards to you both

Fania

Original: aerogram (typescript) with printed letterhead and handwritten postscript from Fania Scholem; Theodor W. Adorno Archive, Frankfurt am Main.

I am confirming to you, and thus indirectly to Ms. Olbrich as well, that I have received the three volumes of Schelling: On the 23rd of November 1962, Adorno's secretary, Elfriede Olbrich, wrote the following to Scholem: "Dear esteemed Professor Scholem, please permit me to explain briefly, on Professor Adorno's behalf, why I sent the Schelling collection to you in this somewhat circuitous way. Professor Adorno wanted to ensure that the three volumes were safely on their way and to have the assurance that they would reach you. Registered packages to Israel may weigh only up to 1,000 grams; however, each of the volumes weighed more than two pounds. Accordingly, I had to send the package to you as an insured parcel, with a customs declaration and export papers. With the friendliest regards, your very devoted [Elfriede Olbrich]." Typescript (carbon copy): Theodor W. Adorno Archive, Frankfurt am Main.

the Schoenfließ family tree: Scholem's spelling. Walter Benjamin's mother, Pauline Schoenflies (1870–1930), was descended from the German-Jewish Schönflies–Hirschfeld family from Neumark and Posen, which included famous artists and scholars such as the classical archeologist Gustav Hirschfeld (1847–1895) and the mathematician Arthur Moritz Schoenflies (1853–1928). Scholem conducted extensive genealogical research into Benjamin's family history. See Scholem, "Ahnen und Verwandte Walter Benjamins" [Walter Benjamin's ancestors and relatives], and the reference in the note to letter no. 6 in this volume.

the first cousin of Gertrud Kolmar: The poet Gertrud Kolmar, née Käthe Chodziesner (1894–1943), was the daughter of Elise Schoenflies (1872–1930), who was Pauline Schoenflies's sister and Walter Benjamin's aunt (see Scholem, "Ahnen und Verwandte Walter Benjamins," p. 149).

In Tiberias, I will study the Aramaic translation of the Sermon on the Mount: The northern Israeli city of Tiberias is situated on the Sea of Galilee, close to the Mount of Beatitudes, where – according to Christian tradition – Jesus of Nazareth held his Sermon on the Mount (Matthew: 5–7).

125 ADORNO TO SCHOLEM, FRANKFURT AM MAIN, 18.12.1962

PROF. DR. THEODOR W. ADORNO

FRANKFURT AM MAIN
KETTENHOFWEG 123
18 December 1962

Dear Scholem,

A thousand thanks for your letter.

It would be nice if, at some point, you could return Mr. Belmore's abomination for my archive.

I've known for a long time that Gertrud Kolmar, who, in actuality, had a tongue twister of a name, was Benjamin's first cousin. I think he once wrote something about her poems on city crests.

I'm glad that you both continue to be well. Matthias Thomae was very sad that he couldn't reach you.

These days, I am deeply engaged with your "Unhistorical Aphorisms" on Kabbalah. It hardly requires any guesswork to know that this matter is especially important to me. Apart from everything else, there is probably no other text that you've written which displays such a deep theoretical connection to Benjamin – especially to the theses on the philosophy of history. Then again, it's an inhumanly difficult text, and, although I am indeed accustomed to a lot, I would not presume to have understood it completely; this is also probably not even possible without knowledge of the original texts. Nevertheless, the piece is extraordinarily meaningful to me, and also to Gretel, and it would be of great importance, indeed, if you could, at some point, fully unfold the speculative-dialectical connections which you've hit on the head with a hammer. Maybe I'll have a chance to formulate a few questions and observations concerning your text, which I would then communicate to you.

We're both quite well; the situation with Gretel's foot is also much better. Yesterday, I finished the first draft of my piece on Heidegger's language; but this means that the real work is only just beginning. In the meantime, I still stand facing a mountain, above all with a view to questions of structure, since, as never before in my life, I went, frenziedly, headlong into dictation. Vis-à-vis the things that are of concern in this work, and, above all, in my book on dialectics, I view everything else that has come from me at this point as mere side dishes. Of these, Suhrkamp has presumably sent you my sociology of music.

All that is cordial from us both, also to Fania,

your loyal

Adorno

Original: typescript with printed letterhead; Gershom Scholem Archive, The National Library of Israel, Jerusalem.

Benjamin . . . once wrote something about her poems on city crests: In her second collection of poems, Gertrud Kolmar drew inspiration from the crests of Prussian provinces, collectable images of which were included, at the time, in packages of HAG coffee. See Gertrud Kolmar, *Preußische Wappen* [Prussian crests] (Berlin: Rabenpresse, 1934). Benjamin tried, repeatedly, to have Kolmar's poems published. In 1928 he published "Zwei Gedichte von Gertrud Kolmar" [Two poems by Gertrud Kolmar] in the Easter supplement to *Die Literarische Welt*, "Das Große Feuerwerk" [The great firework] and "Apfel" [Apple], along with an introduction, which stated his intention "to make the reader's ears chime in ways that German women's poetry has not caused them to since Annette von Droste." See Benjamin, *Gesammelte Schriften IV: Kleine Prosa / Baudelaire Übertragungen* [Minor prose / Baudelaire translations], ed. Tillman Rexroth (Frankfurt am Main: Suhrkamp, 1991), pp. 803–4.

"Unhistorical Aphorisms": The first nine unhistorical aphorisms were published as "Zehn unhistorische Sätze über Kabbala" [Ten unhistorical aphorisms on Kaballah], in *Geist und Werk: Aus der Werkstatt der Autoren des Rhein-Verlages zum 75. Geburtstag von Dr. Daniel Brody* [Spirit and work: from the workshop of the Rhein Verlag's authors on the 75th birthday of Dr. Daniel Brody] (Zurich: Rhein, 1938), pp. 209–15. See David Biale, "Ten Unhistorical Aphorisms on Kabbalah: Text and Commentary," *Modern Judaism*, 5/1 (February 1985), pp. 67–94.

the first draft of my piece on Heidegger's language: Adorno is referring to *The Jargon of Authenticity*.

sociology of music: See Adorno, *Introduction to the Sociology of Music*, trans. E. B. Ashton (London: Seabury Press, 1976).

126 SCHOLEM TO ADORNO
JERUSALEM, 3.1.1963

Jerusalem, on the 3rd of January, 1963

Dear Adorno,

First of all, my best wishes for the new year.

I'll return the results of Belmore's literary efforts to you by regular post.

By agreeing to have the unhistorical aphorisms on Kabbalah printed, I have decisively sinned. In keeping with what I say in one of the aphorisms, I naturally assumed that nobody would take notice of them anyway, and that the best way to hide them would be to house them in a printed venue like such a commemorative volume. Now you want a commentary – what are you thinking? Such things existed only in the olden days, when authors wrote their own commentaries, and, if they were clever, these said the opposite of what was said in the texts. I will guard myself against getting into hot water here. One credo that applies to my aphorisms is: every man for himself. The angel who is set over spiritual conception is generally known as Laila – that means night. One would have to ask this angel what he makes of such a proposition.

I, for my part, have just produced something far more comprehensible by rendering into German an old Hebrew piece from 14 years ago. This way my readers will have fewer headaches.

I have not received a book from you on the sociology of music. I wish you the best of luck for the completion of your study on Heidegger. If someone eats their way through this mountain of millet, I can only admire it. I am expecting great profit and insight from this reading, which is more than you can expect from the Scholemian writings, at least their dialectical parts, which must be read, rather, according to the old phrase: unsettle yourselves.

In the meantime, all that is cordial and best wishes for your wife's recovery

from your

Gerhard Scholem

Original: aerogram (typescript); Theodor W. Adorno Archive, Frankfurt am Main. First published in Gershom Scholem, *Briefe II: 1948–1970*, ed. Thomas Sparr (Munich: C. H. Beck, 1995), p. 91.

In keeping with what I say in one of the aphorisms: Scholem's second unhistorical aphorism on the Kabbalah begins as follows: The public-ness of the main works of the old kabbalist literature is the most significant guarantee of their secret." David Biale, "Ten Unhistorical Aphorisms on Kabbalah: Text and Commentary," *Modern Judaism*, 5/1 (February 1985), p. 72.

The angel who is set over spiritual conception is generally known as Laila – that means night: "Laila" is the Hebrew word for night. Scholem is alluding to the following passage of Talmud:

> R. Johanan stated: It is forbidden to perform one's marital duty in the daytime. What is the scriptural proof? That it is said, Let the day perish wherein I was born, and the night wherein it was said: "A man-child is brought forth." The night is thus set aside for conception but the day is not set aside for conception. Resh Lakish stated: [The proof is] from here: But he that despiseth His ways shall die. As to Resh Lakish, how does he expound R. Johanan's text? – He requires it for the same exposition as that made by R. Hanina b. Papa. For R. Hanina b. Papa made the following exposition: The name of the angel who is in charge of conception is "Night," and he takes up a drop and places it in the presence

of the Holy One, blessed be He, saying, "Sovereign of the universe, what shall be the fate of this drop? Shall it produce a strong man or a weak man, a wise man or a fool, a rich man or a poor man?" Whereas "wicked man" or "righteous one" he does not mention, in agreement with the view of R. Hanina. For R. Hanina stated: Everything is in the hands of heaven except the fear of God, as it is said, and now, Israel, what doth the Lord thy God require of thee, but to fear etc. And R. Johanan? – If that were the only meaning, Scripture should have written, "A man-child is brought forth" why then was it stated, "was brought forth a man-child"? To indicate that the night is set aside for conception but the day is not set aside for conception. (Babylonian Talmud, Tractate Niddah, 16b)

an old Hebrew piece from 14 years ago: Scholem is probably referring to his contribution to the commemorative volume issued on the occasion of Adorno's 60th birthday. See letter no. 118 in this volume.

127 ADORNO TO SCHOLEM, FRANKFURT AM MAIN, 17.4.1963

PROF. DR. THEODOR W. ADORNO

FRANKFURT AM MAIN
KETTENHOFWEG 123
17 April 1963

Dear Scholem,

Today I am coming to you with two questions.

First: could you tell me as precisely and reliably as possible when Benjamin's piece on Hölderlin, the comparison of "Dichtermut" [The Poet's Courage] and "Blödigkeit" [Timidity] was written? The biographical sketch by Podszus in the big edition says 1914–1915, but it's important to me that you verify this. The thing is that I have agreed to give this year's keynote address, on the philosophical problems of Hölderlin interpretation, at the meeting of the Hölderlin Society in Berlin in May. I will, of course, pay due attention to Benjamin's text. It now appears to me that there are some striking similarities, chiefly linguistic, between Benjamin and Heidegger – the latter's favorite term concerning Hölderlin is "the poeticized" [*das Gedichtete*] – and my planned critique of Heidegger stems precisely from the difference revealed by these similarities. As will immediately be evident to you, this difference concerns the concept of the mythical: Heidegger holds that, for Hölderlin, the mythical has the last word; Benjamin, by contrast, shows that, for Hölderlin, the mythical is dialectical. It is hardly negligible that I incontestably present the priority of certain Benjaminian categories, although I'd like to leave the question open as to whether Heidegger knew Benjamin's work (which seems unlikely to me). I'd be grateful to you for a quick word, best sent perhaps to Berlin, where I'll be staying at the Hilton Hotel from the 21st to the 26th.

This brings me to my second question. In the context of the "Berliner Begegnungen" [Berlin Encounters] – I did not come up with this title – I will be speaking on Schoenberg's *Moses und Aron*. The affair is very prestigious; Auden and Madariaga will give the parallel lectures. The Schoenberg text is finished. I've invested a lot of effort in it. I'd be especially pleased if you would accept the dedication of this work to you. It is set to appear in a journal and then in a collection of my so-called musical writings. I know you might argue that music is far removed from your area of expertise; but, at the same time, even in subject matter alone, I feel that, of all my writings, this piece is closest to yours. Moreover, I hold to the superstition that, if only one is properly at home in one area, one essentially understands what is happening in another. In short, you'd be making me very happy; however, I do not want to go ahead without first obtaining your *placet*.

May I ask, by the way, how things are going in your section of the Benjamin letters? Unseld is starting to prod, and it would be nice, in any case, if we could finish in time for the book to come out next year. As regards our part, I can promise this with confidence.

I found Mr. Belmore's essay awful, but, in view of your appeal, I do not want to start a quarrel. Why can't someone like that at least have the decency to remain silent if he hasn't got anything to say.

To you and Fanya all the best, also from Gretel,

your old
Adorno

Original: typescript with printed letterhead; Gershom Scholem Archive, The National Library of Israel, Jerusalem. An excerpt of this letter appears in translation in *Gershom Scholem: A Life in Letters*, ed. and trans. Anthony David Skinner (Cambridge, MA: Harvard University Press, 2002), p. 392.

Benjamin's piece on Hölderlin, the comparison of "Dichtermut" [The Poet's Courage] and "Blödigkeit" [Timidity]: See letter no. 7 and the relevant note in this volume.

keynote address . . . at the meeting of the Hölderlin Society: Adorno's lecture "Parataxis: Zur späten Lyrik Hölderlins" [Parataxis: on Hölderin's late lyrical poetry] was given at the annual meeting of the Hölderlin Society in Berlin on the 7th of June 1963. An expanded version was first published as "Parataxis: Zur späten Lyrik Hölderlins," *Neue Rundschau*, 75/1 (1964), pp. 15–46. See "Parataxis: On Hölderlin's Late Poetry," in *Notes to Literature*, Vol. 2, trans. Shierry Weber Nicholsen (New York: Columbia University Press, 1992), pp. 109–52.

In the context of the "Berliner Begegnungen" [Berlin encounters] . . . I will be speaking on Schoenberg's Moses und Aron: Adorno's lecture, held in April 1963, was published as "Sakrales Fragment: über Schoenbergs *Moses und Aron*," in *Quasi una Fantasia* (Frankfurt am Main: Suhrkamp, 1963), pp. 306–38. See "Sacred Fragment: Schoenberg's 'Moses und Aron,'" in *Quasi Una Fantasia: Essays on Modern Music*, trans. Rodney Livingstone (London: Verso, 1998), pp. 225–48.

Auden: The English poet W. H. Auden (1907–1973) lived in Berlin in 1929. In 1935 he married Erika Mann, Thomas Mann's daughter, to enable her emigration from Germany. In 1939 he moved to the United States. He became an American citizen in 1946 and split his time between England and the US. Along with Elliott Carter, Frederick Goldbeck, Dragotin Gostuski, and Josef Rufer, he formed part of the panel discussing Adorno's lecture.

Madariaga: The Spanish politician, writer, and literary scholar Salvador de Madariaga (1886–1978) had been professor of Spanish literature at the University of Oxford since 1927. From 1931, during the time of the Second Spanish Republic, Madariaga was active as a politician, serving as ambassador in Paris and the United States, and as education minister, among other roles. In 1936 he returned to the University of Oxford. The particulars of his contribution to the event have not been verified.

accept the dedication of this work: Adorno's essay in *Quasi una Fantasia* contains a dedication "To Gershom Scholem." See "Sacred Fragment," p. 225.

128 SCHOLEM TO ADORNO
JERUSALEM, 22.4.1963

Jerusalem, on the 22 of April, 1963

Dear Adorno,

I am replying immediately to your letter of the 17th of April, which arrived this afternoon.

W. B.'s Hölderlin essay originated in late 1914 or, at the very latest, by the first of March 1915. It's the only thing he wrote during the first period of the war. I received it from him as a gift in July 1915. That's the source of the date in Podszus's biographical sketch. Benjamin gave a few (not more than a half-dozen) copies to friends and acquaintances, some of whom he named to me over the course of time. I have no reason to suspect that Heidegger was among these, or that he had any second-hand familiarity with the work. I have also noticed the coincidence in their use of the concept of the poeticized [das Gedichtete]. In any case, you can be sure of these dates.

I gladly accept the dedication of your lecture on Schoenberg's *Moses und Aron*. Maybe there's some way to make it apparent that, while

I unfortunately understand nothing of music, I do know something about Judaism. I will accept this as an advance payment, so to speak, until [you produce] a critique of a philosophical-Kabbalistic concept, such as *tsimtsum*, for which I will gladly sign myself up as a sacrificial offering.

I'm sitting down to the Benjamin letters. Should I finish them, I'll bring them with me to Europe, where I plan to go on the 27th of August. I will probably spend all of September in Copenhagen, but would gladly make a stopover in Frankfurt on the way back. I cannot come to Sils.

To explain my far-reaching leniency with respect to Belmore, I'd just like to comment that we must be clear about the deep shock that must have been caused by W. B.'s very abrupt severing of all contact with the friends from his youth. Among [this group of friends], Belmore is the very softest. I have a letter from another member of the same group of Benjamin's Jewish schoolmates at the Kaiser Friedrich Gymnasium, whom I contacted about material, which really sets the record as far as brusqueness and bitterness goes. Belmore is quite cooperative, which is more than one can say about the others; all this time he's been searching through his wife's apparently extensive and totally disorganized estate, and he recently promised to send me a manuscript that he found there, "Conversation on Love," which may be by W.B. – a stylistic analysis will readily clear this up. In my interactions with these friends of youth from the *Anfang* circle, I am developing the virtues of a lamb's patience, which I otherwise pre-eminently lack.

I hope soon to receive [copies of] my lecture from last year's Eranos conference on the concept of tradition. You will easily recognize me in it, even if, on this occasion, I bit off more than I could chew, to the extent that this is even possible in the case of the Kabbalah. Three weeks ago in the *Neue Zürcher* [*Zeitung*], the old Buber published the pitiful response of a helpless windbag to my critique of his Hasidic interpretations. I am currently deliberating whether there's even any sense in replying.

I'm sending this letter to Frankfurt, since it won't reach you in time in Berlin. With cordial regards,

yours,

G. Scholem

Original: aerogram (typescript); Theodor W. Adorno Archive, Frankfurt am Main. First printed in Gershom Scholem, *Briefe II: 1948–1970*, ed. Thomas Sparr (Munich: C. H. Beck, 1995), pp. 93–4. An excerpt of this letter appears in translation in *Gershom Scholem: A Life in Letters*, ed. and trans. Anthony David Skinner (Cambridge, MA: Harvard University Press, 2002), pp. 392–3.

W. B.'s Hölderlin essay originated in late 1914 or, at the very latest, by the first of March 1915: Later Scholem recalled in more detail the circumstances surrounding the writing of Benjamin's Hölderlin essay: "On October 1 he spoke about Hölderlin and gave me a typewritten copy of his essay 'Zwei Gedichte von Friedrich Hölderlin' [Two poems of Friedrich Hölderlin], which contained a profoundly metaphysical analysis, written in the first winter of the war, 1914–1915, of the two poems 'Dichtermut' [Poet's courage] and 'Blödigkeit' [Timidity]. Only later did I realize that this gift was a sign of his great trust in me." See Gershom Scholem, *Walter Benjamin: The Story of a Friendship*, trans. Harry Zohn (New York: NYRB Classics, 2003), p. 23.

I will accept this as an advance payment, so to speak, until [you produce] a critique of a philosophical-Kabbalistic concept, such as tsimtsum: The Kabbalistic concept of *tsimtsum*, Hebrew for contraction, compression, or drawing in, is a central term in the Lurianic Kabbalah (see letters nos. 15 and 58 in this volume). The concept refers to God's self-contraction and the creation of a mystical space in which creation first became possible. See Scholem, "Schöpfung aus Nichts und Selbstverschränkung Gottes" [Creation out of nothing and the self-contraction of God], in *Über einige Grundbegriffe des Judentums* [On some fundamental concepts in Judaism] (Frankfurt am Main: Suhrkamp, 1970), pp. 53–89, esp. pp. 84–9; see also *Major Trends in Jewish Mysticism* (Jerusalem: 1941; rev. edn., New York: Schocken, 1995), pp. 260–4.

another member of the same group of Benjamin's Jewish schoolmates: Possibly a reference to Franz Sachs, whose letter to Scholem has been lost. In his response of the 5th of April 1963, Scholem writes: "I do not share your view, or indeed your scepticism, that publishing these letters [of Benjamin's] has nothing to offer. . . . I too have been preoccupied with the question as to why, around the time that I first got to know him, he withdrew so radically from everything that had hitherto been of central importance to him. I had the opportunity of witnessing this rupture from a vantage point of great personal intimacy. In our 25 years of friendship, I had many experiences, both good and bad, with him. Interacting with him was not always easy. Nevertheless, for my part, I have retained a very different image of him than you." See Scholem, *Briefe II: 1948–1970*, ed. Thomas Sparr (Munich: C. H. Beck, 1995), p. 92.

"Conversation on Love": See Walter Benjamin, "Conversation on Love," in *Early Writings: 1910–1917*, trans. Howard Eiland et al. (Cambridge, MA: The Belknap Press of Harvard University Press, 2011), pp. 139–43. Scholem gave a date of "circa 1913" for this text by Benjamin.

last year's Eranos conference on the concept of tradition: See letter no. 111 in this volume.

the pitiful response: On 31.3.1963 Martin Buber published a rejoinder to Scholem's critique, titled "Einiges zur Darstellung des Chassidismus" [Reflections on the presentation of Hasidism] in the literary supplement of the *Neue Zürcher Zeitung* (see letter no. 106 in this volume). Buber's essay

"Zur Darstellung des Chassidismus" [On the presentation of Hasidism] was published in the journal *Merkur* in February 1963; it contains a condensed version of Buber's response to critical comments by Scholem's student Rivkah Schatz-Uffenheimer. See Martin Buber, "Zur Darstellung des Chassidismus," *Merkur*, 17/180 (February 1963), pp. 137–46. Repr. in Buber, *Werke*, Vol. III: *Schriften zum Chassidismus* [Writings on Hasidism] (Heidelberg: Lambert Schneider, 1963), pp. 975–88. The full critique and the full response were published together in a single volume as part of the series "Philosophen des 20. Jahrhunderts" [Philosophers of the 20th century], ed. Paul Arthur Schlipp and Maurice Friedmann, *Martin Buber* (Stuttgart: Kohlhammer, 1963). In this volume, which has been translated into English, see Rivkah Schatz-Uffenheimer, "Man's Relation to God and World in Buber's Rendering of the Hasidic Teaching," in *The Philosophy of Martin Buber*, ed. Paul Arthur Schlipp and Maurice Friedman (La Salle, IL: Open Court, 1967), pp. 403–34; and, in the same volume, Buber, "Replies to my Critics, Section IX: On Hasidism," pp. 731–41. Another statement on this issue, entitled "Noch einiges zur Darstellung des Chassidismus" [Some more thoughts on the presentation of Hasidism], appears in *Werke*, Vol. III, pp. 991–8.

129 SCHOLEM TO ADORNO
JERUSALEM, 18.6.1963

Jerusalem, on the 18 of June 1963

Dear Adorno,

I'm making use of a hot summer's day to tell you that I am essentially finished with my part of the Benjamin correspondence, so I will be able to bring a revised copy of the edited manuscript to Europe. All outstanding problems can then be discussed there, when – as I hope – I'll be in Frankfurt for a few days on my way back from Copenhagen around the beginning of October. The problem will be whether we can succeed in convincing Unseld to accept the text that I have prepared without further cuts. Namely, it is quite long. I am preparing a course of retreat, to the extent that a reduction is necessary, by selecting around 100 pages – that is, complete letters – that would have to be left out. That would be a great pity, of course; but I have to contend with such a possibility. Either way, I will bring everything that I've worked on with me. It's about 550 typed pages. I did the notes, and very little remains to be looked up bibliographically. I kept my comments as brief as possible. This is confidential and just for your information: from my experience with Unseld, it seems to me that, if he likes the material in question, one can obtain his consent, in a favorable hour, even in the case of far-reaching accommodations. I'm hedging my bets on this. Since we won't be seeing each other in Sils this year, I'm counting on you being in Frankfurt around this time. We can catch up on all the overdue celebrations then. The volume I'd promised to contribute to the "Bibliothek Suhrkamp" series is actually coming out this year, about which I myself am the most surprised. It's planned for August, and I have, in fact, already seen the proofs. You will probably see the volume before I do.

Cordial regards to you both,

yours,

G. Scholem

Original: aerogram (typescript); Theodor W. Adorno Archive, Frankfurt am Main.

The volume I'd promised to contribute to the "Bibliothek Suhrkamp" series: Scholem is referring to his first publication with Suhrkamp – *Judaica*, which appeared in August 1963 as volume 106 of the "Bibliothek Suhrkamp" series.

130 SCHOLEM TO ADORNO
JERUSALEM, 28.7.1963

28 July 1963

Dear Adornos,

We would gladly and with pleasure accept the invitation to a good dinner on this festive occasion. But Mrs. Prof. Scholem will be in Jerusalem this year, tending to the hearth, whereas Mr. Prof. Scholem, who is named on the invitation, will be in Copenhagen on the 11th of September of this year, and will thus be significantly impeded! This is really a pity; but what is to be done?! Helicopters are provided only for heads of state; and, despite what might be expected of a man in my profession, I cannot magically appear on the roof of the Frankfurt Society for Commerce and Trade.

The menu, guest list, and all the speeches will reach me, if necessary, by telegraph at the Hotel Codan in Copenhagen. Before that, I will be in Ascona for ten days from the 25th of August. I hope to see you in Fr. on the way back from C.

In the same post, I am sending you my last Eranos lecture on the concept of tradition, with the certain expectation that, more than ever, you will get your (dialectical) money's worth with me. This is the third of my lectures on Judaism, and I flatter myself that I have concealed several things in it, as is fitting, even though it is expressed with crystal clarity. This is why I permit myself to send it to you, even in the mountains.

Cordial regards to your wife and to you,

yours,

Gershom Scholem

Original: aerogram (manuscript); Theodor W. Adorno Archive, Frankfurt am Main.

the invitation to a good dinner on this festive occasion: The invitation to Adorno's sixtieth birthday party, issued to Gershom and Fania Scholem, is not preserved in Scholem's archive.

Eranos lecture on the concept of tradition: See letter no. 111 in this volume.

131 SCHOLEM TO ADORNO
COPENHAGEN, 9.9.1963

Copenhagen, 9.IX.'63

Dear Adorno,

These lines are merely intended to convey my best wishes to you and your wife on your birthday. For the second half of life, which you are beginning, I wish that you may pursue your work to your satisfaction and find enjoyment in it – an enjoyment that, judging from what I know, your work to date has already brought you. I regret, once more, that my lecture plans here do not permit me to be in Frankfurt on this day, to see how a philosopher's birthday takes place. I am missing out on all of it, including the celebratory speech and declaration of friendship by Horkheimer, which I would have liked to hear. But, in exchange, I am counting on our meeting in the first week of October.

With cordial regards

yours,

Gerhard Scholem

Hotel Codan
Copenhagen
St. Annae Plads

Original: manuscript; Theodor W. Adorno Archive, Frankfurt am Main.

132 ADORNO TO SCHOLEM, FRANKFURT AM MAIN, 23.9.1963

PROF. DR. THEODOR W. ADORNO

FRANKFURT AM MAIN
KETTENHOFWEG 123
23 September 1963

Dear Scholem,

A thousand thanks for the letter. We missed you, as you can imagine; but you were all the more present in spirit, not least to me, through your turn of phrase "cashing in," which I repeated to myself as an effective antidote against the onset of full-blown narcissism. Incidentally, everything went humanely, amicably, and without abominations. I think that what can be said of this celebration is the best that can be said of any such occasion: that the official aspect did not bring more humiliation than is implied by the concept of the official (you see that I am simply not a nominalist, and I know that you are of the same mind).

In the meantime, with the exception of a few small things that remain outstanding, I have finished working on the folio of Benjamin letters that were allocated to me. There won't be much for us to decide on, except, of course, a few matters of principle regarding what will require annotation and what won't. Where notes are still pending, they won't be difficult to provide. All in all, my section should be easier, if anything, than yours, since it falls into a considerably later period, which is quite well documented and less affected by the forgetfulness that has befallen some of the people with whom Benjamin communicated before the First War. Incidentally, I am very happy about the theoretical content touched on in the letters.

So, I am expecting you here on the 2nd of October and would ask for your prompt confirmation. On the 1st I am flying back from Berlin, where I have what to do for a few days.

For now, let me just add my thanks for your extraordinarily beautiful and substantial contribution to the *Zeugnisse* [Testimonies]. I am very happy it's in there, for more than one reason, as you know. You will find that the commemorative volume, for the most part, contains things that are much better than what one expects from commemorative volumes; and this is precisely how it was planned from the start.

My *Hegel: Three Studies* is coming out any day now. If Unseld doesn't send it to you right away, you will of course receive it from me. I view the fact that your volume of *Judaica* is now also included in the "Bibliothek" as strengthening a position that is particularly important for me, also within this series. A second edition of my Mahler book has become necessary of late.

Until very soon, a thousand thanks, once more, and all the best from Gretel,

your loyal
Adorno

Original: typescript with printed letterhead; Gershom Scholem Archive, The National Library of Israel, Jerusalem.

contribution to the *Zeugnisse* [Testimonies]: See See letter no. 118 and the relevant note in this volume.

Hegel: Three Studies: Adorno's book was first published as Vol. 38 of the "edition suhrkamp" series in 1963. See *Hegel: Three Studies*, trans. Shierry Weber Nicholsen (Cambridge, MA: MIT Press, 1993).

Mahler book: See letter no. 92 and the relevant note in this volume.

133 ADORNO TO SCHOLEM
FRANKFURT AM MAIN, 29.10.1963

PROF. DR. THEODOR W. ADORNO

FRANKFURT AM MAIN
KETTENHOFWEG 123
29 October 1963

Dear Scholem,

I am enclosing a transcript of an astonishing letter from Hansi Schoen, which might interest you.

At the same time, I might also remind you once more that you were going to send me a letter to Hannah Arendt, which would once again be of burning interest to me.

I returned from Tuscany safe and sound and in a state of genuine relaxation.

The music book with the piece dedicated to you on *Moses und Aron* is not out yet; you will, of course, receive it without delay.

All that is cordial to you and Fanya, also from Gretel,

always yours,
Adorno

Original: typescript with printed letterhead and a transcript of the letter from Hansi Schoen, dated 21.10.1963; Gershom Scholem Archive, The National Library of Israel, Jerusalem.

a transcript of an astonishing letter from Hansi Schoen: The transcript of the letter from the 21st of October reads:

> Dear Teddy,
> Only now – after almost three years – have I strength enough to send you a sign of life, if nothing else. It is meant, above all, to explain that I

went out into the world as a restless wanderer; that I spent one year in Australia at Nina's; that I couldn't settle down anywhere, but that I have now found a nice little apartment here, and that I very much want to see my old friends – or at least to hear from them. I sincerely hope to see you again sometime soon so that I can try to explain our Ernst's response to you and to some other old friends.

I read the *Frankfurter Allgemeine* every day so I know how well you are doing, and I am aware of your many great successes. This makes me very happy. I have not heard from Gerhard Scholem for some time – when are the Benjamin letters coming out? Yesterday I saw Paul Tillich on television. Do you remember the funny fancy dress party to which you came dressed as Napoleon? Paul was there too, in a word: all of us. Those were some good years, right?

Please convey my regards to your dear wife 'Swan Neck,' and many good wishes to you both.

sgd. yours, Hansi

[P.S.:] I'll tell you why I went back to using my maiden name when, hopefully, I see you again.

The original letter reads: "Countess J. Rogendorf von Mollenburg / Flat 16, Fitzjohn's House / Fitzjohn's Avenue / London, N.W.3., England / formerly: Hansi Schoen."

a letter to Hannah Arendt: Adorno is presumably referring to Scholem's letter from 23/24 June 1963, which contains a critical response to Arendt's book *Eichmann in Jerusalem*. See Arendt, *Eichmann in Jerusalem: A Report on the Banality of Evil* (New York: Faber, 1963); see also *The Correspondence of Hannah Arendt and Gershom Scholem*, ed. Marie Luise Knott, trans. Anthony David (Chicago: University of Chicago Press, 2017), pp. 201–5.

134 SCHOLEM TO ADORNO
JERUSALEM, 1.11.1963

האוניברסיטה העברית בירושלים
THE HEBREW UNIVERSITY, JERUSALEM

FACULTY OF HUMANITIES — הפקולטה למדעי הרוח

1 Nov. 1963

Dear Adorno,

The letter from Hansi Schoen, the copy of which you sent me, pleased me greatly, and I would urge you to answer her in a friendly way. Somehow, her bitter phase (as happens to many of us) seems to have dissipated, and I guess she is seeking contact with Ernst Schoen's friends. Incidentally, I just wrote to her a week ago to update her on what we've decided regarding W. B.'s letters.

I am enclosing the correspondence with Hannah Arendt, which has been published in the *N.Z.Z.* You will understand why I thought it was quite superfluous to reply to her letter publicly. Every reader can immediately see how things stand.

Permit me to note that the Adorno commemorative volume did not arrive here, nor have any offprints. Would it be possible, through Miss Olbrich, to follow up?

In Rome, I was, on two occasions, with Belmore for relatively long periods of time – very educational.

Now, back to work.

Cordial regards to you both

yours,

Gerhard Scholem

Original: manuscript with printed letterhead; Theodor W. Adorno Archive, Frankfurt am Main.

135 ADORNO TO SCHOLEM
FRANKFURT AM MAIN, 7.11.1963

PROF. DR. THEODOR W. ADORNO

FRANKFURT AM MAIN
KETTENHOFWEG 123
7 November 1963

Dear Scholem,

Kindest thanks for your letter of the 1st of November and for the correspondence with Mrs. Ahrendt. The latter merely confirmed the old antipathy that I have felt for this woman since our youth – for her boundless ambition and her intellectual neophytism. She is right about only one thing: she has never been a leftist intellectual. Sure enough, her background is also not in German philosophy. She is a student of Jaspers.

I wrote to Hansi Schoen in the friendliest way right after receiving her letter. For my part, I hold no grudge against her; the whole affect came from her side alone. Surely, Benjamin had few friends who were as loyal and reliable as Ernst Schoen.

Regarding the commemorative volume, this will probably be sent out only along with the offprints. I'll take care of it, of course.

From one line of yours, I take it that, *in natura*, Mr. Belmore made an equally problematic impression on you as he did on me. Had I known that you were in Rome, I would have put you in touch with a few intellectuals who would have been of interest to you. Meanwhile, I went to Tuscany for a 14-day holiday. It was indescribably beautiful, and I am now, to a certain degree, armed to face the new semester. Horkheimer is in America.

All that is cordial to you both, also from Gretel,

yours,

Adorno

Original: typescript with printed letterhead; Gershom Scholem Archive, The National Library of Israel, Jerusalem.

Mrs. Ahrendt: Adorno's spelling.

She is right about only one thing: she has never been a leftist intellectual: In his letter of the 23rd of June 1963, Scholem criticizes Arendt for "the heartless, the downright malicious tone [she] employ[s] in dealing with the topic that so profoundly concerns the center of our life. There is something in the Jewish language that is completely indefinable, yet fully concrete – what the Jews call *ahavath Israel*, or love for the Jewish people. With you, my dear Hannah, as with so many intellectuals coming from the German left, there is no trace of it" (*The Correspondence of Hannah Arendt and Gershom Scholem*, ed. Marie Luise Knott, trans. Anthony David (Chicago: University of Chicago Press, 2017), p. 202). Arendt responded on the 20th of July 1963, "Your letter contains a number of uncontroversial claims – uncontroversial because they are quite simply wrong. . . . I do not belong to the "intellectuals coming from the German left" (ibid., p. 205).

She is a student of Jaspers: Hannah Arendt wrote her doctoral thesis on Augustine's concept of love at the University of Heidelberg in 1928 under the supervision of the philosopher and psychiatrist Karl Jaspers (1883–1969). See Hannah Arendt, *Love and Saint Augustine* (Chicago: University of Chicago Press, 1998). Jaspers's *Existenzphilosophie* is a central object of Adorno's critique in *The Jargon of Authenticity*. See *The Jargon of Authenticity*, trans. Knut Tarnowski and Frederic Will (London: Routledge & Kegan Paul, 1973), pp. 20–7, 63–76.

136 SCHOLEM TO ADORNO
JERUSALEM, 17.11.1963

האוניברסיטה העברית בירושלים

THE HEBREW UNIVERSITY, JERUSALEM

FACULTY OF HUMANITIES הפקולטה למדעי הרוח

Jerusalem, on the 17th of November, 1963

Dear Adorno,

I thank you for your letter, which I have, unfortunately, misplaced at the moment. Hopefully I have not forgotten anything important. I will wait to see if the commemorative volume and the offprints turn up one day. I'm very glad that you wrote to Hansi Schoen. We'll see . . .

I'm enclosing a copy of my notes to Dr. Unseld, which I drew up as the minutes of our discussion on the 3rd of October. In the meantime, incidentally, I found out something about Felix Noeggerath's biography during a fortuitous or providential encounter with Friedrich Podszus at the Café Odéon in Zurich, where I also found out the fact, unknown to us all, that Noeggerath passed away in Munich a mere 2 years ago. It is really unbelievable how much we did not know! Had I any idea, I would have visited the man in Munich before it was too late. Podszus offered to inquire in Munich whether there are any letters from W. B. in N.'s estate.

Meanwhile, please don't freeze to death in Frankfurt. Here it is still nice and warm. For today, cordial regards to you both,

from your

G. Scholem

Original: typescript with printed letterhead; Theodor W. Adorno Archive, Frankfurt am Main.

Felix Noeggerath: The writer and publisher Felix Noeggerath (1885–1960) had been friends with Walter Benjamin since 1925. He was born in New York and studied philosophy, Indology and Indo-Germanic languages in Munich. He received his doctoral degree in 1916 from the University of Erlangen, with a thesis entitled *Synthesis und Systembegriff: Ein Beitrag zur Kritik des Antirationalismus* [Synthesis and the concept of system: a contribution to the critique of anti-rationalism]. Later he worked as a translator and, for some time, as the co-owner of, and author for, a publishing house specializing in children's books. Benjamin stayed with Noeggerath during his visits to Ibiza in 1932 and 1933. See Scholem, "Walter Benjamin und Felix Noeggerath," first published in *Merkur*, 35/393 (1981), pp. 134–69; repr. in: Scholem, *Walter Benjamin und sein Engel* [Walter Benjamin and his angel] (Frankfurt am Main: Suhrkamp, 1983), pp. 78–127; see also *The Correspondence of Walter Benjamin 1910–1940*, ed. Theodor W. Adorno and Gershom Scholem, trans. Manfred R. Jacobson and Evelyn M. Jacobson (Chicago: University of Chicago Press, 1994), pp. 191–3.

137 SCHOLEM TO ADORNO JERUSALEM, 22.12.1963

Jerusalem, on the 22nd of December, 1963

Dear Adorno,

Right on time for a Jewish Christmas gift, I can now deliver the results of efforts that have been strenuous, lengthy, and mostly futile:

an authoritative recipe for creating the world-famous Jewish dish, cholent. I obtained it with the help of a lady from Israeli diplomatic circles, who, for her part, drew on American-Jewish-Russian sources. I wish you *bon appétit*. If I'm not mistaken, the recipe is intended for 5 people; but this remains to be verified experimentally.

With best wishes for your stomach in 1964,

I remain devotedly

yours

G Scholem

Recipe: see enclosed.

I still have not received offprints for the 2 contributions to your commemorative volume. Is there really nothing to be done here??

Original: typescript with handwritten postscript and an enclosed recipe, which has been lost; Theodor W. Adorno Archive, Frankfurt am Main.

cholent: Cholent (Hebrew: *chamin*, meaning "warm") is a stew traditionally prepared by Jewish people for Sabbath lunch. The dish, which consists mainly of meat, potatoes, beans, and pearl barley, is cooked on Friday morning, before the start of the Sabbath, and is simmered on a low heat until lunchtime on Saturday. The recipe sent to Adorno by Scholem has not been preserved.

138 ADORNO TO SCHOLEM
FRANKFURT AM MAIN, 22.1.1964

PROF. DR. THEODOR W. ADORNO

FRANKFURT AM MAIN
KETTENHOFWEG 123

on the 22nd of Jan. 1964

Professor Dr. Gershom Scholem
28 Abarbanel Street
Jerusalem / Israel

Dear Scholem,

Please accept my most heartfelt, albeit badly delayed, thanks for your letter of the 22nd of December, and for the Jewish Christmas present. Unfortunately, I have not been able to try it yet, since my theologically unschooled physician has put me on a diet that prohibits me from enjoying just these kinds of delicacies. Let us hope that this taboo, which has a venerable prehistory – found already in Empedocles – will be breached, finally, by the reversal from mysticism into enlightenment.

Surely, in the meantime, you've received the offprints of the commemorative volume. You know that I especially enjoyed your contribution. The Benjamin text interested me above all because of the way that it is almost the contradiction of his later work. It goes to show how much even his intellectual development involves the negation of what originally moved him.

The Frankfurt share of the Benjamin notes, meanwhile, is done – short and, I'd like to think, quite satisfactory. How are things at your end? I would imagine that all that is left now is the question of how to think about a preface, which, admittedly, raises considerable problems.

For my own part, in the meantime, I have now split off the first major draft of *The Jargon of Authenticity* from my other philosophical *work in progress*,* which should be beneficial for both projects. The *Jargon*, which, in itself, is a small book, stands complete in its penultimate version, and I hope that the revisions won't require too much additional effort. It was terribly difficult to get to grips with this matter. Nevertheless, I didn't let it get me down. Among other things, I am currently writing something on Kracauer, which will be broadcast on the radio. Between [concern for] the truth, the recognition of an outstanding potential, critique, and consideration for an excessively sensitive friend, I felt that I needed to walk on eggshells. The broadcast will be aired by Hessischer Rundfunk on the 7th of February at 10 pm. The stuff will also surely be printed somewhere. The expanded version of the essay on Hölderlin will come out in the February issue of *Neue Rundschau*. The first part consists of ironclad attacks against Heidegger, whereas the second part, I would like to think, is made up of more pleasant matters. Needless to say, you will receive an offprint straight away. At present, I'm back to the main business, *Negative Dialectics*, and I'm dictating the kind of supplements that are more important than what is to be supplemented. I still have to write two chapters and an introduction, and then I'll finally have this ambitious project behind me.

Unfortunately, Horkheimer has now retired in earnest and has, more or less, withdrawn to Montagnola. Habermas, whom you also know, has, through my undertaking, been appointed and has accepted.

All that is cordial to you and Fanja, also from Gretel,

your old

Adorno

* Original in English.

Please let me know if you've received *Quasi una Fantasia*. The volume contains my text on Schoenberg's *Moses und Aron*, which is dedicated to you. I'm very curious to hear your reaction. Despite the musical theme, I imagine that there is enough in it that pertains to you. Please excuse the many errors in this letter. It was written by a secretary who is not at all used to my ways.

Original: typescript with printed letterhead and handwritten postscript; Gershom Scholem Archive, The National Library of Israel, Jerusalem.

this taboo . . . a venerable prehistory: Adorno is apparently referring to Empedocles' dietary prescription: "Wretches, utter wretches, keep your hands from beans!" See Jonathan Barnes, *The Presocratic Philosophers* (London: Routledge & Kegan Paul, 1979), pp. 79, 97.

the Benjamin text: Adorno is referring to Walter Benjamin's essay "On the Program of the Coming Philosophy" (1917–18), which was included in the commemorative volume for Adorno. along with introductory remarks by Gershom Scholem. See Benjamin, "Über das Programm der kommenden Philosophie," in Max Horkheimer, ed., *Zeugnisse: Theodor W. Adorno zum 60. Geburtstag* [Testimonies: for Theodor W. Adorno on his 60th birthday] (Frankfurt am Main: Europäische Verlagsanstalt, 1963), pp. 33–44 (see letter no. 118 in this volume); see also Benjamin, "On the Program of the Coming Philosophy," in *Selected Writings*, Vol. 1: *1913–1926*, ed. Marcus Bulow and Michael W. Jennings (Cambridge, MA: The Belknap Press of Harvard University Press, 1996), pp. 100–10.

split off the first major draft of The Jargon of Authenticity *from my other philosophical* work in progress: *The Jargon of Authenticity* was originally intended as a part of *Negative Dialectics*. Adorno comments on his decision to split this text of from the rest of the project in the "Author's Note" accompanying the published version of *The Jargon of Authenticity*:

> The author conceived the *Jargon of Authenticity* as part of the *Negative Dialectic*. However, he finally excluded that text from the latter work not only because its size grew disproportionate to the other parts, but also because the elements of linguistic physiognomy and sociology no longer fitted properly with the rest of the plan. The resistance against intellectual division of labor requires that this division of labor should be reflected on and not merely ignored. Certainly in intention and in theme the *Jargon* is philosophical. As long as philosophy was in line with its own nature, it also had content. However, in retreating to the ideal of its pure nature, philosophy cancels itself out. This thought was only developed in the book which was then still unfinished, while the *Jargon* proceeds according to this insight without, however, grounding it fully. Thus it was published earlier, as a kind of propaedeutic. (*The Jargon of Authenticity*, trans. Knut Tarnowski and Frederic Will (London: Routledge & Kegan Paul, 1973), pp. xix–xx)

something on Kracauer, which will be broadcast on the radio: Adorno's lecture on Kracauer was broadcast by Hessischer Rundfunk on the 7th of February 1964. It was later published as "Der wunderliche Realist: Über Siegfried Kracauer," in *Neue Deutsche Hefte*, no. 101 (September/ October 1964), pp. 17–39; see also "The Curious Realist: On Siegfried Kracauer," in *Notes to Literature*, Vol. 2, trans. Shierry Weber Nicholsen (New York: Columbia University Press, 1992), pp. 58–75.

expanded version of the essay on Hölderlin: See letter no. 127 in this volume and the relevant note.

Habermas: The sociologist and philosopher Jürgen Habermas (b. 1929) had been Adorno and Horkheimer's assistant at the Institute for Social Research since 1956. In 1961 he completed his *Habilitation* in Marburg under the supervision of Wolfgang Abendroth. The work was titled *Strukturwandel der Öffentlichkeit: Untersuchungen zu einer Kategorie der bürgerlichen Gesellschaft* [The structural transformation of the public sphere: an inquiry into a category of bourgeois society]. See Habermas, *The Structural Transformation of the Public Sphere: An Inquiry into a Category of Bourgeois Society*, trans. Thomas Burger and Frederick Lawrence (Cambridge, M.A.: MIT Press, 1989). In 1964, Habermas was appointed to Horkheimer's old position as a professor of philosophy and sociology at the Goethe University in Frankfurt am Main.

139 SCHOLEM TO ADORNO
JERUSALEM, 9.2.1964

האוניברסיטה העברית בירושלים
THE HEBREW UNIVERSITY, JERUSALEM

FACULTY OF HUMANITIES — הפקולטה למדעי הרוח

Jerusalem, on the 9th of
February, 1964

Dear Adorno,

Your letter of the 22nd of January arrived a few days before your new book, *Quasi una Fantasia*. Your writings have, in the meantime, taken on such impressive proportions that I will soon have to drop out of the competition. In German [materials], at any rate, I'm well and truly "set up" for some time. I thank you kindly for the dedication of the piece on Schoenberg. I read the article with great interest, especially where I was not limited by my utter ignorance of the technical-musical matters. I hope to hear *Moses und Aron* somewhere, one of these days, so I can make some sense of it. Your reflections on this opera, and on contemporary sacred music, are very impressive. Whether or not you can really disprove the possibility of such music,

I do not know. After all, it cannot be predicted where, and in what forms, the tradition of the sacred will find expression in our world. I wouldn't want to concede that it is impossible *a priori*. The contradiction that you point out between the musical-dramatic element and the element of the sacred makes sense to me, of course. I also won't venture to judge, given my lack of knowledge, whether Schoenberg in fact saw his opera as ritual music. The question remains as to whether there are ritual practices today which still have enough life to engender an authentic music. Jewish music seems, overall, to be something that is downright inconceivable, which fits exactly with your description of it as an image of the imageless. To the extent that I was able to follow you, and insofar as I have understood the discussion of these things, everything that bears the pretence of Jewish music, as such, is labeled with a big question mark. What is Jewish here amounts, time and time again, to the occult. And surely it is to be found somewhere. I am less convinced by your speculation about the subterranean, mystical tradition among modern Jews than I am by your observations on myth and image within the music. I can only imagine this under Jungian hypotheses; and by these I am not exactly convinced. This affinity to a mystical tradition would more likely have to be sought in some structure in the productivity of the Jews that you named than in some historical thread, however thin. I cannot believe in such a thread, especially given what I know about the history of Moravian and Bohemian Jews in the 19th century.

I'm sorry that your health does not permit you to try the Jewish theological recipe. It seems our efforts were in vain!

To my delight, I have, in the meantime, received the offprints. Of Benjamin's essay, one might truly say that, in fact, it represents the pure antithesis of his later intentions. But what first grounds his dialectical turn, as you correctly point out, is precisely the sharp focus of his as yet unbroken faith in the possibility of a system; and I wouldn't presume to answer the question as to whether his genius as a commentator is what led him to the dialectic, or whether the dialectic that was inherent in him determined his genius as a commentator.

I am still thinking about the possibility of writing a few pages for the preface to the letters. This will depend on the attempt. You may recall that we kept the option open of both writing something, if we can manage it. On the other hand, the collection could easily be sent off for typesetting, which will undoubtedly take a while, even if the question of the preface – or prefaces – is not yet resolved. By the way, there is a chance, even if I can take it only as quite marginal, that the university will send me to Europe for a few days to attend to a certain matter. If that happens, it will be during the next 14 days, and it is likely that I'd be in Frankfurt for half a day *en route*. But I can only hope that nothing will come of this sensitive mission, which apparently was – or will be – intended for me.

For the past 6 weeks, we've had an uninterrupted wintery cold snap; it's so rainy and stormy that it feels like we might as well be in Europe. We haven't had a winter like this for years.

Cordial regards to your wife and you, also from Fania,

yours,

Gershom Scholem

Original: typescript with printed letterhead; Theodor W. Adorno Archive, Frankfurt am Main. First published in Gershom Scholem, *Briefe II: 1948–1970*, ed. Thomas Sparr (Munich: C. H. Beck, 1995), pp. 114–15. An excerpt of this letter appears in translation in *Gershom Scholem: A Life in Letters*, ed. and trans. Anthony David Skinner (Cambridge, MA: Harvard University Press, 2002), pp. 404–5.

Whether or not you can really disprove the possibility of such music: Adorno writes the following on the impossibility of sacred music:

> It is in this positive sense that *Moses und Aron* is a fragment and it would not be extravagant to attempt to explain why it was left incomplete by arguing that it could not be completed. . . . The impossibility which appears intrinsic to the work is, in reality, an impossibility which was not intended. It is well known that great works can be recognized by the gap between their aim and their actual achievement. The impossibility we have in mind is historical: that of sacred art today and the idea of the binding, canonical, all-inclusive work that Schoenberg aspired to. ("Sacred Fragment: Schoenberg's *Moses und Aron*," in *Quasi Una Fantasia: Essays on Modern Music*, trans. Rodney Livingstone (London: Verso, 1998), pp. 226–7)

image of the imageless: In his text, Adorno applies the Jewish idea of the Old Testament interdiction against making images to Schoenberg's music: "The absolute which this music sets out to make real, without any sleight of hand, it achieves as its own idea of itself: it is itself an image of something without images – the very last thing the story wanted. The Jewish prohibition on making images which forms the centre of the text also defines the approach of music." See Adorno, "Sacred Fragment," pp. 229–30.

your speculations about the subterranean, mystical tradition among modern Jews: Scholem is referring to the following passage in Adorno's essay:

> We may legitimately ask what produced the conception of this work in light of such immense difficulties, which may be compared to those experienced twenty years before in connection with *Die Jakobsleiter*. . . . Of course it was Schoenberg's own individual make-up that provided the critical impetus. His parents do not seem to have been orthodox in their beliefs, but it may be supposed that the descendant of a family from Bratislava, Jews living in the Leopoldstadt, and anything but fully

emancipated, was not wholly free of that subterranean mystical tradition to be found in many of his contemporaries of similar origins, men such as Kraus, Kafka and Mahler. (See Adorno, "Sacred Fragment," p. 232)

Jungian hypotheses: On the relation to Carl Gustav Jung, see letter no. 25 in this volume.

sensitive mission: Not verified.

140 ADORNO TO SCHOLEM
FRANKFURT AM MAIN, 17.2.1964

PROF. DR. THEODOR W. ADORNO

6 FRANKFURT AM MAIN
KETTENHOFWEG 123
17 February 1964

Dear Scholem,

Very sincere thanks for your letter and for your response to my Schoenberg essay; it is of extraordinary importance to me.

On the question of the possibility of sacred music, my thinking is more circumspect than perhaps came through in this piece. An *a priori* denial is far from my mind; but it is quite telling that one of this epoch's greatest composers did not succeed in this matter, despite applying himself to it with extraordinary seriousness and at the height of his strength. The attempt to determine the elements of this impossibility also casts light on the possibility as such. Whether or not *Moses und Aron* can be understood as a ritual work, in the strict sense, remains debatable, by the way. That it was ultimately staged as an opera speaks in favor of your view that it isn't. I, for my side, would note that it is infinitely far removed from the very idea of a scenic work; rather, through a process of complete recasting, it utilizes every possible element of the European tradition of sacral music – much more so, it seems to me, than the operatic tradition. Even if this work were not sacred, in an authentic sense, wouldn't that be bound up with the problem of sacred art today? It would seem to me that, in the present day, the only possibility of salvaging sacred art and its philosophical truth-content lies in its unflinching migration into the profane; you must also be inclined to this view, I would think. This is exactly what we should talk about sometime.

As to the question of a subterranean mystical tradition, you can believe me that I am far from suggesting any affinity with Jung. After all, the core of his teaching – the archaic images – is a moment in Freud's thought, and the latter even went so far as to postulate something like a – necessarily collective – form of hereditary memory, especially in his *Moses* text. Jung's falsity lies less in his individual insights, which are often very fruitful, than in their isolation from his overall construction, through which they acquired their reactionary, falsifying character. But what I said about this aspect of the Jewish tradition was meant to be far more modest. I simply reiterated my observation that a whole group of Jews from this generation, who hailed from the regions of Bohemia and Moravia – Kraus, Kafka, Schoenberg, perhaps also Freud, and, above all, Mahler – harbored traces of this mystical tradition (God knows where they got it from), as well as its radical metamorphosis through secularization. Heaven knows you are better equipped than I am to offer an explanation for this.

It would be very good if we could discuss the problem of the preface to the Benjamin volume soon. I would only ask that you please give me plenty of notice regarding your dates – by telegraph, if need be – since the next fourteen days are going to be insanely tight for me, with countless exams and administrative duties. I am also going to Münster from the 27th to the 29th of February.

Although there's still plenty left to do, I have turned a corner with *The Jargon of Authenticity*, my, as it were, linguistic-philosophical book. You may have seen the extract in *Neue Rundschau*. My Hölderlin text should come out any day now; you'll receive it shortly, of course.

To you and Fanya all the best, also from Gretel,

your loyal

Adorno

Original: typescript with printed letterhead; Gershom Scholem Archive, The National Library of Israel, Jerusalem.

Jung . . . the core of his teaching – the archaic images: See C. G. Jung, *The Collected Works of C. G. Jung*, Vol. 9 (Pt I): *Archetypes and the Collective Unconscious*, ed. and trans. Gerald Adler and R. F. C. Hull (Princeton, NJ: Princeton University Press, 1981).

a moment in Freud's thought: See Sigmund Freud, *Moses and Monotheism*, trans. Katherine Jones (New York: Vintage Books, 1955).

the extract in Neue Rundschau: Passages from the first part of *The Jargon of Authenticity* had already been published in 1963. See *Neue Rundschau*, 74/3 (1963), pp. 371–85.

141 SCHOLEM TO ADORNO
JERUSALEM, 13.7.1964

13 July 1964

Dear Adorno,

It's been ages since I've heard from you – then again, there was a 4-week postal strike here in the spring, and who knows how much was lost in that.

Will we see you this summer? My wife and I will be at the Hotel Tamaro in Ascona from the 17th to the 30th of August. We're going there directly this time, not via Sils. Then, I will be in Frankfurt until the 6th of September, and again from 10th to the 15th of September, roughly, where, on Sept. 2nd, I'll be contending with an author's evening for the Suhrkamp Verlag, which Unseld asked me to attend. I fear that you won't be back by then – will you?? At any rate, it would be good if you could take these dates into account when making your plans. Of course I'm prepared to make an appearance on your birthday as a well-wisher (now that it has been made known to me), although I suspect that you will seek out some quieter hideaway on this day.

I had hoped – it now seems, in vain – to be able to read the proofs of the letters in F. But this now seems to be out of the question.

I hope you are both well. As I may have already mentioned in a previous letter, I intend to retire this coming spring so that I can live in keeping with my inclinations and disinclinations.

Write soon!

Cordial regards to you both

yours,

G. Scholem

Original: aerogram (manuscript); Theodor W. Adorno Archive, Frankfurt am Main.

I intend to retire this coming spring: Scholem retired in 1965 after 40 years as a professor of Jewish mysticism at the Hebrew University in Jerusalem. Nevertheless, he stayed on as vice-president of the university during the years following (until 1968) and as president of the Israeli Academy of Sciences (1968–74).

142 ADORNO TO SCHOLEM
FRANKFURT AM MAIN, 20.7.1964

PROF. DR. THEODOR W. ADORNO

6 FRANKFURT AM MAIN
KETTENHOFWEG 123
20 July 1964

Dear Scholem,

Very sincere thanks for your letter.

It's a terrible pity, of course, that we won't see each other in Sils Maria this time – we're going there on the 30th of July. But things will work out in Frankfurt. We are staying up there until the 6th of September, but then we'll be back in Frankfurt and can get together at ease and make further headway on the Benjamin letters. You and Fanya are already most cordially invited to my birthday on the 11th. It's wonderful that we can spend it together. The sad thing, though, is that I will miss your reading at Suhrkamp. Is the 2nd of September really a good date? I doubt that many people will come around this time. If it were possible to move it to a date between the 10th and the 15th, that would probably be in the interest of everyone involved.

In other news, the Benjamin letters are still being held up, simply on account of internal delays with the publisher, which Unseld is blaming on Mr. Boehlich; but, with our joint intervention, these should easily be overcome. Meanwhile, Mr. Tiedemann has written a dissertation, which takes as its task nothing less than a construction of sorts of the Benjaminian philosophy. The work, considering its immense difficulties, can only be described as extraordinary. He is now producing a second draft on the basis of my very thorough annotations, and I believe that, by the time you are here, this will already be at your disposal. Through this work, some rather gratifying prospects for the *Arcades* have been revealed, but the latter is such a delicate little plant that I would still rather not touch it at all.

This coming Friday, I have invited Jonas, who will speak on Heidegger and theology in the Philosophy Department. Kracauer, who is here at the moment, set this up. I'm very curious; hopefully what he says will be less Heidegger-friendly than the gnosis book.

I myself have been working prodigiously. The book version of *The Jargon of Authenticity*, 140 pages for the "edition suhrkamp" series, is currently made up and being revised, and the third volume of *Notes to Literature* is finished. But this is all more or less amusement. The main thing, the book on dialectics, is also coming along well: I have only one of the projected parts and the introduction left to write. Then there's still the endlessly difficult task of supplementation and integration, of course. *Sauf imprévu*, it should finally be finished over the course of the coming year. The title has now been decided: it will be called, quite simply, *Negative Dialectics*.

The *sauf imprévu* is no mere phrase, by the way. I have been quite unwell physically. I had a very serious heart ailment, and I think that, had my physician not treated me so energetically, I would have had a heart attack. That the causes may, at first, have been psychogenic hardly changes the somatic picture. I have managed to recuperate somewhat during the past four weeks. My cardiogram is also looking much better, and I hope that I will fully recover in Sils – especially since the doctor explicitly said that he has no concerns regarding the high altitude.

Maybe we can telephone sometime between Sils and Ascona? Either way, at the very latest [we will see each other] here on the 10th of September.

All that is cordial to you both, also from Gretel,

yours ever,

Adorno

Original: typescript with printed letterhead; Gershom Scholem Archive, The National Library of Israel, Jerusalem.

Mr. Tiedemann . . . dissertation: See letter no. 68 in this volume and the relevant note.

gratifying prospects for the Arcades: This presumably refers to Adorno's belief that a "readable text" could be produced from the notes and drafts of the *Arcades Project*.

Jonas . . . on Heidegger and theology . . . the gnosis book: The philosopher Hans Jonas (1903–1993) studied in Freiburg and Marburg under Martin Heidegger, among others. In 1928 he completed his doctorate under Heidegger's supervision with a dissertation entitled *Der Begriff der Gnosis* [The concept of gnosis]. During this time, Jonas became friends with Hannah Arendt. In 1933 he immigrated to London, where he became acquainted with Scholem. In 1934, the first volume of his book *Gnosis und spätantiker Geist* [Gnosis and late-antique spirit] was published. He immigrated to Palestine in 1934, where he taught at the Hebrew University in Jerusalem and became part of Scholem's circle of friends. From 1940 to 1945 he was a soldier in the British Army, as part of the Jewish Brigade group, then from 1948 to 1949, he was a soldier in the Israeli Army. In 1949 he moved to Montreal and in 1955 to New York, where he was appointed to a professorship at the New School for Social Research. In 1979, Jonas published his influential book *Das Prinzip der Verantwortung: Versuch einer Ethik für die technologische Zivilisation* (Frankfurt am Main: Insel, 1979). See Jonas, *The Imperative of Responsibility: In Search of an Ethics for the Technological Age*, trans. Hans Jonas and David Herr (Chicago: University of Chicago Press, 1985).

the third volume of Notes to Literature: The third volume came out in 1965, as Vol. 146 of the "Bibliothek Suhrkamp" series. Among other things, it contained the aforementioned lectures on Kracauer and Hölderlin.

143 SCHOLEM TO ADORNO
JERUSALEM, 25.7.1964

האוניברסיטה העברית בירושלים
THE HEBREW UNIVERSITY, JERUSALEM

25.7.1964

FACULTY OF HUMANITIES הפקולטה למדעי הרוח

Dear Adorno,

I am sorry to hear that your health has been poor. With tripled urgency, I wish you a good rest and recovery in Sils. Of course I can call you from Ascona once, or three times.

Fanja is not coming to Germany; from Ascona she will be going with a group to Spain for 3 weeks, and then I'm meeting her in Strasbourg.

Unseld is in Scandinavia from the 6th to the 14th of September, which made the earlier date necessary; otherwise, of course, I would have had nothing against a later date. Also, at the time, the venue was only available on the 2nd.

Do you think that it would be possible to organize a small event, something like last year's, at the Institute on the 13th or 14th of September? If so, I could discuss the same social issues that I treated last autumn with respect to the Hasidim, but with a focus on the Kabbalah instead: "Social Aspects of the Kabbalah" (in particular, in the Safed period).

I'll keep the evening free on the 11th of September to accept your invitation.

It's a shame that we won't be able to speak with Unseld together, unless, of course, he's back, and available, by the evening of the 14th. I have to leave on the 15th.

All that is cordial and a good rest, with compliments to your lady wife

yours,
Scholem

Original: manuscript with printed letterhead; Theodor W. Adorno Archive, Frankfurt am Main.

a small event, something like last year's: As becomes clear in the subsequent letter, Scholem is referring to an *Arbeitsgemeinschaft* [working group], a small seminar.

"Social Aspects of the Kabbalah": Whether or not this seminar took place could not be verified.

144 ADORNO TO SCHOLEM FRANKFURT AM MAIN, 28.7.1964

PROF. DR. THEODOR W. ADORNO

6 FRANKFURT AM MAIN
KETTENHOFWEG 123
28 July 1964

Dear Scholem,

Sincerest thanks for your letter.
Very briefly today on account of the extreme pressure of my last days here: I would of course be delighted for you to hold another seminar [Arbeitsgemeinschaft] at the Institute covering social aspects of the Kabbalah, in particular, during the Safed period. The most suitable date would be Monday the 14th of September around 4 in the afternoon.

I am very much looking forward to seeing you. As for the matters that remain to be discussed with Unseld, you can either meet with him yourself, or, to the extent that these things concern me, you can brief him so that I can finalize things when I speak with him again.

All that is cordial, and see you very soon,

yours,

Adorno

Original: typescript with printed letterhead; Gershom Scholem Archive, The National Library of Israel, Jerusalem.

145 SCHOLEM TO ADORNO JERUSALEM, 5.1.1965

Jerusalem, on the 5th of January, 1965

Dear Adorno,

I received your new book, *The Jargon of Authenticity*, shortly before the end of our first trimester. I brought it with me to Tiberias, where I vacationed for a few days, and I'd now like to thank you for it. I read it with great pleasure. Your analysis of the disintegration of language in existentialism is very impressive. Some of your claims in it remain inscrutable to me, unfortunately; for instance, when you speak of the societal basis for the semblance of immediacy in the *Jargon*, p. 65, or your denunciation of dignity, p. 132. Don't take this the wrong way, but, given the acuity of your analysis and the plethora of jargon at your disposal, you could have dispensed with unfair quotations, such as the one (p. 65) about "the notorious poverty which is the great inward gleam of the spirit." In Rilke's case, this verse appears in a completely legitimate context – not in a poem about the poverty of the proletariat, that is, but about the poverty of St. Francis. I don't know what is supposed to be notorious about this definition of poverty in Rilke's verse, other than in its polemical misuse initiated by Kurt Hiller; and, God knows, he is not exactly a scrupulous source. I recall having discussed dignity with you once before in Sils. Your sensitivity against this concept is incomprehensible to me.

On p. 83, shouldn't it say "in which the Jew Georg Simmel was given a rap on the knuckles"? If I understood you correctly, your sentence implies a criticism of Simmel put forward by certain people, not a "pat on the back," either in recognition or condescension (at any rate, I cannot think of an instance of the latter in Simmel's case).

I was especially impressed by your discussion of the "encounter" [Begegnung]; surely, though, the shift in the meaning of this word must be older?

The jargon of the existentialists merely replaced that of the neo-Kantians, which was already in tatters. This is also the theme of the beadle's poem, presented in the Department of the Philosophy of Religion at the University of Muri in the year 1918:

Terror drives many a theory
Through ceremonious *termini*
Every problem, be it death or the numeral
Is treated as transcendental.

For now, I wish you and your wife all good things for the New Year – above all, health and the strength to work. See you again someplace.

Cordial regards
yours,
Gerhard Scholem

Original: aerogram (typescript); Theodor W. Adorno Archive, Frankfurt am Main. First published in Scholem, *Briefe II: 1948–1970*, ed. Thomas Sparr (Munich: C. H. Beck, 1995), pp. 119–20.

when you speak of the societal basis for the semblance of immediacy in the Jargon:

> The overall appearance of the immediate, which comes to a head in inwardness – now merely a specimen – makes it unusually hard for those who are steadily exposed to the jargon to see through it. In its second-hand primalness they actually find something like contact, comparable to the feeling in the fraudulent National Socialist *Volk*-community which led people to believe that all kindred comrades are cared for and none is forgotten: permanent metaphysical subvention. The social basis for this is clear. Many instances of mediation in the market economy, which have strengthened the consciousness of alienation, are put aside in the transition to a planned economy; the routes between the whole and atomized individual subjects are shortened, as if the two extremes were near to one another. (Adorno, *The Jargon of Authenticity*, trans. Knut Tarnowski and Frederic Will (London: Routledge & Kegan Paul, 1973), p. 76)

your denunciation of dignity, p. 132:

> The jargon of authenticity is ideology as language, without any consideration of specific content. It asserts meaning with the gesture of that dignity by which Heidegger would like to dress up death. Dignity, too, is of an idealistic nature. . . . In these sentences dignity certainly plays a role as the dignity of being, and not of men. Yet the solemnity of these sentences differs from the solemnity of secularized burials only through its enthusiasm for irrational sacrifice. Combat pilots may have spoken in exactly this way when they returned from a city just destroyed by bombs and drank champagne to the health of those who did not return. Dignity was never anything more than the attitude of self-preservation aspiring to be more than that. The creature mimes the creator. (Adorno, *The Jargon of Authenticity*, pp. 160–1)

"the notorious poverty which is the great inward gleam of the spirit":

> Whatever wants to remain absolutely pure from the blemish of reification is pasted onto the subject as a firm attribute. Thus the subject becomes an object in the second degree, and finally the mass product of consolation: from that found in Rilke's 'Beggars can call you brother and still you can be a king' to the notorious poverty which is the great inward gleam of the spirit. (Adorno, *The Jargon of Authenticity*, p. 73)

Rilke's verse: Rilke's verse reads as follows: "For poverty is luminous from within . . ." See Rainer Maria Rilke, "Third Book: The Book of Poverty and Death," in *The Book of Hours*, trans. Susan Ranson (Rochester, NY: Camden House, 2008), p. 179.

Kurt Hiller: The lawyer and writer Kurt Hiller (1885–1972) was engaged in pacifist politics and was associated with the sexologist Magnus Hirschfeld's Wissenschaftlich-humanitäres Komitee [Scientific-Humanitarian Committee] in Berlin. Hiller parodies Rilke's poem on poverty in his collection *Der*

Unnennbare: Verse 1918–1937 [The unnamable: poems 1918–1937], which was published in Beijing in 1938.

On p. 83, shouldn't it say "in which the Jew Georg Simmel was given a rap on the knuckles"?: "The growth climate of this hostility to cultural philosophy is that academic climate in which they admonished the Jew Georg Simmel, on the grounds that, at least in intention, he absorbed himself in that concretion which the systems were forever only promising. Thus he transgressed a taboo of traditional philosophy which busies itself, if not with the fundamental themes of occidental metaphysics, at least with the question of their possibility." (Adorno, *The Jargon of Authenticity*, pp. 97–8)

I was especially impressed by your discussion of the "encounter" [Begegnung]:

> The very desire to purify the word "encounter," and to reinstate it through strict usage, would become, through unavoidable tacit agreement, a basic element of the jargon, along with purity and primalness – an element of that jargon from which it would like to escape. What was done to "encounter" satisfies a specific need. Those encounters which counteract themselves because they are organized, those encounters to which good will, busy-body behavior and canny desire for power tirelessly exhort us, are simply covers for spontaneous actions that have become impossible. People console themselves, or are being consoled, by thinking that something has already been done about what is oppressing them when they talk about it. Conversation, after having been a means of becoming clear about something, becomes an end in itself and a substitute for that which, in terms of its sense, should follow from it. The surplus in the word "encounter" – the suggestion that something essential is already occurring when those ordered to gather converse together – that surplus has the same deception at its center as the speculation on being helped in the word "concern." Once that word meant a sickness. (Adorno, *The Jargon of Authenticity*, pp. 78–9)

This is also the theme of the beadle's poem, presented in the Department of the Philosophy of Religion at the University of Muri in the year 1918: Regarding the "University of Muri," see letter no. 36 in this volume and the relevant note; see also: letter no. 41 in this volume (Benjamin's *curriculum vitae*). The "beadle" at "the Department of the Philosophy of Religion at the University of Muri" means Gershom Scholem. In 1928 he self-published his poem "Das amtliche Lehrgedicht der philosophischen Fakultät" [The official didactic poem of the faculty of philosophy].

146 SCHOLEM TO ADORNO
JERUSALEM, 1.3.1965

1 March 1965

Dear Adorno,

I haven't heard anything from you in a long time. How are you? I'm concerned that you are struggling with your health.

I would like to believe that the new issue of *Neue Rundschau* with my lecture on Walter Benjamin has now come out, but, as yet, I haven't received it.

The occasion for these lines, aside from the above inquiries, is that today, at a street vendor in Jerusalem, the "Edition Suhrkamp" version of Benjamin's "Critique of Violence" (which Suhrkamp didn't send me) fell into my hands. I must say that I find the afterword by Herbert Marcuse to be a bit much – a classic example of the cold perversion of texts that were apparently too hard for him to digest. (It apparently completely escaped him that the "Critique of Violence" was written under the inspiration of anarchism!) I have absolutely no use for the sorts of phrases that are being thrown around here; there's too much trickery involved. It's a real shame. These texts, even their titles, would have deserved a more unsullied commentary.

In the same shot, I also bought Lefèbvre's *Probleme des Marxismus heute* [Current problems of Marxism]. I'd just like to know how this man uses his new "realistically" Marxist method to explain his <u>own</u> earlier writings, which I possess, and which are all characterized by the most servile Stalinism, despite having not been written under a reign of terror. And who is Mr. Alfred Schmidt who plugs this opus?

Kind regards to your wife and you,

from your

Gerhard Scholem

Original: aerogram (manuscript); Theodor W. Adorno Archive, Frankfurt am Main. First published in Gershom Scholem, *Briefe II: 1948–1970*, ed. Thomas Sparr (Munich: C. H. Beck, 1995), pp. 126–7.

my lecture on Walter Benjamin: Scholem's lecture on Walter Benjamin was held at the Institute for Social Research in Frankfurt am Main and at the Leo Baeck Institute in New York in 1964. It was first published in English as "Walter Benjamin," in *Leo Baeck Yearbook*, 10/1 (1965), pp. 117–36. It was reprinted as: Scholem, "Walter Benjamin," in *On Jews and Judaism in Crisis*, ed. Werner J. Dannhauser (New York: Schocken Books, 1976), pp. 172–97.

Benjamin's "Critique of Violence": See Benjamin, *Zur Kritik der Gewalt und andere Aufsätze, mit einem Nachwort versehen von Herbert Marcuse*

[On the critique of violence and other essays, with an afterword by Herbert Marcuse], which appeared in the "edition suhrkamp" series as no. 103 (Frankfurt am Main: Suhrkamp, 1965). Scholem noted the following on the first page of the afterword in his copy: "A classic example of the cold perversion of texts that were apparently too hard for him to digest! Far too much trickery! Poor author W[alter] B[enjamin] – your texts would have deserved a more unsullied commentary!"

Lefèbvre's Probleme des Marxismus heute: See Henri Lefèbvre, *Probleme des Marxismus heute, deutsch und mit einem Nachwort versehen von Alfred Schmidt* [Problems of Marxism today, translated into German with an afterword by Alfred Schmidt], which appeared in the "edition suhrkamp" series as no. 99 (Frankfurt am Main: Suhrkamp, 1965).

And who is Mr. Alfred Schmidt who plugs this opus?: The philosopher Alfred Schmidt (1931–2012) was a student of Adorno and Horkheimer's. In 1960 he completed his doctoral thesis, *Der Begriff der Natur bei Marx* [The concept of nature in Marx], which was published in the book series of the Institute for Social Research in 1962. In 1972 he became Jürgen Habermas's successor as professor of philosophy and sociology at the University of Frankfurt. From 1985 to 1996, Schmidt was one of the editors of Horkheimer's collected works. See Schmidt, *The Concept of Nature in Marx*, trans. Ben Fowkes (London: Verso, 2013).

147 ADORNO TO SCHOLEM
FRANKFURT AM MAIN, 17.3.1965

PROF. DR. THEODOR W. ADORNO

6 FRANKFURT AM MAIN
KETTENHOFWEG 123
17 March 1965

Dear Scholem,

Kindest thanks for your letter of the 1st of March, which I'm finding upon my return from Paris. Despite the German lectures and the French seminars that I committed to give at the Sorbonne, I thought that I might be able to rest to some degree while there, so I foolishly went immediately after the end of term, with the result that I returned in a state of total exhaustion and, again, with a battered heart. You can hardly imagine the sheer weight that came crashing down on me. As if that wasn't enough, it now turns out that I sustained a mild concussion, from which I'm only gradually recovering, after running head first into an all too invisible glass door. So I ask you to please be lenient with me.

The matter of Marcuse's afterword to the little Suhrkamp volume has its strange backstory, indeed. He sent me his draft with a request to revise it so that I might consider it publishable. After I did so, I received a message informing me that both the volume and the afterword had already, in the meantime, been published. This was no less strange to me than the fact that Unseld had made an arrangement with Marcuse without consulting me first. God knows, I am not claiming a monopoly on Benjamin, but surely, in such matters, there are certain imponderables. Unfortunately I must agree with your verdict on the afterword. What's even worse is his misinterpretation of the concept of dialectics at a standstill and of the theses on the philosophy of history in general. But what can one do? After all, Marcuse is an old friend of mine who is now in the precarious position faced by all émigré professors in America who are approaching the age of retirement. I simply would like to avoid any public controversy so as not to cause him harm; I'm sure you understand this. As I say, in substance I was just as appalled as you.

In Paris, I met, among others, with Bonnasse, who translated your piece on Benjamin, and who is a loyal and cultured man. I also had a long conversation with the old Marcel Jouhandeau, who remembered Benjamin well. Overall, the days in Paris were exceedingly rich; only, they went significantly beyond my physical capacities.

In the meantime, Gretel has intervened with Suhrkamp, since the proofs of the letters still haven't arrived. She received a slightly grumpy response from Boehlich, although this leads me to conclude that the intervention helped. Nevertheless, given this delay, it is a mystery to me how the volume is supposed to come out in time for the book fair. In any event, I neither can nor want to read proofs in August in Sils Maria, at any cost; I will have to be strict in abstaining from doing any work, including things of a technical nature. I intend to draft my part of the preface as soon as I receive the proofs and have leafed through them to my heart's content; this is, as it were, the precondition for my plan. Perhaps you're further along with what you intend.

In spite of all this, I jumped right back into working on my book. I still hope that I might finish it this year, although I don't know if I'll manage. There are simply too many external distractions – faculty and committee meetings, above all – which are piled on my back.

Presumably you've heard that we've been spared Mr. Ehrlich, after all. The matter is, once again, as they say in America, *wide open.**

I only hope that you are doing better than I am. On the 1st of April, Gretel and I are going to the Parkhotel Brenner in Baden-Baden for

* Original in English.

fourteen days to recuperate in earnest. Keep your fingers crossed for us.

To you and Fanja all that is cordial, also from Gretel,

your loyal

Adorno

What are your plans for the summer? We are going to Sils Maria again.

Original: typescript with printed letterhead and handwritten postscript; Gershom Scholem Archive, The National Library of Israel, Jerusalem.

The matter of Marcuse's afterword to the little Suhrkamp volume has its strange backstory, indeed: In a note on a letter from Adorno to Horkheimer, dated 30.9.1964, the background to Marcuse's afterword to "Critique of Violence" is explained in detail with reference to Adorno's correspondence with Marcuse: "The Marcuse–Benjamin affair is exceedingly murky." Marcuse, who, "in a moment of weakness in Frankfurt (after a few drinks at the Suhrkamp reception)," declared his readiness to write the afterword to Benjamin's volume of essays, did, in fact, send his manuscript to Adorno for insight and corrections. Due to a series of misunderstandings, however, the volume had already gone to print by the time Adorno was able to deliver his numerous suggestions for revision to Marcuse. Accordingly, they could not be integrated. See *Theodor W. Adorno / Max Horkheimer: Briefwechsel IV, 1950–1969*, ed. Henri Lonitz and Christoph Gödde (Frankfurt am Main: Suhrkamp, 2006), pp. 731–3.

misinterpretation of the concept of dialectics at a standstill and of the theses on the philosophy of history in general: In his afterword to the Benjamin volume, Marcuse writes: "The 'shock' of immobilization [*Stillstellung*] also applies to the question of what is to be done with regard to organizing activities and organizational matters. . . . If the revolution is to be messianic, it cannot remain oriented within the continuum. Which does not mean that one must wait for a Messiah. For Benjamin the Messiah would be exclusively constituted by the will and the conduct of those who are suffering under the established order, the oppressed: in class struggle." See Herbert Marcuse, "Afterword to Walter Benjamin's *Critique of Violence*," in *Marxism, Revolution and Utopia: Collected Papers of Herbert Marcuse*, Vol. 6, ed. Douglas Kellner and Clayton Pierce (London: Routledge, 2014), pp. 126–7. In a letter to Marcuse, dated the 4th of December 1964, Adorno writes: "What I find quite significant is the overall misunderstanding of the concept of arrest [*Stillstellung*], which is connected to Benjamin's theory of dialectics at a standstill. It does not involve anything like withholding judgment or, indeed, the abolition of the arrested concept. I think that here the emphasis is really misplaced. Moreover, I still think that some of the formulations sound too coarsely revolutionary, and I would advise you to redact these once again." Quoted in *Theodor W. Adorno / Max Horkheimer: Briefwechsel IV*, p. 732.

Bonnasse: Regarding Pierre Bonnasse (Missac), see letter no. 78 and the accompanying notes.

Marcel Jouhandeau: Walter Benjamin became acquainted with the Catholic author Marcel Jouhandeau (1888–1979) during his time in Paris. Benjamin elaborates on his visit with Jouhandeau in an entry from his "Paris Diary," dated 6.1.1930. See Benjamin, "Paris Diary," in *Selected Writings*, Vol. 2.1: *1927–1930*, ed. Michael W. Jennings, Howard Eiland, and Gary Smith (Cambridge, MA: The Belknap Press of Harvard University Press, 2005), pp. 339–40.

Mr. Ehrlich: See letter no. 118 and the relevant note in this volume.

148 SCHOLEM TO ADORNO JERUSALEM, 23.3.1965

Jerusalem, 23 March 1965

Dear Adorno,

Many thanks for your letter, which I am answering right away. I am dismayed to hear that you're having heart troubles again. Apparently you are either unwilling or incapable of budgeting your energy, although this would be absolutely advisable. I'm not exactly lazy either, but if I were to trifle with my strength the way you do, I'd be inviting all manner of devils to take hold of me. I sincerely advise you not to let it come to that. *And take it easy.** I didn't know that Marcuse is already close to retirement. I wish him all the best, and I know how you regard him. But he rubbed me the wrong way with his "*loose talk*."† I'm glad to hear that you had the same reaction, even if it's only "for internal use," which is understandable.

I'm also waiting for the proofs of the Benjamin letters. As for your question regarding my summer plans, I believe it is not impossible that we could meet for a couple of days in Sils Maria. I might be able to come up for a few days before I go to California on the 2nd of September. But this year I declined to attend the Eranos conference, since I simply can't make time for the intensive preparations required to give a lecture. If I do come to Sils, I would therefore be coming directly from Jerusalem. Incidentally, it's quite plausible that I could be in Frankfurt for a few days on my way back (in late October), so I think we'll see each other this year, and I can only hope to find you in complete health. I have no complaints on my end at the moment.

* Original in English.

† Original in English.

With cordial regards and all best wishes for your rest and recuperation, and due compliments to your lady wife.

Yours,
G. Scholem

Original: aerogram (typescript); Theodor W. Adorno Archive, Frankfurt am Main.

California: In September 1965, Scholem gave a public lecture at the University of Judaism, then the West Coast branch of the Jewish Theological Seminary of America, in Los Angeles. Further details were not verified.

149 ADORNO TO SCHOLEM
FRANKFURT AM MAIN, 22.4.1965

PROF. DR. THEODOR W. ADORNO

6 FRANKFURT AM MAIN
KETTENHOFWEG 123
22 April 1965

Dear Scholem,

Kindest thanks for your letter of the 23rd of March. In the meantime, we spent fourteen days in Baden-Baden. With plenty of fresh air and lots of sleep, we are both well rested, so I am facing the semester with some composure. I'm taking the liberty of starting my metaphysical lectures late, on the 11th of May.

Meanwhile, I've received a sizeable stack of Benjamin proofs, all of which fall exclusively within your jurisdiction. Nevertheless, I read them carefully and allowed myself to correct a handful of print errors, and also added "sic" where necessary, as you have done elsewhere. But of course, you alone have the final say about everything in these letters.

The ones to Schoen have to be sent to poor Hansi, whose visit here yielded a quite lamentable outcome, even though I supported her with the radio station as best as I could.

It has to be said of the correspondence that Benjamin was no exception to the rule that the level and quality of letters is always also determined by its addressee. The ones to you and, to a lesser degree Schoen, are, of course, infinitely superior to the ones to Belmore, Carla Seligsohn, and the others from the youth movement [*Jugendbewegten*]. I did notice that the relationships outlined in the letters before 1917 are not always entirely intelligible – perhaps you were a little too ascetic in your explanations, even though your motivation was highly understandable. It is not clear, for instance, what caused the rift with Grete Radt, what the nature of his relationship to

Carla Seligsohn was, and what the case was with Jula Cohn. Above all, though, it is unclear what drove him ultimately to break with his friends from the Freie deutsche Jugend [Free German Youth], aside from the rather general motive that, after a certain point, these people had nothing more to say to him, as it were. Presumably you kept quiet about these matters out of discretion, which I understand all too well. (À propos discretion: did you receive the third volume of *Notes to Literature*? In the piece on Karl Kraus there is a passage on the concept of discretion and its dialectic). So I hesitate to push you to add a few explanations here and there. Instead, I would like to encourage you – time permitting – to write an essay on Benjamin's youth in order to really explain these matters. The names of living people could, for the time being, be enciphered. Such an essay seems to me to be demanded precisely by the idea, which you emphatically expressed, that one must also transmit a clear image of Benjamin the person. And, of course, you would be the only person who could write such a text. The fact that one could thus protect Benjamin from posthumous defamations, such as those put forward by Belmore – even if Belmore might have been the offended party in this case – would be a byproduct not to be scorned.

Once again, I find myself up to my ears in the book on dialectics, in the most difficult sections, and occasionally I am seized by despondency; but I hope that, in the long run, my stubbornness will prove to be greater than my stupidity. On the side, a few smaller pieces have resulted: some reflections on philosophical thinking, which will soon be published, a school essay on the occasion of Ernst Bloch's 80th birthday, in which I compare Simmel's piece on the handle with Bloch's piece on the pot, and an open letter on the occasion of Horkheimer's 70th birthday, which you may have seen in *Die Zeit*. By the way, Horkheimer was rather unwell – he had two thromboses in his arm and this apparently affected his lung. It all seems to be more or less better now, but I still can't shake an uneasy feeling. On his 70th birthday Gretel and I visited him in Montagnola.

Of all my impressions from Paris, the most enduring ones were of the conversations with Beckett – not only do I view him as an author of the highest rank, but he also achieves an identity of life and work the likes of which I have never in my life seen before. What do you make of this phenomenon? Surely he must be of interest to you too, under the aspect of a nihilistic mysticism, or, rather, a mysticism of *nihil*. By the way, he has a Protestant background, even though he is Irish. He told me that the mythologizing tendencies of Joyce, with whom he was friends, are quite alien to him.

If all goes well, by no later than the 1st of August we will once again be enjoying the *pomp funèbre* at the Waldhaus, and I look forward to seeing you with all my heart. I turned down an invitation to speak in Salzburg during the first days of August; so there will be hardly any postponement.

To you and Fanya all that is cordial, also from Gretel,

your old

Adorno

B.'s early statement about Hegel moved me greatly. It is astonishing that he innervated something as central as the constellation of the mystical and the violent. It is no less astonishing that he apparently underestimated the immense truth content of Hegel's philosophy.

Original: typescript with printed letterhead and handwritten postscript; Gershom Scholem Archive, The National Library of Israel, Jerusalem.

my metaphysical lectures: In the summer of 1965, Adorno held a series of lectures, titled "Metaphysics: Concept and Problems," which includes considerations that were later included in the "Meditations on Metaphysics" section of *Negative Dialectics*. See Adorno, *Metaphysics: Concept and Problems*, ed. Rolf Tiedemann, trans. Edmund Jephcott (Stanford, CA: Stanford University Press, 2001).

poor Hansi, whose visit here yielded a quite lamentable outcome, even though I supported her with the radio station as best I could: Mrs. Schoen, the widow of Ernst Schoen, attempted, unsuccessfully, to claim a pension from the radio station where her husband had worked as the program director from 1925 to 1933.

[*Jugendbewegten*]: Adorno's phrase literally translates as "those moved by youth." It is a play on the German word *Judendbewegung* (youth movement).

Carla Seligsohn: Adorno's spelling. Carla Seligson (1892–1956) was married to Benjamin's friend Herbert Belmore from 1917.

Grete Radt . . . Jula Cohn: See letter no. 70 and the relevant note in this volume.

a passage on the concept of discretion . . . the piece on Karl Kraus:

> Kraus' hatred of the press is the product of his obsession with the demand for discretion. The bourgeois antagonism is manifested even in the latter. The concept of privacy, which Kraus honors without criticism, is fetishized by the bourgeoisie and becomes "my home is my castle." Nothing, on the other hand, neither what is most holy nor what is most private, is safe from the exchange principle. Once concealed delight in the forbidden provides capital with new opportunities for investment in the media, society never hesitates to put on the market the secrets in whose irrationality its own irrationality is entrenched. (Adorno, "Morals and Criminality: On the Eleventh Volume of the Works of Karl Kraus," in *Notes to Literature*, Vol. 2, trans. Shierry Weber Nicholsen (New York: Columbia University Press, 1992), pp. 40–57, here, p. 43)

some reflections on philosophical thinking: On the 9th of October 1964 Adorno gave a lecture on Deutschlandfunk radio. The published version included a dedication to Herbert Marcuse on the occasion of his 70th birthday. See Adorno, "Anmerkungen zum philosophischen Denken," *Neue deutsche Hefte*, no. 107 (October 1965), pp. 5–13; see also "Notes on Philosophical Thinking," in *Critical Models: Interventions and Catchwords*, trans. Henry W. Pickford (New York: Columbia University Press, 1998), pp. 127–34.

a school essay on the occasion of Ernst Bloch's 80th birthday: See Theodor W. Adorno, "Henkel, Krug und frühe Erfahrung," in *Ernst Bloch zu Ehren: Beiträge zu seinem Werk* [In honour of Ernst Bloch: contributions on his work], ed. Siegfried Unseld (Frankfurt am Main: Suhrkamp, 1965), pp. 9–20; see also Adorno, "The Handle, the Pot and Early Experience," in *Notes to Literature*, Vol. 2, trans. Shierry Weber Nicholsen (New York: Columbia University Press, 1992), pp. 207–19.

an open letter on the occasion of Horkheimer's 70th birthday: Adorno's open letter to Max Horkheimer, written on the occasion of the latter's 70th birthday on 14.2.1965, was first published as "Offener Brief an Max Horkheimer" [Open letter to Max Horkheimer] in *Die Zeit*, 12 February 1965, p. 32; repr. in *Gesammelte Schriften 20.1*: *Vermischte Schriften* [Miscellaneous Writings], ed. Rolf Tiedemann et al. (Frankfurt am Main: Suhrkamp, 1986), pp. 155–63.

conversations with Beckett: In March of 1965, Adorno met with Samuel Beckett in Paris. It was the third of at least six personal meetings between Adorno and Beckett. In the Theodor W. Adorno archive, there is a letter from Adorno to Beckett, dated the 1st of March 1965, in which Adorno announces his arrival in Paris and suggests a meeting at the Hotel *Pont Royal*.

B.'s early statement about Hegel: In a letter to Scholem, dated 31.1.1918, Benjamin writes: "The Hegel I have read, on the other hand, has so far totally repelled me. If we were to get into his work for just a short time, I think we would soon arrive at the spiritual physiognomy that peers out of it: that of an intellectual brute, a mystic of brute force, the worst sort there is: but a mystic, nonetheless." See *The Correspondence of Walter Benjamin 1910–1940*, ed. Theodor W. Adorno and Gershom Scholem, trans. Manfred R. Jacobson and Evelyn M. Jacobson (Chicago: University of Chicago Press, 1994), pp. 112–13.

150 SCHOLEM TO ADORNO
JERUSALEM, 2.5.1965

Jerusalem, on the 2nd of May, 1965

Dear Adorno,

Enclosed you will find a letter simultaneously addressed to you, Unseld, and Boehlich regarding the Benjamin corrections. You will see from it that Boehlich has rather left us in the lurch. He hasn't looked at or corrected a single one of the issues I queried. What was I to do other than make a fuss? I tried hard to stay very conciliatory; but this is in no way alright. Please push for an immediate meeting with these gentlemen, and for a response to me. Right after I received the first proofs, I handwrote a letter to Boehlich, in which I flagged the main issues. However, there was no reply; nor did I receive a second set of proofs. I am now reading the second *batch** of letters from 1919 to 1922.

We are under no obligation to provide Hansi with the letters to Schoen, as I have also written to her. The written agreement that she and I drew up merely stipulates that we will present her with the biographical notes and remarks concerning Ernst Schoen (this will not only concern factual matters, naturally). I also have nothing against it, of course, if you wish to send her the letters to Schoen that we've included; although, if you do, the corrections I've made would have to be included (obvious print and typographic errors in the manuscript, which do not reflect the originals).

Regarding your remarks on my notes: I handled all matters concerning Benjamin's relationships with women with the utmost reserve, in part through lack of knowledge and in part out of due discretion. You are mistaken if you think that I know much about these things. I do not know what caused the rift with Grete Radt, who was introduced to me as his bride. I can only suspect that it was caused by the renewed encounter with Dora. Discretion prohibits me from saying what happened with Jula Cohn. She is still alive and I am presently engaged in correspondence with her. His relationship to Carla Seligson was exactly as it appears in the letters – moved by youth [jugendbewegt] and marked by a cautious eroticism, which, however, came to no effect. The most it ever amounted to was a kiss during a ball. The general motive that drove him to break with his friends from the youth movement is crucial. I don't know of any particular circumstance, except in the case of Belmore, who, during my visit in Rome, gave me a detailed description of his last meeting with W.B. in July of 1917, which was not totally devoid of a diabolical element. I don't believe that my knowledge is sufficient to write an essay on Benjamin's youth, as you wish.

I thank you sincerely for sending the 3rd volume of your *Notes to Literature*, the majority of which I was unfamiliar with. I am reading it with the liveliest sympathy. For my part, I have nothing to show for myself – just a short review of a recently published German translation of a book by Agnon, which is coming out in the next issue of

* Original in English.

Neue Rundschau. You should also get your hands on this book, and Ms. Gretel even more so. But who is to say whether you'll have the requisite leisure for it, for instance on a Shabbat and a Sunday? Do you read as slowly as I do, or is the ability to read a book quickly one of the many gifts with which you have been blessed? In this case, I could only envy you.

I made a reservation at the Hotel Margna in Sils Maria for the last week of July, just in case, and I hope to see you and your wife there. However, I must ask you absolutely not to mention this to any third parties. The reason for this is that I excused myself from the Eranos conference this year, and I wouldn't want word to get out that I am actually in Switzerland at the same time. After it's all over, it won't matter. I am planning to go to California directly from Sils, but I am counting on the possibility of stopping off in Frankfurt for a few days on my way back. By the way, you missed me in Frankfurt this *weekend*.* That is, I was supposed to be flown out to Berlin in a mad rush to take part in a radio discussion, hosted by Norddeutscher Rundfunk, with Messrs. Günther Grass and Heinrich Böll on Germany taking up diplomatic relations with Israel. I would have accepted the invitation, except the people, who frenetically called here during the Passover holiday, were unable to find my address – I was at the seaside with my wife for a few days and nobody could remember the name of the hotel where we were staying! So, I was a hair's breadth away from coming to Germany for 5 days. Like a true *angelus ex machina*, I would have dropped to you from the plane.

Now that I'm re-reading them, I find that Benjamin's letters read wonderfully and have a lot to offer. Cordial regards to you and your wife.

Yours,

Gerhard Scholem

So far I have not read anything by Beckett!
I do <u>not</u> know your letter to Horkheimer from *Die Zeit*! Do you have a copy?

Original: typescript with handwritten postscript and a copy of Scholem's letter to Adorno, Unseld, and Boehlich, dated 2.5.1965 (see letter no. 151 in this volume); Theodor W. Adorno Archive, Frankfurt am Main.

the letters to Schoen: According to a marginal note in Elfriede Olbrich's hand, the letters were sent to Hansi Schoen without corrections.

* Original in English.

a short review of a recently published German translation of a book by Agnon: Scholem's review of the German translation of S. J. Agnon's novel *Ore'ah Noteh Lalun* [A guest for the night], published by S. Fischer in Frankfurt am Main in 1964, appeared in *Neue Rundschau*, no. 2 (1965), pp. 327–33. He wrote: "The Hebrew original was published in 1939, two years before the German murder of the Jews began, which physically destroyed the community that is described here. The subject of this book is the fact that this community was hopelessly disintegrated – the dying of a Jewish city before it was drenched in blood" (p. 328).

151 SCHOLEM TO SIEGFRIED UNSELD, WALTER BOEHLICH AND ADORNO
JERUSALEM, 2.5.1965

Copy for Adorno

Jerusalem, on the 2 of May, 1965

To:
Suhrkamp Verlag, Dr. S. Unseld
and Mr. Boehlich
Prof. Adorno

Esteemed gentlemen,

I am writing this letter to all three of you in the hope that you might consult with each other and notify me of the outcome immediately.

I realized with great consternation that my remarks on certain questions arising from the Benjamin proofs – which I sent, in part to Adorno and in part to Boehlich – have remained unanswered, and I thought it best to refer you once more to these questions and to insist that something must be done to avoid a big fuss.

1. I told you after receiving the proofs of the first 48 letters that I need two sets of proofs, so that I can keep one, in order to check the corrections. I cannot return my corrections before I receive a second set of everything that I have been sent to date. Meanwhile, I received an additional 47 proofs (not continuously paginated, but again numbered 1–47) without my previous comments having been taken into consideration, and once again as a single copy.

2. I must know, unequivocally, to whom I should send the corrections, and who is responsible for overseeing their implementation, and, above all, who is responsible for factoring in the comments made therein. We cannot proceed like amateurs in this matter.

3. I made the corrections without reading the manuscript, as I wasn't sent one. In case of doubt, I can, thank God, consult the originals of the letters addressed to Kraft and myself, since I have

them here. Indeed, in several cases, my verification of these has led to improved readings of difficult passages. However, in the case of the letters to Belmore, I don't have this option, since the gentleman demanded that his letters be returned. I have photocopies of the letters to Schoen. My corrections of these letters thus stem from insight into the original texts, and, if there is any doubt, they should supersede the print manuscript, which I do not have. In other cases, especially when preparing further corrections, I will aim to consult the originals wherever possible.

4. I am, of course, reading the sections that I have edited with particular care, but I think it's only right that Adorno and I each read the other's parts as well. Somebody will have to coordinate the evident corrections and the remaining questions that each of us flags when reviewing the other's work. Moreover, somebody has to make sure that the changes are incorporated. Who will that be?

5. Unfortunately an error has occurred in the numbering of the letters. There are two letters with the number 40; accordingly, after this point, every number must be increased by one. Wouldn't it be better to do this directly in the manuscript, to spare us from having to do it in the proofs? Hopefully there aren't more letters without numbers.

6. My main concern has to do with the notes. We had agreed that Mr. Boehlich would look over the notes and coordinate them. As I emphasized during our last meeting, there were several occasions where I was unable to verify quotes. As such, I formulated the notes as questions or simply added question marks because I assumed that Mr. Boehlich would send somebody to the library, or would, at any rate, take care of the text in these notes. Unfortunately this did not happen, and in several places the notes simply mirror my questions, rather than reflecting a text that can be printed. I highlighted this in my corrections. But what will happen now?? Will Mr. Boehlich look over the notes and rewrite them as necessary, i.e. will he insert the relevant information or add comments along the lines of "not verified"? See, for example, the note at the end of the letter to Ernst Schoen in the proof labelled H 9a. Why was it not addressed? I assumed, naturally, that Mr. Boehlich would duly answer all of the questions raised in the notes during his final revisions of the overall manuscript.

7. I inserted question marks in several passages where I was unsure and also wasn't certain what the manuscript says. The missing information can be verified, in part, with an atlas, e.g., no. 15: is the place called San Martino di Castrazzo or di Castrozza?

8. Does someone in your office make any preliminary corrections before we receive the proofs, and do we receive the proofs after the preliminary corrections have been integrated? Judging from the

current proofs, which contain some mysterious print errors, I'm assuming that nobody makes such preliminary corrections. Is that alright?

9. Until now, the first 100 galley proofs all fall under my editorship and so all the notes are mine. Soon, however, with the letters to Rang and Hofmannsthal, the sections that fall under Adorno's editorial domain will begin. Will Mr. Boehlich look over and coordinate these sections, as agreed, so as to avoid repetitions?

10. When handing over the manuscript, I also gave you an envelope containing a number of letters that we had set aside when, after initially reviewing the material, we faced spatial constraints. Since we then settled on a more generous scope for the book, and determined that issues of space would not be decisive, we had agreed that these letters would be included in the relevant places. I have a feeling that this did not happen. Am I mistaken? Were some of the letters included after all? Or were they not even looked at? I would urgently ask you to consider this matter and keep me apprised. The letters in question primarily include some addressed to Belmore and several to me.

11. I will be in Israel until mid-August at the latest. Is it certain that the corrections will be done by then?

I would be very grateful, my dear colleagues, if you could respond to these points and, more importantly, if you could make the necessary arrangements that follow from them. As soon as I receive a second set of the proofs, I will send my corrected proofs by registered airmail to the person of your determination.

Could you please send me Stefan Benjamin's home address?

With cordial regards and in the hope of your quick reply,

yours,

G. Scholem

Original: typescript with Scholem's handwritten remark: "Copy for Adorno"; Theodor W. Adorno Archive, Frankfurt am Main.

152 ADORNO TO SCHOLEM
FRANKFURT AM MAIN, 12.5.1965

PROF. DR. THEODOR W. ADORNO

6 FRANKFURT AM MAIN
KETTENHOFWEG 123
12 May 1965

Dear Scholem,

Just a few intermittent words for now: I called Unseld right away about the edition of the letters; however, he said that he hadn't received your letter yet – or, at any rate, he hadn't read it – so we'll have to continue to be patient. If things go wrong, it won't be on me.

Believe me when I say that my inquiries concerning Benjamin's youth weren't motivated by nosiness or indiscretion – you and I seem to take a similar view of such matters, and I am as averse to digging around in people's private affairs as you are. But since you wanted to paint a personal picture of Benjamin through the selection of the early letters – you know that my feelings on this point were a bit different from yours – I only thought it would be important to flesh out the notes at least to such an extent that the uninformed reader might have a sense of what is going on. Even Gretel and I found it very difficult, at times, to make sense of the letters from Benjamin's youth, and we're hardly neophytes. I'd therefore like to ask you to consider, once more, if something might be done on this front as you're preparing your corrections.

One more thing: it would really be a shame, from our perspective, if you were to come to Sils Maria only during the last week of July. Because of countless, and, for the most part, very tedious university commitments, I'll be stuck here until the end of the semester on the 31st of July, so I won't be available in Sils before the 1st of August. If it's not too much trouble, I'd be grateful if you could revise your plans.

I'll be in touch as soon as I've heard from Unseld, or, indeed, as soon as I've organized the meeting you suggested.

Until then, very cordially

yours,

Adorno

Original: typescript with printed letterhead; Gershom Scholem Archive, The National Library of Israel, Jerusalem.

153 ADORNO TO SCHOLEM FRANKFURT AM MAIN, 20.5.1965

PROF. DR. THEODOR W. ADORNO

6 FRANKFURT AM MAIN
KETTENHOFWEG 123
20 May 1965

Dear Scholem,

I am eating my way through the Benjamin letters slowly, since, like you, I have not been blessed with the gift of quick reading. I've also corrected all manner of print errors and noted spelling mistakes, which I thought could be corrected without sacrificing precision. I still haven't gotten hold of Unseld. He's out of town!

I'm writing to you today, once more, for technical reasons. As you'll recall, we had originally decided to leave out all forms of address. It emerges now, upon re-reading the letters, that there is a distinct incongruity between the rather abrupt leap into each letter at the beginning, and the closing words, which are often very elaborate. Since the latter unquestionably belong to the letter's substance, and are also quite varied, they can under no circumstances be left out. My suggestion would be to restore the forms of address [at the start of each letter]. I believe that the visual impression of the proofs should be enough to convince you of this proposal. If I have your consent, I will aim to get Unseld's as well.

Besides this, I just wanted to ask if you wouldn't find it advisable to print your poem on the *Angelus* (your handwritten copy of which I am safeguarding, by the way) in the same place in the correspondence where it first appeared? This would, for one thing, foster an understanding of all of the passages that refer to this poem, including the equivocations about the planned journal; however, it would also do justice to the poem itself, which is not merely of intrinsic significance but was also important for Benjamin.

I was especially pleased that Benjamin had already seen through Heidegger after reading his *Habilitation* and, indeed, in the most decisive [aspect]: namely, as a *faiseur*. In the case of this man, everything – absolutely everything – can be explained out of a will to power and a highly developed technique of intellectual domination. The purity of the matter is completely lacking in him. And Benjamin noticed this in the mandarin style of Heidegger's first publication on the philosophy of language. *Ceterum censeo*, I suggest that we add a footnote, upon the book's first mention, to point out that the work, which Heidegger had ascribed to Duns Scotus, in fact is not the latter's at all, but is Thomas of Erfurt's. After all, such things can bring one joy.

Please write soon.

On Friday I'll be going to Berlin for a few days, where I'll be giving some lectures, but I'll be back on Monday. I'm making good progress with my work. I'm currently more vexed with the faculty than is good for my health, but such is the price I pay to get some things done that I consider worthwhile.

Most cordially, also from Gretel, and also to Fanya,

yours,

Adorno

Original: typescript with printed letterhead; Gershom Scholem Archive, The National Library of Israel, Jerusalem.

your poem on the Angelus: Scholem's poem "Gruß vom Angelus" [Greetings from the Angelus] was written for Walter Benjamin's birthday. It includes the dedication: "For Walter, on the 15th of July 1921." The poem refers to Paul Klee's painting *Angelus Novus*. Thesis IX from Benjamin's "On the Concept of History" cites the poem as its motto. See Walter Benjamin, *Selected Writings*, Vol. 4: *1938–1940*, ed. Howard Eiland and Michael W. Jennings (Cambridge, MA: The Belknap Press of Harvard University Press, 2006), pp. 392–3. Scholem included the poem in his notes to Benjamin's letter, dated 25.7.1921. See *The Correspondence of Walter Benjamin 1910–1940*, ed. Theodor W. Adorno and Gershom Scholem, trans. Manfred R. Jacobson and Evelyn M. Jacobson (Chicago: University of Chicago Press, 1994), pp. 184–5. See also: letter no. 110 in this volume.

that Benjamin had already seen through Heidegger after reading his Habilitation: In a letter to Scholem, dated circa 1.12.1920, Benjamin wrote the following: "I have read Heidegger's book on Duns Scotus. It is incredible that anyone could qualify for a university position on the basis of such a study. Its execution requires *nothing* more than great diligence and a command of scholastic Latin, and, in spite of all of its philosophical packaging, it is basically only a piece of good translation work. The author's contemptible grovelling at Rickert's and Husserl's feet does not make reading it more pleasant. The book does not deal with Duns Scotus's linguistic philosophy in philosophical terms, and thus what it leaves undone is no small task." See *The Correspondence of Walter Benjamin 1910–1940*, p. 168.

a footnote: No such note was included in the edition of Benjamin's letters (see letter no. 155).

more vexed with the faculty than is good for my health: Adorno is alluding to the appointment of Ludwig von Friedeburg to a professorship in sociology. The administrative difficulty arose from the fact that the Faculty of Social Sciences stipulated that the position was "to be defined as [a professorship] in philosophy and sociology" (Theodor W. Adorno / Max Horkheimer: *Briefwechsel* IV, 1950–1969, ed. Henri Lonitz and Christoph Gödde (Frankfurt am Main: Suhrkamp, 2006), p. 754.

154 SCHOLEM TO ADORNO
JERUSALEM, 28.5.1965

Jerusalem, on the 28th of May, 1965

Dear Adorno,

Enclosed you will find a copy of my letter to Boehlich, sent at the same time as my letter to you. (It is also intended for presentation to Unseld.) You will see from it that I was surprised to receive, as a gift from Jula Cohn, some papers of Benjamin's that were still in her possession. This was the result of my sending her my lecture on W. B. in the *Neue Rundschau*. She wrote me a very nice letter and invited me to visit her. She had apparently long since destroyed all of Benjamin's letters apart from the ones she sent me. The four letters, which could be included without difficulty, simply by leaving out one sentence, are very beautiful, and intimately emotional. I completely omitted two love letters, of course. She wrote to me to say that this is all that she has left by way of letters (14 in total). At the same time, she gave me an extremely valuable gift, namely, the original manuscript of the essay on the *Elective Affinities* (which was, understandably, originally dedicated to her) – indeed, a most precious manuscript – as well as a number of poems which he addressed to her.

As I expressed in my letter to Boehlich, I agree with your suggestion to reintroduce the forms of address, in case you can push this through in an editorial meeting. Frankly, it's all the same to me, since the forms of address are rarely of particular personal interest, whereas the closing formulations often say much more. At any rate, you have my approval, and you can refer to it with Unseld and Boehlich.

I have no objections to your suggestion of printing the poem "Gruß vom Angelus" [Greetings from the Angelus] in the place where it is first mentioned. Even today, I still like this poem – I recently re-read it – especially when I imagine the picture as it was hung at my place in Munich. In this case, too, please proceed in coordination with the gentlemen from the publishing house. My corrected proofs have now all been sent to Boehlich.

Although I was aware of the fact that the topic of Heidegger's *Habilitation* didn't really derive from Duns Scotus but, rather, from a pseudo-Duns, I didn't mention it because it didn't seem relevant to me in this context.

In your discussion with the publishers, please emphasize the matter of the volume's publication date, which I laid out in my letter to Boehlich. The book should only come out after it has been properly proofread. As I can surmise from Boehlich's letters, he wants to do the inspection and supplementation of the notes, which I highlighted in my complaint, and which he was to take care of, based only on the galley proofs, that is, prior to the page makeup. In itself, this will cause a considerable delay. Given the circumstances, I am of the opinion that it would be best, as I suggested, to look through the page proofs in Frankfurt in late October. If only they'll be done by then!!

In any event, the book will not be out in time for the autumn book fair – there can be hardly any doubt about that. Hence, it makes no difference whether it comes out two or three months sooner or later. Besides, the volume is hardly suitable as a confirmation gift or for putting under a Christmas tree.

Having now read some 170 proofs one after another, I find that the overall impression made by the letters is quite splendid. What he gives us is as much a lively commentary on himself as it is an extension of his opus, in many directions. The intensification that occurs from the, as it were, "harmless" letters of his youth becomes exceptionally clear.

What you write about my stay in Sils Maria must be due to a misunderstanding of – or a typo in – my previous letter. In fact, I meant that I wanted to spend the last week of August with you, not the last week of July. So there's no problem. I'd only ask that you treat this plan confidentially, for the time being, and for good reason. Nobody besides my wife knows of this intention of mine.

Have I, as I believe, sent you a copy of my letter to Mr. Schloesser from the commemorative volume for Margarethe Susman? You didn't confirm it. It was important for me to know that this brilliant document reached your hands. Its legitimate place was at the opening of my *Judaica* volume. A long, angry response to it, which does not mention me, appeared last week, in the form of a horridly apologist essay about the Jews and the Germans, in the Hamburg paper *Die Zeit*. It was penned by our philosophical colleague Mr. Arnold Metzger in Munich. I've got half a mind to ask Marion Dönhoff to print my letter from the commemorative volume [in her paper]. I know Metzger from his time in Jerusalem in 1933/34.

Cordial regards to you both, also from my wife, who, unfortunately, is ill

yours, G. Scholem

Original: typescript, including a copy of Scholem's letter to Walter Boehlich, dated 28.5.1965 (carbon copy of typescript with Scholem's handwritten corrections); Theodor W. Adorno Archive, Frankfurt am Main. First published in Gershom Scholem, *Briefe II: 1948–1970*, ed. Thomas Sparr (Munich: C. H. Beck, 1995), pp. 132–4, and 134–5 (the letter to Boehlich).

a copy of my letter to Boehlich, sent at the same time as my letter to you:

Copy for Adorno
Jerusalem, on the 28th of May, 1965
Dear Mr. Boehlich,
I have looked over the new batch of proofs and am returning them to you by registered airmail. In several places, I also marked up the letters to Rang and Hofmannsthal, which Adorno worked on, where his reading seemed doubtful to me, and where I was convinced that the original texts said something else.

Here and there, I added some annotations to the letters addressed to me – references, etc. I would ask you to pay close attention when you go through the materials in case anything needs amending.

The numbering will presumably have to be redone for the next set of proofs. I have just received a number of letters from Mrs. Jula Radt, formerly Jula Cohn, which are almost all from the period between late

1925 and early 1927. I have selected five of them and I am enclosing numbered copies here along with the proofs. I would ask that you and Adorno look them over. They are very interesting, as they convey a sense of his life in Paris during his first long stay in 1926, as well as giving a very nice impression of Moscow, and of Ibiza in 1933. I'd be strongly in favor of including them. I struck a line from one of the letters which was too personal. For the same reason, I did not feel justified in including other letters from this period, although it is a pity that such personal tones as prevail in his letters to this woman cannot be made audible in this volume. However, the tone of the letters I've selected is also very personal and beautiful. From 1926, I previously had only three letters to myself and one to Hofmannsthal, so these make for a welcome and content-rich addition. These letters, of course, will have to be numbered sequentially, and I would recommend that somebody from the publishing house read through the corrections of these additional proofs before the page makeup is done. For the letter that is to be inserted in proof no. 145, if it is to be included, some editorial remarks on the people mentioned in it would have to be added. I cannot provide these from here. This means, for example, Princess Bassiano and Count Pourtalès, as well as Groethuysen, who, to my knowledge, appears for the first time in this letter. We would then have to use the relevant note from a subsequent letter here.

Prof. Adorno raised the question as to whether it wouldn't be better to restore the forms of address that we've removed. Should you decide to do so, I just want to say expressly that I have no objections. I suspect that the total number of letters to appear in the book will be around 300. This would mean extending the original plan by no more than 250 lines – that is, by fewer than 10 pages. For this price, it seems worth restoring the original forms of address in full. At any rate, I agree to whatever you decide about this matter.

I assume that the 167 proofs that I've received so far make up roughly half of the total (or even more than that). On this basis, I predict that the correction of the galley proofs could be completed by August, but I believe that we have to reckon with the fact that the page makeup and final printing will only come under wraps in the autumn months. I'll be on the road between the 15th of August and the end of October, and, given the uncertainty of my address during this trip, I can't guarantee that I'll be able to work on corrections to the page makeup during this period. On the other hand, I think it's absolutely necessary for me to look over the final proofs. I could probably do this best if I stopped off in Frankfurt for a few days in the second half of October on my way back from America. I'm sure that, in the case of such a publication, with its great documentary significance, it makes little difference whether the book comes out in September 1965 or in January–February 1966, as long as it is assured to come out around this time. What should be avoided at all costs are errors caused by rushing the typesetting (such as we saw in the numerous typos in the first edition of Benjamin's *Schriften*). Since Adorno is also going on holiday from the 1st of August, you can deduce the implications yourself. But precisely in the case of such a delay, it is especially urgent that I see the final proofs in Frankfurt, i.e. they must be finished by then. I ask you, please, also to show this letter to Dr. Unseld, and I hope to hear from you soon. I have also sent a copy of this letter to Adorno.

With cordial regards,

[Scholem]

lecture . . . in the Neue Rundschau: Scholem is presumably referring to his lecture on Walter Benjamin, which was given in Frankfurt and New York in 1965, and which was published in the *Neue Rundschau*. See letter no. 146 in this volume.

The four letters . . . are very beautiful, and intimately emotional: The volume of Benjamin's letters edited by Adorno and Scholem, and published in 1966, contains five letters to Jula Radt-Cohn. See *The Correspondence of Walter Benjamin 1910–1940*, ed. Theodor W. Adorno and Gershom Scholem, trans. Manfred R. Jacobson and Evelyn M. Jacobson (Chicago: University of Chicago Press, 1994), pp. 292–3, 295–7, 298–9, 310–11, and 422–4. Additional letters were included in the later edition of Benjamin's correspondence: see *Walter Benjamin: Gesammelte Briefe III, 1925–1930*, ed. Henri Lonitz and Christoph Gödde (Frankfurt am Main: Suhrkamp, 1998), pp. 80–2, 125–7, 129, 137–41, 150–5, 166–7, 170–5, 221–4, 227–8, and 245–7.

a copy of my letter to Mr. Schloesser . . . Margarethe Susman: In a letter dated 25.9.1962, Manfred Schloesser (b. 1934), head of the Agora Verlag, invited Scholem to contribute a piece to a commemorative volume honoring the writer Margarete Susman (1872–1966) on her 90th birthday. Scholem had initially declined the invitation; however, following Schloesser's persistent requests, he explained his decision in an open letter, which was included in the collection. In it, he states:

> Dear Mr. Schloesser, I am in equal measure honored and embarrassed by your invitation to contribute to a commemorative volume for Margarete Susman. I see no other way but to explain the nature of this embarrassment to you and, by extension, to the prospective readers of the planned volume. The announcement of this volume, which you kindly sent me, states that it is "not only intended as an homage but equally as a document of a German-Jewish conversation that is indestructible at its core." Nobody could be more confounded by such an announcement than I. For as much as I am prepared to pay homage to the venerable Margarete Susman, a figure to whom I am connected by more than mere opinion – shared or otherwise – I must decisively decline the invitation; the invitation, that is, to nourish the illusion of a "German-Jewish conversation that is indestructible at its core," which is unfathomable to me, and which, according to you, this collection is supposed to support.

Scholem's open letter was first published in *Auf gespaltenem Pfad: Festschrift zum neunzigsten Geburtstag von Margarete Susman* [On a split path: commemorative volume on the occasion of Margarete Susman's 90th birthday], ed. Manfred Schloesser (Darmstadt: Erato-Presse, 1964), pp. 229–32. It was reprinted as "Wider dem Mythos vom deutsch–jüdischen Gespräch" [Against the myth of the German–Jewish dialogue], at the beginning of *Judaica II*, the second volume of Scholem's *Judaica* series with Suhrkamp (Frankfurt a.M., 1970), pp. 7–11. See "Against the Myth of the German–Jewish Dialogue," in *On Jews and Judaism in Crisis*, ed. Werner J. Dannhauser (New York: Schocken Books, 1976), pp. 61–4.

essay about the Jews and the Germans in the Hamburg paper Die Zeit: On the 21st of May 1965, *Die Zeit* ran an article by the philosopher Arnold Metzger (1892–1974) titled "Der Dialog zwischen Deutschen und Juden: Haben die Beziehungen der beiden Völker die Hitlerjahre überdauert?" [The dialogue between Germans and Jews: did the relations between the two nations survive the Hitler years?] (p. 32). Metzger both poses the question and offers a response:

> Is there an intimate connection between the Germany of National Socialism and the Germany that brought forth great philosophy and art? What is the nature of this relation? Where is this relation located? Even today, this question has hardly been thought through. I want to pose it in connection with the special relationship that obtained between Jews and Germans before Hitler destroyed it – a peculiar, unique, and, I would dare to say, spiritual relationship, which is rooted in Germany as in no other country. I want to speak of the Jews' love for Germany. It spans history, and, despite the horrendous atrocities perpetrated on Jews by Germans, I believe that it lives on today – even if we hardly dare to utter this thought. . . . Germany was for all the worlds' Jews – not just those from Germany – the land of Kant and Goethe, to name only these two. Indeed, perhaps no other nation gave the world such noble apostles of humanity. Nobody exalted the idea of humanity beyond all national ties as magnificently as Lessing and Herder.

Regarding the German–Jewish dialogue, Metzger writes: "I spoke initially about the symbiosis between Germanness and Jewishness. It was destroyed. But it cannot founder. Because, strictly and essentially speaking, it was not a dialogue between two different nations or two essentially different races, but between two different attitudes towards the world. And, moreover, despite all of the differences between the partners in this conversation, it was a dialogue marked by a common disposition towards the world, aimed at the realization of a human community of peace. Even under Hitler, this dialogue never ceased."

I've got half a mind to ask Marion Dönhoff to print my letter from the commemorative volume [in her paper]: Countess Marion Dönhoff (1909–2002) was the editor in chief and co-publisher of *Die Zeit*. Under National Socialism, she was active in the anti-fascist resistance movement around Claus Schenk, the Count of Stauffenberg. As such, she was indirectly involved in the attempted coup of the 20th of July 1944. In his letter to Dönhoff, dated the 28th of May 1965, Scholem writes that, in his view, Metzger's essay is a "highly unfortunate concoction . . ., which strikes a completely phony and untrue note at the outset of what could possibly be a new era of improved relations between Germans and Jews – and coming from a Jew, no less!" Scholem asked Dönhoff to print his open letter to Schloesser from the commemorative volume for Margarete Susman in *Die Zeit*: "I think that the readers of *Die Zeit* should be allowed to consider a different view of the situation as well." Scholem's letter to Dönhoff is included in Scholem, *Briefe II: 1948–1970*, ed. Thomas Sparr (Munich: C. H. Beck, 1995), p. 136. However, his open letter was not published in *Die Zeit*.

I know Metzger from his time in Jerusalem: Arnold Metzger, who was of Jewish descent, was Edmund Husserl's assistant in Freiburg during the 1920s. His *Habilitation*, *Phänomenologie und Metaphysik* [Phenomenology and metaphysics] could not advance his academic career in 1933. From 1935 to 1937 he taught philosophy at the Hochschule für die Wissenschaft des Judentums [Higher Institute for the Science of Judaism] in Berlin. In 1938 he immigrated to Paris, in 1940 to England, and in 1941 to the US. After the war he returned to Germany, where, in 1952, he was named honorary professor of philosophy at the University of Munich.

155 ADORNO TO SCHOLEM
FRANKFURT AM MAIN, 10.6.1965

PROF. DR. THEODOR W. ADORNO

6 FRANKFURT AM MAIN
KETTENHOFWEG 123
10 June 1965

Dear Scholem,

Kindest thanks for your letter of the 28th of May.

In the meantime, Stefan Benjamin, who authenticated the illustrated books from the nineteenth century that I found, sent me a message informing me that Dora Sophie died last year. I presume you also were unaware of this – anyway, it moved me greatly.

The same letter indicates that the collection of children's books, which we thought was lost, was rescued and is apparently in Stefan's possession; may he keep it together.

I took the opportunity to inquire once more about the materials that allegedly stayed behind in San Remo and which would now, by rights, belong to him. Incidentally, all manner of new things by Benjamin seem, in the meantime, to be coming to light. There is even a Benjamin archive in the Eastern Zone. Both the Suhrkamp Verlag and Tiedemann will look into it (Taubes took on Tiedemann as his assistant, promising to secure his *Habilitation*. The conditions were very favorable; I couldn't stop Tiedemann). The German Department at the University of Giessen has, moreover, supposedly acquired an array of Benjaminiana at an auction in Amsterdam. I will contact their department head and try to obtain photocopies, at least.

While I was studying the proofs (I have eaten my way through proof no. 168), I was deeply disturbed to discover that Benjamin's unsuccessful attempt to pass his *Habilitation*, which was due to the fact that Schultz passed him off to the aesthetics department, coincided precisely with my absence from Frankfurt. I was studying composition with Berg in Vienna at that time. Had I been here, and had Benjamin – whom I already knew quite well by that time – discussed the matter with me, then I can say with some degree of certainty that everything would have turned out differently, and the consequences would have been incalculable. You may be interested to know that the letter of June 1928 from Königstein falls during the days that Benjamin visited Gretel and me there (where I was recovering from a terrible car accident). It's not mentioned in the letter. These days are unforgettable to me because it was in Königstein that Benjamin first read us passages from the *Arcades Project* – passages that were to remain unsurpassed in their freshness and in the brilliance of their approach.

One of Benjamin's letters, the first to refer to the tension between a theological element and a Marxist one, is a response to a letter from you, which I don't know, but which, I think, we ought to include in the book. Please make the necessary arrangements for this, and please also insert your beautiful Angelus Novus poem wherever you think it belongs. Kindest thanks in advance.

I am very happy to hear that you received more material from Jula Cohn.

As for the forms of address, I wouldn't proceed according to any set principle. My suggestion would be to leave out forms of address where they don't contribute anything significant and to include them where they add value. I'll gladly forego the reference to the false Duns Scotus; it is just that, in the case of Heidegger, who presents himself as so scholastically erudite, it is especially amusing.

With regard to the publication date, I am quite in agreement with you. A few months make no difference if we can be sure that the text appears in a form that we can vouch for. This is imperative to me as well, especially in light of the haste with which I had to complete the *Schriften* at the time.

That you will be in Sils will not be revealed to anyone.

I did not receive a copy of your letter to Mr. Schloesser from the commemorative volume for Susman. Either you didn't send it, or it's been lost. So please send it to me! Nor do I know Mr. Metzger's response. However, I do know the man himself, from ages ago. He is one of the most revolting, miserable people I've ever met, and I can imagine, *a priori*, the tenor of what this chap wrote to you. If only as confirmation, it would thus be important to me to know his unholy text.

I am still working with great verve on my book, although I'm always happy when – after a few weeks of animalistic immersion – I have some excuse to get my head out of it and gain some distance. So, now to write a few theses on the concept of tradition for the new journal put out by Insel. You'll also get to see these soon.

To you both all the best, also from Gretel,

your old

Adorno

Original: typescript with printed letterhead; Gershom Scholem Archive, The National Library of Israel, Jerusalem.

the illustrated books from the nineteenth century . . . the collection of children's books, which we thought was lost: See Ingeborg Daube, "Katalog der Kinderbuchsammlung Walter Benjamins" [Catalogue of Walter Benjamin's collection of children's books], in *Walter Benjamin und die Kinderliteratur: Aspekte der Kinderliteratur in den zwanziger Jahren, mit dem Katalog der Kinderbuchsammlung* [Walter Benjamin and children's literature: aspects of children's literature in the twenties, including a catalogue of the children's books], ed. Klaus Doderer (Weinheim: Juventa, 1988), Preface, pp. 247–82.

materials that allegedly stayed behind in San Remo: After 1934, Walter Benjamin often stayed with his ex-wife Dora in San Remo. See letter no. 104 in this volume. No manuscripts of Benjamin's were found in San Remo.

a Benjamin archive in the Eastern Zone: In 1957, the central archive of the GDR in Potsdam received materials that had been confiscated from Benjamin's Paris apartment by the Gestapo, and which had been stored in Upper Silesia and brought to Moscow by the Red Army after the end of the war. In 1972 they were given to the Akademie der Künste [Academy of Arts] in East Berlin. See Erdmut Wizisla, "Irrfahrt einer Hinterlassenschaft: Die Moskauer Nachlaßteile Walter Benjamins" [The odyssey of an inheritance: the Moscow portion of Walter Benjamin's estate], in *Kulturgüter im Zweiten Weltkrieg: Verlagerung – Auffindung – Rückführung* [Cultural goods during the Second Word War: displacements – discovery – recovery], ed. Uwe Hartmann (Magdeburg: Koordinierungsstelle für Kulturgutverluste, 2007), pp. 313–28; *The Correspondence of Walter Benjamin and Gershom Scholem, 1933–1940*, ed. Gershom Scholem, trans. Gary Smith and Andre Lefevere (New York: Schocken Books, 1989), pp. 4–5. See also letter no. 199.

Tiedemann will look into it . . . I couldn't stop Tiedemann: From 1965 to 1967, Rolf Tiedemann worked as a research assistant at the Hermeneutics Department, which was part of the Faculty of Philosophy at the Freie Universität Berlin. The department was led by the scholar of religious studies, Jacob Taubes. Tiedemann did not complete his *Habilitation* under Taubes.

an array of Benjaminiana *at an auction in Amsterdam*: In 1965, the German Department at the University of Giessen acquired an extensive collection of letters, manuscripts, books, and offprints from Walter Benjamin's estate, which had belonged to his friend Martin Domke. The items were purchased at an auction held at the antiquarian bookshop, Mansfield Book Mart H.E. Heinemann in Montreal, Canada (not Amsterdam as Adorno claims). See Irmgard Hort and Peter Reuter, eds, *Aus mageren und aus ertragreichen Jahren: Streifzug durch die Universitätsbibliothek Giessen und ihre Bestände* [The lean years and the fruitful ones: a foray into the university library at Giessen and its holdings] (Giessen: Universitätsbibliothek Giessen, 2007), p. 233. See also letter no. 10 in this volume.

Benjamin's unsuccessful attempt ... the aesthetics department: In 1923, Walter Benjamin submitted his *Habilitation*, *Origin of the German Trauerspiel*, to the University of Frankfurt. In his essay "Walter Benjamin," Scholem describes the event as follows: "For more than two years Benjamin worked to attain habilitation as a *Dozent* (lecturer) in modern German literature at Frankfurt University, encouraged at first by the head of the department, Professor Franz Schultz, who promptly backed out as soon as he received the thesis, covering his retreat with polite maneuvers. He and the head of the Aesthetics Department, Professor Hans Cornelius, complained in private that they did not understand a word of the work. Yielding to strong pressure, Benjamin unfortunately agreed to withdraw the thesis, which was sure to be rejected." Gershom Scholem, "Walter Benjamin," in *On Jews and Judaism in Crisis*, ed. Werner J. Dannhauser (New York: Schocken Books, 1976), p. 184. See also the editorial remarks accompanying the German edition of Benjamin's *Ursprung des deutschen Trauerspiels*: *Gesammelte Schriften I: Abhandlungen* [Treatises], ed. Rolf Tiedemann and Hermann Schweppenhäuser (Frankfurt am Main: Suhrkamp, 1991), pp. 895–902. See also Burkhardt Lindner, "Habilitationsakte Benjamin: Über ein 'akademisches Trauerspiel' und über ein Vorkapitel der 'Frankfurter Schule' (Horkheimer, Adorno)" [Benjamin's *Habilitation* file: on an "academic mourning play" and the chapter prior to the Frankfurt School," in *Walter Benjamin im Kontext* [Walter Benjamin in context], ed. Burkhardt Lindner (Königstein im Taunus: Athenaeum, 1985), pp. 324–41.

my absence from Frankfurt: From March until August 1925 Adorno lived in Vienna, where he studied composition with Alban Berg and piano with Eduard Steuermann. See Stefan Müller-Doohm, *Adorno: A Biography*, trans. Rodney Livingstone (Cambridge: Polity, 2005), pp. 83–94. See also *Theodor W. Adorno / Siegfried Kracauer: Correspondence 1923–1966*, ed. Wolfgang Schopf, trans. Susan Reynolds and Michael Winkler (Cambridge: Polity, 2020), pp. 8–71.

the letter of June 1928 from Königstein: Benjamin's letter to Scholem, dated 2.6.1928, is included in *The Correspondence of Walter Benjamin 1910–1940*, ed. Theodor W. Adorno and Gershom Scholem, trans. Manfred

R. Jacobson and Evelyn M. Jacobson (Chicago: University of Chicago Press, 1994), pp. 336–7.

One of Benjamin's letters: See Benjamin's letter to Scholem, dated 17.4.1931 – a response to Scholem's letter from Jericho, dated 30.3.1931: *The Correspondence of Walter Benjamin 1910–1940*, pp. 376–8. See also: letter no. 43 in this volume.

a few theses . . . for the new journal put out by Insel: Adorno's theses first appeared in the *Inselalmanach auf das Jahr 1966* [Insel almanac for the year 1966] under the heading "Über Tradition" [On tradition]; they were later included in Adorno, *Ohne Leitbild / Parva Aesthetica* [Without a guiding image / parva aesthetica] (Frankfurt am Main: Suhrkamp, 1967), repr. in Adorno, Gesammelte Schriften 10.1, ed. Rolf Tiedemann et al. (Frankfurt am Main: Suhrkamp, 2003), pp. 423–31. See "On Tradition," trans. Aaron Bell, *Telos*, no. 94 (1992), pp. 75–82.

156 SCHOLEM TO ADORNO
JERUSALEM, 20.6.1965

Prof. Theodor Adorno
Frankfurt am Main.

Jerusalem, on the 20 of June, 1965

Dear Adorno,

Many thanks for your letter of the 10th of June. I received it upon my return from Buber's funeral, along with an invitation from *Merkur* in Munich asking me to comment on the deceased in a commemorative essay. I promptly declined, telling them that, unfortunately, I feel quite unable, for a German readership, to treat the question of Buber's spiritual epiphany and the reasons for his enormous success with the Germans, as well as his complete failure with the Jews. Between you and me, that's a topic for dialectical sociologists. Incidentally, it fell to me to deliver the eulogy – I said to my wife, Fania: tell me three points that I can discuss without saying things that are directly untrue. I credit myself greatly for having succeeded at this. Thanks to Fania!

The news that Dora Benjamin died last year was, in fact, unknown to me, and I am greatly saddened by it. My last meeting with her, in May 1961, deeply disturbed me, due to the image of complete decay that she presented. I couldn't bring myself to visit her again after that.

If Tiedemann is going to Berlin, as you write, then how will he put together the biographical notes for the volume of Benjamin's correspondence? I understood from Boehlich's letters that this was the plan. And how can Tiedemann assist Taubes if the latter has a professorship in Jewish studies? The expert is astonished and the layman wonders.

Jula Cohn has given me permission to include in the volume the letters to her that I selected, copies of which I sent to Boehlich. I'm very curious as to how my reunion with her will go. She also wrote to tell me that the letters to her brother Alfred are still at her sister-in-law's. However, the latter is Walter Benjamin's first fiancée, and I was repeatedly informed that she wants to hear nothing more of him, nor anything connected to him. Maybe someday she'll change her mind. The letter from me to which Benjamin was responding, and which first mentions the tension within him between the theological and the Marxist element, no longer exists, so I cannot include it. The other two letters from 1931 have already been included, as you know.

I sent you a copy of my letter to Mr. Schloesser by registered mail three days ago. I'm quite sure I've sent it to you before. Metzger's essay (which does not name me but which is clearly intended as a response to my letter) appeared in *Die Zeit* about 4 weeks ago. It's a ghastly document.

Surely, I gave you a copy of my Eranos lecture on the concept of the tradition of commentary last year. It contains the most precise formulations of which I am capable on revelation and tradition. In 1932, when I first put them to paper, directed against Mr. Schoeps, Walter Benjamin greeted them with unreserved approval. By the way, I wonder why I haven't been sent the new Suhrkamp journal. They really could've made the effort.

For now I send cordial regards and am looking forward to a happy reunion in Sils,

yours,
Gerhard Scholem

Original: aerogram (typescript); Theodor W. Adorno Archive, Frankfurt am Main. First published in Gershom Scholem, *Briefe II: 1948–1970*, ed. Thomas Sparr (Munich: C. H. Beck, 1995), pp. 139–41. An excerpt of this letter appears in translation in *Gershom Scholem: A Life in Letters*, ed. and trans. Anthony David Skinner (Cambridge, MA: Harvard University Press, 2002), pp. 412–13.

Buber's funeral: Martin Buber died on 13.6.1965. He was buried the following day at *Har HaMenuchot*, the main Jewish cemetery in Jerusalem.

an invitation from Merkur ... *commemorative essay*: In his response to the editor of *Merkur*, Hans Paeschke, Scholem wrote the following: "For the time being, and if at all, I would be able to comment on Buber only in Hebrew and for a Hebrew readership. Unfortunately I feel quite unable, for a German readership, to treat the question of Buber's position, his spiritual epiphany, and the reasons for his enormous success with the Germans, as well as his complete failure with the Jews. It's a very, very broad field. I find it difficult to explain myself on this matter in the form of a letter. These questions greatly move many of us, and we will somehow have to reckon with it, albeit in a Jewish forum." See Scholem, *Briefe II: 1948–1970*, p. 287 (note).

it fell to me to deliver the eulogy: Scholem's eulogy for Martin Buber was not published.

157 ADORNO TO SCHOLEM
FRANKFURT AM MAIN, 22.6.1965

PROF. DR. THEODOR W. ADORNO

6 FRANKFURT AM MAIN
KETTENHOFWEG 123
22 June 1965

Dear Scholem,

Kindest thanks for your letter.

As you can imagine, I have also been plagued by God and the world – but especially the latter – with requests to write something about Buber; and, just like you, I declined. Certainly, I do not want to be ungrateful to this man, to whom I owe my first conception of Hasidism, however problematic it may be. But since one fateful day, some forty years ago, when Horkheimer and I had a terrible falling-out with him, nothing has changed in my decisive rejection of his philosophy – a philosophy that definitely belongs to the context of the darkest German ideology. After *The Jargon of Authenticity* and a few other pleasantries on B[uber] that I have written, I hardly need to emphasize the degree to which I agree with your position. The reasons that he – like Gollancz – serves as the opposite of a scapegoat in Germany are all too evident. I can't help but see the old Susman in much the same context – a woman whose moral flab, so to speak, melted in the messianic flame and was rendered into appearance. I can hardly imagine anything worse than these figures, who supplied elements of truth to the lie. Don't even get me started about Susman's poems.

For the record, I am in complete agreement with your response to Mr. Schloesser, which most certainly didn't reach me the first time around. Given what happened, even the words "German–Jewish conversation" are enough to make one sick. It's the simple truth that such a conversation never took place. Even the so-called great Germans, like Kant and Goethe, wrote things that now appear like firewood being dragged to Hus's stake by the little old woman. It's a truly abysmal irony that the German interest in Judaism qua Judaism, as opposed to individual Jewish figures, has set in only now that there are no more Jews there.

If I returned in spite of this, I can give nothing but individual reasons: the possibility to work – for a time – without constraint or oversight. In this regard, I want to say to you that I was truly devastated by what you wrote in your letter to Benjamin, namely that his attempt at a collective identification bears a far greater danger than any suffering caused by loneliness. This is to say nothing of your subsequent formulation on suicide. Despite the difference between your views on materialism and mine, my response to him was always the same. I also considered Benjamin's love for materialism to be unfortunate, with respect to both materialism and his own philosophy. In the end, though, both points seem to coincide. I am very happy that some of your great letters on the materialism debate will now be contained in the collection.

As for the biographical notes to the Benjamin letters, it looks like Boehlich will have to seize the fountain pen himself. It's not all that urgent. We, Gretel and I, have dutifully read all the proofs that we've received to date – roughly 180 of them – and we intend to carry on working on them until the end of July. However, in August, I am neither able nor willing to do any work, no matter how light or pleasant it may be. I simply need the time to rest. My heart has been giving me more and more trouble over the past few weeks.

As concerns Taubes: in addition to his professorship in Jewish studies, he has another position, I'm not exactly sure which kind, in the field of "hermeneutics," *whatever that may be*,* and I suspect that he has attached Tiedemann to himself through this second position. By the way, I have to say that recently Mr. T. acted very decently on a number of occasions. Peter Szondi, for instance, wouldn't have been promoted without him; and, at present, he is putting his weight behind one of my students, Haag, with considerable vigor. The problem seems to me to be that he overestimates his capacity for influence and thereby kills it. But we'll have to wait and see.

Herbert Marcuse and Kracauer will both be visiting me here, almost at the same time. Perhaps the former can finally take the latter down a peg; he'd certainly deserve it.

Perhaps in Sils I can read you some of my own stuff on tradition and cognition. The passages are from the "Metaphysical Reflections" that will form the end of my book, which is progressing quickly now, in what's actually in the final stage of editing. The fact that I will actually be able to finish the book only became clear very late, i.e. after my return from Baden-Baden in April. Before this, I kept dodging a

* Original in English.

decisive issue, namely the problem of non-identity. However, I feel that what I've produced on this point is now presentable. My health permitting, the manuscript should be ready to go to print by next spring at the latest.

Unseld is being remarkably stingy with the new journal. I was given a copy, but at the same time I was told to purchase a subscription, since Suhrkamp can't afford to hand out authors' copies for free this time. I'll protest this with my particular brand of graciousness when an opportunity next presents itself, and be sure to include you in my protest.

What is the likelihood of your visiting in Frankfurt after Sils Maria?

All that is cordial, also to Fanya, the squarer of the circle, and also from Gretel,

your old

Adorno

Original: typescript with printed letterhead; Gershom Scholem Archive, The National Library of Israel, Jerusalem.

since one fateful day . . . a terrible falling-out with him: Not verified.

After The Jargon of Authenticity *and a few other pleasantries on B[uber] that I have written*: According to Peter von Haselberg, Adorno invented the term "religious Tyrolean" to describe Buber (see Stefan Müller-Doohm, *Adorno: A Biography*, trans. Rodney Livingstone (Cambridge: Polity, 2005), p. 20). In *The Jargon of Authenticity*, Adorno wrote: "Ever since Martin Buber split off Kierkegaard's view of the existential from Kierkegaard's Christology, and dressed it up as a universal posture, there has been a dominant inclination to conceive of metaphysical content as bound to the so-called relation of I and thou. This content is referred to the immediacy of life. Theology is tied to the determinations of immanence, which in turn want to claim a larger meaning, by means of their suggestion of theology: they are already virtually like the words of the jargon. In this process, nothing less is whisked away than the threshold between the natural and the supernatural." See *The Jargon of Authenticity*, trans. Knut Tarnowski and Frederic Will (London: Routledge & Kegan Paul, 1973), p. 16.

like Gollancz: The British-Jewish publisher Victor Gollancz (1893–1967) was the head of the Victor Gollancz publishing house and the founder of the Left Book Club. He was a committed enemy of the National Socialist regime; however, later in life he became very critical of the idea of collective German guilt. He spoke out against the expulsion of the so-called Sudeten Germans – that is, Germans living in territories that became Czechoslovakia – and against the treatment of the Germans by the allies. By the same token, he was critical of the expulsion of Palestinians after the 1948 war and supported the appeals for aid made by Palestinian refugees.

what you wrote in your letter to Benjamin . . . formulation on suicide: Adorno is referring to Scholem's letters from 30.3.1931 and 6.5.1931, which draw a connection between the materialism debate, theology, and Benjamin himself. In the first letter, Scholem writes the following to Benjamin:

> As long as you write about the bourgeois for the bourgeois it can be all the same, I might even say totally irrelevant, to the *genuine* materialist as to whether you have the desire to surrender to the illusion of being in agreement with him. On the other hand, in dialectical terms, he should actually have every interest in strengthening you in this illusion, since your dynamite could presumably be, to him as well, recognizably more potent on "that" terrain than his. . . . He has no use for you in his own camp since the purely abstract identification of your spheres would necessarily be exploded there with the first steps you took toward the center. (*The Correspondence of Walter Benjamin 1910–1940*, ed. Theodor W. Adorno and Gershom Scholem, trans. Manfred R. Jacobson and Evelyn M. Jacobson (Chicago: University of Chicago Press, 1994), p. 375)

The second letter then states: "You write, make a counterproposal. I can only suggest that you acknowledge your genius, which you are currently so hopelessly attempting to deny. Self-deception turns all too easily into suicide, and God knows your suicide would be too high a price to pay for the honor of correct revolutionary thinking. Your desire for community places you at risk, even if it is the apocalyptic community of the revolution that speaks out of so many of your writings, more than the horror of loneliness. I am indeed ready to put greater stake in that than in the imagery with which you are cheating yourself out of your calling" (ibid., p. 379).

As concerns Taubes . . . he has another position: The Institute for Jewish Studies at the Freie Universität Berlin was founded as part of the negotiations leading to Jacob Taubes's appointment. He served as the Institute's director until 1979. In addition to this, he chaired the hermeneutics division within the Department of Philosophy at the Freie Universität Berlin.

Peter Szondi: The literary scholar Peter Szondi (1929–1971) was born in Budapest. In 1944 he was interned at the Bergen-Belsen concentration camp. He was freed and sent to Switzerland as part of the Kasztner agreement. After studying in Zurich and Paris, he completed his doctoral thesis, *The Theory of Modern Drama*, in Zurich in 1954 and his *Habilitation* at the Freie Universität Berlin in 1961. In 1965 he received tenure and was appointed director of the newly founded Institute for Literary Studies and Comparative Literature at the Freie Universität Berlin (today it is named after Szondi). In 1968 Szondi was a visiting professor at the Hebrew University in Jerusalem. In 1971 he was appointed to a professorship in comparative literature at the University of Zurich. In October of that year he committed suicide in Berlin.

one of my students, Haag: Karl-Heinz Haag (1924-2011) received his doctorate in 1951 under the supervision of Max Horkheimer with a work entitled *Die Seinsdialektik bei Hegel und in der scholastischen Philosophie* [The dialectic of being in Hegel and in scholastic philosophy]. He completed his *Habilitation*, titled *Kritik der neueren Ontologie* [Critique of recent ontology] in 1961. Both have been reprinted in Haag, *Kritische Philosophie:*

Abhandlungen und Aufsätze [Critical philosophy: treatises and essays] (Munich: Edition Text + Kritik, 2012).

on tradition and cognition . . . from the "Metaphysical Reflections": See the third 'Meditation on Metaphysics' in Adorno, *Negative Dialectics*, trans. E. B. Ashton (London: Routledge, 1973), pp. 368–73.

158 SCHOLEM TO ADORNO JERUSALEM, 5.7.1965

5 July 1965

Dear Adorno,

A technical request for help concerning one of W.B.'s letters, proof no. 192 (letter 177). Could you please ask your wife to check with Egon Wissing, whose address I don't have, whether he remembers the correct name of the lady who lived at the apartment on Prinzregentenstrasse before W. B. (Boch? Bloch? I can't make it out). Wissing lived in the same building, after all, and I remember him saying once that he had arranged the apartment transfer.

I'd like to get the name right, if possible.

Kind regards

yours, G. Scholem

Original: aerogram (manuscript); Theodor W. Adorno Archive, Frankfurt am Main.

the correct name of the lady: From the summer of 1930 until his emigration, Benjamin lived in the studio of Eva Boy at Prinzregentenstrasse 66. See Benjamin's letter to Boy, dated the 14th of November 1930, in *Walter Benjamin: Gesammelte Briefe III, 1925–1930*, ed. Henri Lonitz and Christoph Gödde (Frankfurt am Main: Suhrkamp, 1998), p. 555, as well as the note on p. 556.

159 ELFRIEDE OLBRICH TO SCHOLEM
FRANKFURT AM MAIN, 8 JULY 1965

PROF. DR. THEODOR W. ADORNO

6 FRANKFURT AM MAIN
KETTENHOFWEG 123
8 July 1965

Dear esteemed Professor Scholem,

Professor Adorno has asked me to send you a copy of the response he received from the Piper Verlag. It seems to confirm what Mr. Adorno already suspected: that the translation of *Sodom et Gomorrhe* never existed.

Mr. Adorno sends his cordial regards.

Respectfully,
your very devoted
Elfriede Olbrich

Copy:

Professor Dr. Theodor W. Adorno

6 Frankfurt am Main
Kettenhofweg 123

Munich, on the 7th of July, 1965
Dr. B/kre

Most esteemed Professor,

Please excuse the late response to your friendly request. Unfortunately we had to wait for the return of Mr. Piper's long-time secretary in order to investigate the issue further. We believed that she, more than anyone else, would be able to advise in the matter of Proust and Benjamin, respectively. Unfortunately, I must inform you that our investigation yielded no trace of the papers in question. In 1937, Dr. Robert Freund, Mr. Reinhard Piper's erstwhile partner, left the firm and emigrated to America (he died in New York in 1952). Upon Freund's departure, the R. Piper & Co. Verlag transferred to him the translation rights to the work of several foreign authors, including Marcel Proust. Dr. Freund obtained the works SWANN'S WAY and THE GUERMANTES WAY. No reference to SODOM ET GOMMORRHE could be found.

With best regards,
your devoted

O. F. Best
(Dr. Otto F. Best)
R. PIPER & CO. VERLAG
Editorial Office

Original: typescript with printed letterhead and a copy of the response from the Piper Verlag; Gershom Scholem Archive, The National Library of Israel, Jerusalem.

160 GRETEL ADORNO TO SCHOLEM
FRANKFURT AM MAIN, 23.7.1965

PROF. DR. THEODOR W. ADORNO

6 FRANKFURT AM MAIN
KETTENHOFWEG 123
23 July 1965

Dear Mr. Scholem,

I wrote to Egon Wissing right away and today I received his response: he has no idea of the name of the woman whose apartment Benjamin had sublet. I'd simply refer to her as Mrs. or Miss B.

I am very much looking forward to seeing you and Fanja in Sils Maria. See you soon.

With the most cordial regards,
always yours,
[Gretel Adorno]

Original: typescript (carbon copy); Theodor W. Adorno Archive, Frankfurt am Main.

161 SCHOLEM TO ADORNO
JERUSALEM, 26.12.1965

26 December 1965

Dear Adorno,

How are you, and, above all else, how is your wife? Did the treatment help with the ulcer? And may I also take this occasion to wish you continued, or just renewed, good health for the year 1966?

Besides this festive (?) occasion, I have another reason for contacting you today: I intend to accept an invitation to Berlin (to attend, as an audience member, a symposium on Kafka from the 17th to the 19th of February). I want to use this opportunity to make a small detour to Frankfurt in the interest of the Benjamin letters, in order to see you, and also because I have to pass through town anyway. It seems most likely to me that I'll stop in F. on my way back, though it's possible that it will be the other way around. For me it would work better on the trip back.

In the meantime, cordial regards to you both
yours,
Gershom Scholem

Original: aerogram (manuscript); Theodor W. Adorno Archive, Frankfurt am Main.

162 ADORNO TO SCHOLEM
FRANKFURT AM MAIN, 3.1.1966

PROF. DR. THEODOR W. ADORNO

6 FRANKFURT AM MAIN
KETTENHOFWEG 123
3 January 1966

Dear Scholem,

Kindest thanks for your letter. We've had all manner of health-related problems recently. Gretel had a regular ulcer, which was completely cured through skilful care. However, she also had to undergo surgery to remove a polyp in her throat. The whole business was difficult, especially because of an anaesthetic, which aggravated her stomach again. But thankfully it all went well and the polyp turned out to be totally harmless. I feel boundlessly reassured, and Gretel is doing much better. As for me, I am making good headway with my book, but I'm not exactly as fresh as dew; in all seriousness, I am overworked to the limits of what I can bear. However, I've arranged to go on leave for the next two semesters, so everything is looking a little bit lighter.

Despite our constant pressure, I still cannot report any progress regarding our book. The good Mr. Boehlich claims that he hasn't gotten to it yet and so it drags on interminably. So much the better, then, that you'll be here in February; I'm sincerely looking forward to it. If you could be so kind, please inform me of the exact dates of your visit as soon as possible, since mid-February is the worst time here on account of countless exams, and I want to make arrangements early so that we can spend ample time together.

I expect to hear from you soon, and remain, in the meantime, with the kindest regards from Gretel, also to Fanja,

your old and loyal
Adorno

Original: typescript with printed letterhead; Gershom Scholem Archive, The National Library of Israel, Jerusalem.

163 SCHOLEM TO ADORNO
JERUSALEM, 3.2.1966

Jerusalem, on the 3rd of February, 1966

Dear Adorno,

Unfortunately, I too have now taken ill and must cancel my trip to Berlin. It's nothing serious, but under no circumstances should I embark in 14 days on a trip abroad in the unpredictable February weather. Instead, I plan on stopping off in Frankfurt for two days from the 16th to the 18th of March on my way to the USA. We could then discuss matters together, as well as with the people at Suhrkamp, although, as you can appreciate, these conversations will take place in completely different registers. By then I should be completely recovered, as long as I conduct myself normally. I would like to know if I can count on you and Mr. Boehlich to both be in Frankfurt around this time. Otherwise there is no sense in my coming to Frankfurt. There's a non-stop flight from Tel Aviv to Frankfurt each Wednesday which I would take. Please be so kind and let me know as soon as possible; I have to arrange my ticket for the long trip. Due to illness, that's all for today.

With cordial regards to you both,

yours,

G. Scholem

I'm also writing to Boehlich via the same post.

Original: aerogram (typescript) with handwritten postscript; Theodor W. Adorno Archive, Frankfurt am Main.

164 ADORNO TO SCHOLEM
FRANKFURT AM MAIN, 8.2.1966

PROF. DR. THEODOR W. ADORNO

6 FRANKFURT AM MAIN
KETTENHOFWEG 123

8 February 1966

Dear Scholem,

A thousand thanks for your letter. I am very sad that you are unwell, of course, and I sincerely hope that it is actually nothing serious. On the other hand, I am glad that your visit is somewhat delayed, since mid-February is so untenably busy here that I was worried that we wouldn't be able to find a quiet moment for us at all (I didn't put it so blatantly in my last letter). In March, this shouldn't be a problem. I'll be in Brussels during the first few days of March, and from the 25th I'll be going to Baden-Baden for relaxation. Between the 16th and the 18th I may be lying in bed at home under treatment, but that certainly wouldn't stand in the way of us being together.

Let me also add that I am just as outraged as you are by the delay in preparing the page makeup of the Benjamin letters. We've intervened countless times and all we have achieved thereby is to anger Mr. Boehlich. He's a very decent man with many [good] qualities, but he's overburdened – whether in actuality or only in his head. That is to say, we'll be entirely of one mind on this point.

Wishing you a complete and speedy recovery and all that is cordial to you both, from us both,

your old
Adorno

Original: typescript with printed letterhead; Gershom Scholem Archive, The National Library of Israel, Jerusalem.

Brussels: Adorno gave a series of lectures on the sociology of music in Brussels.

165 SCHOLEM TO ADORNO
JERUSALEM, 25.2.1966

Jerusalem, February 25, 1966

Dear Adorno,

These lines are merely to confirm that I will be arriving in Frankfurt at noon on Wednesday the 16th of March, and that I will be staying at the Park Hotel. On Friday, I'll be flying on to America. I am counting on seeing you and your wife on Wednesday afternoon or evening. Perhaps you could ask your secretary to set up a meeting with the powers that be at Suhrkamp; or, if you prefer not to take part in such a meeting, perhaps she could arrange a get-together between me and Suhrkamp / Boehlich / Unseld. We can discuss the rest in person. I hope that you will both have recovered from all your ailments by the time we meet. Please arrange with the dwellers of the Marxian heaven for the sun to shine on the 16th of March – that is, in case you don't maintain any diplomatic relations with the other heavenly inhabitants. I would rather rely on the old angels, especially since I recently looked back over Marx's pages on the Jewish question, which, once again, almost made me vomit. The Talmud states that the keys to making it rain were not even entrusted to (Kafka's?) angels. However, the same Talmud also states that, on the Day of Atonement, as the high priest in Jerusalem entered the holiest of holies, he implored God with particular vigor not to heed the prayers of the tourists (who had asked for good weather) – a purely materialist consideration in the interest of the conditions of agricultural production. So, one has a choice between these Talmudic utterances about the weather and its masters. On this note, I remain faithfully yours

with cordial regards,

G. Scholem

Original: aerogram (typescript); Theodor W. Adorno Archive, Frankfurt am Main.

The Talmud . . . the keys to making it rain: Here Scholem is alluding to two different books of the Talmud. See Babylonian Talmud, *Tractate Ta'anit*, 2a:

> R. Johanan said: Three keys the Holy One blessed be He has retained in His own hands and not entrusted to the hand of any messenger, namely, the Key of Rain, the Key of Childbirth, and the Key of the Revival of the Dead. The Key of Rain, for It is written, The Lord will open unto thee His good treasure, the heaven to give the rain of thy land in its season, The Key of Childbirth, for it is written, And God remembered Rachel, and God hearkened to her, and opened her womb. The Key of the Revival of the Dead, for it is written, And ye shall know that I am the Lord, when I have opened your graves. In Palestine they said: Also the Key of Sustenance, for it is said, Thou openest thy hand etc. Why does not R. Johanan include also this [key]? – Because in his view sustenance is [included in] Rain.

See also Babylonian Talmud, Tractate Yoma, 53b:

> AND HE UTTERED A SHORT PRAYER IN THE OUTER HOUSE: What did he pray? Raba son of R. Adda and Rabin son of R. Adda both reported in the name of Rab: "May it be Thy will, O Lord our God, that this year be full of heavy rains and hot." But is a hot year an advantage? – Rather: If it be a hot one, let it be rich in rain. – R. Aha the son of Raba concluded the prayer in the name of R. Judah [thus]: May there not depart a ruler from the house of Judah, and may the house of Israel not require that they sustain one another, and permit not the prayers of travellers to find entrance before you.

166 GRETEL ADORNO TO SCHOLEM
FRANKFURT AM MAIN, 2.3.1966

PROF. DR. THEODOR W. ADORNO

6 FRANKFURT AM MAIN
KETTENHOFWEG 123
2 March 1966

Dear Mr. Scholem,

Since Teddie has gone to Brussels to give some lectures, I am writing to you today to make sure that it all works out with our meeting.

I'll be expecting you for dinner at our place shortly after 7pm on Wednesday the 16th of March. I've told a few other people too. We are both very much looking forward to seeing you.

I reminded Unseld of the Benjamin letters just two days ago, but he only shrugged his shoulders and said that he also couldn't get Böhlich into gear. I fear that you may have to enlist a higher-ranking Prince of Darkness to sort this out.

To you and Fanja all the best,

always yours,
Gretel Adorno

Original: typescript with printed letterhead; Gershom Scholem Archive, The National Library of Israel, Jerusalem.

Böhlich: Gretel Adorno's spelling.

167 GRETEL ADORNO TO SCHOLEM
FRANKFURT AM MAIN, 18.4.1966

Dr. Gretel Adorno

6 Frankfurt am Main
Kettenhofweg 123
18 April 1966

Professor Dr. Gershom Scholem
Hebrew Union College
Cincinnati, Ohio 45220

Dear Mr. Scholem,

Hansi Schoen sent us the corrected version of the *curriculum vitae*. She added a few words. Teddie takes particular exception to the word "poet." Now, I wanted to ask if you could possibly talk Hansi out of this, or if you think we should swallow it *tel quel*.

I hope that you are doing well in Cincinnati and that you're making good progress with your work.

Baden-Baden was very nice, and we really managed to relax. We are going to Prague for a week now. After that, Teddie will be in Bremen for three days, in Vienna from the 14th to 21st of May, and then he's going to Berlin around the 23rd of June.

Very cordial regards from us both,

yours,

Gretel A

Original: typescript; Gershom Scholem Archive, The National Library of Israel, Jerusalem.

Hansi Schoen sent us the corrected version of the curriculum vitae: The index of correspondents in the 1966 edition of Benjamin's letters contains the following entry on Ernst Schoen: "Schoen, Ernst (1894–1960). Musician, poet, and translator. WB's schoolmate and later friend. Since his youth, in contact with the family of the composer Busoni. Lived primarily in Berlin; later in Frankfurt as head of broadcasting until 1933. In England from 1933 to 1952, then in Berlin again. WB published "Ein Gespräch mit Ernst Schoen" [A conversation with Ernst Schoen] in the *Literarische Welt* (August 30, 1929). Only the letters WB wrote to him before 1921 are preserved." See *The Correspondence of Walter Benjamin: 1910–1940*, ed. Theodor W. Adorno and Gershom Scholem, trans. Manfred R. Jacobson and Evelyn M. Jacobson (Chicago: University of Chicago Press, 1994), p. 643.

Prague: Adorno's trip to Czechoslovakia lasted from the 22nd to the 29th of April and took him to Prague, Brno and Bratislava. In Prague, probably on the 26th of April, he gave a lecture entitled "Soziologie und empirische Forschung" [Sociology and empirical research] at the Philosophy Department of the Charles University. This lecture forms the basis of an essay with the same title that was later published in the volume *Sociologica II*. See Adorno, "Sociology and empirical research," in *The Adorno Reader*, ed. Brian O'Connor (Oxford: Blackwell, 2000), pp. 174–92. On the 27th of April, Adorno gave a lecture at the Janáček Academy in Brno entitled "Formprinzipien der zeitgenössischen Musik" [Formal principles of contemporary music], and on the 28th of April he gave a lecture on "Gesellschaft" [Society] at the Sociological Society. He repeated the lecture "Formprinzipien der zeitgenössischen Musik" in Bratislava on the 28th of April before the Association of Slovak Composers. It couldn't be verified with certainty whether he also repeated the lecture "Sociology and Empirical Research" in Bratislava.

Bremen: A televised conversation with Hans Otte on "Der musikalische Adorno" [The musical Adorno] had been planned for the 4th of May. A letter from the network [to Adorno], dated 14.2.1967, states: "Your conversation with Otte (recorded during your last visit to Bremen in May of last year) has, in the meantime, been scheduled for broadcasting on Channel 3." The exact date of the broadcast and the title of the show were not verified. On the 5th of May, Adorno gave a lecture at the Bremer Kunsthalle titled "Über einige Schwierigkeiten in der Auffassung neuer Musik" [On some difficulties in the understanding of new music]. See Adorno, "Difficulties," in *Essays on Music*, ed. Richard Leppert, trans. Susan H. Gillespie (Berkeley: University of California Press, 2002), pp. 644–80. The lecture was recorded by Radio Bremen for the series "Pro Musica Nova" and was presumably broadcast on the 6th of May. Adorno also read parts of his "Meditations on Metaphysics" on the radio. See Adorno, *Negative Dialectics*, trans. E. B. Ashton (London: Routledge, 1973), pp. 361–84, 393–8, 405–8. The readings were broadcast on the 5th of May 1966. On the 5th or 6th of May, Adorno also recorded a reading of his lecture "Kulturkritik und Gesellschaft" [Cultural criticism and society], which was aired posthumously in his honour on 6.8.1971. See Adorno, "Cultural Criticism and Society," in *Prisms*, trans. Samuel Weber and Shierry Weber (Cambridge, MA: MIT Press, 1981), pp. 146–62.

Vienna: During the "Europa-Gespräch" [Europe Conversation] about "Stagione – oder Ensembleoper" [Stagione or Ensemble Opera], which took place at the Palais Pálffy, Adorno took part in a panel discussion on the 16th of May at the invitation of the Austrian Society for Music. Other panelists were Hans Hotter, Hermann Juch, Rolf Liebermann, Herbert Schneiber, Erwin Thalhammer, and Helmut A. Fiechtner. On the 17th of May, Adorno read parts of his newly published book, *Negative Dialectics*, at the invitation of the Zentralsparkasse [central savings bank] of the municipality of Vienna, in their institutional building. On the 18th of May he gave another lecture at the Palais Pálffy, this time at the invitation of the Austrian Society for Literature which was published as "Funktionalismus heute." See "Functionalism Today," trans. Jane Newman and John Smith, in *Oppositions: Journal for Ideas and Criticism in Architecture*, no. 17 (1979), pp. 30–41.

Berlin: On the 23rd of June Adorno gave a lecture entitled "Die Kunst und die Künste" [Art and the arts] at the Akademie der Künste in Berlin. See "Art and the Arts," in *Can One Live After Auschwitz?*, ed. Rolf Tiedemann, trans. Rodney Livingstone (Stanford, CA: Stanford University Press, 2003), pp. 368–87.

168 SCHOLEM TO GRETEL ADORNO
CINCINNATI, 22.4.1966

HEBREW UNION = JEWISH INSTITUTE OF RELIGION
UNDER THE PATRONAGE OF THE UNION OF AMERICAN HEBREW CONGREGATIONS

CINCINNATI — CLIFTON AVENUE – CINCINNATI, OHIO 45220
NEW YORK
LOS ANGELES
JERUSALEM

22 April '66

Dear Gretel Adorno,

Sincere thanks for your letter!

After careful deliberation, I suggest – in the interest of the good cause, and in God's name – letting the lines about Ernst Schoen remain as Hansi rewrote them. (It could have been much more difficult!!) Let's just swallow it!

Has there been any progress with Boehlich???? In keeping with the *timetable** we drew up in Fr., *I am waiting*.†

Most esteemed lady, please don't forget that I intend to come to Fr.[ankfurt] from the 18th to the 22nd of June. We had a big symposium here on "*Mysticism and Society*,"‡ with your humble servant as chief pontificator. Perhaps the Institute would be interested to hear my lecture on this topic?

I am doing very well, knock wood; I'm living here under the most pleasant of circumstances. I'm even having fun with my course on the theology of Sabbatianism (for future Reform rabbis), and I hope that you won't have any complaints regarding my appearance.

Cordial regards to you both,

yours,

Gerhard Scholem

Original: aerogram (manuscript) with printed letterhead; Theodor W. Adorno Archive, Frankfurt am Main.

Ernst Schön: Scholem's spelling.

a big symposium: Scholem gave a talk, entitled "Mysticism and Society," at the "symposium" organized by the Frank Weil Institute at the Hebrew Union College in Cincinnati. See Scholem, "Mysticism and Society," *Diogenes*, 15/58 (1967), pp. 1–24.

my course: Not verified.

* Original in English.
† Original in English.
‡ Original in English.

169 SCHOLEM TO GRETEL ADORNO
CINCINNATI, 12.5.1966

HEBREW UNION = JEWISH INSTITUTE OF RELIGION
UNDER THE PATRONAGE OF THE UNION OF AMERICAN HEBREW CONGREGATIONS

CINCINNATI — CLIFTON AVENUE – CINCINNATI, OHIO 45220
NEW YORK
LOS ANGELES
JERUSALEM

Dear Gretel Adorno,

I'm just reading the corrections on pp. 640–700. Regarding p. 663, I'd like to suggest that you add an annotation with the precise date for the conversation in the Schweizerhäuschen (in Königstein??). Surely it would be important to know this. (And, *entre nous*, the two of you should write down your attempts to recollect this historic conversation!) Was this in 1928/9? (Before the Brecht period, judging from how the letter unfolds? Asja Lacis was in Germany in 1929, but not in 1928, as far as I can make out?

Who is Lenia, on p. 666? If it's [Lotte] Lenia, then why not add her first name in square brackets?

Who is Mrs. Favez, on p. 667? There'd be room for a note on this page! p. 674: *Höllenphantasmagorie*!

Cordial regards to you both

yours G.S.

Original: aerogram (manuscript) with printed letterhead, date in accordance with postmark; Theodor W. Adorno Archive, Frankfurt am Main.

conversation in the Schweizerhäuschen: In his letter to Adorno from Paris, dated 31.5.1935, Benjamin describes his relation to the Institute for Social Research at the end of the 1920s in connection with the development of his *Arcades Project*: "What brought about the end of this epoch were the conversations I had with you in Frankfurt, and especially the 'historical' conversation in the little Swiss house [*Schweizerhäuschen*] and, after that, the definitely historical one held around the table with you, Asja, Felizitas, and Horkheimer. It was the end of rhapsodic naïveté." See *The Correspondence of Walter Benjamin 1910–1940*, ed. Theodor W. Adorno and Gershom Scholem, trans. Manfred R. Jacobson and Evelyn M. Jacobson (Chicago: University of Chicago Press, 1994), p. 489. A note explaining the significance of this "historic conversation" was not included.

[Lotte] Lenia: Scholem's spelling. The actress and singer Lotte Lenya (1898–1981) appeared in a number of plays written by Bertolt Brecht and Kurt Weill. In 1926 she married Kurt Weill. After she and Weill divorced in 1933, she was engaged to Max Ernst from 1935. The line in Benjamin's letter to Adorno, to which Scholem is referring, states: "I would like to see

Lotte Lenya, as well as Max Ernst. If you can arrange something, you can be assured of my consent." See *The Correspondence of Walter Benajmin*, p. 491.

Mrs. Favez: Juliane Favez was the secretary of the Geneva division of the Institute for Social Research, which was founded in 1932. During the years of exile, she stayed in contact with Walter Benjamin, especially regarding financial matters.

Höllenphantasmagorie!: Scholem is pointing out a typographical error in Adorno's letter to Benjamin, dated 2.8.1935, in which Adorno uses the term, *Höllenphantasmagorie* [phantasmagoria of hell] in reference to Benjamin's exposé of his *Arcades Project*. See Benjamin, *The Arcades Project*, ed. Rolf Tiedemann, trans. Howard Eiland and Kevin McLaughlin (Cambridge, MA: The Belknap Press of Harvard University Press, 1996), pp. 1–14. The letter is printed in *The Correpondence of Walter Benjamin*, pp. 494–503. See also *The Complete Correspondence of Walter Benjamin and Theodor W. Adorno, 1928–1940*, ed. Henri Lonitz, trans. Nicholas Walker (Cambridge, MA: Harvard University Press, 2001), pp. 104–14 (esp. p. 106).

170 ADORNO TO SCHOLEM
FRANKFURT AM MAIN, 21.9.1966

PROF. DR. THEODOR W. ADORNO

6 FRANKFURT AM MAIN
KETTENHOFWEG 123
21 September 1966

Dear Scholem,

My in-depth knowledge of your interest in marginal phenomena of this sort has inspired me to send you a carbon copy of my response to Buber-Honig, as distinguished from Honig-Buber. I replied to him in a friendly fashion, but I remained steadfast in my refusal to lend my name to this cause.

Since I don't have your current address, I'm simply writing to you in Jerusalem. Tomorrow I'll be flying to Berlin for a few days. Towards the end of next week, I'll be going to Italy, via Switzerland, where I finally hope to get some rest. In addition to everything else, meanwhile, I came down with a bad case of the flu, but I feel sufficiently restored to risk this adventure.

The Benjamin recollections published in *MONAT* appear quite decent and should cast a favorable light on the letter book.

All the best for Fanya and the most cordial regards to you, also from Gretel,

your

Adorno

Original: typescript with printed letterhead and a carbon copy of Adorno's letter to Camille R. Honig, dated 13.9.1966; Gershom Scholem Archive, The National Library of Israel, Jerusalem.

a carbon copy of my response to Buber-Honig: Adorno's response, dated, 13.9.1966, to Camille R. Honig, the founder and president of the International Martin Buber Society in London, reads:

> Esteemed Mr. Honig,
> With sincere thanks, I acknowledge receipt of your letter and the material on the Martin Buber Society, which you were so kind as to send me. I found it waiting for me upon my return from holiday.
>
> Please understand that I wish neither to serve nor even to appear as one of the vice-presidents. For this, [I have] two reasons. For one thing, I cannot, as a matter of principle, belong to any organization that uses my name without obtaining my prior consent. But then I also have reasons with regard to content. I am highly critical of Buber's thought, and I have expressed this repeatedly – most recently, in a very open manner, in my book *The Jargon of Authenticity* (1964). Frankly, I find it hard to imagine that you've read any of my own work; otherwise you would have scarcely had the thought to include me in your organization, as a decided critic of Heidegger's philosophy, to which, after all, Buber was quite close. Nor could you have expected that, despite all personal respect for Buber, I would have been able to lecture on the deceased. I have reason to believe that he himself would have been just as strongly opposed as I am to the prospect of my playing a role in this organization.
>
> I would ask you to please remove my name from the list of vice-presidents, as you have apparently done in the case of Ernst Simon, who actually was quite close to Buber.
>
> Much obliged, your sincerely devoted
> Th. W. Adorno

(Carbon copy of typescript; Theodor W. Adorno Archive, Frankfurt am Main).

Italy: Adorno travelled via Milan, and was in Naples from the 6th to the 10th of October, in Palermo from the 10th to the 14th, and in Rome from the 14th to the 24th. On the 5th of October he gave a lecture at the Goethe Institute in Milan entitled "Zum Begriff der Gesellschaft" [On the concept of society]. On his return journey, he repeated this lecture at the Goethe Institute in Rome. While in Naples he gave a lecture at the Istituto Francese entitled "Médiations des contenus sociaux par la musique" [Mediation of social contents through music], which he repeated on the 11th of October in Palermo and on the 17th of October at the Goethe Institute in Rome. See Adorno, "Mediation," in *Introduction to the Sociology of Music*, trans. E. B. Ashton (New York: Seabury Press, 1976), pp. 194–218.

The Benjamin recollections published in MONAT: Adorno's piece on Benjamin, entitled "Erinnerungen" [Recollections] was first published in *Der*

Monat, 18/216 (1966), pp. 35–8. See also Adorno, *Gesammelte Schriften 20.1: Vermischte Schriften* [Miscellaneous Writings], ed. Rolf Tiedemann et al. (Frankfurt am Main: Suhrkamp, 1986), pp. 173–8.

171 GRETEL ADORNO TO SCHOLEM
FRANKFURT AM MAIN, 1.11.1966

INSTITUTE FOR SOCIAL RESEARCH
AT THE JOHANN WOLFGANG GOETHE
UNIVERSITY

FRANKURT A.M.
SENCKENBERG-ANLAGE 26
TELEPHONE: 772147 & 772195

1 Nov. 1966

– Dr. Gretel Adorno –

Dear Mr. Scholem,

In response to my request, Egon Wissing has informed me that – despite the fact that he lived next door to Benjamin at the time – he also had no idea about his suicidal intentions. If anything, Benjamin had an aversion to morphine, although he did, on occasion, speak about wanting to end it all if there was no longer a way forward.

I am enclosing a photograph of Asja Lacis from the archive.

Teddie has returned safely, and very inspired, from his Italian journey.

I hope you are both safe and sound in Jerusalem.

With the most cordial regards, also to Fanja,

always yours,

Gretel A.

Original: typescript with printed letterhead; Gershom Scholem Archive, The National Library of Israel, Jerusalem.

Benjamin . . . suicidal intentions: In late July of 1932, upon his return from Ibiza, Benjamin rented a "dying room" in Nice, which he describes as at an "*impasse* with *vue sur le parc.*" See *Walter Benjamin: Gesammelte Briefe IV, 1931–1934*, ed. Henri Lonitz and Christoph Gödde (Frankfurt am Main: Suhrkamp, 1998), p. 115.

photograph of Asja Lacis: See figure 57 in *Walter Benjamin, 1892–1940: Eine Ausstellung des Theodor W. Adorno Archivs Frankfurt am Main in Verbindung mit dem Deutschen Literaturarchiv Marbach am Neckar* [Walter Benjamin, 1892–1940: an exhibition by the Theodor W. Adorno Archive, Frankfurt am Main, in cooperation with the Deutsches Literaturarchiv Marbach am Neckar], ed. Rolf Tiedemann, Christoph Gödde and Henri Lonitz (*Marbacher Magazin* no. 55/ 1990), p. 165.

172 SCHOLEM TO ADORNO
JERUSALEM, 7.11.1966

Jerusalem, 7.11.1966

Dear Adorno family,

I am happy to be able to sit at my desk again, having put my long journey behind me. Meanwhile, I hope that you are also happily reunited and that you are both enjoying renewed good health. In the meantime, I am awaiting the microfilms from Potsdam, which I was told to expect in November or December. Hopefully it will actually work out! The harmlessness or integrity of those in charge is attested to by the fact that they didn't destroy Benjamin's will. I have found a letter here, among the ones addressed to me, that was written two days after the will and the suicide note to Wissing, evidently directly after he had given up on the idea.

Many thanks for the photo of Asja Lacis. I have been unsuccessfully racking my brains over what this lady's erotic attraction may have been. This will remain, once more, in ever familiar incertitude.

Perhaps Agnon's Nobel Prize will move you to read one of the immortal German translations of his works? I would recommend the collection of stories published by Manesse, titled *Im Herzen der Meere* [In the heart of the seas], although I suggest that you initially skip the titular story.

I have made inquiries with Ernst Simon about Mr. Honig of the Buber Society. He is a highly dubious figure. At least half of the people named on his letterhead got there without being consulted. In a word: the man's a fraud. Alas, Mr. Jakob Taubes' epilog to the Overbeck volume from the Insel collection also falls into this category. I couldn't resist inspecting these significant pages for their content. Thank God you're not saddled with him.

With cordial regards,

always your

old Scholem

Original: aerogram (typescript); Theodor W. Adorno Archive, Frankfurt am Main.

microfilms from Potsdam: On 10.10.1966 Scholem visited the Deutsches Zentralarchiv in Potsdam, the central archives of the GDR, to view the Benjamin estate located there. The following day he left a handwritten note with the relevant department requesting that microfilms of the materials be sent to him:

> The undersigned, Prof. G. Scholem, Vice-President of the Israel National Academy of Sciences and Humanities, resident at 28 Abarbanel St.,

Jerusalem (Israel), hereby requests microform images of the following materials from the estate of Walter Benjamin. I request that the following files be photographed in full (microfilm) – numbered according to (index) card nos.: 1, 5, 10, 12, 14, 19, 21, 22, 27, 30–32m, 36 to 38m, ~~47~~.

The materials in questions include Walter Benjamin's correspondence (also including my own letters to him), and two files of handwritten notes (37–38) plus his will.

I would ask for the material to be sent to the German Academy of Sciences in Berlin for the attention of President W. Hartke. The academy has declared itself willing to bear the costs.

I intend to use these materials for private study. I was Walter Benjamin's closest friend and am one of the editors of the collection of his letters, which is forthcoming with the Suhrkamp Verlag.

Prof. G. Scholem
Potsdam, 11 October 1966.

I have found a letter here . . . the suicide note to Wissing: Benjamin's unsent letter to Egon and Gert Wissing, which contained his will, was written on the 27th of July 1932 in Nice. See *Walter Benjamin: Gesammelte Briefe IV, 1931–1934*, ed. Henri Lonitz and Christoph Gödde (Frankfurt am Main: Suhrkamp, 1998), pp. 117–22. Benjamin had written to Scholem on the previous day and then again on the 7th of August, this time from Poveromo. For the former, see *Walter Benjamin: Gesammelte Briefe IV, 1931–1934*, pp. 111–13. For the latter, see *The Correspondence of Walter Benjamin and Gershom Scholem, 1932–1940*, ed. Gershom Scholem, trans. Gary Smith and Andre Lefevere (New York: Schocken Books, 1989), p. 16. Neither letter makes any reference to suicidal intentions.

Agnon's Nobel Prize: In 1966, the Israeli writer Shmuel Yosef Agnon (1888–1970) received the Nobel Prize for literature alongside the poet Nelly Sachs (1891–1970). He was the first Hebrew-language author to receive this prize. Agnon was born in Buczacz (Galicia) and immigrated to Palestine in 1907. He lived in Germany from 1914 to 1924, and he became acquainted with Scholem during this period in 1917. They remained close and lifelong friends. Alongside this letter, the Adorno Archive contains a clipping from the *Jerusalem Post – Week-End Magazine* from 9.12.1966, pp. 3–4, in which the following text was printed: "Prof. Gershom Scholem reminisces on AGNON – MAN INTO ARTIST. Portrait of the author as a young man," an English translation of Scholem's speech, delivered on 16.11.1966, on the occasion of Agnon being awarded the Nobel Prize. At the top, Scholem noted by hand: "(Original was written in Hebrew)." The German version appeared under the title "Agnon in Deutschland. Erinnerungen" [Agnon in Germany: Memories] now in: Scholem, *Judaica 2*, pp. 122–132. In the bibliographic reference, Scholem writes: "This speech was originally given in Hebrew as part of a celebration held in honour of the Nobel Prize winner, Agnon, at the house of the President of Israel on the 16th of November, 1966. The slightly expanded version appeared [in German] in: *Neue Zürcher Zeitung*, the 12th of February 1967" (p. 229). See Scholem, "Agnon in Germany:

Recollections," in *On Jews and Judaism in Crisis*, ed. Werner J. Dannhauser (New York: Schocken Books, 1976), pp. 117–25.

Im Herzen der Meere: See S. Y. Agnon, *In the Heart of the Seas*, trans. I. M. Lask (Madison: University of Wisconsin Press, 2004).

Ernst Simon: The Israeli philosopher and educationalist Ernst Akiva Simon (1899–1988) was one of the most important figures in the establishment of the Israeli educational system. He was born and studied in Berlin and completed a doctorate on Hegel and Ranke at the University of Heidelberg in 1923. Until his immigration to Palestine in 1928, he was involved in Franz Rosenzweig's Freies jüdisches Lehrhaus [Free Jewish House of Learning], in Frankfurt. In 1934 Simon returned to Germany for one year to work with Martin Buber at the Mittelstelle für jüdische Erwachsenenbildung [the Jewish Centre for Adult Education]. In 1939 he became a lecturer in the history and philosophy of pedagogy at the Hebrew University in Jerusalem, where, in 1950, he became professor of pedagogy. Simon belonged to the inner circle of Scholem's friends.

Mr. Jakob Taubes' epilog to the Overbeck volume: Scholem's spelling. See Jacob Taubes, "Entzauberung der Theologie: Zu einem Porträt Overbecks" [The disenchantment of theology: towards a portrait of Overbeck], in Franz Overbeck, *Selbstbekenntnisse* [Confessions] (Frankfurt am Main: Insel, sammlung insel 21, 1966), pp. 7–27.

173 ADORNO TO SCHOLEM FRANKFURT AM MAIN, 15.11.1966

PROF. DR. THEODOR W. ADORNO

6 FRANKFURT AM MAIN
KETTENHOFWEG 123
15 November 1966

Dear Scholem,

Kindest thanks for your letter of the 7th of November.

As you know, right before her return journey, Fanja and I were able to get together with Inge Bachmann in Rome. It was an especially lovely noon, for me, at any rate.

In the meantime, the two volumes of letters have come out and I am very happy about it. All sorts of calamities occurred with the index of persons; the lady responsible for it (incidentally, a student of mine, who used to study with Bloch – a very talented girl) had it appended, typeset, and printed without consulting me first. I myself am primarily affected by the resulting horrors. Especially embarrassing, of course, is that my father's name – Wiesengrund – is incorrectly denoted as Adorno. I'm going to put together an index of the print errors, and it looks like Unseld will take it upon himself to ensure that it is included in the volume.

For the record, I want to inform you that Ernst Bloch is outraged, even though God knows that everything seriously insulting to him was eliminated. He is using his fair wife as a mouthpiece for his indignation, who, as soon as her power base is at stake, is as sensitive as she is lacking in basic humanity toward others. I think that neither you nor I should react to this matter unless Ernst writes to us directly. In that case it would be good if we deliberated together about what to do – if anything. Incidentally, Ernst didn't call me during his last visit, giving the strange reason that he didn't want to impose on me to have to be together with him and his wife.

Meanwhile, I have hired an assistant for the Philosophy Department – someone towards whom Taubes had put out his feelers, but whom he deemed to be too unreliable. It's truly a blessing that I don't have to contend with him here. I haven't brought myself to read the Overbeck epilogue yet, even though Unseld had good things to say about it.

Since, in addition to Habermas, I have managed to get Friedenburg and Mitscherlich on the faculty, the situation here has become quite respectable. This could also be advantageous when we make an appointment in Jewish studies. It goes without saying that Mr. Funkenstein, who keeps sending me clammy application letters, is out of the question.

Judging from his interminable letters, Mr. Honig seems to be more of a fool than a fraud; in terms of the effect, this amounts to more or less the same thing.

Agnon, by the way, is not unknown to us. We had already read some stories by him early on, in the twenties or early thirties, and we were very impressed. We owe the recommendation to Benjamin.

All that is cordial and best wishes to you both, also from Gretel,

always yours,

Adorno

Original: typescript with printed letterhead; Gershom Scholem Archive, The National Library of Israel, Jerusalem.

Fanja and I were able to get together with Inge Bachmann in Rome: The writer Ingeborg Bachmann (1926–1973) lived in Italy from 1954. In 1959 she gave the Frankfurter Poetik-Vorlesungen [the Frankfurt Lectures on Poetics] at the Goethe University in Frankfurt on the "Problems of the Contemporary Lyric."

index of persons . . . student of mine: Not verified.

an assistant for the Philosophy Department: Adorno is referring to Henrich von Nussbaum. Whether or not Nussbaum actually took this position was not verified.

Friedeburg: After studying at the Universities of Kiel and Freiburg, the sociologist and politician Ludwig von Friedeburg (1924–2010) contributed to the analysis of the Gruppenexperiment [group experiment] at the Institute for Social Research. He completed his doctorate in Freiburg in 1951 with a thesis entitled *Die Umfrage als Instrument der Sozialwissenschaften* [The survey as an instrument in the social sciences]. After a period at the Allensbach Institute for Opinion Polling, between 1951 and 1954, he headed the Department for Empirical Research at the Institute for Social Research, from 1955 on. In 1960 he completed his *Habilitation*, entitled *Sozialforschung im Industriebetrieb und Gesellschaftstheorie* [Social research in industrial enterprises and social theory]. From 1962 to 1966 he was professor of sociology and director of the Institute of Sociology at the Freie Universität Berlin. He then returned to Frankfurt in 1966, where he taught sociology and became director of the Institute for Social Research. Between 1970 and 1974 he was the culture minister for Hesse. From 1975 to 2001 he was executive director of the Institute.

Mitscherlich: Alexander Mitscherlich (1908–1982) was a psychoanalyst, social psychologist, physician, and writer. He studied history, art history and philosophy at the University of Munich; however, in 1932 he was forced to abandon his dissertation after Karl Alexander von Müller, the anti-Semitic successor of his deceased Jewish doctoral supervisor, Paul Joachimsen, refused to continue supervising the projects of his predecessor's students. Mitscherlich went on to study medicine in Berlin and became active in the resistance movement, for which he was wanted by the Gestapo. Subsequently, Mitscherlich immigrated in 1935 to Switzerland, where he continued his medical studies. During an illegal visit to Germany in 1937, he was arrested by the Gestapo and detained for eight months. In 1941 he completed his doctoral thesis, *Zur Wesensbestimmung der synästhetischen Wahrnehmung* [towards a determination of the essence of synaesthetic perception], under the supervision of Viktor von Weizsäcker. Thereafter he worked as a neurologist at the University of Heidelberg. In 1952, Mitscherlich became adjunct professor of psychosomatic medicine at the University of Heidelberg. In 1960 he founded the Sigmund Freud Institute in Frankfurt am Main, whose director he remained until 1976. From 1966 to 1973 he was professor of psychology at the University of Frankfurt.

Funkenstein: Amos Funkenstein (1937–1995) was an Israeli philosopher and historian. After completing his studies at the Hebrew University in Jerusalem, he went to Berlin in 1958. In 1964 he completed his doctorate at the Freie Universität Berlin with a thesis entitled *Gegenwartsbestimmung, Heilsplanbegriff und Entwicklungsgedanke im Geschichtsdenken des hohen Mittelalters* [Determination of the present, the concept of a salvation plan, and the idea of development in the historical thought of the High Middle Ages]. During this time, Funkenstein taught at the Institute for Jewish Studies at the Freie Universität Berlin, of which Jacob Taubes was the director. In 1967 he became a lecturer in history at the University of California, Los Angeles. At the end of the 1970s he also taught at the University of Tel Aviv, where he co-founded the Cohn Institute for the History and Philosophy of

Science and Ideas. In 1986 he moved to Stanford University, where he was professor of Jewish culture and history. In 1991 he moved to the University of California, Berkeley. In 1995 he received the Israel Prize for Jewish History.

174 SCHOLEM TO ADORNO
JERUSALEM, 29.11.1966

Jerusalem, 29.11.1966

Dear Adorno,

Many thanks for your letter of the 15th of November. Fania told me about her lunch with you in Rome, and since I already know quite a lot about you, I mainly grilled her – on several aspects – about Ingeborg Bachmann. She was not particularly taken with her! I can't really comment, as I haven't yet met the lady.

In the meantime, I've also compiled a few print errors in the volume of letters and sent them to Unseld so that he can perhaps include them in a list. I find that the volume has, all in all, been extraordinarily well revised, and there seem to be only a few objective errors. I saw the index of persons in the corrections phase; however, I didn't see the final proofs. Accordingly (in quite a number of places), I could correct only those entries that I knew about from the get-go. For example, it slipped my attention, alas, that Oskar Wiesengrund was your father – an error that I would have otherwise corrected immediately. In case you get hold of any interesting reviews, perhaps you could send them my way.

What you've communicated regarding Ernst Bloch's outrage can't really come as a surprise. In the conversation we had with Boehlich, we agreed that he would probably have been offended no matter what we printed, and that there was a limit to how much we would have to take his feelings into consideration, although we certainly did. Incidentally, I haven't heard anything more on this matter, and I know nothing of the form in which he or his wife gave expression to his outrage. Could you please enlighten me a bit about this? Since Unseld is such a gentleman, he hasn't said a word about it to me, and I am assuming that he shouldered the blame.

I am going to Rome for a week to ten days at the beginning of January. Would you, by chance, be down there at the same time? Has the issue of the *Neue Rundschau* with my essay on Jews and Germans already come out? And what do you say about the text by Golo Mann, if one can even call these scribbles a text? I haven't received the issue to date and have begun to wonder about it.

With cordial regards from one home to another,

your old G. Scholem

Original: aerogram (typescript); Theodor W. Adorno Archive, Frankfurt am Main. First published in Gershom Scholem, *Briefe II: 1948–1970*, ed. Thomas Sparr (Munich: C. H. Beck, 1995), pp. 156–7.

the issue of the Neue Rundschau *with my essay on Jews and Germans*: Scholem's lecture was given on the 2nd of August 1966 at the plenary meeting of the World Jewish Congress in Brussels, which was dedicated to the theme of "Jews and Germans." The plenary featured two Jewish and two German keynote speakers. The lecture first appeared as "Juden und Deutsche," *Neue Rundschau*, 77 (1966), pp. 547–62. An English translation was published as "Jews and Germans," in *Commentary* (November, 1966), pp. 31–8.

text by Golo Mann: See Golo Mann, "Zur Geschichte der deutschen Juden" [On the history of German Jews], *Neue Rundschau*, 77 (1966), pp. 563–73.

175 ADORNO TO SCHOLEM
FRANKFURT AM MAIN, 1.12.1966

PROF. DR. THEODOR W. ADORNO

6 FRANKFURT AM MAIN
KETTENHOFWEG 123
1 December 1966

Dear Scholem,

Kindest thanks for your letter.

I discovered the horrors in the index of persons right away. It's especially embarrassing that my father appears as "Oskar Adorno." Nobody had shown me the index, although Unseld has half-promised that a small list of print errors would be drawn up and added to the book.

Regarding the Bloch issue, I haven't learned anything new since I told you about the matter. In my opinion, we don't need to do anything on this front, since he hasn't contacted either of us directly.

As for Rome, I can only note with deep regret that it will be impossible for me to travel there in January. However, you should not miss the opportunity of meeting with both Iris von Kaschnitz and Ingeborg Bachmann. Their addresses are as follows:

Iris von Kaschnitz
Via Vittorio, 3

Ingeborg Bachmann
Via Bocca di Leone, 60
Telephone: 681344

The issue of *Neue Rundschau* supposedly came out last week, although I haven't as yet received a copy; yesterday, a reminder was sent. It's also supposed to contain a piece by me, a lecture on functionalism that I gave at the Deutscher Werkbund in Berlin a year ago. It would be nice if we were both in it together.

Perhaps you've heard that Kracauer died. He was physically somewhat shaky when I saw him in the summer, to be sure, but he was exceptionally alert mentally. In spite of everything, his death has affected me to an extraordinary degree. After all, he is the oldest friend of my youth – if not my childhood – and I owe him so much that it lets me forget some of what hurt me in later years. It is really just like the verse by Karl Kraus: "What has the world made of us." If I compare Kracauer's potential with what he became and what he accomplished, the balance is somewhat sad. What is to blame is the fact that, in his work, he was never able to get away from himself – a lack of self-forgetting, of generosity, which was also carried over into intellectual matters. It was precisely this fixation with his own ego that wound up turning against this ego. I wrote a short obituary for the *Frankfurter Allgemeine Zeitung*, which I am enclosing.

I'm currently facing much more aggravation here than is good for me, for which the political situation is partly to blame. Although this misfortune is inanimate, I evidently lack the resilience I used to have when coping with such matters.

In the meantime, I have finished a little book of essays on aesthetics and the sociology of art, which is due to appear in the "edition suhrkamp" series under the title *Ohne Leitbild / Parva Aesthetica* [Without a guiding image / parva aesthetica]. *Negative Dialectics* is now out, although, as yet, I have only my personal copy. Of course, you'll receive the volume from the publisher.

All that is cordial from your

well and truly old

Adorno

Original: typescript with printed letterhead; Gershom Scholem Archive, The National Library of Israel, Jerusalem.

Iris von Kaschnitz: The translator Iris Schnebel-Kaschnitz (1928–2014) was the daughter of the poet Marie Luise Kaschnitz (1901–1974) and the classical archeologist Guido Kaschnitz von Weinberg (1890–1958). Kaschnitz von Weinberg worked at the German Institute of Archeology in Rome from 1923 to 1931. In 1941 the couple moved to Frankfurt, where Kaschnitz von Weinberg had been appointed to the chair of classical archeology. Adorno was friends with Marie Luise Kaschnitz, who held the visiting professorship in poetics at the University of Frankfurt in 1960. Adorno's essay "Titles: Paraphrases on Lessing" is dedicated to her. See *Notes to Literature*, Vol. 2, trans. Shierry Weber Nicholsen (New York: Columbia University Press, 1992), pp. 3–11. An entry from Adorno's dream notes, dated the 13th of April 1962, describes a dream in which Marie Luise Kaschnitz appears. A copy of this entry, bearing a dedication to Scholem, is contained in the

Scholem Archive (see the relevant note to letter no. 115 in this volume). It reads as follows: "I was due to sit an exam, an oral exam in geography. I was the only person to do this out of a large number of examinees, probably in the entire university. I was told that this was a privilege thanks to my other achievements. I was to be examined by Leu [Kaschnitz]. My task was to define exactly what area had been occupied by a particular, precisely delimited district in an older description of the city of Rome, a grey, soft-cover octavo volume." See *Dream Notes*, ed. Christoph Gödde and Henri Lonitz, trans. Rodney Livingstone (Cambridge: Polity, 2007), pp. 65–6. The line "I was to be examined by Leu" in the copy sent to Scholem was changed to "I was to be examined by Leu Kaschnitz" in the published edition. After the death of her husband in 1958, Marie Luise Kaschnitz often lived in Rome, where she became friends with Ingeborg Bachmann. After Adorno's death, Kaschnitz dedicated two poems to him, entitled "Th. W.A." See Marie Luise Kaschnitz, "Th. W.A.," in *Gesammelte Werke*, Vol. 5: *Die Gedichte* [The poems], ed. Christian Büttrich and Norbert Miller (Frankfurt am Main: Suhrkamp, 1985), pp. 463, 723.

lecture on functionalism: Adorno's lecture "Zum Problem des Funktionalismus heute" [On the problem of functionalism today] was given at the meeting of the Deutscher Werkbund in Berlin on the 23rd of October 1965. It was first published as "Funktionalismus heute" in *Neue Rundschau*, 77/4 (1966), pp. 585–600. It was then absorbed into *Ohne Leitbild / Parva Aesthetica* [Without a guiding image / parva aesthetica] (Frankfurt am Main: Suhrkamp, 1967), now in Theodor W. Adorno: Gesammelte Schriften, Vol. 10.1, ed. Rolf Tiedemann et al. (Frankfurt am Main: Suhrkamp, 2003), pp. 375–95. See "Functionalism Today," in *Oppositions: Journal for Ideas and Criticism in Architecture*, no. 17 (1979), pp. 30–41.

Kracauer died: Siegfried Kracauer died in New York on the 26th of November 1966 from complications following a bout of pneumonia.

verse by Karl Kraus: Adorno is referring to Kraus's poem "Lilacs": "Now I know, despite everything, that it is spring again. / I did not see it for so much night / And for a long time I did not think it. / Now I notice for the first time, the lilac is already blooming. / How did I find the secret again? / I had been robbed of it. / What has the world made of us! / I turn around – there blooms the lilac. / And I thank God; He created me anew, / As He created again all the splendour. / Awakened to gaze upon it once more, / I remain standing. The lilac still blooms." See Karl Kraus, *Poems*, trans. Albert Bloch (Boston: Four Seas, 1930), p. 38.

a short obituary: Adorno's obituary, titled "Siegfried Kracauer tot" [Siegfried Kracauer dead], was published in the *Frankfurter Allgemeine Zeitung* on the 1st of December 1966 (p. 20). The piece was later revised and reprinted as "Vorwort" [Preface], in: *Die nicht mehr schönen Künste: Grenzphänomene des Ästhetischen* [The no-longer fine arts: marginal phenomena of the aesthetic], ed. Hans Robert Jauß (Munich: Fink, 1968), pp. 6–7. Also in *Gesammelte Schriften 20.1: Vermischte Schriften* [Miscellaneous Writings], ed. Rolf Tiedemann et al. (Frankfurt am Main: Suhrkamp, 1986), pp. 194–6.

much more aggravation here ... political developments: In a letter to Horkheimer, dated the 8th of December 1966, Adorno describes his chagrin with the political direction taken by the German Social Democratic Party, SPD, since the enaction of the Godesberg program in 1959. The program hastened the party's transformation from a socialist workers' party to a centrist peoples' party and its embrace of a free-market economy and national defence: "Perhaps you remember that some time ago, I harboured a plan to write a critique of the Godesberg program," Adorno wrote.

> But I am having serious doubts as to whether it is the right time. If one were to attack the SPD today – and such a piece would have to amount to an attack, no matter how one went about it – then this would provide grist to the mills of all those undermining democracy, which has been severely shaken. ... But now a good number of people associated with us ... are of the view that, in light of the Grand Coalition, the time to write such a thing is now. Only an extremely incisive, critical self-reflection could help the SPD not to completely wear itself out in this alliance. I must confess to you that my political instinct has abandoned me – I no longer feel at all as confident in my political judgment as I did earlier and as long as we were together. On the one hand, it is obvious that a Grand Coalition will endanger the SPD's almost certain prospects of electoral victory in 1969, and that, as a result, the party will embark on a right-wing, conservative course *á la* [Franz Josef] Strauß, conceived of as a rescue from neo-Nazism, but quite similar to that from which it purports to be rescuing. On the other hand, I regard the Grand Coalition as a genuine opportunity for the transition to a two-party system, as you envisage it, and thus the elimination of the NPD [National Democratic Party of Germany], which, despite all appeasements, I judge just as severely as you. As non-durable as the Grand Coalition may well be, and as alarming as its implications are, the present situation seems to me to pose such an acute threat that what is more immediate, temporally speaking, deserves to be prioritized. And, in light of this, I hesitate to write anything about Godesberg. But such massive pressure is being put on me that it won't be easy to resist, especially since it was originally my idea. If we could write such a piece together, the whole matter would maybe look different; but presumably there is little chance of that right away. And I in no way want to do this *à fond perdu*; either something like this is published immediately, or it is doomed from the outset. Please give me some wise counsel, and it would be kind if you wouldn't procrastinate on this. (*Theodor W. Adorno / Max Horkheimer: Briefwechsel IV, 1950–1969*, ed. Henri Lonitz and Christoph Gödde (Frankfurt am Main: Suhrkamp, 2006), pp. 782–4

Negative Dialectics: Adorno's book *Negative Dialectics* was first published in November 1966. The initial print run was 4,000 copies.

176 SCHOLEM TO ADORNO
JERUSALEM, 9.12.1966

9 December 1966

Dear Adorno,

Have you also received the impudent, or merely resentful, letter from Taubes? I wrote to Unseld (I'm not responding to T.), informing him that of course *Halbjahr* [semi-annual] is a typographical error, which is supposed to say *Halljahr* [jubilee] – no doubt about it, and when he's right, he's right. Everything else is mere chatter. It really illustrates how admiration becomes hate when it is not reciprocated. The interpretation of my note on p. 180 is quite fantastical (referring to that which would not have been discernible from the letters under discussion[)]. As if the Russian girlfriend hadn't constantly come up before in ways that made her sufficiently identifiable! I'm the one that's been "led down the garden path"? I had letters from Dora about the situation all along!

From T's style, you can sufficiently realize why I wanted nothing to do with this excrescence, and why I still want nothing to do with him now. (He even learned the Aby Warburg quote from me!)

Do you respond to such things?

I was unaware of Kracauer's death! Many thanks for sending your obituary, which I found <u>very</u> interesting. (I have only read little of K.)

I'm enclosing a rejoinder to a veritably reptilian journalistic feat (recently printed in a local newspaper), in which it's insinuated that I thwarted Buber's appointment to Jerusalem. This kind of thing easily becomes gossip. I want to have this clarification published somewhere visible in Germany, since the book that is mentioned therein will surely find buyers in Germany. But where? Perhaps you could see to it that it's printed in the *Frankfurter Hefte*?

Most cordial regards,

yours,

G. Scholem

I've taken note of the addresses of the Roman ladies.
But who is <u>Iris</u> Kaschnitz?
A daughter of the poet?
Have I met her before?

Original: manuscript; Theodor W. Adorno Archive, Frankfurt am Main.

letter from Taubes: On the 5th of December 1966, Jacob Taubes wrote to Siegfried Unseld to thank him for sending the collection of Benjamin's essays, entitled *Angelus Novus*, as well as the two volumes of collected letters. The letter, a carbon copy of which was sent to Adorno, states:

Regarding the letters: you know that they have been keenly awaited by some. Their expectation was not disappointed. In these letters, Benjamin comments on his work in most illuminating ways. Many passages in the [book on the] *Trauerspiel* became clear to me only through the reference to Rang. I dedicated a whole week to the letters, and if I now have some meager suggestions for possible improvements, please treat them as thanks for your gift. . . . If I compare Benjamin's letters to Rosenzweig's, which were published by Schocken in 1935, I can hardly make out any improvement in the editorial technique. Have a look at the Rosenzweig letters and try to attain the same editorial standard (Scholem knows them well, since he appears in them several times – at an important juncture, he is described as a "nihilist" who always has to have the last word.) . . . And now, for the most important matter, concerning letter 288 to Fritz Lieb: This is the only letter of which I've seen the original, since one of my students brought it to the publishing house via Szondi. It numbers among the letters that Scholem "worked on." Although, generally speaking, Scholem knows how to handle manuscripts, and although he surely knows Benjamin's handwriting better than anyone else, I dare to question his reading. The sentence states: "I ask myself whether there might not perhaps be a kind of world-historical *Halbjahr* [semi-annual], in which, instead of the unfree, demons rejoice in their existence, and whether we might not have entered upon such a period." I don't know what Scholem had in mind in the case of this world-historical *Halbjahr*. Perhaps he is privy to some kind of esoteric knowledge? Perhaps this world-historical semi-annual period is part of the secret doctrine of the Central and State University of Muri? But how can the Protestant theologian Fritz Lieb be expected to know about this secret doctrine? Would it not be more revealing to call to mind the biblical "*Halljahr*" [jubilee]? . . . I may be mistaken, but my reading seems more reasonable, unless Scholem has some kind of special source, which speaks of a "world-historical semi-annual period" – I, for one, do not know of any such mystical source. Since I don't like to exercise criticism behind people's back, I've permitted myself to send a copy of this letter to the editors. Who is right should be decided in Frankfurt and Jerusalem. As Aby Warburg said, God resides in the detail. It would be a pity if Benjamin's historico-philosophical doctrine of a world-historical jubilee were lost because of a misreading by Scholem. (Carbon copy of typescript: Theodor W. Adorno Archive, Frankfurt am Main)

The interpretation of my note on p. 180 is quite fantastical: In the aforementioned letter of the 5th of December 1966, Taubes writes: "The second note following letter no. 180 is pernicious. The name of the Russian girlfriend is not disclosed. Presumably it's Asja Lacis! One senses the editors' censure for having been led down the garden path. The explanatory remarks accompanying these letters are hardly the appropriate forum for this kind of reckoning." In the letter cited by Taubes (letter 180, dated the 1st of August 1928), Benjamin writes the following to Scholem: "Dear Gerhard / My trip to Palestine is a settled matter, as is my intention to strictly observe the course of study prescribed by

Your Hierosolymitan Excellency. Let me moreover avow that the awestruck undersigned will be able to read the alphabet common to the country before he sets foot on the soil of Eretz Israel. . . . The date of my arrival . . . may have to be delayed until mid-December. This will depend first of all on whether I can make up my mind to complete the Arcades project before I leave Europe. Second, on whether I get together with a Russian woman friend in Berlin in the fall. Neither question has been decided as yet." See *The Correspondence of Walter Benjamin 1910–1940*, ed. Theodor W. Adorno and Gershom Scholem, trans. Manfred R. Jacobson and Evelyn M. Jacobson (Chicago: University of Chicago Press, 1994), p. 339 (translation slightly modified). With reference to the "Russian woman friend," Scholem writes the following in note 2: "Whose appearance on the scene had more to do with the developments of the next two years than was evident in the letters to Jerusalem." See *The Correspondence of Walter Benjamin*, p. 341.

He even learned the Aby Warburg quote from me: In 1977 Taubes published an article on Scholem entitled "Der liebe Gott steckt im Detail: Gershom G. Scholem und die messianische Verheißung" [God is to be found in the detail: Gershom G. Scholem and the messianic promise] (see letter no. 73 in this volume), in which he wrote:

> Since without opposition, Gershom Scholem, or at least his work, is advancing into the void and fading out, only a critique can bring it back to spiritual life. While such a critique will not be exercised here, its rudiments will be indicated within Scholem's own work. For nothing of his undertaking would be understood unless it is recognized that this dialectical head contains an utterly ironic mind. . . . Kabbalah is, in the eminent sense, "oral teaching": dialogue in diction and contradiction. Made "fixed" as tradition, it leaves behind only a corpse of words and concepts. Gershom Scholem knows all about this "difficulty" in his undertaking. He practices the trade of philosophy with the utmost seriousness in order to eliminate unauthorized persons and readings; but not without a shot of jocularity or despair. He immerses himself in each detail: Aby Warburg's motto, "God is to be found in the detail," is one of his favorite expressions. He wants, in the first place, to draw no distinction between small and big, since as long as we can locate its trace, nothing that ever took place will be lost. (Taubes, "Der liebe Gott steckt im Detail: Gershom G. Scholem und die messianische Verheißung," *Die Welt*, 10 December 1977, p. 27; reprinted in *Der Preis des Messianismus: Briefe von Jacob Taubes an Gershom Scholem und andere Materialien* [The price of messianism: letters from Jacob Taubes to Gershom Scholem and other materials], ed. Elettra Stimilli (Würzburg: Könighausen & Neumann, 2006), pp. 25–31).

a rejoinder to a veritably reptilian journalistic feat (recently printed in a local newspaper): The details of the publication in a local Israeli newspaper were not verified. However, in his book *Zwiesprache mit Martin Buber* [Dialogue with Martin Buber] (Munich, 1966), the Israeli journalist and writer Schalom Ben-Chorin wrote the following:

> The Orthodox . . . didn't want to grant a man like Buber the right to lecture on 18th century, East-European Jewish Pietism. On the other hand, here too a contradiction became apparent in the sober scholarship. It was Gershom Scholem, professor of Jewish history at the Hebrew University in Jerusalem, who rejected Martin Buber's interpretation of Hasidism as subjective and unscholarly. Scholem's rejection of Buber's interpretation of Hasidism went hand in hand with their lifelong friendship. . .; but it was precisely Buber's genius that remained suspect to Scholem, the historian and philologist. With professorial distance, Scholem sensed in Buber the poet whom he revered and respected, but whom he did not want to see at the lectern discussing Hasidism. He charged him with an all too subjective selection, thus describing Buber's method as unscientific. We have named Scholem . . . only as a representative of the wider, non-Orthodox rejection of Buber. Of course he was not the only one. Orthodox rabbis as well as rationalist professors marginalized Buber as an academic teacher. (Quoted from Gershom Scholem, "Martin Bubers Berufung nach Jerusalem: Eine notwendige Klarstellung" [Martin Buber's appointment to Jerusalem: a necessary clarification], *Frankfurter Hefte*, 22/4 (1967), pp. 229–31; here p. 230)

I want to have this clarification published somewhere visible in Germany: Scholem's clarification was published as "Martin Bubers Berufung nach Jerusalem. Eine notwendige Klarstellung" [Martin Buber's appointment to Jerusalem. A necessary clarification] in *Frankfurter Hefte*, 22/4 (1967), pp. 229–31. It also appeared as "Eine notwendige Klarstellung" [A necessary clarification], in *Mitteilungsblatt, Wochenzeitung des Irgun Olej Merkas Europa*, 34/48 (1966), p. 4. Finally, it was published under the same title in *Neue Zürcher Zeitung*, on the 9th of December 1966, p. 9.

177 ADORNO TO SCHOLEM
FRANKFURT AM MAIN, 16.12.1966

PROF. DR. THEODOR W. ADORNO

6 FRANKFURT AM MAIN
KETTENHOFWEG 123
16 December 1966

Dear Scholem,

Kindest thanks for your letter.

Taubes had also sent me a carbon copy of his letter to Unseld. I understand nothing of the *Halljahr* [jubilee] matter; other than that, I found his letter to be fatuous, quarrelsome, and apparently inspired by a wish to strike you in precisely the area that should give him greatest cause to feel ashamed compared to you. It's been clear to me that your verdict on him was correct ever since he revealed himself – in an almost stirring manner – through his duplicity with regard to Buber. The sole reason that I maintain quasi-diplomatic relations with him – although I by no means wish to rationalize it – is that he is one of the very few people at the Freie Universität – in many ways a disagreeable institution – who is unambiguously – at least politically – on the left. As such, he has, so far, proven himself to be reliable in matters of university strategy. His girlfriend, Margherita Brentano, is very decent, and, accordingly, he treats her badly. She has just published an outstanding essay on the crisis of the German universities in a special issue of the journal *Magnum*, edited by Ulrich Sonnemann – "Die verlorenen Paradiese der Deutschen" [The lost paradises of the Germans]. I warmly recommend to your attention this entire exceedingly remarkable journal. It may well be the strongest criticism of the overall conditions in West Germany that has, to date, been put forth by non-communists – and, for precisely this reason, it is all the more powerful. I responded to the copy of Taubes' letter with a few non-committal words.

You'll find further details on Kracauer in the third volume of my *Notes to Literature*, which contains the essay "Der wunderliche Realist" [The curious realist]. Apparently his widow did not think it necessary to respond to my essay or the letter that accompanied it. Clearly, she found that I didn't offer up enough frankincense to him. During the second half of his life, Kracauer became truly possessed by a guardian devil, which was capable of steering him in such a way that no criticism – and, indeed, no self-criticism – could get close. Consequently, he had an almost unblemished sense of self-satisfaction, and that doomed him, intellectually. Nothing will remain of his later work, and almost nothing will remain of his earlier work, as I had to convince myself when I tried to facilitate one or another publication. At the same time, he really was innately gifted, and I owe him a great debt of gratitude, which is all that remains, as I amicably swallow all the upset that I had with him over decades, which, at times, assumed truly grotesque forms.

I quite liked your essay on the Buber matter; I will send it to Kogon with the request that he print it in full.

Iris von Kaschnitz is the daughter of Leu (the poet). She is a charming, and by the way, highly intelligent person, and we are as close to her as we are to her mother. You really shouldn't miss [the opportunity of meeting] her. By the way, did I tell you that I was recently in the apartment of a young composer in Rome, located in the middle of the former ghetto, where I learned its harrowing history during the last war?

Judging from the immediate responses I've heard, the feedback on the book of letters has been quite friendly. I haven't seen any reviews yet, but I wouldn't be surprised if the volumes turned out to be a considerable success, also commercially. Meanwhile, *Berlin Childhood*, for which I'd presaged the same, remains puzzlingly unknown.

Would you please be so kind as to let me know whether you have, in the meantime, received the *Negative Dialectics*? If not, I'll follow up.

All the best to you and Fanja, also from Gretel – we're both quite well, although we currently have more aggravation with the Institute and otherwise than we would care for.

Always yours,

Adorno

Another letter from Taubes. The dominant impression is of something clammy, to a degree that I have rarely experienced in intellectual matters. [How awful] that one is nevertheless dependent on cooperation with this sort.

Original: typescript with printed letterhead and handwritten postscript; Gershom Scholem Archive, The National Library of Israel, Jerusalem.

his duplicity . . . with regard to Buber: It is unclear what Adorno is referring to. For Jacob Taubes' writing about Buber, however, see his "Martin Buber and the Philosophy of History," in *From Cult to Culture: Fragments Toward a Critique of Historical Reason*, ed. Charlotte Elisheva Fonrobert and Amir Engel (Stanford, CA: Stanford University Press, 2010), pp. 10–27.

Margherita Brentano: The philosopher Margherita von Brentano (1922–1995) studied history, German and English in Berlin and Freiburg im Breisgau. In 1948 she completed her doctorate under the supervision of Martin Heidegger with a thesis titled *Die Bedeutung des "ἕν" als Grundbegriff der aristotelischen Metaphysik* [The significance of the "ἕν" as a basic concept of Aristotelian metaphysics]. In 1956 she became assistant to Wilhelm Weischedel in the Department of Philosophy at the Freie Universität Berlin, where she was subsequently appointed to a professorship in philosophy in 1972. In 1967 she married Jacob Taubes, whose first wife, Susan Taubes (to whom he was married from 1949 to 1961), committed suicide in 1969. Alongside her academic activities, and in connection with them, Margherita von Brentano was an avid political activist in the struggle against fascistic and anti-Semitic tendencies in post-war Germany, as well as campaigning for the equality of women at German universities. See her *Akademische Schriften* [Academic writings], ed. Peter McLaughlin (Göttingen: Wallstein, 2009).

essay on the crisis of the German universities: The final issue of the journal *Magnum*, published by DuMont, was dedicated to the theme of "Die verlorenen Paradiese der Deutschen" [The lost paradises of the Germans]; it contained Margherita von Brentano's essay "Politikum wider Willen: Zur Gegenwärtigen Lage der Universität" [Politicized against their will. The contemporary state of universities], in which she discusses a series of controversial university reforms in Germany, arguing that "the state and society are under the impression that the universities cannot carry out their reforms, and, thus, they want to impose these upon them. . . . As such, they are breaching the border between the public and the republic of scholars from the outside, whereas protests, demands, and student actions are breaching it from the inside. The universities in the Federal Republic have become politicized, albeit 'against their will.'" See *Magnum: Die Zeitschrift für das moderne Leben*, no. 59 (November, 1966), pp. 24–5, 82–9. The quotation above is taken from p. 24.

I responded to the copy of Taubes' letter with a few non-committal words: On the 8th of December 1966 Adorno wrote the following to Taubes: "As for the issue surrounding *Halljahr / Halbjahr* [jubilee / semi-annual], I really couldn't say one way or the other. Presumably you sent a copy to Scholem. He will surely respond to this point. *Prima vista* it is, of course, equally improbable that Benjamin had Luther's Bible translation in mind as the Kabbalah" (carbon copy of typescript: Theodor W. Adorno Archive, Frankfurt am Main).

The curious realist: See letter no. 138 and the relevant note in this volume.

Kogon: The journalist, sociologist, and political scientist Eugen Kogon (1903–1987) was arrested numerous times as an opponent of the National Socialist regime in the period between 1936 and 1938. In 1939 he was deported to the Buchenwald concentration camp. In 1945, when Kogon was placed on a list of persons whom the SS planned to execute, he was smuggled out of the camp in a crate by the camp's physician. His book *Der SS-Staat: Das System der deutschen Konzentrationslager* [The SS state: the system of the German concentration camps] was published in 1946. During the same year, Kogon and the journalist Walter Dirks co-founded the *Frankfurter Hefte*, a leftist, Catholic journal covering politics and culture. Kogon, who actively promoted the establishment of a European republic, was appointed to a professorship in political science at the Technical University of Darmstadt in 1951.

a young composer: Adorno is referring to Sylvano Bussotti (b. 1931), who lived on Via del Portico d'Ottavia in the former Jewish ghetto in Rome. Bussotti met Adorno through his former partner, the composer Heinz-Klaus Metzger.

178 ADORNO TO SCHOLEM
JERUSALEM, 4./5.1. 1967

4/5 Jan. 1967

Dear Adorno,

Your magnum opus has just arrived – my sincere thanks and simultaneous congratulations! I'm travelling to Rome tomorrow, so I will only be able to begin reading it later. (By the way, I wrote to the two ladies that you mentioned – are they mutually compatible?) I will be in Rome until 12.1. at the Hotel Astor on Via Tevere 5. Hopefully there's sunshine!

In haste, to you both
cordial regards and wishes
for 1967
yours,
G. S.

Original: aerogram (manuscript); Theodor W. Adorno Archive, Frankfurt am Main.

179 ADORNO TO SCHOLEM
FRANKFURT AM MAIN, 10.1.1967

PROF. DR. THEODOR W. ADORNO

6 FRANKFURT AM MAIN
KETTENHOFWEG 123
10 January 1967

Dear Scholem,

Kindest thanks for the lines. Hopefully you have arrived well and installed yourself in Rome. If you have a good dinner at one of the local establishments in Trastevere, and if you're better able than I was to bear the overwhelming noise, then spare a friendly thought for me.

The ladies, Iris Kaschnitz and Ingeborg Bachmann, are on excellent terms and you can absolutely make plans to do something with both of them together. As it happens, they live very close to each other, in near proximity to the Spanish Steps.

You also shouldn't miss the chance of meeting Iris's cousin, the Baron Marschall von Bieberstein. He is the director of the Goethe Institute in Rome – a truly delightful human being. (When I gave a lecture in Naples recently, he came especially from Rome.) By the way, he has a Jewish or half-Jewish wife.

I get the impression that the Benjamin letters are having a tremendous impact. The *Frankfurter Rundschau* printed a very thorough and positive, if somewhat fatuous review – a full newspaper page in length. What is remarkable is the disparity between Benjamin's current aura and the lack of understanding of his philosophy. But the authority of intellectual matters and the degree to which they are adequately comprehended tends, in many cases, to diverge.

Gretel and I are doing quite well and I am back to working with renewed vigor. I hope to keep up these efforts to do my bit, so long as, in the course of these efforts, I notice no signs of complete senility in myself. We will see whether these efforts don't, in fact, speed up the process of becoming senile. That, too, is a bit of dialectic.

Most cordially, as ever

yours,

Adorno

Original: typescript with printed letterhead; Gershom Scholem Archive, The National Library of Israel, Jerusalem.

The Baron Marschall von Bieberstein: Michael Freiherr Marschall von Bieberstein (1930–2012) was, successively, the director of the Goethe institutes in Rome, Paris, and Madrid.

Frankfurter Rundschau printed a . . . review: On the 7th of January 1967, Wolfram Schütte reviewed Benjamin's *Briefe* [Letters] and the collection *Angelus Novus: Ausgewählte Schriften* [Selected writings] in a piece entitled "Trümmer, Bausteine und Vorstufen: Das verzweifelte Exil Walter Benjamins – Zur Edition seiner Briefe und des *Angelus Novus*" [Rubble, building blocks and precursors: the desperate exile of Walter Benjamin – on the edition of his letters and *Angelus Novus*]. Schütte sums up his review with the following observation: "Walter Benjamin's work and life – they come together in a series of epiphanies of hope, the promise of which has only been imperfectly redeemed. He, however, did redeem what he promised, and indeed far beyond, to the extent that he was able to wring it from his life and times. His work remains a fragment, his life absurdly and pointlessly destroyed – yet, it can stand alongside the most important things that this time produced. Just as his thinking could not dispense with the concepts of future and utopia, so the future will not be able to dispense with his work, insofar as it conceives of remembrance not in the manner of a museum but, rather, as a productive act. Only then will his 'desperate exile' come to an end."

180 ADORNO TO SCHOLEM
FRANKFURT AM MAIN, 31.1.1967

PROF. DR. THEODOR W. ADORNO

6 FRANKFURT AM MAIN
KETTENHOFWEG 123

31 January 1967

Dear Scholem,

To my delight, I just received confirmation from Kogon that he will print your essay on the matter of Buber's appointment to Jerusalem in the *Frankfurter Hefte*. I wanted to inform you right away, so that you don't commit, out of ignorance of this acceptance, to possibly giving the piece to someone else.

May I also ask if you've had a chance to glance at *Negative Dialectics*? This time I'm terribly curious about your reaction.

The Benjamin letters seem to be finding ever-greater resonance. The *Süddeutsche Zeitung* ran a very long and very friendly response by Günter Blöcker, who is otherwise quite reactionary. Presumably you've already gotten to see it.

All good wishes for Fanja – hopefully she's doing better.

All the best to you both, also from Gretel,

always yours,

Adorno

Original: typescript with printed letterhead; Gershom Scholem Archive, The National Library of Israel, Jerusalem.

The Süddeutsche Zeitung *ran a very long and very friendly review by Günter Blöcker*: The review appeared in the weekend edition of the *Süddeutsche Zeitung* (28/29 January 1967) under the heading "Instrument seiner Gedanken" [Instrument of his thoughts]. The journalist and writer Günter Blöcker (1913–2006) was initially a director and dramaturge in Hanover, Potsdam, and Berlin. From 1945 he was a full-time freelancer, who worked primarily as a literary critic and essayist.

All good wishes for Fanja: The notification of Fania Scholem's illness does not appear to have survived.

181 SCHOLEM TO ADORNO JERUSALEM, 6.2.1967

6.2.1967

Dear Adorno,

Sincere thanks for your message regarding the *Frankfurter Hefte*. Did you send them my address here so that they might forward me an author's copy when it comes out?

I have only just been able to begin reading your book and have now finished the preface – in which the reader has yet to bite the bullet, if one is to listen to your warning. Of course, I'll write to you once I've covered more ground! Much in what I've seen so far has stirred my thoughts and concerns, although for the time being I can only suspect what's around the corner. The final pages of the Introduction are easier to parse than the preceding ones. (Who, may I ask, is the author of the lovely line on p. 54: "Only thoughts which cannot understand themselves are true"? I presume I would approve, if only I understood it.[)]

All that is cordial to you both

yours,

G. Scholem

Original: manuscript; Theodor W. Adorno Archive, Frankfurt am Main.

the author of the lovely line on p. 54: See Adorno, *Negative Dialectics*, trans. E. B. Ashton (London: Routledge, 1973), p. 48. Adorno is, in fact, quoting a line from his own *Minima Moralia*. See *Minima Moralia: Reflections from Damaged Life*, trans. Edmund Jephcott (London: Verso, 1974), p. 192.

182 SCHOLEM TO ADORNO
JERUSALEM, 1.3.1967

Jerusalem, 1 March 1967

Dear Adorno,

As you can see, I have let quite some time elapse, *nolens volens*, before getting in touch to let you know that I have finished reading *Negative Dialectics* – no easy feat for the poor Scholem – and now I can finally thank you in the proper way – namely, after having read the book and also racking my brains over it. Needless to say, I was especially drawn to and engaged with the first half of the book, and, for equally understandable reasons, to the third part of the "Models." The connection to your Husserl book was, of course, very clear to me, and, at the same time, helpful for grasping your intention.

If you permit me to sum up my opinion in a single sentence, it would be that I've never read such a chaste and self-restrained defence of metaphysics. Starting from a place where the defence of metaphysics must have appeared as hopeless and Don Quixotesque as indeed it did to some of your predecessors, you embarked on a sally, the vigor and determination of which I can admire. The attempt not only to break out of the Hegelian dialectic – the age-old wisdom that the negation of the negation is the positive – without letting oneself be seduced by false affirmations, of the sort that lie so close to the inherited Hegelian dialectic; moreover, to extract this new metaphysical approach precisely through recourse to Marxism – that is truly an undertaking worthy of tribute. Provided one concedes your materialist thesis, the battle you wage to rescue metaphysics is nothing short of admirable. Of course, such a materialist starting point also gives you the advantage of being able to produce the factuality of your metaphysical investigations, since this has to be contained in the objects from the outset. However, it is neither clear nor evident to me if your basic premise can be described as materialist in anything other than a nominal sense (as an "anti-Idealist" thesis). Whether or not such a connection to metaphysics is possible from a radically materialist position is, surely, questionable. I see your problem as follows: even after the theory of class struggle has exploded, precisely in and through its application, and hence been rendered philosophically irrelevant in our own historical period when it comes to grounding our real experience (to say nothing of an analysis of its legitimacy in other periods, where it hasn't yet been put to the test) – can it still be possible to use these categories, after their alleged historical carrier has failed?

I don't know if I'm mistaken in assuming that the moment of necessity in isolating Marxist categories from the theory of class struggle is behind what you and Horkheimer call Critical Theory. Your readers must have noticed that you don't express yourself on this point with complete clarity. Here and there, class structure still comes up as some kind of *hypokeimenon* for certain sets of relations, albeit rarely, and, as it were, only in a minor key, without the fanfare granted to it by to it by more dyed-in-the-wool Marxists. Please excuse the *catabasis eis allo genos* in my images. At no point in your book is it clear why it is, or should remain, attached to the Marxist theory of history. For me, as someone who has absolutely no use for the materialists' categories, what remains highly dubious and hardly feasible in reality, is the question of the transition from being – from social being in its totality, as a decisive category in your way of reading – to consciousness. If I have understood you correctly, then it is here that the hypothesis of mediation by the totality of the social process comes up – a hypothesis that is supposed to establish the true connection between being and consciousness, and which plays the role of a *deus ex machina* whenever you make use of it. The presupposition of this mediation, however, is a hypothesis or a matter of faith, since there is no concrete instance where it could be shown precisely what this mediation actually consists of and why it produces these phenomena of consciousness and not others. It was precisely this point that seemed so indigestible to Marx's readers; and unfortunately, as far as I am concerned, the deductions of the young Lukács did not make it any more illuminating. All Marxists, insofar as they do not (as 'vulgar Marxists'?) dispense with such mediation and attempt instead to establish the direct reflection of social being in consciousness (whereby, of course, they must make hopeless fools of themselves, *ut figurae docent*) have stopped at the thoroughly metaphysical thesis that such total mediation, conceived of as the explanatory ground of every phenomenon, exists; a thesis that cannot be substantiated concretely, nor, if you wish, abstractly, with reference to the workings of consciousness. As I mentioned above, this is the article of faith that one has to grant you if one wants to follow your line of thought. The metaphorical character and the lack of persuasive power in Marx's famous chapter on commodity fetishism is extremely illustrative and characteristic of this central weakness in philosophical-dialectical materialism. The fascination that this chapter has exerted on intelligent people in the past fifty years is in no way supported by the stringency of its exposition. This is also how I feel in your case, when I find you piously, as it were, repeating the alas unproven claims concerning the connection between the exchange process and processes of abstraction in consciousness – as if any one of your predecessors had ever gone beyond imagery and dubious analogies to clarify this connection. I don't want to deny *a priori* that ideas and categories could have a social content; what is not clear to me is the claim that there actually could be method that allows one rigorously to deduce this. But presumably this is one of the things that your reader will have to grant you in advance. I find your critique of the philosophy of immanence to be serious and illuminating, especially where it appeals to the non-identical moment in the object of cognition. But the leap from the non-identical to the socially mediated is accomplished more readily through your faith than through my skepticism, which paradoxically turns the usual discourse about faith and skepticism on its head. This transition, in your critique, from the non-identical as such to that which is exclusively socially mediated is not always clearly expressed. This is true, for example, of some lines of yours about the transcendental illusion, which, in themselves, are highly interesting to me. What you mean here can be envisaged as a possibility, but it is not clear how this illusion is related to the actually or putatively underlying genetic processes, beyond a general assertion. I derived great pleasure from your suggestion that, by dispensing with the theory of class struggle, Marxism must no longer be seen as a scientific credo but, rather, as a perpetually open question. Surely this is the most heretical formulation of historical materialism, and, justifiably, it is this heretical moment in your materialist philosophy that will be most striking to readers. I've jotted down a lovely line on p. 368 as a motto for some future lectures of mine on mysticism: the *totum* is the totem. We may yet see eye to eye on this watchword!

By the way, I might also add that the connection between myth and mysticism in the doctrine of being – truly one of your most striking dialectical moments, at least in my view – follows only indirectly from your critique of Heidegger. One could just as easily deduce it directly.

We'll surely have an opportunity to discuss the particulars in person. I expect that I will be in Europe during June, since my wife has to be in Zurich to undergo some rather complicated orthopedic surgery. I will accompany her to Europe and use the opportunity to make excursions to London and Oslo. I will probably also come to Frankfurt, or else we could meet in Zurich one weekend. How long my wife will have to stay there will depend on the success of the follow-up treatment; it may even take a few months.

I thank you, again, for your book and for all that it has brought me. The labor of the concept in which you rightly expect your readers to engage is not wholly lost on me. Please write soon to let us know how you're doing, and most cordial regards to you both.

Your old

Gershom Scholem

Original: typescript; Theodor W. Adorno Archive, Frankfurt am Main. First published in Gershom Scholem, *Briefe II: 1948–1970*, ed. Thomas Sparr (Munich: C. H. Beck, 1995), pp. 177–80.

the third part of the "Models": See Adorno, "Meditations on Metaphysics," in *Negative Dialectics*, trans. E. B. Ashton (London: Routledge, 1973), pp. 361–408.

the connection to your Husserl book: See Adorno: *Against Epistemology – A Metacritique: Studies in Husserl and the Phenomenological Antinomies*, trans. Willis Domingo (Oxford: Blackwell, 1982).

the deductions of the young Lukács: See Georg Lukács, "Reification and the Consciousness of the Proletariat," in *History and Class Consciousness: Studies in Marxist Dialectics*, trans. Rodney Livingstone (London: Merlin Press, 1971), pp. 83–222. See also letter no. 96 in this volume.

Marx's famous chapter on commodity fetishism: Scholem is referring to the section on "The Fetishism of Commodities and the Secret Thereof." See Karl Marx and Friedrich Engels, *Marx & Engels Collected Works*, Vol. 35: *Capital*, Vol. 1 (London: Lawrence & Wishart, 1996), pp. 81–93.

claims concerning the connection between the exchange process and processes of abstraction in consciousness: "Despite the preponderance of the object, the thingness of the world is also phenomenal. It tempts the subjects to ascribe their own social circumstances of production to the noumena. This is elaborated in Marx's chapter on fetishes, truly a piece from the heritage of classic German philosophy. Even its systematic motive survives in that chapter: the fetish character of goods is not laid to a subjectively errant consciousness, but objectively deduced from the social *a priori*, the exchange process" (Adorno, *Negative Dialectics*, pp. 189–90).

lines . . . about the transcendental illusion:

> The delusion that the transcendental subject is the Archimedean fixed point from which the world can be lifted out of its hinges – this delusion, purely in itself, is indeed hard to overcome altogether by subjective analysis. For contained in this delusion, and not to be extracted from the forms of cogitative mediation, is the truth that society comes before the individual consciousness and before all its experience. The insight into the fact that thinking is mediated by objectivity does not negate thinking, nor does it negate the objective laws that make it thinking. The further fact that there is no way to get out of thinking points to the support found in non-identity – to the very support which thought, by its own forms,

> seeks and expresses as much as it denies it. Still transparent, however, is the reason for the delusion that is transcendental far beyond Kant: why our thinking in the *intentio obliqua* will inescapably keep coming back to its own primacy, to the hypostasis of the subject. (Adorno, *Negative Dialectics*, p. 181)

I've jotted down a lovely line on p. 368: "The totum is the totem. Grayness could not fill us with despair if our minds did not harbor the concept of different colors, scattered traces of which are not absent from the negative whole. The traces always come from the past, and our hopes come from their counterpart, from that which was or is doomed" (Adorno, *Negative Dialectics*, pp. 377–8).

the connection between myth and mysticism in the doctrine of being: "The celebration of senselessness as sense is mythical; so is the ritualistic repetition of natural contexts in symbolic individual actions, as if that made these contexts supernatural. Categories such as *Angst* – of which, at least, we cannot stipulate that they must be everlasting – are transfigured into constituents of Being as such, into things superior to that existence, into its *a priori*" (Adorno, *Negative Dialectics*, p. 119).

183 ADORNO TO SCHOLEM
FRANKFURT AM MAIN, 14.3.1967

PROF. DR. THEODOR W. ADORNO

6 FRANKFURT AM MAIN
KETTENHOFWEG 123
14 March 1967

Dear Scholem,

I thank you most sincerely for your long letter, which, as you can imagine, moved me greatly. Coincidentally, I discovered it on my desk just as I was reading an essay by Heissenbüttel. In it, he accuses me, in a rather unpleasant manner, of having suppressed Benjamin's Marxism, which he seems to view – alongside Brecht's – as being the Marxism of Marx himself. One simply doesn't have it easy in this world.

The intention to rescue metaphysics is indeed the central one in *Negative Dialectics*. I'm very glad that this has come across and that you are well disposed towards this attempt. Of course, our differences stem from the relation to materialism. I am not so naïve as to deceive myself, to suit my own purposes, by diminishing the weight of what you bring to bear in your letter. I would like nothing more than the opportunity to discuss these matters with you in earnest in June, as I've long wished to do. On the other hand, I don't want to postpone the discussion for quite so long, and would like at least to indicate some of my initial reactions.

If I understand myself correctly, which is certain of no thinker – I myself coined the good Hegelian saying that only those thoughts that do not understand themselves are true – then I precisely have not presupposed any materialist thesis in this work. On the contrary, my aim was to undermine the assumption of something given, which, after all, also belongs to the ontological mode of thinking. In other words, the attempt is made to reach materialism, in a very specific sense, not to set out from it. This occurs in the second main part, which I'd ask you to consider from this perspective. It seems to me that what does justice to the concept of materialism – at least once one has escaped the spell of identity – is what I have, in the immanent, epistemological discussion, called the preponderance of the object; and this can't be imagined as a crude assertion, but is presented very delicately, namely, only within the dialectic. The weighty arguments that, I believe, I have advanced against idealism present themselves beyond the spell, and as stringently materialist. This means, however, that such materialism is not conclusive; it is neither a worldview, nor something fixed. To me, it is this path to materialism – a path that is totally different from any dogma – that seems to warrant that affinity with metaphysics (I would have almost said theology), which you rightly recognized as the book's central concern.

As far as the theory of class struggle is concerned, this is no article of faith. It's definitely not connected with the vulgar metaphysics of the proletariat, which proved itself most definitely not to be the carrier of world spirit. What is thereby excluded is the orientation of materialism toward what happened in the East, where, for bad philosophical reasons, namely that one must have something that one can hold on to, they still adhere to this [vulgar metaphysics]. What I intend is a materialism directed against the official doctrines, heretical through and through. From this vantage point, I hope it will appeal to you.

On the other hand, it is my conviction that the theory of class struggle itself – once one disassociates it from the complex of communist rule – remains indispensable for the construction of history and, with it, philosophy. What is called dialectics seems to me in reality to be nothing other than this: the equation of the principle of identity and the principle of domination wants to get this across. Nothing could be further from this anti-ontological book than an ontological determination of the relation between being and consciousness. Insofar as I believe that there is anything to say on this matter, which neither falls short of philosophy nor lends itself to ideological abuse, it may be found in the latter sections of the second part. Also, regarding the thesis on the mediation through totality, I would like to think that, with everything that was said about the spell, I get somewhat further than you grant me. But precisely this should really be the subject of our discussion when we meet. Until then, all that remains for me is to rejoice in our *unio in haeresia*. And, in the meantime, you may concede to the heretic that he has no materialist faith.

A little collection of my aesthetic essays, *Ohne Leitbild* [Without a guiding image] is coming out soon. It's a kind of exhalation after what was and is the arduous struggle of the big book, not only for its readers. It goes without saying that you'll be sent the little one promptly. (I haven't received my copies yet!)

I'm unhappy to hear that Fanja is still unwell. Today I can do nothing more than to wish you both all the very best.

I am worried about resuming my lectures, which do rather uproot me from my things. But if someone has a profession, one must also perform it, after all.

All that is cordial to you both, also from Gretel,

your loyal

Adorno

I saw Szondi a few days ago and found him to be in fine fettle. He and Lexi seem to be much happier together than they want to let on in front of the astonished public. Apparently, they both think that they are obliged to put up with each other, whereas, in truth, they simply like each other. I was in Dhaun for a few days for a conference organized by the Studienstiftung, which essentially focused on *Negative Dialectics*. I was quite impressed with the event, above all because of the astounding degree of understanding from beyond my group of students.

Original: typescript with printed letterhead; Gershom Scholem Archive, The National Library of Israel, Jerusalem.

essay by Heissenbüttel: Adorno's spelling. See Helmut Heißenbüttel, "Vom Zeugnis des Fortlebens in Briefen" [Evidence of living on in letters], *Merkur*, 21/3 (1967), pp. 232–44.

preponderance of the object: See Adorno, *Negative Dialectics*, trans. E.B. Ashton (London: Routledge, 1973), pp. 183–6.

Szondi . . . and Lexi: Peter Szondi and Alexandra Kluge (1937–2017) were close friends. They met through Adorno.

a conference organized by the Studienstiftung: The event, whose theme was "Aufklärung und Mythos im Denken der Gegenwart" [Enlightenment and myth in contemporary thought], took place at the residential adult education centre at Castle Dhaun from the 5th to the 10th of March.

184 SCHOLEM TO ADORNO
JERUSALEM, 6.4.1967

Jerusalem, 6.4.1967

Dear Adorno,

Kind thanks for your letter of the 14th of March. I hope that, sooner or later, we will have the opportunity to discuss the questions that are raised therein. God willing, I'll be in a position to dart over there from Zurich sometime in June, or you might come here at some point. We are waiting for confirmation of the date of Fania's surgery, and of course, as concerns further arrangements, I am entirely dependent on this in every respect. I expect to be in Zurich until roughly the 4th of July, with an interruption from the 18th to the 23rd of July, when I have to be in Oslo. I am postponing further discussion of these matters until then.

Werner Kraft gave me the issue of *Merkur* with the essay by Heissenbüttel, which contains a remarkable mix of topsy-turvy logic, some arguments that may – in part – be worth hearing, and completely misguided psychologizing. The attack on you seems to have been especially close to his heart. The different assessment of the letters and their author, which I've seen in the reviews to date, is extraordinarily uplifting. I received two unimaginably angry letters from our old friend Belmore, the content of which you can guess. I wrote a very long letter to Hartung about his review in *Die Zeit*, to which I just received an evasive response.

Although I don't have any copies available, I certainly don't want to miss satisfying the dark sides of your nature by pointing out the publication of my long speech on Buber. It's due to appear in the literary supplement of the *Neue Zürcher Zeitung* on the 2nd and 8th of April. It shouldn't be difficult for you to get your hands on a copy. The few author's copies I have been promised are sent out by regular mail, and won't arrive until the end of April.

That's all for today. Unfortunately we cannot count on Fania's condition improving until she has surgery; and it remains to be seen how things go afterwards – there can be no prognosis.

Meanwhile, please accept cordial regards to you both, and wishes for good work, even after returning to the lectern.

Your old
Gerhard Scholem

Original: aerogram (typescript); Theodor W. Adorno Archive, Frankfurt am Main.

angry letters from our old friend Belmore: The letters could not be identified.

Hartung about his review in Die Zeit: See Rudolf Hartung, "Der Mann, der von vielem absah: Die Briefe Walter Benjamins" [The man who abstained from many things: Walter Benjamin's letters], *Die Zeit*, 10 February 1967.

long speech on Buber: Scholem's lecture "Martin Bubers Auffassung des Judentums" [Martin Buber's conception of Judaism] was given at the Eranos conference in 1966. It was first published in *Eranos-Jahrbuch 1966*, Vol. 35: *Schöpfung und Gestaltung* [Creation and formation], ed. Olga Fröbe-Kapteyn (Zurich: Rhein, 1967), pp. 9–55. It was reprinted on the 2nd and 9th of April 1967 in the Sunday issue of the *Neue Zürcher Zeitung*. (An abridged version was included in the international edition of the *NZZ* on the 1st and 8th of April 1967. See "Martin Buber's Conception of Judaism," in *On Jews and Judaism in Crisis: Selected Essays*, ed. Werner J. Dannhauser (New York: Schocken Books, 1976), pp. 126–71.

185 ADORNO TO SCHOLEM
FRANKFURT AM MAIN, 14.4.1967

PROF. DR. THEODOR W. ADORNO

6 FRANKFURT AM MAIN
KETTENHOFWEG 123
14 April 1967

Dear Scholem,

My sincere thanks for your letter, which I received today upon my return from Vienna, where Gretel and I spent a couple of exceedingly gratifying weeks – in the frequent company of Lotte Tobisch. At the same time, I received a letter from Heißenbüttel, in which he seems disposed to grant me at least the possibility of a rectification. What a load of nonsense. At any rate, after a conversation with Unseld, I think that the real object of his aggression is not me, but the publisher. It seems to me, however, that his attack contains so many factual inaccuracies that it should be possible, with Tiedemann's help, to thoroughly rectify the matter. It's curious that the effort to establish Benjamin as a philosopher is met with such resistance by friend and foe alike. [It is hard to fathom] what all these people imagine philosophy to be.

Would it be possible for you to send me the letters from Mr. Belmore? It's probably not worth having them photocopied, but I would quite like to read them. I'd be in favor of giving the man a frightful smack on the muzzle, if I weren't afraid that he might cause difficulties over the publication of the letters to him in case of a new edition. What do you think?

Regarding your Buber speech in the *NZZ*, I'll get in touch with them right away. And, while we're on the topic of Zurich – I hear that a position in philosophy has opened up there. It would mean a great deal to me if my student Haag were to get it. You know him too – and if you don't remember him clearly, just read his contribution to the *Zeugnisse* [Testimonies] dedicated to me, which will give you an idea of the man's quality. Quite aside from his intellectual prowess, his knowledge of philosophy is universal – from Aristotle to Duns Scotus to Hegel. Since you have considerable influence in Zurich, may I ask that you intervene on Haag's behalf – for instance with Werner Weber, or one of the people there with whom you are close? I can't think of anyone better than him.

As far as Fanja is concerned, I can only keep my fingers crossed. And I'm not so thoroughly imbued by the views of her relative, Freud, that I would refrain from sending my good wishes.

I sincerely hope that we will see each other in July. Keep in mind that I'll be in Berlin on the 7th to recite my little piece on Goethe's *Iphigenia*. Our summer plans this time are still quite vague.

The transition from the Viennese milieu to the lectern is not entirely easy, but I hope I'll manage it somehow. The past few weeks did us a world of good, if only because of the pleasure in variation. At the same time, they were quite tiring because of an excess of so-called social obligations.

Most cordially, also from Gretel, and to Fanja,

your old

Teddie Adorno

Original: typescript with printed letterhead; Gershom Scholem Archive, The National Library of Israel, Jerusalem.

upon my return from Vienna: The Adornos spent two weeks in Vienna with the intention mainly of relaxing. Adorno did, however, give a few lectures during this time. He writes about his stay in Vienna in the following piece: "Wien, nach Ostern 1967" [Vienna, after Easter 1967], in *Ohne Leitbild / Parva Aesthetica* [Without a guiding image / parva aesthetica] in Adorno, *Gesammelte Schriften* 10.1, ed. Rolf Tiedemann et al. (Frankfurt am Main: Suhrkamp, 2003), pp. 423–31.

Lotte Tobisch: Adorno was friends with the Austrian actress Lotte Tobisch von Labotýn (1926–2019) for many years. They corresponded extensively. See *Theodor W. Adorno / Lotte Tobisch: Der private Briefwechsel* [The private correspondence], ed. Bernhard Kraller & Heinz Steinert (Graz: Droschl, 2003).

a letter from Heißenbüttel: In a letter dated the 10th of April 1967, Heißenbüttel wrote to Adorno in response to the latter's reaction to his *Merkur* essay (see letter no. 201 in this volume): "Dear Professor Adorno, / Please excuse my late reply to to your exceedingly friendly letter (I was traveling and then came down with the flu). In it, you rightly demonstrate a series of discrepancies in my essay on the selection of Walter Benjamin's letters. Of course these need to be rectified. I too am eager to ensure that everything is correctly presented. Perhaps I am more one-sided in this regard than you, since I am concerned mainly with a few aspects of the fragments comprising the *Arcades Project*. I am of the opinion that the position of the theses "On the Concept of History" would have to be determined by a further comparison" (typescript, Theodor W. Adorno Archive, Frankfurt am Main).

with Tiedemann's help: For information on Rolf Tiedemann's essay on the Benjamin debate, see letter no. 200 and the reference there.

my student Haag ... his contribution: See letter no. 157 and the relevant note in this volume. As is apparent from his letters to Adorno, Jacob Taubes, in his capacity as professor of philosophy at the Freie Universität Berlin, actively sought to have Haag appointed to a position at the Institute, albeit unsuccessfully. *His contribution*: See Karl Heinz Haag, "Das Unwiederholbare" [The unrepeatable], in *Zeugnisse: Theodor W. Adorno zum 60. Gerburtstag* [Testimonies: for Theodor W. Adorno on his 60th birthday], ed. Max Horkheimer (Frankfurt am Main: Suhrkamp, 1963), pp. 151–61, reprinted in Haag, *Kritische Philosophie: Abhandlungen und Aufsätze* [Critical philosophy: treatises and essays] (Munich: Edition Text + Kritik, 2012), pp. 97–107.

Werner Weber: The journalist and literary scholar Werner Weber (1919–2005) was editor of the art, literature and science desk at the *Neue Zürcher Zeitung* from 1946–1973, of which he became the department head in 1951. From 1973 to 1987 he was professor of literary criticism at the University of Zurich.

her relative, Freud: Gershom Scholem's second wife, Fania Scholem (née Freud), was "a somewhat distant relative belonging to the Galician branch of the Freud family," as Scholem notes in his correspondence with Benjamin. See *The Correspondence of Walter Benjamin and Gershom Scholem, 1933–1940*, ed. Gershom Scholem, trans. Gary Smith and Andre Lefevere (New York: Schocken Books, 1989), p. 24.

my little piece on Goethe's Iphigenia: Adorno's lecture "Zum Klassizismus von Goethes *Iphigenie*" [On the classicism of Goethe's *Iphigenie*] first appeared in *Neue Rundschau*, 78/4 (1967), pp. 586–99. See Adorno, "On the Classicism of Goethe's *Iphigenie*," in *Notes to Literature*, Vol. 2, trans. Shierry Weber Nicholsen (New York: Columbia University Press, 1992), pp. 153–70.

186 ADORNO TO SCHOLEM
FRANKFURT AM MAIN, 22.5.1967

PROF. DR. THEODOR W. ADORNO

6 FRANKFURT AM MAIN
KETTENHOFWEG 123
22 May 1967

Dear Scholem,

These hasty lines are meant only to say how much I am thinking of you, and how much I hope that it won't come to a war with the Arabs. Freud wants to prohibit good wishes, which he sees merely as an archaic remnant of a belief in the power of thought. However, I, for one, sense nothing in his prohibition but bourgeois coldness – a stoicism which, by dint of its sheer rationality, ultimately kills its reasonable purpose. Allow me, then, to keep my fingers crossed.

All that is cordial from your
loyal Adorno

May I ask you for the letter from Belmore – ?

Original: typescript with printed letterhead and handwritten postscript; Gershom Scholem Archive, The National Library of Israel, Jerusalem.

that it won't come to a war with the Arabs: The Six-Day War between Israel, Egypt, Jordan, and Syria lasted from the 5th until the 10th of June 1967. The situation between Israel and the Arab states, which had been very tense since the war in 1948 and the Suez Canal crisis in 1956, had escalated in the preceding months. On the 15th of May 1967, the Israeli day of independence, the Egyptian military forcibly crossed the Suez Canal onto the Sinai peninsula, which had been guarded by troops from the UNEF (United Nations Emergency Forces) since the Suez crisis. Following the withdrawal of the UNEF troops from the peninsula, as well as the closure to Israeli ships of the Straits of Tiran along the peninsula, Israel launched a massive attack on Egyptian airfields. At the same time, the Israeli Air Force attacked targets in Jordan, Syria, and Iraq – countries, whose armies had been preparing for war. The Six-Day War led to great losses on all sides. The occupation of regions in the Gaza strip, the West Bank, the Sinai peninsula, the Golan Heights, and East Jerusalem had radical geo-political consequences, which continue to be felt in the region today.

Freud wants to prohibit good wishes, which he sees merely as an archaic remnant of a belief in the power of thought: "The motives, which lead men to practise magic: they are human wishes. All we need to suppose is that primitive man had an immense belief in the power of his wishes. The basic reason why what he sets about by magical means comes to pass is, after all, simply that he wills it. To begin with, therefore, the emphasis is only upon his wish." See Sigmund Freud, "Totem & Taboo," in *The Standard Edition of the Complete Psychological Works of Sigmund Freud*, Vol. XIII: *1913–1914*, ed. and trans. James Strachey and Anna Freud (London: Hogarth Press, 1955), p. 83.

187 SCHOLEM TO ADORNO
JERUSALEM, 27.5.1967

Saturday, 27.5.

Dear Adorno,

I thank you sincerely for your lines, which arrived on Friday in the midst of a very difficult situation. On Sunday I am supposed to fly to London to speak at the university. If shooting does not break out before my departure, I will make the trip because of the urgent wish of the Israeli embassy there. If this letter is postmarked from London, it will mean that I am there, since a letter from Israel would arrive much later. If a war does break out, heaven only knows whether I'll fly back right after my lecture (Tuesday evening) and cancel all my other plans, or whether I'll go to Zurich on Thursday as planned (where Fania is to arrive on the 5th of June). I am prepared for both possibilities.

You may be able to reach me by telephone at the hotel in the mornings before 9 or in the late evening.

Clive Hotel, Juniper 2233.

In case I stay in Europe, I'll contact you from Zurich (there: Hotel Urban, Tel. 32 70 52).

If, at the last minute, I don't fly at all, you may not hear from me right away.

In haste and with cordial regards, yours

G. Scholem

Original: manuscript; Theodor W. Adorno Archive, Frankfurt am Main. First published in Gershom Scholem, *Briefe II: 1948–1970*, ed. Thomas Sparr (Munich: C. H. Beck, 1995), p. 185. An excerpt of this letter appears in translation in *Gershom Scholem: A Life in Letters*, ed. and trans. Anthony David Skinner (Cambridge, MA: Harvard University Press, 2002), pp. 423–4.

in the midst of a very difficult situation: The Straits of Tiran were closed to Israeli ships on the 22nd of May. On the 25th of May, Egypt prompted Syria, Jordan, Saudi-Arabia, and Iraq to station troops at Israel's borders. On the 26th of May, the Egyptian president Gamal Abdel Nasser called for the destruction of Israel.

188 ADORNO TO SCHOLEM
FRANKFURT AM MAIN, 6.6.1967

PROF. DR. THEODOR W. ADORNO

6 FRANKFURT AM MAIN
KETTENHOFWEG 123
6 June 1967

Dear Scholem,

Kindest thanks for the letter.

I am writing today just to let you know how much we are thinking of you, and how – quite aside from our friendship – these thoughts aren't limited to the private sphere, but intend, rather, the whole. Presumably you wound up staying in Israel, and this concerns me for two reasons: first, because of the perilous situation there and, second, because of the possible postponement of Fania's surgery, for which there's probably an urgent need.

We know that you've got other things on your mind these days, but if you could at least send us a little card we'd both be sincerely grateful.

All the best, also from Gretel

In loyal friendship

yours

Teddie Adorno

Original: typescript with printed letterhead; Gershom Scholem Archive, The National Library of Israel, Jerusalem.

because of the perilous situation: The Six-Day War had erupted on the previous day, the 5th of June 1967. The city of Jerusalem was severely affected.

189 SCHOLEM TO ADORNO
ZURICH, 14.6.1967

Dear Adorno, I will arrive in Frkfrt. from Copenhagen on Friday, 23.6 around noon. Thank you kindly for making the guest room at the Institute available to me. Please have arrangements made for a 2-night stay.

In case you are going to be at Glück's on Friday evening, perhaps you could ask G. if we could all be there together. In case Unseld is in F., I'd be glad to meet with him on Saturday evening. I'll see whether this is the case.

For the time being, just a quick update: Fania is doing quite well, given the circumstances. More on this in person.

I'll be in Oslo from 18.6: Stefanhotellet, Rosenkrantz plass 1.

Cordial regards to you both,
yours G.S.

Original: postcard (manuscript), no date given, dated by postmark; Theodor W. Adorno Archive, Frankfurt am Main.

190 ADORNO TO SCHOLEM
FRANKFURT AM MAIN, 15.6.1967

PROF. DR. THEODOR W. ADORNO

6 FRANKFURT AM MAIN
KETTENHOFWEG 123
15 June 1967

Dear Scholem,

Kindest thanks for the card.

I think it would be easiest if you were to come with us to Glück's place on Saturday the 24th. His brother Franz (Adolf Loos's editor, whom I know quite well from Vienna) will also be there with his wife. Glück is currently away, but I will make the necessary arrangements with him.

You will find everything waiting for you at the Institute. Of course, because of the lack of service personnel, our guest room doesn't offer the same degree of comfort as a hotel, but at the very least you'll have a bathroom and some quiet.

We had lunch with Unseld yesterday and I mentioned our arrangement to him; I think he'll have time for you on Friday evening. Perhaps it'd be best if you confirmed this with him directly.

I am heartily glad that Fania is doing well, under the circumstances. Please send her my kindest regards. And to both of you the most cordial regards, also from Gretel, from

your
Adorno

Original: typescript with printed letterhead; Gershom Scholem Archive, The National Library of Israel, Jerusalem.

Glück's ... brother Franz: After completing his doctorate in 1923, the historian of art and literature Franz Glück (1899–1981) worked for the Viennese publishing house Schroll & Co., which he directed from 1945 to 1949. From 1949 to 1967 he was the director of the city of Vienna's museums. In 1962 Glück edited the collected works of the Austrian architect Adolf Loos (1870–1933), which were published by the Herold Verlag in Vienna and Munich.

191 ADORNO TO SCHOLEM
FRANKFURT AM MAIN, 18.9.1967

PROF. DR. THEODOR W. ADORNO

6 FRANKFURT AM MAIN
KETTENHOFWEG 123
18 September 1967

Dear Scholem,

Werner Weber from the *Neue Zürcher Zeitung* has invited me to write a piece on the occasion of your seventieth birthday. I would like to do this all the more since I cannot contribute anything to the commemorative volume being planned in your honor on account of the fact that I'm simply unable to deliver something pertaining to Jewish studies. One may be able to bring owls to Athens, but one certainly can't bring anything Boeotian to Jerusalem; and this is precisely the difficulty with the prospective piece for the *NZZ*. It simply isn't my place to say anything authoritative about the authoritative things that you have said. I could speak only of my experiences and impressions and – above all – of my lack of specialist knowledge. But I don't want to do this without your prior approval, since I can imagine that you might be embarrassed if something about you were to appear in print that is so clearly devoid of any objective competence. I personally believe that so much shared substance has crystallized between us over the years that the risk isn't too great; but I'd like to get your opinion on the matter first.

Things are going quite well at our end; we were really able to recuperate in western Switzerland. We hope that Fanja is well on the road to recovery.

I had some trouble recently with a paranoid man – a foreign anti-Semite, as it happens – who threatened me with murder in an extortive way. I believe he had it in him to carry out his plans. He singled me out without having ever seen me, and presumably without having ever read a word of what I've written. As of three days ago, he's behind bars. I expect he'll be deported from Germany once he's been convicted and has served his sentence. Since he expressed the intention of traveling to Israel in his letters, I will tell you his name, just in case, so that you can take protective measures: he's called K.J. S.-B., and he has an Ecuadorian passport.

Gretel and I send very cordial regards to you both. Do send a word soon.

Your old and loyal
Adorno

Original: typescript with printed letterhead; Gershom Scholem Archive, The National Library of Israel, Jerusalem.

to write a piece on the occasion of your seventieth birthday: Adorno's piece, "Gruß an Gershom G. Scholem Zum 70. Geburtstag: 5. Dezember 1967" [Greetings to Gershom G. Scholem: For his 70th birthday, 5 December 1967] appeared in the *Neue Zürcher Zeitung* on the 2nd of December 1967 (p. 20). The piece was later included in *Gesammelte Schriften 20.2: Vermischte Schriften* [Miscellaneous Writings], ed. Rolf Tiedemann et al. (Frankfurt am Main: Suhrkamp, 1986), pp. 478–86.

I cannot contribute anything to the commemorative volume being planned in your honor: The Israeli scholar of religion Raphael Jehuda Zwi Werblowsky (1924–2015) asked Adorno to contribute a piece for a planned commemorative volume marking the occasion of Gershom Scholem's 70th birthday. The piece was to be on a theme pertaining to the history of religion, the philosophy of religion, or Jewish studies. On the 17th of July 1967 Adorno wrote to Werblowsky to thank him for the invitation and added the following: "In terms of content, I have two suggestions. I am planning to write something on the volume of poems by Paul Celan – the greatest lyric poet living today and, at the same time, a very eloquent Jew. If I succeed at this, I would be delighted to dedicate this piece to Scholem and to contribute it to the commemorative volume. My only stipulation is that this wouldn't preclude publication in Germany. Otherwise, the second volume of my musical writings, *Quasi Una Fantasia*, contains an essay on Schoenberg's *Moses und Aron*, which is dedicated to Scholem. Perhaps this piece could be included in the commemorative volume? I don't expect that more than a handful of people would have seen the volume and this text in Israel" (carbon copy of typescript: Theodor W. Adorno Archive, Frankfurt am Main).

K.J. S.-B.: The man, who had immigrated to Germany from South America, initially sent Adorno letters in 1965, in which he praised his work and asked for professional and intellectual advice. In 1967 he wrote again from Africa, asking Adorno to help him make contacts in Israel with the intention of gaining employment there. Upon his return to Germany, the man complained to Adorno, in another letter, that after the war all academic positions were given to Jews, whereas a "Volksdeutscher" [ethnic German] like himself was unable to find work, even though he hadn't personally murdered any Jews. Drawing on a number of anti-Semitic clichés, and with reference to Israel's expulsion of Palestinian refugees, in June 1967 the man threatened to murder Adorno if he didn't help him secure an academic position in Israel or in Germany. Finally, in a telegram to Adorno, he professed his intentions of going to Jerusalem and committing murderous attacks. Following his arrest, he wrote to Adorno from prison. Out of pity, Adorno then dropped the charges against him. The man's name has been abbreviated here for reasons of privacy. See Editor's Introduction p. xxxiii.

192 SCHOLEM TO ADORNO
JERUSALEM, 21.9.1967

21 Sept. '67

THE ISRAEL ACADEMY OF SCIENCES & HUMANITIES

Dear Adorno,

I'm happy to hear from you, all the more so considering the threats against you that you wrote about, and the unexpected hassles that they brought into your life. Accordingly, all the best! Fanja is very gradually getting better. I will join her in Zurich on the 22nd of October and we will return together a week later – she will require many months of care and treatment, however, the malady itself has been eradicated. Perhaps we'll see each other this week after all? I'm not quite sure, of course, if I'll be able to come to Frankfurt; it will depend on F. and on the circumstances.

Regarding your question about the *NZZ*, I say: you have my blessing, just in case, beyond any "lack of competence," it's fun for you. In Potsdam I read a letter you wrote to W. B. in '38, in which you wonderfully describe our first encounter – I was seriously tempted to transcribe it! No time, unfortunately. So please, *go ahead*.* Should you require any dates or factual information, feel free to ask me! "Postcard sufficient." I'm sure you'll come up with the rest yourself. In any case, you should have all of my German writings, including the piece on the Jews and the Germans. My Zurich speech on Israel appeared in last month's issue of *Monat* (August). It's important to me that you know it. In my most recent opuscule, *Mysticism and Society*, by contrast, our spheres well and truly intersect. The offprints arrived two days ago, and I'll send you a copy by airmail. If its commitment to a dialectical treatment of religious conditions, including the so-called unmediated ones, makes sense to you, then I'll be happy. However, should you find a fly in the ointment, please feel free to pull it out!

That's all for today! See you soon and cordial regards to you both,

your old

G. . .olem, so to speak!

Original: aerogram (manuscript) with printed letterhead; Theodor W. Adorno Archive, Frankfurt am Main.

The Israel Academy of Sciences & Humanities: Scholem served as vice-president of the Israel Academy of Sciences & Humanities from 1962 to 1968 and as president from 1968 to 1974.

* Original in English.

a letter you wrote to W. B. in '38, in which you wonderfully describe our first encounter: Scholem is referring to Adorno's letter to Benjamin dated the 4th of March 1938. See *The Complete Correspondence of Walter Benjamin and Theodor W. Adorno, 1928–1940*, ed. Henri Lonitz, trans. Nicholas Walker (Cambridge, MA: Harvard University Press, 2001), pp. 248–54, here p. 248.

my German writings, including the piece on the Jews and the Germans: See letter no. 174 and the relevant note in this volume.

My Zurich speech on Israel: Gershom Scholem's speech on Israel first appeared as "Rede über Israel" [Speech about Israel], *Der Monat*, 19 (August 1967), pp. 5–8; repr. in *Judaica 2* (Frankfurt am Main: Suhrkamp, 1970), pp. 47–54.

my most recent opuscule, Mysticism and Society: See letter no. 168 and the relevant note in this volume.

193 ADORNO TO SCHOLEM
FRANKFURT AM MAIN, 28.9.1967

PROF. DR. THEODOR W. ADORNO

6 FRANKFURT AM MAIN
KETTENHOFWEG 123
28 September 1967

Dear Scholem,

A thousand thanks for your letter.

My potential murderer is under lock and key. I don't know if and when he'll stand trial. Should he actually have the intention of gracing Israel with a visit, I'll inform you in good time.

I'm very glad that the plan for the NZZ appeals to you. I followed up on your reference to my 1938 letter to Benjamin in which I describe my meeting with you, and – would you believe it? – Gretel had a copy in her filing cabinet! "The Goy is orderly." I have to say, I had my fun with this document, and, with your permission, I'll make it the basis for my essay in some form or another. Once the latter has been written, published, and read by you, I'll send you a copy of the letter. I still have to see which aspects of my far-flung readings of your works I can include in my essay without imposture.

It's wonderful that Fanja is slowly, but decisively, getting better. I'll be away again for one or two days around the 20th of October, but after that I'll be here, and of course it'd be wonderful if you both could visit.

My book is coming along nicely, at least insofar as this can be said of something that is nourished by the experiences of an entire lifetime, as well as a relatively reliable memory. Aside from this, I've got a few smaller projects on the go, as usual, including the introduction to the first German edition of a rather unknown book by Durkheim, which I think has turned out quite well. I am trying to deploy the strength, which I reproduced during the holidays, as effectively as I can in the subsequent months.

A thousand good wishes for Fanja, and all the best, also from Gretel,

your loyal

Teddie

Original: typescript with printed letterhead; Gershom Scholem Archive, The National Library of Israel, Jerusalem.

My book is coming along nicely: Adorno was working on his *Aesthetic Theory*.

including the introduction to the first German edition of a rather unknown book by Durkheim: See Adorno, "Einleitung zu Emile Durkheim, *Soziologie und Philosophie*" [Introduction to Emile Durkheim's *Sociology and Philosophy*], in Durkheim, *Soziologie und Philosophie* [*Sociology and Philosophy*], trans. Eva Moldenhauer (Frankfurt am Main: Suhrkamp, 1967), pp. 7–44. See also: *Gesammelte Schriften 8: Soziologische Schriften 1* [Sociological writings 1], ed. Rolf Tiedemann et al. (Frankfurt am Main: Suhrkamp, 2003), pp. 245–79.

194 SCHOLEM TO ADORNO
JERUSALEM, 13.10.1967

13 Oct. 1967

Dear Adorno,

Unfortunately I won't be able to make an excursion to Fr. after all, since I'll be staying in Zurich these few days with Fania. On the 29th of Oct. I am flying back with her to Israel. From 22.10 we'll be at the Hotel Urban in Z.

Sincere thanks for your letter. I'm currently writing a very long encyclopedia entry on the Kabbalah, for which I've sold myself, for transparent motives. Now I have to make the best of it.

Did you receive [the copy of] *Mysticism and Society* that I sent you?

All the best to you both

yours

Gerhard Scholem

Original: manuscript; Theodor W. Adorno Archive, Frankfurt am Main.

a very long encyclopedia entry on the Kabbalah: See "Kabbalah," in *Encyclopaedia Judaica*, Vol. 10 (Jerusalem: Keter Publishing; New York: Macmillan Company, 1972), pp. 489–653.

195 ADORNO TO SCHOLEM
FRANKFURT AM MAIN, 7.11.1967

PROF. DR. THEODOR W. ADORNO

6 FRANKFURT AM MAIN
KETTENHOFWEG 123
7 November 1967

Dear Scholem,

It's a terrible pity that we missed each other this time. I am all the happier that Fanja is genuinely doing so much better.

Today I want to ask for your advice on a somewhat difficult matter. The president of the Bundestag, Gerstenmaier, has invited the Israeli Germanist, Kurzweil, to Germany to hold some lectures. An attempt to organize something with the Germanists here has failed, although I cannot quite see why. Now Franz Böhm has turned to me, asking if it would be possible for me to arrange something at the Institute. This is a bit tricky, however, since the subject area of Kurzweil's lectures makes it hard to justify hosting him here. Moreover, since, as you know, our budget has been cut, we can no longer finance guest lectures. This could possibly be remedied with the help of Mr. Gerstenmaier, or the organization Inter Nationes, which has close ties to the Federal Foreign Office. Kurzweil also has a reputation for being "difficult," which could just as well speak for him or against him. I'd like to help in this matter, but, at the same time, I don't want to incur the displeasure of the person I'm trying to help, as so often happens. I am asking you now if you could let me know, first, how you evaluate Kurzweil as a scholar; next, if you believe that something can be done on this front, given that no good deed goes unpunished; and, finally, what you think of the idea in general. Kindest thanks in advance.

I am dictating this letter under enormous pressure, hence the brevity.

All the best to you both, also from Gretel,

your old

Teddie Adorno

Original: typescript with printed letterhead; Gershom Scholem Archive, The National Library of Israel, Jerusalem.

Gerstenmaier: The Protestant theologian and politician Eugen Karl Albrecht Gerstenmaier (1906–1986) was arrested for his involvement in the attempt to assassinate Hitler on the 20th of July 1944. In 1949 he became a member of the Bundestag for the Christian Democratic Union of Germany, the CDU. He was the longest-serving president of the Bundestag, having served from 1954 to 1969.

Kurzweil: The literary scholar and rabbi Baruch (Benedict) Kurzweil (1907–1972) was one of Israel's most important literary critics. He was born in

Moravia and studied at a yeshiva in Frankfurt, where he was trained as a rabbi. At the same time he studied at the University of Frankfurt, where, in 1933, he completed his doctorate with a thesis titled *Die Bedeutung bürgerlicher und künstlerischer Lebensform für Goethes Leben und Werk, dargestellt am Faust 1. Teil* [The significance of bourgeois and artistic ways of life for Goethe's life and work, presented with reference to Faust, part I]. Subsequently he worked as a teacher in a Jewish high school in Berlin until his emigration to Palestine in 1939. Kurzweil settled in Haifa, where he worked as a high school teacher until being appointed to a professorship in Hebrew literature at Bar-Ilan University in 1955. He committed suicide in 1972. Kurzweil was an outspoken critic of the secularizing tendencies in modern Hebrew literature, in which he saw a loss of connection to the Jewish tradition. Against this backdrop, he also criticized Scholem's interpretation of Jewish history, especially his assessment of Sabbatianism. See Scholem's letter to Kurzweil, dated the 4th of December 1959, in *Briefe II: 1948–1970*, ed. Thomas Sparr (Munich: C. H. Beck, 1995), pp. 50–2. An excerpt of this letter appears in translation in *Gershom Scholem: A Life in Letters*, ed. and trans. Anthony David Skinner (Cambridge, MA: Harvard University Press, 2002), pp. 374–5.

Franz Böhm: The lawyer and economist Franz Böhm (1895–1977) studied law and political science, after serving as a soldier in the Jordan Valley and the Dead Sea, among other places, as part of the Asia corps during World War I. He completed his doctorate in 1932 and his *Habilitation* in 1933. In 1936 he published a text entitled *Die Ordnung der Wirtschaft als geschichtliche Aufgabe und rechtsschöpferische Leistung* [The order of the economy as a historical task and legally foundational achievement]. The text appeared as part of a series, initiated by Böhm, titled "Ordnung der Wirtschaft" [The economic order]. During the 1930s he actively fought the discrimination against Jews and offered legal representation to many. In 1940 his license to teach was revoked on account of his criticism of the Nazi regime. In 1945 he was appointed to a professorship in Freiburg and later in Frankfurt. From 1953 to 1965 he was a member of the Bundestag for the Christian Democratic Union of Germany, the CDU. In this capacity, he advocated for dialogue between Germany and Israel. From 1955 to 1965 he served as the deputy chair of the reparations committee in the Bundestag. Franz Böhm was chairman of the board of the Institute for Social Research.

Inter Nationes: The Inter Nationes association, which was founded in 1952 on the initiative of chancellor Konrad Adenauer, serves to promote German culture abroad.

196 SCHOLEM TO ADORNO
JERUSALEM, 10.11.1967

10 Nov. 1967

Dear Adorno,

Regarding your questions about Kurzweil, this also concerns me personally: namely, K. has a kind of paranoia with respect to me. For many years (since 1957), he's been tirelessly writing essays directed against me (I own eight). Therein he debunks me as a nihilist, a demonologist, an *associate** of half-Nazis (Eranos!!), a preacher (!!!) of myth, a secularist, as having succumbed to parochial ideas of secular Zionism, as a historicist, etc., etc.; and, moreover, as someone who, instead of engaging in the orgies of the Sabbatians, orgiastically celebrates an empty "intellectual game" with Judaism, and strives to replace "the" Jewish religion with the Science of Judaism (in other words, the man is an existentialist = pious), and some other nonsense and 1/4-truths.

His essays, which I never responded to, are bursting with hate = love (that's what's behind all of this), distortions and highfalutin chatter about the danger I pose – a danger that it is his calling to warn people about, precisely because, as the most significant scholar of Judaism in recent years, and as an ingenious nihilist, I am doubly and triply dangerous. His last essay (published in October 1967) practically falls all over itself.

His principle for interpreting my work is this: every utterance I make about a historical phenomenon of Judaism is an esoteric credo of my own secret "historiosophy," which needs to be combatted. It would be the pinnacle of absurdity to allow him, of all people, to speak at your Institute. He is throwing around essays directed against me left and right. Moreover, since he tends to fall out with anyone on any occasion, and for no good reason, I cannot advise that you become involved with him – if you heard that he's difficult, this is an *understatement*;† he suffers from a persecution delusion, and regards me as a spider that crouches at the center of the system. As a critic of modern Hebrew literature, he is quite able; as a polemicist, he is an imitation of Kraus. I give him enough material for half a lifetime! At the moment, he is attempting to contrast my parochial Zionism with Benjamin's Marxism. He (but also I!) could truly tell you a lot about this!!

I am partisan when it comes to K.; nevertheless, this doesn't dissuade me from decidedly advising you not to open [the doors of] your Institute to him.

* Original in English.
† Original in English.

Most cordial regards to you both,
yours
Gerhard Scholem

Original: aerogram (manuscript); Theodor W: Adorno Archive, Frankfurt am Main.

essays directed against me: On 25.9.1957 and 25.10.1957, Baruch Kurzweil published two articles in the newspaper *Haaretz*, under the heading

”הערות ל‹שבתי צבי› של גרשם שלום“

[Remarks on Gershom Scholem's *Sabbatai Sevi*]. In these articles, he rejects Scholem's interpretation of Sabbatianism and sharply criticizes his views on Jewish historiography. See

ברוך קורצווייל, ”במאבק על ערכי היהדות“, תל אביב 1969, עמ' 99–134,

[Baruch Kurzweil, *In Struggle for the Values of Judaism* (Jerusalem and Tel Aviv: Schocken Books, 1969), pp. 99–134].

his last essay: Scholem is probably referring to:

ברוך קורצווייל, ”על גבולות סמכויותיה של ההיסטוריה“, בתוך: במאבק על ערכי היהדות,
ירושלים ותל אביב, תש"ל, עמ' 83–166.

[Baruch Kurzweil, "On the limits of history's jurisdiction," in *In Struggle for the Values of Judaism* (Jerusalem and Tel Aviv: Schocken Books, 1969), pp. 166–83].

Scholem noted the following on the first page of the book:

”דוגמא למופת לשנאה המקלקלת השורה. ועל כגון אלה אענה?“

["An example of the hatred that ruins the row. Am I really supposed to respond to this sort of thing?"]

197 ADORNO TO SCHOLEM
FRANKFURT AM MAIN, 16.11.1967

PROF. DR. THEODOR W. ADORNO

6 FRANKFURT AM MAIN
KETTENHOFWEG 123

16 November 1967

Dear Scholem,

Most heartfelt thanks for your letter.

Obviously, I put a stop to the matter with Kurzweil right away. My instincts aren't half bad in these things. It wasn't easy though – at the behest of Gerstenmaier, Franz Böhm had thrown his weight behind the plan with characteristically long-winded enthusiasm, and it was very time-consuming to talk him out of it. Nevertheless, I suceeded – but not to the extent that Mr. Kurzweil, who seems to be from Frankfurt originally, has entirely surrendered his plan to invade these parts; there's a probable threat that he'll come this spring. It's obvious that I would have clashed with him immediately.

Hopefully Fanja's convalescence is proceeding in a satisfactory way; please keep me updated about this.

All the best to you both, also from Gretel,

your loyal

Teddie Adorno

Original: typescript with printed letterhead; Gershom Scholem Archive, The National Library of Israel, Jerusalem.

198 ADORNO TO SCHOLEM
FRANKFURT AM MAIN, 5.12.1967

PROF. DR. THEODOR W. ADORNO

6 FRANKFURT AM MAIN
KETTENHOFWEG 123

5 December 1967

Dear Scholem,

By the time these lines reach you, I hope that you'll have read my profuse congratulations in the *NZZ*. I'd like to reiterate these in the form of a synthesis: "Mazel und Broche" (is that how the saying goes?) and "ad multos annos" (here I feel more confident). I hardly need to tell you that my good wishes include the selfish hope that you continue to be productive, and that you visit Europe frequently. Above all else, I wish Fanja good health. Naturally, my good wishes are also Gretel's. It really is a pity that, just as four years ago we couldn't be together to celebrate my sixtieth birthday, now we cannot be together to celebrate your seventieth. The idea that you are seriously supposed to be seventy is quite unbelievable.

Today I merely want to add one thing: amid all the to-ing and fro-ing that occurred as I was correcting the congratulatory piece, some nonsense found its way in. I'd ask you to set it right immediately. Column 3, line 12 (from the bottom), should not read "to all" but, rather, "much of what attracted other peoples' scorn and paranoid delusions," etc. The philological cells in your eyes will have undoubtedly spotted this already; but I wouldn't want you to think that I was being sloppy on such a festive occasion.

In loyal and friendly affinity

always yours

Teddie Adorno

Original: typescript with printed letterhead; Gershom Scholem Archive, The National Library of Israel, Jerusalem.

"Mazel und Broche": Yiddish: good luck and a blessing.

Paragraph 3, line 12 (from the bottom), should not read "to all" but, rather, "much of what attracted other peoples' scorn and paranoid delusions," etc.: Adorno's text reads as follows: "In contrast to that which is exemplified by Maimonides' philosophy, Scholem is attracted to the Jews' nocturnal history. That is to say, he is drawn to that which has attracted other peoples' scorn and paranoid delusions, that which is eagerly denounced, within Judaism, by Orthodox and Liberals alike." See Adorno, "Gruß an Gershom G. Scholem. Zum 70. Geburtstag, 5 Dezember 1967" [Greetings to Gershom G. Scholem: For his 70th birthday, 5 December 1967], in *Gesammelte Schriften 20.2: Vermischte Schriften* [Miscellaneous Writings], ed. Rolf Tiedemann et al. (Frankfurt am Main: Suhrkamp, 1986), pp. 478-86, here p. 485–6.

199 SCHOLEM TO ADORNO JERUSALEM, 8.12.1967

Jerusalem, 8 December 1967

Dear Adorno,

Although the *NZZ* has not given up the old custom of sending their specimen copies by regular mail, Dr. Weber's secretary, who got to know and appreciate me, suddenly had second thoughts and sent me another copy by air mail. So, yesterday I came into possession of your essay, for which I thank you heartily. I read your remarks with the greatest interest, both those from thirty years ago – which aren't half bad – and those from today. I was especially pleased by your praise of my unceremoniousness, which is a quality that means a lot to me. It will appeal to your dialectical sensibility when I tell you that my sympathies extend not only to the heterodox but also to the orthodox. Much in my writing has sought to dialectically establish the connections between these two spheres. While you are right to point out that I have said much about the secularization of mysticism – and, what is more, of religion – it should also be noted that I see secularization not as something definitive but, rather, as one of those ever-changing forms. You know very well that I am anything but an atheist, and that my religious conviction is tightly bound up with my historical insights. Indeed, you allude to this yourself at one point in the latter part of the text. Regarding another remark of yours: by the theses on Messianism do you mean my "Unhistorical Aphorisms on Kabbalah," which I very deliberately hid in an inaccessible place? Because I cannot remember having published any theses on messianism as such, even if, privately, I wrote many of these in my notebooks. I hope we will have ample opportunity to discuss these matters, and in the meantime I thank you wholeheartedly for the conviction that these lines express. I only wish that all of what you say in praise of my character were true. I may need this when I face the final judgment – if not before – and surely that is an occasion that's hard to miss. Until then, I'll take pleasure in the dream in which I appeared to you. What I told you in it is really well worth listening to. The occult origins of "Fox, you've stolen the goose" are truly crying out to be discovered by someone like me.

For now, please accept the best wishes for you both from your sentimental Leviathan (if there can be such a thing) and implausible birthday boy,

Gershom Scholem

P.S. – I just received your letter, kindest thanks. Nothing goes down in the newspapers without typos. I've corrected the infiltrating error.

Last night, to my delight, I discovered that Kafka, in a letter from 1916, had very favorable things to say about Mr. Scholem and his radical views (the letter was addressed to his fiancée, who had written to him about me). I didn't realize that I was granted honors by Kafka as early as 1916. The editors, who can't tell heads from tails, identified me as the humorist Scholem Aleichem!! How am I to cash in my honor?!

Original: typescript with handwritten postscript and enclosed manuscript of Scholem's text "Scholem und Sholem Alechem"; Theodor W. Adorno Archive, Frankfurt am Main. First published in Scholem, *Briefe II: 1948–1970*, ed. Thomas Sparr (Munich: C. H. Beck, 1995), pp. 191–2. An excerpt of this letter appears in translation in *Gershom Scholem: A Life in Letters*, ed. and trans. Anthony David Skinner (Cambridge, MA: Harvard University Press, 2002), p. 426.

I was especially pleased by your praise of my unceremoniousness: In his piece "Gruß an Gershom G. Scholem" [Greetings to Gershom G. Scholem], Adorno writes the following: "His way of responding calls to mind the grumpy modesty of musicians when, on occasion, they are obliged to speak of that which moves them, but which defies words. This demeanor is heightened, in Scholem's case, by virtue of a wellspring of originary and very kind-hearted unceremoniousness." See "Gruß an Gershom G. Scholem. Zum 70. Geburtstag," in *Gesammelte Schriften 20.2: Vermischte Schriften* [Miscellaneous Writings], ed. Rolf Tiedemann et al. (Frankfurt am Main: Suhrkamp, 1986), p. 484.

my religious conviction is tightly bound up with my historical insights: Adorno had written the following: "His immersion in a body of literature, which, at the time that he began working on it, was deemed apocryphal – even within Judaism – is only conceivable as the result of his having been directly affected by the kabbalistic texts. Everything seems to suggest that his own nature was designed for the most exposed theologoumena; that the mystical sparks must have been kindled within him. . . . If I am not gravely mistaken, Scholem became a historian of the Kabbalah – the word itself means tradition and thus implies history – because he understood its content as historical essence; as such, he believed that he could only speak of it in historical terms. Such historical truth can only be grasped at the farthest extreme from its origin, precisely in consummate secularization" ("Gruß an Gershom G. Scholem" pp. 483–5).

"Unhistorical Aphorisms on Kabbalah": See letter no. 125 and the relevant note in this volume.

take pleasure in the dream in which I appeared to you: Adorno's piece "Gruß an Gershom G. Scholem" concludes with the following lines: "I had a dream some time ago, which seems to me to be an apt parable for Scholem, whom I wish a long and happy life with these inadequate words. He supposedly told me: 'There is an old Nordic legend in which a knight abducts a girl using a rope ladder made of silk; all manner of difficulties follow from this. This legend is the basis of the German folk song '*Fox, you stole the goose*'" ("Gruß an Gershom G. Scholem," p. 486).

that Kafka, in a letter from 1916, had very favorable things to say about Mr. Scholem and his radical views: Scholem's letter to Adorno was accompanied by a typescript, with Scholem's handwritten corrections, titled "Scholem und Scholem Alechem." The piece was published in the *Neue Zürcher Zeitung* on the 12th of January 1968 and states the following:

> Recently, for my birthday, I received Franz Kafka's letters to his bride, Felice Bauer – one of the last major Kafka documents that was still outstanding. What could delight and surprise any reader of Kafka more than finding himself referred to in the letters – and approvingly, no less? On the 22nd of September 1916, Kafka writes the following to his bride about a debate at the *Jüdisches Volksheim* [Jewish People's Home] in Berlin:
>
> "The discussion you describe is typical; theoretically I am always inclined to favor proposals such as those made by Herr Scholem, which demand the utmost, and by so doing achieve nothing. So one simply mustn't appraise such proposals and their value by the actual result laid before one. Incidentally, I think this is generally applicable. Actually, Scholem's proposals in themselves are not impracticable." (pp. 703–704).*
>
> Apparently the editors of the volume could not quite figure out who was meant by such a Mr. Scholem and they proceeded to identify me with the famous Yiddish humorist Scholem Aleichem (not in the text, but in the index); however, it should surely have been inexplicable to them how the classical Yiddish author, recently deceased in America, was supposed to have contributed to a debate at the *Jüdisches Volksheim* in Berlin during the First World War. Of all people, Scholem Aleichem, who spent his whole life poking fun at radical exuberance, is supposed to have made suggestions that demand the utmost and hence, at the same

* See Franz Kafka, *Letters to Felice*, ed. Erich Heller and Jürgen Born, trans. James Stern and Elisabeth Duckworth (New York: Schocken Books, 1973), p. 505.

time, nothing?! The all-or-nothing Scholem was, in fact, me as a young student. On the 7th of September 1916, Siegfried Lehmann, director of the *Volksheim*, had given a lecture titled "Das Problem der jüdisch-religiösen Erziehung" [The problem of Jewish-religious education] which Kafka refers to in his letter of the 18th of September 1916. I attended this lecture, which provoked my sharp opposition, because I sensed in it a lack of seriousness. It fancied itself as an interpretation of Buber's interpretation of Hasidism, without any knowledge of historical Judaism, as I formulated it in my diary at the time. On the 16th of September, a heated exchange about the lecture took place at the *Volksheim*, principally between Lehmann and me. It was during this debate that I made the suggestions – demanding the utmost, though by no means impracticably so – which Felice Bauer, who was present, evidently reported to Kafka. These radical suggestions entailed focusing less on literary chatter than on the sources. This discussion led to a fierce exchange of letters between Lehmann and me, a correspondence that is still in my possession. Perhaps it would thus be advisable to differentiate between Scholem and Scholem Aleichem?" (Gershom Scholem, "Scholem und Scholem Alechem," *Neue Zürcher Zeitung*, 12 January 1968, p.13a)

Scholem also writes of this incident in his memoir. See *From Berlin to Jerusalem: Memories of my Youth*, trans. Harry Zohn (New York: Schocken Books, 1980), pp. 78–80. Kafka's letter to Felice Bauer was first published in Kafka, *Briefe an Felice Bauer und andere Korrespondenz aus der Verlobungszeit* [Letters to Felice Bauer and other letters from the period of engagement], ed. Erich Heller and Jürgen Born (Frankfurt am Main: Fischer, 1967), pp. 703–4. The index mistakenly identifies "Mr. Scholem" as Scholem Alechem (p. 781). Subsequent editions of the letters, including the English translation cited above, rectified the error.

200 ADORNO TO SCHOLEM
FRANKFURT AM MAIN, 31.1.1968

PROF. DR. THEODOR W. ADORNO

6 FRANKFURT AM MAIN
KETTENHOFWEG 123
31 January 1968

Dear Scholem,

Perhaps you are aware that, based on some nonsense published by Heissenbüttel, a war is being waged against the Benjamin edition – against us all – by a vulgar Marxist leaflet that goes by the name of *alternative*. Today, I only wanted to ask you if you would possibly be prepared to write a few words in my defence in this matter, since I am being defamed in the most unimaginable manner. The decisive thing would not be formalities, or correcting the lies that are being spread about me, principally by a certain Ms. Brenner; rather, it would be important if you, as the most qualified authority in these matters, would very strongly emphasize my philosophical credentials in matters pertaining to Benjamin. Should you feel inclined to follow my suggestion and to support me publicly, then I would see to it that you'd receive all of the requisite materials, in case you do not have them already. Above all, this means a text by Tiedemann, which is highly decent!

You're probably seeing a lot of Peter Szondi these days; please send him my most heartfelt regards.

Gretel and I are doing quite well, aside from the idiotic trouble with the Benjamin affair. The rough draft of my next big book is complete, and, despite the aggravation, I am also getting a lot done otherwise.

Hopefully Fanja has fully recovered now; perhaps you'd be so kind as to write and let me know.

To you and her all that is cordial, also from Gretel

your old and loyal
Teddie Adorno

Original: typescript with printed letterhead; Gershom Scholem Archive, The National Library of Israel, Jerusalem.

a war is being waged . . . by a vulgar Marxist leaflet that goes by the name of alternative: The journal *alternative: Zeitschrift für Literatur und Diskussion* dedicated a double issue (nos. 56/57, October/December 1967) to Walter Benjamin's writings and their literary legacy. It thus continued the discussion about Benjamin's literary legacy that was started by the publication of Heißenbüttel's article in *Merkur* (no. 21, 1967). In her introduction to the issue, the editor, Hildegard Brenner, writes the following:

> Walter Benjamin, destitute and forcibly exiled since 1933, took his own life while fleeing from fascist thugs in 1940. The posthumous fame achieved by his work is due to the efforts of the Suhrkamp Verlag and, above all, to Theodor W. Adorno, who – upon returning to Germany – prepared the editions of Benjamin's selected works and letters (the latter with Gershom Scholem). Adorno, who, along with Max Horkheimer, co-directed the Institute for Social Research (then in New York) was, at the time, engaged in a controversy with Benjamin – a stipend holder from the Institute. Adorno's double role, as both an opponent in this controversy and as Benjamin's editor, is problematic. To this day, it gives rise to ceaseless speculations about whether the edition, in fact, conceals the differences between them.
>
> With the publication of the two-volume collection of letters, the charge that the literary estate had been manipulated was raised publicly – most pointedly by Helmut Heißenbüttel. . . . The materials collected in the Benjamin archive in Frankfurt are marked as "private property" (Tiedemann, 1965, p. 212). Adorno justifies this with reference to a letter from Benjamin sent from the internment camp at Lourdes. Very

belatedly, it became known that a substantial part of Benjamin's estate is publicly accessible in the state archive of the GDR at Potsdam. The fact that these papers include Walter Benjamin's only known will could create a new legal situation that might support the public usage of the Frankfurt holdings as well (p. 185).

Ms. Brenner: In 1964, the literary scholar Hildegard Brenner (b. 1927) took over the editorship of the journal *Alternative: Blätter für Lyrik und Prosa* and changed the journal's name to *alternative: Zeitschrift für Literatur und Diskussion*. She was co-editor of the journal until 1982. From 1971 to 1978 she was professor of literature and German studies at the University of Bremen.

Above all, this means a text by Tiedemann, which is highly decent!: See Rolf Tiedemann, "Zur 'Beschlagnahme' Walter Benjamins oder Wie man mit der Philologie Schlitten fährt" [On the "confiscation" of Walter Benjamin, or how to play fast and loose with philology], *Das Argument*, 10/46 (1967), pp. 74–93. In his article, Tiedemann refers to the issue of *alternative* dedicated to Benjamin, as well as Heißenbüttel's critique of the selected correspondence. Among other things, he presents a table juxtaposing the arguments put forth by Heißenbüttel and *alternative* with factually accurate accounts of the situation. Tiedemann concludes his article as follows: "There remains much to debate about Marxism: both about Benjamin's Marxism, which is problematic enough, and about the Marxism of the Marxist, which is no less problematic. What is not debatable, though, is the Marxism of the *alternative*, for it isn't one. It is a bizarre form of leftist opportunism which unsuccessfully attempted to enter into a coalition with philology" (p. 93).

You're probably seeing a lot of Peter Szondi these days: Peter Szondi was visiting professor of literature at the Hebrew University in Jerusalem from January to April 1968 (see letter no. 157 in this volume). Szondi wrote the following to Gershom and Fanja Scholem after he left Jerusalem at the beginning of April 1968: "I had a wonderful time with you and I was touched that you so calmly, lovingly, and ironically put up with my unstable mood, for which Israel is not to blame." See Peter Szondi, *Briefe*, ed. Christoph König and Thomas Sparr (Frankfurt am Main: Suhrkamp, 1993), p. 247.

201 SCHOLEM TO ADORNO
JERUSALEM, 8.2.1968

Jerusalem
8.2.68

Dear Adorno,

Your letter concerning the Benjamin quarrels, which I received a few days ago, concerned me greatly; less because of its substance – I'm aware of the facts through the issue of *alternative* (which I own) – than because of the strong emotional response that it appears to have provoked in you. I did not take the whole matter anywhere near as seriously as you did. This includes the essays by Heißenbüttel and Peter Hamm, which are, in part, blatantly malicious and written with the intention of hurting you. To the extent that you saw fit to answer such things at all, of course, I would have thought it right of you to respond to Heißenbüttel's insinuations, which began this whole thing. The letter you sent him was far too gentle. However, as things stand, it surely wouldn't be right to testify to your philosophical legitimacy as a reader of Benjamin. This would seem very misguided to me since nobody doubts that this is not what lies at the centre of the attack; above all, because one can – *bona fide* and legitimately – disagree on the interpretation of Benjamin's thoughts and writings as much as about the assessment of his biography. On this point, it absolutely cannot be a case of positing some particular reading as conclusive or "official," as your detractors write – even if one of us were to consider it as necessarily correct. You yourself have never done so in your writings. The malice lies in other allegations, among which the philosophical is only relevant at the point where you – grotesquely – appear as an anti-Marxist who found Benjamin's Marxism unsuitable, rather than as a Marxist to whom Benjamin's Marxism appeared insufficiently thought through. The fact – which is, indeed, on record – that, from our very different vantage points, we converged on some of our objections to Benjamin's statements, or to his basic *approach**, as we have formulated it, has made it possible for your detractors to confound matters in a way that is convenient for them. That is, they have jumbled my criticisms, which admittedly come from an avowed non-Marxist, and yours, which are those of an avowed Marxist; and they have done so in a manner that allows certain phrases, such as those directed against me by Heißenbüttel, suddenly to apply to you – for instance in the last piece that I received from Werner Kraft: an essay by W. Schütte, published in the *Frankfurter Rundschau*. I don't believe that, in this matter, it would be seriously significant, or even tactically prudent, for me to comment on your objective philosophical qualifications. I neither believe that you need such a recommendation nor that your critics have any doubts in this regard. In truth, several things are being confused here. I see three lines of attack. Of these I feel genuinely competent to comment only on one, about which there can be no controversy; there is another line of attack, however, where legitimate disagreement is possible.

1. Objections against your editing and selection of Benjamin's writings. On this point you are accused of being tendentious, by apparently omitting things in the original edition of Benjamin's writings in order to push the Marxist essays into the background.

In fairness, I cannot comment on this, except – should it be necessary – by saying that I saw, and probably approved, the list of texts suggested for inclusion (to the extent that I recall). At the time, though, Suhrkamp's limit of 1,200 pages for the final edition would have weighed significantly on the considerations as to what should be included. As far as I recall, I explicitly approved the selection. I was not consulted on the edition and selection of subsequent publications of Benjamin's writings. As for related attacks, such as the charge that you did not allow Benjamin's texts to be published unaltered (as claimed in *alternative*, p. 197): only you, or someone who knows the texts in question, can comment on this. Perhaps Tiedemann has already done so in the response that you mention, which I don't yet know.

2. Attacks on the edition of letters and the allegedly tendentious process both of selection and commentary. Here Heißenbüttel's remarks are very careful, ambiguous, and hypothetically general. Namely, he refrained from positing any concrete restrictions of an objective sort in the selection process; rather, he put forward the thesis that, for both of us, the confrontation with Benjamin was still, to this day, so alive that it carried through to the preface and also prevailed in the fact that we included certain important letters to Benjamin that were critical of him. This argument, in itself, is debatable, but then he makes particular claims about the specific coloring that you impart to your interpretation of Benjamin, which he attacks, but which are in no way directly related to his polemic against the mode of selection. The lines on p. 240 of Heißenbüttel's *Merkur* essay are decisive for this point. There's a hodgepodge of very different claims here: malicious ones, such as the suggestion of a "reinterpretation, whereby the surviving, controversial correspondent enforces his view." This carefully but intangibly insinuates that you or I suppressed Benjamin's rejoinders to our criticisms, although the author was careful not to say this explicitly – and factually, this claim is entirely untrue. Or other claims, such as the one that you or I interpret Benjamin's body of work as a continuity, which he deems to be impermissible. In fact, we both do interpret Benjamin's work as a continuity, each in our own very personal ways. In my opinion, the attempts by Heißenbüttel, Hamm, and others to argue the converse [i.e., that Benjamin's work takes a turn after his adoption of Marxism] are quite unconvincing and surely also, in part, factually inaccurate; but, as such, they are debatable. This could very well be the subject of an objective discussion – a kind of disputation or symposium, or some

other format. I believe that I've said what I think on this matter in my *Neue Rundschau* essay. You too have said your piece at several points, using formulations that I wouldn't always back fully, although that is irrelevant for the polemic in question. Hamm was the first to vulgarize Heißenbüttel's views in his piece in the *Frankfurter Hefte*. Without providing any kind of evidence of his own, he made out as if Heißenbüttel had proven, or otherwise made it seem probable, that the selection of the letters was subject to anti-Marxist censorship – something that, in truth, Heißenbüttel was careful not to do. The mendacious claims made subsequently in the issue of *alternative* are based on Hamm; they too do not provide any concrete evidence that specifically Marxist statements were omitted from the letters.

3. The attack on the interpretations of Benjamin proffered by the "harmonists" and reactionaries, which presumably means you and me. For the most part, these attacks bracket me out, as someone who – for obvious reasons – is of little concern to the authors and, as such, is not the target of their *ressentiment*. Rather, the attacks are directed principally against you. In particular, they seem to express a long pent-up rage and deep *ressentiment* at your lack of Marxist activism, and possibly at your place in German intellectual life more generally. The lack of sympathy for Brecht's influence on Benjamin, which we both hold in common, presumably played a significant role here. The whole discussion [about Brecht's influence on Benjamin] is, however, by its nature, legitimate, and could still take place, even if all the misrepresentations and perversions that Tiedemann has probably addressed in his response were to be eliminated, or if they hadn't been put into play at all. To tell you the truth, the quality of Benjamin's writings in his last ten years is such that I'm convinced that it's not possible to advance a conclusive interpretation of these sometimes very vaguely formulated thoughts. Even within the issue of *alternative* itself, the contributors present radically inconsistent interpretations. The essay by Holz, for example, keeps the continuity of Benjamin's thinking firmly in view, and even defends it (just as you and I do, although he doesn't name us explicitly). As such, it differs radically from the other published contributions.

What do I conclude from all this? If the Suhrkamp Verlag is interested in clarifying the spurious accusations directed against the edition of Benjamin's letters, for which I know myself to be in part responsible, then there are plenty of ways to handle this. In my estimation, the best solution would be to stage something like a public panel discussion about the edition of the letters, in which the two of us would face one of the gentlemen who are spreading these accusations. In the first instance, one would have to invite Mr. Heißenbüttel, in order to force him to respond unambiguously to a number of clearly formulated questions regarding what exactly is entailed by his allegations against the volume of letters. If the framing were to be broader, I could equally well imagine a conversation about the interpretation of Benjamin more generally. But this is not a matter in which your, or mine, or the Suhrkamp Verlag's integrity and reputation are at stake. I could also imagine such a conversation being broadcast on the radio. In any case, if my presence were desired, then such an event would have to take place at a time when I am in Europe, or, more specifically, in Frankfurt. In this case, I could pay for an ad hoc trip to Frankfurt with the prospective fee from a broadcaster or a possible subsidy from Suhrkamp – I wouldn't want to profit from such an engagement. It would have to be ascertained whether the Hessischer Rundfunk and, above all, the publishers would be sufficiently interested to make such a 3 or 4 day trip desirable and and therefore feasible. I'd welcome it if you could explore this option for me, for which I would gladly make myself available. Either way, it would be good if you could send me Tiedemann's essay for reference. If the general interest among the intelligentsia is really so great, then presumably other broadcasters would also air such a debate. By the way: if an acceptable representative of the opposing party cannot be found, because they are trying to avoid a direct confrontation with us, then one could also invite an independent discussant – that is, somebody who's not involved in the polemics in question. Surely such a person should exist.

I haven't spoken out publicly about the claims made in *alternative* regarding the Benjamin estate and similar matters, since I didn't want to adversely impact the prospect of the Suhrkamp Verlag or myself receiving copies – in part or in full – of the materials collected in Potsdam. If I publicly declare that the archive in Potsdam hasn't followed through on the assurances they gave me, and that they haven't responded to my letters at all, then naturally the chances of obtaining the materials that I saw there at the time are nullified. Anyway, I did tell Boehlich that the publisher should demand photographs of all the materials. Of course, the question is whether the publisher's specific stake in Brecht and his connections to East Berlin could conflict with their stake in Benjamin. I don't think that the GDR people have anything to gain by referring to Benjamin's will, since it would force them to admit that both the will and the accompanying suicide note to Egon Wissing explicitly name me as the real, "legitimate" heir – not only in terms of the right of disposition but also materially speaking.

Obviously they will never hand over the materials; and, unless they explicitly admit this, there's no way of forcing them to do so. If I were to take legal measures, which, in the interest of the matter, I cannot do, they would no doubt refer to some law which stipulates that culturally significant materials – and Benjamin's estate could easily be declared as such – cannot leave the territory of the GDR. Stefan is by no means named the executor of the estate in the will, but is designated, rather, as the inheritor of Benjamin's library – at least insofar as the books are not specifically bequeathed to other friends who are named therein. I am to be granted total disposition over the estate and any income generated from it. This also explicitly includes the estate of the Heinle brothers. Of course Benjamin did not expect any such income from the writings that had been published as of 1932. He did request, however, that I entrust part or all of his estate to the Hebrew University. Naturally, Mrs. Heise's guarded silence on these matters fueled Mr. Schütte's ignorance, as well as his false assumptions. Nevertheless, it is clear that publicly debating the will won't help our efforts to obtain the materials from Potsdam.

That's all for today. Szondi is staying on the top floor of our building, where a two-room apartment has just become available. We see him every day.

I may be in Europe at the start of June – that is, if I wind up taking part in a meeting of the Union Academique Internationale in Brussels on the 10th of June, since they would cover my travel expenses. I am not planning to leave here before then. In that case, I could stop off in Frkft. on Friday and Saturday (7–8 June) to discuss all relevant matters with you and the people at Suhrkamp – even if you don't think that the plans I outline above are feasible or advisable.

An earlier meeting to discuss any of the above would have to be agreed upon with a view to my *timetable** here.

If Tiedemann's essay has come out in the meantime, I'd ask you to send it to me by airmail.

In the meantime, all that is cordial to you both.

Yours,

Gerhard Scholem

The methods employed by *Alternative* or P. Hamm vividly remind me of Kurzweil's polemics against me.

Original: typescript / manuscript; Theodor W. Adorno Archive, Frankfurt am Main.

* Original in English.

Peter Hamm: See Peter Hamm, "Unter den Neuerern der Wichtigste" [The most sigificant among the innovators], *Frankfurter Hefte*, 22/5 (1967), pp. 359–64.

The letter you sent him was far too gentle: On the 14th of March 1967 Adorno had written the following to Helmut Heißenbüttel:

> Dear Mr. Heißenbüttel,
> I found your essay on Benjamin's letters upon returning from a conference held by the *Studienstiftung* [(German national) academic foundation] in Dhaun, and you won't be surprised to learn that it caused me quite a shock. The fact that, on reflection, I was not as hurt as one ought to be, if one is not a saint, has a simple reason. I believe that the passages referring to difficulties between Benjamin and me genuinely stem from misunderstandings, which I can easily clear up. . . . What is central, however, is a clarification of the misconception that I somehow wanted to suppress Benjamin's Marxist and Brechtian things. The truth of the matter is that, at the time, I had only a limited scope for the two-volume edition of the writings. Since Benjamin entrusted me with managing his literary estate, all I could do was to include in the edition those things that seemed most important to me. If I'd had anything else in mind, even the slightest retouching, then surely I would have never given my permission for the separate publication of the texts relating to Brecht; nor would I have co-edited the collection of letters. Surely that speaks for itself.
>
> As for the Baudelaire essay, which I criticized at the time: I am currently preparing it for publication in the *Neue Rundschau*. My criticism notwithstanding, the original essay was not printed in the *Zeitschrift für Sozialforschung*; what was finally printed there was not a corrected version but something else entirely. I believe that when the original piece is published, there will be no doubt as to why I criticized it.
>
> You seem to suspect that, for whatever reasons, I wanted to suppress Benjamin's Marxist intentions. However, my motive in this controversy was far more complex. While, on the one hand, I defended Benjamin's metaphysical impulses against himself, I tried, on the other hand, to defend dialectical materialism against him – which he seemed to me to be misconstruing by way of a short-circuit. Not only him, but also Brecht. I consider myself to be an exacting connoisseur of Marx's work, which you implicitly concede. As such, I could not overlook the fact that, while Benjamin was committed to Marxism, he hadn't understood the essential content of Marx's theory. God knows, I have a sufficiently high estimation of Brecht's merits; but his ignorance of Marxism – down to the best-known things, such as the theory of surplus value – was quite indescribable. Neither of them had studied Marx's works in earnest. Rather, to adapt what Hobbes once said about religion, they had swallowed it like a pill. In contrast to the materialist dialectic as a theory, their Marxism seemed heteronymous and irrational to me, which is precisely what I found worrisome. Had Benjamin really gained an understanding of the latter, it would have improved his own conception of

> Marxism. . . . My suggestion would be for you and me to debate these matters on the radio, thus giving me a chance to set the record straight. . . . With respect to the theoretical side of things, I might ask you to have a look at *Negative Dialectics*. It marks the attempt to express both metaphysical and materialist intentions in a way that is as radically free from all idealism as can be imagined. Paradoxically enough, at the same time that I read your essay, I received a letter from Scholem, in which he polemicizes, in a friendly way, against my book's materialism. (Carbon copy of typescript: Theodor W. Adorno Archive, Frankfurt am Main)

W. Schütte . . . in the Frankfurter Rundschau: See Wolfram Schütte, "Eingriffe? Es geht um Walter Benjamin" [Interventions? Concerning Walter Benjamin], *Frankfurter Rundschau* no. 16, 19 January 1968, p. 8. Schütte claimed that "the publication of Walter Benjamin's far-flung writings was not only deficient; it was deliberately only partially published in order to advance an 'esoteric' interpretation that is accessible only to a circle of initiates." Schütte's piece was reprinted in the April/June edition of *alternative* in 1968 (p. 86). The issue polemically continued the debate surrounding Benjamin in view of plans for the publication of a critical edition of his writings.

the charge that you did not allow Benjamin's texts to be published unaltered (as claimed in alternative, p. 197): Two versions of Benjamin's text "Theorien des deutschen Faschismus: Zu der Sammelschrift *Krieg und Krieger*, herausgegeben von Ernst Jünger" (1930) [Theories of German fascism: on the collection of essays *War and Warrior*, edited by Ernst Jünger (1930)] appear on p. 197 of the Benjamin-themed issue of *alternative*. Under the heading "Text Rekonstruktionen" [Textual reconstructions], the editors included a passage from the original version of the text, which was first published in the journal *Die Gesellschaft* in 1930, alongside an abridged version, which was reprinted in *Das Argument* in 1964. The editor of *alternative* writes that, in the later version, "the final line of the text was omitted following pressure from the archive in Frankfurt." The passage printed in *alternative* reads:

> The war that this light exposes is as little the "eternal" one which these new Germans now worship as it is the "final" war that the pacifists carry on about. In reality, that war is only this: the one, fearful, last chance to correct the incapacity of peoples to order their relationships to one another in accord with the relationship they possess to nature through their technology. If this corrective effort fails, millions of human bodies will indeed inevitably be chopped to pieces and chewed up by iron and gas. But even the habitués of the chthonic forces of terror, who carry their volumes of Klages in their packs, will not learn one-tenth of what nature promises its less idly curious but more sober children, who possess in technology not a fetish of doom but a key to happiness.

The omitted final lines read: "They will demonstrate this sobriety the moment they refuse to acknowledge the next war as an incisive magical turning point, and instead discover in it the image of everyday actuality. And they will demonstrate it when they use their discovery to transform this war into civil war, and thereby perform that Marxist trick which alone is a match for this sinister runic nonsense." See Walter Benjamin, "Theories of German Fascism: On the Collection of Essays *War and Warrior*, edited by Ernst Jünger," in *Selected Writings*, Vol. 2.1: *1927–1930*, ed. Michael W. Jennings, Howard Eiland and Gary Smith (Cambridge, MA: The Belknap Press of Harvard University Press, 2005), pp. 312–21. The passage above is taken from pp. 319–21. On Adorno's response, see letter no. 202 in this volume.

The lines on p. 240 of Heißenbüttel's Merkur *essay*: p. 240 of Heißenbüttel's essay reads: "In the Preface, the materialist method is reinterpreted as a vague image category: the non-binding nature of interpreting the work aphoristically is thus accepted, the late historical-political themes are immediately reinterpreted in light of the early theological ones, etc. The work appears through a reinterpretation, whereby the surviving, controversial correspondent enforces his view."

my Neue Rundschau *essay*: See Gershom Scholem, "Walter Benjamin," *Neue Rundschau*, Vol. 76 (1965), pp. 1–21; repr. In *Judaica 2* (Frankfurt am Main: Suhrkamp, 1970), pp. 193–227. For an English translation, see Scholem, "Walter Benjamin," in *On Jews and Judaism in Crisis*, ed. Werner J. Dannhauser (New York: Schocken Books, 1976), pp. 172–97. See also letter no. 146 in this volume.

The essay by Holz: See Hans Heinz Holz, "Philosophie als Interpretation: Thesen zum theologischen Horizont der Metaphysik Benjamins" [Philosophy as interpretation: theses on the theological horizon of Benjamin's metaphysics], in *alternative*, nos. 56/57 (October/ December 1967), pp. 235–42.

a public panel discussion: Adorno noted "main point" in pencil next to these words.

I'd welcome it if you could explore this option for me, for which I would gladly make myself available: A radio broadcast of Adorno and Scholem discussing Walter Benjamin never took place.

since I didn't want to adversely impact the prospect of . . . receiving copies . . . of the materials collected in Potsdam: See Scholem, "Preface," in *The Correspondence of Walter Benjamin and Gershom Scholem, 1932–1940*, ed. Gershom Scholem, trans. Gary Smith and Andre Lefevere (New York: Schocken Books, 1989), p. 5. See also Scholem, *Walter Benjamin: The Story of a Friendship*, trans. Harry Zohn (New York: NYRB Classics, 2003), pp. 245–6.

suicide note to Egon Wissing: See Walter Benjamin's letter, written in Nice and dated the 27th of July 1932, in *Walter Benjamin: Gesammelte Briefe IV, 1931-1934*, ed. Henri Lonitz and Christoph Gödde (Frankfurt am Main: Suhrkamp, 1998), pp. 117–22.

the estate of the Heinle brothers: See letters nos. 11 and 41 in this volume. The estate of the Heinle brothers, which Benjamin had to leave behind in

Berlin in 1933, has mostly been lost, aside from a handful of letters and manuscripts.

Mrs. Heise: The Benjamin themed issue of the journal *alternative* includes an interview by the editor, Hildegard Brenner, with the literary scholar Rosemarie Heise (1927–2014). At the time, Heise was researching the parts of Benjamin's literary estate that were stored at the central archive of the GDR, in Potsdam. Heise was the editor of the journal *Junge Kunst*, the publication of the central committee of the Freie deutsche Jugend [Free German Youth] in the GDR, as well as the journal *NDL*, the publication of the Deutscher Schriftstellerverband [Association of German Writers] in the GDR. From 1972 to 1976 she was a research associate in the department of performing arts at the Akademie der Künste [The academy of arts] in East Berlin. In 1971 she edited and published the first edition of Benjamin's writings in the GDR: Walter Benjamin, *Das Paris des Second Empire bei Baudelaire* [The Paris of the Second Empire in Baudelaire], (Berlin and Weimar: Aufbau, 1971). Rosemarie Heise was married to Wolfgang Heise (1925–1987), one of the most important philosophers in the GDR.

202 ADORNO TO SCHOLEM
FRANKFURT AM MAIN, 20.2.1968

PROF. DR. THEODOR W. ADORNO

6 FRANKFURT AM MAIN
KETTENHOFWEG 123
20 February 1968

Dear Scholem,

Please accept my sincerest thanks for your letter, which shows such a degree of love in the thoroughness with which you respond to the campaign concerning Benjamin that it has truly done me good.

You are certainly right in saying that my response to Heißenbüttel was too gentle. To account for this, I can only note the fact that he and I had a very friendly relationship for quite some time. Among other things, I had secured the lectureship in poetics for him here. Besides, he backed down in his letter, and granted me the possibility of responding to the matter at hand. However, I did not take him up on his offer – probably because I had the instinct that I'd be entering into a treacherous situation if I were to defend myself in a matter that is so unfounded and absurd that it offers no grounds for a defence. Of course, it never occurred to me to establish my own view of Benjamin as the official one, in a Bayreuthian manner. Nevertheless, I think that the question of what Benjamin's Marxism was about is decidable. I completely agree with you that the polemic stems from rancor over the fact that I'm not running around shouting Ho Chi Minh, rather than from any genuine, objective interest in Benjamin.

Meanwhile, the *Frankfurter Rundschau* published a concise and superb essay by Tiedemann – a retort to the last piece by Schütte. I'd almost like to believe that his response has settled this side of the matter. The short essay, if anything, is better and more effective than the long one, which is coming out in *Argument* in early March. As far as I know, however, a further attack is looming from the most unexpected direction, namely a piece by Hannah Arendt in *Merkur*; but I'll take that as it comes.

As to what the best course of action is now, we discussed this at a very long meeting at Unseld's place last Friday. In addition to Unseld, the participants were Tiedemann, Schweppenhäuser, my teaching assistant Kulenkampff, the outstanding Germanist Mautz, Boehlich and Michel from Suhrkamp, and, finally, Gretel and myself. With the exception of Boehlich, the dominant view was that it would be wrong of me to meet for a discussion with the likes of Brenner. This is consistent with my own reaction. By extension, this also applies to you, of course. The unanimous opinion was that a public panel discussion on the edition of the letters would not be opportune at present. Should the situation change, making it necessary after all, then it could surely be organized during your visit to Europe. I myself will be in Switzerland from mid-July to the 20th of August before returning here; these dates could be negotiated, I assume. By contrast, a public discussion with our adversaries should take place on the Boehlich "level," as it is known locally.

Presumably you've gotten to see Tiedemann's little essay. I've asked him to send you the longer one right away.

Interest in the whole affair is, in fact, considerable, but it's motivated more by sensationalism than by the matter at hand. The only real difficulty I see concerns an aspect of Benjamin's attitude during his later years, especially after his emigration, to which you allude. He always maintained, in conversations with me, and surely with you as well, that he had absolutely no intention of letting go of his original, theological, and speculative-metaphysical motives, which probably found their most brilliant documentation in the first *Arcades* draft. This is confirmed even when one reads the historical-philosophical theses (Heinz Klaus Metzger wittily remarked to Tiedemann: it's just as well that the word dialectical materialism is frequently mentioned in the theses, since this mention is the only relation to materialism that in any way manifests itself in the theses). On the other hand, I don't think it's impossible, and perhaps it's even probable, that Benjamin – where his somewhat childlike strategy dictated – expressed himself as a hardened revolutionary in cruder terms to others, especially to

Brecht and Lacis, than he did to us. That's what these ladies and gentlemen may be referring to. It's not without its charm that a letter from Brecht now confirms my reasons for excluding the Fuchs essay from the collection at the time, namely: that Benjamin himself had a rather negative view of this essay. Brecht defended the essay against Benjamin and thus posthumously contributed to my defence. Another *trouvaille* of Tiedemann's is that, of all the pieces that Benjamin wrote on Brecht, the latter published only a single one – and this he honored only after endless hemming and hawing. You know that I've long been of the opinion that, while, on the one hand, Benjamin was in a certain thraldom vis-à-vis Brecht, on the other hand, he feared him; and he rightly sought, above all, to stave off Brecht's influence on his central works. That too remains to be documented by Tiedemann. Tiedemann recently spent a considerable amount of time with Mrs Lacis in East Berlin. However, she is subject to the clouding of her memory, evidently as a result of being imprisoned under Stalin, and she said some rather confused things. Nevertheless, Tiedemann seems to have convinced her not to provide any more support to Brenner. She seems to conflate all manner of occurrences: for instance, she credits herself with the fact that Benjamin went to Moscow instead of Jerusalem, but she in no way acknowledges – or remembers – that this was a visit of only a few weeks. After all, it is significant in this context that, while Benjamin intended to stay in Europe – a tragic error – ultimately, he decided to go to America and not to Russia. I specifically recall that he thought no differently than we did about the trials that were already taking place in Russia at the time.

During the big meeting at Unseld's place, a plan was drawn up for the new edition, the brunt of which will be borne by Tiedemann and his wife. Of course, you and I will also be involved – if only to avoid the impression that the publisher wants to disavow us. However, we will be spared the difficult philological questions surrounding the edition. You will receive a memorandum on the state of affairs soon.

I want to take this opportunity to encourage you to do something in connection with Benjamin, which no one but you could accomplish. It concerns Benjamin's relationship to Jewish mysticism. There can be no doubt that Benjamin, at least during his earlier period – up to and including the text about the translator – assumed Jewish mystical teachings as binding for his own work. They alone can provide the key to the theological writings from his youth, which, in part, are truly hermetic. For this purpose, however, one would really have to have insight into the Kabbalistic theorems that Benjamin drew on. Here, if I may permit myself to speak in terms of *Negative Dialectics*, no one but you would be able to lay the cards on the table. A piece of this sort would probably be the most important contribution imaginable for the interpretation of Benjamin, so I want to animate you, with all the vigor at my disposal, to consider this undertaking. For my part, I have taken it upon myself to write a a supremely encumbered philosophical introduction to the planned volume made up of the materials from the *Arcades* complex, edited by Tiedemann, as soon as the preparations are sufficiently advanced. Arguably, this is what, properly speaking, remains for me to do in this regard. I can hardly resist the impression that there is a peculiar analogy between the manner in which the late Benjamin accepted Marxism *hook and sink*,* as it were, and his earlier relationship to the Kabbalah, a source that was also not available to him first hand. It strikes me that this may be the place wherein the secret of this thinking lies buried.

Please send our warmest regards to Peter Szondi. A rumor is making the rounds here which suggests that Peter is negotiating a professorship in Jerusalem. Its source is Ernst Simon, whose brother I saw almost daily in Vienna. I would be very sad if he were to leave, but at the same time I can imagine that such a step would actually be for him something like the end of a permanent situation of emigration, which must be hard for him to bear. Needless to say, this remark is intended only for you, not for him.

To you and Fanja all the best, also from Gretel

your loyal

Teddie Adorno

Original: typescript with printed letterhead; Gershom Scholem Archive, The National Library of Israel, Jerusalem.

the lectureship in poetics: In 1963, Helmut Heißenbüttel held the endowed visiting professorship in poetics at the University of Frankfurt. His lectures were collected in Heißenbüttel, *Über Literatur* [On literature] (Olten and Freiburg im Breisgau: Klett-Cotta, 1966). A second edition was later published as *Über Literatur und Frankfurter Vorlesungen* [On literature and Frankfurt lectures] (Munich: DTV, 1972). See also Heißenbüttel, *Über Benjamin* [On Benjamin] (Frankfurt am Main: Suhrkamp, 2008).

Frankfurter Rundschau ... *essay by Tiedemann*: On the 7th of February 1968, the *Frankfurter Rundschau* published Rolf Tiedemann's essay "In Sachen Benjamin: Vorläufige Entgegnung eines Benjamin-Mitherausgebers" [Concerning Benjamin: preliminary response from a Benjamin co-editor]. The article served as a response to the pieces by Wolfram Schütte and Siegfried Unseld ("Zur Kritik an den Editionen Walter Benjamins" [On the critique of the Walter Benjamin editions], 24.1.1968); to the editorial team of the *Frankfurter Rundschau* ("In Sachen Benjamin" [Concerning Benjamin], 25.1.1968); and to the editorial team of the journal *alternative* ("In Sachen

* Original in English.

Benjamin: Entgegnung der Zeitschrift *alternative* auf Siegfried Unselds Darstellung" [Concerning Benjamin: response from the journal *alternative* to Siegfried Unseld's portrayal], 29.1.1968). In this essay, Tiedemann confronts some of the accusations made by the editors of the journal *alternative*, especially the charge that the collected writings contain "numerous omissions" which were supposed to have unilaterally determined and willfully manipulated Benjamin's image. Moreover, it confronted the claim that the will, which had been found in the central archive of the GDR in Potsdam, changed the legal status of Benjamin's estate (see letter no. 172 in this volume and Editor's Introduction, p. xxxvii in this volume). As Tiedemann wrote, the suggestion that "the 1932 will shows that Benjamin wished to make his materials public is incorrect. It is correct that the will names Gershom Scholem as the heir of the literary estate with the explicit right to manage it. It is true, moreover, that, shortly before his death, Benjamin put in writing his wish for Adorno to act as the custodian of his estate – a wish that was honored by Benjamin's son. Finally, it is correct that, since the 1955 edition of the *Schriften* (see p. xxvii in that volume), Scholem and Adorno have cooperated on the edition of Benjamin's work."

The short essay, if anything, is better and more effective than the long one, which is coming out in Argument in early March: See letter no. 200 in this volume.

Hannah Arendt in Merkur: See Hannah Arendt, "Walter Benjamin I: Der Buckelige" [Walter Benjamin I: The hunchback], *Merkur*, 22/238 (January/February 1968), pp. 50–60; "Walter Benjamin II: Die finsteren Zeiten" [Walter Benjamin II: The dark times], *Merkur*, 22/239 (March 1968), pp. 209–23; "Walter Benjamin III: Der Perlentaucher" [Walter Benjamin III: The pearl diver], *Merkur*, 22/240 (April 1968), pp. 305–15. An expanded version of these essays was later published as "Walter Benjamin: 1892–1940," trans. Harry Zohn, in *Men in Dark Times* (San Diego: Harcourt, 1968), pp. 153–206.

my teaching assistant Kulenkampff: In 1969, Arend Kulenkampff (b. 1936) completed his doctoral thesis, titled *Antinomie und Dialektik: Zur Funktion des Widerspruchs in der Philosophie* [Antinomy and dialectics: on the function of contradiction in philosophy]. A book based on his thesis, bearing the same title, was published by J. B. Metzler of Stuttgart one year later.

the outstanding Germanist Mautz: The literary scholar and writer Kurt Mautz (1911–2000) had been a student of Adorno's in Frankfurt in the period before 1933. In 1936 he completed his doctorate at the University of Giessen with a thesis titled *Die Philosophie Max Stirners im Gegensatz zum Hegelschen Idealismus* [Max Stirner's philosophy in contrast to Hegel's idealism]. After the war he worked as an adjunct lecturer and high school teacher in Frankfurt and Mainz and wrote studies on Georg Heym, Adalbert Stifter, and expressionism, as well as novels and poems.

Michel: The writer Karl Markus Michel (1929–2000) worked at the Institute for Social Research from 1955 to 1958. From 1961 he was an editor for the Suhrkamp Verlag.

Heinz Klaus Metzger: The music theorist Heinz-Klaus Metzger (1932–2009) had studied composition, first in Paris, with Schoenberg's student Max Deutsch, and later at the Städtische Akademie für Tonkunst [Municipal Academy for Musical Arts] in Darmstadt with Rudolf Kolisch. He got to know Adorno in 1950, when he took part in the Darmstadt (formerly Kranichstein) *Ferienkurse für Neue Musik* [Summer Courses for New Music]. He and Adorno corresponded extensively. From the 1950s, Metzger worked as a music critic, in which capacity he promoted a radical concept of progress in music.

Fuchs essay: See Walter Benjamin, "Eduard Fuchs, Collector and Historian," in *Selected Writings*, Vol. 3: *1935–1938*, ed. Howard Eiland and Michael W. Jennings (Cambridge, MA: The Belknap Press of Harvard University Press, 2002), pp. 260–302. Brecht's letter to Benjamin (c. April/ May 1937) reads as follows: "I re-read your study of Eduard Fuchs and I liked it even better this time. You may take this nonchalantly, but I think that it's precisely your moderate interest in the subject that has made this piece so economical. There is no decoration here, but everything is decorous (in the good old sense of the word) and the spiral is never elongated through a mirror. You always stay on topic, or the topic stays on you." See Bertolt Brecht, *Werke*, Vol. 29: *Briefe 2: 1937–1949*, ed. Günter Glaeser et al. (Frankfurt am Main: Suhrkamp, 1998), p. 29.

Tiedemann and his wife: The literary scholar Hella Tiedemann-Bartels (1936–2016) co-edited the edition of Benjamin's *Gesammelte Schriften* [Collected Writings]. Together with Rolf Tiedemann and Hermann Schweppenhäuser, she edited the third volume, *Kritiken und Rezensionen* [Critiques and reviews], in 1972. From 1984 to 2001, Tiedemann-Bartels was adjunct professor in the Department of General and Comparative Literary Studies at the Freie Universität Berlin. See Scholem's letter to Hella Tidemann-Bartels from the 5th of October 1972 in Scholem, *Briefe III: 1971–1982*, ed. Itta Shedletzky (Munich: C. H. Beck, 1999), p. 36.

up to . . . the text about the translator: See Walter Benjamin, "The Task of the Translator," in *Selected Writings*, Vol. 1: *1913–1926*, ed. Marcus Bullow and Michael W. Jennings (Cambridge, MA: The Belknap Press of Harvard University Press, 1996), pp. 253–63.

the planned volume made up of the materials from the Arcades *complex, edited by Tiedemann*: The two-volume edition of *Das Passagenwerk* [The Arcades Project] was first published only in 1982, thirteen years after Adorno's death.

203 SCHOLEM TO ADORNO
JERUSALEM, 29.2.1968

Jerusalem, 29.2.1968

Dear Adorno,

I received your letter of the 20th of February with pleasure. I will express my thoughts regarding the Benjamin edition in a letter to Unseldt, of which I'll send you a copy. I have various comments on the matter, and, before I commit to anything, I suspect that further discussion with the publishers will be required whenever I am next in Europe. It's entirely possible, albeit not certain, that I will be in Germany for a few days during the second half of May, at which point we could get together in Frankfurt for a day. Unfortunately you don't mention whether you'll also be in Sils in August, where we could meet with greater leisure.

Regarding Hanna Arendt's essay, it will be best to reserve judgment until the whole thing is out. In the first piece one finds, intermingled, an addiction to originality (Benjamin is not a philosopher!!!), misunderstandings, and debatable claims of the sort that can, at any rate, be discussed. As is so often the case with her writing, the first characteristic predominates. Obviously the essay was carefully completed before the new smear campaign began; that much is clear from the annotations, which were evidently added afterwards. I would have expected the essay to strike a far more spiteful tone in its treatment of you – I was actually surprised – but perhaps the worst is yet to come. I find Heißenbüttel's latest pages to be far more scandalous. I intend to write to Mr. Paeschke, who sent me a copy, about the outrageous statement concerning your "zeal to publish."

What you write about Tiedemann's conversations with Asja Lacis is interesting. Her memory is totally muddled. She's making associations that are out sync with any chronology. Benjamin went to Moscow in 1926, when the question of Jerusalem was still by no means pressing – it first became serious in the summer of 1927. As Tiedemann told me, she also made completely nonsensical claims about Benjamin's supposed publications in Russia. It's no wonder, given her lot.

As to your wish that I write something about Benjamin's relation to Jewish mysticism, you've already made this suggestion to me several times; I remember that we had a conversation about this topic once before in Sils. It seems highly doubtful to me that the Kabbalah is the key to the theological writings from his youth, but I would be happy to discuss this with you again in more detail.

I conveyed your regards to Szondi. I don't think there's anything to the rumors that he's negotiating a professorship in Jerusalem. That's something I would know. There would be interest in him here, but I do not believe that it would be reciprocated. Some kind of dark drive within him gave him the positive momentum – which is otherwise highly unusual for him – to come here. But he is surrounded by such an air of isolation, of unwillingness to step outside of himself – such a tendency toward depression, and a lack of direct engagement with things – that it weighs on those of us who deal with him frequently. Others notice it too. This appears to be the onset of a dreadful, deeply rooted feeling of guilt, exacerbated precisely by contact with a Jewish society, toward which he feels guilty, since he was saved – at the expense of others, he feels – on the famous Kastner train of 1944. This eats at him more than one might think. He finds it hard to open up to others. Nearly the only time he speaks to us with passion is when he discusses the student affairs in Berlin. Next week he and I are traveling to Tiberias, where I will show him some of the Kabbalistic holy sites. Some of it is bound to sink in somehow. Surely this can't be formulated any less determinately. In short, he's a highly gifted, complicated, and thoroughly unhappy man. This is just between the two of us.

Cordial regards to you both

yours,

Gerhard Scholem

A copy of the letter to Unseld is enclosed.

Original: typescript, with a copy of Scholem's letter to Siegfried Unseld, dated 29.2.1968; Theodor W. Adorno Archive, Frankfurt am Main. An excerpt of this letter appears in translation in *Gershom Scholem: A Life in Letters*, ed. and trans. Anthony David Skinner (Cambridge, MA: Harvard University Press, 2002), pp. 432–3.

Unseldt: Scholem's spelling.

Hanna: Scholem's spelling.

Heißenbüttel's latest pages: Heißenbüttel published another statement on the continuing debate surrounding the reception of Benjamin in a section titled "Marginalien" [Marginalia], in the same issue of *Merkur* that contains the first part of Hannah Arendt's three-part Benjamin essay. See *Merkur*, 22/238 (January/ February 1968). Under the title "Zu Walter Benjamins Spätwerk" [On Walter Benjamin's late work] (pp. 179–85), he charges that, "despite his zeal to publish," Adorno is unwilling to make public Benjamin's "draft for a definition of art in the 20th century" which is said to lie hidden in the texts on Baudelaire.

saved . . . on the famous Kastner train of 1944: Scholem's spelling. Peter Szondi and his family were saved from the concentration camp at Bergen-Belsen as part of the "Kasztner agreement." Rudolf Kasztner was the leader of the Jewish organization *Va'adat Ha-Ezrah ve-ha-Hatzalah be-Budapesht* [Budapest Aid and Rescue Committee] from 1941 to 1945. An agreement between him and Adolf Eichmann enabled a selection of several thousand Hungarian Jews from Bergen-Belsen to be "bought out" and brought to Switzerland in exchange for trucks and other goods.

copy of the letter to Unseld:

Dear Mr. Unseld,
Thank you very much for your letter of the 23rd of February and for the transcript of the conversation on the 16th of February about the new edition of Benjamin's works. I have a lot to say about this edition, both about matters of principle and about technical aspects, and I fear that it won't be possible to explain these points sufficiently well in writing. I think it's urgently necessary for us to meet in Frankfurt to discuss these issues – as soon as I am in Germany. This might be the case as early as mid to late May. As things stand, I cannot commit to or promise anything; though, needless to say, I will gladly support you to the best of my ability. As for matters of principle: the way things stand, I am not sure whether anything that exists in print can be left out of such an edition, aside from collaborative translations completed with others. Perhaps you can convince me otherwise, but on this point I have deep reservations. As for the proposed titles: *Sämtliche Schriften* [Complete writings] or *Gesammelte Werke* [Collected works] – in contrast to the participants in your discussion, I would opt for *Sämtliche Werke* [Complete works]. This concerns not only the collection of reviews, in which the most unknown and forgotten material will be emphasized, but also the Baudelaire translations, which under no circumstances may be left out, as well as the radio lectures, radio plays, and novellas. I think that it would be disastrous to establish a principle of selection from the outset, which would quickly run into trouble. I am equally skeptical about the exclusion of diaries, to the extent that they have survived.

I am firmly of the opinion that only a chronological ordering of the materials can serve as the principle of publication for the various volumes in the collection. Under no circumstances should this principle be breached with respect to publication dates. The problem almost exclusively arises in the case of his writings up to 1927; thereafter, almost everything he wrote more or less coincides temporally with the date of publication. Essays of which there are several versions should, insofar as the differences are significant, be printed sequentially or in parallel to one another. Only relatively small divergences should be noted in the editorial apparatus. For instance, I would include both French versions of the Bachofen essay. I would also, at some point, print a German translation of the original French manuscript – in numerous places the Germanisms in his French are what allow Benjamin's intention to shine through.

I have reservations about describing his prose essays as "Lesestücke" [Reading passages]. This is a heading that I do not like at all. As for the scope: no limits should be prescribed at the outset. In the case of the letters, there can be no doubt that the edition was harmed by the fact that we were able to increase the scope only toward the end. We would have worked quite differently had we known from the start that we could have included more. For the *Arcades* book, in case there's any doubt, or a decision needs to be made, I would opt to include Benjamin's original texts over the excerpts that he collected from German and French authors. In my opinion, a situation in which such a decision would have to be made should be avoided by increasing the scope of the projected edition.

I cannot yet determine the cost of xeroxing the manuscripts that are in my possession. Conceivably, I could also bring certain pieces to Germany with me so that you can have them copied during my visit. I can't say anything specific on this point yet.

By the way, I'd like to join Adorno in his decision to forego any payment for my possible involvement. The only costs that you might incur on my behalf would be for transcripts, photocopies, or possible travel expenses.

What is meant by my involvement in the edition of the early writings would have to be clarified. I am no believer in "supplementary volumes" outside of the Benjamin edition. I also want to declare my diverging opinion regarding the radio lectures. Given Benjamin's genius in all matters relating to children, I believe that it is inconceivable to leave out his 20 or so lectures for the children's program, which are presently in Potsdam. Despite the fact that he wrote these lectures with the left hand, as it were, they nonetheless bear the unmistakable mark of his spirit – occasionally, in the most remarkable ways. I have read some of them. That is enough, for today, dear Mr. Unseld, to give you a rough view of my position. Also, for your information, I sent another reminder to the archive in Potsdam today repeating my request, first and foremost, for photos of my letters. I'm curious as to whether I'll receive a response. (Carbon copy of typescript: Theodor W. Adorno Archive, Frankfurt am Main)

204 SCHOLEM TO ADORNO
JERUSALEM, AFTER 7.3.1968

Dear Adorno,

Here's a <u>copy for you</u>, if you like.

Original: typescript with a copy of Scholem's letter to Hans Paeschke of the 7th of March, 1968; Theodor W. Adorno Archive, Frankfurt am Main.

copy for you: Scholem wrote:

> Dear Mr. Paeschke,
> Thank you very much for sending the first part of Hanna Arendt's essay. If possible, I hope you will also send me the subsequent parts by

airmail. I cannot yet make out what it's driving at. On closer inspection, the hypothesis that W. B. was not a philosopher amounts to little more than a reformulation – addicted to its own sense of originality – of what I (and Adorno) described more accurately in the opposite terms. I consider this to be little more than gimmickry. This is what comes out of most of her polemics (although some of them are surely up for debate). What is one to make of such a grotesque phrase as the one suggesting that we were of the opinion that W. B. "stopped thinking deeply, in an incomprehensible (to us) manner?" This is refuted in every document. But she seems to have a taste for such sonorous expressions, even if, when it comes to giving them a precise determination, they suddenly lose their meaning.

The charges against Tiedemann are entirely due to her (H.A.'s) own imprecision. For instance, consider the claim on p. 57: the entry in the index of the collected letters names Adorno as one of the present directors of the Frankfurt Institute, not as the director of the Institute in Geneva or New York during the 1930s, which he wasn't (as she would have precisely known had she looked into the matter). These polemics seem to crop up across the board – nobody wants to look too closely. One gets the impression that years of pent-up anger at Adorno, which must have some deeper reasons, are now being vented.

Why, in a German journal, must H. A. quote an English translation of my essay on Benjamin from the *Neue Rundschau*?? Is the *N.R.* not available to her?

Of course, the contrast between H. A.'s estimation and the polemic by Heissenbüttel, coming from the opposite corner, is amusing. I don't know my way around the new German literary landscape, with its intricate entanglements and *ressentiments* – perhaps this is why I am less of a target – but surely you will grant me a certain sense for tone; and I have to say that, quite aside from the objective value of his deductions, Heissenbüttel's tone is repulsive to me. I already felt this way about the semi-encoded insinuations in his first review, which also took aim at Adorno (I was only incidental here, since I am hardly a target for the up-and-coming defenders of Marxism). The misreadings and carefully formulated allegations effected therein surprised me even then. In addition to the recent publication of Heissenbüttel's second attack, the further coarsening of the conversation by new disputants reveals the general direction in which things are going. To be frank: I am very surprised that you, who have frequently published pieces by Adorno in *Merkur*, allowed the sentence on Adorno's "zeal to publish" (p. 184) to go to print. I do understand that it cannot be your business to check whether the information provided by your contributors is correct in every case, but are you not struck by this line's malicious tone? It gave me a jolt. Such wording gives a deeper insight into an author. One can legitimately disagree about interpretations of Benjamin's writings, and, when it occurred to me to publish a selection of letters, I sincerely thought that I was providing material for just such a discussion; and this is precisely because Benjamin's letters provide a running commentary on his life and work (it is completely untrue that the letters were censored[)]. I shudder when I read what has been done with them, however.

I will likely be in Germany for a few days in the third week of May, by invitation of the German-Israeli Society. If (as appears to be the plan) they host an event in Munich, during which I am to give a (harmless) lecture, then this would present a good opportunity for us to have a conversation. The dates are not up to me. I have merely indicated the period during which I am available. I would be very happy if this could be arranged.

With best regards,

Your very devoted Gershom Scholem.

(Carbon copy of typescript; Theodor W. Adorno Archive, Frankfurt am Main)

205 ADORNO TO SCHOLEM
FRANKFURT AM MAIN, 14.3.1968

PROF. DR. THEODOR W. ADORNO

6 FRANKFURT AM MAIN
KETTENHOFWEG 123
14 March 1968

Dear Scholem,

Please accept my most heartfelt thanks for your letter of the 29th of February, for the copy of your note to Unseld, and, *last but not least*,* for the copy of your letter to Paeschke. It is no exaggeration when I say that few things have brought me as much joy as the latter. It is not customary for men of our age to say such things, but this testimony of spontaneous solidarity touched me to the core – and you can believe me that I haven't exactly been spoiled with solidarity throughout this appalling affair. It is scarcely imaginable how suddenly alone one is when one becomes embroiled in a situation like this. It is just like the Latin phrase: *tempora si fuerint nubila, solus eris*. I am severely handicapped by the fact that certain decisive things cannot be said by me but must be said on my behalf by others. Horkheimer will also spring into action, of course. I am enclosing a short essay from the *Frankfurter Rundschau*, which I hope will bring a provisional end to the matter, at least as far as pragmatic issues are concerned. As for the substantive questions surrounding the interpretation of Benjamin, I have arranged with the *Neue Rundschau* that I will write a detailed response as soon as Mrs. Arendt's essay is known to me in full. Among all the atrocities that she committed, I almost find the attack

* Original in English.

on Tiedemann to be worse than the one on me; it is so flagrantly unjust. Before any of these things were published, Paeschke wrote me a letter, oozing with friendliness, asking to set up a meeting with me and generously promising to provide ample room for a rejoinder. Naturally, I rejected both offers. At that point, I received a second, totally unexpected letter from him, which was abject and regretful. What a bootlicker.

Regarding the letter to Unseld, all I can say is that of course I am grateful for every additional piece by Benjamin that is included in the collection. I don't know the things he wrote for children. If you think they are so important, then we should include some specimens, at any rate. Then again, I fear that, for the most basic material reasons, certain limits will be set for the scope of the thing, and I do think that, in this case, we should concentrate on the essential. Above all, this means that the wish to show Benjamin from as many different sides as possible must not be realized at the expense of more decisive things. I think it is especially important in this regard that the early theological writings that are in your possession appear as completely as possible – even if we run the risk of being slandered again. I do not know whether it will be possible to print different versions of texts alongside each other. In principle, this would certainly be desirable; however, it must not occur at the cost of other, more important things, which might otherwise not be published. Last but not least, one will have to rely on Benjamin's own *votum* here – regarding the late period (certainly, since 1933), I know pretty well how he judged his own stuff, with considerable sovereignty, by the way. Perhaps the diaries could be published separately, like the letters.

"Lesestücke" [Reading passages] is a working title. It is, of course, not what this volume will be called; if need be, it could be titled "Kleinere Prosa" [Minor prose], although that would also have to be discussed. I too am in favor of including the Baudelaire translations; and I also believe that there's not much to be hoped for from supplementary volumes (of the sort found in the Brecht edition). Unlike you, however, I do think that we should try to print the *Arcades* material in full, if possible. After all, the underlying idea is that the montage of materials makes up the thing itself (whether that would have, in fact, been possible is a different question). At least these materials, already so carefully organized by Benjamin, will sparkle. Final decisions on the matter can only be made, however, once Tiedemann has progressed much further with the *Arcades* convolutes.

I am very well aware of the reasons that you are hesitant to write about the Kabbalah-Benjamin complex. By the way, it occurs to me that there is a peculiar analogy between the early Benjamin's relation to Jewish mysticism and the late Benjamin's relation to Marxism.

In both cases, it seems as though his metaphysical-epistemological longing, as well as his insight that tradition itself is a constituent element of philosophy, led him to bind himself to quasi-authoritative texts without having fully thought them through, and without having even, in a higher sense, studied them. I know, all too well, what difficulties this resulted in for the late Benjamin. You'll be all the more aware of what it meant for the early one. Rather than encouraging you to write something contentual *ad vocem* Benjamin and the Kabbalah, which would indeed be riddled with problems, my actual idea was much more for you to write something about this complex in a very general sense. I cannot shake the feeling that, as things stand, the early writings are left hanging without your commentary. Benjamin would have been the first to highlight the dubiousness of theological positions, detached from their standing within tradition. I don't know if I was able to clarify what I mean, but there can be no doubt that this concerns a desideratum of the highest order. Moreover, I believe that, once you and I are no longer around, there will simply be no one left who is capable of expressing these things adequately.

By the way, I may use the occasion [of my response to Arendt] to say something that has remained unsaid throughout the whole controversy over the two-volume edition: namely, that the requisite selection, which needed to be made, was probably optimal to ensure the quality of the selected materials. Needless to say, the attempt to turn Benjamin into a "critic" instead of a philosopher is utter nonsense. What is this woman's idea of philosophy! Well, it's clearly that of the gentlemen, Heidegger and Jaspers. I will make that a central point of my response.

I am very glad that you'll be here in May. As far as my schedule is concerned, I have to be in Kiel on the 24th and 25th. Hopefully it won't cause you too much trouble to plan ahead in such a way that these aren't the very days that you will be here; on this occasion we really must be together unstintingly.

With regards to our vacation, the thing is this: just like last year, we are not going to Sils. Two years ago, the food at the Waldhaus absolutely did not agree with Gretel, and the Kienbergers made no effort to provide an adequate diet for her condition. We can't move down to the village because they cannot accommodate our old bachelor habit of taking two adjoining en suite rooms. Moreover, I find it to be too loud down there, and as I get older the sensitivity of my musician's ears is steadily increasing. Last year we found very adequate lodgings in Crans, and the town itself is also pretty; but it really is too far down, and, above all, there are not enough really long walking trails. As such, we've decided to go to Zermatt this time. We've already made reservations. The incomparable merit of this place, as you may or may not know, is that cars are not permitted there. This makes for heavenly quiet. We are heading there around July 15th, right after the semester ends. We're likely to stay between five and six weeks, just as we used to do in Sils.

There has been a reconciliation of sorts with Ernst Bloch. I saw him at Unseld's place on Friday, after a lecture of his, which I skipped. Unfortunately the crowd was quite large. He told me that his book on materialism and theology, or whatever that stuff is called, contains a major attack on *Negative Dialectics*; however, he apparently intends to soften it somewhat, given the smear campaign against me. As a representative of utopia he felt compelled to do something against negativity. I think it's sad that a spirit of such richness has shrunk to such an impoverished dichotomy. On the other hand, his behavior in the matter surrounding Benjamin has been very friendly, and it hardly seems right to fight with him any longer, since the signs of age-related decline cannot be missed. Oftentimes what he says – even in public – lacks any coherence. Madame was friendly in a sour kind of way. As a precaution, Gretel didn't come along. I couldn't help but apply to him, behind his back, the title of a farce by Nestroy: *Der konfuse Zauberer* [The confused magician]. It's simply a *statement of facts*.*

In other news, I recited my little piece about Borchardt in Zurich a few weeks ago, and also read a few lovely poems by him. You will find all of this in a collection that I edited, which does not conceal his problematic sides but attempts to rectify the shameful repression of his work. I am letting my book rest for a few weeks, which may not be so bad for it. I am in up to my ears with the organization of the big sociology conference, and especially with the preparation of my keynote address on the theme of "Spätkapitalismus oder Industriegesellschaft" [Late capitalism or industrial society]. Besides this, I am very busy writing a comprehensive introduction to a collection, forthcoming with Luchterhand, which will document the controversy on dialectics and positivism in sociology. It is shaping up to become a highly accountable *declaration of intention*.† I am not displeased with all of this, however, since it allows me to gain a certain distance from the, as yet, somewhat formless draft of my book on aesthetics. As I wrote to you, I finished it, which means, of course, that now the real work is just beginning. I'm not in the best of shape, physically, not least as a result of the attacks. But we can only go to Baden-Baden after the conference, on the 12th of April, and then for only ten days.

What you say about Peter Szondi doesn't exactly sound encouraging

* Original in English.

† Original in English.

– I am really quite worried about him. When you give him my regards, please also tell him that, from the outset, he was more astute in his judgment of Heißenbüttel than I was. By the way, Bloch's son is in Israel. He's working on a Kibbutz, and, according to Bloch, it's done him a world of good and has really regenerated him. Apparently he wants to stay there permanently. Have you come across him there? He always made a very good impression on me. Speaking of sons – Stefan issued me with a new, extremely gracious, power of attorney and – what is more important – by so doing, he declared his conviction that what I have done to date with regard to Benjamin has, by all means, been for the benefit of his father.

As far as Asja Lacis is concerned, I have the same impression as you. Have you heard back from Potsdam, by the way? I rather doubt it.

This really has become something of an epistle. But there was so much to say – please forgive me. And a thousand thanks once more!

To you and Fanja all the best, also from Gretel,

your old and loyal

Teddie Adorno

Original: typescript with printed letterhead; Gershom Scholem Archive, The National Library of Israel, Jerusalem.

tempora si fuerint nubila, solus eris: The Latin verse "Donec eris felix, multos numerabis amicos: tempora si fuerint nubila, solus eris" comes from Ovid's *Tristia*, Book I, chapter IX, verse 5. The standard English translation reads: "So long as you are secure you will count many friends; if your life becomes clouded you will be alone." Ovid, *Tristia & Ex Ponto*, trans. Arthur Leslie Wheeler (Cambridge, MA: Harvard University Press, 1990), p. 45.

Horkheimer will also spring into action: No public statement by Horkheimer is known.

a short essay: See Adorno, "Interimsbescheid" [Interim reply], *Frankfurter Rundschau*, 24/9 (6.3.1968), p. 12. Repr. in *Gesammelte Schriften 20.1: Vermischte Schriften* [Miscellaneous Writings], ed. Rolf Tiedemann et al. (Frankfurt am Main: Suhrkamp, 1986), pp. 182–6.

Paeschke wrote me a letter: On 29.2.1968, Adorno responded thus:

> Dear Mr. Paeschke, I received your gracious letter of the 15th of February, along with the issue of *MERKUR*. Given the relationship, up to this point, between the journal and myself, the least you could have done would have been to send me the contributions from Mrs. Arendt and Heißenbüttel before they came out. I could have corrected some of the serious errors they contain; for instance, the suggestion that I was the director of the Institute for Social Research in America, a role that I

assumed only after my return to Germany in 1949. In light of these two essays, and a string of others published by MERKUR in recent years, it may be better to speak of an open animosity on the part of the editorship than of a *conspiration du silence*. I do not think that, under the circumstances, a conversation between you and me would do much good. I reserve the right to determine whether, where, and how, I will respond. (Carbon copy of typescript: Theodor W. Adorno Archive, Frankfurt am Main)

Paeschke's letter to Adorno of 15.2.1968 includes the line that Adorno must view Paeschke "in light of a *conspiration du silence*." (Original: typescript; Theodor W. Adorno Archive, Frankfurt am Main).

the diaries: Adorno is referring to Benjamin's notebooks, which occasionally contain diary-like entries. Benjamin's early diaries have been lost.

Needless to say, the attempt to turn Benjamin into a "critic" instead of a philosopher is utter nonsense: In the first part of her essay, Arendt refers to Benjamin as "the most important critic of the time." See Arendt, "Walter Benjamin I: Der Bucklige" [Walter Benjamin I: the hunchback], *Merkur*, 22/238, issues 1 and 2 (January/February 1968), p. 61. Moreover, she writes: "The philosophy of Walter Benjamin – that hardly does him justice. Although he studied philosophy, he thought as little of it as Goethe did. Of the four books that he began, but never finished, in the time leading up to the Hitler catastrophe, not one of them could in any sense be called philosophical or theoretical – even at the time, he described them as 'the real sites of wreckage or catastrophe'" (pp. 58–9). A modified version of this essay was incorporated into a longer piece, which exists in English; see Arendt, "Walter Benjamin: 1892–1940," trans. Harry Zohn, in *Men in Dark Times* (San Diego: Harcourt, 1968), pp. 153–206.

Kiel: Carla Henius and Adorno gave a concert together in Kiel on the 24th of May 1968. The programme included Schoenberg's *George Lieder*, Op. 15, "Das Buch der hängenden Gärten" [The book of the hanging gardens]; Anton Webern's *George Lieder*, Op. 4; and Adorno's *George Lieder*, Op. 7., which he accompanied himself. The "conversational concert" was preceded by Adorno's lecture "George," as well as his improvised concert introduction to Schoenberg's *Lieder*. See, "Stefan George," in *Notes to Literature*, Vol. 2, trans. Shierry Weber Nicholsen (New York: Columbia University Press, 1992), pp. 178–92. On the 26th of May, Adorno gave a lecture titled "Reflexionen über Musikkritik" [Reflections on music criticism] at the Kieler Schauspielhaus. The artistic director of the Schauspielhaus was Carla Henius's husband, Joachim Klaiber. See Adorno, "Reflexionen über Musikkritik," in *Gesammelte Schriften 19: Musikalische Schriften 6* [Musical writings 6], ed. Rolf Tiedemann et al. (Frankfurt am Main: Suhrkamp, 1984), pp. 573–91.

the Kienbergers: The married couple Rolf and Rita Kienberger (1917–1994; 1926–2006) ran the Hotel Waldhaus in Sils Maria, where Theodor and Gretel Adorno used to spend their summer vacations.

Ernst Bloch ... his book on materialism and theology: See Ernst Bloch, *Atheism in Christianity: The Religion of the Exodus and the Kingdom*, trans. J. T. Swann (New York: Herder & Herder, 1972), pp. 230–1.

Bloch ... lecture: Not verified.

the title of a farce by Nestroy: *Der konfuse Zauberer oder Treue und Flatterhaftigkeit* [The confused magician or loyalty and fickelness] (1832) is the title of a magic play [Zauberspiel] by the Austrian playwright, actor and opera singer Johann Nestroy (1801–1862).

little piece about Borchardt: See Rudolf Borchardt, *Ausgewählte Gedichte: Auswahl und Einleitung von Theodor W. Adorno* [Selected poems: selected and introduced by Theodor W. Adorno] (Frankfurt am Main: Suhrkamp, 1968). An English translation of Adorno's introduction appears in Adorno, "Charmed Language: On the Poetry of Rudolf Borchardt," in *Notes to Literature*, Vol. 2, trans. Shierry Weber Nicholsen (New York: Columbia University Press, 1992), pp. 193–210.

sociology conference ... my keynote address: Adorno's address, titled "Spätkapitalismus oder Industriegesellschaft? Einleitungsvortrag zum 16. Deutschen Soziologentag" [Late capitalism or industrial society? Opening lecture for the 16th German Sociologists' Conference] (1968) was first published in *Spätkapitalismus oder Industriegesellschaft? Verhandlungen des 16. Deutschen Soziologentages* [Late capitalism or industrial society? proceedings from the 16th German Sociologists' Conference], ed. Theodor W. Adorno (Stuttgart: Ferdinand Enke, 1969), pp. 12–26. An English translation, by Fred Van Gelder, appears in *Modern German Sociology*, ed. V. Meja, D. Misgeld, and N. Stehr (New York: Columbia University Press, 1987), pp. 232–47.

comprehensive introduction to a collection, forthcoming with Luchterhand: Adorno is referring to the volume *Der Positivismusstreit in der deutschen Soziologie* [The positivist dispute in German sociology]. See the relevant note to letter no. 110 in this volume.

Stefan issued me with a new, extremely gracious, power of attorney: On 18.1.1968, Stefan Benjamin wrote the following to Adorno: "Would it be appropriate if I send you a power of attorney, at least to do what is no longer possible for my father: to declare my solidarity with you?" (Typescript; Theodor W. Adorno Archive, Frankfurt am Main). On 22.1.1968 Adorno responded: "Given everything that has happened, it is a consolation in the truest sense that you – as the one who is most legitimately entitled – are so clearly and unambiguously committed to me, and I would like to thank you from the bottom of my heart. Nothing more gratifying could happen to me than if you actually wanted to send me this power of attorney: it would also remove the last remnant of legitimation from this nonsense." (Carbon copy of typescript; Theodor W. Adorno Archive, Frankfurt am Main). On 1.2.1968, Stefan Benjamin sent Adorno the power of attorney to manage his father's estate.

206 SCHOLEM TO ADORNO
JERUSALEM, 29.3.1968

29 March 1968

Dear Adorno,

Many thanks for your long letter, which I cannot respond to properly right now. I am definitely counting on our meeting in Frankfurt, where I will be from the 10th to the 13th or 14th of May. I suggested to Unseld that we have another Benjamin meeting on the 11th of May, for which I am attempting to have Szondi brought in from Berlin. I am being awarded an honorary doctorate from the University of Zurich in late April, and I intend to stay in Switzerland for a few days, since it is too much to go back for the Israel anniversary on the 2nd of May.

I am enclosing a copy of another letter to Paeschke of *Merkur*, which will surely meet with your approval.

The little Szondi took off this morning. It is my belief that the effect that this visit had on him is yet to show itself. He's not at peace with himself; otherwise he would find it much easier to decide where he belongs. Everyone was very taken with him here.

Cordial regards to you both

your old

Gerhard Scholem

Original: manuscript with an enclosed copy of Scholem's letter to Hans Paeschke, dated 24.3.1968.

copy of another letter to Paeschke: On the 24th of March 1968, Scholem wrote the following to Hans Paeschke:

> Copy for Adorno
> PERSONAL
> Jerusalem, 24 March 1968
> Dear Mr. Paeschke,
> For a possible discussion regarding my reservations about contributing to your journal, I think it would be beneficial if I said a few things concerning a line from the sequel to H. Arendt's essay in *Merkur* (p. 215), which you were kind enough to send me recently. What alienated me from Arendt since her Eichmann book (in which this method of arrogant and brash insolence is exercised *ad nauseam*) is her adoption of a totally false tone, through which she transforms circumstances that are faultless or perhaps also (often enough) exciting or poignant into vulgarities.
>
> You are undoubtedly familiar with Walter Benjamin's published letters, which document his years of hand-wringing over the (ultimately unrealized) plan to learn Hebrew. Nevertheless, you saw fit to print in

Merkur the truly shameful, not to say, nasty, sentence – for which the author [Arendt] must be held accountable – that W.B. was ready, or thought he was "to study Hebrew for 300 marks a month if the Zionists thought it would do them some good, or to think dialectically, with all the mediating trimmings, for one thousand French Francs if there was no other way of doing business with the Marxists" (p. 215).* As someone who witnessed these exact events first hand, and who was also personally involved in documenting these experiences in great detail in the edition of the letters, what am I to say to such a view of this life? I don't want to conceal anything from you: I repudiate this. I knew Hannah Arendt when she was a socialist or a half-communist and I knew her when she was a Zionist. I am amazed at the light-years of distance from which she speaks, with sovereign detachment, about movements that once touched her deeply. This capacity is not available to me, and, to tell you the truth, I don't believe this sovereignty in her either. It barely conceals a bitter *ressentiment*, which shines forth in everything she's written on Zionism and Zionists, including what she says in this essay. It's not his thinking that is supposed to have drawn him, however problematically, to these two positions (the Hebrew one and the Marxist one); nor is he supposed to have wanted to learn Hebrew or to think like a Marxist: what is supposed to have counted was 300 Marks per month or, respectively, (what was then) 1,000 Francs. Indeed, one can read the letters like this, as I have learned from this essay; but I despise those who read this way.

Any platform that promotes such disputes has no attraction for me, and, regardless of your favourable opinion of my independence, I can well understand Adorno if he wishes to avoid your journal. You speak of the limited possibilities open to an editor. You are probably right. But what I cannot believe is that you are incapable of excluding despicable, mean tricks.

With melancholy sentiments, your very devoted Gershom Scholem.

207 ADORNO TO SCHOLEM
FRANKFURT AM MAIN, 5.4.1968

PROF. DR. THEODOR W. ADORNO

6 FRANKFURT AM MAIN
KETTENHOFWEG 123
5 April 1968

Dear Scholem,

I am responding to you in a rush, under the manic pressure of preparations for the 16th German Sociologists' Conference, which will finally mark the end of my presidency of this society, just to

* See Hannah Arendt, "Walter Benjamin: 1892–1940," trans. Harry Zohn, in *Men in Dark Times* (San Diego: Harcourt, 1968), p. 180.

thank you for your lines, and most especially for the copy of your second letter to Paeschke.

I also find that the passage by Arendt in which she openly accuses Benjamin of corruptibility (while, at the same time, accusing me of sophistry) is the worst thing that this vile woman has written so far. It is of extraordinary significance that you, as someone who is not immediately under attack, should speak out so forcefully in this matter. I am curious as to whether Paeschke will respond to you. If he does, I'd be very grateful if you could send me a copy of the letter. I would have it photocopied and sent back to you right away.

In the meantime, Tiedemann's really outstanding response came out in *Argument*. I presume you have this text; I explicitly asked Tiedemann to send it to you right away. *Alternative* has announced a sequel on this matter, and they had the nerve to ask me if I would make one of Benjamin's manuscripts available to them. I will grant them this request so that they cannot say that I'm perpetrating an academic monopoly of the archive, but with the condition attached that they cannot publish it, since the rights belong to Suhrkamp. I believe that you also agree with this.

I am very glad that you will be here on the 11th of May and I have reserved the date for a meeting with Unseld.

I am not doing too well at the moment, since I'm suffering from the most terrible bout of sleeplessness, apparently due to being totally overworked. I'll have to spend the *weekend** in bed if I am to make it through the conference, for which I have to give the opening address, among other things. I am, nevertheless, in very good spirits, otherwise.

Please give us word as to whether Fanja has fully recovered. Leu Kaschnitz recently underwent a similar operation, which seems to have gone quite well, although she will have to go back for a second surgery sometime soon. It is probably for exactly the same thing.

All that is cordial,
always yours
Teddie Adorno

Original: typescript with printed letterhead; Gershom Scholem Archive, The National Library of Israel, Jerusalem.

the passage by Arendt in which she openly accuses Benjamin of corruptibility (while, at the same time, accusing me of sophistry): In her *Merkur* essay, Arendt writes: "As clear as it was to Benjamin that his situation as an émigré in Paris offered him no material perspectives or possibilities to publish, and that this provided reason enough to 'be docile to the suggestions of the Institute [for Social Research],' it was equally evident to him that his

* Original in English.

friendship [with Brecht] constituted an absolute limit to docility. Certainly, he could be diplomatic. He himself viewed his late letters to Adorno and Horkheimer as models of diplomacy" (p. 62).

Tiedemann's really outstanding response came out in Argument: See letter no. 200 and the relevant note in this volume.

208 SCHOLEM TO ADORNO
ZURICH, 2.5.1968

2.5.1968

Dear Adorno,

I intend to come to Frankfurt on the 10th of May (until the 14th?) and I am expecting the meeting arranged with Unseld to take place on Saturday afternoon, as planned.

I will be at the Hotel Urban in Zurich until Wednesday morning. (327052)

Shall we spend Friday evening together?

Cordial regards to you both

yours, G. S.

Original: manuscript; Theodor W. Adorno Archive, Frankfurt am Main.

209 ADORNO TO SCHOLEM
FRANKFURT AM MAIN, 6.5.1968

PROF. DR. THEODOR W. ADORNO

6 FRANKFURT AM MAIN
KETTENHOFWEG 123
6 May 1968

Dear Scholem,

kindest thanks for your letter. I am very much looking forward to seeing you. Unfortunately I am not available on Friday – I committed a long time ago to giving a lecture on the radio that evening, and the afternoon is filled with exams. We will only be able to meet on Saturday. It's very good of you to make yourself available for this meeting.

All that is cordial, also from Gretel,

yours,

Teddie Adorno

Original: typescript with printed letterhead; Gershom Scholem Archive, The National Library of Israel, Jerusalem.

a lecture on the radio: On the 10th of May Adorno presented his lecture "Probleme der Musikkritik" [Problems of music criticism] on the Hessischer Rundfunk for the Westdeutscher Rundfunk.

210 SCHOLEM TO ADORNO
JERUSALEM [?], 24.7.1968

24.7.1968

Dear Adorno,

I am writing in great haste. Heartfelt thanks for the Volkswagen memorandum concerning W.B.

Please don't forget that I am coming to Frankfurt for one week from the 8th of September in order to view B's papers at the Institute. Gretel and I agreed that I'd be able to access the materials then.

Our addresses are as follows:

6–18 August	Margna, Sils Maria
19–31 August	Hotel Tamaro, Ascona
1–8 September	Zurich, Hotel Urban

Where exactly can I reach you?

See you again in F. or before?

Cordial regards, also to your wife

yours,

G. Scholem

Original: manuscripts; Theodor W. Adorno Archive, Frankfurt am Main.

Volkswagen memorandum: For the edition of Walter Benjamin's *Gesammelten Schriften* [Collected Works], the editors and the Suhrkamp Verlag applied for financial support from the Volkswagen Foundation. Walter Boehlich wrote the memorandum for the Volkswagen Foundation on the 8th of July 1968. Adorno looked it over and made corrections. On the 15th of July 1968 it was submitted to Dr. Hubert Flitner, the head of the Volkswagen Foundation. The "Memorandum für eine neue Walter Benjamin-Ausagabe" [Memorandum for a new Walter Benjamin edition] is contained in *"So müßte ich ein Engel und kein Autor sein": Adorno und seine Frankfurter Verleger: Der Briefwechsel mit Peter Suhrkamp und Siegfried Unseld* ["So I would have to be an angel, not an author": Adorno and his Frankfurt publishers: the correspondence with Peter Suhrkamp and Siegfried Unseld], ed. Wolfgang Schopf (Frankfurt am Main: Suhrkamp, 2003), pp. 637–41.

211 ADORNO TO SCHOLEM
ZERMATT, 9.8.1968

Hotel Bristol
9.VIII.1968

Dear Scholem, we are sitting up here in the steadily changing weather, relaxing energetically, and thinking very much of you. We'll be back in Frankfurt by the end of the month, most certainly from the 8th of September on. We received a very encouraging letter from the Volkswagen Foundation; things are looking good. Obviously, you can look through everything. In the meantime, I've received microfilms of all the letters to Gretel and me from the archive in Potsdam, which is hard to believe. Up here, I'm shutting everything out. Ahead of me lies a sabbatical semester, during which I hope to wrap up the aesthetics book. All the best and see you very soon!
Most cordially, also from Gretel,
yours Teddie Adorno
All the best to Fanja!

Original: postcard (manuscript), "6703 Zermatt / Das Matterhorn 4478 m."; Gershom Scholem Archive, The National Library of Israel, Jerusalem.

212 ADORNO TO SCHOLEM
FRANKFURT AM MAIN, 7.11.1968

PROF. DR. THEODOR W. ADORNO

6 FRANKFURT AM MAIN
KETTENHOFWEG 123
7 November 1968

Dear Scholem,

I'd like to thank you from the bottom of my heart for the truly magnificent gift for my 65th birthday, with which you brought me immense joy. And this is in no way diminished by the fact that the commemorative volume made me embarrassingly aware of just how much I don't know. Even if one concedes a degree of legitimacy to the division of labor, as one must, there is so much in all of this that I really ought to know, that I conceive it as an injustice not to know, regardless of whether an instance of general human insufficiency is expressed thereby. I was really made aware of all of this during my work on the aesthetics book, which led me unexpectedly, but all the more forcefully, to the question of the ban on images [Bilderverbot].

Aside from the desperately intense work on my book, and a trip to Austria, where I spent a lot of time with Lotte, talking with her about everything concerning her, my silence during the last weeks is caused by a degree of aggravation that goes beyond what I believe I can cope with emotionally. It came from the most diverse sides: from Helene Berg, a friend from my youth (the widow of the composer about whom I just wrote a small book); from the widow of the composer Hanns Eisler; from a *Habilitation* candidate of mine, who behaved as shamefully towards me as only Taubes did towards you; and, above all – and this is where the fun ends – from Ernst Bloch. What he did to me is so truly mean that it defies explanation. In Unseld's estimation, which makes sense to me, it's an act of revenge for the passages directed against him in Benjamin's letters, although, of course, neither you nor I wrote those. As Habermas thinks, a considerable dose of professional jealousy may also have been involved, although I'm usually hesitant to impute this as a motive. The whole thing is so outrageous that I really must ask you to have a look at the passage in question: pp. 324–325 in his book *Atheism in Christianity*. That the whole book is nonsense; that Bloch's spirit has been reduced to spite; that nothing of his communism remains but the common, changes nothing in this matter. Worst of all, I now have to listen to all sorts of people telling me that I'm being too sensitive. As if, in God's name, an instrument like me could function, or even be possible at all, without such sensitivity. It's especially painful that none of my friends have, as yet, reacted in a way that is really noticeable, except for Habermas, who has refused to meet with Bloch again. Of course, the breech is final; and I'd be inclined, if the opportunity presents itself, to compose for him the infernal galop that he once exalted. But please look at it yourself and form your own judgment.

Otherwise, things are going well – although this otherwise is, in the Hegelian sense, truly abstract. Work is progressing steadily, and it seems that I have overcome the deadlock in one of the most difficult places in the book. Incidentally, with respect to aesthetics, the presentational problems are not without objective interest. These consist precisely in the fact that, while the sequence from first to last is almost indispensable for a book, it has proven to be so incompatible with the matter at hand that an arrangement, in the traditional sense, such as I have pursued until now (also in *Negative Dialectics*) has proven to be impracticable. As such, the book has to be written in quasi-concentric, equally weighted, paratactic sections, arranged around a focal point, which they bring to expression through their constellation. Now, that sounds pretty nice, but it's tremendously hard to execute. Please keep your fingers crossed for me.

Bonnasse, to whom we owe a debt of gratitude regarding Benjamin's estate, but who is gradually becoming a nuisance, would like to know more about the French report that you mentioned, "Notes sur les *Tableaux parisiens*" [Notes on the *Tableaux parisiens*]. He would like to know whether Benjamin expressly wrote such an essay, or whether it is merely a compilation of parts from other texts. Since I am unable to satisfy his insistent requests, I would be sincerely grateful if you could spare the time to write to him.

Otherwise, there is only this to report: that against my intentions, as if under a kind of compulsion, I have drafted something entirely different: a series of theses on subject and object, with which I've been extremely occupied. It will likely be included in the volume *Stichworte* [Keywords], which Suhrkamp wants to publish next autumn, and for which I have plenty of material; a kind of sequel to *Eingriffe* [Interventions].

At least I had a radiant and warm autumn in Vienna and Graz, followed by a few uncommonly colorful, if also exhausting days in Munich.

By the way, I met Schweppenhäuser's protégé Rexroth and was favorably impressed. He wants to lecture on fundamental problems of Benjamin's aesthetics in Schweppenhäuser's seminar.

There have been some difficulties with Uri Rapp, who is quite conceited and does not grasp what is expected of a doctoral thesis, on the so-called problem of roles, under my supervision. However, Ms. Schmidt, whom you know, has managed to steer him a little bit. In a few weeks, he wants to present a plan for his thesis that is more satisfactory than the first attempt, which was, for me, a rather unpleasant mix of superficiality and cleverness. If, when you get a chance, you could write me a line with your assessment of this man, I'd be grateful.

Fortunately, Gretel is doing quite well; and as regards me, with all the manure that I'm burdened with, and that is being flung at me, including endless obligations with exams, I am astonished at how little it has covered me, and at how much I've still been able to keep my head free.

Please be so kind as to write me soon.

To you and Fanja all the best, also from Gretel,

always yours,

Adorno

Once again, I have found an ideal wife or girlfriend for Peter Szondi; but how can one arrange things in such a way that he doesn't get his back up? I got to know her in Munich, together with Alexander Kluge, to be specific, at the house of a friend of mine.

Original: typescript with printed letterhead and printed postscript; Gershom Scholem Archive, The National Library of Israel, Jerusalem.

the truly magnificent gift for my 65th birthday: Not verified.

aesthetics book . . . ban on images: Adorno is referring to the following passage, which probably came to him during his work on the Borchardt collection: "The Old Testament prohibition on images has an aesthetic as well as a theological dimension. That one should make no image, which means no image *of* anything whatsoever, expresses at the same time that it is impossible to make such an image. Through its duplication in art, what appears in nature is robbed of its being-in-itself, in which the experience of nature is fulfilled. Art holds true to appearing nature only where it makes landscape present in the expression of its own negativity; Borchardt's 'Verse bei Betrachtung von Landschaft-Zeichnungen geschrieben' [Verses written while contemplating landscape drawings] expressed this inimitably and shockingly." See Adorno, *Aesthetic Theory*, ed. Rolf Tiedemann and Gretel Adorno, trans. Robert Hullot-Kentor (London: Continuum, 2002), pp. 67–8.

a trip to Austria . . . Lotte: Adorno had gone to Vienna to present his monograph on Berg, which had been published by the Viennese publisher Elisabeth Lafite. An English translation was published as *Alban Berg: Master of the Smallest Link*, trans. Juliane Brand and Christopher Hailey (Cambridge: Cambridge University Press, 1991). Subsequently, Adorno travelled to Graz on the invitation of Harald Kaufmann, the founder and director of the Institut für Wertungsforschung [Institute for the study of valuation]. While there, he presented the lecture "Konzeption eines Wiener Operntheaters" [Conception of a Viennese operatic theatre] in the ceremonial hall of the Music Academy. The following year, the lecture was published in the second issue of the journal *Studien zur Wertungsforschung*. See Adorno, *Gesammelte Schriften 19: Musikalische Schriften 6* [Musical Writings 6], ed. Rolf Tiedemann et al. (Frankfurt am Main: Suhrkamp, 1984), pp. 496–515. Adorno also took part in radio programs on several occasions during this trip.

a degree of aggravation: Adorno is referring, on the one hand, to the escalating confrontations with the student movement. The students demanded declarations of solidarity from Adorno, such as his public intervention on behalf of Fritz Teufel, who was facing criminal charges, as well as his participation in demonstrations. Adorno did not want to meet these demands. On the other hand, he was disappointed at the reception of his monograph on Berg. After Helene Berg had declined to write a foreword for the book and refused to grant permission to print a part of the unfinished Third Act of *Lulu*, she did not come to Vienna for the book launch on the 22nd of October. Adorno complained to the publisher, moreover, about the book's lack of presence in German bookshops.

Helene Berg: Helene Berg (1886–1976) was married to the composer Alban Berg since 1911. After her husband's death in 1935, she became the heiress and executor of his estate. She founded the Alban Berg Stiftung [Alban Berg Foundation] in 1968.

the widow of the composer Hanns Eisler: Stephanie Eisler was the third wife of the composer Hanns Eisler (1898–1962). After his death, she was involved in the publication of his collected works. See Hanns Eisler, *Gesammelte Werke*, founded by Nathan Notowicz and edited by Stephanie Eisler and Manfred Grabs (Leipzig: Deutscher Verlag für Musik, 1982). In 1944, Adorno and Hanns Eisler had co-authored a study on the theory of film music, *Composing for the Films*, which was published in New York by Oxford University Press. The first German-language edition of this book, which introduced Eisler's unilateral alterations, in departure from the original English edition, was published by the East Berlin publisher Bruno Henschel & Sohn in 1949. In 1969, Adorno prepared a German edition based on the original text, titled *Kompositionen für den Film* (Munich: Rogner und Bernhard, 1969), which was which was published only after Adorno's death. See Adorno and Eisler, *Composing for the Films* (London: Continuum, 2005).

a Habilitation candidate of mine, who behaved . . . shamefully towards me: Not verified.

pp. 324–325 in his book Atheism in Christianity: Adorno is referring to the following passage:

> There is no room here for any exaggeration or isolation in the treatment of evil, as was the fashion in the all too elevated cult of despair, or in Adorno's jargon about the 'nonactuality of the good.' And metaphysics also goes much further than the mere grumbling and grousing we have spoken about, with its purely negative dialectics which both Marx and Hegel were forced to relativize, so far removed was it from the real class-struggle, so remote from being so much as an 'algebra of revolution.' . . . The power of this pre-ordained confidence manifests itself within the clerical apparatus in the hierarchy of ownership and the ownership of the hierarchy, and this has precisely the same effects as defeatism – the revolution is suppressed. Neither of the two exaggerations, however – the one stemming from idle negativity, the other from guaranteed positivity, leaves the narrow confines of a space which, for Nietzsche, had been burst asunder by atheism. (Ernst Bloch, *Atheism in Christianity: The Religion of the Exodus and the Kingdom*, trans. J. T. Swann (New York: Herder & Herder, 1972), pp. 230–1)

Infernal galop: Not verified.

Bonnasse: Pierre Missac was preparing the publication of two pages with texts by and on Benjamin for inclusion in an issue of *Le Monde des Livres*, which came out on the 31st of May 1969. For this purpose, Missac also translated Adorno's piece "A l'écart de tous les courants" [Away from all currents]. See Adorno, *Gesammelte Schriften 20.1: Vermischte Schriften* [Miscellaneous Writings], ed. Rolf Tiedemann et al. (Frankfurt am Main: Suhrkamp, 1986), pp. 187–9.

"Notes sur les Tableaux parisiens*"*: At the invitation of Paul Desjardins in May 1939, Benjamin took part in the Decades of Pontigny where he spoke freely on the *Tableaux parisiens*. A typescript of the "Notes" was drafted,

based on notes made by the host. See Benjamin, *Gesammelte Schriften I.2*, ed. Rolf Tiedemann and Hermann Schweppenhäuser (Frankfurt am Main: Suhrkamp, 1974), pp. 740–8. Scholem apparently heeded Adorno's request and wrote to Missac. An echo of his letter can be discerned in Missac's letter to Adorno, dated the 19th of November 1968: "In the meantime, I have heard from Scholem, who confirms that he does not have copies of the Benjamin texts collected in Frankfurt. From his letter, I conclude that he has absolutely no objections to my viewing these manuscripts. He added that the 'Notes sur les *Tableaux parisiens*' are in a large file in box no. IV/4. . . . Do you think it might be possible for me to come to you on Saturday, the 14th of December, to view these documents?" (typescript: Theodor W. Adorno Archive, Frankfurt am Main).

a series of theses on subject and object . . . in the volume Stichworte: See Adorno, "On Subject and Object," in *Critical Models: Interventions and Catchwords*, trans. Henry W. Pickford (New York: Columbia University Press, 1998), pp. 245–58.

Schweppenhäuser's protégé Rexroth: Tillman Rexroth (1942–1979) was the editor of the fourth volume of Benjamin's *Gesammelte Schriften.*

Uri Rapp: The Israeli sociologist Uri Rapp (1923–1993) studied under Adorno, among others. In 1971 he completed his doctorate at the University of Konstanz. See Uri Rapp, *Handeln und Zuschauen: Untersuchungen über den Theatersoziologischen Aspekt in der menschlichen Interaktion* [Acting and watching: investigations into the theatrical-sociological aspect of human interaction] (Darmstadt: Luchterhand, 1973). From 1965 he was lecturer in the sociology of theatre at the University of Tel Aviv.

Ms. Schmidt: From 1964 to 1970, the sociologist Regina Becker-Schmidt (b. 1937) was a research associate at the Institute for Social Research. In 1970 she completed her doctorate with a thesis entitled *Geschichte und Geschichtsphilosophie im Elitebegriff: Soziologische Modellanalysen von Elitetheorien* [History and the philosophy of history in the concept of the elite: sociological model-analyses of theories of the elite]. From 1972 until her retirement in 2002, she was professor of sociology and social psychology at the Gottfried Wilhelm Leibniz University in Hannover. She co-authored a volume published by the Institute for Social Research. See Regina Schmidt and Egon Becker, *Reaktionen auf politische Vorgänge: Drei Meinungsstudien aus der Bundesrepublik* [Reactions to political processes: three opinion studies from the Federal Republic] (Frankfurt am Main: Europäische Verlagsanstalt, 1967).

an ideal wife or girlfriend for Peter Szondi: Adorno may be referring to the actress Hannelore Hoger (b. 1942), whom he met in Munich, as appears to be suggested by a passage from a letter to Alexander Kluge dated the 31st of October 1968, which reads: "It saddens me that I was unable to converse more with Miss Hogar that evening, but she sat there silently observing, while I gushed on like a waterfall, God knows why. Please apologize again to her on my behalf" (Carbon copy of typescript; Theodor W. Adorno Archive, Frankfurt am Main).

Alexander Kluge: The writer and director Alexander Kluge (b. 1932) completed his doctoral studies in law at the University of Frankfurt in 1956 with a thesis titled *Universitäts-Selbstverwaltung* [Self-governance of the university]. Subsequently he became the legal advisor of the Frankfurt Institute for Social Research and a confidante of Adorno's. As a director, he became one of the most important representatives of New German Cinema during the 1960s, with films including *Abschied von Gestern* [Yesterday girl] (1966). At the same time, Kluge published theoretical and socio-political writings as well as prose texts. In 1973 he was awarded an honorary professorship at the University of Frankfurt.

213 ADORNO TO SCHOLEM
FRANKFURT AM MAIN, 18.11.1968

PROF. DR. THEODOR W. ADORNO

6 FRANKFURT AM MAIN
KETTENHOFWEG 123
18 November 1968

Dear Scholem,

I have received an invitation from the music department of the *National Council of Culture and Art in Tel Aviv*.* The dates and conditions – to the extent that they are as yet clear – are still causing some difficulties, but of course the invitation is very tempting. However, I'd have to know about the nature and standing of the institution that has issued the invitation. I could only come if it's top-notch, so to speak, and doesn't in some way rank below the University. You will surely understand this, and I'd be very grateful indeed for your input and advice.

While Hannah Arendt thought it was fine to attack me in her introduction to the English-language Benjamin selection, you come off better this time. I don't know whether I'll respond at all. Perhaps remaining silent would be more economical, psychologically.

A few days ago, Ernst Simon came to our place for an evening meal (in which he didn't actually participate; for ritual reasons he consumed only two eggs and some cheese, and we felt very guilty). It was lovely to see him, and your ears must have been burning.

Yesterday we saw Peter Szondi again for the first time in quite a while.

I'm making good progress on my book, although incomparably more slowly than I would have thought, partly on account of the countless distractions – especially an unimaginable load of exams – and partly

* Original in English.

because of the reasons indicated in my previous letter. I must wait and see if my head is thick enough to push through.

All that is cordial, also to Fanja, and also from Gretel

always yours,

Adorno

Original: typescript with printed letterhead; Gershom Scholem Archive, The National Library of Israel, Jerusalem.

invitation from the music section of the National Council of Culture and Art in Tel Aviv: The invitation was issued by Yeshayahu Spira (1903–1986), the assistant director general of the council.

Hannah Arendt ... her introduction to the English-language Benjamin selection: Arendt's essay on Benjamin, first published in three parts by the journal *Merkur*, appeared in a modified, English-language version as the introduction to the collection of Benjamin's writings that she edited herself. See "Introduction: Walter Benjamin, 1892–1940," in *Walter Benjamin, Illuminations: Essays and Reflections*, ed. Hannah Arendt (New York: Schocken Books, 1968), pp. 1–51. See also letters nos. 76 and 215 in this volume.

214 ADORNO TO SCHOLEM
FRANKFURT AM MAIN, 22.11.1968

PROF. DR. THEODOR W. ADORNO

6 FRANKFURT AM MAIN
KETTENHOFWEG 123

22 November 1968

Dear Scholem,

I am writing in haste to share with you the delightful news that the Volkswagen Foundation has agreed to support the Benjamin edition with the increased figure of 120,000 DM [German marks], which I had requested. A letter to me is apparently on its way. An expert appraisal from Peter Szondi seems to have helped greatly. Sometimes we professors aren't as unworldly as the children of this world would have it.

All that is cordial to you and Fanja, also from Gretel,

yours,

Adorno

Original: typescript with printed letterhead; Gershom Scholem Archive, The National Library of Israel, Jerusalem.

An expert appraisal from Peter Szondi: No further details have been determined.

215 SCHOLEM TO ADORNO
JERUSALEM, 25.11.1968

האוניברסיטה העברית בירושלים
THE HEBREW UNIVERSITY OF JERUSALEM

FACULTY OF HUMANITIES הפקולטה למדעי הרוח

Jerusalem, 25.11.1968

Dear Adorno,

I have received three letters from you in the past two weeks: one regarding Bloch, another regarding Tel Aviv, and a third about the Benjamin funding. First of all, I congratulate us on the success with Volkswagen, which should help put the edition on a firm footing. I expect to be able to come to Frankfurt myself for two weeks in the spring so as to push forward with reviewing the documents for selection purposes. I just have to find a suitable date. Perhaps you could ask Miss Olbricht to find out when in the spring the regular technical trade show takes place, since there are no hotel rooms to be found at that time.

This brings me to your second question, namely, regarding your trip to Israel. Here I have to take a step back first.

Over the course of this year, the rector of the university and I repeatedly discussed the possibility of inviting you and Horkheimer – or each of you individually – for one or more lectures. The rector, Rotenstreich, who is himself a philosopher, seemed very interested in this possibility. At the same time, it is difficult for us to compete if another government agency is willing to pay for your trip – if only because of our financial situation. When I received your letter, I thought – and discussed the idea with Rotenstreich – that perhaps we could combine your invitation from the *Council of Culture and Art** with the university's interests, enabling you to come speak to us (in English, which is generally understood here) as a guest of the university in Jerusalem for a few days. However, in the meantime, I have made inquiries with Doctor Spira of Tel Aviv, the authority responsible for your invitation. In itself, the department is not half bad. In musical matters, it is actually the only worthy entity – with the exception of the Musicology Department at the Jerusalem university – that can bring someone from abroad in a befitting manner. It's a board that is convened by the

* Original in English.

Minister of Education and Culture,* which is activated from time to time on an ad hoc basis, e.g., in your case. Neither the rector nor I see any reason why you should turn down such an invitation on the grounds of the council's status. However, Dr. Spira told me over the phone that the idea would be to invite you to come during the *Musical Festival*,† in August or September, to give two lectures in Tel Aviv and one in Jerusalem, which would be organised by the council. Now, unfortunately, this rules out the possibility of any coordination and cooperation with the university, since it is closed and, as such, no guest lectures take place – to say nothing of the fact that there are no students around, who would otherwise flock to hear a man of your standing speak. Even more unfortunately, these dates would rule out the possibility of your spending time with us. You won't hold it against me if I tell you that I am counting on your first visit to Israel taking place during a time when I'll be here. I'm sure that would be important to both of us. However, (a) the first half of August will be fully consumed by a congress of scholars of Judaism from around the world, and (b) thereafter, in mid-August, I'll be travelling to Switzerland and will likely be staying in Europe for the whole of September, during which time I also expect to be in Frankfurt for fourteen days to see to the Benjamin material – the second visit this year within the framework of our plan. If you accept the invitation to the festival, then all of this will fall away – in particular, the possibility of being invited to our place and of spending time with the Scholems. At most, Fania would be here by herself, although that too is <u>not</u> certain.

Dr. Spira did, however, mention another possibility, namely that you could come independently of the festival. In this case, a coordination could be established between the university and this institution. – and much more, if you are interested. The rector wants to discuss this with Dr. Spira, a friend from his youth, in the coming days, and he believes that they will be able to reach an agreement. If you were interested in such an arrangement, then the rector would invite you, in the name of the university, to hold something like two lectures during your visit, possibly a philosophical one and one on music theory. He would, in this case, write to you in Frankfurt.

But such a visit only makes sense during the semester. The "Easter holidays" in Jerusalem are from mid-March (roughly 14.3.) to mid-April (13.4.). The summer semester ends on the 20th of June. So the question is whether you think it's possible to plan your visit – and I am assuming that Gretel would also be accompanying you – during this time frame.

* Original in English.

† Original in English.

In case an arrangement [with the council] isn't possible, there is still the question, independent of this, as to whether the university could not invite you separately, e.g., within the framework of an exchange visit of Frankfurt professors to Jerusalem (in correlation to the previous year's visit of Jerusalemites to Frankfurt). In the latter context, Rotenstreich told me that the university wanted to invite Horkheimer.

So that's the situation, and the various possibilities it entails. I am outlining this in detail so that you might indicate your preferences, especially in case the university is unable to agree to a joint invitation with the council. If you are unable to come at all this spring, then we would, in any case, have to consider a later date, during the next academic year, for a possible invitation from the university.

At any rate, I would consider a trip to Frankfurt in the spring only at a time when you are also there, at least for part of it.

I haven't seen the English-language selection of Benjamin's writings. Is the introduction different from the *Merkur* essay? The latter was reworked so that its polemical thrust was all but eliminated and published in the *New Yorker* on the 19th of October. I was sent a copy. I wouldn't respond unless it gets the facts totally wrong. In matters of interpretation, everyone must seek heaven in their own fashion. Truth will separate itself from error in the course of time.

A visit for dinner by such a strictly kosher gentleman as Ernst Simon is downright epochal. I am very glad to hear that it also turned out to be enjoyable. I believe he's returning to Israel in a week.

Regarding the Bloch matter, I would like to say – having read the relevant text, at least as far as you're concerned, as well as some other passages – that if I were in your position, I would stay calm. The jab at you is not nice – it is even a little malicious – and, without a doubt, it is an act of revenge of some kind. Moreover, there is poor Bloch's sense that, as a prophet of hope, it is incumbent on him to represent "the positive" over and against the destructive negativity of so-called hopelessness. It could have been much worse, and, if I may, I hope that I can caution you not to take this matter to heart. As you correctly note, the book is nonsense. The title is completely inadequate, calculated purely for the sake of sensationalism. All of the heretics, whom the book treats so thoroughly, were (God knows!) anything but atheists; they would have died from laughing at the notion that God does not exist. I find it difficult to work my way through all of this chatter, which is mostly second-hand. In any event, Bloch's own dictum applies to the enthusiastic readers of his opus: "the one devours everything that is served to him, even if it is not tasty." (p. 58). What annoys me about Bloch – although, of course, he's not alone in this – is the insouciance with which he plagiarizes Jung, whom he finds unappealing, but who wrote some remarkable things on Job.

What does Your Highness think of the goings-on at the Suhrkamp Verlag, about which we heard so much during Unseld's visit? How should we proceed on this?

I must conclude for today, with cordial regards to you both, also from my lady wife

your

old

Gershom Scholem

Original: typescript with printed letterhead; Theodor W. Adorno Archive, Frankfurt am Main.

Miss Olbricht: Scholem's spelling.

Bloch's own dictum: In the aphorism "selber hoch hinaus" [to fly oneself high], Ernst Bloch wrote: "The one devours everything; even if what was and is given to him is not tasty. The other demands that the cooking improve and is not afraid to check that everything is in order. After all, he will have to pick up the bill himself. He does not feel honored when he is told that it was prepared for him long ago and from on high. Anything can be too much precisely by becoming too little." See Bloch, *Atheismus im Christentum: Zur Religion des Exodus und des Reichs* [Atheism in Christianity: on the religion of the Exodus and the Kingdom] (Frankfurt am Main: Suhrkamp, 1968), p. 57. This aphorism is omitted from the standard English translation: *Atheism in Christianity: The Religion of the Exodus and the Kingdom*, trans. J. T. Swann (New York: Herder & Herder, 1972).

goings-on at the Suhrkamp Verlag: Scholem is referring to an uprising of the editors, who demanded greater worker participation and a socialization of the publishing house.

216 ADORNO TO SCHOLEM
FRANKFURT AM MAIN, 11.12.1968

PROF. DR. THEODOR W. ADORNO

6 FRANKFURT AM MAIN
KETTENHOFWEG 123

11 December 1968

Dear Scholem,

Today, I wish simply to confirm, with heartfelt thanks, that I've received your friendly and detailed letter of the 25th of November, and I apologize for not having responded sooner. But all hell has literally broken loose here with a Walpurgis Night of the students, in which the pseudo-revolution is spinning out of control in the most ludicrous actions. Although they have not yet occupied the Institute, they have occupied the seminar building: they're disrupting all classes, they've chased Habermas out of his office, and they are committing atrocities to which one can only be reconciled through complete helplessness and naïveté. You will understand that, under these circumstances, I have not been able to formulate a cogent thought.

I just want to tell you that I am sincerely thankful for the prospect of being invited to the university in Jerusalem, and that of course I will come only when you are there. Indeed, the most compelling reason for my visit, above all, would be the possibility of spending time there with you. I haven't responded to the council yet, and I'd be very grateful if you could excuse my silence to them on account of the absurd situation here. Such a visit is inconceivable, by the way, before 1970. I have, of course, been thoroughly wrenched from the continuity of writing, and work on my book has come to a halt. I've had to abandon the idea of completing it during my sabbatical term, and I cannot engage myself in any ambitious undertakings until it reaches a stage where all that remains to do is what film directors call the *fine cut.**

So far there has been no physical violence, but, given the way that things are escalating, anything is possible. I mention this only in case you should find yourself in a situation in which you have to write an obituary for me, or else you have to make representations to a higher authority on my behalf.

The one good thing in all of this is that I've quite forgotten about Bloch. It is old news that he steals [*klaut*] from wherever he can. (The typo "glaubt" [*believes*] was profound!)

The situation with Unseld seems to have mostly calmed down; however, it was a terrible blow for him. He is exceedingly fragile, as is so often the case with people who outwardly seem so strong and energetic.

Bonnasse continues to be a nuisance.

I hope I'll soon be in a condition to write to you properly.

For today, all that is cordial to you both, also from Gretel,

your old and loyal

Teddie Adorno

Original: typescript with printed letterhead; Gershom Scholem Archive, The National Library of Israel, Jerusalem. See Rolf Tiedemann (ed.), *Frankfurter Adorno Blätter V* (Munich: Edition Text + Kritik, 1998), pp. 86–7.

The typo: Adorno typed *glaubt* [believes] and changed it, by hand, to *klaut* [steals]. The subsequent sentence was added by hand.

* Original in English.

217 ADORNO TO SCHOLEM
FRANKFURT AM MAIN, 6.2.1969

Dear Scholem, [I am sending you] this merely as a small sign, amidst the horrible turbulence with the students. Needless to say, I'd ask you to treat this letter with the utmost discretion!

Most cordially, also from Gretel and
also to Fanja

yours, Teddie Adorno

Original: manuscript written on a carbon copy of the typescript of a letter to the director of the Volkswagen Foundation; Gershom Scholem Archive, The National Library of Israel, Jerusalem.

this: In his letter to the director of the Volkswagen Foundation, Adorno expressed his support for the plan to publish an edition of Franz Rosenzweig's works. Ernst Simon and Gershom Scholem were to be the editors.

218 ADORNO TO SCHOLEM
FRANKFURT AM MAIN, 26.2.1969

PROF. DR. THEODOR W. ADORNO

6 FRANKFURT AM MAIN
KETTENHOFWEG 123
26 February 1969

Dear Scholem,

Stefan Benjamin was here yesterday. It was a surprise, so everything had to be improvised. I had to give a lecture in the evening at the *Hochschule für Musik* [Music Academy] and we were only able to meet afterwards, along with a group of people who were certainly stimulating but somewhat removed from Stefan's interests. Nevertheless, I was extremely moved to see him again. You'll be pleased to learn that Stefan was able to salvage his father's collection of children's books. As for the two legendary suitcases in San Remo, we are trying to come up with a way of obtaining these without scaring the current owners (who are, by all accounts, as suspicious as they are lax in matters of ownership), just in case our probing causes them to destroy any letters – if any actually still exist. Stefan made a likeable and friendly impression on Gretel and me.

Today I want only to inform you of the following: between the 1st and the 15th of April, Gretel and I will go on a desperately needed interim vacation. Of course, it would be a catastrophe if you were to show up during that time, so I want to urge you sincerely to make arrangements in such a way as to ensure that I will be here when you are.

Good work is being done on the [Benjamin] edition, and a meeting is scheduled for early March, at which point we should be much further along than at our first meeting. You know that I plan to write a lengthy introduction to the *Arcades Project* as soon as Tiedemann's edition is reasonably close to finished; it is set to be a supremely encumbered text. I wish you would consider, once more, whether you might not draw up something similar for the theological writings from his youth. I still stand by my thesis that Benjamin's central motives have been preserved, secularized, in his materialist phase. My God, why else would he have so fascinated us?

During the past few months I have worked on my book with a degree of stubbornness and doggedness that you can hardly imagine, and I have made good progress on the – for me, pivotal – second draft. I won't waste the remaining five weeks. The fact that I have, nonetheless, fallen behind on what I'd set out to achieve during my sabbatical term is due to the student protests. Not only did they rob me of a disproportionate amount of my time; they weighed so heavily on me that I could not muster any of that halcyon cheerfulness that Nietzsche recommends for ambitious authors. The song "Hang the Professors," which I had to listen to repeatedly, is not exactly conducive to such cheerfulness. Nevertheless, the ostrich policy has, once again, proven to be very useful.

I recently saw Peter Szondi. He was very kind, but certainly not yet out of his depression.

Health-wise, we have so far managed to get through the bad season quite well, thanks to a timely vaccination against the Hong Kong flu. Hopefully Fanja continues to be well. Mrs. von Kaschnitz, who was suffering from a similar condition, but who chose another mode of surgery, is, unfortunately, still severely impaired in her ability to walk.

To you both, all that is cordial, from
your old and loyal
Teddie Adorno

Original: typescript with printed letterhead; Gershom Scholem Archive, The National Library of Israel, Jerusalem.

collection of children's books: See letter no. 155 in this volume.

the two legendary suitcases in San Remo: See letter no. 10 and the relevant note in this volume.

the halcyon cheerfulness that Nietzsche recommends for ambitious authors: Presumably Adorno was thinking of the following passage from "The Case of Wagner": "They are quite right, these German youths, considering what they are like: how *could* they miss what we others, we *halcyons*, miss in

Wagner – *la gaya scienza*; light feet, wit, fire, grace; the great logic; the dance of the stars; the exuberant spirituality; the southern shivers of light; the *smooth* sea – perfection." See Friedrich Nietzsche, "The Case of Wagner," in *The Birth of Tragedy & The Case of Wagner*, trans. Robert Kaufmann (New York: Vintage, 1967), p. 178.

219 SCHOLEM TO ADORNO
JERUSALEM, 7.3.1969

Jerusalem, 7.3.1969

Dear Adorno,

I have to respond to you on several points. I was very happy to learn that Stefan Benjamin visited you. Your reference to the two legendary suitcases in San Remo, which evidently thus still exist, is truly stimulating to the imagination, and I hope that something can be done on this front. Why wouldn't it be possible for Stefan himself to go there and speak with these people? Is it a question of money? Did he explain to you why Dora, for her part, could never be persuaded to take such a step?

As for my visit: I can confirm that, unless something unexpected comes up, I will be in Frankfurt in September for a further review of the Benjamin estate – specifically from the 1st to the 10th of September and again from the 21st of September until the 4th of October, at the latest. I have to interrupt my visit because of the trade fair, during which time all the hotels are booked, so I will use this as an opportunity to take another small trip. So, we will surely have the chance to speak in depth. It's quite important that I have access to the papers on the 1st of September, and that you or Gretel are present. But I'm counting on this. An earlier appearance from me in Germany is not to be expected.

For your book on aesthetics, I wish you lots of energy and the power to work. I am amazed at all that you project out of yourself. For me, getting my thoughts out – if I have any – is like pulling teeth. You could certainly use some halcyon cheerfulness – this much is clear to me – and I am astonished at what I read from time to time about the conditions at German universities. I am not familiar with the lyrics to "Hang the Professors." Aside from three or four representatives of this species that I know and like, I wouldn't have any objections to this demand, although – if it came down to it – I'd probably resist putting it into action.

Now for the important question of your visit to Israel: I am writing to you after consultation with Dr. Spiro and with Rotenstreich, who is still rector until the 1st of July.

The date of September '70 is completely out of the question. The university is closed between the 1st of July and the end of October. I am also away in September. Based on the university calendar, we have identified two periods that would be best for your visit to Israel, during which you could give two lectures at the university in addition to those in Tel Aviv, or other obligations.

(1) The period between the 20th or 21st of December and the 31st of December 1969 or early January 1970 would work very well. It would already be the Christmas vacation there, so you wouldn't need any special dispensation to take time off, while our first trimester runs until the 1st of January 1970, so the students would still be here. In addition, our presence would be guaranteed then, so all of our criteria are fully met.

(2) Also, if you can, there would be a possibility of a ten-day stretch between the 18th of January and the 20th of March 1970 – i.e. during the second trimester. If, for instance, you were to come to Tel Aviv a little bit earlier, during the holidays here between the two trimesters, say on the 14th or 15th of January, then you could easily speak in Jerusalem on 19th or 20th of January. We don't know, of course, whether this still falls during your long Christmas break or whether you would need to take a few days off for this purpose.

These are the two concrete possibilities that I would ask you to decide between. The spring, unfortunately, is not an option, since, as you say, you have all but bindingly accepted an invitation to Princeton at this time. The current rector cannot make plans for late 1970. If you tell Dr. Spiro or me (or ideally both of us) that you are prepared to come during one of these times, then the rector will issue you an official invitation to give two lectures, and perhaps a seminar with some of our students, if you feel so inclined. One of the lectures at the university would be philosophical in character, the other musical-philosophical or musicological, and they would be held in the relevant departments. It's also conceivable that the lectures would take place within a broader framework, although this depends somewhat on the themes. You cannot assume that the students speak German, so you should aim to lecture in English. The projected lectures for Dr. Spiro, however, can be held, in part, in German. I think he suggested one in German and one in English, although he's surely written to you in the meantime about this. I don't expect that you'll have any difficulty making yourself understood in English in front of students. Their level of English is not overwhelming, but it's at least good enough. Your appearance here would be a momentous occasion, and I hope that we've finally arrived at some suggestions that will make this possible.

The rector is keen to know as soon as possible what we should plan for. The *National Council** and Dr. Spiro would cover your travel expenses; the cost of your stay would be split between Spiro and the university. Although we cannot pay for Gretel's travel, we can cover expenses for both of you during your stay. I am hoping for a favourable answer from you.

I haven't heard a word from Peter Szondi since his return to Europe. I'm chalking it up to his depressive disposition, but who knows what's really behind it. He's always moaning that the preparation of his classes takes up all of his time, so I don't want to disturb him. That's all for today. Most cordial regards to you both, also from Fanja

yours, Gershom Scholem

Original: typescript; Theodor W. Adorno Archive, Frankfurt am Main.

Dr. Spiro: Scholem's spelling of Spira.

an invitation to Princeton: See the following letter in this volume.

220 ADORNO TO SCHOLEM FRANKFURT AM MAIN, 21.3.1969

PROF. DR. THEODOR W. ADORNO

6 FRANKFURT AM MAIN
KETTENHOFWEG 123
21 March 1969

Dear Scholem,

After having not heard from you for some time, I was very happy to receive your letter. I was starting to worry that something was wrong, or that the situation, which is really unpleasant, was weighing too heavily on you. My response was delayed by a few days because, just as the winter was coming to an end, I unexpectedly came down with the flu, which, exhausted as I already am, affected me more than it properly should have.

As far as the legendary suitcases in San Remo are concerned, it is in no way clear whether they exist at all. Of course, like you, I also asked why Stefan doesn't just go there himself. He told me that he'd already been there once, and that the new owners of the Villa Verde met him with intense suspicion. He fears that if he were to show up there again, the people would destroy the suitcases out of a fear that they might lose them (the cases themselves, not the contents) – that is, if the contents haven't been destroyed a long time ago. His view

* Original in English

was that, if anyone could do anything, it would be an Italian. We are thinking of a close acquaintance of mine, a certain Professor Cases, who used to hold a high-ranking position at the Einaudi publishing house, and we want to try to win him over for our plan. After Stefan indicated to me that his relationship with his mother was by no means good, I did not ask him about Dora's reasons for not looking into this matter herself.

Regarding your dates here: I will be in Venice from the 5th to the 9th of September. I received a very tempting invitation from there, and I had to accept after the hosts unexpectedly agreed to my financial terms. I have nothing planned for the period between the 21st of September and the 4th of October. So we will find plenty of time to be together. We must be very careful in all matters relating to the Benjamin archive (in the very drastic sense of keeping it under lock and key!) because one of the so-called revolutionary student groups – the "Kinderläden" in Berlin – have repeatedly voiced the intention of looting or robbing the archive, which is why we brought it into safe custody, and we do not want to part with the key to this safe place under any circumstances – especially since one cannot even trust one's own assistants anymore (this doesn't mean Tiedemann and Schweppenhäuser, of course, but it does mean a student of the latter's, who is nice enough and even seems to be quite loyal, but who is nonetheless a member of the the SDS [Socialist German Student League]. Such things as these also don't help to make life pleasant.

Unfortunately, I cannot relay to you the lyrics of the Professor song in their entirety, since I've never heard more than the ingenious first line. Given the author's apparent powers of imagination, I don't think it extends much further.

Now, for the most important thing, or at least that which is currently causing the most problems: the date of our trip to Israel. What are here the Christmas holidays of 1969/70 won't work – I most urgently need these weeks for my book on aesthetics: for revisions to the final draft, if everything goes well – and it almost certainly looks as though things will not go so well, and that I'll have to spend these measly fourteen days still tinkering with my text. Before I have this behind me, I will not have the inner freedom and peace that I will need for this journey, which is, of course, eminently encumbered for me.

Unfortunately, the second period that you propose, from the 18th of January to the 20th of March 1970, is also no good. The semester here runs until the middle of February; it's Horkheimer's 75th birthday on the 14th of February, which I must, under all circumstances, spend in Montagnola; and then, long before I received the invitation to Israel, I agreed to lead the so-called Gauss Seminar at Princeton for six weeks. I cannot withdraw from this. So, I must ask you, once again, to consider whether an arrangement could be made, if not for the end of the year, then at least for the fall or late summer of 1970 (i.e. for September). I'd gladly agree to give a lecture on philosophy and another on the philosophy of music in the respective departments, and to hold a seminar with the students afterward, if this is desired. Of course, I don't expect the students to sit through a lecture in German and I'm prepared to do the whole thing in English. Naturally, it's easier for me to speak about difficult and nuanced matters in German than in English, but I would under no circumstances want to make a false step. One mustn't forget for a second what happened, especially if one lives in Germany.

I'm satisfied with the material arrangements that you propose, including the fact that I will be covering Gretel's travel expenses. It matters at least as much to her as it does to me to make this plan possible. It is purely a question of the dates.

It still needs to be established whether the topic of the philosophical lecture should be drawn from the orbit of *Negative Dialectics* (for instance, the "Meditations on Metaphysics") or from the aesthetic *work in progress*.* Regarding the musical side of things, I think it would be good if I spoke on either Mahler or Schoenberg (I'd prefer the latter since, in Israel, he seems to be less well known than Mahler!). Of course, my lecture wouldn't be biographical or musicological-historical in the conventional sense but, rather, musical-philosophical, in the manner that is particular to me.

Celan called a few days ago and conveyed Peter Szondi's regards from Paris. Incidentally, the latter appears to have taken a very strange turn, which I find worrisome: namely, toward the kind of pedantry that surpasses what is common, even among German professors; I can hardly explain this other than in psychiatric terms – as an obsessional neurosis, and one can only hope that it isn't worse than a neurosis. I'm also familiar with his tune that the preparation of his classes leaves him no time for his work. While I don't blame him for this, I do regard it with alarm. My God, where would we have gotten if we'd behaved so primly?

I've made good progress with my book on aesthetics, *tant bien que mal*, albeit not as much as I had hoped. I'll soon be finished working through the text in detail, which involved countless elaborations. For me, this second stage is the decisive one. The third stage, which remains outstanding, will involve determining the final organization of the whole, which will, once again, pose the greatest difficulties. Don't think that this comes easily to me. It's only the first drafts that

* Original in English.

are written relatively quickly, mainly so that I can have something to gnaw on. Nothing remains where it was initially and the effort that follows is unspeakable. Sometimes all I long for is peace and endless sleep; but I fear that this won't happen for me until it's final. On the other hand, I have the strange compulsion actually to say what I think I have to say, without any great illusions about the objective necessity, and without any at all about the immediate effect.

In the meantime, Horkheimer was here. An official new edition of *Dialectic of Enlightenment* is coming out in the autumn with Fischer, and together we've hatched a new preface for it.

I hope that Fanja is doing quite well – I'd like to assume that this is the case since you aren't saying anything to the contrary. Please send her our most cordial regards.

All the best, also from Gretel,

your old

Teddie Adorno

Original: typescript with printed letterhead; Gershom Scholem Archive, The National Library of Israel, Jerusalem.

Villa Verde: The guest house run by Benjamin's ex-wife, Dora, was called Villa Verde (see letter no. 104 in this volume).

Professor Cases, who used to hold a high-ranking position at the Einaudi publishing house: The Italian Germanist and cultural critic Cesare Cases (1920–2005) worked, among other things, as a translator and editor of German literature and philosophy for the Turin-based publishing house Einaudi. Cases was also professor of German literature at the universities in Cagliari, Pavia, and Turin. It has not been determined whether Cesare Cases took any actions in San Remo.

Venice: The "L'XI Corso Internationale D'Alta Cultura" [11th international course in high culture] on the theme of "La critica forma caratteristica della civiltà moderna" [The critical form characteristic of modern civilization], took place from the 6th to the 27th of September at the Fondazione Giorgio Cini. The program announced two lectures to be held by Adorno on the 6th and the 8th of September, on the themes of "La critica musicale" [Music criticism] and "Critica della cultura e società" [Critique of culture and society]. After Adorno's death, Adorno's lectures were read aloud in their Italian translation.

Gauss Seminar at Princeton: The Gauss Seminars in Criticism, which offer a platform for discussing contemporary issues in the humanities, have taken place at Princeton University since 1949. Traditionally, distinguished scholars are invited to lead them. Past speakers have included Hannah Arendt, Erich Auerbach, Jürgen Habermas, Herbert Marcuse, and Paul Tillich.

Celan: The lyric poet Paul Celan (1920–1970) was born in the Romanian town of Czernowitz. During the German occupation of the city, Celan was first forced into the local ghetto and later into a labor camp. His poems frequently refer to his parents' death at a concentration camp in Transnistria. Peter Szondi first introduced Celan to Adorno in 1959. Celan committed suicide in April of 1970, a few months after his first visit to Jerusalem. Adorno's essay "Valéry's Deviations" (1960) is dedicated to him. See Adorno, "Valéry's Deviations," in *Notes to Literature*, Vol. 1, trans. Shierry Weber Nicholsen (New York: Columbia University Press, 1991), pp. 137–73. See also "Theodor W. Adorno and Paul Celan, Briefwechsel 1960–1968" [Theodor W. Adorno and Paul Celan, Correspondence 1960–1968], ed. Joachim Seng, *Frankfurter Adorno Blätter VIII* (Munich: Edition Text + Kritik, 2003), pp. 177–200.

An official new edition of Dialectic of Enlightenment: Adorno and Horkheimer's *Dialectic of Enlightenment* was first published by Querido Press in Amsterdam in 1947. The book was still available during the 1960s and was widely disseminated through pirated editions after 1968. In 1969, after Horkheimer had resisted the idea for a long period, the authors decided to have it reissued by S. Fischer Verlag in Frankfurt am Main. In the 1969 Preface to the new edition, they write: "We do not stand by everything we said in the book in its original form. That would be incompatible with a theory which attributes a temporal core to truth instead of contrasting truth as something invariable to the movement of history. The book was written at a time when the end of the National Socialist terror was in sight. In not a few places, however, the formulation is no longer adequate to the reality of today. All the same, even at that time we did not underestimate the implications of the transition to the administered world." *Dialectic of Enlightenment*, ed. Gunzelin Schmid Noerr, trans. Edmund Jephcott (Stanford, CA: Stanford University Press, 2002), pp. xi–xii; here, p. xi.

221 SCHOLEM TO ADORNO
JERUSALEM, 20.4.1969

Jerusalem 20.4.1969

Dear Adorno,

I waited to respond to your letter of the 21st of March because the rector was away, and I needed to follow up with him about some of the things we'd been discussing.

Firstly, regarding my Frankfurt plans: I hope that we can make arrangements so that I can have access to the papers even while you are in Venice, and that, during these days, the key to the ward where you are keeping the papers might be delivered into my loyal hands. As an old reactionary of solid character, I should be more reliable than your assistants in the SDS [Socialist German Student League]. I naturally want to maximize my time, so as to be able to make positive suggestions about which pieces to include. As I've already written to you, I intend to be in Frankfurt from the 1st of September, and I'd be grateful if you could take note of this.

I wish you all the best for your book on aesthetics. As far as the new edition of *Dialectic of Enlightenment* is concerned, I recently read an outraged denunciation of the reactionary character of this book of yours, its relapse into irrationalism, myth, and other similar things – all of which gives the creeps to a genuine adherent of the Enlightenment, which this author imagines himself to be. This seems, more or less, in keeping with the current intellectual fashions, and I couldn't help but smirk, given my own experiences in the field of Enlightenment studies. It was inevitable that you should also be accused of "*Trahison des clercs*."

I haven't heard anything from Peter Szondi since last summer, nor has he responded to my letters. I don't see what else I can do here.

Now, for the possible dates, or non-dates, of a trip to Israel with lectures at the university: Unfortunately, your specifications do not leave us any possibility of welcoming you here during the academic year '69–'70. According to what you have indicated, the dates that I proposed are out of the question, and there are no others. The next academic year ends in June of 1970, and the rector, whose term ends this June, tells me that it is impossible to commit his successor to anything beyond the following year (1969–70), especially since you can't make an unequivocal commitment to a reasonable date. September '70 coincides with the holidays here. There is nothing else I can do but wait for us to discuss other possibilities in person when we see each other in September. I'm very sorry that your literary plans and other travel commitments make an arrangement for the next academic year impossible. At most, it remains for you and Dr. Spira of the National Council to agree on a tour of music lectures at some other time, independent of the university and of my own scheduling – I cannot rule out that I will be in America for two or three months in the fall of 1970. Since I don't yet know who the new rector will be, I cannot take any further steps at this time. The question of dates must therefore be postponed for the time being.

Do you happen to have Celan's address in Paris? I'd like to send him something.

I hope that you have conquered your bout of flu and that you are now able to meet the challenges posed by your work, as well as those posed by confrontations with the revolutionary "Kinderläden," and other similarly progressive institutions of the Zeitgeist, with renewed freshness. Every visitor who comes to Israel from Europe or the U.S. is enviously astonished at the unscathed idyllic relations that we have with our students, which are unparalleled in the world. But, then again, the Nation of Israel is also unparalleled; and with this humble remark, I will conclude. My devotion to you and your wife, until the outbreak of the Marcusean revolution.

Your old

Gershom Scholem

Original: typescript; Theodor W. Adorno Archive, Frankfurt am Main.

an outraged denunciation: not verified.

"*Trahison des clercs*": Scholem is alluding to a 1927 essay of that title by the French writer and philosopher Julien Benda (1867–1956). See Julien Benda, *The Treason of the Intellectuals*, trans. Richard Aldington (New York: Routledge, 2017).

Do you happen to have Celan's address in Paris?: There is no letter from Scholem in Celan's estate. Scholem's estate contains one letter from Celan to Gershom and Fania Scholem which was written on the 20th of October 1969, immediately after Celan's visit to Israel.

confrontations with the revolutionary "Kinderläden": Scholem is alluding to a recently published collection of various texts by Walter Benjamin, under the title, "Eine kommunistische Pädagogik. Spielzeug und Spielen. Anleitung für eine revoutionäre Erziehung" [A communist pedagogy: toys and play. Instructions for a revolutionary education] (Berlin West: Zentralrat der sozialistischen Kinderläden [central committee of the Socialist Kinderläden, 1969)].

222 ADORNO TO SCHOLEM
FRANKFURT AM MAIN, 29.4.1969

PROF. DR. THEODOR W. ADORNO

6 FRANKFURT AM MAIN
KETTENHOFWEG 123
29 April 1969

Dear Scholem,

This is just to acknowledge your very friendly letter; a reasonable answer is out of the question during the *tohu va'vohu** at present. The dear students have broken up one of my lecture courses under scandalous circumstances. I do not know whether I will resume it during the current semester or how I will handle my teaching in the future. Although all of this is just a kind of inanimate misfortune, it is plenty aggravating nonetheless.

Today I want nothing more than warmly to recommend my friend Ulrich Sonnemann to you. He is in Israel for a few weeks, and he will

* *Tohu va'vohu*: (also tohu wa'bohu) Biblical Hebrew (Gen. 1:2): chaos, formless and void. The term has been taken up within German, meaning chaos.

be contacting you, on my suggestion. He is one of the few people who, at a mature age, and in complete freedom, has decisively approached what Horkheimer and I stand for intellectually, and to which I know that you are also deeply attached. Incidentally, Sonnemann is a cousin of the deceased Heinrich Simon from the *Frankfurter Zeitung*. I think you will get along well with him, and I thank you in advance for every minute that you devote to him.

Most cordially, also from Gretel, and to Fanja

always yours,

Teddie Adorno

Original: typescript with printed letterhead; Gershom Scholem Archive, The National Library of Israel, Jerusalem.

The dear students have broken up one of my lecture courses under scandalous circumstances: On the 22nd of April, Adorno was beset by three female students who bared their breasts. He fled the auditorium and canceled his lectures and seminars.

Ulrich Sonnemann: The philosopher and psychologist Ulrich Sonnemann (1912–1993) was born in Berlin. After being persecuted and detained in the Gurs internment camp in southwestern France, he was able to escape to the USA in 1941. Following military service, he was appointed in 1949 to a professorship at the New School for Social Research. In 1955 he returned to Germany, where he worked as a freelance writer in Munich until 1969. His book *Negative Anthropologie: Vorstudien zur Sabotage des Schicksals* [Negative anthropology: preliminary studies on the sabotage of fate] was published in 1969 by Rowohlt Verlag of Reinbek/Hamburg. In 1974 Sonnemann was appointed to a professorship in social philosophy at the Gesamthochschule in Kassel. Adorno writes the following in the Preface to *Negative Dialectics*: "Ulrich Sonnemann is working on a book, which is supposed to be entitled *Negative Anthropology*. Neither he nor the author knew beforehand about this coincidence. It refers to a compulsion in the material itself." See Adorno, *Gesammelte Schriften 6: Negative Dialektik/Jargon der Eigentlichkeit*, ed. Rolf Tiedemann et al. (Frankfurt am Main: Suhrkamp, 1970), p. 11. The passage is omitted in the standard English translation of *Negative Dialectics*. See also Adorno's piece dedicated to Ulrich Sonnemann, "Marginalia to Theory and Praxis," in *Critical Models: Interventions and Catchwords*, trans. Henry W. Pickford (New York: Columbia University Press, 1998), pp. 259–78. Finally, see Adorno, "Zu Ulrich Sonnemanns *Negativer Anthropologie*" [On Ulrich Sonnemann's *Negative Anthropology*], in *Gesammelte Schriften 20.1: Vermischte Schriften* [Miscellaneous Writings], ed. Rolf Tiedemann et al. (Frankfurt am Main: Suhrkamp, 1986), pp. 262–3.

Heinrich Simon from the Frankfurter Zeitung: From 1906, the journalist and publisher Heinrich Simon (1880–1941) worked at the *Frankfurter Zeitung*, which was founded by his grandfather Leopold Sonnemann. In 1934 he had to abandon his position and escape from Germany, via Paris, to Tel Aviv, where he became the director of the Palestine Philharmonic Orchestra.

223 ADORNO TO SCHOLEM
FRANKFURT AM MAIN, 14.5.1969

PROF. DR. THEODOR W. ADORNO

6 FRANKFURT AM MAIN
KETTENHOFWEG 123
14 May 1969

Dear Scholem,

After responding to your letter of the 20th of April only with a request to welcome my friend Sonnemann, I wanted at least to send you a few more words today.

My plans for the late summer are as yet unclear, apart from the days in Venice. However, I will certainly be here at the end of August, and it's not entirely impossible that I'll still be here on the 1st of September.

As far as the Benjamin Archive is concerned, you will surely come to an understanding with Gretel, who is guarding the hoard of the Nibelungen. In the meantime, the "Kinderläden" are publicly frothing with anger at the secretion of the archive, as you well know.

I was impeded in my work on the aesthetics book as a result of the horrors here, but I've since resumed it. Aside from that, I've written a pair of prolegomena for an essay collection in the style of *Eingriffe* [Interventions] (it is to be called *Stichworte*); these only need the final revision. Today I received the first proofs for the new edition of *Dialectic of Enlightenment*. Incidentally, there are growing indications that the students don't want to break with me entirely, so it's conceivable that I'll soon resume lecturing in some form or other.

The question of the dates for my trip to Israel is truly – I would have almost said – a cross. September 1970 looks to be free and suitable, but of course there's no possibility of a blank check from the new rector. To go to Israel independently of the university doesn't seem to me to make sense, and if you weren't there, the whole trip would, in any case, be pointless.

Celan's address is: 78 rue de Longchamp, Paris 16^{e}. It hasn't changed, at least as far as I'm aware. Incidentally, although he is not angry with me at the moment, an evening we had with him was a little tedious and forced.

I don't want to conceal this from you, but I ask for your discretion: the relationship to Marcuse has become extraordinarily strained after – contrary to his own desire of coming here without a great media circus – he suddenly made a public discussion with the students one of the conditions of his visit, which makes an arrangement with the Institute impossible. If I am properly informed, his wife threatened to join the students in protest against him if he did otherwise. Strange are the ways of men.

Most cordially, as always, also for Fanja, and also from Gretel,

your old

Teddie Adorno

Original: typescript with printed letterhead; Gershom Scholem Archive, The National Library of Israel, Jerusalem.

a pair of prolegomena: The dialectical prolegomena, "On Subject and Object" and "Marginalia to Theory and Praxis" may be found in *Critical Models: Interventions and Catchwords*, trans. Henry W. Pickford (New York: Columbia University Press, 1998), pp. 245–58 and 259–78 respectively.

Marcuse ... his wife: Inge Marcuse (née Werner, 1910–1973) married Marcuse in 1956 after the death of her first husband, Franz Neumann.

224 GRETEL ADORNO TO SCHOLEM
FRANKFURT AM MAIN, 26.6.1969

Frankfurt am Main, on the 26th of June 1969

Dear Gerhard Scholem,

Sincere thanks for your lines from the 24th of June.

Our schedule is as follows: we leave here on 22nd of July and we arrive in Zermatt on the 23rd. We anticipate staying there until roughly the 26th of August. Teddie will probably not go to Venice until around the 3rd or 4th of September, so you could still catch him here if you arrive by the 31st of August.

With respect to the archive, I've already arranged with the student, Mr. Rexroth, who always does retrievals from the safe, to be available to us here without fail on Monday, the 1st of September. So you should have no difficulty gaining access to the Benjamin archive.

I am very much looking forward to your visit and I wish you and Fanja all the best for the summer.

We will be staying at the Hotel Bristol in Zermatt.

Very cordial regards to you both

yours,

Gretel

Original: typescript; Gershom Scholem Archive, The National Library of Israel, Jerusalem.

your lines from the 24th of June: Scholem's letter of this date has not been preserved.

225 GRETEL ADORNO TO SCHOLEM
FRANKFURT AM MAIN, 9. AUGUST 1969

THEODOR W. ADORNO
geb. 11. September 1903

ist am 6. August 1969 sanft entschlafen.

In tiefster Trauer
Margarete Adorno
geb. Karplus

Frankfurt/Main, Kettenhofweg 123, 9. August 1969

Die Beerdigung findet am Mittwoch, dem 13. August 1969,
um 11 Uhr auf dem Frankfurter Hauptfriedhof statt.
Es wird gebeten, von Beileidsbesuchen abzusehen.

Theodor W. Adorno
b. 11 September 1903

passed away peacefully on the 6th of August 1969.

In deepest sorrow
Margarete Adorno
née Karplus

Frankfurt/Main, Kettenhofweg 123, 9 August 1969

The funeral will take place on Wednesday the 13th of August 1969,
at 11 a.m. at the Frankfurt Main Cemetery.
Please refrain from condolence visits.

Original: card with obituary notice; Gershom Scholem Archive, The National Library of Israel, Jerusalem.

226 GRETEL ADORNO TO SCHOLEM FRANKFURT AM MAIN, 9.10.1969

PROF. DR. THEODOR W. ADORNO

6 FRANKFURT AM MAIN
KETTENHOFWEG 123
9 October 1969

Dear Mr. Scholem,

I'd like to thank you, once again, for coming right away from Jerusalem to Frankfurt.

I am also enclosing an appraisal by Kornfeld and Klipstein, as well as a copy of the letter to Stefan Benjamin. The value of the piece seems, in fact, to lie somewhere between 50,000 and 100,000 Marks. Rudolf Hirsch immediately estimated it at 80,000 Marks.

I haven't heard from Unseld yet about the insurance, but he's currently very busy with the book fair.

With best wishes for Fanja,
always yours,
Gretel Adorno

Original: typescript with printed letterhead; Gershom Scholem Archive, The National Library of Israel, Jerusalem.

from Jerusalem to Frankfurt: Theodor W. Adorno passed away on the 6th of August 1969 during his vacation in the Swiss municipality of Zermatt. Scholem was present for the funeral at the Frankfurt Main Cemetery on the 13th of August.

an appraisal by Kornfeld and Klipstein: After Adorno's death, Gretel Adorno asked Dr. Eberhard W. Kornfeld for an evaluation of the *Angelus Novus* painting by Paul Klee, which, according to Benjamin's will from 1932, was to go to Scholem. Kornfeld was one of the most renowned collectors and auctioneers of Klee's work and the owner of the Galerie Kornfeld & Co. in Berne (formerly Galerie Kornfeld und Klipstein).

227 SCHOLEM TO GRETEL ADORNO JERUSALEM, 27.10.1969

Jerusalem, 27.10.1969

Dear Gretel,

Kind thanks for your lines and for the appraisal by Kornfeld, which I arranged through a friend in Zurich. In the meantime, I'm waiting to hear from Stefan Benjamin, who wanted to use the last week of October to try to visit his aunt in Berlin and to get at the papers in

Potsdam. If I don't hear from him, then I will contact him directly sometime in November. It is likely that, in the meantime, he will have discussed how to proceed in this matter with his lawyer. As for the painting, I might suggest that one of the people consulted thus far be invited to take a trip to Frankfurt to view the original. This suggestion imposes itself after reading the three letters that you have received thus far.

Please write to me, when you get a chance, to let me know what you are doing and how you have been. I was very glad to see you recently and I hope to see you again soon. Fania sends cordial regards, as does

Your

Gerhard Scholem

Would you do me the kindness of dropping the "Mr."? Thanks in advance!

Original: aerogram, typescript with handwritten postscript; Theodor W. Adorno Archive, Frankfurt am Main.

Stefan . . . his aunt in Berlin: Hilde Benjamin (1902–1989) was the wife of Georg Benjamin. From 1953 to 1967 she was the minister of justice in the GDR.

The three letters: not determined.

228 GRETEL ADORNO TO SCHOLEM FRANKFURT AM MAIN, 11.11.1969

11 November 1969

Dear Gerhard Scholem,

A thousand thanks for your lovely lines.

Today I am sending you Suhrkamp's statement of how much Stefan Benjamin received from 1951 to September 1969. With the new edition, the amount will increase significantly.

To date, I've heard nothing from Unseld regarding insurance for the *Angelus Novus*.

With the most cordial regards, also to Fanja,

always yours, [Gretel Adorno]

Original: carbon copy of typescript; Theodor W. Adorno Archive, Frankfurt am Main.

229 GRETEL ADORNO TO SCHOLEM
FRANKFURT AM MAIN, 15.12.1969

15.12.1969

Dear Scholem,

Unseld made inquiries about how to best insure the painting and found out that it would be easiest if I simply raised the coverage of my household insurance to 100,000 DM [German marks], with the explicit instruction that this increase is intended to cover the *Angelus Novus*. I made this arrangement right away.

Have you heard anything from Stefan Benjamin about the will in the meantime?

I hope that you are both in good health, and I wish you all the best for the New Year.

All the best,
always yours, [Gretel Adorno]

Original: carbon copy of typescript; Theodor W. Adorno Archive, Frankfurt am Main.

will: Gretel Adorno is presumably referring to Benjamin's 1932 will (see letter no. 110 and the relevant note in this volume).

230 SCHOLEM TO GRETEL ADORNO
JERUSALEM, 20.12.1969

Jerusalem, 20 Dec. '69
28 Abarbanel St.

Dear Gretel,

I thank you sincerely for your note and for your new year's wishes, which we reciprocate in the same spirit.

I've heard nothing from Stefan for three months now. I'll write to him soon, since he must have had sufficient leisure during this lengthy period of time *to make up his mind** as to how he actually wants to handle this matter. He was, in the meantime, in East Berlin – that was his plan, at least, for the end of October. If I hear something, you will definitely find out about it.

Around the 16th of March, I am going to give a lecture at University College London, and I may be able to speak with St. B. while I am there. If I can't stop off in Frankfurt on my return trip, I'll pass

* Original in English.

through no later than the beginning of May, since I'll have to come to Europe for three or four days, once again for academy-related business. Apart from this, I'll be here until mid-August, 1970.

All that is cordial,
yours,
Gerhard Scholem

Original: manuscript; Theodor W. Adorno Archive, Frankfurt am Main.

Stefan . . . East Berlin: See the following letter in this volume.

lecture: Not verified.

231 SCHOLEM TO GRETEL ADORNO
JERUSALEM, 5.3.1970

5 March 1970

Dear Gretel,

Thank you very much for your last message. Here's how things stand with me: I intend to pass through Frankfurt for a few days, from the 23rd to the 25th of March, on my return trip from London, where I'm traveling on the 16th of March to give a lecture. I'd be very happy if we could spend one of the two evenings together. Perhaps you can arrange with Unseld which of the two evenings you'd like for yourself? And maybe you could also see if there's anything that would make a meeting of our committee of three necessary or desirable?

I'd also be prepared to meet with Mr. Rexroth during this time, in case he has any questions or problems that I could assist him with.

Stefan just wrote to me to say that, due to illness, he couldn't go to Berlin after all, and that – with the help of a lawyer from West Berlin – he hired a lady in East Berlin to take measures at the archive in Potsdam. Maybe I'll bring the letter with me. Stefan seems to have something like angina pectoris.

In the hope of a seeing you again soon, most cordial regards, also from Fanja,

from your
Gerhard Scholem

Original: manuscript; Theodor W. Adorno Archive, Frankfurt am Main.

your last message: Not preserved in Scholem's estate.

Mr. Rexroth: See the relevant note to letter no. 212 in this volume.

232 GRETEL ADORNO TO SCHOLEM
FRANKFURT AM MAIN, 12.3.1970

PROF. DR. THEODOR W. ADORNO

6 FRANKFURT AM MAIN
KETTENHOFWEG 123
12 March 1970

Dear Scholem,

It would be very nice if you could come to Frankfurt on your way back from London. I just have to tell you, unfortunately, that I stupidly broke my tibia three weeks ago, and have been in the hospital until now; however, I should be discharged and allowed to go home tomorrow.

If the committee of three were to meet, it would probably be best if you and Unseld came to me, since I can't move and won't be able to do so for several more weeks.

Meanwhile, Miss Olbrich has contacted Mr. Rexroth to inform him that you'll be here between the 23rd and the 25th of March.

I have, in the meantime, received a handwritten list of the materials in the archive at Potsdam from Alfred Sohn-Rethel, which he drew up when he was there. I hope it's complete.

With the most cordial regards to you both,
always yours,
Sgd. Gretel Adorno

p.p. and with best regards,
Elfriede Olbrich

Original: typescript with printed letterhead; Gershom Scholem Archive, The National Library of Israel, Jerusalem.

Alfred Sohn-Rethel: The philosopher and sociologist Alfred Sohn-Rethel (1899–1990) belonged to the wider circle of the Frankfurt School, although he was never a member of the Institute for Social Research. He was born in Paris and grew up partly in Berlin. He studied economics, philosophy, history, and sociology at the University of Heidelberg, where he completed his doctorate in 1928. He left Germany in 1936, going first to Lucerne, then to Paris, and, in 1937, to Oxford, where he was in contact with Adorno. During and after the Second World War, Sohn-Rethel remained in London, where he worked in adult education. His influential book *Geistige und körperliche Arbeit* [Intellectual and manual labor] was published by Suhrkamp in 1970. In 1972 he became visiting professor at the University of Bremen, where he was appointed to a full professorship in 1978. In the spring of 1965, Sohn-Rethel was able to view the part of Benjamin's estate that was held at the Deutsches Zentralarchiv in Potsdam, which consisted of the papers that Benjamin left behind in his Paris apartment after he fled, which had subsequently been confiscated by the Gestapo. On the 24th of April, 1965, he reported to Adorno about his visit, "for which no more than a day . . . was made available." See *Theodor W. Adorno and Alfred Sohn-Rethel: Briefwechsel, 1936-1969*, ed. Christoph Gödde (Munich: Edition Text + Kritik, 1991), pp. 142–6.

233 SCHOLEM TO GRETEL ADORNO
JERUSALEM, C. LATE MARCH 1970

Dear Gretel, by Airmail

I hope you are feeling better now? I received your letter of the 12th of March. I hope to see Rethel's notes from Potsdam when I'm back in Fr. (maybe even this spring).

Cordial regards from Fanja and me, and get well soon
yours, Gerhard Scholem

Original: postcard, manuscript, with indecipherable postmark, "The Hebrew University, Jerusalem"; Theodor W. Adorno Archive, Frankfurt am Main.

234 GRETEL ADORNO TO SCHOLEM
FRANKFURT AM MAIN, 15.7.1970

Frankfurt, on the 15th of July 1970

Dear Scholem,

Mr. Rexroth has meanwhile compiled all the hashish material, and also, unfortunately, promptly turned it over to Mr. Unseld. The stuff is of entirely disparate quality, and I have serious reservations about whether it should be published. It would require a very comprehensive afterword, in which Benjamin's other works as well as his hashish literature are referred to in general terms. Mr. Unseld hasn't looked at it yet, but unfortunately he's much too interested in it. I don't think we'd be doing Benjamin any favors if we were to publish it now, when hashish has become topical. I'd be grateful if you could also raise your concerns to Unseld when you get the opportunity.

I'm back to spending mornings at the Institute, and can move myself forward with a cane, which means, thank God, that I'm no longer quite so dependent.

To you and Fanja all the best,
always yours,
Gretel Adorno

Original: typescript; Gershom Scholem Archive, The National Library of Israel, Jerusalem.

all the hashish material: In 1972, Tillman Rexroth edited a volume titled *Über Haschisch*, which contains Benjamin's prose texts, protocols, and reports on his experiments with drugs, along with an Introduction by Hermann Schweppenhäuser. See Benjamin, *On Hashish*, ed. Howard Eiland (Cambridge MA: Belknap Press of Harvard University Press, 2006). In the summer of 1932, Benjamin counted the "truly exceptional book about hashish" that he planned to write – alongside the *Pariser Passagen* [Paris Arcades], the *Essays zur Literatur* [essays on literature], and *Deutsche Menschen* [German men and women] – as one of the four books that he had given up the hope of ever completing and publishing (see Benjamin's letter to Scholem of the 26th of July 1932 in *The Correspondence of Walter Benjamin and Gershom Scholem: 1932–1940*, trans. Gary Smith and Andre Lefevere, Cambridge MA: Harvard University Press: 1992), pp. 14–15.

235 SCHOLEM TO GRETEL ADORNO
NEW YORK [?], 14.10.1970

14 Oct. 1970

Dear Gretel,

Fania and I are coming to Frankfurt on Sunday, the 25th of Oct., and, if at all possible, we would like to see you in the afternoon or evening – whichever suits you. Perhaps [we] could take you out for dinner?

Please notify us at the Hotel Urban, Zurich, Stadelhoferstraße, where we will be arriving from New York on Tuesday morning (the 20th of Oct.).

We are looking forward to seeing you and hope to find you with your health restored.

We'll be at the Parkhotel in Frkft.

All that is cordial
yours,
Gerhard Scholem

Original: manuscript; Theodor W. Adorno Archive, Frankfurt am Main.

236 GRETEL ADORNO TO SCHOLEM
FRANKFURT AM MAIN, 19.10.1970

Frankfurt on the 19.10.1970

Dear Scholem,

I am very much looking forward to seeing you again.

It's very nice of you to want to invite me out to dinner; I'll be at the Parkhotel at seven thirty.

Very cordially

always yours, [Gretel Adorno]

Original: carbon copy of typescript; Theodor W. Adorno Archive, Frankfurt am Main.

Index

Page references in italics indicate mentions in the editor's annotations. Page references in brackets indicate disguised or indirect mentions of a subject or work.